NO LONGER AN ISLAND

NO LONGER AN ISLAND

Britain and the Wright Brothers,
1902–1909

ALFRED GOLLIN

Stanford University Press
Stanford, California
1984

Stanford University Press
Stanford, California

© 1984 by Alfred Gollin
Originating publisher: William Heinemann Ltd,
London

First published in the USA by
Stanford University Press,
1984

Manufactured in Great Britain

ISBN 0-8047-1265-4
LC 84-51314

This book is dedicated
to the Memory
of
My Parents

Contents

Acknowledgement and Author's Preface

I have to acknowledge the gracious permission of Her Majesty The Queen to publish a document from the Royal Archives, reproduced in the text. In this connection I must also express my thanks to the Librarian at Windsor Castle, Sir Robin Mackworth-Young, for his courtesies. He and his staff were generous in the assistance they gave.

Thousands of documents in the Public Record Office in London were examined and I wish to record my appreciation of the help provided by the staff of that great institution.

In the Library of Congress in Washington, D.C., I examined the papers of Octave Chanute and the huge number of documents preserved in the collection known as The Papers of Wilbur and Orville Wright. Three officers of the Library – Dr Marvin McFarland, Dr John C. Broderick, Chief, Manuscript Division, and Dr Paul T. Heffron, Acting Chief – all helped in this phase of the work.

The late Sir Geoffrey Harmsworth assisted me in a long correspondence and in several meetings in London. He saw to it that I could examine the collection of Lord Northcliffe's Papers, preserved in the British Library.

In the House of Lords Record Office (H.L.R.O.) several collections of papers were examined. For the purposes of this history, material in the Beaverbrook and Bonar Law Papers was exploited.

I have to thank Lord Esher for permission to publish a number of documents preserved in the Esher Papers at Churchill College, Cambridge. The staff there were courteous and helpful.

The Papers of Arthur Lee, later Lord Lee of Fareham, were examined in the Courtauld Institute in London where Mr Michael Doran showed me every consideration. I also consulted there the privately printed three-volume work by Lee, *A Good Innings*.

Documents from the private correspondence of J. L. Garvin, in my personal possession, were also used in the work.

The Papers of R. B. Haldane, later Viscount Haldane of Cloan, were examined in the National Library of Scotland. In Edinburgh, Mr Alan Bell of the Department of Manuscripts was extremely helpful.

I have also to thank the officials of the British Library, those of its Newspaper Library at Colindale, and the librarians in the University of California, Santa Barbara.

Mr H. E. Scrope of Vickers Limited kindly furnished me with a copy of his privately printed book, *Golden Wings, The Story of Fifty Years of Aviation By the Vickers Group of Companies*.

The use I made of all this material is indicated in the footnote references in the text. My object, with the footnotes, has been to demonstrate exactly how these sources were exploited.

I must also express my sincere thanks to the John Simon Guggenheim Memorial Foundation, and especially to its President, Dr Gordon Ray; to the American Council of Learned Societies; and to the National Endowment for the Humanities for the financial assistance that helped me to complete the work. The Chancellor of the University of California, Santa Barbara, Dr Robert Huttenback, provided support and assistance.

Several officers connected with the Royal Air Force showed great interest and offered splendid encouragement while this work was in preparation. The late Sir John Slessor, Marshal of the Royal Air Force, was nothing less than an inspiration. He showed his interest in a long correspondence and in spirited conversations at his home, Rimpton Manor, near Yeovil in Somerset. The late Air Chief Marshal Sir William Elliot, at one time Commander-in-Chief, Fighter Command, offered advice and assistance in several ways. He once wrote to me "there is a great need and scope for what you want to do, and in more than one respect there is a great deal to be said for the task being undertaken by an American". Group Captain E. B. Haslam, formerly Head, Air Historical Branch, Ministry of Defence, London, assisted me in every way he could and I wish to record my thanks to him. I also received marvellous support and encouragement from Dr John Tanner, the Director of the Royal Air Force Museum at Hendon. He furnished the most generous help at every phase of the work and I must express my gratitude for all that he did.

I also wish to acknowledge my gratitude to a great historian, George Dangerfield. He urged me forward in the most enthusiastic way while the work was in preparation. My dear friend Mr Maurice H. Smith, formerly of H.M. Customs and Excise, provided invaluable help. He read and commented on each chapter in a way that could have been done by no one else. I owe him a great debt. Mr John Grigg, the distinguished biographer of Lloyd George, intervened with decisive effect at one stage in the pre-publication developments. I should like this fact to be placed upon the record. My dear wife, Valerie, sustained me at every phase of the work. It would not be possible to express adequately, my appreciation for all she did.

I wish also to thank Mrs Gill Coleridge; and Messrs David Godwin and

Roger Smith of William Heinemann Ltd. Mr G. C. Jones was kind enough to prepare the index.

Some of the materials exploited in this book were first published in my article "The Wright Brothers and the British authorities, 1902–1909", *English Historical Review* XCV, No. 375 (April 1980); and some were also published in articles in the American scholarly journal *Albion*. They are reproduced here with the permission of the editor.

Several years ago I was engaged in research in Stanley Baldwin's collection of Papers, preserved in the University Library at Cambridge. A phrase I kept coming across in his correspondence was "the Air Defence of Great Britain". They were very interested in British Air Defence in those days, the 1930s.

I knew that Air Chief Marshal Sir Hugh Dowding, the first Air Officer Commanding-in-Chief, Fighter Command, had fought a defensive battle in 1940 which demonstrated nothing less than his genius. I knew also that after Hitler, in violation of Germany's treaty obligations, announced the existence of a German Air Force in 1935, many British diplomatic decisions were influenced by the fear of a German air attack upon their country. It seemed to me, in my innocence of the subject, that I could write a quick little book dealing with the years 1935–1940 to illustrate these developments. It took quite some time but I discovered, eventually, that some people in Britain had been afraid of an air attack or an air invasion of their country since 1908, and even earlier. I had stumbled upon a theme of very great importance in British life in the present century. I learned that the first government to approach the brothers, Wilbur and Orville Wright, about their invention, the aeroplane, was the British Government. I decided, in Sherlock Holmes's great phrase, to try and "open the matter up". The result was that, after a good deal of research, I came to the remarkable conclusion offered in the first paragraph of this history.

Department of History,   Alfred Gollin
University of California,
Santa Barbara

CHAPTER 1

The Wright Brothers

Winston Churchill's famous speech – The Battle of Britain –
When did it begin? – Safety against Invasion – "England is
No Longer an Island" – Wilbur and Orville Wright – The
Wright family – The Wright Cycle Company – Their in-
terest in Aeronautics – Octave Chanute – He would not
keep a secret – The Wright brothers at Kitty Hawk – The
Kill Devil Hills – Wilbur Wright's Lecture – Chanute's
actions – The wind-tunnel – Sturdy Independence of the
Wright brothers – The glider of 1902 – Intervention of B. F.
S. Baden-Powell

I

In June 1940 Winston Churchill made a famous speech to the House of
Commons. In it he sought to prepare his countrymen for a terrible ordeal.
He wanted them to ready themselves to withstand the shock of a German
invasion of England. It was expected that the invasion would be preceded
by a terrific air attack upon the United Kingdom, launched from bases in
France and the Low Countries by the German Air Force. In his speech
Churchill said: "What General Weygand called the Battle of France is
over. I expect that the Battle of Britain is about to begin." Churchill even
told his audience that the fate of Christian civilization itself turned upon
the outcome of the battle. According to the official reckoning the tactical
phase of the Battle of Britain began on 10 July 1940. However, if this
impending attack was of such supreme significance a longer view of the
matter should be taken; and it may be asked – properly – When did the
Battle of Britain really begin? A not unreasonable answer is that the
Battle of Britain began when the Wright brothers flew.

No goverment paid more attention to the early activities of Wilbur and
Orville Wright than did the British Government. Indeed, the first government to attempt to purchase their invention, the aeroplane, was the
British Government. Even before the Wrights succeeded in perfecting a
powered aeroplane, at a time when they had won a slight measure of fame

1

for themselves as accomplished glider pilots, a spy travelled from Britain to their home in Dayton, Ohio, in December 1902, in order to interview them about their work and about their accomplishments in the air.

There was good cause for this extraordinary British vigilance and interest in the early years of the present century. For ages past the British had always been concerned with what Arthur Balfour, the prime minister of that day, rightly called "this eternal and most important question of our safety against invasion". Until this time the British had defended their island home from all threat of invasion by controlling, with their fleets, the far and narrow seas. Command of the oceans was the dominating and vital factor of all British strategy and of British life itself. So long as the British Navy ruled the seas they could, as Sir John Fisher, one of their great admirals, told them, "sleep quiet in your beds". It is for this reason that the Royal Navy always occupied such a unique place in their thoughts, calculations, and affections. All observers were aware of these peculiar and particular sentiments. A foreigner, the great French historian, Halévy, remarked of the Navy in this very period that: ". . . the habit of counting upon the protection of her navy was so deeply ingrained in the British mind that it had become an instinct. England was in love with her navy." The British point of view in this regard was stated concisely by Sir Walter Raleigh in his classic official history, *The War in the Air*. He wrote: "The British navy is a great trust, responsible not so much for the progress of the nation as for its very existence".[1]

Now, however, some few men in Britain began to see the possibility of fundamental changes, however remote, in the strategic condition of their country. It was realized, though certainly not universally, that as soon as an efficient flying machine made its appearance England lay open to an invasion from the air, that her traditional reliance upon the Navy and seapower was no longer so valid as it had been in what was looked upon as the dawn of a new age, the air age. As one contemporary expressed it when he learned of what he believed to be the first successful aeroplane flight: "England is no longer an island".[2] In connection with this formidable novelty Sir Walter Raleigh wrote in his official history: "It is not extravagant to say that the 17th of December 1903, when the Wright brothers made the first free flight through the air in a power-driven machine, marks the beginning of a new era in the history of the world".[3]

---

[1] For Halévy's comment see his *History of the English People in The Nineteenth Century* (London, 1952), vol. VI, p. 582. For Raleigh's see Sir Walter Raleigh, *The War in the Air* (Oxford, 1922), vol. I, p. 3, hereafter cited as Raleigh, *The War in the Air*.

[2] The contemporary, as we shall see, was the great newspaper magnate, Lord Northcliffe.

[3] Raleigh, *The War in the Air*, p. 1.

It has been well said of Wilbur and Orville Wright that they changed the nature of human life on this planet. Man had aspired to fly for thousands of years. It was the Wright brothers who realized this dream of the ages. One admirer has pointed out that many people look upon their feat "as the most remarkable single achievement in the history of invention".[1] But the magnificence of their work has too often been taken for granted. Their creation was so stupendous that we tend, at times, to forget its high significance. Even worse, serious historical errors have been committed in recounting their story. These errors have had grievous consequences for any proper or accurate understanding of the origins of the British Air Services. Worse still, controversy has always been associated with their names. Some of those who have written about the Wrights praised them as few figures in history have been praised; but others condemned them in the harshest terms. Their genius aroused fierce enmity and brooding hostility. This attitude resulted in even more serious errors of historical interpretation which have, in their turn, concealed the truth about the earliest history of Britain's Air Forces.

In his official history Sir Walter Raleigh wrote of the Wrights' invention that: "When it was thrice offered to the British Government, between the years 1906 and 1908, it was thrice refused, twice by the War Office and once by the Admiralty".[2] This statement was incorrect in several important particulars but nearly every subsequent work concerned with British aviation history followed it in its errors, sometimes with serious historical consequences. This false view of the relationship between the British Government and the Wrights even found a place in the official archives. In a document prepared for the Cabinet by the Air Staff in 1937 Raleigh's statement about the Wrights was repeated in the following terms: "their invention had been refused . . . twice by the British War Office and once by the Admiralty . . . "[3]

There were results even more serious than this official lapse. When Percy B. Walker, a famous British aviation authority, was asked to prepare an authorized history of the Royal Aircraft Establishment, that great scientific institution which has been called "the cradle of British aviation", he produced a tremendous and powerful contribution to aeronautical history. However, his impressive book was marred by a curious, bitter and unrelenting antagonism to Wilbur Wright. He believed he had discovered in Wilbur's correspondence with the British authorities "indications of incipient paranoia" and "neurotic imbalance". These were cruel charges to level against one who had contributed so much to

[1] John Evangelist Walsh, *One Day at Kitty Hawk* (New York, 1975), p. 9, hereafter cited as Walsh, *One Day at Kitty Hawk*.

[2] Raleigh, *The War in the Air*, pp. 70–71.

[3] Cab. 21/524. "The Unified Air Force", undated, and docketed "Not to be circulated without reference to A.M."

human history and to the development of mankind. Furthermore, basing his opinion upon the incorrect details contained in *The War in the Air* Walker blamed the Wright brothers for Britain's failure to secure the Wright aeroplane. He called this failure a "tragedy" and he argued that "the universality of unsuccessful negotiation does bear out the belief that subconsciously the Wright Brothers did not want to sell their aeroplane; and especially does this appear to have been so in the course of the negotiations with Britain".[1] But we have to observe, in this introductory part of our study, that the exchanges between the Wright brothers and the British authorities were entirely more complicated than these official and authorized histories allowed.

Britain's negotiations with the Wrights present a record of lost opportunities and missed chances. In these developments time was a vital factor. The British failed to act positively until it was too late for them to act at all; until the secrets and unique accomplishments of the Wrights had been made available to the entire world. The American Government, for its part, made similar or even worse mistakes. They, too, neglected opportunity when it was presented to them in the years between 1905 and 1907. In 1909 this American failure to secure exclusive rights to the secrets of the Wright aeroplane was made public. There was popular outcry and expression of outrage in the United States. The story was revealed in the Sunday edition of *The New York Times* of 6 June 1909. The language of this newspaper account reflected the brashness and crudeness of the American journalism of that day. Nevertheless, the strictures it contained might have applied with equal force to the conduct of the British Government when it, too, lost genuine advantages in its competition with other nations. The *New York Times* article stated:

> HOW AMERICA LOST THE WRIGHT AEROPLANE
> . . . Here is the story of how the American Government lost the opportunity of controlling and owning absolutely the most effective war weapon invented since the discovery of gunpowder. It is the story of how the lethargy or mental stigmatism of a Government department deprived the American people from leading the world in methods of attack and defense . . .

If the Americans were thus remiss we have to notice that the British were even more inattentive to their country's needs when they failed to avail themselves of what the Wright brothers offered. Few Americans at that time were worried about an invasion of the United States. The

[1] See Percy B. Walker, *Early Aviation at Farnborough, The History of the Royal Aircraft Establishment*, vol. II, p. 62, hereafter cited as Walker, *Early Aviation at Farnborough*.

British, however, were genuinely concerned with such a possibility in the early years of the present century. For them, the appearance of vehicles that could fly through the air simply compounded their "eternal" problem – the problem of "safety against invasion".

It follows that any serious history of the Air Defence of Great Britain must begin with an account of these noble young Americans, at once heroes and men of genius.

II

Wilbur and Orville Wright, who were to solve problems the best minds of the world deemed insoluble, were the sons of Milton Wright, of Dayton, Ohio, a bishop in the United Brethren Church. Wilbur was born in 1867, and Orville in 1871. There were, in the Wright family, two older brothers and a younger sister. These Wrights were proud of their ancestry. A maternal grandfather, John Koerner, was so bitterly opposed to the militarism and autocracy of his native Germany that he left the country in 1818 and settled in Virginia. On the paternal side they could trace their line back to a John Wright who had purchased Kelvedon Hall in Essex in 1538. Another ancestor, Samuel Wright, removed from England in 1636 and established himself at Springfield, in Massachusetts.

Bishop Wright exercised a remarkable influence upon his family. He urged his children to think and to act independently and to value their own considered judgements. This resulted in a noteworthy strength of character which impressed many of the great men they met in later life. The bishop was a man of strict and high principle. Wilbur and Orville never drank or smoked and if it could be avoided they refused to do any work on Sundays. Milton Wright taught his children to respect others and to act in such a way that they could always respect themselves.

Both parents regularly encouraged the children to challenge accepted beliefs and ideas. The mother, Susan Koerner Wright, was blessed with a marvellous ability to understand how mechanical things worked. It was said in the family that "she could mend anything". These gifts were passed on to her children. The Wright family was marked out by a dry sense of humour that enabled them to laugh at themselves or at almost any predicament in which they might find themselves. Although their father was a man of moderate means they believed they had been endowed with "special advantages". Orville Wright once explained in this connection that: ". . . we were lucky enough to grow up in a home environment where there was always much encouragement to children to pursue intellectual interests; to investigate whatever aroused curiosity. In a different kind of environment our curiosity might have been nipped long before it could have borne fruit."[1]

Wilbur was a good student and a fine athlete. His trim and spare build enabled him to excel in a number of athletic activities. By 1885, when he was in his nineteenth year, his course seemed to be set. He was planning to attend the Yale Divinity School and become a minister, like his father. But then tragedy struck and ruined his life. He was playing hockey when a wildly swung stick was smashed into his mouth with stunning force. The blow knocked out nearly all his upper front teeth and many of the lower ones. Lips and gums were shattered. After a doctor had attended him the boy staggered home with his head swathed in bandages. The results of the mishap were grievous. Although false teeth restored his face after a time, there were complications. He began to suffer from a chronic stomach disorder which refused to respond to treatment. Even worse, he became convinced that his heart had been weakened and that it would soon fail him. He sank into a deep melancholy and refused to leave the house. In his opinion his shining future was now a thing of the past. This almost total seclusion lasted for several years and during all that time Wilbur Wright was not gainfully employed. He devoted himself to work around the house and to reading. When his mother became mortally ill he looked after her with great tenderness until she died but in his wretchedness and misery he withdrew from the world and remained almost a recluse, a cause of deep concern to his father and to the other members of the closely knit family.

Orville followed more lively pursuits during these years. He was restless and energetic. He looked forward to a career in business. He was interested especially in journalism and in printing. Gradually and by slow degrees Wilbur began to show a brotherly concern in his activities. By 1889 the new "safety bicycle", a machine with both wheels of the same size, was becoming popular in the United States. Orville bought one and was soon a keen competitor in nearly all the bicycle races and track competitions that took place in the city of Dayton. Wilbur also purchased a bicycle. He too attended the competitions but only as a spectator.

In 1892 the brothers, who were well aware of the fact that they were mechanics of first-class quality, decided to open a shop for the sale of bicycles. The business was a success. They determined not merely to sell or repair bicycles but to design and build machines of their own creation. As the fortunes of the Wright Cycle Company improved Wilbur and Orville opened a joint bank account. Each could deposit or withdraw money from it without consulting the other. There began to develop a

---

[1] See Fred C. Kelly, *The Wright Brothers* (London, 1944), p. 27, hereafter cited as Kelly, *The Wright Brothers*. Kelly's biography was "authorized" by Orville Wright.

relationship remarkable even for brothers. This singular closeness of mind and spirit would lead eventually to the invention of the aeroplane.

Wilbur was the first to become interested in the problem of human flight. In 1894 he read an article about a brilliant German engineer, Otto Lilienthal, who had succeeded in making hundreds of flights with a glider of his own invention. Unfortunately, these pioneering experiments ended in a disaster in 1896 when Lilienthal was killed in a gliding accident. The news of his death quickened Wilbur's latent interest in aeronautics; and he soon involved Orville in discussion and analysis of Lilienthal's achievements. They began to seek out, in Dayton's libraries, books on the subject of flight.

They also learnt of the work of a distinguished American scientist, Professor Samuel Pierpont Langley, the Secretary of the Smithsonian Institution. Langley believed in the possibility of successful flying machines, and he hoped to construct one. In pursuit of his goal, after years of thought and experiment, he built a small model which he called an "aerodrome". It was powered by a tiny steam engine. In May 1896 this unmanned device managed to fly through the air for more than a minute and Langley, in the following year, published an account of it in a popular journal.

As their reading and discussions continued the Wright brothers became convinced that human flight was possible; and that they wanted to play some part in achieving it. They had already arrived at some tentative conclusions about the mistakes Lilienthal had made. Then, in May 1899, a decisive step was taken. Wilbur decided to begin upon a systematic study of aeronautics and human flight. In his businesslike way he wrote a letter to the Smithsonian Institution in Washington in order to obtain exact information about what was already published in this field. The letter reflects the straightforward approach he adopted in beginning his great adventure. He wrote:

> . . . I am about to begin a systematic study of the subject in preparation for practical work to which I expect to devote what time I can spare from my regular business. I wish to obtain such papers as the Smithsonian Institution has published . . . and if possible a list of other works in print in the English language. I am an enthusiast, but not a crank in the sense that I have some pet theories as to the proper construction of a flying machine. I wish to avail myself of all that is already known and then if possible add my mite to help on the future worker who will attain final success. I do not know the terms on which you send out your publications but if you will inform me of the cost I will remit the price.[1]

[1] The letter is printed in the marvellous work of Marvin McFarland ed., *The Papers of Wilbur and Orville Wright* (New York, 1972), vol. I, pp. 4–5, hereafter cited as McFarland, *The Papers of Wilbur and Orville Wright*.

III

The authorities at the Smithsonian responded to Wilbur's request by sending him a number of pamphlets which they had published, and a list of books appropriate to his concerns. The brothers, who had already spent a considerable amount of time in observing the actions of birds in the air, now embarked upon a careful, detailed and intense examination of all that had been attempted or accomplished in the field of aeronautics.

One early reaction to this corpus of literature was a feeling of awe that some of the most capable minds in history had grappled with the problem of flight. They also learned from their reading that in the past decade or two several professional engineers, in Europe and in the United States, had become interested in the question. Some of these technical experts had built and experimented with various kinds of aircraft; and had published exact details of their researches and investigations. Although none had succeeded completely many believed that a flying machine could be constructed eventually. From these prodigious studies the Wrights gained, as they later put it in a classic article published in *The Century Magazine* for September 1908, "a good understanding of the nature of the flying problem".

Characteristically they came to a number of definite conclusions as a result of their analysis of the literature. They decided, as they explained it in their *Century Magazine* article, that in the field of aviation there were "two schools".

The first, represented by such men as Professor Langley, was chiefly concerned with questions of power, thrust and lift. These men wanted to construct a machine that would rise into the air by brute force even though they had little or no idea how they would control it once it was in flight. A second school, represented by Otto Lilienthal and his followers, adopted a different approach to the problem. These pioneers were mainly concerned with control in the air. They believed that a glider was the vehicle that would enable them to learn how to ride the air successfully – how to fly. By practice with a glider, the men of this school reckoned, they would encounter and learn how to overcome the actual problems of navigation in so unfamiliar a medium as the air. When the principles of successful flight were learnt and mastered, but not before, the advocates of this approach were prepared to add an engine to a machine they could already fly.

The sympathies of the Wright brothers were with the latter school. Their frugal, efficient, and puritanical nature would not permit them, as they put it in their article, "the wasteful extravagance of mounting delicate and costly machinery on wings which no one knew how to manage".

The Wrights came to the further conclusion that Otto Lilienthal had made the greatest advances in the art and technology of gliding flight. But they decided also that he had perished because his methods of flight control and the way he sought to maintain the balance of his machine in the air were entirely inadequate for his purpose.

When Lilienthal flew in his glider he found that the air was seldom uniform in its motion and that a sudden gust might lift one wing higher than the other. His problem was to restore equilibrium to the glider before it fell to the earth. He did so by shifting his body weight from side to side in an attempt to counteract the forces of the wind. The Wrights, for their part, rejected this method as unsound. They wanted to substitute for it a mechanical system that would enable the pilot to restore balance and equilibrium at will. "In order to meet the needs of large machines", they wrote in the *Century Magazine* article, "we wished to employ some system whereby the operator could vary at will the inclination of different parts of the wings, and thus obtain from the wind forces to restore the balance which the wind itself had disturbed".

It was at this stage of their reflections that the genius of the Wright brothers began to assert itself. It seemed to them that if they applied this concept of a compound surface for the wings, and extended it to supplementary adjustable shapes in the form of elevators and rudders, they could create a system of aircraft control of genuine promise. Wilbur Wright took the lead in these developments. In August 1899, in order to see if their theories would work in practice, he built a five-foot biplane kite with wings that could be "warped", or twisted, at the tips. The "warping" was controlled from the ground by means of cords and short sticks. When the kite was flown in a field near Dayton it proved to be an instant success. Wilbur could direct its performance in the air, almost at will. The Wrights realized that plenty of problems and mysteries still confronted them in their quest but they understood, as well, that they now possessed a control system superior to anything that had been achieved before.

IV

The next step followed at once. They now decided to build a large man-carrying glider. This phase of their researches was planned with exquisite care. The new glider would require a testing area of very considerable size. Moreover, the testing-ground would have to be in a place where there were steady winds, and owing to the mortal hazards involved, a relatively smooth surface would also be indispensable. In November 1899 Wilbur began a correspondence with the United States Weather Bureau in order to obtain details about wind velocities in the Chicago area; and to find out if there were any government publications that contained such information.

The brothers also decided to take another important step. In May 1900 Wilbur wrote a letter to Octave Chanute, the foremost authority on aeronautics in the United States. We must mark Chanute well. He played an important and recurring part in our story.

Octave Chanute was a civil engineer of outstanding achievement. He was born in Paris in 1832 but emigrated to the United States with his parents when he was six years of age. Chanute began his professional career humbly, as an ordinary railroad worker, but he soon rose to become an engineer of remarkable abilities. In time he became responsible for the construction of rail lines that extended from Chicago to Texas. He designed, and completed in 1869, the famous Kansas City Bridge which spanned, for the first time, the treacherous Missouri River. In 1867 he won a competition for the design of the Union Stockyards of Chicago, and supervised their construction. In 1873 Chanute was appointed chief engineer for the Erie Railroad. He also concerned himself in the building of the "elevated railroads" of New York City. In 1880 he developed an interest in the study of wood preservation and began to build a number of wood-preserving plants, chiefly to serve railroads; and this business became his chief professional occupation in the later phases of his life.

Chanute had been interested in aeronautics for some years but his concern developed into fascination in 1875. In that year he visited Europe and there took particular notice of the work and theories of an Englishman, Francis Herbert Wenham, a well-known marine engineer and an early member of the Aeronautical Society of Great Britain. Wenham believed firmly that artificial flight by man was possible; and he predicted it would be achieved by systematic scientific study. Chanute was intrigued by his concepts and ideas. In the 1880s he launched a campaign to awaken the interest of other American engineers in the subject of flight. He lectured, almost without respite, to engineering societies, scientific associations, and to students at engineering colleges.

By 1889 Chanute found he possessed the money, and also the leisure, to devote himself to this new interest. He embarked upon a prolific correspondence with all those interested in aeronautics, in every part of the world. He also engaged in a systematic course of reading and undertook the task of classifying all the aeronautical information then in existence. In 1891 he began to write a series of articles for the *Railroad and Engineering Journal*; these papers resulted in the appearance of his classic book, *Progress in Flying Machines*, which was published in 1894. The book was at once a history of attempts to solve the flying problem and also, as a result of his analysis of successes and failures, a valuable guide for anyone who proposed to make further advances in these spheres.

Chanute, as a result of the information he acquired, came to recognize the quality of Otto Lilienthal's achievements and decided, in 1896, to experiment with machines of the Lilienthal type, at Dune Park, some fifty miles from Chicago. There, in company with a number of associates, he made definite but incomplete advances in the art of flying.

By May 1900, when Wilbur Wright approached him, Octave Chanute was in his sixty-ninth year. He was, at this stage of his life, a kind and generous old man but he was no longer the keen-minded technician of his youth. His scientific abilities had been dulled with the passage of time.[1] Nevertheless, a curious desire still flickered and burned in his breast. It was not simply that he was garrulous. He wanted to be recognized by his peers as the man who knew everything about the latest developments in the world of aeronautics. He hoped to learn the exact details of the most recent experiments; and to report the results to anyone prepared to listen to him. Chanute was in the grip of this singular ambition. In his case it took the form of what may only be called a fierce determination to tell all he had learnt of the work of others, even if they were not yet ready to reveal it themselves. He would not keep a secret.

In the early stages of the warm relationship that grew up between them and Chanute, the Wright brothers were not especially worried about secrecy. It took them some time to realize that they had secrets to protect. In their enthusiasm they informed Chanute of almost everything they did, or planned to do. Later, when they grasped the fact that they were making scientific and technical progress that was unique, they became concerned with the older man's restless desire to reveal the details of their innovations; but they found they were usually unable to stop him. He wrote or spoke about them to experts in France and in Germany; and he also reported their achievements to his correspondents in Great Britain.

His activities in this regard may be illustrated by an example. It is known that Chanute travelled to Paris in the spring of 1903. By that time the Wright brothers had made the most astonishing advances in their work. There he delivered an illustrated lecture and later wrote articles about their accomplishments for an audience of French experts – and rivals. After his lecture, in preparation for his articles, he wrote to Augustus Moore Herring, an engineer he employed to assist him in his aeronautical experiments, in order to ask him to prepare exact drawings of his gliders, which could not fly well, and also drawings of the Wright brothers' glider, which could.

On 17 May 1903 Chanute wrote to Herring: "I . . . enclose my check for $35 in settlement of balance for your services . . . The drawings which I want are for the French Aviators. I found them much interested in our gliding machines and promised to send them detailed plans of the multiple wing, the two surfaced, and the Wright glider. If you are too busy

---

[1] See in this connection the conclusions of a modern authority, Harry Combs, *Kill Devil Hill* (Boston, 1979), p. 125, hereafter cited as Combs, *Kill Devil Hill*.

to make them soon, I will have the drawings made here . . ."[1] The
comment of a brilliant aviation authority about the first of Chanute's
articles, published in France in August 1903, is pertinent to the present
account and analysis: "This article is one of the most important documents in aviation history; for it was here that the Wrights' . . . glider was
first presented visually to the world, through both general arrangement
drawings (plan, side-elevation, and front-elevation), and one excellent
photograph."[2]

V

Octave Chanute replied in the most courteous terms to Wilbur's letter of
May 1900. After offering advice and encouragement he suggested various
places that might prove suitable for their proposed gliding experiments.
Eventually, after correspondence with the United States Weather
Bureau the Wrights selected the hamlet of Kitty Hawk in North Carolina
as their experimental ground. This area, they were told by the authorities,
was subject to steady breezes and it possessed almost endless stretches of
sand. These factors were of particular significance in their planning. The
Wrights were keenly aware of the hard fact that when the time came for
them to sail aloft in their man-carrying glider they would be risking their
lives. Lilienthal's fate was one they kept in their minds whenever they left
their workshop for the field of action and trial.

In September 1900 Wilbur travelled to Kitty Hawk and began to
assemble the parts of the large glider they had built in the previous month.
Orville arrived later and then the experiments commenced.

The chief object of their excursion was to test the efficiency and range
of the controls they had devised for the glider; and also to obtain practice
in their use. The experimental method was worked out with some care.
They planned to fly the glider first as a man-carrying kite. It was to be
tethered to a small wooden tower they called a "derrick". Free flight in
the air would be entirely too dangerous in the first stages of this novel
enterprise. Gliding flight would be attempted only after Wilbur, the pilot,
had gained some experience in working his machine in the air when it was
still held fast to the derrick. The results of these 1900 trials were mixed.
The wings of the glider were clearly deficient in the lifting power their
calculations had led them to anticipate. But their control of the machine
in the air was even better than they had dared to expect. In flight the glider

---

[1] Octave Chanute Papers (Library of Congress): O. Chanute to Herring, 17
May 1903.
[2] Charles Harvard Gibbs-Smith, *The Rebirth of European Aviation, 1902–
1908: A Study of the Wright Brothers' Influence* (London, 1974), p. 71, hereafter
cited as Gibbs-Smith, *Rebirth of European Aviation*.

responded beautifully to the control systems they had incorporated in its construction. Owing to the deficiencies shown by their wings they were unable to gain the amount of practice they had hoped for but their new system of balance inspired them with genuine confidence for the future. They resolved to build another glider and to return with it to Kitty Hawk in the following year.

As a result of these experiences in the field the Wright brothers were stimulated to advance even further toward the fulfilment of their dream, the creation of a vehicle that a man might fly in the air. Nothing minor could now serve to satisfy their purpose. They proposed, after excited discussion, to build a machine that would be more than twice the size of anything ever contemplated by Lilienthal or Chanute, and nearly twice the size of the glider designed by Percy Pilcher, an outstanding British aeronaut and engineer who had lost his life in a gliding accident in 1899. These predecessors always believed that certain death must follow any attempt to fly a glider of the size planned by the Wrights; but Wilbur and Orville reckoned that their new control system would enable them to manipulate the huge surfaces in perfect safety.

In November 1900 Wilbur sent Octave Chanute a detailed account of their experiments and experiences at Kitty Hawk. In his courteous and civil way he congratulated the brothers, heartily, upon their successes. He wrote also: "I have lately been asked to prepare an article for *Cassier's Magazine*, and I should like your permission to allude to your experiments in such brief and guarded way as you may indicate".[1] After hesitation and qualification Wilbur agreed to this request and the article was published, eventually, in June 1901.

In constructing the wings for their new glider the Wrights depended, in good part, upon the calculations of Otto Lilienthal, which they read in translation.[2] While this work was going forward, in June 1901 Chanute came to Dayton in order to meet the brothers. Their friendship, based until this time upon correspondence, was now strengthened by personal contact. Indeed, after this meeting Chanute hoped to join the brothers' researches with his own, in one way or another. Eventually, it was arranged that two of his associates would stay with them, at his expense, in their camp at Kitty Hawk in order to help them in any way that they could, and also to test one of Chanute's gliders which would be assembled there. The associates were George Spratt and E. C. Huffaker. Chanute

---

[1] See McFarland, *The Papers of Wilbur and Orville Wright*, p. 45.

[2] Aviation historians sometimes disagree about the part played in this work by the Wrights' sister, Katharine. One way in which she helped them was to enlist the aid of the local high school teacher, William Werthner, who translated passages "in current German aeronautical publications, especially several by Lilienthal . . ." See Professor William Werthner, "Personal Recollections of the Wrights" in *Aero Club of America Bulletin*, July 1912, vol. 1, p. 13.

took good care to explain to the brothers that Spratt was "discreet concerning other people's ideas. Huffaker I consider quite reliable. I mention this as you told me you have no patents".[1] Chanute was so impressed with the Wright brothers that after a time he, too, visited them in their remote camp, in August 1901, and took several photographs of their new glider in flight.

The trials of the glider took place in July and August 1901 at the Kill Devil Hills, a cluster of sand dunes four miles south of Kitty Hawk. To their great surprise, this new machine proved to be a bitter disappointment to its inventors. Once again, the lifting power of the wings was shown to be inadequate. But on this occasion problems of control that had not appeared before also made themselves evident. The glider did not respond in the manner expected of it. Wilbur risked his life in repeated attempts to penetrate these mysteries. In the course of one flight the glider suddenly plunged into the ground and he suffered bruises to his nose and eye. After modifications to the wings some splendid glides were finally achieved so that Chanute, the expert authority in these matters, was able to assure the brothers that their results were better than any that had ever been attained before. Nevertheless, gloom now dominated their outlook.

There was good reason for this change of view. The Wright brothers now began to suspect that the published calculations of Lilienthal, and all other authorities, were incorrect. It followed that if no reliance could be placed upon them there was no genuine theoretical basis for the design of wings. The Wrights came to the conclusion that they might be forced to reject all previous aerodynamic theory expressed in quantitative terms. Such a possibility, after their years of hard work, appalled them. The enormity of their task now seemed overwhelming. On the journey home from Kitty Hawk Wilbur told Orville: "Not within a thousand years would man ever fly". In their *Century Magazine* article they described the new situation concisely: "The experiments of 1901 were far from encouraging . . . we saw that the calculations upon which all flying machines had been based were unreliable, and that all were simply groping in the dark. Having set out with absolute faith in the existing scientific data, we were driven to doubt one thing after another, till finally, after two years of experiment, we cast it all aside . . . Truth and error were everywhere so intimately mixed as to be undistinguishable."

Despite his great disappointment Wilbur quickly recovered from the depression which settled upon him after his frustrating experiences at the Kill Devil Hills in the summer of 1901. In a short time the enthusiasm of the brothers was revived; and they set to work again to try and solve the technical problems which had plagued them there. Chanute, from his

[1] See McFarland, *The Papers of Wilbur and Orville Wright*, p. 65.

home in Chicago, proved a constant source of encouragement. Then, on 29 August 1901, after talking with some members of the Western Society of Engineers, he wrote to Wilbur and invited him to address that body on the subject of his gliding experiments. Chanute, as president of the Society, promised also that Wilbur's lecture would be published in its official transactions. Here, indeed, was a challenge for the recluse of only a few years earlier. At first Wilbur proposed to decline the invitation but his sister cajoled him into accepting it. His sense of humour helped him in his preparation of the talk. When he was asked by Orville and his sister whether the lecture was to be "witty or scientific" he quipped that "he thought it would be pathetic before he got through with it! . . ."[1]

Wilbur Wright's lecture to the Western Society of Engineers, delivered in Chicago on the evening of 18 September 1901, and published in the *Journal* of the Society in December of that year, was a triumph. It has been called "one of the most significant aeronautical lectures ever delivered". It has been "reprinted and quoted as often as any other article ever written on the subject of flying".[2]

On that September evening Wilbur was introduced to the company by President Chanute. This introduction was later published, for all to see, together with the address itself. In his opening remarks Chanute, an authority of international distinction, told the audience of the Wright brothers: "These gentlemen have been bold enough to attempt some things which neither Lilienthal nor Pilcher nor myself dared to do. They have used surfaces very much greater in extent than those which hitherto had been deemed safe, and they have accomplished very remarkable results, part of which it was my privilege to see on a visit which I paid to their camp about a month ago."[3]

Wilbur began his talk in the boldest manner possible. There was no sign of hesitation or doubt in the message he delivered to the assembled engineers. He explained to his audience that there were three general classes of difficulties that still obstructed the "pathway to success" in the building of a successful flying machine. The first of these concerned the

---

[1] McFarland, *The Papers of Wilbur and Orville Wright*, p. 95
[2] For these comments see the extremely important article by J. Laurence Pritchard, "The Wright Brothers and the Royal Aeronautical Society" in the *Journal of the Royal Aeronautical Society*, vol. 57, No. 516, December 1953, p. 756, hereafter cited as Pritchard, *The Wright Brothers and the Royal Aeronautical Society*; and Kelly, *The Wright Brothers*, p. 63.
[3] See "Some Aeronautical Experiments" by Mr. Wilbur Wright with introduction by President Chanute in the *Journal of the Western Society of Engineers*, vol. VI, no. 6, December 1901. The subsequent quotations from Wilbur's lecture are taken from this source. The lecture was also reprinted in the annual *Report* of the Smithsonian Institution in 1902. Chanute called it a "devilish good paper, which will be extensively quoted". See for this McFarland, *The Papers of Wilbur and Orville Wright*, p. 168.

construction of the sustaining wings; the second related to the generation and application of the power required to drive the machine through the air; and the third was concerned with the balancing and steering of the machine after it was actually in flight. He claimed that the first two of these categories of problems were already "to a certain extent solved". He emphasized, however, that "the inability to balance and steer still confronts students of the flying problem. . . . When this one feature has been worked out", he concluded, "the age of flying machines will have arrived for all other difficulties are of minor importance". In order to illustrate his point Wilbur went on to say:

> . . . If I take this piece of paper, and after placing it parallel to the ground, quickly let it fall, it will not settle steadily down as a staid, sensible piece of paper ought to do, but it insists on contravening every recognised rule of decorum, turning over and darting hither and thither in the most erratic manner, much after the style of an untrained horse. Yet this is the style of steed that men must learn to manage before flying can become an everyday sport.

Wilbur proceeded to tell his listeners of the historic work of Lilienthal, Pilcher, and Chanute; and then he went on to recount the technical details of his and Orville's more recent experiments with their gliders. He carefully suggested that their calculations in the area of wing design now differed from those of Lilienthal. He emphasized, at the end of his discourse, that the way forward in these early stages of the art lay not with the advocates of powered flight, like Professor Langley, but only with the operators of gliding machines who could learn how to increase their knowledge and skill while they were flying in the air.

Octave Chanute was so pleased with this lecture that he ordered three hundred offprints of it when it was published, in December 1901. "One half is to be sent to you", he told Wilbur, "and I will distribute the remainder among my foreign and domestic correspondents".[1]

Thus, owing to Chanute's actions, all those interested in the developing science of aeronautics, in every part of the world, were made aware of the pioneering achievements of the Wright brothers; and of the direction in which they proposed to advance in order to develop a powered aeroplane that could navigate successfully in the air.

---

[1] McFarland, *The Papers of Wilbur and Orville Wright*, p. 184.

VI

When the Wrights returned from Kitty Hawk in the late summer of 1901 they were full of doubt about the validity of Lilienthal's calculations; and, as a result of their recent experiences in the field they also mistrusted all the other published calculations dealing with wing construction. Indeed, at this stage of their course they realized that they were confronted by two sets of problems which still had to be solved before their goal could be won. In the first place they had to design and build an efficient wing that would provide their machine with sufficient and adequate aerodynamic lift; secondly, the old problem of the control of their aircraft in flight still remained with them. When Wilbur returned from his visit to Chicago they began a joint attack in these areas of inquiry. Orville once remarked of their cooperative efforts: "I can remember when Wilbur and I could hardly wait for morning to come to get at something that interested us. *That*'s happiness."[1]

They now embarked upon a series of scientific experiments that enabled them to establish fundamental principles which had never been grasped before. They built a wind-tunnel, of their own design, and in it they tested more than two hundred types of wing surfaces. They discovered that the published figures dealing with these surfaces were, indeed, incorrect; but as a result of their meticulous testing they were able to compile original and valid tables of figures of their own. They now possessed knowledge that no one else had ever had before. These wind-tunnel experiments made it possible for them to abandon empirical methods of construction in building the wings for their famous glider of 1902. This work in their laboratory enabled them to design a machine that could lift itself into the air. At every stage of the way Octave Chanute was kept informed of these developments. He wrote to them: "It is perfectly marvellous to me how quickly you get results with your testing machine. . . . You are . . . better equipped to test the endless variety of curved surfaces than any body has ever been . . ."[2]

As the nature of their scientific advances was made clear to him Chanute became fascinated. He was also generous. From time to time he offered the Wrights funds of his own in order to provide them with the time they needed to pursue their research. In each case these kindly offers were refused. Chanute had devoted much of his life to aeronautics. When he recognized the quality of the Wright brothers' achievements he made a remarkable proposition. In December 1901 he wrote to Wilbur:[3]

---

[1] Fred C. Kelly, "Traits of the Wright Brothers" in *Technology Review*, vol. 51, June 1949, p. 504.
[2] McFarland, *The Papers of Wilbur and Orville Wright*, p. 156.
[3] *Ibid.*, p. 183.

I very much regret in the interest of science that you have reached
a stopping place, for further experimenting on your part promises
important results . . . If however some rich man should give you
$10,000 a year to go on, to connect his name with progress, would
you do so? I happen to know Carnegie. Would you like for me to
write to him? In any event . . . I hope that you will prepare a paper
. . . so that your discoveries shall not be lost to others. I would take
pleasure in presenting such a paper either to the Western Society of
Engineers, or to the American Association for the Advancement of
Science, of which I happen to be a member . . .

Chanute now encountered the sturdy independence of the Wright
brothers which was to have an effect later, when they dealt with the agents
of their own government and with those of foreign powers. Wilbur
replied that he had thought about a career in science but that it would be
entirely too dangerous for him to neglect his business since such neglect
might wreck it. He expressed his appreciation for the offer, but he refused
to accept it. He planned to gain his object in his own way.

In addition to their wind-tunnel experiments the Wright brothers also
worked on the other problem that still concerned them, the problem of
control in the air. They understood that they had made tremendous
advances in this area but they realized also that their achievements were
still not enough for the true and absolutely controlled flight they were
seeking to attain. In 1901 when they had tried to turn their glider in the air
it had become unmanageable. They now added a vertical rudder or tail to
the machine and hoped it would help them solve this problem. The new
glider they prepared for the trials of 1902 incorporated these various
changes. It was even larger than the huge machine of the previous year.

The Wrights left Dayton in August 1902 and established themselves in
their old camp near the Kill Devil Hills. The gliding tests began in
September. The first glides with the new machine were made only a few
feet above the ground but as the work continued it became clear that the
lifting power of the new wings was exactly what they had predicted. The
machine soared across the sands in longer and longer flights.

The control problem was not solved so easily, however. As long as the
brothers flew in straight lines the glider responded adequately. When
they attempted a steep turn in the air there were desperate troubles.
Eventually they achieved genuine control when turning in the air by
coupling the rudder to the wing-warping device. This arrangement
required a very high order of skill from the pilot but they found that the
adjustments they made served their purpose perfectly. In September and
October 1902 the brothers made nearly one thousand gliding flights in
which they proved the effectiveness of the various devices they had
invented for the control of their machine in so unfamiliar an element as

the air. It has been well said of this achievement that the "basic elements of control, universal in all subsequent airplanes, were now embodied in the Wrights' glider".[1] They had triumphed at last. Their almost unwavering perseverance had enabled them to overcome every obstacle. All that remained for them to do was to fit an engine to their machine.

Early in October Octave Chanute arrived in the camp, accompanied by his assistant, Augustus M. Herring. He was astonished by the quality of the Wrights' performances in the air. When he left about ten days later their achievements dominated his mind. Upon his return home Chanute found a letter awaiting him from one of his many aeronautical correspondents. In this case the writer was Major B. F. S. Baden-Powell, Scots Guards. This letter was to set up a train of remarkable events that proved to be of genuine significance in the development of Britain's Air Services. Major Baden-Powell explained to Chanute, in his letter, that he had not written to him for several years because he had been away at the front during the South African War. His letter stated:[2]

> 32 Princes Gate
> London S.W.
>
> Sept. 27th 02
>
> Dear Sir
> It is a very long time since you have heard from me, I having only lately returned after nearly 3 years active service in South Africa.
> I have now returned to be as keen as ever about aeronautics, and intend if I get the opportunity, to set to work to conduct some big experiments.
> I hear that a Mr. Wright has been doing some good work in America. Do you know of any full account being published of his experiments?
> . . . We should always be very glad of any notes of what is going on in America . . .
>
> Yours faithfully,
> B. Baden-Powell

---

[1] See the excellent work of Lloyd Morris and Kendall Smith, *Ceiling Unlimited* (New York, 1953), pp. 38–9, hereafter cited as Morris and Smith, *Ceiling Unlimited*.

[2] Octave Chanute Papers, B. Baden-Powell to Chanute, 27 September 1902.

CHAPTER 2

How the British Learned of the Wrights and their Achievements

Major B. F. S. Baden-Powell – His military career – His interest in aeronautics – His man-lifting kites – He corresponds with Chanute – Professor Langley – Percy Pilcher – The St Louis World's Fair – Chanute's letter about the Wrights – A Presidential Address – Patrick Young Alexander – He travels to Dayton – "he may have some secret connection with the Government" – The need to protect secrets – Percy Walker's bizarre charges – The temptation of Octave Chanute – The Wrights build an engine – They design propellers – Their sense of humour – The failure of Professor Langley – Octave Chanute tells all – His correspondence with Alexander – He arranges to meet Alexander – Alexander makes a mistake – "the age of the flying machine had come at last" – Chanute reports the results – Colonel Capper becomes interested.

I

At the time he wrote to Octave Chanute Major Baden Fletcher Smyth Baden-Powell was a soldier of some considerable experience; and already a leading figure in the early development of British military aviation. He was a member of a well-known Victorian family. His father, the Reverend Baden Powell, had been Savilian Professor of Geometry in the University of Oxford. The father was at once a theologian of genuine eminence and also a distinguished, if controversial, scientist. The real power in the family, however, lay with the mother. Henrietta Grace Smyth Powell was the daughter of an admiral and a grand-niece of Nelson. In 1860 when her husband died she demonstrated a remarkable devotion to his memory by changing the family surname to Baden-Powell; and insisted so vigorously upon the new form that some of her relatives began to call her "Old Mrs Hyphen". One of Baden-Powell's more famous brothers was Robert Stephenson Smyth Baden-Powell, the hero of the defence of Mafeking in the Boer War, and later founder of the Boy Scout Movement.

The Baden-Powell who is our concern was educated at Charterhouse. In 1882 he joined the Scots Guards and two years later he saw active service with the Guards Camel Corps on the Nile. In 1888 he became A.D.C. to Sir Anthony Musgrave, the Governor of Queensland; and in the following year he joined a punitive expedition that was sent to New Guinea. After further service in Queensland Baden-Powell returned to his regiment and was present at a number of the famous engagements of the South African War including Belmont, Modder River, Magersfontein, Paarderberg, and also the relief of Mafeking. Early in life he developed a passionate interest in aeronautics. He believed firmly in its military value and did all he could to impress his superiors with the soundness of this opinion.

The problem with Baden-Powell was that while he had built up an international reputation in aeronautics it was one he did not deserve. He was an enthusiast possessed of an energy that was truly astonishing. Tirelessly he experimented, wrote and lectured on the subject of aviation but he lacked the technical training and ability to make or even recognize genuine or original contributions. He looked upon himself as an inventor. Among the things he tried to "invent" in the course of his lifetime were a new type of bicycle; a motor-driven aeroplane; various man-lifting kites; and dirigibles. He was not especially successful in these technical forays but his enthusiasm, especially in the field of aeronautics, never faltered.

As a young man in 1880 he joined the Aeronautical Society of Great Britain. The membership of this distinguished body was made up, in good part, of professional engineers who believed in the possibility of successful mechanical flight. Indeed, the Aeronautical Society of Great Britain was the first engineering organization in the world to exhibit a serious interest in the aeroplane. When the society was founded in 1866 the Duke of Argyll became its president and a number of eminent scientists joined its Council. In this way the entire subject of aeronautics was given a respectable standing that it had not attained before. In time, some of the finest and most celebrated engineers in Britain took part in its activities and deliberations. The Society sponsored lecture series and aeronautical exhibitions. It published its famous *Annual Reports* which contained the most trustworthy and accurate information in articles of a consistently high quality.

For some years the Society flourished but after a time it suffered a serious decline in interest, and in membership. It was Baden-Powell who was responsible for a dramatic revival of its fortunes. He became secretary and as a result of his tireless efforts the organization sprang into renewed life. It may be said, accurately, that in 1897 he "refounded" the Aeronautical Society of Great Britain. While he was on active service in South Africa, in gratitude for his earlier contributions he was selected as the Society's president, *in absentia*. He thus attained for himself a position of genuine eminence and distinction in the world of aeronautics.

Baden-Powell was convinced that the proper application of aeronautic-al knowledge could serve the technical purposes of the British Army in a number of ways. In 1894, with this object in mind, he constructed and began to experiment with a number of man-lifting kites which were designed to carry an observer into the air so that he could survey distant enemy positions. The military value of these kites lay in the fact that they could be raised aloft in breezes or winds that were too strong to permit the employment of the more familiar captive observation balloons. In 1894 at the Pirbright Camp, near Aldershot, Baden-Powell, short in stature, with a sturdy figure and a heavy military moustache, vigorously carried out a number of experiments with his kites. The tests met with a certain measure of success so that the authorities at the War Office developed an interest in the work. Nevertheless, Baden-Powell's particular design was looked upon as a failure because, in the words of one technical expert, "the kites from time to time made separate dangerous sideways somersaults".[1]

By this time Baden-Powell had begun to correspond with a number of aeronautical authorities in various parts of the world. One of his Amer-ican correspondents was Octave Chanute, in a letter to whom in May 1896 he described his kites. Later he revealed a measure of disappointment, and discontent, with his superiors, writing to Chanute: ". . . I can only speak from experience of our own Govt. & can . . . say that they are most unsatisfactory . . . They will apparently have nothing to say to any invention (1) unless it is proved to be thoroughly successful & practical in all respects or (2) you have sufficient private influence with the officials concerned to get them to take an interest in the matter. But I have complaints from all sides of inventors who cannot get the authorities to look at their inventions. Our Government, as far as I know never undertakes to complete any invention or carry out any ideas suggested to them. More's the pity."[2]

By 1898, with good cause, both men became seriously interested in the practical development of powered aeroplanes for military purposes. In that year the United States Government decided to appropriate large sums of money for such work. Early in the year diplomatic relations between Spain and the United States became particularly tense and it was expected that war between the two countries would follow as a result of their disagreements about conditions in Cuba. President William

---

[1] Harald Penrose, *British Aviation, The Pioneer Years 1903–1914* (London, 1967), p. 44, hereafter cited as Penrose, *British Aviation, The Pioneer Years.*

[2] Octave Chanute Papers, B. Baden-Powell to Chanute, 2nd October 1896. These remarks were made with particular reference to the prospects of a "flying machine" if it were offered to a European government.

McKinley had been impressed earlier by the partial successes of Professor Samuel Pierpont Langley's model "aerodromes". As a result of his initiatives a joint board made up of officers of the Army and Navy was appointed with instructions to examine Langley's steam-powered models. Eventually, and in consequence of the president's directives, the United States Army's Board of Ordnance and Fortifications invited Professor Langley to undertake the construction and testing of a full-sized flying-machine. The American authorities did not believe that Langley could at once furnish them with a practical engine of war but they did feel that his experiments could lead to the development of a military aircraft that might, in time, take its place in the American arsenal.

Eventually these bold arrangements were secured, and Professor Langley, in the course of the year 1898, received two allotments of $25,000 each, in order to carry out the enterprise. Although a standard aviation history has declared that the project remained a secret until 1903, this was not the case. Reports about it were published in both the American and the British Press, and Major Baden-Powell seized on them as soon as they appeared. On 17th December 1898 he wrote to Chanute and enclosed in his letter a cutting from the *Pall Mall Gazette*, dated 5 December. *The Pall Mall Gazette* article stated:

> The United States Government is going to be the first to experiment with flying machines, as distinct from balloons, for reconnoitring and military purposes. A sum of 25,000 dols. has just been apportioned for this purpose by the Board of Ordnance and experiments are to be made by General Greely with the scientific assistance of Professor Langley, the most distinguished authority on aeronautics across the Atlantic.

In his letter Baden-Powell enquired of Chanute: ". . . Is the enclosed paragraph correct? It looks like a good beginning."[1]

Exciting developments were also taking place in Britain. A few days later Baden-Powell wrote to Chanute again in order to tell him about the work of Percy Pilcher, the brilliant British disciple of Lilienthal, who was to perish in a gliding accident only a few months later. Pilcher has been called "the only man who by temperament, training and achievement could have anticipated the Wrights in powered flying". He knew Baden-Powell well and the major, in his letter, informed Chanute of the status and condition of his experiments:[2]

[1] Octave Chanute Papers, B. Baden-Powell to Chanute, 17 December 1898. The standard aviation history that stated the project remained secret is the excellent work of Morris and Smith *Ceiling Unlimited*, p. 4.
[2] Octave Chanute Papers, B. Baden-Powell to Chanute, 26 January 1899. The reference to Pilcher's great ability is in Gibbs-Smith, *Aviation*, p. 26.

I presume . . . that you have not done anything more yourself with your gliding machines – which seems a pity. Pilcher still talks of applying a small engine & screw propellor to his gliding machine – and indeed *has* both for he showed them to me the other day – but he is so busy on other things that he has been unable to fit the thing up. . . .

II

When Major Baden-Powell left England for the war in South Africa this correspondence with Chanute came to an end for a time. Upon his return from the scene of action it was expected of Baden-Powell that he would, after a reasonable interval, deliver his presidential address to the Aeronautical Society of Great Britain. This sturdy, upright, and honest Victorian soldier who had served with camels on the Upper Nile and who had fought in the field in the last great colonial war of the British Empire, had now become involved in technical areas which were, simply put, beyond his reach. He was not equipped to explain, in detail, to a company of professional engineers and scientists, the latest advances, accomplishments, or innovations in the field of aeronautics. He planned, therefore, to survey the most recent developments for his audience and to call to their attention, in general terms, the work of different aeronautical experimenters, in various parts of the world. In these circumstances he was very glad to take up, once again, his interrupted exchanges with Octave Chanute, the great American authority in this field.

Octave Chanute, for his part, was delighted to receive Baden-Powell's letter of 27 September 1902 enquiring about "a Mr. Wright" who "has been doing some good work in America". At this time Chanute had become involved in the preparations for a great World's Fair, known as the St Louis Exhibition, which was to be held in 1904 at the direction of President Theodore Roosevelt, to celebrate the centennial of the purchase of the Louisiana Territory from Napoleon. As a part of the World's Fair it was proposed to hold, at St Louis, an International Aeronautical Congress; and the Fair's authorities asked Chanute to assist them in making the proposal known to aeronauts in every part of the world. In the autumn of 1902, therefore, Chanute's mind was occupied with the prospects of this St Louis Exhibition, and also with the recent achievements of Wilbur and Orville Wright at the Kill Devil Hills near Kitty Hawk.

Major Baden-Powell was not, of course, Chanute's only correspondent in Great Britain. In March 1902, before the Wrights had gone to Kitty Hawk and to their great triumphs of that year, Chanute had written about them to Alexander McCullum, another member of the Aeronautical

Society of Great Britain. In his letter Chanute described the methods employed by the Wrights when they warped the wings of their glider and he also explained how they were able to land their machine safely. He told McCullum that the Wrights had made genuine advances in their work but his letter ended on a note of caution. He explained to McCullum: "The Wrights have no intention of adding a motor yet. They will try more gliding experiments next autumn, when vacation time comes."[1]

Now, however, after the Wrights had completed their marvellous experiments of 1902, Chanute wrote of them to Baden-Powell in entirely different terms. In his letter he informed Baden-Powell of the planned Aeronautical Congress at St Louis; he mentioned Wilbur Wright's address to the Western Society of Engineers, delivered in the previous December; and he added startling new information that was certain to excite all those in Britain interested in the development of powered flight.

This letter turned out to be a document of tremendous significance in the history of early British military aeronautics. Chanute wrote to Baden-Powell:[2]

> Chicago, ILL. Oct. 21st 1902
> B. Baden-Powell
> 32, Princes Gate. London S.W.
>
> My dear Mr Baden Powell.
> I am very glad that you are back from S. Africa, and to get once more in touch with you. I received your letter of Sep 27th upon my return from witnessing this season's gliding experiments of the brothers Wright. They have made a very considerable advance since last year and now glide at angles of 6° to 7°, sustaining 125 to 160 lbs. per *net* horsepower. I mail separately Mr. Wright's paper of last year (he will write another this year) and a copy of the rules for the St. Louis contests in 1904.
> Wright is now doing nearly as well as the Vulture, is not far from soaring flight, and I am changing my views as to the advisibility of applying a motor . . .
>
> Faithfully yours
> O. Chanute

Octave Chanute's letter contained exactly the kind of information Major Baden-Powell required for the preparation of his presidential

---

[1] Octave Chanute Papers, O. Chanute to Alex McCullum, 4 March 1902. Part of this letter is printed in J. Laurence Pritchard, *The Wright Brothers and the Royal Aeronautical Society*, p. 747.

[2] Octave Chanute Papers, O. Chanute to B. Baden-Powell, 21 October 1902. A copy of this letter is printed in J. Laurence Pritchard, *The Wright Brothers and the Royal Aeronautical Society*, p. 751.

address. This oration was delivered to the membership of the Aeronautical Society of Great Britain on 4 December 1902. In his remarks on that occasion Baden-Powell discussed recent aeronautical developments and also the future of aerial navigation. He mentioned Count Zeppelin's "monster air ship" which was being tested in Germany. Although Zeppelin had made some progress with his design Baden-Powell concluded that it could not yet be "considered a practical success". He also touched upon the work of Alberto Santos-Dumont, a young Brazilian living in Paris, who was experimenting with navigable balloons in that city. While he had flown a number of times Baden-Powell pointed out that "unfortunately the actual results carry us . . . little beyond what was accomplished twenty years before".

He turned next, in his discourse, to the subject of "flying machines proper" and described the recent experiments that had been made with them. He spoke of the work of Professor Langley, and of the German Wilhelm Kress, and about the large machine built in Australia by Lawrence Hargrave.

He then mentioned the achievements of Wilbur and Orville Wright. "In America", he said, "Mr Wilbur Wright and his brother have been making wonderful progress with gliding machines . . ." Baden-Powell went on to read out to the assembled engineers parts of Octave Chanute's letter to him of 21 October. He commented on Chanute's information that: "I think this is a most remarkable statement and there really seems no reason why such experts, having attained proficiency in the delicate art of balancing themselves according to the various puffs and currents of the air, should not be able to soar away on the wings of the wind and remain indefinitely in mid air".

In his address Major Baden-Powell, speaking as a professional soldier, also offered the company his opinion of what the future might hold when a "practical flying machine" was developed at last. He said: "One can scarcely imagine any invention which could have a greater effect on the conduct of warfare . . ."[1]

In the audience on that December evening was a curious and remarkable man. His name was Patrick Y. Alexander, a prominent member of the Aeronautical Society of Great Britain. Patrick Alexander made it his business to investigate personally the latest developments in aeronautics wherever they took place, in any part of the world.

He was so interested by what Major Baden-Powell said about the Wright brothers that he left London, almost upon the instant, and travelled to Dayton, Ohio, in order to interview Wilbur and Orville

[1] Parts of Baden-Powell's talk are reproduced in Pritchard, *The Wright Brothers and The Royal Aeronautical Society*, pp. 746ff. The address was also reprinted by the Smithsonian Institution.

Wright about their experiments. Such was Alexander's ardour and keenness in the matter that he actually called upon the Wrights in their home in Dayton during a family holiday on Christmas Eve, 1902, only three weeks and one day after Baden-Powell had spoken of their latest achievements in his Presidential Address to the Aeronautical Society in London.

As a result of this singular initiative Alexander was now able to tell his friends in the British Army what the Wright brothers had actually accomplished, and what they planned for the future.

III

Patrick Young Alexander's father was an engineer of distinction and one of the founders of the Aeronautical Society of Great Britain. In the latter part of his life the father became manager of the famous Cammell's Steel Works at Sheffield. The older man saw to it that his son gained an early apprenticeship in the business of rolling steel plates and in learning the rudiments of industrial chemistry. One of his friends once wrote of him: "Mr Patrick Alexander was brought up in an atmosphere of armaments, Naval programmes, and scientific developments generally".[1]

In time Alexander inherited his father's life savings of some £60,000 which made him a wealthy and independent man. He soon became known for his extraordinary generosity. He gave his money away to needy inventors in various fields of endeavour. He was especially helpful to any aeronautical pioneer who required financial support in order to continue his researches. He became known as the "patron of flight in all its forms" and as a "prophet of aviation".

Alexander had a theory. It was his belief that few men could expect to live beyond the age of fifty. Since he had no dependants he thought he could spend his money as he chose and in time, as a result of this conviction, he exhausted his capital by giving it away in prizes designed to encourage aviation and in gifts to educational institutions. This prodigality resulted in genuine good fortune for many impecunious inventors but unfortunately for Patrick Alexander he found, when about fifty years of age, that his inheritance had been expended. He became a bankrupt and existed thereafter, for many years, on funds supplied to him by his friends, and from a small salary he received from the United Services College, an institution he had presented with a gift of £10,000 only a short time before.

The great love of Alexander's life was aviation. Although his interests also embraced industrial chemistry, the manufacture of armour plate,

[1] Major C. C. Turner, *The Old Flying Days* (New York, 1972), p. 11.

syntonic telegraphy, and meteorology he was dominated by a powerful desire to play some role in the early development of aeronautics. In the 1890s he made a number of balloon ascents. In 1894 he jumped from a hot air balloon, and descended with the aid of a parachute. He engaged in various aeronautical experiments of his own. He was a confirmed traveller. In his enthusiasm he made it his business to meet and know all the aeronautical pioneers of his day. He travelled all over the world in order to establish personal contacts with these men. He visited Otto Lilienthal and Count Zeppelin in Germany. He travelled to Russia and spoke with aeronautical authorities there. He made a journey to Peking. In England he knew Hiram Maxim, Wenham, and Pilcher. When he learned of the brilliant work of the Wright brothers he determined to add these Americans to the list of his acquaintances.

It may be mentioned here, so that we can have a fuller understanding of the man, that after the Wright brothers flew successfully in public, in 1908, Alexander believed that his work in aviation had been completed. He then developed a new interest. The subject of his new concern was levitation. However, as one of his friends wrote of this novelty, "no record has been left of any success he may have achieved in this field".[1]

In order to arrange an interview with Wilbur and Orville Wright in December 1902 Alexander, upon his arrival in the United States, first introduced himself to Octave Chanute, whom he had not met before. Chanute, at this time, was in a position to tell his visitor a great deal. Shortly before Alexander appeared upon the scene Wilbur Wright had informed Chanute of his and Orville's plans for the immediate future. On 11 December 1902 Wilbur told Chanute: "It is our intention next year to build a machine much larger and about twice as heavy as our present machine. With it we will work out problems relating to starting and handling heavy-weight machines, and if we find it under satisfactory control in flight, we will proceed to mount a motor."[2]

When Alexander met Chanute at his home in Chicago it was arranged that a letter of introduction should be prepared for him by Chanute so that he could call upon the Wrights who had not known of him before. On 19 December Chanute wrote to Wilbur Wright: "Permit me to introduce Mr. Patrick Alexander, of England, one of the leaders in aeronautical investigations, who desires to meet you while in this country. I feel sure that you will be as much pleased to make his acquaintance as I have been myself."[3]

Chanute was correct in his assumption that the Wright brothers would

[1] Griffith Brewer, *Fifty Years of Flying* (London, 1946), p. 123.
[2] McFarland, *The Papers of Wilbur and Orville Wright*, p. 290. See also Kelly, *Miracle at Kitty Hawk*, p. 86.
[3] McFarland, *The Papers of Wilbur and Orville Wright*, p. 291.

be pleased to meet Patrick Y. Alexander. He made the most pleasant impression upon his hosts in Dayton. Some time after this initial encounter Wilbur told Chanute of Alexander: ". . . we were much pleased with him so far as his brief visit last year enabled us to make his acquaintance. We both liked him very much."[1]

In this way a friendship was struck up. Alexander, as we shall see in the further course of this history, made a number of visits to Dayton and he also saw to it that he met the Wright brothers elsewhere, as well. With the passage of time, however, the Wrights' attitude changed. In July 1908 Wilbur Wright wrote to Chanute of Alexander that "He is certainly the strangest man I have ever known".[2]

There was good reason for these altered impressions. As their friendship developed Wilbur and Orville Wright began to suspect that Alexander was not merely a casual visitor to their home. They decided that he was working secretly for the British Government. In 1907 Wilbur Wright prepared a confidential memorandum which summarized the negotiations which had taken place between the Wrights and the British Government. In this memorandum Wilbur recalled Patrick Alexander's visit to Dayton in December 1902. The memorandum made clear that the Wrights believed Alexander was connected, in some way, with the British Government:[3]

MEMORANDUM BY. W. WRIGHT, ESQ.

WRIGHT BROTHERS' ENGLISH NEGOTIATIONS.

In 1902 Mr. Patrick Alexander, a supposedly wealthy English amateur, visited us at Dayton. It is suspected that he may have some secret connection with the Government. . . .

During these negotiations we have been visited at somewhat frequent intervals by Mr. Alexander and feel convinced that he has some connection with the Government and that the Government has some reason for his watching very closely what we are doing.

When Alexander, his visit completed, left the United States in order to return to London in December 1902 Chanute wrote to him in civil terms to say: ". . . If I do not see you again, I bid you good bye, and I remain very pleased to have made your acquaintance".[4]

Patrick Y. Alexander, however, had no intention of allowing his new association with Chanute to lapse. He recognized the older man as a

[1] *Ibid.*, p. 355.
[2] *Ibid.*, p. 906.
[3] Wright Brothers' Papers (Library of Congress), "Memorandum by W. Wright, Esq." dated 8 February 1907.
[4] Octave Chanute Papers, Chanute to Alexander, 26 December 1902.

fountain of information about the Wright brothers that he would not neglect in the future.

IV

As soon as Wilbur and Orville Wright returned to Dayton after their brilliant achievements at the Kill Devil Hills in 1902 they began to carry out plans, already fixed upon before they left Kitty Hawk, to advance their work to its final phase. They understood the time had come to bring their years of experiment to a conclusion. They would build a power-driven aeroplane.

They now knew that they possessed, in their glider of 1902, a machine they could fly and control in the air. As a result of their work in the laboratory they knew also, after the field trials of 1902, that they could calculate in advance the performance of any machine they chose to build, and that they could do this with a scientific accuracy impossible before this time. In these circumstances they believed that only two problems remained to bar their way forward. They had to obtain an engine suitable for their purpose; and they had to discover some means of converting the horsepower it produced into propulsive thrust that could carry their machine aloft, and keep it there.

However, it may be observed for the purposes of the present history, that it was at this time that another set of problems began to bear upon the activities of the Wrights. At this stage of their course they became increasingly aware of a new development. They found they now had to protect the secrets of their work from American and foreign rivals.

In December 1902 Professor Langley, experimenting still with his "aerodrome", approached Octave Chanute in order to learn more about what the Wrights had achieved. He was especially interested in "their means of control". He told Chanute: "I should be very glad to have either of them visit Washington at my expense, to get some of their ideas on this subject . . .". Even Chanute, who liked and respected Professor Langley, felt that this request, or offer, was "cheeky". He at once sent the Wrights his own advice: "I think you had better patent your improvements."[1] A few months later Chanute informed Wilbur that one of his correspondents, a keen glider pilot named Captain Ferdinand Ferber, a French artillery officer, believed the Wright "system" was "ahead of all the others" and for that reason he wanted to purchase "your 1902 machine . . .".[2]

These were merely early examples of the many, repeated, attempts

---

[1] McFarland, *The Papers of Wilbur and Orville Wright*, p. 290 and n. 4.
[2] *Ibid.*, p. 299.

that were made in the next few years to obtain from the Wright brothers, by one means or another, the fruits of their labours in the workshop, in the laboratory, and in the field. Not unnaturally, Wilbur and Orville responded by trying to preserve their secrets. From this time the Wright brothers learned that they had to be vigilant, and very cautious in their dealings with anyone interested in their invention. Their attitude was a straightforward one. They wanted to safeguard their secrets until they could sell what they alone had created and thus win for themselves the recognition and also the financial rewards they believed their genius, bravery, and devotion had earned.

While this attitude might seem to be a prudent and reasonable reaction by men who had made discoveries that had eluded everyone else for centuries past, it has resulted in the levelling of the most severe charges against the Wright brothers, and especially against Wilbur Wright. For example, Percy B. Walker, in his authorized history of the Royal Aircraft Establishment, *Early Aviation at Farnborough*, sought to show that the authorities in the British War Office who tried, a few years later, to purchase the Wright aeroplane were the most "patient men" who only failed in their efforts because of the obsessive and even diseased desire for secrecy shown by the Wrights in the negotiations. As we shall see later, these charges were bizarre. Nevertheless, Walker wrote of the exchanges between the British Government and the Wrights:[1]

> . . . the men at the War Office strove hard to persuade the Brothers to show a vestige of reason, and never gave up until the whole affair simply petered out after years of fruitless effort.
>
> A new theory is now put forward by me to account for the failure of the negotiations . . . It is maintained that Wilbur had a deep-rooted psychological resistance to anyone possessing his precious aeroplane, even having a look at it . . . in time Wilbur's attitude assumes paranoiac proportions. First one attaché and then another . . . are refused permission to see the aeroplane their country wishes to buy. Admonishment by his old and trusted mentor, Octave Chanute, over his intractability with the British, produces no response . . .

The end of 1902 and the beginning of 1903 when the Wrights realized that they had to protect their discoveries from competitors was a period that produced yet another important development in their lives. It was at this time that Chanute, himself, began to abuse their trust and the friendly relationship which had been established between them.

When Patrick Alexander made his hurried visit to the United States in order to meet the Wrights, Chanute was preparing for a European tour of

[1] Walker, *Early Aviation at Farnborough*, vol. II, p. xv.

his own. His object in making this journey was to arouse European interest in the aeronautical section of the forthcoming St Louis Exposition. Early in January 1903 Chanute sailed from Boston, in company with his daughters, and visited Egypt. He then travelled to a number of European cities, including Paris and London. On 2 April he delivered a lecture in Paris before a distinguished company of men who were interested in the development of aeronautics in France. He later told the Wrights of this talk, which inspired the French to hasten on their own experiments with aeroplanes, that: "Our friend Mr Patrick Alexander came over from London to hear me spout, and sends his best respects to you".[1]

Chanute did not tell them, however, that during this visit to France he tried to reveal all their secrets to his hosts; and that he also allowed the Frenchmen to believe that the Wright brothers were not original workers but that they were merely his pupils and that he was their teacher, mentor, and guide.

Although no verbatim text of Chanute's lecture of 2 April exists, C. H. Gibbs-Smith, the British aeronautical expert, carefully examined the comments made on the lecture by two Frenchmen who heard it and wrote about it in the French technical Press a few days later. Gibbs-Smith concluded from his examination of these articles: ". . . it is hard indeed to feel that Chanute did not make these quite outrageous claims . . . With all due charity, one can only conclude that this fine old man, finding himself in . . . the romantic country of his birth . . . succumbed to the temptation of acting the part of inspirer . . . and mentor of the Wrights".[2]

Chanute succumbed to a similar temptation when he visited England shortly afterward. In England he went to see the Reverend J. M. Bacon, a clergyman, who was very interested in "scientific" ballooning. Bacon's daughter, herself a prominent lady balloonist of the day, wrote of Chanute in her memoirs:[3]

> I see again the courteous, keen-eyed, white-haired old American gentleman, sitting at our table and telling us, in modest, matter-of-fact tones, of a gliding machine of his own design, on which two young men were even then accomplishing most successful flights . . . He said they were brothers of the names of Orville and Wilbur Wright.

The Wright brothers, of course, did not know what Chanute told the Reverend Bacon and his daughter. But it was in this period that they first experienced some annoyance with their old friend. Years later when their

[1] McFarland, *The Papers of Wilbur and Orville Wright*, p. 304.
[2] Gibbs-Smith, *The Rebirth of European Aviation*, p. 62.
[3] Gertrude Bacon, *Memories of Land and Sky* (London, 1928), p. 129.

warm association at last broke apart there was a bitter quarrel and Wilbur wrote angrily to Chanute: ". . . we also have had grievances extending back as far as 1902, and on one occasion several years ago we complained to you that an impression was being spread broadcast by newspapers that we were mere pupils and dependants of yours . . ."[1]

These experiences – with Professor Langley, Captain Ferber, and Chanute – which took place at the end of 1902 and the beginning of 1903 were early examples of the kind of incidents that served to put the Wright brothers upon their guard when the time came for them to try and sell their invention, the aeroplane.

V

At first the Wrights believed it would be a simple matter to acquire an engine for the flying machine they proposed to build. In December 1902 they sent letters to a number of automobile firms and to manufacturers of petrol engines setting out the specifications for the type of petrol engine they required. In those days, however, the engine building firms were very competitive and for that reason they tried to keep their latest designs and advances as secret as possible. The Wrights received several replies to their letter but none was satisfactory.

Undaunted, these remarkable young men determined to build an engine themselves. They had already built a small, air-cooled, one-cylinder petrol engine to operate the machinery in their workshop and they decided now to construct a larger one for their "power flyer", as they called it. Orville was given the task of designing the engine while their mechanic, Charlie Taylor, who looked after the bicycle shop when they were away, did the actual machine work involved. The motor was finished in the short period of six weeks and was tested first in February 1903. Thereafter it went through several further developments and when the design proved adequate for their purpose it was taken to Kitty Hawk at the end of September, when all the labours of the Wrights were at last put to the proof.

It may be mentioned, as an example of the kind of hostility the Wrights sometimes provoked during their lifetime and later, that when Len Deighton, years afterward, wrote his book *Fighter, The True Story of the Battle of Britain*, he stated of Charlie Taylor's contribution to the building of this engine: "They could not use a motor-car engine, because all contemporary ones were too heavy by far. It was their assistant, an unsung hero named Charles Taylor, who took only six weeks to build a

---

[1] McFarland, *The Papers of Wilbur and Orville Wright*, p. 984. The letter is dated 29 January 1910.

lightweight petrol engine from scratch . . . His engine was based upon an earlier gas engine design by Lenoir but that does not alter the fact that Taylor was more important as a pioneer of powered flight than were the Wright brothers."[1]

While their engine was being built one further problem remained for solution. The Wrights had now to design a propeller that could furnish the thrust necessary to maintain their machine in flight. Naturally enough, no reliable corpus of data on air propellers was available to them but Wilbur and Orville reckoned they could learn how propellers operated by studying books on marine engineering. It seemed to the Wrights that when they grasped the theory of marine propellers they could easily adapt this knowledge to the task which confronted them. In accord with their usual practice they repaired to the Dayton Public Library and there obtained a number of books that dealt with the subject of marine engineering. They were shocked to discover, however, that no corpus of theory dealing with marine propellers existed. All the formulae concerned with marine propellers were based upon experiments, and on observation. Exact knowledge of the working of a screw propeller, though it had been in use for more than a century, was lacking. The Wrights realized at once that the rough calculations which were entirely adequate for marine screws could not serve at all when it came to the construction of a propeller to be used in a power-driven aeroplane.

This entirely unexpected challenge struck the Wright brothers with an almost stunning force. Once again, they found themselves confronted by the unknown. In this instance, however, there was no time to attack the problem by a process of trial and error. If they were to return to Kitty Hawk to experiment with their powered aeroplane before the winter gales set in and made flying impossible, it would be necessary for them to devise a theory or a formula that would allow them to understand the way in which propellers worked. Months were spent in probing the theoretical intricacies of the problem. Eventually, they mastered this new difficulty and as a result of the theory they worked out they were able to fashion highly proficient propellers of their own design, devices that were, in fact, a model of efficiency for that time. A British expert later wrote of this phase of their work: "Of such stuff is genius made!"; and a modern American authority stated that their calculations in this new area ". . . are nothing short of miraculous . . . it was genius . . . of the theoretical quality of Leonardo, Kepler, Copernicus, Einstein . . .".[2]

---

[1] Len Deighton, *Fighter, The True Story of the Battle of Britain* (London, 1977), p. 82.

[2] The British authority is J. Laurence Pritchard, *The Wright Brothers and the Royal Aeronautical Society*, p. 764. The American is Harry Combs, *Kill Devil Hill*, pp. 184–5.

By April 1903 two propellers were completed in the Dayton workshop. The Wrights decided to employ two propellers for the flyer because, by this means, they could obtain a reaction against a greater quantity of air; and because the propellers, designed to rotate in opposite directions, would thus neutralize each other's torque and gyroscopic effect. A single propeller, it was realized, would tend to pull to one side. L. M. Wainwright, President of the Diamond Chain Company of Indianapolis, became interested in the Wrights' transmission problem. He furnished them with valuable technical advice about the chains they used, which ran over sprockets, and carried the power of the engine to the propellers. Early in June 1903 the motor and propellers were completed, and then the construction of the aeroplane itself was begun.

All this brilliant scientific and technical work was carried out in that spirit of modesty and good humour which so marked out and characterized the Wright brothers. In June 1903 Orville wrote to Dr George Spratt, Chanute's young associate who had stayed with them earlier in the camp at Kitty Hawk, to say: "Isn't it astonishing that all these secrets have been preserved for so many years just so that we could discover them!! Well, our propellers are so different from any that have been used before that they will have to either be a good deal better, or a good deal worse." Orville also cautioned his friend: "Please do not mention the fact of our building a power machine to anybody".[1]

While this work was going forward in Dayton Professor Langley continued to experiment with his government-sponsored "aerodrome". On 17 July Chanute suddenly flashed word to Wilbur that Langley was at last ready to test his "man-carrying machine". The Wrights, despite this spur, were unable to hasten forward their own preparations. Late in August Wilbur explained to Chanute that owing to unexpected delays they would not be able to leave for Kitty Hawk until the latter part of September. In fact it was not until 23 September that the Wrights departed from Dayton and began their long journey to the Kill Devil Hills, there to test their "power flyer" for the first time.

It was only after the brothers had already settled into their camp in North Carolina that Professor Langley decided that all his arrangements were at last complete. On 7 October 1903 at Widewater, in Virginia, on the Potomac River southeast of Washington, D.C., Langley caused his machine to be launched, by catapult, from a runway fixed to the top of a specially designed houseboat. The result was a disaster. "Aerodrome" and pilot were hurled along the rails of the runway and fell, almost upon the instant, into the waters beneath. The pilot barely escaped with his life while the Langley machine was hoisted from the river, a complete and total wreck.

[1] McFarland, *The Papers of Wilbur and Orville Wright*, pp. 313–15.

By 16 October Wilbur Wright learned of this tragic failure. From his remote camp at the Kill Devil Hills he wrote to Chanute: "I see that Langley has had his fling and failed. It seems to be our turn to throw now, and I wonder what our luck will be. We still hope to see you before we break camp."[1]

Shortly before this time Wilbur was told by Chanute that Patrick Y. Alexander was planning another visit to the United States. Now Chanute informed him that Alexander, fully aware of these latest aeronautical developments in the United States, had left England and was hastening across the Atlantic in the fast passenger liner *Kronprinz Wilhelm*. Chanute hoped he would be able to obtain an invitation for Alexander so that he, too, could be present in the camp at Kitty Hawk when the Wright brothers at last availed themselves of their "turn to throw".

VI

While the Wright brothers were designing and assembling the component parts of their "power flyer" Octave Chanute was also busy, in his own sphere. In April 1903 he left Paris and travelled to London where he made the personal acquaintance of many of those in Britain who were interested in aeronautics. Patrick Y. Alexander saw to it that he met Major Baden-Powell and other enthusiasts during the course of this visit. When Chanute returned to the United States he began a regular correspondence with some of those he met in England; in particular, he now corresponded on a regular basis with Patrick Alexander. On 19 May Chanute wrote to Alexander to thank him for "the many courtesies which I received from you while in Europe . . ." and in June, in response to Alexander's request, Chanute sent him information about current aeronautical developments in the United States.[2]

These American developments were significant. At the end of August 1903 Alexander suddenly informed Chanute that he now planned yet another visit to the United States. In response, Chanute told Alexander all he knew of the activities of Professor Langley, and of those of the Wright brothers also:[3]

> . . . Langley has been having a devil of a time . . . He went to his experimental station on the Potomac July 15th, and within the next week he ought to have flown; but first his house boat was blown away. When towed back, he undertook to test his model machine

[1] *Ibid.*, p. 364.

[2] Octave Chanute Papers, Chanute to Alexander, 19 May 1903; and 18 June 1903.

[3] Octave Chanute Papers, Chanute to Alexander, 10 September 1903.

and that plunged into the water . . . Then he got his big machine ready, and at the first attempt at a launch the gasoline motor gave out. At the second attempt the port propeller slewed out of its orbit and wrecked itself . . . Upon this being repaired the starboard propeller flew to pieces . . . I am really sorry for Langley and I quite appreciate his desire to experiment in secret.

The Wrights have been delayed at home by various affairs, and have not gone to their experimental grounds this year. When they do, the Season will be very short and I may not go at all. . . .

Shortly afterward, on 12 September, Chanute told Wilbur Wright of Alexander's planned visit: "I have a letter from Mr. Alexander, saying that he expects to be in this country the last week in October. He told me in London that he might go to Japan. Have you heard from him?" After this innocent question Chanute added: "I have not led him to believe that he would be welcome to see your experiments, and nobody knows, from me, what you propose to do this year." Wilbur Wright responded to this in the most straightforward way: "We were glad to learn that Mr. Alexander is thinking of visiting this country again. Orville and I had made a firm resolve that Dr. Spratt and yourself should be the only visitors in camp this year up to the moment of actual trial. We have so much to do, and so little time to do it in. However, if Mr. Alexander's trip should occur at a time that would make it at all practicable to invite him to camp we shall certainly do so . . . We will consider the matter further when we see how things progress in camp."[1]

In this way, as a result of Octave Chanute's initiative, the man the Wright brothers later looked upon as a secret agent of the British Government secured an invitation, however tentative, to be present in their camp at the Kill Devil Hills where the first successful powered aeroplane flight in the history of the world was made, some three months later.

Meanwhile, despite his statements to the contrary, Octave Chanute continued to supply Alexander with all the information about the Wrights that he possessed. When the Wright brothers despatched the various parts of their aeroplane to Kitty Hawk, from Dayton, their goods had to pass through the freight depot of the Northern and Southern Railroad, at Elizabeth City, North Carolina. On 16 September this depot was destroyed in a fire and it was feared, incorrectly, that the Wrights' possessions might have been damaged or ruined when the building burnt down. A few days later, on 23 September, Chanute wrote to Alexander about this fire, and about the latest activities and plans of the Wrights:[2]

[1] For these exchanges see McFarland, *The Papers of Wilbur and Orville Wright*, pp. 354–5.
[2] Octave Chanute Papers, Chanute to Alexander, 23 September 1903.

I think the Wrights left yesterday for Kitty Hawk, but I am afraid
that they will have a disappointment. They have been getting out
parts for a new machine, and had shipped them forward in advance.
Now, I see by the press despatches that the freight house at Elizabeth
City North Carolina, has been burned with all its contents, but I hope
that Wright's things have not yet reached there. . . .

By the end of September the Wrights had settled in at their camp near
the Kill Devil Hills. During October they repaired their old shed at the
site and also built another. In addition, they made a number of practice
glides on their 1902 machine in order to prepare themselves for the major
test that lay ahead. Chanute told them, at this time, that because of some
difficulties with his wood-preserving business he might not be able to visit
them in their camp. During these days of preparation Wilbur kept
Chanute informed of all they were accomplishing, and of their hopes for
success with the "power flyer". On the 16th he told Chanute: ". . . we
will have done something before we break camp".[1]

On 23 October Dr Spratt arrived at the camp in order to be with his
friends at the moment when all their labours were at last brought to a
culmination. And on the next day Octave Chanute wrote two letters. In
one he explained to Wilbur that owing to all the delays which had
occurred at the Kill Devil Hills, he might "be able to be present at your
trials". He added: "I now expect to go to Washington, where I have other
business. I will stop at the New Willard's Hotel. Please advise me there by
letter or wire whether to visit you. Do not hesitate to say so if you would
rather not have me come, and give me also your views as to a visit from
Mr. Alexander. He wrote me that he would sail from Cherbourg on the
Kronprinz Wilhelm, which is due in New York on the 27th. I am writing
him to meet me in Washington . . . but I have not advised him that you
are at Kitty Hawk, nor hinted at your plans . . . It is a marvel to me that
the newspapers have not yet spotted you."[2]

Chanute also wrote to Alexander on 24 October in order to arrange to
meet him when he arrived in Washington:[3]

> I hope you got my letter at Cherbourg. I hurried back from
> Southern Illinois in the hope of going on to New York to meet you,
> but that now turns out to be impossible.
>
> Please wire me as soon as you arrive, and advise me of your
> proposed movements.
>
> I expect to be in Washington D.C. on the 2nd or 3rd of November,

---

[1] McFarland, *The Papers of Wilbur and Orville Wright*, p. 364.
[2] *Ibid.*, p. 372.
[3] Octave Chanute Papers, Chanute to Alexander, 24 October 1903.

and would be very glad to meet you there . . . I stop at the New Willard Hotel.

I have quite a number of interesting things to talk over with you, so will not write them now.

On 28 October Chanute sent a telegram to Alexander who had, by this time, arrived in New York. The telegram stated:[1]

WELCOME ACROSS. I MAY NOT REACH WASHINGTON TILL THE THIRD.

A few days later Chanute's arrangements were completed successfully when Wilbur Wright sent him a telegram of his own, from Kitty Hawk. Wilbur's telegram declared:

YOURSELF AND MR. ALEXANDER WELCOME AFTER NOVEMBER FIFTH. BRING ABUNDANT BEDDING.[2]

Despite Chanute's clear and explicit instructions, however, Alexander failed to meet him in Washington. For this reason Chanute, on 6 November, repaired alone to the Wright brothers' camp in North Carolina. Alexander actually arrived at Chanute's hotel in Washington but only to leave a note, explaining that he had to hurry off to Boston in order to meet Major Baden-Powell, the British delegate to the Aeronautical Section of the St Louis World's Fair. Alexander, with a priceless opportunity in his grasp, chose to rush off in an entirely wrong direction. Chanute later explained the details of this mishap, or blunder, to one of his German correspondents, Major Hermann Moedebeck, author of a contemporary little treatise entitled *The Pocket Book of Aeronautics*, published first in Germany, and later in an English edition which appeared in 1907. Chanute told Moedebeck of this misadventure shortly after he returned from his visit to the Kill Devil Hills:[3]

I missed seeing Mr. Alexander on his passage through this country. We had an appointment in Washington for Nov. 3rd, but on my arrival I found a note that he had been called to Boston to meet the British delegate to the St. Louis Expn, and from Boston he went to Chicago, St. Louis & San Francisco while I was East with Wright. I have a letter from San Francisco stating that he is sailing for New Zealand . . .

[1] Octave Chanute Papers, Chanute to Alexander, 28 October 1903, Telegram.
[2] McFarland, *The Papers of Wilbur and Orville Wright*, p. 376.
[3] Octave Chanute Papers, Chanute to Major Moedebeck, 27 November 1903.

In this letter Chanute also alerted the major to the fact that the Wright brothers were on the verge of great accomplishments, telling him: "You may be prepared to receive some very interesting news as to the performance of these gentlemen."

It thus came about that Patrick Alexander, the aeronautical enthusiast, with the opportunity of a lifetime in his hand, failed to seize it. Chanute believed, for a considerable period of time, that Alexander was outraged by this turn of events; and that the unpleasant feeling rankled for years. He was genuinely upset by Alexander's attitude. At first he decided that Alexander was annoyed with him because of this miscarriage in their plans. Later Chanute came to believe that Alexander was angry with him because of their differences in a joint venture upon which they had embarked, the translation into English of Major Moedebeck's *Pocket Book*. It is most probable, however, that Chanute's first impression was the correct one. Years later, in 1907, the distressed old man wrote to Alexander of these developments:[1]

> . . . I think that you are "disgruntled" and for two years I have been wondering what it is about. When first you returned from your trip around the world I imagined it due to annoyance at having been unable to see the first tests of the Wright motor machine, but now I think it may be because I induced you to translate the Moedebeck Pocket book . . .
>
> Now, for whatever I may have said, or done, or omitted to do, I sincerely beg your pardon. I cannot bear to have a cloud between us. . . .

VII

Early in November the Wright brothers started upon the final phase of their work when they began the task of fixing the engine to its assigned place on the glider. There followed a series of mechanical problems which resulted in the appearance of inefficient lock-nuts, loose sprockets, and cracked or broken propeller shafts. The weather turned cold. There were storms. On 5 November George Spratt decided to abandon his friends in their camp, convinced they were confronted by nothing less than a disaster. On the day after his departure Chanute arrived but for most of the time he was with them the weather was so inclement they were forced to sit indoors, talking of hopes, plans and future aspirations. On the 12th Chanute departed the camp and the Wrights were at last left to themselves, to continue with their final preparations.

On 28 November, well behind their original schedule, the morning was

---

[1] Octave Chanute Papers, Chanute to Alexander, 21 May 1907.

spent in testing the engine. Suddenly another cracked propeller shaft was discovered. In consequence it was at once decided that Orville should return to Dayton in order to make entirely new shafts of solid tool steel, more durable than the tubular ones which had been unable to withstand the shocks of premature or missed explosions in the engine. When he was returning to Kitty Hawk with the new propeller shafts Orville read in a newspaper that Professor Langley had regrouped and regathered his own forces for a second trial of his machine. Orville learned that on 8 December 1903 at Arsenal Point, near Washington, the Langley "aerodrome" had been launched again; as it was leaving the track, however, there occurred a complete collapse of the frame and the "aerodrome", already reduced to wreckage, dropped into the waters below.

By 14 December Wilbur and Orville were at last ready. On that day their power machine was drawn out of its shed. A signal was hoisted to alert their neighbours at Kitty Hawk, and at the Kill Devil Hill Life Saving Station. Then, in the company of Bob Westcott, John T. Daniels, Tom Beacham, W. S. Dough, and Uncle Benny O'Neal, the engine was given its final test. A coin was tossed to decide which of the brothers would make the first trial, and Wilbur won. The machine was placed in the starting position and then under Wilbur's hand it rushed along its track, rising some fifteen feet into the air, only to stall and gradually sink back to the earth.

This misadventure was no disappointment to the Wright brothers. It illustrated another of the problems that confronted them. They had not merely to invent and design the various parts of the aeroplane but they had also to learn how to fly it when no one had any experience of the art and when the responses of the machine, owing to lack of practice with the controls, were nothing less than a mystery. Wilbur blamed this failure on himself and decided the trouble had resulted from his own error in judgement in turning up too suddenly, as soon as the aeroplane left the track. On the day after this adventure he sent a telegram to Bishop Wright, anxiously awaiting the result in Dayton, at once assuring him that success was certain and urging him also to keep quiet about what was taking place.

Three days after this original trial the Wrights attacked the problem again. On this occasion it was Orville's turn to mount the machine. He, too, found control of the front rudder quite difficult but he managed to fly through the air, for a brief period. On this 17 December 1903 the Wrights made four successful controlled flights, the longest lasting for nearly a minute. As they wrote later in a statement prepared for publication in the newspapers, after these flights "we at once packed our goods and returned home, knowing that the age of the flying machine had come at last".

As soon as they were able the Wright brothers flashed word of their success, by telegram, to their family in Dayton; and when the news was received there Katherine Wright at once sent a telegram to Octave Chanute in order to inform him. Meanwhile, a local newspaper in the vicinity of Kitty Hawk, the Norfolk *Virginia-Pilot*, published an account of the flights in its edition for 18 December 1903. The account was incorrect in many of its details. It claimed, for example, that the Wrights had flown a distance of three miles when the fact was that the longest of their flights was only eight hundred and fifty-two feet. This report in the *Virginia-Pilot* was copied by some newspapers in the United States and in Europe, but it was ignored by others. Major Baden-Powell, far away in London but ever vigilant in the cause of British aviation, reacted almost at once. On 23rd December 1903 he wrote to Chanute:[1]

> . . . What is this I read in the daily papers about the brothers Wright having made a machine fly 3 miles? Is there any truth in this?

VIII

When Octave Chanute learned of the success of the Wright brothers he sent them his congratulations. He also enquired about when they would be ready to make the details of their achievement public knowledge. Wilbur sharply told him, in reply, and for a good reason we shall examine later, that they were not yet prepared to furnish pictures or descriptions of their machine or their methods to anyone. However, since the newspapers continued to publish incorrect stories about what had occurred on 17 December, the Wrights prepared an accurate factual statement of their own, dated 5 January 1904, and sent it to the Associated Press. When their statement was published in the Dayton *Press* they clipped out copies of it and mailed them to various friends and associates.

Chanute read the Associated Press statement when it was published in his own local newspaper, the Chicago *News*. Now he too began to send copies of it to his various correspondents in different parts of the world. Indeed he now launched upon a regular campaign to alert all his friends to what had taken place at those far-off sand hills on the bleak North Carolina coast. He sent several copies of the Wright statement, together with explanatory letters, to his correspondents in England so that the aeronautical authorities there were soon aware of the exact details of what the Wright brothers had achieved. He wrote twice to Major Baden-Powell and sent him a copy of the Wright statement. He also wrote to Herbert Wenham, the British pioneer who had done so much to increase his own interest in aviation. When he sent a copy of the

[1] Octave Chanute Papers, B. Baden-Powell to Chanute, 23 December 1903.

statement to Wenham he declared: "To you, who first called attention to the possibility of artificial flight . . . I send the first correct account which has been published of the achievement of the Wright brothers. It is a beginning, and if no accident occurs it may lead to practical results . . ."[1]

Chanute sent the fullest and most detailed of his accounts to Patrick Y. Alexander who had returned to England in January 1904, after a journey round the world. Chanute began his letter by telling Alexander about the invitation the Wrights had extended to him, in the previous November:[2]

> I was very sorry not to find you in Washington, but it turned out for the best. The Wrights had built a new apparatus, provided with a motor and propellers, and were to test it November 5th. They had made a firm resolve that, besides themselves, none but the surgeon & myself should be present. I had written to obtain an invitation for you but did not dare advise you. On my arrival in Washington I found a telegram inviting *you* to the camp, but it was yourself who had flown instead of the Wrights.

He then proceeded to supply details of the Wright success, and about their attitude after it:

> I got to the camp on the 5th, only to find that on the preceding day the propeller had been twisted off the shaft in a test. It had to go to Dayton to be rebrazed. On its return the shaft itself was twisted in two, and two new shafts had to be forged and turned at Dayton.
>
> Finally on the 17th of December (I could not stay so long) the first dynamic flight in history took place. I enclose herewith a clipping in which the Wrights state what they did do. It is a first success which cannot be pursued on account of weather. The Wrights are immensely elated. They have grown very secretive and nobody is to be allowed to see the machine at present so that your chance is gone . . .
> I have not seen them and letters are now very scarce. They delayed over a year after I first advised them to apply for patents, and I suppose that now they have the inventor's tremors that their secrets will be divulged.

Chanute completed his budget of news by reporting on Professor Langley's work:

> Langley tried his machine again Dec. 8th and failed in consequence of an accident to his launching gear. A dinner is to be given him in New York tomorrow, which is the right thing to do . . .

---

[1] Octave Chanute Papers, Chanute to Wenham, 9 January 1904.
[2] Octave Chanute Papers, Chanute to Alexander, 18 January 1904.

As a result of this letter from Chanute, and its enclosure, no one in Britain now possessed more information about the Wright brothers and their aeroplane than Patrick Alexander. And exactly at this time Alexander began to tell all he knew of the Wrights to a friend, Brevet Lieutenant-Colonel John Edward Capper, R.E. Colonel Capper had only recently returned to England from active service in South Africa. He had been summoned home for a good reason. The authorities at the War Office wanted him to take charge of a unit known as the Balloon Sections, in the Aldershot Command. The chief concern of this unit was military aeronautics.

During the South African War the British Army had benefited greatly by the performance in the field of its captive balloon units. It has been said that British military ballooning in South Africa was one of the few bright spots in an otherwise dismal and disappointing campaign. Now that the war was over it was recognized in the War Office that the time had come for reorganization and for further serious thought about the future of military aeronautics.

In consequence of these conclusions a Committee on Military Ballooning was established, and Capper appointed its Secretary. In those days, the reader should understand, the term "Military Ballooning" was generally understood in British Army circles to encompass all forms of aerial activity including, in addition to balloons, kites, airships, and also aeroplanes, or flying machines. The final report of this committee was printed in January 1904. But the news of what the Wrights had done, which was received at almost exactly the same time, made many of its conclusions entirely obsolete. No member of the committee was more aware of this development than Colonel Capper.

A British expert who knew several of his country's aeronautical pioneers, and who was allowed access to the most secret and confidential documents dealing with this early period of aeronautical history, later wrote of this time, January 1904: ". . . the dynamic Capper had seized on the report of flight by the Wrights as an event opening a vista of magnificent importance . . . Capper was eagerly discussing flying machines at every opportunity – particularly with 36-year-old Patrick Young Alexander . . ."[1]

John Capper had already distinguished himself on active service. He was now about to demonstrate, in his new post, capacity of the highest order in the field of military administration. In this way a mind that was entirely more capable than those of Alexander, the wealthy amateur, and Major Baden-Powell, the military enthusiast, began to come to grips with the issue of the invention of the Wright brothers and how it might be made to serve the purposes, needs and requirements of the British Army.

[1] See Harald Penrose, *British Aviation, The Pioneer Years*, p. 57.

CHAPTER 3

The British Authorities Approach the Wright Brothers

New plans of the Wright brothers – They plan the conquest of the Air – Their unscrupulous competitors – Augustus Moore Herring, a scoundrel – The envy of Chanute – A forged article in the Press – The need for caution and vigilance – Reaction in the United States – Samuel and Godfrey Cabot – The jealousy of the French – The Reaction that occurred in Britain – Major Baden-Powell congratulates the Wrights – He publishes News of their Success – Publication in the *Aeronautical Journal* – Leo Amery's brilliant Insight – Development of a practical Aeroplane – Formidable technical Problems – The Huffman Prairie – Octave Chanute informs Patrick Alexander – Difficulties of the Wright Brothers – How they solved them – Colonel Capper visits Dayton – The Balloon Factory and the Balloon Sections – Colonel Templer's ambition – Capper ordered to visit the United States – His preparations – He meets Chanute – He alerts his Superiors at Aldershot – He meets the Wright Brothers – His Report of the Mission – His Special Recommendations – He decides England must not "be left behind" – His plans for the Future.

I

Wilbur and Orville Wright returned to their father's home in Dayton after the long railway journey from North Carolina in a glow of personal pride and satisfaction. Alone, they had succeeded in the task to which they had first put their hands years before, in 1899. They had achieved what has been called "the miracle of the ages", and "man's most noble accomplishment". Only a few years later an enthralled contemporary, in seeking to describe what they had done for humanity, wrote of them: "When every King now reigning shall have been forgotten, the story of these amazing men will be a tale that will be part of the legends of the nations and that will be told to inspire children in their earliest years with the thought of noble deeds and grand achievements for the enlargement of the power of our race".[1]

At the end of December 1903 the Wright brothers entertained a more sober view of their situation. At that moment they were entirely aware of what they had accomplished but they understood, also, that a completely new and intricate phase of their work now loomed before them. They had been the first men to fly a heavier-than-air machine but this, as they knew, was merely a beginning, little more than the starting-point in a new quest, which was nothing less than the conquest of the air.

A great deal of research and much dangerous experiment still lay ahead if they were to develop their "power-flyer" into a practical aeroplane that could be used for any of a variety of civilian or military purposes. They now planned to build a more sophisticated machine than its predecessor, one similar in size, but heavier in weight, with a more powerful engine, and equipped with new and improved control systems.

In addition, and in accord with this new outlook, they realized also that they were mere novices in the art or craft of piloting a powered aeroplane. Before they could present their invention to the world as a practical device of such value that it could win them fortune and fame, which they wanted, they would have to increase their skill as pilots by such prolonged practice in the air that they would be able to exert a mastery over the machine that had been entirely unattainable in their pioneering but brief and hectic powered flights over the North Carolina sand dunes.

These altered and enlarged horizons now determined their new course. Before their great success of December 1903 their chief object had been to become the first men in history to fly and to control a heavier-than-air machine in flight. They had realized from the outset that such an achievement, if carried to the kind of conclusion they now planned for themselves, could lead to distinction, renown, glory and wealth. Until this time, however, such feelings had been suppressed or held firmly in check by men who had been raised from boyhood to believe in the virtues of strict self-control, by men who would not lightly or openly indulge such hopes, even among themselves.

When Wilbur left Dayton for his first visit to Kitty Hawk his family had looked upon the excursion as a holiday that might serve to improve his health after so many years of sickness and seclusion. Not one of the Wrights was then prepared to admit any concern over the possible success or failure of Wilbur and Orville's experiments. Indeed, Wilbur Wright took care to make clear to his father, the bishop, that he regarded the Kitty Hawk adventure of 1900 as a "pleasure trip pure and simple", a mere vacation from which he hoped to return "heavier and stronger than

---

[1] The contemporary was the distinguished British journalist, H. Massac Buist. See his article "The Human Side of Flying" in *Flight*, 13 March 1909.

I left". But he was so close to his father he also confided to him at that time: "It is my belief that flight is possible and, while I am taking up the investigation for pleasure rather than profit, I think there is a slight possibility of achieving fame and fortune from it".[1]

Now, in December 1903, the possibility was much more than "slight". After their triumph at Kitty Hawk entirely new prospects and vistas opened before the Wright brothers. Moreover, as a result of their accumulated experiences of the past few years they knew exactly what was still required of them, and exactly what remained for them to do in order to fulfil their destiny.

These reflections were rapidly translated into action. When the Wrights returned from Kitty Hawk a number of bicycles were in their Dayton workshop, in various stages of construction. Some of these, their stock, were finished and sold but no new ones were built. Moreover, it was at this time that they began to turn the routine work of the shop over to Charlie Taylor, their mechanic. The Wright brothers were now determined to devote as much of their time as was required to the construction of a new powered aeroplane and to those experiments and practice flights that would enable them to become skilled and proficient pilots, masters of the air.

Months earlier, in March 1903, they had applied for basic patents in order to place upon the record the details of their scientific accomplishments. Early in 1903, however, after seeking technical advice in Dayton, they consulted H. A. Toulmin of Springfield, Ohio, a patent attorney, in order to put their case in his hands. Thus protected, they were ready to begin upon a new programme of research and development. In January 1904 they began to build an entirely new machine. The aeroplane that had been flown at Kitty Hawk was never used by them again, even for test purposes.

II

Even before the Wrights were able to start work in 1904 there occurred the first of a number of incidents which served to alert them to the unscrupulous competitors, and hangers-on, they could expect to encounter in this new phase of their career.

The reader will recall that Octave Chanute, from time to time, had induced the brothers to permit some of his associates to join them in their camp during their various field trials in North Carolina. One of these, Dr George Spratt, had become their friend. They developed a hearty dislike for another of Chanute's assistants, E. C. Huffaker, because he was an

---

[1] Wilbur's letter is reproduced in Kelly, *Miracle at Kitty Hawk*, p. 27.

incompetent and lazy worker, and a man of slovenly personal habits. In 1902 when he visited their camp Chanute had brought with him the third of these helpers, the engineer Augustus Moore Herring.

It is fair to say that Augustus Herring was a scoundrel. He may well be called the villain of early aeronautical history. While he was in camp with the Wrights he certainly saw their famous glider of 1902 but he made no contribution whatsoever, either to its construction or in its trials. Nevertheless, on 26 December 1903 Herring brazenly wrote to the Wright brothers claiming that he had arrived at an independent solution of the problem of heavier-than-air flight. He proposed a partnership between himself and the brothers in which each would possess a one-third interest.

Herring claimed also that he had already been offered a significant sum of money for his "rights" to interference suits against the Wrights. By means of this last statement he informed Wilbur and Orville that he was prepared to challenge them on the issue of the priority of their invention, and that substantial amounts of money were involved in his challenge. Most probably, Herring, who had invented nothing of any genuine significance, hoped that the Wright brothers would seek a compromise with him in order to avoid the tedious, lengthy, and expensive litigation in the courts which he now threatened to bring down upon them.[1]

This act of December 1903 was not an isolated incident in Augustus Herring's career. He betrayed Chanute, his employer and patron, when he tried to claim that he had devised and invented one of the older man's gliders. He boasted, also, to anyone who would listen to him, that he owned patents for a successful heavier-than-air flying machine, when all that he really possessed were patent applications which were of no monetary or scientific value at all. Later, by referring to these supposed patents, and by other means also, Herring managed to outfox Glenn Curtiss, the American aeronautical pioneer, a slippery customer in his own right, who rashly entered into a business relationship with him in order to form the ill-fated Herring-Curtiss Company, a firm that was doomed from the start because Herring was never able to perform for it in the way he had promised at the beginning of their negotiations.

In 1907 when the United States authorities advertised for tenders for the construction of a practical aeroplane that could be used for military purposes, Herring sent in a bid that was fixed, deliberately, at a price lower than that submitted by the Wright brothers. His idea was to win the contract for himself, by this means. Since he did not know how to construct a machine that could fly he planned to sublet his contract to the Wrights, for a commission. He was insolent enough to travel to Dayton in order to make this proposal to the brothers but they rejected it, disgusted at his shamelessness.

[1] The details of Herring's letter are published in McFarland, *The Papers of Wilbur and Orville Wright*, p. 413, n. 2.

At the end of 1903 and early in 1904 Herring conducted a number of interviews with American and European journalists in which he suggested that he had devised or created almost everything of value in the developing art and technology of aeronautics. When Major Moedebeck published one of these notices in his periodical, the *Illustrierte Aeronautische Mitteilungen*, Chanute warned him that he was giving prominence to a "man who attempted blackmail".[1]

The Wright brothers' triumph of December 1903 also provoked the envy of Chanute himself; and this development made even more intense their feeling that they now had to be prudent, vigilant, alert and cautious if they were not to be cheated of what they had recently come to look upon as their just rewards. Early in January 1904 when he learned of Herring's letter to the Wrights, Chanute wrote to them in order to express his amazement at Herring's "impudence" in asking for a third part of their invention. In this same letter Chanute also referred to the statement about their flights at Kitty Hawk they had recently sent off for publication in the newspapers. In his letter he quoted one of the sentences of their statement, underlining one word in it: "All the experiments have been conducted at our expense, without assistance from *any* individual or institution". Chanute then added the following: "Please write to me just what you had in your mind concerning myself when you framed that sentence in that way".[2]

To this request, or enquiry, the Wright brothers chose to return a mild reply. It was clear to them that Chanute had already conceived the idea, which was entirely mistaken, that he had made some vital or significant technical contribution to the development of their successful powered aeroplane. The brothers explained to Chanute that the object of their statement was to justify their desire to preserve the secrets of their work. Unlike Professor Langley, they declared, they had received no public funds to support them during all their years of research and experiment. Therefore, they were under no obligation to reveal anything to anyone: "We had paid the freight", Wilbur wrote to Chanute, "and had a right to do as we pleased".

However, much more lay behind the choice of words in their statement for the Press. The Wrights had written the statement in the way that they did because a number of American and foreign newspapers had suggested that they were Chanute's pupils; and that he had supported them with his own funds, as a benefactor, so that they could complete their experiments. As the Wrights were aware, Chanute never made any attempt to

---

[1] *Ibid.*, p. 434.

[2] The material in this and the following two paragraphs is based upon information and comment in McFarland, *The Papers of Wilbur and Orville Wright*, pp. 414ff.

correct these mistaken and erroneous impressions. They believed that unless something was done these misstatements might develop into permanent misconceptions that could eventually deprive them of the credit, and the profit, of their discoveries. As Marvin McFarland, editor of *The Papers of Wilbur and Orville Wright* put it: "The genuineness of their friendship for Chanute . . . is plainly evidenced by the fact that they kept their reproaches to themselves . . ." Nevertheless, by early 1904 they had recognized and were annoyed by the older man's attitude.

Almost immediately after these exchanges took place the Wright brothers were made the victims of a forgery. An unprincipled journalist, or writer, named D. A. Willey published an article in a New York periodical, the *Independent*, on 4 February 1904. The article, entitled "Experiences of a Flying Man", was presented to the public as the work of Wilbur Wright. This was simply not the case. Willey falsely claimed he possessed a letter from Wilbur which authorized him to write the piece. Actually Willey had used material from a couple of Wilbur's published lectures and from some Press reports. He had also been in correspondence with Chanute for a period of months in order to obtain details and photographs from him but he fooled Chanute completely about the purpose of his various requests for information.

The Wright brothers, jealous for their own reputations, would not tolerate such actions. Wilbur at once wrote a wrathful letter to the editor of the *Independent* in order to complain to him of his paper's "unmitigated impudence"[1] in publishing such an article. The *Independent*, in a subsequent issue, apologized for its mistake but the Wrights and Chanute, also, were so angry and annoyed by what had taken place that Chanute declared himself willing "to spend some money" in order to have Willey punished in the courts.

It seems clear that by the beginning of 1904 Wilbur and Orville Wright were forced to realize that they would no longer be able to carry on as ordinary private citizens. In their own minds their great achievement at Kitty Hawk was still tentative and incomplete. Nevertheless, it was now obvious that there were plenty of unscrupulous people who were ready to exploit for their own benefit what they had done, with their approval or in defiance of it.

III

It is certain that the proverbial man in the street was not especially concerned by what had taken place at the Kill Devil Hills at the end of December 1903. Nevertheless a number of vigilant observers in various countries were fascinated by what had occurred there.

[1] See Kelly, *Miracle at Kitty Hawk*, pp. 129–130.

In the United States two brothers, Samuel and Godfrey Lowell Cabot, wealthy and influential members of a distinguished Boston family, were very interested by the Wright brothers' achievement of powered flight. Each of these men communicated with the Wrights in order to congratulate them or to enquire if their new invention could be put to commercial use.

Samuel Cabot contacted Chanute, by telegram, as soon as the news of the Wright brothers' success was published in the Press. As early as 19 December 1903, in reply to the telegram, Chanute sent Samuel Cabot exact details of the Wright "flyer". He wrote to Cabot: "There are yet no good accounts that I have seen of the Wright apparatus. It is like their 1902 machine, but larger being 40 ft 4 ins across by 6 ft 6 in wide and two surfaces 6 ft 2 in apart. It is provided with a 10 Horse power motor, by the side of the aviator, and 2 screw propellers 8 ft 6 in diameter in the rear. A pair of sleds take the shock of landing. It is started by resting the centre on a rolling platform which runs upon a single plank set edgewise and shod with iron; men running at the side and keeping the machine evenly balanced. The enclosed rough sketch will give you the idea . . ."[1]

A few days later Samuel Cabot offered, through Chanute, to provide the Wright brothers with money. Chanute responded to the offer by sending Cabot more information:[2]

> . . . The newspapers are quite wrong about the performance of the Wrights. It was no more than I wrote you in a former letter, which by the way please keep confidential, as the Wrights have determined to give no pictures nor descriptions, nor statements of methods for the present. They are in no need of money, but I will transmit to them your kind intimation.
> . . . It is going to take some time to develop the machine so that it will be safe to attempt long flights. There will be breakages of various parts until this "one horse shay" is equally strong in all its parts, and there may be personal accidents. We hope for the best but counsel prudence . . .

Meanwhile the Wrights themselves sent an account of their flights at Kitty Hawk to Godfrey Cabot, Samuel's brother. He was so impressed by the intelligence he received from them that he decided upon a bold step. He at once approached a relative, one of the most powerful politicians in the United States, the famous Senator Henry Cabot Lodge, who was a close friend of President Theodore Roosevelt. Godfrey Cabot suggested to the senator that the United States Government should begin to pay attention to what the Wright brothers had done. He informed him about

[1] Octave Chanute Papers, Chanute to S. Cabot, 19 December 1903.
[2] Octave Chanute Papers, Chanute to S. Cabot, 1 January 1904.

the flights of 17 December and explained: "It seems to me that this may fairly be said to mark the beginning of successful flight through the air by men unaided by balloons. It has occurred to me that it would be eminently desirable for the United States Government to interest itself in this invention . . ."[3]

Senator Lodge passed this letter on to the United States War Department but the officials there decided to ignore it. For some time they had been the victims of savage criticism and denunciation, in the national Press and in the Congress itself, because they had furnished Professor Langley with so much money for his ill-fated experiments. This campaign of ridicule and censure was so bitter that, in the opinion of Langley's friends, it broke his spirit and eventually caused his death a few years later.

For their part, the military bureaucrats in the War Department, condemned once for squandering public funds in support of the ridiculous and impracticable dreams of a professor, had now learnt the value of prudence in such matters. They did nothing. Langley's failures had demonstrated what every practical man already knew. They proved that heavier-than-air flight was impossible. In this way, it may be observed, the United States Government missed an opportunity to become the first government in the world to secure control of an aeroplane that could fly successfully in the air.

There was a different and more violent reaction in France. There, the news of the Wrights' success produced outbursts of envy that have been described as "almost hysterical". French aviation circles were now shaken by spasms of chauvinism of the kind that were so characteristic of life in the Third Republic.

There had existed in France, for generations, a tradition of scientific interest in the possibility of human flight which stretched back to the Montgolfier brothers, pioneers who had successfully flown a hot-air balloon as early as June 1783. More latterly, however, Frenchmen who were concerned with heavier-than-air flight had been inspired by the work of the Wrights, although some of them regularly sought to deny any such influence. Nevertheless, Captain Ferdinand Ferber of the French Army, their pioneer in gliding flight, depended for valid technical information upon Octave Chanute who freely sent him material about the Wrights' aeronautical devices whenever he could. Moreover, after Chanute spoke in Paris in April 1903 and then published a number of illustrated articles about the technical achievements and advances of the Wright brothers, the French were provided with the information that enabled them, in the words of one expert authority, to begin upon the

---

[1] His letter, dated 31 December 1903, is printed in Kelly, *Miracle at Kitty Hawk*, pp. 122–3.

"true revival of aviation in Europe" which was "due directly to the Wright brothers".[1]

Early in 1904 the Frenchmen decided there was still time for them to beat the Wrights in the race to produce a practical and successful powered aeroplane. There were exhortations to French engineers in speeches and in published articles to triumph yet over their American rivals, for the honour of France and the glory of the Republic.

An article that appeared in the technical publication *L'Aérophile*, in its issue for December 1903, reported the cry of alarm of Ernest Archdeacon, an enthusiast, who asked: "Will the homeland of the Montgolfiers have the shame of allowing that ultimate discovery of aerial science to be realized abroad?"; and also the plea of Captain Ferber, a man who owed so much to the Wrights, who declared: "The aeroplane must not be allowed to be perfected in America". Later, the same journal published the speech of Victor Tatin, the aeronautical patriot, in its edition for February 1904. He said: "Shall we someday have to read in history that aviation, born in France, was only successful because of the labours of the Americans, and that only by servilely copying them did the French thereafter obtain any results . . ."

The Wright brothers professed to feel only amusement at these strident outbursts and exhortations but Chanute paid more attention to them. In one of those budgets of news which he now sent, almost on a regular basis, to Patrick Y. Alexander, Chanute informed his friend of what the Wright brothers were planning to do in the immediate future and also expressed his surprise at the fact that the English seemed less interested in these developments than were the French. Chanute told Alexander:[2]

> I was glad to learn by your letter of Jan. 29th that you were safely home. You must have received the next day mine of the 18th giving you an account of the success of the Wrights with a dynamic machine. I am surprised at the fact that it has been so little mentioned in the English papers, while the French press is full of it . . . Mr. Wright . . . will resume his experiments as soon as the weather will permit, say in May, and if the patents are made safe will later give public exhibitions. . . .

IV

We must turn now, in our history, to the reaction of the British when they learned of what had taken place at Kitty Hawk in December 1903.

[1] Gibbs-Smith, *The Invention of the Aeroplane*, p. 54.
[2] Octave Chanute Papers, Chanute to Alexander, 16 February 1904.

It is necessary to pause first, however, in order to point out that this reaction is a matter of very genuine significance in any study dealing with the early history of Britain's Air Service. The subject is at once intricate and complicated; and it will be dealt with more fully as the present work proceeds. For the moment, however, the reader should bear in mind that when the Wright brothers offered to sell their invention to the British War Office in 1905, their offer was refused. Years later a prominent British aeronautical expert, Percy B. Walker, in seeking to defend this decision of the authorities at the War Office, wrote of them in his History: "How could the War Office face the nation after committing them to an invention which they had never seen, and which was claimed by two bicycle-makers as far away as Dayton in the United States of America?"[1]

It is not suggested here, at this stage of the present exposition, that the British authorities were in error in failing to acquire the Wright invention in 1905. Instead, we have to begin to establish, at this point in our narrative, that the Wrights were not merely two unknown "bicycle-makers" at the time they gave the War Office authorities the opportunity to purchase their aeroplane. By 1905, as we shall see, enough was known about them, and their work, in British technical and military circles, to make Percy Walker's comment misleading, and also invalid.

Beginning in January 1904 the Wright brothers, and Chanute also, communicated with several members of the Aeronautical Society of Great Britain. Indeed, one of the society's officials wrote later, with pride, that the society's members were more interested in the accomplishments and successes of the Wrights than were their contemporaries in the United States, where the pioneering work was actually being done. Years after these events J. L. Pritchard, Secretary of the (Royal) Aeronautical Society, in a formal tribute to the Wrights, stated in the text of his survey of their work: "Here is set down the story of the unprecedented achievement of the Wright Brothers, their impacts on, and relationships with, those members of the one-time Aeronautical Society of Great Britain who knew them and were aware of the reality of their genius . . ." He added: "The experiments made and the results obtained during the years 1904–5 are largely given here in letters from the Wrights and Octave Chanute to members of the Society who were taking a much livelier interest than was being taken in America at the time."[2]

On 7 January 1904 Orville Wright sent Major Baden-Powell, President of the Aeronautical Society of Great Britain, a clipping containing the statement the Wrights had prepared for publication in the Press. Orville explained that the clipping "gives an authentic account of the recent trials

---

[1] Walker, *Early Aviation at Farnborough*, vol. II, p. 44.
[2] J. Laurence Pritchard, *The Wright Brothers and the Royal Aeronautical Society*, p. 742; and p. 767.

of our successful Flyer".[1] On the same day, and acting entirely upon his own, Chanute sent Baden-Powell a copy of the same clipping: "The Wrights", he told Baden-Powell, "have been hesitating about publishing *anything* concerning their recent flights with a dynamic machine. They made their minds up yesterday, and I sent you the result . . ."[2]

Major Baden-Powell has sometimes been criticized severely, in the historical literature, because it seemed that he did not at once appreciate the high significance of what the Wright brothers had achieved at the end of December 1903. This was not the case. On 18 January 1904 he wrote to Orville Wright in order to congratulate him, in civil and even warm terms, upon what had been done:[3]

> I am very much obliged to you for so kindly sending me an account of your experiments. I was very anxious to hear the truth, having seen various vague accounts in the papers. Allow me to offer my congratulations on your important success. . . .
>
> I am looking forward to a trip to the United States in September, when I shall hope to have the honour of meeting you.

Major Baden-Powell, who owned a number of periodical publications in addition to his other interests, decided to print the Wright statement in one of them. When he thanked Chanute for the information he had sent, the major wrote: ". . . I am . . . much obliged for the cutting about Wrights' machine. I had however just got a letter from Mr. Orville Wright, in which he enclosed a similar account. You may see that I have put it into 'Knowledge & Scientific News'. This paper, by the way, is getting along very well now . . ."[4]

A few months later, in April 1904, even more serious attention was paid to the accomplishments of the Wright brothers when a long article about their work was published in *The Aeronautical Journal*, the official organ of the Aeronautical Society of Great Britain. This periodical was one of the most respected technical publications in the world. The article, entitled "The Experiments of the Brothers Wright", was divided into two parts. Part one, "With Gliding Machines depending upon Gravity for their Motive Power", described the Wrights' experiments with their gliders and referred to the brothers as "these intrepid aviators". Part two of the article was entitled "With the Power Flyer. – Communicated by Mr. Orville Wright". This section of the article was the prepared statement Orville had sent earlier to Major Baden-Powell. *The Aeronautical*

[1] *Ibid.*, p. 768.

[2] Octave Chanute Papers, Chanute to Baden-Powell, 7 January 1904.

[3] Wright Brothers' Papers, B. Baden-Powell to Orville Wright Esq., 18 January 1904. For a critical comment on Baden-Powell's acumen at this time see Gibbs-Smith, *The Rebirth of European Aviation*, p. 139.

[4] Octave Chanute Papers, B. Baden-Powell to Chanute, 14 February 1904.

Journal called the statement "a true and authentic account". The final paragraph of the Wright brothers' statement left British technical readers in no doubt about the high claims that were being made. It declared of their powered flights of 17 December at Kitty Hawk:

> Only those who are acquainted with practical aeronautics can appreciate the difficulties of attempting the first trials of a flying machine in a 25-mile gale . . . we were determined, before returning home, to know whether the machine possessed sufficient power to fly, sufficient strength to withstand the shock of landings, and sufficient capacity of control to make flight safe in boisterous winds, as well as in calm air. When these points had been definitely established, we at once packed our goods and returned home, knowing that the age of the flying machine had come at last.

Meanwhile, man's new ability to fly was noticed in an entirely different forum. The technicians of the Aeronautical Society of Great Britain were not the only ones in England to reveal a remarkable alertness at this time.

By the early years of the present century, some men in Britain were becoming frightened and uneasy. The blunders of the South African War had disclosed to all the world the incapacity of the British Army and the incompetence of the British War Office. As a result, many politicians and journalists began to fear for the future of their country. In the opinion of some of these thinkers the war had revealed and made obvious a serious decline in British power and strength. Men wondered if Britain was still capable of maintaining and defending the Empire.

In response to this gloomy attitude there also grew up in England a movement that aimed to work a reversal of these trends, and this loss of confidence, by exploiting the country's resources in new and more efficient ways. There were still patriots and optimists in the land.

As a matter of course these ideas were accompanied by other reflections. There occurred, at this time, a good deal of speculation about Britain's destiny. The strategy Britain should adopt in order to maintain the supremacy she had enjoyed for centuries became a subject for sharp debate. Leo Amery, a brilliant young journalist and politician of the day, was a leader in the intellectual circles that concerned themselves with such matters. As early as January 1904 Amery began to think about man's ability to fly in the air as a new factor to be taken into account when the fate of Britain, and the Empire, was discussed.

At the end of January 1904 Amery attended a meeting of the Royal Geographical Society, in London. The principal speaker of the evening was a distinguished strategical thinker, the eminent geographer, and Director of the London School of Economics and Political Science, Halford Mackinder. At the meeting Mackinder delivered a talk, "The Geographical Pivot of History", which became famous. His ideas were later taken up in Germany by General Karl Haushofer, and by Adolf Hitler.

Mackinder believed in the strategic significance of what he called the great "Heartland". By Heartland Mackinder meant the whole north European-Asiatic plain, which stretched eastward from the Elbe river to Vladivostock. He argued that when this vast Heartland was at last developed industrially and agriculturally and knit together by a modern system of railways its productive power would be so great that it could overwhelm any other national or international combination of powers.

In the discussion which followed Mackinder's talk Amery challenged these views. As an Imperialist and an ardent believer in Britain's future, Amery said: ". . . it is now a question of railway-mobility as against sea-mobility. I should like to say that sea-mobility has gained enormously in military strength to what it was in ancient times . . . What I was coming to is this: that both the sea and the railway are going in the future – it may be near, or it may be somewhat remote – to be supplemented by the air as a means of locomotion . . . and when we come to that, a great deal of this geographical distribution must lose its importance, and the successful powers will be those who have the greatest industrial basis. It will not matter whether they are in the centre of a continent or an island; those people who have the power of invention and of science will be able to defeat all others".[1]

Years later, after a lifetime of service to the State, Amery explained in his *Autobiography* that his purpose on that January evening in 1904 was to qualify Mackinder's argument by suggesting that "air power might yet, in the hands of the more highly industrialised powers, redress the balance". He pointed out also that he had offered this comment "a very few months after the brothers Wright had made their first flight at Kitty Hawk . . ."[2]

V

While these developments were taking place in various parts of the world the Wright brothers began upon a programme of further research and experiment. They knew exactly what they wanted to do. Their object was to devise a practical aeroplane. They were no longer satisfied by their

---

[1] See "The Geographical Pivot of History" a talk read at the Royal Geographical Society, January 25, 1904, and published in *The Geographical Journal*, No. 4, April 1904, vol. XXIII, p. 441.

[2] L. S. Amery, *My Political Life* (London, 1953), vol. I, p. 229. The reader should notice that Amery made his comment a very few *weeks* after the Wrights had flown. The comment was published a few months later in April and for this reason, in all probability, Amery made the slight mistake that is to be found in the text of his *My Political Life*.

great success at Kitty Hawk, however significant it was. In their opinion the flights of December 1903 were merely a first step. They had fashioned a machine that could lurch into the air and sustain itself there for a time. Now they proposed to improve upon their original design in order to create a vehicle that could be used effectively for sport, commerce, or in the military sphere.

In addition, they were determined to gain so much practice with their new aeroplane that they would become skilled pilots. The aim was to learn how to control their machine in flight at all times and in all circumstances. Although they were prudent men they were prepared to risk their lives on each occasion that they left the ground in the course of the experiments they now planned to carry out; for it was only in this way, dangerous though it was, that they would be able to come to grips with those mysteries of powered flight that still remained for their solution.

Wilbur and Orville understood they were confronted by formidable technical enquiries. For example, their experiences at Kitty Hawk had taught them their machine was oversensitive in control. They had been unable to regulate the horizontal course of the aeroplane as it flew. The Kitty Hawk flights had been marked out by uncontrollable undulations in the air. The aircraft rose and fell in flight and, despite every effort, they had been unable to correct this heaving up and down as they rushed over the sands. The reason for these aberrations was that their forward elevator, or "horizontal rudder" as they called it, was too evenly balanced. It produced a very significant reaction whenever it was manipulated. In their inexperience they had over-controlled the elevator on each of the powered flights. They realized that this and other flaws in their arrangements would have to be corrected.

In constructing the new machine in 1904 the Wrights introduced a number of general changes in design in order to make it perform more efficiently. The new "Flyer" was heavier and more sturdy than its predecessor. The camber of the wings was modified in order to obtain greater speed in the air. They decided more power was essential and they began, as a result, the construction of three new petrol engines. The capacity of the petrol tank was increased so that the new aeroplane would be able to remain aloft for longer periods of time.

While this work was going forward Octave Chanute sometimes complained to his friends that the Wright brothers had become very secretive. This was not entirely accurate. In March 1904 Wilbur informed Chanute that the brothers were hard at work preparing for the spring season of experimental flights. He told him the new machine would be the same size as the old one, that it would be heavier, that the gearing of the engine would be changed so that additional weight could be carried and that the speed in flight would be increased to about forty miles per hour. A day after Wilbur sent this budget of information Patrick Y. Alexander wrote to Chanute in order to find out what the Wrights were doing with their new aeroplane. Chanute replied at once so that his friend would remain fully informed: "I have your enquiry 15th inst. concerning the Wright machine. Nothing is to [be] added now to what I have already sent you. The weather is still too cold to resume experimenting . . . and I do not believe the Wrights will get at it before May . . ."[1]

The Wrights now decided they would have to find a field in the immediate vicinity of Dayton for the trials of the new aeroplane. Further journeys to Kitty Hawk at this stage of the work would consume too much time and cost too much money. The area around the city was examined and a cow pasture belonging to Torrence Huffman, president of the Fourth National Bank of Dayton, was selected.

This field, variously known to the local inhabitants as the Huffman pasture or Huffman prairie, was hardly ideal for their purpose but it was the best site available. It was some one hundred acres in extent and bordered, on two sides, by high trees. The pasture was near Simms station, a halting place on an electrified interurban railway line that ran between Dayton and Springfield. When the Wrights approached Torrence Huffman to enquire if they could rent the pasture for their trials and experiments the banker revealed a certain largeness of outlook. He told them they were welcome to use the place free of any charge provided only that they drove his cattle and horses to a safe place before each of their experimental flights began.

As the preparatory work neared a conclusion but before any flights were attempted Wilbur Wright invited Chanute to witness their trials, whenever his engagements would allow him to visit them at the Huffman prairie. Wilbur also promised to keep Chanute informed of any developments of significance that might occur in this pre-flight period of preparation.

This was most welcome news for Octave Chanute. Although the Wrights did not know it, Chanute was very pleased to be taken into their confidence in this way, at this juncture.

The older man had developed a genuine respect and fondness for Patrick Alexander. It was exactly at this time, however, that he began to become aware of certain difficulties in their relationship.

Chanute hoped to carry on an amicable correspondence with his friend in England but Alexander now demonstrated an obvious reluctance to exchange letters in the way Chanute desired. Alexander, in his correspondence, confined himself to a single topic. He wrote only to find out about the progress being made by the Wright brothers. He sent such a letter of enquiry to Chanute on 15 March. A few weeks later Chanute complained to him: "I have received nothing from you since your brief

[1] Octave Chanute Papers, Chanute to Alexander, 28 March 1904.

note of enquiry of March 15 . . ." On the same day, 6 May 1904, Chanute also wrote to Major Moedebeck in order to grumble about Alexander's strange conduct: ". . . I have had only very brief notes from Mr. Alexander (Jan 28th & March 15th) since his return from his trip around the world, enquiring what the Wrights were doing. In point of fact they are building a new machine, and hope to get it done – some time this month . . ."[1]

Despite this difficulty in his personal affairs Chanute made certain his friends in England realized that he was still in very close contact with the Wright brothers. A few days later, on 9 May, he wrote to Major Baden-Powell in order to tell him: ". . . Wright brothers expect to resume experimenting in about ten days. There will, of course, be many delays and breakages, but I expect them to attain very good results".[2]

VI

Octave Chanute was entirely correct in these predictions and expectations. By the latter part of May the Wright brothers were at last ready to try their new aeroplane in the field.

They faced an awesome challenge. At Kitty Hawk they had managed a number of straight-line flights, "powered-straights" as they were to be called by future generations of pilots. But at the Huffman pasture the goal was entirely different. The experiments there were designed to achieve complete control in the air when a variety of manoeuvres was attempted. They were now determined to learn how to fly circles and figures of eight in the air. Until such evolutions were mastered completely they would not possess a machine of practical utility. As they began upon this new quest they could only guess at the further mysteries and subtleties of flight that still awaited them.

When all was prepared the Wrights informed every newspaper in Dayton that they would attempt to fly at the Huffman prairie, on 23 May 1904. Several journalists, friends, and neighbours appeared at the field in order to witness the novelty. Unfortunately, the wind was not strong enough to permit a flight but an attempt was made, nevertheless, in order not to disappoint the invited guests. The machine ran along its starting track and slid off at the end of it without rising into the air. The trial was repeated on the next day when the aeroplane managed to glide in the air for about sixty feet but then dropped to the ground. These failures were

[1] Octave Chanute Papers, Chanute to Alexander, 6 May 1904; and Chanute to Major Moedebeck, 6 May 1904.
[2] Octave Chanute Papers, Chanute to Baden-Powell, 9 May 1904. See also Pritchard, *The Wright Brothers and the Royal Aeronautical Society*, p. 771.

only the first of many to occur during the experiments of 1904. It took the Wrights some time to realize that conditions at the Huffman pasture were so different from those prevailing at Kitty Hawk that radical changes would have to be made before they could launch their machine into the air and expect it to stay there for a significant period of time.

Chanute reported these disappointing results to Patrick Y. Alexander early in June. By that time he had become seriously concerned by Alexander's attitude. He wondered if he had offended his friend in some way. He gave expression to these feelings in a letter to Alexander, dated 2 June. He also took care to keep Alexander informed about the Wrights and the progress of their work.[1]

> I have just received your letter of May 20th and it expresses such profound disgust with things in general that I am alarmed about you. Has your health failed, or have you met with some losses, or have I unwittingly offended you?
>
> I have puzzled over the fact that I have received but two brief notes (more enquiries) from you since you got back home five months ago, and I cannot think of anything that I have written you that could possibly give offence. Should there be anything I beg of you to advise me.
>
> . . . The Wrights have been experimenting again without any great results, but are to try again in a few days.

Shortly after Chanute wrote to Major Moedebeck: "Pray tell me, confidentially, what is the matter with Mr. Alexander. I am quite at a loss about him."[2]

While Wilbur and Orville struggled to overcome the technical difficulties that plagued them at the Huffman prairie the Aeronautical Society of Great Britain again singled them out for notice. An article that mentioned their achievements appeared in *The Aeronautical Journal*, the organ of the society, in July 1904. In form the article was a review of a lecture, "Aerial Navigation", read by Octave Chanute before the American Association for the Advancement of Science on 30 December 1903. Chanute's paper had been printed in the *Popular Science Monthly* for March 1904 and was taken up by *The Aeronautical Journal* in July. According to the review in *The Aeronautical Journal*: "There is . . . no opinion of the progress in the engineering of balloons and aeroplanes that we so much value as that of Mr. Octave Chanute . . ." Having thus affirmed Chanute's credentials the review then reproduced his opinion of the Wright brothers "whose flying machine was successfully tested on December 17". According to *The Aeronautical Journal* "Mr. Chanute

---

[1] Octave Chanute Papers, Chanute to Alexander, 2 June 1904.
[2] Octave Chanute Papers, Chanute to Moedebeck, 9 July 1904.

considers that too much praise cannot be awarded to those gentlemen".

During the course of this summer the Wright brothers discovered that the atmospheric conditions at the Huffman pasture were quite different from those at Kitty Hawk. Moreover, the speed of the prevailing breezes at their new field was found to be very much lower than that of the winds they had encountered on the Carolina shore.

In order to gain flying speed it was necessary for their machine to rise into the teeth of the wind. However, at the Huffman pasture the wind shifted regularly, and there were frequent unpredictable lulls. The aeroplane had to race along a track, of the Wrights' own design, in order to become airborne, but whenever the wind changed its direction the launching track had to be laid all over again so that it would conform with the new conditions. This entailed exhausting and time-consuming work. There was also great danger. On occasion the wind shifted at the moment of launching. The result was a crash. Unless the problem could be solved the Wrights, as a matter of course, faced frequent damage to the machine and regular injury to themselves.

Their mechanical ingenuity proved equal to the difficulty. Wilbur and Orville were firm believers in the American dictum that obstacles exist to be overcome. They decided, after weeks of frustration, that they needed a starting device that would render them independent of the wind, fitful as it was, an instrument that would furnish them with sufficient initial velocity to leave the ground whenever they desired to do so.

They designed a catapult powered by a falling weight. A pyramidal tower of tall poles was erected at one end of the launching track. Inside the pyramid a heavy weight was lifted to the top and linked to the aeroplane by a system of ropes and pulleys. When the weight was released and crashed to the ground the Flyer was hurled forward on its track with such speed that it leapt into the air. This device was tried for the first time on 7 September 1904. It was an instant success. From that moment the fortunes of the Wright brothers began to change. They could launch their machine whenever they chose, even in a dead calm.

Notable results now followed. Gradually, as they gained in experience, the brothers were able to extend their time in the air. A great step was taken on 20 September when the first circular flight was completed successfully. On 9 November 1904 Wilbur flew for more than five minutes, circling the Huffman prairie four times, and covering a distance of more than three miles. A few weeks later Orville performed a similar feat.

These flights of 1904 were all made at very low heights, sometimes a mere ten feet above the ground, so that if a crash occurred there would be a reasonable chance to survive it. The object was not to establish endurance or altitude records but to learn how to fly. One aeronautical problem was not solved during the 1904 season. The machine tended to stall and fall out of control whenever a tight turn was attempted. This difficulty was not fully overcome until the autumn of 1905. Nevertheless, at the end of 1904 the Wright brothers were delighted with their achievements and were convinced they now possessed a machine they could develop into a practical aeroplane.

Early in October Wilbur urged Octave Chanute to come to the Huffman prairie so that he could at last observe for himself what he had dreamt of for so many years, an aeroplane manoeuvring in flight and performing evolutions in the air at the direction of its pilot. On 15 October 1904 Chanute responded to the invitation and travelled to the field, where he witnessed a flight.

A few days later another visitor, a stranger, arrived in Dayton. He was not allowed to see the aeroplane in the air or on the ground. However, the Wright brothers invited him to their home where, despite their caution and vigilance, they showed him every courtesy. They spoke to him at some length about their experiments; they permitted him to examine one of their motors; and they allowed him to see several photographs of their aircraft in flight.

This visitor was Colonel Capper. He had travelled from his headquarters in the Aldershot Command to the United States in order to observe the aeronautical section of the St Louis Exhibition. Before he left London he had been "briefed . . . on the current state of the art . . . in the United States"[1] by his friend, Patrick Y. Alexander. As a result, when the exhibition at St Louis was over, and before he returned to England, Colonel Capper made a special journey to Dayton for the sole purpose of meeting Wilbur and Orville Wright.

VII

The decision to send Colonel Capper to the United States was made in the War Office, in Whitehall, in July 1904. It was the duty of the high military authorities there to decide upon the aeronautical policy of the British Army.

The orders and general instructions of the War Office in this sphere of military activity were carried out and put into effect by two separate organizations stationed, at this time, in the Aldershot Command. These two institutions were known as the Balloon Factory and the Balloon

---

[1] The phrase is in Penrose, *British Aviation, The Pioneer Years*, p. 58. The reader should bear in mind that Penrose knew these British aeronautical pioneers, and that when he prepared his history the British authorities allowed him access to many secret and confidential documents dealing with the subject of early military aeronautics.

Sections. In the course of time the first of these bodies developed into the famous Royal Aircraft Establishment and the second became the Royal Air Force.

Despite its archaic name the Balloon Factory, by 1904, was involved in all forms of aerial activity. It was concerned with the construction of kites, gliders, and dirigible airships, as well as with military observation balloons. By this period the men in charge of the Factory were also thinking about aeroplanes for the use of the British Army. In addition, the establishment was more than a mere factory. Research into and development of all kinds of aerial vehicles were also carried out. The Balloon Factory was controlled directly by the War Office in London. Despite its geographical situation it was not looked upon as an integral part of the local Aldershot Command.

The officer in charge was known officially as the Superintendent of the Balloon Factory. In 1904 the Superintendent was Colonel James Lethbridge Brooke Templer, a hard-riding militia officer belonging to the King's Royal Rifles, and known as a pioneer in the construction and employment of military observation balloons, a man regarded by his contemporaries as "a great leader and the grand master of the ballooning art".

Colonel Templer was an enthusiast. For decades he had devoted his life to this area of military action. It was his great hope and ambition to make the British Army "air-minded" and to provide it with an efficient Air Arm. Such was his devotion that he spent a great amount of his private fortune in pushing this work forward, sometimes with the support of his military superiors, and sometimes without it.

Colonel Templer was stockily built and he wore a heavy military moustache. It was his habit to wander through the sheds of his Factory to make certain all was in order and to see that his instructions were being carried out to the letter. On these visits or inspections he regularly carried, in his old-fashioned way, a snuff-box in one hand and a large coloured handkerchief in the other. It was Templer who had been responsible, in good part, for the orders which summoned Colonel Capper home from South Africa to take up command of the Balloon Sections, at Aldershot. He looked upon Capper as his successor, as the officer who would continue the work he had begun as far back as 1878.

For their part, the Balloon Sections were military units under the direct control of the General Officer Commanding at Aldershot. These units were manned chiefly by officers and soldiers of the Royal Engineers. Their task was to train troops in the use of aerial vehicles of all kinds, to take part in peacetime manoeuvres, and to be ready to perform in the field on active service in time of war. It may be mentioned here that as a result of various reorganizations the name of the Balloon Sections was altered to Balloon Companies, in April 1905, and in April 1906 the unit was designated the Balloon School. Throughout these changes Colonel Capper remained as "Commandant".

By the early summer of 1904, owing to the activity and energy of Octave Chanute, everyone in Britain interested in aviation had been made aware of the St Louis World's Fair, and its aeronautical section. After consultation with Capper, Colonel Templer decided that a great deal would be learned if a British officer could attend the World's Fair since aeronauts from the "whole of the civilised world" were expected to be there, demonstrating machines and devices of every kind. In June 1904 Templer suggested to the War Office that Colonel Capper should be sent on such a mission. He prepared his recommendation in brief but forceful terms:[1]

From the
SUPERINTENDENT BALLOON FACTORY,
To the
SECRETARY,
WAR OFFICE, HORSE GUARDS,
WHITEHALL, S.W.

Aldershot. 27th June, 1904.

Sir,

St. Louis World's Fair

I have the honour to recommend that a Military Ballooning Officer be specially deputed to attend the above Fair for a month or six weeks in September and October next. It is undoubted that there will be the latest things in aeronautics, and an immense amount to be learnt there.

I would recommend that Lieut.-Colonel Capper, R.E., who has offered his services, should be deputed for this duty.

I have the honour to be,
Sir,
Your obedient Servant,
J. Templer
Colonel
S.B.F.

A month later, on 28 July, the War Office agreed to this request. Colonel Capper at once began his preparations for the journey. His first step was to consult with Patrick Y. Alexander so that he could obtain from him letters of introduction to various American aeronautical experts. Capper believed that Alexander's assistance in furnishing him with such letters was vital to the success of his historic mission. When he

---

[1] Air 1/728/176/3/17A. Templer to Secretary, War Office, 27 June 1904. See also Walker, *Early Aviation at Farnborough*, vol. II, p. 3.

returned to Aldershot after the mission was completed he prepared an official report for the War Office. In it he explained to his superiors:[1]

> Before leaving England I was, through the courtesy of Mr. P. Y. Alexander, a gentleman who is probably better acquainted personally with all interested in aeronautics in Europe and America than any other living individual, given a number of letters of introduction to various gentlemen who are interested in Aeronautics, and whom I might hope to see in St. Louis, or might visit if they lived within reasonable distance of my route. . . .
>
> . . . I wish to invite attention to the fact that without Introductions I should have had difficulty at St. Louis and elsewhere in America in obtaining information, and in finding out where to obtain it, whilst thanks to the Introductions given by a civilian friend I was everywhere treated with great openness by those who are working on aeronautical subjects, and was able to go direct to the right people.

Alexander supplied Capper with letters to a number of American professors engaged in aeronautical experiments. In addition he gave him letters of introduction to Professor Langley, Octave Chanute, and "Messrs. W. & O. Wright, Dayton".

Colonel Capper decided it would be prudent, and also beneficial, if he informed the American authorities of his planned visit to their country. At the end of August he sent a formal letter to the United States Consul-General in London:[2]

> Sir,
>   Having been deputed by His Majesty's Government to visit the St. Louis Exhibition, I would be extremely obliged if you would put me in the way of obtaining any papers that will be of assistance to me while travelling in the United States of America, and will permit me to take uniform, etc., and a sufficiency of clothing free into the country, where I shall only be for some six weeks to two months.
>   I am, Sir,
>   Your obedient Servant
>
> Balloon Factory,
> Aldershot   Lieut.-Colonel,
> 31.8.04   Commanding Balloon Sections, R.E.

Thus prepared, armed with his letters of introduction supplied by Patrick Y. Alexander and with other appropriate documents, and accom-

---

[1] See Air 1/1608/204/85/36. "Aeronautics" prepared by J. E. Capper, Bt. Lieut.-Colonel, R.E., and dated "Aldershot, 15.12.04".

[2] Air 1/728/176/3/17A. Capper to United States Consul-General, 31 August 1904.

panied by his wife, Colonel Capper sailed from Liverpool on board the R.M.S. *Lucania* on 10 September 1904. He arrived in New York a week later. On the day before his ship docked he wrote a letter to the Wright brothers to inform them of his visit to St Louis and to tell them he might be able to travel to Dayton in order to see them. Patrick Alexander's letter of introduction to the Wrights, dated 20 August 1904, was despatched at this time. It explained to them: "My friend Lt. Col. Capper, C.B., R.E., is visiting America and will also go to St. Louis, and he would very much like to have a talk with you".[1]

VIII

Colonel Capper's first significant act after his arrival in the United States was to seek out Octave Chanute. He knew that Chanute, a fountain of aeronautical information, would be delighted to tell him about the technical work in aeronautics being carried on in every part of the country. He arranged to travel to Chicago as soon as he could do so. There, he spent a good deal of time with Chanute who graciously provided him with details about his own gliding machines; and with information about the Wright brothers' aeroplane, as well.

Capper proceeded next to St Louis, as his duty required, and at once began to study the aeronautical exhibits which were displayed or demonstrated at the World's Fair. As we shall see in the next chapter he made a careful note of everything to be seen but his general impression was one of disappointment. Although he learned a good deal Capper decided that the quality of the exhibits at St Louis was not especially high. While he was at the exhibition he met Major Baden-Powell and a number of German, French, Russian and American aeronautical authorities, some military men and others who were civilian experts.

Chanute had earlier informed several of his British friends that the Wrights might appear at the World's Fair in order to demonstrate their successful aeroplane but Capper was sorry to learn that the brothers had decided, after weeks of reflection, not to enter their machine in any of the competitions. He took good care, however, to keep in close touch with them. When Wilbur Wright, in response to his letter written on the *Lucania*, invited him to visit Dayton he replied at once in order to accept; and to express his opinion of the aeronautical section of the World's Fair:

[1] Wright Brothers' Papers, Alexander to the Wrights, 20 August 1904. The best published account of Capper's trip is in Walker, *Early Aviation at Farnborough*, vol. II, pp. 6ff. However, a critical analysis of Walker's entire presentation is in Alfred Gollin, "The Wright brothers and the British authorities, 1902–1909" in *The English Historical Review*, vol. XCV, April 1980, No. CCCLXV, pp. 293ff.

"I am much obliged to you for your kind letter and invitation to visit you. I hope to do so later, and to let you know about the time shortly. At present I am rather uncertain as to the date to which I will stay here. The aeronautical show here is somewhat disappointing, but there is something to learn, and I hope that the congress may lead to an enlarged knowledge on the subject."[1]

Capper understood he would be required to prepare a formal and official report of his American visit for the War Office upon his return to England. However, while he was still in St. Louis he decided he had already discovered information of such military significance that he should at once alert his superiors in Aldershot.

He therefore wrote a letter, dated 2 October 1904, and despatched it to Aldershot, most probably to his senior colleague at the Balloon Factory, Colonel Templer. In his letter he described the balloons and airships he had seen at the exhibition, and also mentioned one of Chanute's man-carrying gliders that had been demonstrated there.

However, he had not been excited by the performance of these aeronautical devices. His military ardour had been aroused by the information he had collected dealing with the work of the Wright brothers.

In the letter he sent to Aldershot Capper suggested that unless the British Army itself began to experiment with aeroplanes it would be left behind in the military applications of the new technology. He urged that an "experimental school" for the purpose should be established in England. He wrote:[2]

> . . . The Wrights are not coming here. They are keeping quiet till perfect, but have sent me an invitation to go to see them at Dayton, which I shall do. It is undoubted that they have made a flight of half a mile with a motor attached to their glider, and are working on a larger machine with which they intend to try extended flight. A few earnest workers are working over here. I hope to see more in Washington and elsewhere, and when the problem of mechanical automatic stability is solved, machines will fly and with very little danger. I feel convinced myself the time is near, and that we must have a proper experimental school in England, or we shall be left behind . . .

In these circumstances Capper made certain the Wright brothers were kept informed of his activities. On 17 October he told Wilbur that he

---

[1] Wright Brothers' Papers, Capper to Wilbur Wright, 27 September 1904.
[2] Air 1/728/176/3/17A. Capper's letter, dated 2 October 1904. It was most probably sent to Templer but the physical condition of this document is such no positive identification of the recipient is possible.

proposed to arrive in Dayton on the 23rd. He made clear to him that:
". . . my only object in stopping at Dayton is to make acquaintance with
you and your brother".[1]

IX

The meeting between Wilbur and Orville Wright and Colonel Capper was
a cordial one. It might be expected that a first encounter between a
high-ranking British officer of that period and a couple of American
bicycle-makers would be marked out by a certain stiffness of manner,
upon the one side or upon the other. This was not the case. The honesty
and straightforwardness of Wilbur and Orville worked an instant effect.
Capper was genuinely impressed by the character of his hosts. The charm
of the Wright family and household also played a part. Indeed Mrs
Capper, who accompanied her husband on the journey to Dayton,
became friendly with the brothers and with their sister Katharine, who
lived with them; and this friendship lasted for years.

Wilbur Wright later recorded some significant details of the meeting. In
1907, in his confidential memorandum, mentioned earlier, he wrote:[2]

> In 1904 Colonel J. E. Capper, Chief of the Aeronautic Depart-
> ment of the British [War] Department visited us in Dayton and
> requested us, when we felt that our machine had been brought to a
> practical stage, to give Great Britain the first chance. We told him
> that we were not yet ready to talk business.

Capper made his own impressions clear to his superiors when he
prepared his formal report for the War Office in December, after his
return to England. This report must be looked upon as one of the
important documents of early British aeronautical history. In the section
of his report entitled *"Wright's Flying Machine"* he declared:[3]

> At Dayton I visited Messrs. O. & W. Wright, who have for the past
> five years been carrying out experiments with a double decked
> Gliding Machine.

[1] Wright Brothers' Papers, Capper to Wilbur Wright, 17 October 1904. See
also Walker, *Early Aviation at Farnborough*, vol. II, p. 16.

[2] Wright Brothers' Papers, "Wright Brothers' English Negotiations", 8 February 1907.

[3] Air 1/1608/204/85/36. "Aeronautics". Visit to United States of America in
Sept. to Novr. 1904, by Brevet Lieutenant-Colonel J. E. Capper, C.B., Commanding Balloon Sections, Royal Engineers. The report is dated "Aldershot
15.12.04". All further references to this report, in the present chapter, are taken
from this source.

These experiments have been very generally successful, so much so as to lead them to construct a large glider which would carry both one operator and a motor driving fan propellers. In December last they succeeded in keeping the machine in the air for 59 seconds, and since then they have made further experiments which have induced in them both a very strong confidence that they will shortly without difficulty be able to compass journeys of considerable length.

Both these gentlemen impressed me most favourably; they have worked up step by step, they are in themselves well educated men, and capable mechanics, and I do not think are likely to claim more than they can perform.

Colonel Capper's report continued with a statement that has been called by a British aeronautical authority "one of the most significant in British aviation history":[1]

They were most courteous, showed me their motor of which they do not desire any particulars at present made public, and also gave me, in confidence, certain particulars of their machine and of the work they have actually done, illustrated by photographs taken of the machine in different conditions of flight, which have satisfied me that they have at least made far greater strides in the evolution of the flying machine than any of their predecessors.

The report placed great emphasis upon the Wrights' confidence in themselves and in their creation:

They would not commit themselves to any definite statements, but were of opinion that within a few months they may be in a position to make their knowledge more public, and to show practically the measure of success they have reached.

Colonel Capper concluded this section of his report in a separate paragraph which he entitled "*Military Importance*". His conclusion was designed to cause excitement and to evoke the interest of his military superiors:

The work they are doing is of very great importance, as it means that if carried to a successful issue, we may shortly have as accessories of warfare, scouting machines which will go at a great pace, and be independent of obstacles of ground, whilst offering from their elevated position unrivalled opportunities of ascertaining what is occurring in the heart of an enemy's country.

[1] The authority is Walker, *Early Aviation at Farnborough*, vol. II, p. 18. He prints several parts of Capper's report though his text varies slightly from that preserved in the Public Record Office.

He sought also to warn the War Office authorities that opportunity for their country was slipping away. He wrote of the development of flying machines: "England is very backward. There are strong hopes of success in this direction, and such success, with at any rate small machines, may come much earlier than is generally anticipated, and America is leading the way, whilst in England practically nothing is being done."

Capper was genuinely excited by what he had discovered on his American tour. His ambition and his patriotism, alike, had been set aflame as a result of his experiences in the United States. He therefore concluded his report with a number of "Special Recommendations". He sought, by means of these "Recommendations", to exert some influence upon the entire aeronautical policy of the War Office. In particular, he suggested that an "experimental school", the idea he had first touched upon when he was in St Louis, should be established in England. He wrote:

Special Recommendations

What has perhaps struck me more than anything else is the want of a proper experimental school, organised under the War Office, but free for the greater part of the year from Military duties, for the carrying out of such experiments as are necessary to determine the conditions which a dirigible balloon or flying machine must fulfil to be successful, and for collating information on the subject. . . .

Such a school should be furnished with proper instruments, and with a small experimental laboratory recognised as such. The annual expenditure on such a school need not be large, especially as the personnel could be furnished from among the officers and men of the Balloon Sections; but it would be necessary that officers showing any special talent for the work should be kept to it for considerable periods. . . .

He also recommended the creation of a technical library at Aldershot.

Further, I would advocate the gradual formation of a Government library at Aldershot of all works which bear on the subject of aeronautics . . . Our English publications are very scanty, and I know of hardly any which belong to the Government. Foreign literature on the subject is greater in quantity and better in quality. I could find but little of real interest among the works in the British Museum when I tried to improve my knowledge of the subject in 1903. . . .

Contact with others will assist us in judging as to what works are worthy of occupying a position in such a library . . .

Further, such contact with other workers must lead to great economies both of time and money, in saving us from making experiments in directions which have elsewhere proved profitless . . .

Colonel Capper finished his report with an appeal to his superiors, urging that the work he had begun with his visit to the United States, should be allowed to continue, and to expand:

> We have made a start now in the direction of contact with others, largely owing to my deputation to St. Louis, and I trust that such contact may be brought closer, and that all the officers of the Balloon Sections may be encouraged to obtain further general knowledge on aeronautical subjects, by the facilities above recommended.
>
> J.E.C.
Bt. Lieut.-Colonel, R.E.
>
> Aldershot
> 15.12.04.

In later years Colonel Capper's mission to the United States came to be regarded as a matter of such high importance in the history of British military aviation that a number of myths about it began to appear in the historical literature. Several incorrect accounts of his adventure were published in various monographs or articles whose quality commands respect. This resulted in serious misinterpretation of the aeronautical policy adopted by the British War Office in the earliest days of successful powered flight.

For example, one distinguished authority who was allowed to see the report of 15 December 1904 stated that in it Colonel Capper recommended to the War Office "that a machine should be bought from the Wright brothers without delay".[1] However, Capper made no such recommendation in his report.

He had certainly been fascinated by the Wright brothers when he met them in Dayton. He learned there that they had flown and were preparing to build an even more efficient flying machine in the immediate future. He asked them, as Wilbur Wright's memorandum reveals, to "give Great Britain the first chance" whenever they were ready to sell their invention. He was very interested in the secrets of their scientific and technical work. He would have been delighted if the British Government could have purchased a Wright aeroplane in 1904.

Nevertheless, he did not recommend such an acquisition in his report. Colonel Capper was too prudent a military administrator and too cautious a public servant to act in such a bold way.

However, he was determined, after his American visit, to do what he

---

[1] The authority is Harald Penrose. See his *British Aviation, The Pioneer Years*, p. 65.

could to make certain the British Army would not "be left behind" in these awesome new developments in aeronautics. In order to secure such a result he recommended that the War Office should strike out by itself and establish an experimental school and laboratory; that a technical library should be built up; that his officers in the Balloon Sections should be encouraged to devote themselves to the study of aeronautics; that all these innovations should be concentrated in the Aldershot Command.

Colonel Capper believed his American mission had enabled Britain to make "a start" in these developments. When he returned to Aldershot his goal was to see to it that this work was continued. He wanted the British Army to be put in a position that would enable it to forge ahead on its own in the field of aviation and aeronautics. Furthermore, he wanted to be the man who organized, controlled, and carried out these novel departures that would result, if all went well, in the creation of an efficient and modern Air Arm for his country.

CHAPTER 4

The Wright Brothers Approach the British

Colonel Capper's determination – Early balloonists and
military application – English ballooning enthusiasts – The
Royal Engineer Committee – Captain James Templer –
The Balloon Equipment Store – Bechuanaland Expedition
– The Suakin Expeditionary Force – A Balloon Section is
Authorized – Templer appointed Superintendent – The
South African War – Colonel Arthur Lynch's Lecture –
Provision for six Balloon Sections – Dirigible Balloons –
Samuel Cody and his Kites – Recommendations of the
Committee on Ballooning – Colonel Capper's Report –
Personality and qualifications of Colonel Capper – Tech-
nical Training Balloon Sections – A remarkable letter from
Wilbur and Orville Wright – Capper Speaks to the Aero-
nautical Society – The Wright triumphs of 1904 – Their
Course of Action – They write to Capper – Patrick Alexan-
der again – His remarkable "contact" – Wilbur and Orville
write to Congressman Robert Nevin – The Negative Reply
of the U.S. War Department – Its significance – The
Advantages of Treating with the British Government –
Apprehension and Caution of the Wright Brothers – Their
letter Arrives in England.

I

When Colonel Capper returned to England in November 1904 after his
visit to the United States he was excited by what he had learned
there about the Wright brothers and their aeroplanes. Nevertheless, his
energy and his ambitions were not confined to the subject of aeroplanes.

Capper was a serious student of the military art. He knew that the
British Army of that day already possessed a formidable record in the
sphere of military aeronautics and he was determined to improve upon it,
in several directions. At the end of 1904 the authorities at the War Office
and in the Aldershot Command were interested in the technical possibili-

ties of captive balloons, dirigible airships, man-lifting kites, gliders, and aeroplanes.

Colonel Capper had now made up his mind to play a vigorous part in the development of all these various aeronautical devices, by study and by experiment, so that his country would be prepared to hold its own in any future warlike actions that might take place in the air.

The earliest balloonists who began to meet with some measure of success in the late eighteenth century had been quick to advocate the military potential of their balloons. They believed balloons could perform valuable service as aerial scouts or that they could be used to drop bombs on cities or troop encampments.

Few professional soldiers, however, were prepared to pay serious attention to the balloonists. In 1793, for example, one of the Montgolfier brothers proposed to destroy the city of Toulon, then in revolt against the Republic, by dropping more than fourteen tons of explosive on the town from a balloon. The Republican armies in France occasionally used hydrogen balloons but Napoleon was not impressed by devices of this kind. When it was suggested to him in 1808 that he might invade England with a fleet of Montgolfier balloons he at once rejected the idea as an impossible operation of war.

In 1849 the Austrians employed hot air balloons in order to drop explosives on Venice. The Austrian Army held the city under siege but the range of its guns was not enough to bring the place under effective conventional fire. The Austrians formed a number of "balloon battalions" to drop bombs weighing more than thirty pounds from Montgolfier balloons. Although the physical destruction caused was not great it was said that these attacks from the air produced a serious effect upon the morale of the besieged townspeople.

During the Italian campaign of 1859 the French military employed a professional balloonist who made several ascents in order to try and spy out the enemy's positions. His efforts were not judged to be entirely successful and the balloonist was forced to sue the French Government in an attempt to collect all the monies he believed were owing to him for his exploits.

In the wars of the first part of the nineteenth century balloons of various kinds found sporadic employment in several European armies. During the American Civil War, however, the Union forces used them more extensively in order to direct artillery fire and to reconnoitre Confederate encampments and positions. The Confederates, in reply, sought to construct their own balloons and used anti-aircraft guns in attempts to bring down the balloons of their enemies. European military observers who visited the United States during the war were not especially impressed by the efficiency of the balloons.

Technical and popular interest in them was revived during the siege of

Paris in 1870 when the French resorted to balloons to send letters to the provinces from their besieged capital. Between the end of September 1870 and January 1871 some three million letters were despatched from Paris for destinations in other parts of France. Men were also carried out of the town in this way. Gambetta made his escape by means of a balloon ascent and was able to prolong the struggle against the Prussians for a time, as a result. Bismarck was not pleased by these novelties of aerial warfare. He informed the French authorities that balloonists who fell into the hands of his troops would be treated as spies. Other measures were also adopted by the besiegers. Alfred Krupp built a number of balloon or anti-aircraft guns. These were small cannon mounted on pedestals and carried in wagons. Several of these Krupp guns saw action during the siege. After 1870, slowly and by degrees, a number of balloon units were established as regular formations in the various European armies.

II

In England, ballooning enthusiasts urged the military exploitation of their devices throughout the nineteenth century. In 1818 a keen patriot who lived in Cheshire published a pamphlet in which it was proposed that balloons, each carrying hundreds of pounds of explosives, could be used to attack vessels in harbour. Such ships, it was argued in the pamphlet, would find it difficult to avoid assaults of this kind because they would be unable to manoeuvre out of the way in the close confines of a port. In 1846 the British Government subsidized experiments with a bomb-dropping balloon but the results did not impress the officers assigned as observers.

During the 1860s the War Office authorized more serious experiments with balloons at Aldershot and at Woolwich but the authorities decided eventually not to recommend the establishment of a balloon unit in the British Army. The successful employment of balloons during the siege of Paris, however, aroused renewed curiosity about them. In 1870 an organization called the Royal Engineer Committee was resuscitated so that the War Office would be in a position to refer to it, upon a regular basis, questions about new inventions and improvements in articles of equipment that might be adopted for use by the Army. One of the first matters submitted to the attention of this Royal Engineer Committee was a request to investigate the possibility of using balloons with the Army in the field. A few experiments with balloons were duly carried out but they produced no dramatic result so that official interest in the subject lapsed for a period of several years.

This situation was changed in 1878. At that time James Templer, a young captain in the 2nd Middlesex Militia, began to exert a significant influence. Captain Templer was an experienced amateur balloonist and a man of great energy and determination. He possessed an ample private fortune which he was prepared to expend freely in order to advance the cause of ballooning in the British Army. He built a balloon called the *Pioneer* and practised with it at Woolwich Arsenal. He proceeded to train several officers of the Corps of Royal Engineers in the use of balloons. His various experiments and his programme of training were successful. As a result of his work the War Office decided to make a small sum available for further study and practice. At the same time the authorities took care to state that the balloon was not yet recognized as an item of official equipment for the Army.

During the years that followed a few further experiments were carried out at Woolwich Arsenal. Then in 1882 the War Office decided that the Balloon Equipment Store, as the Woolwich establishment was called, should be transferred to the School of Military Engineering at Chatham. There, under the direction of the Royal Engineer Committee, several officers and men were trained to experiment with balloons and also to practise with them in the field. In the words of the acknowledged expert in this area of military history: "This decision may be regarded as the first step taken in the direction of forming a balloon section as a recognised part of the Army".[1] The officers and sappers at Chatham now began to carry out separate but related functions. They experimented with various methods of generating hydrogen for the balloons and they also sought to find out the best means of constructing balloon envelopes. In addition they were trained in the management and handling of these devices in the field. They were trained to employ balloons in aerial reconnaissance, signalling, and in photography.

By 1884 when an expedition was sent to Bechuanaland to pacify the country a captive balloon detachment was included in its order of battle. The balloons were employed in the field and valuable experience in their use was gained as a result. In the following year balloons proved their military value in a more dramatic campaign.

In 1885 an expeditionary force was sent to the port of Suakin in the Eastern Sudan, the scene of bitter fighting between British and Egyptian troops and the famous dervish leader, Osman Digna. James Templer commanded the balloon detachment that accompanied this Suakin expeditionary force.

His balloons rendered outstanding service, in several ways. On one occasion in March 1885 one of the balloons was used to accompany a camel convoy that supplied a British column which had been pushed out into the desert in order to harry the dervishes and thus break down the power of Osman Digna in the region of the port. In earlier actions the

---

[1] See the classic work of C. F. Snowden Gamble, *The Air Weapon* (Oxford, 1931), p. 63, hereafter cited as Snowden Gamble, *The Air Weapon*.

Arabs had regularly attacked such convoys but the balloon made so significant an impression upon them in this instance that no shots were fired and not a single camel load of the convoy was lost. Balloons were also sent to outlying villages, where they observed and reported the movements of the dervish forces.

The great Departments of State in Britain seldom act with unseemly haste. The next forward step in these aeronautical developments was not taken until 1887. In that year the War Office appointed Major Templer as "Instructor in Ballooning". He was gazetted to the post on 1 April and the position was formally recognized and provided for in the Army Estimates for the year.

In the summer of 1889 a balloon detachment was ordered to Aldershot to take part in manoeuvres and while it was there it attracted the favourable notice of Lieutenant-General Sir Evelyn Wood, Commander of the Aldershot Division, who was impressed by the ability of an officer in a balloon to spy out, with unprecedented accuracy, the details of an "enemy" encampment. General Wood recommended to the War Office that the Balloon Establishment should be transferred from Chatham to Aldershot so that it could cooperate more closely and upon a regular basis with the troops who were trained there. Eventually the War Office concurred in this recommendation.

An important step in the history of British military aeronautics was taken in 1890 when a Balloon Section was formally authorized as a unit in the Corps of Royal Engineers, in the Army Estimates for that year. The unit was established with a strength of three officers, three sergeants, and twenty-eight rank and file sappers while the sum of £600 was also allotted as the salary for the Instructor. Further amounts were allocated for stores, maintenance of the establishment, various other contingent expenses and for the construction of a new school and depot.

Until this time the shop where British Army balloons were constructed, known as the Balloon Factory, had been quartered in the St Mary's Barracks at Chatham. Now, however, the War Office decided to move the Balloon Factory to Aldershot where the troops of the Balloon Section were serving. As the years passed the work of the Factory was so expanded that a further administrative reorganization became necessary. In 1897 the War Office created a new post – "Superintendent of the Balloon Factory". Almost as a matter of course James Templer was appointed to the place.

When this change was made the Officer-in-Charge of the Balloon Section took over the task of instructing the troops who handled the balloons in the field. He reported directly to the Officer Commanding Troops and Companies at Aldershot. Templer, although he continued in close association with these sappers and their officers, was now more concerned with research and with the construction and development of new types of balloons and new ancillary equipment for them. He was responsible for the proper execution of his duties to a high military official in the War Office in London, the Inspector-General of Fortifications.

At about this time the authorities in the War Office began to show some interest in man-lifting kites which could be operated, for a variety of purposes, in winds or breezes that were too dangerous for the employ-ment of captive balloons. Captain Baden-Powell convinced his superiors that the kites possessed military value. After trials and experiment it was decided that they, too, should be included in the equipment of the Balloon Section; and that the sappers of the Section should be trained to use them in the field.

III

The Balloon Sections, Royal Engineers, went to war in 1899 when the campaign against the Boers began in South Africa. Several balloon units were assembled in England and despatched to the various fronts, at intervals, as the fighting continued. A Balloon Section served with some distinction during the siege of Ladysmith. Another was employed by Lord Methuen at Magersfontein. Lord Roberts used captive balloons in his victorious advance of 1900. Winston Churchill, who was present during this triumphant march into Boer territory, later compared the balloon he had seen there with "the pillar of cloud that led the hosts of Israel".[1]

Although several British commanders were very critical of the balloons in action others were favourably impressed. Balloons were variously employed, on several fronts, in signalling; in directing the fire of gun and howitzer batteries; and in observing the deployment and movement of enemy forces.

The highest leadership of the British Army was very interested in the performance of these balloons during the war. This fact is borne out by the existence of a curious and remarkable document, preserved in the official archives. The document is a translation of a lecture delivered in Paris by Colonel Arthur Lynch of the Boer Army. His lecture was published originally in *l'Aéronaute* of April 1902 under the title: "The role of English Military Balloons in the South African War, by Colonel Arthur Lynch of the Boer Army". Dockets attached to the translation reveal that it was read by the Superintendent of the Balloon Factory; by the Inspector-General of Fortifications; and by the Commander-in-Chief himself, Field-Marshal Lord Roberts, the revered hero of the Boer War. As we shall see later in this history Lord Roberts, a brilliant soldier, was

---

[1] Quoted in Thomas Pakenham, *The Boer War* (New York, 1979), p. 444.

genuinely interested in the development of aeronautical devices for military purposes.[1]

Arthur Lynch, the lecturer, was an Australian. He was educated in his own country, in Europe, and in England. When the South African War broke out he travelled there as a correspondent for some English periodicals. His sympathies, however, were on the Boer side. He soon enlisted in their service and saw action with their 2nd Irish Brigade in Natal. As his lecture in Paris revealed he discovered a great deal about British military balloons during the course of the war. He told his audience of French aeronauts: "The balloons have been of great utility to the English at various places, above all at Ladysmith, Colenso, Modder River and Fourteen Streams . . . I take this occasion to say that the English flatter themselves, and perhaps with reason, that they possess the best balloon service of all the armies of the world. Certainly they never draw back from the necessary expense, and they are always the first to make use of all the new inventions in the world of aerial navigation."

Lynch explained the tactical value of the balloons in some detail. He said: "As all the world knows, in actual warfare with smokeless powder it is very difficult to determine the actual position either of a battery or of a body of infantry which attacks you suddenly. One is struck without the satisfaction of knowing who is one's adversary, or from whence the blow came. But the observations made by the help of a balloon have often permitted the English to note exactly the position of a battery, of a laager, of a camp of troops, or of military works, or even movements preparatory to a regular assault. . . ."

In his lecture he made very clear the powerful effect the balloons exerted upon the Boers:

"Therefore the Boers took a dislike to the balloons. All the other instruments of war were at their command. They had pieces of artillery superior to for the most part, and better served than those of the English; they had all the telegraphic and heliographic apparatus; but the balloons were a symbol of a scientific superiority on the side of the English which seriously disquieted them."

Colonel Lynch also revealed in his lecture that the Boers had attempted an aerial attack of their own against their British enemies. He explained the failure of this novel effort in his own amusing way:

"On the side of the Boers, as I have said, there was no balloon, but an American inventor arrived one day with a project which he called an 'eye-opener'. That comprised an immense kite, with which he flattered

---

[1] The translated lecture, with its dockets, is preserved in W.O. 32/6062. See also Air 1/1608/204/85/36. There is some discussion of Lynch's lecture in Walker, *Early Aviation at Farnborough*, vol. I, pp. 34ff.

himself he would photograph the English positions, let fall dynamite, and if necessary, hoist a man into the air.

"He chose a day for his experiments when there was a strong wind, but, unhappily for the 'eye-opener', the wind was so violent that the cord broke, and the kite, free from its bridle, flew off almost into the town of Ladysmith. After this experience the Boers did not attach much importance to ideas of this kind."

Colonel Lynch ended his remarks by emphasizing his belief in the military value of balloons. He said: "To sum up my impressions: I believe that the balloon is of the very greatest value in many military operations, above all in sieges, and in that instance as much to the besieged as to the besiegers. There are other possible developments, and I foresee that the role of this arm is destined to become of ever-increasing importance . . ."

Balloons were not the only aerial devices used by the British Army during the South African War. The frequent strong winds they encountered made it necessary for them to employ kites as well for reconnaissance and also to carry the aerials of wireless telegraphic sets high into the air. Major Baden-Powell played some part in these activities. When he returned to England at the end of the war he sent an account of his experiences to Octave Chanute. He wrote:[1]

> . . . I am afraid my Kite experiences in South Africa were very primitive and not worth recording. Of *course* our Govt. refused to send out any Kite equipment, and yet directly I got out Lord Methuen asked me if I would not get a photo of the lines at Magersfontein with a Kite. So I set to work to rig up a thing of such materials as I could get in camp. I got it up one day for trial in camp & let it out 800 yds. with camera attached – but, unfortunately for me, the enemy "cleared" before I got all in good working order. We also tried several experiments with wireless telegraphy, but without very satisfactory results . . .

IV

Even before the South African War came to an end some military leaders in Britain were convinced that aeronautical developments could not be ignored by a modern and efficient Army. Other high-ranking soldiers disputed this point of view and saw little of military value in the new technology.

Nevertheless, in the Army Estimates for the financial year 1901–1902

---

[1] Octave Chanute Papers, B. Baden-Powell to Chanute, 24 November 1902. Baden-Powell told this story to Snowden Gamble at a later date. See his *The Air Weapon*, p. 81.

provision was made for six Balloon Sections, five of them to be completely operational. This, in its turn, meant that the Balloon Factory had to be
moved from its cramped quarters at Aldershot to a more spacious site
where greater numbers of balloons, with their ancillary trappings and
equipment, could be constructed. Eventually, the new home of the
Balloon Factory was established at Farnborough, in Hampshire, a place
described many years later by Air Chief Marshal Sir Philip Joubert de la
Ferté as "the cradle of British aviation".

An entirely new phase in these aeronautical developments began at
exactly this time. The German and French authorities had been ex-
perimenting for some years with dirigible or navigable airships but the
British War Office had regularly refused to sanction trials with this type of
aircraft. When Colonel Templer returned from active service in South
Africa early in 1901 he was determined to find out about these airships. At
the end of the year he travelled to Paris in order to meet Alberto
Santos-Dumont, the brave young Brazilian who lived and worked there.
In October 1901 Santos-Dumont had managed to fly around the Eiffel
Tower in a navigable airship of his own design. Templer also interviewed
Colonel Charles Renard, the officer in charge of the great French
aeronautical establishment at Chalais-Meudon. Renard refused to allow
Templer to visit the place since he desired to preserve the secrets of
official French aeronautical activity. He did tell him, however, that
the French expected to produce a dirigible balloon in about sixteen
months time.

During his visit Templer also spoke or conferred with other French
aeronautical experts. Thus armed, he prepared a report for the War
Office, in January 1902, which recommended that experiments with
dirigible balloons should be commenced in Britain. The War Office
replied to this recommendation by informing Templer that the vote in the
Army Estimates for 1902–1903 for the Balloon Factory and the Balloon
Sections was to be reduced by one-half, from £12,000 to £6,000. Despite
this harsh blow to his hopes Templer managed, from time to time, to
obtain supplementary grants for the construction of "elongated balloons". The creation of these devices at the Balloon Factory, under his
direction, was looked upon as a first step in the building of a British
military airship.

The British Army also developed a keen interest in kites in this period.
The war in South Africa had demonstrated that kites could sometimes be
used in winds that were too strong for captive balloons. In the pre-war
period Captain Baden-Powell, as we have seen, had attracted the attention of his superiors when he managed to raise men into the air with his
kites. A far more brilliant inventor of kites was a remarkable American,
Samuel Franklin Cody, who sought to interest the War Office in his
"observation kites" in October 1901.

The story of Samuel Cody and early British military aviation is unusual, even bizarre. Cody was born in Birdville, Texas. He began his working life as a cowboy, hunter, and tamer of wild horses. On a visit to England he met a beautiful English girl and married her. From that time he looked upon England as his home.

Cody earned his living in Britain as a professional entertainer who toured the music halls and demonstrated his prowess, before large and appreciative audiences, as a crack shot with rifle and pistol, a lasso expert, and trick rider. He wore, even when he was not on the stage, an outsize cowboy hat, long flowing locks and a goatee beard so that he would resemble his namesake, William Frederic Cody, the famous "Buffalo Bill".

Samuel Cody's hobby was kite-flying. He produced such remarkable results with the kites he invented that he attracted the attention of the War Office and the Admiralty. Eventually Cody, as an employee of the War Office, progressed from the building of kite-systems to the construction of gliders, and also a powered aeroplane. In October 1908 he became the first man to fly a powered aeroplane in the British Isles.

In 1901 and 1902 when Cody sought to attract the attention of the War Office to his kites the authorities there showed only a tepid curiosity in them. In February 1903 Cody, a man who knew how to persevere, approached the Admiralty in the hope that they would take up his offer to demonstrate the military value of his kites. The Admiralty, however, declined to accept his proposal.

Cody, the enthusiast, would not acquiesce in so negative a decision. In March 1903 he informed the Admiralty that he planned to carry out experiments with his kites on the Woolwich Common; and he invited them to send a representative to observe the display. The Naval authorities who were interested in the possibilities of the kites had already asked Major Baden-Powell to furnish them with his expert opinion of Cody's inventions. When he reported that "the kites are good"[1] the situation changed completely. It was decided that a high-ranking officer should be despatched to Woolwich to see exactly what Cody could do.

The officer who observed the kites in action at the Woolwich Common recommended to his superiors that formal naval trials with them should be undertaken. As a result Prince Louis of Battenberg, a brilliant and influential naval officer, at that time Director of Naval Intelligence at the Admiralty, took the matter up with some enthusiasm. He recommended that the Navy should experiment with the kites on a ship at sea and that further trials should be held at Whale Island, the Naval Gunnery School in Portsmouth Harbour.

The Navy was interested in the kites for several reasons. In those early

---

[1] See Walker, *Early Aviation at Farnborough*, vol. I, p. 137.

days of wireless telegraphy it was hoped that a kite might be employed to raise a wireless aerial high in the air, from a ship or from a shore establishment. It was believed, also, that kites might be used to hoist an observer aloft for the purposes of reconnaissance at sea; to transmit light articles from one vessel to another; and to lift a sailor into the air as a "lookout to guard against submarines".[1]

The official naval trials took place at the end of March and early in April 1903. They were moderately successful but Cody spoiled his chances with the Admiralty by asking for very large sums of money for his patents and for the salary he required as a kiting instructor, and designer of kites.

While these naval trials were being carried out the War Office paid careful attention to them. When the Admiralty failed to secure Cody's services the military authorities proceeded to act by themselves. In 1904 Sir John French, the General Officer Commanding-in-Chief at Aldershot, applied to the War Office for permission to study Cody's kites and to report upon them. When this request was approved French directed that the investigations should be carried out by Colonel Capper and his Balloon Sections. In this way the close association between Capper and Cody began.

The first military flight trials of the kites took place at Aldershot in June 1904. They were successful. More than twenty ascents were made. An officer of the Balloon Sections managed to attain a height of 1,300 feet during one of the tests while Capper himself went up to a height of 1,000 feet in another flight. Eventually, Colonel Capper recommended that Cody should be hired by the War Office as a Kiting Instructor. After several limited engagements Cody was appointed, in April 1906, "Chief Kite Instructor" in the British Army.

Under the terms of the arrangement Cody received a salary of £1,000 per year, and free fodder for his horse. As Chief Kite Instructor he trained the sappers of the Balloon School in the operational employment of his kites; and he also designed and supervised the manufacture of kites in the Balloon Factory. By 1906, however, as new technical possibilities opened before them, Colonel Capper and Cody became less interested in the military value of kites. Their minds became fixed upon two other projects: the building of a powered aeroplane for the Army; and the construction of the propulsion system that would be required for the first British military airship.

[1] This phrase is Cody's own. See Walker, *Early Aviation at Farnborough*, vol. I, p. 135.

V

The War Office and the British Army had performed so incompetently during the Boer War that everyone concerned with such matters realized that serious changes and reorganizations were an immediate requirement of the post-war era. Those responsible for the efficiency and preparedness of the Army did not neglect military aeronautics in their considerations.

In June 1903 a Committee on Military Ballooning,[1] which we have noticed in an earlier chapter, was appointed to study the entire subject and to make recommendations about the further development of aeronautics in the British Army. Colonel Capper, as we have seen, was selected as Secretary of this committee. Most of the other members were also officers of proven quality. It may be mentioned that one of them, Brevet Lieutenant-Colonel H. H. Wilson, later became Field-Marshal Sir Henry Wilson, Chief of the Imperial General Staff.

The committee, in carrying out its task, surveyed the achievements of foreign countries in the field of aeronautics and also studied the organization and accomplishments of the Balloon Sections and the Balloon Factory. When a great deal of pertinent information had been collected and analysed the committee then brought forward its recommendations in two reports, an interim report printed in July 1903, and a final report printed in January 1904.

Particular attention was paid to the organization of the Balloon Sections. In place of the six Balloon Sections the committee recommended the establishment of a "Balloon School". The task of this School would be to train classes of officers and soldiers, upon a rotating basis, in the operational use of aeronautical devices. When the course of training was complete the men would be despatched to their units and replaced by others who would, in their own turn, be provided with the instruction that was required. This proposal of the committee was adopted a few years later. In April 1905 the Balloon Sections were renamed the Balloon Companies and in April 1906 these units were formed into the Balloon School with Colonel Capper as its "Commandant".

The members of the committee believed it was urgently necessary for the British Army to obtain possession of a dirigible balloon, or airship. They decided that the Balloon Factory was the place where this military airship should be constructed. When the committee considered the future of the Balloon Factory it recognized the dual nature of the place: it was at once a research establishment and also a factory. In its report the committee set out certain tasks for the Factory. These included: the creation of a dirigible balloon; the construction of an "elongated bal-

---

[1] For the work of this committee see the excellent account in Walker, *Early Aviation at Farnborough*, vol. I, pp. 42ff.

loon"; work with man-lifting kites; the fabrication of smaller balloons that could be used for signalling in the field; the devising of haulage systems that could bring balloons down from the heights; and work with photographic equipment that might be attached to balloons or kites. The committee further recommended that the Balloon Factory should be rebuilt at a new and more spacious site so that there would be ample room to carry out the various commissions and duties that might be assigned to it.

VI

This was the general condition of aeronautics in the British Army when Colonel Templer recommended to the War Office, in June 1904, that Capper should be "deputed to attend" the St Louis World's Fair where he would be able to observe "the latest things" in aeronautics and in aviation.

When Colonel Capper returned to England after his American visit he prepared a report about the excursion for his superiors. We have already taken notice of those sections of the report, dated "Aldershot, 15.12.04", which dealt with the achievements of the Wright brothers; and also the "Special Recommendations" which Capper urged upon the authorities as his suggestions for the further development of aeronautics in the British Army.

The other parts of this report were also significant. They make clear which developments in the new technology were of interest to the contemporary military mind in 1904. Furthermore, during his visit to St Louis Colonel Capper had examined displays of German and French aeronautical equipment as well as American exhibits. He was therefore in a position to offer the War Office and the Aldershot Command a valuable summary and analysis of the achievements of several countries in this field. He wrote in his report:[1]

General Summary

As regards aeronautics I have the following general remarks to offer on my American experiences. –

Captive Balloons.

That we can learn little or nothing in America as regards the construction of, material of, and management of Military Captive Balloons.

---

[1] Air 1/1608/204/85/36. "Aeronautics". "Aldershot 15.12.04".

Dirigible Balloons.

That there is no sign at present of America coming to the front in Dirigible Balloons. France and possibly Germany are making progress: but there is still much to be done in this line, especially in the designing of shapes and screw propellers best suited to give good results . . .

Flying Machines.

England is very backward. There are strong hopes of success in this direction, and such success, with at any rate small machines, may come much earlier than is generally anticipated, and America is leading the way, whilst in England practically nothing is being done.

Kites.

I saw nothing in any way equal to the "Cody" Kite, a set of which is shortly to be procured by our War Office for continued trial.

Meteorological Work.

Our Government affords but little assistance to work done for the study of atmospheric conditions, air currents, etc. Whilst the importance of a thorough knowledge of these in order to safely navigate the air must be admitted, in the same way as a knowledge of the sea, its tides and currents is necessary for the successful sailor, the British Government affords but little assistance. America and most of the great European nations take active part in such experiments – with us it is almost entirely due to the efforts of private individuals that anything at all is done.

We must now look more closely at the personality and qualifications of Colonel Capper because it was at about this time that he began to be recognized as the leading figure in the field of British military aeronautics. It was already realized that Colonel Templer's authority and influence were certain to decline in the period after the South African War; and that Capper would take over the functions and duties which the older man had discharged for so many years.

In the opinion of a technical expert John Capper was now "entering a phase of great mental activity".[1] He was in his early forties. He possessed a voracious interest in aeronautical developments. Indeed, he looked upon it as his military duty to learn everything he could about the progress being made in aeronautics, especially in France and in the United States. Many years later *The Times*, in referring to this phase of his career, wrote of him: "He had a reputation as a scientific soldier whose progressive ideas were often in advance of the times and will be remembered for his pioneer work in the early days of military aeronautics . . ."[2]

[1] Walker, *Early Aviation at Farnborough*, vol. I, p. 44.
[2] *The Times*, 26 May 1955.

Nevertheless, it has been argued that Capper did not merit the reputation he secured for himself. He was a capable soldier and an unusually strict disciplinarian who won and held the respect and loyalty of his men. But he was not a scientist. Indeed, in the opinion of one authority Capper "was regrettably lacking in scientific knowledge and training, and his understanding of mechanical engineering was rudimentary . . ."[1] However, what he did not lack was high administrative ability; devotion to his duty; sustained energy; the physical strength and agility that enabled him to work with his troops and advisers in the field whenever experiments with various aeronautical devices were carried out; and a deep ambition to create an Air Arm that would be worthy of an established place in the organization of the British Army.

When he returned from his visit to the United States it was Capper's task to prepare two reports. We have already examined one of these, his account of the American journey. The second report, written almost immediately after the first was completed, was entitled "Technical Training Balloon Sections".[2] In it Capper explained and described the work carried out by his units during the year 1904. Characteristically, the report contained several recommendations for the more efficient employment of the officers and men involved. Capper, as a military commander, seldom hesitated to offer suggestions to his superiors when he was convinced of the validity of his opinions.

In the report Capper explained that the Balloon Sections had carried out their Balloon Drill – "filling, manoeuvring, and observing" – at Aldershot. One Section was placed on "Special duty" in order to experiment with "Mr. S. F. Cody's kites". Another Section was sent to Lydd where it observed Siege Artillery Fire. A Section was despatched to the Royal Artillery Camp at Larkhill, on Salisbury Plain, where it observed the firing of the Royal Field Artillery and the Royal Horse Artillery. In September a Combined Section was attached to the Defending Force in the Essex Manoeuvres.

The report was not simply an account of the activities of the year. Colonel Capper pointed out to his superiors that the junior officers who served in the Balloon Sections were often sent abroad as soon as they became proficient in their work; and that they were replaced by men who were unfamiliar with the requirements of military ballooning. He made clear, in blunt terms, that not enough officers of the rank of captain were being trained: "On service", he explained, "the Establishment of a Section lays down that a Captain should be in command. There are few Captains . . .

[1] Walker, *Early Aviation at Farnborough*, vol. I, p. 87.
[2] For the details of the report set out in this and the following paragraphs see Air 1/1608/204/85/36. "Technical Training Balloon Sections" dated "Aldershot, January 1905".

who have served with the Balloon Sections for any length of time . . . The result will undoubtedly be that on service, though there is no fear but that all will do their duty, the technical ignorance of the O.C. will make itself felt, and we cannot hope to obtain the best results." He urged that two senior officers should be posted to the Balloon Sections for a period of several years. He also advocated the establishment of formal "Officers' Classes" so that the training of officers could be carried out in the most efficient manner possible.

At exactly the time that Colonel Capper completed this report he received a remarkable letter from Wilbur and Orville Wright. In it they told him they had greatly improved their performances in the air since his visit to Dayton. They were now convinced, they wrote, of the "practicability" of mechanical flight; and had decided the time had come for them to bring their invention to the attention of "military authorities" for consideration.

During his visit to Dayton in October 1904 Capper, as we have seen, had asked the Wright brothers to give Great Britain "the first chance" when their machine had been brought to a "practical stage". At that time Wilbur and Orville had told him they "were not yet ready to talk business". Now, however, their attitude had changed.

Their letter was composed in careful and even cautious tones but it was obvious from it that the Wrights were now prepared to consider the possibility of offering to sell their aeroplane, and their accumulation of scientific knowledge, to the British Government; and that they were asking Colonel Capper what kind of reaction they might expect if they made such an offer to the appropriate authorities in London.

VII

Colonel Capper's report of his American journey was, of course, a highly confidential document. It was prepared in order to inform his military superiors about recent aeronautical developments. Early in December 1904, however, Capper rose at a meeting of the Aeronautical Society of Great Britain so that he could tell a wider audience of his countrymen something of the impressions he had gained at the St Louis Exhibition, and in the United States.

He began by expressing disappointment with the aeronautical display at the St Louis World's Fair. He remarked: "We should . . . very much liked to have seen the Messrs. Wright Bros., and see what progress they had made with their machine . . ." He went on to speak very carefully of other aspects of his American visit. Despite his caution what he said was certain to excite the interest of his listeners. He declared: "I shall be very much surprised if we do not hear from America before long of a gliding machine driven through the air by a motor. I am not at liberty to give any details on the subject, but I shall not be surprised if we hear of that being practically done."

Capper, at this meeting, also gave expression to an attitude that was later to exert a significant influence upon the further development of British military aviation. He said with respect to these aeroplanes whose appearance he predicted: "It seems to me it is rather bad for us to allow the Americans to lead us in that direction".[1]

VIII

Colonel Capper's visit to Dayton in October 1904 was merely an interlude in the Wright brothers' programme of trial and experiment for that year. After his departure Wilbur and Orville set to work again and achieved some astonishing results. On 9 November 1904 Wilbur Wright flew for just over five minutes and covered a distance, in the air, of more than three miles. On 1 December Orville equalled this feat when he flew for nearly three miles in circles round the Huffman pasture in a time of about five minutes, at a speed of thirty-five miles per hour.

During the year 1904 the Wrights had made one hundred and five attempts to fly. With these successes that marked the end of their experimental season they believed, although some technical problems still remained, that they were at last in possession of a machine they could develop into the world's first practical and useful aeroplane. When the brothers arrived at this conclusion they decided also that the time had come at last for them to gather in those rewards in fame and wealth they felt they had earned. They reckoned they could do so if they offered to sell their machine and their scientific knowledge to the United States Government, and also to the British Government.

They now embarked upon a course of action that has sometimes been misunderstood by aeronautical historians. On 3 January 1905, with the *Flyer* safely dismantled and stored away for the winter, Wilbur Wright called at the Dayton home of Congressman Robert M. Nevin, the Republican representative for the Dayton district. Wilbur explained to his Congressman that he and his brother had been experimenting for five years and had recently perfected a powered aircraft that was "fitted for practical use". He sought Nevin's help and advice and asked him to find out if these developments might be a "subject of interest" to the Government of the United States.

The Congressman, in his wisdom, suggested to Wilbur that the

---

[1] The Aeronautical Society met on 2 December 1904. Capper's remarks were published in *The Aeronautical Journal*, January 1905, p. 3.

brothers should write him a letter setting out the details of their marvellous accomplishments; and he promised to take it to William Howard Taft, the Secretary of War, and use it to secure an appointment for them with the appropriate officials in the War Department in Washington.

When Wilbur returned home he and Orville did not make the letter to Congressman Nevin their first order of business. Instead, on 10 January 1905, nine days before they prepared their letter to Nevin, they wrote to Colonel Capper, at his headquarters in the Aldershot Command. In this letter they asked Capper if his government would be interested in purchasing their aeroplane and "the scientific and practical knowledge and instruction we are in a position to impart".

In their letter to Capper the Wrights informed him of the brilliant flights they had made after his visit in the previous October. They declared:[1]

> . . . On the first day of December . . . we made four circuits of the field in four minutes and 53 seconds, covering a distance of almost three miles at a speed of thirty-five miles an hour. Seventy pounds of deadweight, in the form of steel bars, were carried in this flight. A flight of five minutes and four seconds was made a short time before but the speed and distance were not so well ascertained.

Having established the nature of their accomplishments the Wright brothers proceeded to business:

> Though no spectacular performances were attempted, the season's results were so satisfactory that we now regard the practicability of flying as fully established for the special uses to which it will be applied at first. In such a work as that of creating a corps of aviators for military scouting purposes, it is quite probable that more delay

[1] From the copy in the Wright Brothers' Papers. Wright Cycle Company to Lt Col. J. E. Capper, 10 January 1905. See also Walker, *Early Aviation at Farnborough* vol. II, pp. 24–25. Walker remarks of the Wright letter to Capper: "They had previously approached their own Government, but entirely without success". This statement is incorrect. Wilbur Wright had seen Congressman Nevin but no approach to the American Government had been made by the Wrights, at this stage. See also Fred Kelly, *Miracle at Kitty Hawk*, p. 135, who states: ". . . the Wrights wanted to offer it first of all to their own government. Their first step in this direction was a letter to the representative in Congress from the Dayton district". As the above account shows they wrote to Colonel Capper in Aldershot before they wrote to Congressman Nevin. Even Marvin McFarland misinterpreted the Wrights' actions in this connection. He wrote of the Wrights: ". . . they offered the airplane to the United States Government . . . The airplane was to be the exclusive military secret of the United States . . ." See his "When The Airplane Was a Military Secret" in *The Air Power Historian*, vol. II, Number IV, October 1955, p. 75, a classic account.

will be experienced in selecting and properly training the men than in perfecting the details of the machine to a point sufficient to bring flyers within the limit of usefulness. This fact, together with the increasing difficulty of securing the necessary privacy for further experiment, has raised the question in our minds whether the present is not the proper time to bring the matter before military authorities for their consideration. There is no question but that a government in possession of such a machine as we can now furnish and the scientific and practical knowledge and instruction we are in a position to impart, could secure a lead of several years over governments which waited to buy perfected machines before making a start in this line. If we should conclude to make a proposition of this kind, it would probably be on the basis of furnishing for the 1905 season's experiments a machine capable of carrying two men at a minimum speed of thirty miles an hour.

The next paragraph in this letter of 10 January 1905 sought Capper's advice. It stated:

If you think it probable that an offer of such character would receive consideration from your government at this time, we will be glad to give further consideration to matters of details, etc.

Shortly before these intricate developments began Patrick Y. Alexander decided to write a letter of his own to the Wright brothers. The tone of his communication was at once discreet and encouraging. His letter was dated 2 January 1905. It probably arrived in Dayton after the Wright brothers had sent their letter to Colonel Capper but before they composed the missive Congressman Nevin had asked them to send him:[1]

Pinehurst
Maychett   Monday
Farnborough, Hants.   2.1.5

Dear Sirs,
    I wish to thank you very much for your kindness to Lt. Col Capper C.B. R.E. who tells me, through my introduction he much enjoyed his visit and talking over with you the merits of your machine.
    Although the results of the St. Louis Fair may have been disappointing I think it has done good in a way that the matter has more official attention all the world over than was hitherto the case, and people or rather "the man in the street" is more convinced of the practicability of this method of locomotion so much so that more

----

[1] Wright Brothers' Papers, Patrick Y. Alexander to the Wrights, 2 January 1905.

thoughts are given to the possibilities of your machine than any other I know of. . . .

Well, I suppose you have heard I have left Bath and am now living at the above address . . .

Believe me
Very Sincerely Yours
Patrick Y. Alexander

Upon receipt of this the Wrights could only reflect about those in Britain who were giving "more thoughts" to the "possibilities" of their machine. They probably did not realize that when Alexander moved to Farnborough he went to live in the place that was being developed, at just this time, as the centre of British military aeronautics. Indeed, in the following year Patrick Alexander, a civilian, actually worked with the Balloon Companies of the Royal Engineers during their military exercises on the nearby Salisbury Plain. On 6 June 1906 Capper wrote to a friend from the Balloon Factory, Aldershot: "Alexander was here yesterday . . . He is going down to Salisbury Plain in a few days to work with the Balloon Cos. there".[1] Many years later this statement was noticed by Percy Walker when he prepared his authorized history of the Royal Aircraft Establishment. He commented: "Although Patrick Y. Alexander . . . was renowned for his diversity of aeronautical interests, such close contact with British military operations is somewhat remarkable".[2]

Octave Chanute was also active, in his own sphere, in this January of 1905. He kept up his correspondence with Patrick Alexander, now living in Farnborough. On 17 January he wrote to Alexander to tell him how much he had enjoyed meeting Colonel Capper upon the occasion of his American visit; and he emphasized to Alexander his expert opinion that the aerial experiments of the Wright brothers were the most promising of those being carried out in the United States: "I thank you", he wrote, "for introducing Col. Capper, whom I was much taken with. He will have told you that the Wrights are now keeping their experiments secret. I hear of other projects in this country but none very promising."[3]

IX

On 18 January 1905 Wilbur and Orville Wright at last wrote the letter Congressman Nevin had asked them to prepare. In it they declared that they had produced, after years of experiments, a practical flying machine

[1] See Air 1/1613/204/88/17. Capper to J. W. Dunne, 6 June 1906.
[2] Walker, *Early Aviation at Farnborough*, vol. II, p. 187 and *f.n.*
[3] Octave Chanute Papers, Chanute to Alexander, 17 January 1905.

that could move through the air at high speed and that was also capable of landing without being wrecked. They included in their paper details about the successful performances of the machine and also an offer to enter into negotiations with the United States Government for its sale, or for the sale of their technical knowledge and the scientific data they had accumulated during their years of study and practice.

In their letter the Wrights asked Congressman Nevin if he could find out for them "whether this is a subject of interest to our own government . . . as early information on this point will aid us in making our plans for the future".[1] The clear implication was that if their own country was not interested in these proposals they might embark upon negotiations with foreign nations.

Nevin's plan was to take this document to Secretary Taft at the War Department. Unfortunately, the Congressman became ill and was unable to call upon Taft. Instead, the Wrights' letter, together with one written by Nevin, was sent to the War Department's Board of Ordnance and Fortification.

On 24 January Major General G. L. Gillespie, the General Staff officer who was the President of the Board, replied to Nevin in terms that astounded the Wright brothers. The nature of the Wrights' proposal had been misunderstood completely.

Wilbur and Orville Wright had offered the United States Government a machine that could fly through the air. Yet General Gillespie wrote to Nevin: "Referring to your letter of the 21st instant to the Honourable Secretary of War inviting attention to the experiments in mechanical flight conducted by Messrs. Wilbur and Orville Wright, which has been referred to the Board of Ordnance and Fortification for action, I have the honour to inform you that, as many requests are made for financial assistance in the development of designs for flying machines, the Board has found it necessary to decline to make allotments for the experimental development of mechanical flight, and has determined that before suggestions with that object in view will be considered, the device must have been brought to the stage of practical operation without expense to the United States."

A second paragraph of the general's letter declared: "It appears from the letter of Messrs. Wilbur and Orville Wright that their machine has not yet been brought to the stage of practical operation, but as soon as it shall have been perfected, this Board would be pleased to receive further representations from them in regard to it."[2]

---

[1] The letter is printed in Kelly, *Miracle at Kitty Hawk*, pp. 135–6.
[2] Wright Brothers Papers, General G. L. Gillespie to Hon. R. M. Nevin, 24 January 1905. The letter is partially printed, but without the date, in Kelly, *Miracle at Kitty Hawk*, pp. 136–7.

This letter is of significance in any study of early British military aeronautical history because it makes clear that from the latter part of January 1905 the Wright brothers had to face the fact that the American authorities, their own countrymen, were not prepared to consider their proposals seriously – even though they were offered an opportunity to obtain the first successful and practical aeroplane in history. Indeed, a British expert has referred to the various letters the United States War Department sent to the Wright brothers as documents "which came very near the border-line of official insanity".[1]

As patriotic, if hard-headed, Americans Wilbur and Orville were genuinely distressed by the attitude of the military authorities in Washington, D.C. The matter was discussed on several occasions in their correspondence with Octave Chanute in the months that followed. On 1 June 1905 Wilbur explained their feelings to Chanute: "We should be ashamed of ourselves if we had offered our machine to a foreign government without giving our own country a chance at it, but our consciences are clear. At the Christmas holidays we talked with Mr. Nevin . . . and he proposed that we write him a letter containing a general statement of our business, and that he take it to Mr. Taft . . . But owing to sickness he was compelled to turn over our letter without personally seeing Mr. Taft and shortly afterward received the letter from the Ordnance Department which I enclose. As we had made no request for an appropriation, but on the contrary had offered to furnish machines of 'agreed specifications at a contract price' (which offer was entirely ignored), we were driven to the conclusion that the letter of the War Department was intended as a flat turndown. We still think so . . . ."[2]

At this point in his letter Wilbur mentioned his note to Colonel Capper but he did not provide Chanute with its date, 10 January 1905. Chanute might have concluded that the Wrights only wrote to Capper after they received the discouraging letter from General Gillespie. As we have seen, however, they wrote to Capper even before they wrote to Congressman Nevin. Wilbur's letter of the 1st June continued: ". . . It is no pleasant thought to us that any foreign country should take from America any share of the glory of having conquered the flying problem, but we feel that we have done our full share toward making this an American invention, and if it is sent abroad for further development the responsibility does not rest upon us. We have taken pains to see that 'Opportunity' gave a good clear knock on the War Department door . . . If the American Government has decided to spend no more money on flying machines until their

---

[1] Gibbs-Smith, *Rebirth of European Aviation*, p. 191.
[2] The letter is in McFarland, *The Papers of Wilbur and Orville Wright*, pp. 494–5.

practical use is demonstrated in actual service abroad, we are sorry, but we cannot reasonably object. They are the judges."

Chanute responded to Wilbur's account with a most thoughtful reply, perhaps one of the most sagacious letters this inveterate letter writer ever produced. He wrote to his friend: "I am at a loss to understand how the Ordnance Department misconstrued your letter into an application for an appropriation to experiment and assumed that your invention was not brought to the stage of practical operation . . . My first feelings were of mortification and regret that the United States War Department should have extended to you a 'flat turndown' . . . Now that I have cooled down I see some advantages in your being forced to consider the overtures made by Col. Capper for the British Government, because: First, your invention is worth far more to the British than to the United States Government. Second, the British are less hampered than we in appropriating secret service funds, so that you can probably get a better price, and sooner. Third, your invention will make more for peace in the hands of the British than in our own . . . If you close negotiations with England I hope that you will find some way of saving our government from any ill results of its present blunder . . ."[1]

When the Wright brothers decided that the time had come for them to sell their invention they were very nervous and apprehensive. With good cause they were afraid that unscrupulous competitors, despite the existence of their various patents and patent applications, might attempt to steal the fruits of their genius. Moreover Wilbur and Orville, who were men of business, practical and unsentimental, realized also, despite their genuinely patriotic attitude, that they had to protect themselves from the power of governments.

They feared from the first that the American military authorities might be so impressed by the technical possibilities of their machine that the government would confiscate it, together with all their unique scientific data, gained after years of effort, labour, trial, and experiment. Orville Wright once explained their attitude in a letter he sent to the United States Board of Ordnance and Fortification, in Washington. His letter reflects the brilliant and meticulous way in which the brothers had prepared themselves for the task of selling their aeroplane. He wrote to the authorities: "Our course in asking from governments large sums for the first machine has been based upon an impression that governments often appropriate inventions useful in warfare, and tell the inventor to prosecute a claim under the law. But since the inventor, who has claims to prosecute before he has realized any money from his invention, must transfer the principal interest in his invention to capitalists in order to

---

[1] Chanute's letter dated 6 June 1905 is printed in McFarland, *The Papers of Wilbur and Orville Wright*, pp. 496–7.

raise money to prosecute the claims, he does not derive much profit for himself, even after judgement in his favour has been obtained."[1]

In these circumstances, and acting upon this impression, the Wright brothers had made their preparations with very great care. By their design their message to Colonel Capper arrived in England at about the same time that Congressman Nevin received their letter of 18 January 1905, in Washington, D.C.

[1] Orville's letter, dated 30 October 1907, is printed in McFarland, *The Papers of Wilbur and Orville Wright*, pp. 825–6. See also J. H. Parkin, *Bell and Baldwin* (Toronto, 1964), p. 170: "The Wrights, once successful powered flight was achieved, operated in secrecy, in the understandable belief that they were entitled to some financial return for their work. They appreciated, at that early date, that governments were most likely to provide such return, and that in dealing with governments secrets were more valuable than patents". There were further ramifications resulting from this impression of the Wright brothers and these will be dealt with in the next chapter of the present history. See also in this connection Walsh, *One Day at Kitty Hawk*, p. 178: Wilbur's "one abiding concern was that the United States Army might be so impressed . . . that the government would be led to appropriate it whole, to confiscate it, with all the formulations and scientific data . . ."

CHAPTER 5

First Refusal: Colonel Capper's Change of Course

I

In the Aldershot Command Colonel Capper's mind, at the beginning of
1905, was fixed upon captive balloons, Samuel Cody's man-lifting kites,
and the various tasks and duties of his Balloon Sections. His pleasant and
efficient routine was interrupted by the unexpected arrival of the Wright
brothers' letter, on 30 January. Capper, with the ingrained discipline of
his calling, made no immediate reply to Wilbur and Orville Wright.
Instead, he at once forwarded their letter to a superior, the General
Officer Commanding Royal Engineers, Aldershot Command, and requested that he be informed about the answer he might send to his

American friends. He then endorsed their claims in the firmest manner possible: "I wish to invite very special attention", he declared, "to the wonderful advance made in aviation by the Brothers Wright. I have every confidence in their uprightness, and in the correctness of their statements. Taking the latter for granted, it is a fact that they have flown and operated personally a flying machine for a distance of over three miles at a speed of thirty-five miles an hour". Capper proceeded, in his note, to supply his superiors with certain technical aspects of the Wright achievement: "The machine has no gas bag. . . . The fact that it can carry 70lbs . . . of dead weight means that it can carry that amount of fuel etc., and as it has gone for three miles . . . it is merely a question of skill, nerve and endurance of the operator, for it to go 50 or 100 miles . . . or any required distance".[1]

Having presented these endorsements Capper finished his note by urging that he be allowed to answer the Wrights, as soon as possible: "I wish to urge most strongly that I be permitted to answer the letter stating that I think it probable that their offer would receive consideration from His Majesty's Government. I would point out that such an answer would in no way tie His Majesty's Government to anything beyond giving full and due consideration to any offer made by these gentlemen. I cannot but feel that if these gentlemen are prepared to make any reasonable offer, their statement . . . is a true one, and they should meet with every encouragement from us in the interest of progress in our war appliances . . ."

The British authorities, as a result, were now in a position to embark upon a serious attempt to secure for their country the first successful aeroplane in the history of the world.

Aldershot Command, upon receipt of these papers, decided that so remarkable a communication as this one from the Wright brothers involved matters most properly dealt with by a higher authority. For this reason the Wright letter, together with some other documents, was at once sent to the War Office in Whitehall.

We must now glance, however briefly, at the organization of the War Office at this time so that the further course of these exchanges and negotiations may be understood. Profound changes had just taken place in that venerable institution of government.

In the period after the South African War no Department of State was

---

[1] Capper's note is reproduced in Walker, *Early Aviation at Farnborough*, vol. II, p. 26. Walker's account of Britain's negotiations with the Wright Brothers is brilliant; but it is marred by errors of interpretation and by his unwavering hostility to the brothers, especially Wilbur. Moreover, some of the documents he prints differ slightly from those preserved in the Public Record Office in London, and in the Wright Brothers' Papers in the Library of Congress in Washington, D.C. In addition, Walker does not employ footnotes to identify his sources so that students who examine his work can never be clear about them.

more severely criticized for its inadequacies than was the British War Office. Arthur Balfour, the brilliant but politically ill-fated prime minister of the day, was firmly resolved upon organizational reforms and changes so that the War Office would be able to discharge its vital functions with that kind of efficiency which had been so notably absent in the recent hostilities. In November 1903 he appointed a powerful War Office (Reconstitution) Committee, known more familiarly from the name of its chairman as the Esher Committee.

Lord Esher was an eminent military thinker and a strategist of wide outlook. His colleagues were Colonel Sir George Clarke, later Lord Sydenham of Combe, an experienced military administrator, and the more famous Admiral Sir John Fisher, at this time the Commander-in-Chief at Portsmouth and already looked upon as a man who was almost certain to attain the highest rank in his profession.

The members of the Esher Committee were vigorous and resolute men. They would not tolerate the inefficiencies of the past. They were ruthless in their determination to turn the War Office into a modern and efficient establishment. In the past the responsibilities of the Secretary of State for War and the Commander-in-Chief had been poorly drawn up and ill-defined. Rivalry and confusion of effort were the result. The committee recommended that the post of commander-in-chief should be abolished and Lord Roberts, the last holder of this office, was summarily discharged from his place. The committee also recommended the establishment of a board, drawn up on the lines of the Board of Admiralty, to carry out the higher administrative functions of the War Office. This board was called the Army Council.

The Army Council, which came into existence in 1904, was composed of seven members, four military and three civil. The Secretary of State for War was its president and each member of the new organization was allotted certain administrative duties while these again were subdivided and placed under high-ranking officers called Directors. Our concerns lie with the fourth military member of the Army Council, the Master-General of the Ordnance.

In his case he was supplied with two directors, the Director of Artillery and the Director of Fortifications and Works. The duties of the Director of Fortifications and Works included supervision of the Army's aeronautical activities. His directorate was divided into six sections; one of these sections was responsible for the immediate administration of the Balloon Factory and all related aeronautical work. The officer in charge of this section was called the "Inspector of Electric Lights" but he was, as a matter of course, responsible for much more than his rather quaint title suggested.

In 1905 the Director of Fortifications and Works at the War Office was Colonel R. M. Ruck, an officer who was very interested in aeronautics and in aviation. He was later appointed a high official in the Aeronautical Society of Great Britain and during his term as president the Society became, in 1918, the Royal Aeronautical Society.

II

The first action of the War Office was to see to it that a polite letter of acknowledgement, dated 9 February 1905, was sent to the Wright brothers by the Directorate of Artillery. After further reflection and some technical appraisal of the Wright proposal Colonel Ruck quickly ordered one of his officers in the Directorate of Fortifications and Works to write the brothers, on 11 February, in order to ask them to submit a definite offer with respect to what they were prepared to supply. Major H. N. Dumbleton, the officer concerned, also pointed out that the Army Council did not, by this request, bind itself to any further action in the matter. It was only after Dumbleton's letter had been sent that Colonel Capper decided to reply to his friends.

He explained to them that he had felt obliged to consult his government, in the first instance. "Your letter which I was very pleased to receive has been some time unanswered", Capper wrote to the Wright brothers, "as it raised a very important question which I did not think I was justified in answering without directly approaching His Majesty's Government to see what their wishes in the matter might be". He further made clear that the government authorities had now taken charge of the negotiations: "I have, however, just heard that a member of the Government has written directly to you on the subject on which you approached me, and doubtless I shall hear more as to what you are doing in the matter".[1]

Colonel Capper also added his personal congratulations: "It is a thing of which you both may well be proud, and forms a fine ending to the years of practice and trouble that you have taken in the matter; – and there are many who will envy you". He ended his letter by expressing the hope that they might be able "to see more of each other in the future" and by sending his and his wife's "kindest remembrances" to Miss Wright.

By means of this letter Capper made clear to Wilbur and Orville that they now had to deal with the British Government, and that he was no longer directly involved in their transactions. At the same time he showed the brothers that he still entertained the friendliest feelings for them, and for their family, and that he firmly believed in the great achievements they had reported to him.

[1] Wright Brothers' Papers, Capper to the Wrights, 15 February 1905. The letter was written from the Balloon Factory, Aldershot. See also Walker, *Early Aviation at Farnborough*, vol. II, pp. 27–8.

III

It was now the task of the Wright brothers to draw up a detailed and formal reply to the request of the Director of Fortifications and Works in the British War Office. The Dayton brothers knew exactly what they wanted to do and on 1 March 1905 they despatched to London a long letter which they hoped would make their situation clear to the British authorities.

Our understanding of what followed has been complicated by the work of the great British aeronautical authority, Percy B. Walker. In his authorized history of the Royal Aircraft Establishment, *Early Aviation at Farnborough*, he wrote the fullest and most detailed account of these negotiations ever published. In this book he sought to defend the reputation of the War Office authorities responsible for dealing with the Wrights because they have been condemned in the literature for their failure to secure the Wright aeroplane for their country when the opportunity to purchase it was pressed upon them. Walker carried out his purpose by launching, in his history, a vigorous attack upon the personality and mental state of the Wrights. He blamed them for the fact that the negotiations produced no positive result. Wilbur was his particular target. In the interests of historical accuracy and understanding notice must be taken of some of his harsh comments, throughout this stage of our account.

The Wright letter of 1 March began by acknowledging receipt of the letters sent by the Directorate of Artillery and by the Directorate of Fortifications and Works. Walker dismissed this highly important document as: "long and involved, with much of it scarcely intelligible". The brothers wrote:[1]

March 1, 1905

The Secretary, War Office,
London, S.W.

Dear Sir:
   Your communications #84/W/5144.(A.3.) and #84/W/5144 (F.W.5.) have been received. We have found it a matter of some difficulty to formulate a satisfactory proposition for the sale of an aerial scouting machine to the Government of Great Britain, owing to the fact that what we have to offer consists in part of a piece of machinery and in part of expert scientific knowledge. Of these the

---

[1] From the copy in the Wright Brothers' Papers, Wright Cycle Co. to The Secretary, War Office, London, S.W. 1 March 1905. For Percy Walker's comments mentioned above see his *Early Aviation at Farnborough*, vol. II, pp. 30–4.

latter is of much the greater value; but as it is also the part on which both parties to this negotiation would have the greatest difficulty in fixing a value, at this time, it will probably be best for the present to confine the proposition to a machine including with it only such information as would necessarily be disclosed by the machine itself and the needed instruction in its use.

In the next paragraph of their carefully composed letter the Wrights sought to suggest to the War Office authorities the quality of their scientific accomplishments; and the unique opportunities they were offering to the British Government.

Walker commented about this paragraph: "There then follows a vague philosophical rigmarole which marks the beginning of an obsession with what Wilbur regarded as their scientific achievements to the detriment of their unique success in practical application . . ." No one in the world, and there were now several in the field in various countries, had achieved the practical successes in flying gained by the Wright brothers at this stage of aeronautical history; but it must be emphasized that they had not blundered by accident or by chance upon the solution of a problem that had defied some of the most brilliant minds in history. They were, indeed, scientists who had studied, planned, tested and experimented for years until they gained a corpus of knowledge not available to anyone else. They alone could build heavier-than-air machines capable of sustained and controlled powered flight. When they referred to their "expert scientific knowledge" and to its value the Wrights knew exactly what they said, for their accumulation of such knowledge was unique and without precedent. Their paragraph stated:

The expert knowledge of natural laws and original formulas whereby it is possible to compute the elements of flyer(s) of any desired size or speed with as much accuracy and certainty as is the case with steam ships, and some original discoveries relating to the action of screws, which will doubtless prove of value in marine engineering as well as in aeronautics, may be left to future negotiations. Should the British Government prefer to leave the designing and development of various types of aerial apparatus in the hands of private parties, of course these matters would be of no special interest to it; but in case it wished to bring such development under its own control, or to conduct experiments on its own account, this information would be of the greatest value, not only in designing successful machines, but also in detecting the impracticability and impossibility of many proposed plans on which sums aggregating immense amounts might otherwise be wasted.

The Wrights next declared that they were ready to deliver to the British Government a single machine; or a machine and all the scientific knowledge upon which it was based. In making this offer they revealed the extreme care and the sturdy independence of character they had employed in preparing to sell their invention. By their design, in order to preserve their secrets, they had neglected to patent all their original devices so that anyone calling at a Patent Office, in the different countries where they had patents, would be unable to acquire the details of all their discoveries. They explained:

> Although we consider it advisable that any agreement which may be made at present be based upon a single machine and necessary instruction in its use, we would be willing, if desired, to insert in the contract an option on the purchase of all that we know concerning the subject of aviation, including a license to operate our patents. Our British patent 6732 A.D. 1904 covers only some elementary features. The question of patenting other features is at present held in abeyance.

The letter turned next to specific details. Even Walker called this part of it "realistic and practical":

> We are ready to enter into a contract with the British Government to construct and deliver to it an aerial scouting machine of the aeroplane type of the following specifications:
> The said machine to be capable of carrying two men of average weight and supplies of fuel for a flight of not less than fifty (50) miles.
> The speed of said machine when flying in still air to be not less than thirty (30) miles an hour.
> The said machine to be of sufficiently substantial construction to making landings without being broken, when operated with a reasonable degree of skill.

The Wrights turned next to the terms of acceptance. Walker condemned them for what they suggested in this part of their letter; but we will reserve comment upon this aspect of their plans for a later and more appropriate section of our analysis. The Wrights said, in concluding their proposal:

> Before the said machine is accepted by the British Government, and before any part of the purchase price is paid, the constructors shall in the presence of representatives of the British Government demonstrate by trial flights that the specifications have been met, the number of trials to be optional with the constructors.
> The purchase price of the machine shall be determined by the maximum distance covered in a single one of the said trial flights, and shall be computed at the rate of Five Hundred Pounds Sterling for each mile covered; provided that (if) none of the trial flights reaches

a distance of ten miles, the British Government shall not be obliged to purchase or accept said machine.

In case the machine is accepted, personal instruction in the use of the machine will be provided for those who may be selected by the Government, the compensation of said instructor to be fixed at two hundred (200) pounds per month; the services of said instructor to be continued for such period as the Government may elect not exceeding six months, except by consent of both parties.

If the conditions herein outlined meet with the approval of the War Office, we are ready to enter into a formal contract.

Respectfully yours,
(signed) WRIGHT CYCLE CO.

IV

It was now the duty of Colonel Ruck, as Director of Fortifications and Works, to make decisions about this unusual and extraordinary set of offers and proposals. After reading the Wright letter he assumed that a range of fifty miles would be attained in one of their trial flights; and that they were asking the British Government for the sum of twenty-five thousand pounds for a single machine. Colonel Ruck came to another conclusion: "he could see no prospect of being allowed anything approaching this amount by the Government of the day".[1]

In spite of this gloomy opinion Ruck was not prepared to abandon the possibility of securing the Wright aeroplane for the British Army. He decided to refer the entire matter to the Royal Engineer Committee.

By this time the Royal Engineer Committee had become an important and influential advisory body with special responsibility for new inventions and other technical military innovations. After rather lengthy deliberations the president of the Royal Engineer Committee offered its conclusions to Ruck, in a note dated 22 April 1905. In this note the president, writing for the committee, declared that the capabilities of the Wright flying machine were "too uncertain at present to render the conclusion of an agreement advisable". The committee suggested that the British Military Attaché in Washington should be asked to enter into communications with the Wright brothers. In his note the president added a significant sentence: "Should these gentlemen be able at any time to carry out satisfactory flying trials in the presence of the Military

---

[1] See Walker, *Early Aviation at Farnborough*, vol. II, pp. 32–3. The account of the British military authorities' reaction to the Wright proposal, set out above in this section, is based entirely upon Walker's narrative of events at pp. 32–4 of his book. All quotations in this section are drawn from that source.

attaché, the question of an agreement, on terms to be settled, might be taken up".

Colonel Ruck agreed with this advice offered by the Royal Engineer Committee. He, too, wanted to obtain more factual evidence about the capabilities of the Wright machine.

On 27 April he reported to his superior officer, General Sir James Wolfe Murray, the Master-General of the Ordnance, that the course of action suggested by the Royal Engineer Committee was sound: "We cannot", he declared, "negotiate further without considerable risk of getting into trouble and expense without any satisfactory result. At the same time we do not wish to drop the matter, as there are certain features about the invention which show great promise of future development."

The machinery of the General Staff at the War Office was now employed to carry the negotiations further. The authorities sent copies of all the relevant papers to Colonel H. Foster, the British Military Attaché in Washington.

He was ordered to communicate directly with the Wright brothers and to ask them if he could visit Dayton in order to observe their aeroplane in flight. At the same time the Wrights were informed of his proposed visit. On 13 May 1905 R. H. Brade, at that time Assistant to the Secretary of the War Office, sent the Wrights the first formal reply to their letter of the 1st March. He explained to them: ". . . I am commanded by the Army Council to acquaint you that Colonel Foster, the British Military Attaché at Washington, has been asked to visit your works. I am to request that you will give him any necessary information and an opportunity of seeing the machine at work. On receipt of his report a further communication will be sent to you."

When Percy Walker commented on this letter in his history he declared: "Thus, in May 1905, the prospects of an agreement between the British War Office and the Wright Brothers seemed promising . . ." But another distinguished British aeronautical historian, who was also allowed by the authorities to see all these confidential exchanges, came to an entirely different conclusion about Reginald Brade's communication of May 1905. Harald Penrose later wrote in his aviation treatise of the Wright brothers and the War Office: "Before the end of May they received reply that the War Office was unwilling to commit itself to a contract until a representative had first witnessed a demonstration, and that an officer would be sent to see them. Official procrastination had begun."[1]

---

[1] See Walker, *Early Aviation at Farnborough*, vol. II, p. 34; and Penrose, *British Aviation, The Pioneer Years*, p. 68.

V

Colonel Hubert Foster, the British Military Attaché in Washington, was a capable and efficient officer. However, he was not at his post in Washington when the packet of correspondence concerned with the Wright brothers arrived there, with its instructions that he should communicate directly with them and so arrange to visit Dayton in order to observe their machine in flight. His duties required that he should be elsewhere.

In March 1905 Foster had gone on a visit to Mexico and he remained there until October. In this period only one British Military Attaché was assigned both to the United States and to Mexico, and Foster, as a matter of course, found that in carrying out his duties he had to spend some of his time in the latter country.

For this reason Colonel Foster did not communicate with the Wright brothers in any way until November of 1905. During all this time the authorities in the War Office did almost nothing to hasten on this phase of the negotiations that they themselves had instructed Foster to carry out.

No sense of urgency or immediacy was shown by them during all these months, a time when the Wright brothers either approached or were approached by American, French, and Austrian authorities with respect to the aeroplane that they at last perfected in this very period. The Wrights had given the initiative in the matter of the acquisition of the first aeroplane to the authorities in the War Office but the advantage was frittered away during these weeks owing to the leisurely attitude of the Master-General of the Ordnance, the Director of Fortifications and Works, and their high-ranking colleagues in their gloomy rooms in Whitehall.

While they waited for Colonel Foster to make himself known to them the Wright brothers were not idle. They advanced to new heights of achievement and finally solved the last technical problems that had plagued their performances in the latter part of the 1904 season of experiments. Late in May 1905 they began to assemble a new aeroplane. This machine was similar to its predecessors but sturdier in construction. Before they were finished with it, as the weeks of trials continued and improvements were incorporated in its design, they had created what has been called the "first practical powered aeroplane of history".[1]

Aeronautical technicalities were not the only matters to occupy the minds of the Wright brothers at this time. They thought constantly about how to sell their invention without putting at hazard the honours, rewards, and profits they were convinced they deserved.

At the end of May 1905, as a result of their initiative it seemed probable

---

[1] Gibbs-Smith, *Rebirth of European Aviation*, p. 166.

to them that they would soon be able to come to an arrangement with the British Government. Octave Chanute, ever curious about their activities, wrote: "I shall be glad to know where and when you are to resume your practice, and how near you conceive yourselves to be from a practical machine which can be used in war". On 28 May Wilbur sent him a concise reply: "We stand ready to furnish a practical machine for use in war at once, that is a machine capable of carrying two men and fuel for a fifty-mile trip. We are only waiting to complete arrangements with some government. The American government has apparently decided to permit foreign governments to take the lead in utilizing our invention for war purposes. We greatly regret this attitude of our own country, but seeing no way to remedy it, we have made a formal proposition to the British Government and expect to have a conference with one of its representatives at Dayton, very soon. We think the prospect favorable. We have felt serious misgivings regarding the advisability of any further experiments prior to reaching an understanding with some government. At present our machine is a complete secret, but it may not remain so if we attempt further experiments, like those of last year. We have the materials ready so that we could be ready to fly in two or three weeks if we wished to do so".[1]

At this time, also, interest in the achievements of the Wrights began to grow in every part of the aeronautical world. Even before they made their first trial flight of the 1905 season an account of their earlier work was sent, secretly, to the Aeronautical Society of Great Britain by Professor Albert F. Zahm of the Catholic University of America, an engineer who was prominent in those days because of his experiments with a windtunnel and other aeronautical devices.

Zahm had first approached the Wrights in 1902 in order to ask for a copy of Wilbur's address to the Western Society of Engineers, delivered in the previous September. For several years he seemed to be the brothers' friend but he later became an envious and base enemy who did all he could, employing any means, to denigrate them and to deny the authenticity of their achievements. He illustrates the calibre of man Wilbur and Orville sometimes had to deal with in these early years of aviation history.

On 16 June 1905, when he still posed as their friend, Zahm wrote, without the knowledge of the Wrights, to E. Stuart Bruce, the Honorary Secretary of the Aeronautical Society of Great Britain, in order to tell him of what the brothers had done. Zahm's letter contained a startling conclusion which was certain to arouse the interest of everyone in Britain concerned with aeronautics:[2]

[1] McFarland, *Papers of Wilbur and Orville Wright*, pp. 492–4.
[2] The letter is reproduced in J. Laurence Pritchard, *The Wright Brothers and the Royal Aeronautical Society*, p. 771.

I would like to give you a bit of news . . . on condition that it be withheld from the papers till you have it from other sources. I have learned that the Wright Brothers have been experimenting at Dayton, Ohio, with much success; but have induced the local reporters to keep still. They have made 105 flights in a machine carrying one man and 70 lb. of bar iron. The machine is under good control, flies 40 miles an hour, and has made trips of about 3 miles circling about at a height not exceeding 30 or 40 feet. I judge that the 70 pounds of iron can be replaced by gasoline which will enable them to keep on the wing several hours continuously . . . If the above data be true – and I have them from reliable authority – it means that a new epoch in aeronautics is at hand.

VI

As the great work at the Huffman prairie went forward during the summer and early autumn of 1905 the expected visit of the British representative was often in the minds of Wilbur and Orville Wright; but they received no word from him and none from his superiors in Whitehall. On 18 June following a successful engine test Wilbur explained to Chanute that the brothers had decided, after some reflection, to complete the machine and to take the risk of a few private trials so that they could try out, in the air, the new improvements that had been added to it. He also said: "The exact date of meeting with the British representative is not fixed but will probably be within a month".[1]

On 23 June the first trial flight of the new season was made. The brothers at once encountered unexpected difficulties that were not solved for weeks. There were accidents that endangered their limbs and their lives while the machine was damaged on several occasions. Heavy rains turned the pasture into a quagmire which further delayed their progress. Chanute, who followed these developments with very great interest, wrote to Wilbur on the 28th: "Let me know when the British representative turns up. I should like to be present on that occasion".

By this time the Wrights could no longer look forward to an early meeting with Colonel Foster because there had been no communication from him or from any other British official since the previous May when Reginald Brade had written to them from the War Office. On 16 July Wilbur explained to Chanute that one cause of their problems in the air lay in the fact that they had altered the operating handles of the machine and were still unfamiliar with them so that the instant responses required

---

[1] See McFarland, *The Papers of Wilbur and Orville Wright*, p. 498. All further quotations in this section are drawn from pp. 498–521 of this work, unless otherwise noted.

in flight had not yet been acquired by either of the pilots. Wilbur felt confident that their novel arrangements would eventually prove to be successful "but they have cost us several rather unlucky breakages, aggregating several weeks of delay". In these new circumstances the Wrights were no longer so eager for an early visit from Colonel Foster. Wilbur added: "When the British representative comes we will be glad to let you know. We will not hurry matters till we get the machine under proper control."

Octave Chanute continued to follow the technical progress of the Wright trials with the greatest vigilance. He was also very concerned about their relations with the British Government. On 6 September he wrote to Wilbur: "Let me know when you expect the British officer". Wilbur could only reply, on the 17th: "We have had no word from the British War Office since the letter informing us that an officer had been instructed to visit us at Dayton; nor have we written to them. We are waiting for them to move."

Despite this disappointment Wilbur Wright was now caught up in the excitement caused by their remarkable technical advances. He proudly informed Chanute: "Our experiments have been progressing quite satisfactorily, and we are rapidly acquiring skill in the new methods of operating the machine. We may soon attempt trips beyond the confines of the field."

By September the fortunes of the Wright brothers had changed. In 1904 their aeroplane had shown a tendency to stall and fall out of control in tight turns. During a flight on 28 September 1905 Orville discovered the method required to correct this defect and the last mystery confronting the Wright bothers was solved. As Wilbur explained later: "The remedy was found to consist in the more skillful operation of the machine and not in a different construction." The Wrights had also made basic changes in their propellers. An American expert has remarked of this work: "The entire program was in fact extremely complicated; it was beyond the understanding or capacity of any other aspiring pilots or scientists anywhere in the world, who had yet even to match the efficiency of the *first* propellers produced by the brothers."[1]

Wilbur and Orville could now exercise a perfect control over their machine. At the end of September and the beginning of October 1905 they proceeded to embark upon a series of sensational flights.

On 26 September Wilbur flew for more than eleven miles. Their father, Bishop Wright, witnessed the performance. On the 29th Orville flew for almost twenty minutes and covered a distance of twelve miles, in a single flight. On 3 October Orville flew for more than fifteen miles. On 5 October 1905 Wilbur made the longest flight of the year, an excursion that lasted for almost forty minutes, and covered a distance of more than

[1] Combes, *Kill Devil Hill*, p. 246.

twenty-four miles. He only came down when his supply of fuel was exhausted. This was a longer flight than the total of their one hundred and five flights of 1904. The Wright brothers were masters of the air.

During this series of flights the Wrights took care to invite a dozen friends and neighbours to the Huffman pasture so that they could witness these remarkable performances. Until this time only the local farmers, and a few others, had observed their machine in the air. The guests included Katharine Wright, their father, and also the banker, Torrence Huffman himself. Although Wilbur and Orville were still very anxious to preserve as secret the details of their aeroplane they also wanted to be in a position to furnish prospective purchasers with the names of responsible citizens who could testify that what the brothers claimed about their achievements was true.

Some of these witnesses were unable to keep silent about the marvels they had observed. As a result, on 5 October the Dayton *Daily News* published an article reporting that the Wrights were making sensational flights every day. This article was quickly reproduced in the Cincinnati *Post*. Such publicity might attract visitors who were more technically proficient than the selected guests who had come to the Huffman pasture at the brothers' invitation. For this reason the Wrights at once halted their experiments. They still hoped to try for a flight of one hour later in the season, but this did not happen. Indeed, as we shall see later, the Wright brothers did not fly again until 1908.

When Wilbur reported the details of these accomplishments to Octave Chanute the older man was overjoyed by the news. Chanute wrote to his friend: ". . . I am enthused and delighted by what you tell me of your recent advance in performance. I congratulate you and your brother most heartily upon a success as well deserved as it is epoch-making."

VII

By October 1905, following these glowing successes, the Wright brothers, after much calculation, decided the time had come to launch a new campaign of letter writing to try and sell their invention to various governments. They thereupon wrote to the American Secretary of War; to Captain Ferber of the French Army; and shortly thereafter to the British War Office.

The American negotiations ended in failure. These began on 9 October when the Wrights sent a letter to the Secretary of War in Washington. They pointed out in it that their earlier informal offer had met with almost no consideration. They declared: "We do not wish to take this invention abroad, unless we find it necessary to do so . . ."[1]

[1] The exchanges between the Wrights and the American authorities in October 1905 are printed in Kelly, *Miracle at Kitty Hawk*, pp. 148–152.

They explained further that after a contract was agreed upon and signed they were prepared to furnish the American Government with a practical flying machine that could carry an operator and supplies of fuel sufficient for a flight of one hundred miles. They also suggested that the government, by the terms of the contract, would only be required to accept the machine "after trial trips in which the conditions of the contract have been fulfilled". They sought to make clear that the minimum performance of their device during the trial trips was to be a "flight of at least twenty-five miles at a speed of not less than thirty miles an hour". If these distances and speeds were not attained during the trials the government would not be bound to pay them anything, even though a contract had been signed.

This idea of a "contingency contract", as it has been called, was hit upon by Wilbur and Orville in order to protect themselves and the secrets of their invention. In dealing with governments the Wrights were afraid that if they demonstrated their aeroplane to "expert" military officials before a contract was signed these authorities would be able to learn the secret details of the machine's construction, and might then, having gained such vital intelligence, abandon the negotiations, and the brothers, in order to build an aeroplane themselves.

The reader should bear the idea of this "contingency contract" in mind because the outcome of the Wrights' negotiations with the British was very seriously affected by it.

The reply to the Wrights' letter of 9 October was sent by the new President of the Board of Ordnance and Fortification, Major General J. C. Bates. He informed the brothers that the United States Government declined to "make allotments for the experimental development of devices for mechanical flight". Before a contract could be considered, the general explained, it would be necessary for the Wrights to furnish the Board with drawings and descriptions of the machine that would enable its construction to be understood. The Wright brothers, however, were not prepared to divulge any of their secrets to anyone. Even the officials of the United States Government would not, by their design, be allowed to see any blueprints or the machine itself until a formal contract had been signed.

On 19 October they wrote to the president of the Board in order to tell him: "We have no thought of asking financial assistance from the government. We propose to sell the results of experiments finished at our own expense." In this letter the Wrights also stated: "We ought also to know whether you would wish to reserve a monopoly on the use of the invention, or whether you would permit us to accept orders for similar machines from other governments . . ."

The answer, this time, was prepared by Captain T. C. Dickson, Recorder of the Board. It stated that the Board would not "take any

further action on the subject until a machine is produced which by actual
operation is shown to be able to produce horizontal flight and to carry an
opertor". With this, the Wrights reckoned that their American negotiations of October 1905 had come to an unsuccessful end. Octave Chanute
had already volunteered to help in his own way. On 22 October he wrote
to Wilbur: "I am glad to know that you intend to give the American
government another chance to acquire your invention. If I can be of any
help in bringing your achievements to its notice, or to that of the Board,
please command me."[1] Later, Chanute enquired if the brothers would
like him to advise the President of the United States, or some member of
the Congress, about their work; but Wilbur and Orville decided that
the matter should be kept secret because knowledge of the American
refusal would be certain to have a negative effect upon the attitudeof
foreign governments, and would thus complicate their negotiations with
them.

The Wright brothers also approached Captain Ferdinand Ferber of the
French Army in an attempt to arrange a deal with the French Government. Ferber had sought to purchase some of their machines in the past.
On 9 October the brothers wrote to him to inform him of the startling
results achieved during their recent trials in the air. They declared of their
machine: "It is our present intention to offer it to governments for war
purposes, and if you think your government would be interested, we will
be glad to communicate with it."[2]

Ferber, who possessed in full the arrogance which distinguished so
many of the French aeronauts and aviators of this period, replied by
asking the Wrights to name their price for a machine. He added that the
French Government, owing to his recent successes with his own glider,
was no longer interested in paying as much for a Wright aeroplane as it
had been in the recent past. Wilbur, in response, promptly offered to sell
the French an aeroplane for the sum of one million francs.

He also wrote, a bit later, to the French ambassador in Washington to
acquaint him with the fact of these negotiations; and to suggest that he
send a representative to Dayton so that witnesses to their flights could be
interviewed, and an appropriate report about their testimony prepared
for the authorities in the French Ministry of War. Since Captain Ferber's
motorized gliding experiments did not produce the results he had anticipated, or hoped for, these exchanges with the French continued for a
period of several months. When news about them was eventually published in the French and in the English Press the British War Office was
alerted; and, as we shall see, the Wrights' bargaining with France thus

---

[1] McFarland, *Papers of Wilbur and Orville Wright*, pp. 518–19.
[2] For these negotiations with Ferber see McFarland, *Papers of Wilbur and
Orville Wright*, pp. 524–5, n. 2.

became another factor that helped to determine the outcome of their negotiations with the British.

As a part of this October campaign the Wright brothers also wrote to the British War Office, on 19 October. The purpose of this letter was to inform the British that they were now prepared to increase the minimum acceptance range of their proposed trial flights from ten to fifty miles. Moreover, since they had received no communication from any British authority for a period of fully five months this letter was clearly designed to re-establish the contact:[1]

> The Secretary, War Office,   October 19th, 1905
>   London, S.W.
>
> Dear Sir:
>   Under date of March 1st, 1905, we submitted a proposition to furnish to the War Department [*sic*] a flying machine for scouting purposes. We now write to say that recent flights justify us in offering to so amend the proposition as to make the acceptance of the machine dependant upon a trial flight of at least fifty miles, instead of ten miles as specified in the original offer.
>
>   Respectfully yours,
>   Wright Cycle Co.

On the same day Wilbur explained the developing situation to Octave Chanute. He also made clear to him the firmness with which the Wrights held to their "contingency contract" idea: "We are not anticipating an immediate visit from the Britishers as we have no word from them for several months and do not expect anything until we write or stir them up in some indirect way. We should prefer to finish up our experiments for this season before they appear. We have never had any intention of showing the machine in advance of a definite understanding in regard to its purchase. We will give the American government another chance before finally accepting any foreign contract."[2]

VIII

In London, the authorities in the War Office at last began to stir themselves into action of a kind. On 19 October Major William Baker

---

[1] From the copy in the Wright Brothers' Papers, Wright Cycle Co. to The Secretary, War Office, London, 19 October 1905. See also Walker, *Early Aviation at Farnborough*, vol. II, p. 36.

[2] McFarland, *Papers of Wilbur and Orville Wright*, pp. 516–17.

Brown, the Inspector of Electric Lights, asked the Director of Military Operations when they could expect a report from Colonel Foster. He learned that Foster had just returned to Washington from Mexico. When the Wright brothers' letter arrived a reply to it was sent to Dayton, on 11 November. Meanwhile, however, the British authorities had struck out in an entirely new direction.

The Directorate of Fortifications and Works had applied to Colonel J. D. Fullerton, a retired officer of Royal Engineers, for advice about "Flying Machines" that the British Army could build by itself. If Fullerton's suggestions proved to be feasible there would be no need for the War Office to bargain with the Wright brothers, or with anyone else. They would be able to develop an aeroplane of their own, a British Army flying machine. This bold initiative reflected the feelings of several of the officers concerned. They were motivated by a patriotic desire to possess a practical aeroplane of British conception, design, and construction.

Colonel Fullerton was looked upon, by his contemporaries, as an aeronautical authority of distinction. His opinions were respected, and sought after, by all those in Britain concerned with the subject. He had served at Chatham with the Army's Balloon Section and was an active member of the Aeronautical Society of Great Britain. He regularly published technical articles and reviews in its *Journal*. As early as 1892 he had lectured on "Aeronautics" before the Royal United Service Institution. Later, he became secretary of the Aeronautical Society and also editor of its *Journal*. Moreover, he was a man who was firmly convinced of the validity of his own opinions, and seldom hesitated to offer them at meetings of technical societies or in the pages of technical reviews.

On 16 November 1905 Fullerton submitted a report, a remarkable document in the history of early British military aeronautics, "Proposed Experiments in connection with Flying Machines", to the Directorate of Fortifications and Works. This document, nine foolscap pages in length, supplied the authorities with technical information about the airfields that would be required, about methods of testing various surfaces, the construction of model aeroplanes, and also the construction "of a full sized machine to carry a passenger". Moreover, in the report Colonel Fullerton condemned the Wright type of aircraft, a "soaring machine" as he called it, as being "very dangerous".[1]

Colonel Fullerton suggested that certain arrangements would be necessary for the proposed experiments. He pointed out that a large open space, free from obstacles such as houses, trees, or telegraph lines would

---

[1] Air 1/728/176/3/29. "(F.W.4) Proposed Experiments in connection with Flying Machines", dated "16 Nov. 1905" and signed "J. D. Fullerton Lt. Col. R.E. ret." It may be mentioned that Colonel Fullerton's proposals could not have led to the production of a practical aeroplane.

be needed. "Any large open space is suitable", he explained, "but there should be, at least one good straight run, of from ½ to ¾ mile in length, for testing the lifting power of full sized machines".

In order to test the resistance of surfaces to the air a Whirling Table would be required. Workshops would be needed to produce models and full sized machines; and a "few officers & men" would be necessary to assist in taking measurements. The models, driven by rocket motors, would be very useful in all the preliminary phases of the work.

In the report Fullerton identified the Wright aeroplane as a "soaring machine" and went on to state of this "class" of aircraft:

> A great number of soaring machines have been made from time to time, some with motors and some without, and there is no doubt that it is quite possible to make one with a small motor, which will enable a man to fly. But these machines are very dangerous; a great deal of practice is necessary to manage them properly, & practice in the air, is not by any means as easy or as safe as it looks . . . they are very crank and difficult to right, when their normal position is varied.

He urged that the British Army's experiments should be carried out with an entirely different type of aircraft. The War Office authorities reckoned that the Wrights wanted the sum of twenty-five thousand pounds for their aeroplane but in the conclusion of his report Fullerton suggested, in a section entitled "Estimate of Cost", that a British machine could be built for a much smaller sum: "It is extremely difficult to give an accurate estimate of the cost . . . probably if the proposed machine was constructed in the government workshops its costs would not exceed say £500."

It is thus clear that before Colonel Foster requested an interview with the Wrights in Dayton, his colleagues in London had been advised by an expert that the Wright aeroplane was dangerous to fly, and that a British flying machine, built on entirely different lines, could be constructed at a fraction of the cost demanded by the Wright bothers. Two days after Fullerton produced his report Colonel Foster wrote to the Wrights for the first time, from the British Embassy in Washington.

As this situation became more complicated, and more tense, the Wrights embarked upon a new and bolder phase of their campaign to sell their aeroplane to one government or another. They were still determined to preserve their technical secrets but they believed that publicity about their flights of 1903, 1904 and 1905 would provoke curiosity, and thus speed up the course of events. Their particular targets in this new course were the French and British governments. As Wilbur explained to Chanute: ". . . we concluded that too much time was being wasted by

England & France in coming to close quarters, so we decided to apply a mild outside pressure".[1]

The "outside pressure" was applied on 17 November when the Wright brothers wrote to a number of selected correspondents about their successful flights of 1903, 1904, and 1905. At about the same time they decided to "absolve" Chanute from his obligation to keep secret the spectacular results of the 1905 season's experiments. The letters sent on the 17 November were despatched to Carl Dienstbach, New York correspondent of the *Illustrierte Aeronautische Mitteilungen*; to Georges Besançon, publisher of *L'Aérophile*; to Colonel Capper; and to Patrick Y. Alexander of the Aeronautical Society of Great Britain.

Two letters sent to Dienstbach were published in his magazine in February 1906. The letter to Georges Besançon was published in France in November 1905 and became a significant element in a heated controversy that raged in that country over the veracity and reliability of the Wrights' reports about their achievements. The letter to Alexander was read by him at a meeting of the Aeronautical Society of Great Britain on 15 December 1905 and was published in the *Aeronautical Journal* for January 1906. Some of this publicity dealing with the aeronautical accomplishments of the Wright brothers did not, as we shall see, escape the notice of the authorities in the British War Office.

On the day after the Wrights sent off these several communications which they hoped would be published in the various European capitals Colonel Foster at last wrote to them, on 18 November 1905. In the previous May R. H. Brade of the War Office had informed them that the Colonel had been asked by his superiors to visit their "works". Half a year had elapsed since that time but now a direct contact was established. Foster's letter was a model of clarity and military efficiency:[2]

> Dear Sirs,   British Embassy, Washington D.C.
> The British War Office have sent me your letter to them of 10th. Jany. last, and of March 1st. with the view of my entering into communication with you, as the "representative" alluded to in your last.
> I am prepared to visit Dayton to witness a flight as you propose, so as to inform my war office of the fact that your machine makes such a satisfactory flight as to make it desirable for the Government to consider the matter of a contract as suggested by you.
> The actual terms of my instructions are: "Should these gentlemen be able at any time to carry out successful flying trials in the presence of the Military Attaché the question of an agreement, on terms to be settled, might again be taken up".

---

[1] McFarland, *Papers of Wilbur and Orville Wright*, p. 534.
[2] Wright Brothers' Papers, H. Foster to the Wrights, 18 November 1905.

May I therefore ask you if you are ready to shew me a flight, which I would come to witness as soon as you can arrange one? Any time in the next 4 weeks would suit me, but the sooner the more satisfactory for me.

Yours faithfully,
H. Foster
Colonel
British Military Attaché

Washington D.C. Nov. 18th. 1905.

IX

There now began a noteworthy correspondence which was to help decide the fate of Britain's first negotiations to obtain possession of a Wright aeroplane, the only practical flying machine in existence at that time. Indeed, no competitors in any country were to attain the Wrights' levels of proficiency and technical achievement for years to come. Wilbur at once replied to Colonel Foster, on 20 November 1905:[1]

> Your letter of November 18th has been received. We would be pleased to have you visit Dayton at once as you suggest. It is desirable that you should thoroughly satisfy yourself of the truth regarding our flights by an investigation on the spot and personal conference with people who have witnessed them. The flights of October 3rd, 4th and 5th of fifteen, twenty-one, and twenty-four miles respectively, were witnessed not only by farmers living in the neighborhood, but also by a number of prominent citizens of Dayton whom we had invited to be present whose names we will be glad to furnish you.

When Percy Walker sought to analyze this part of Wilbur's letter he referred to "this absurd offer of testimony from local farmers and the élite of Dayton." It may perhaps be mentioned that the Wright aeroplane had been flown near that city and for this reason it does not seem entirely absurd for Wilbur to have suggested that its citizens were the ones who had witnessed the flights, independent witnesses whose names could be furnished to Colonel Foster as a preliminary step in his investigation of the matter.

We come now, in our account, to a crucial development in the negotiations. As we have seen, Wilbur and Orville had carefully planned

---

[1] From the copy in the Wright Brothers' Papers, Wright Cycle Company to Foster, 20 November 1905. See also Walker, *Early Aviation at Farnborough*, vol. II, pp. 38–9.

in advance the way in which they would sell their invention to a government. They had worked out a method to safeguard its secrets during the course of any sale. This occurred when they hit upon the idea of the "contingency contract".

By the terms of this device or tactic a contract with a government would be signed first, before any official representative would be allowed to see the aeroplane, either on the ground or in flight. If the machine could not fly for the distances and at the speeds stipulated in the contract, the government would not be obligated to accept it, and nothing would be lost by either side in the transaction, save for the time expended by the parties concerned.

The Wright brothers and Chanute each believed that the officer sent from the British Embassy would be an "expert"[1] in aeronautics and aviation. They had awaited his appearance for six months. In these circumstances they were not prepared to change the procedures they had fixed upon beforehand, for any reason.

The Wrights were dominated by the idea that they possessed priceless secrets. They would not risk the loss of these secrets by allowing an official observer to examine the aeroplane before a contract was signed. They trusted no one and relied for their success in the venture upon themselves alone. They would not yield on the principle of the "contingency contract".

Indeed, as Colonel Foster's letter made clear to them the British Government, for its part, had committed itself to nothing at all at this stage of the bargaining. For these reasons a resolute Wilbur made clear to Colonel Foster, in terms of unbending firmness, the nature of the "contingency contract" idea – in the next paragraph of his letter of 20 November:

> Of course we can not consent to show the machine to the representatives of any government which is considering the purchase of our knowledge and inventions until we are assured that the terms of sale will be satisfactory. It would be highly injudicious to place ourselves at the mercy of any one by disclosing any part of our secrets with the expectation of arranging satisfactory terms afterward. Moreover, we would find the saleability of the invention greatly reduced, if the construction and operation of the machine should be shown to the military attachés of other governments than the one which should be first in deciding to purchase. As a preliminary to the consummation of a definite contract, we will furnish incontestable evidence that we have done all that we claim to have done. By the

[1] For example, on 16 October 1905 Chanute wrote to Wilbur: "I fancy that you will have soon a visit from the British expert". See McFarland, *Papers of Wilbur and Orville Wright*, p. 515.

terms of the contract not one cent need be paid out by the government until after the machine has fulfilled certain stipulated requirements in a trial trip in the presence of the government's representatives.

This insistence upon secrecy until a contract was signed resulted in a series of classic charges against the Wright brothers. In the production of these denigrations British experts played an important role.

Percy Walker, in his analysis of the "contingency" idea, dismissed it as "Wilburian rigmarole". Another British authority, Oliver Stewart, made an even more grotesque and ignorant statement about the attitude the Wrights assumed in 1905. "To the doubter", Stewart wrote in his *Aviation: The Creative Ideas*, "this attempt to sell something without allowing the buyer to see it in action suggests that the Wrights could not at that time make a powered flight".[1]

Wilbur's letter of 20 November ended with a reasonable and clearly drawn proposal to the British representative:

> Although the machine has already been dismantled, we can, in case an agreement is reached, set up the machine at some retired place and make a flight surpassing those to which we have already referred. We would have put the record much higher before quitting, but for the impossibility of securing privacy for further flights at that time and place.

This was a hard letter. When he received it Colonel Foster had a problem. As a soldier he was bound by the instructions sent to him by his superiors in the War Office. He now wanted the Wright brothers to understand these orders, and to comply with them. On 22 November he at once replied to Wilbur in order to explain his position to them:[2]

> Yours of 20th inst. – There is evidently a certain amount of misunderstanding between us, so I will try & clear the ground by stating very shortly what I want to do, when you will see clearly, I hope, that most of your letter is not quite to the point.
>
> My instructions are very short, & I know nothing of the intentions or wishes of my War Office (beyond what I read in them) as to flying machines.
>
> I am to ask you to shew me your machine doing a satisfactory flight, *after* which the W.O. will enter into negotiations with you, if satisfied.

[1] For Walker's comment see *Early Aviation at Farnborough*, vol. II, p. 39. For Oliver Stewart's ridiculous comment see his *Aviation: The Creative Ideas* (New York, 1966), p. 25.

[2] Wright Brothers' Papers, H. Foster, Colonel, Military Attaché, to the Wrights, 22 November, 1905.

Thus, para I of yours falls through. The W.O. have already had flights *described*, but want me to *see* one for them, as their representative.

Para 2 is also, may I say, unnecessary – I do *not* want to see the details or mechanism, nor am I to report in any way on that, but only to see the machine performing a flight.

This I take it will be quite satisfactory to you, as it will in no way prejudice you. Many people have, you tell me, seen flights on Oct. 3. 4 & 5th. I only want to see one too, as you propose in your last para. I could come to Dayton at any time to see it if you would be good enough to arrange for a flight. Hoping this letter is clear, & will be satisfactory to you, believe me, Gentlemen, Yours faithfully H. Foster Colonel Military Attaché.

Colonel Foster was an unusually patient and diligent officer. On the next day, before he had received any reply he wrote again, in order to make his position absolutely clear. In this letter, dated 23 November, he explained that he was only a representative of the War Office and not an intermediary who could involve himself in any negotiations. His sole purpose in communicating with the Wrights, he said, was to arrange a visit to Dayton so that he could observe their aeroplane in flight:[1]

Re mine of yesterday, _____

To make my letter quite clear I will give you the exact words of my instructions:

"The Committee suggests that the Military Attaché at Washington be requested to enter into communication with Messrs. Wright. Should these gentlemen be able at any time to carry out satisfactory flying trials in the presence of the Military Attaché, the question of an agreement, on terms to be settled, might be again taken up". This is sent to me for action.

All I would therefore ask you is to say whether you will shew me a flying trial, and if you will, to fix a near date. If you do not wish to, I will so inform the War Office, whose representative I am only for the purpose of seeing the trial. I am not their intermediary for negotiations with you, and on that point I would ask you to communicate direct with the Secretary for War, War Office, London.

The Wright brothers, despite this lucid exposition, remained fixed in their determination not to permit Colonel Foster to see their aeroplane until a contract was secured with the British Government. They now understood he had no authority to negotiate with them for such a purpose. They realized that if further progress was to be made they would

[1] Wright Brothers' Papers, Foster to the Wrights, 23 November 1905. See also Walker, *Early Aviation at Farnborough*, pp. 39–40.

have to apply to the authorities in the War Office, once again. Nevertheless, their tenacity in the affair remained undiminished. They would not lightly abandon the possibility of an arrangement with the British.

They decided to reply to Foster in terms that made clear to the British authorities that they were not the only bargainers in the field and that a measure of celerity in coming to a decision, something notably lacking thus far in their conduct, might be advisable if they genuinely wished to secure the aeroplane. In their letter of reply to Colonel Foster they did not mention but hinted at their exchanges with the French Government. Wilbur later explained this tactic to Octave Chanute, at a time when news of their negotiations with the French had been published in Paris: "We wrote Col. Foster . . . that we feared the delay resulting from referring back to the London office the question of whether or not an actual sight of the machine in flight should necessarily precede any discussion of terms would result in the arrival of a crisis in our other negotiations before the British government had made up its mind to proceed. They have no doubt learned from the Paris papers that our hint was not a mere 'bluff' . . ."[1]

The hint was contained in their letter to Colonel Foster, dated 25 November 1905:[2]

> Your letters of November 22nd and 23rd have been received. We sincerely regret that your instructions seem to preclude such immediate investigation at Dayton as we suggested in our letter to you, since the delay in referring the point to the War Office will still further reduce the probability of reaching an understanding on the main issue before it is too late.
>
> At the request of Lt. Colonel Capper we gave the British government the first chance to secure the use of our invention in foreign countries, and did not take up the matter elsewhere until a number of months had passed. But the progress of the later negotiations has been such as to make it possible that a crisis will be reached before the British War Office has all obtainable information before it and is ready to reach a decision as to whether it will take up the flying machine at this time.

It may be mentioned that when Percy Walker reproduced this letter in his *Early Aviation at Farnborough* he left out the significant words "in foreign countries". He then proceeded to attack Wilbur Wright as follows: "The statement that the British government had been given the first chance to purchase is not strictly true since the United States government had been approached earlier. There is no reason to suspect

---

[1] For this letter, dated 13 December 1905 see McFarland, *The Papers of Wilbur and Orville Wright*, p. 534.

[2] From the copy in the Wright Brothers' Papers, Wright Cycle Co. to Foster, 25 November 1905.

deliberate dishonesty on Wilbur's part, however: merely another example of his muddled thinking where business was concerned!'' The muddle in this instance was solely Walker's. His charge was valid if the words ''in foreign countries'' are ignored but they appeared in the letter the Wrights sent to Colonel Foster and it is only in the faulty version, published in his book, that they do not appear.[1]

It was now clear to Colonel Foster upon the one side and to Wilbur and Orville Wright upon the other that they had reached a deadlock in their exchanges. In their situation no further progress was possible. In these circumstances all that remained was for the two parties to report separately to the War Office, in London; and this was done on 28 November. Nevertheless, Colonel Foster found that he could not leave the matter alone.

On 29th November, the day after he reported upon the failure of the negotiations to the War Office, he wrote again to the Wright brothers. In this letter he employed for the first time a phrase that was taken up later, with significant effect, by the high authorities in the Directorate of Fortifications and Works. He asked the Wrights to acknowledge that it would be impossible for any purchaser to negotiate for an invention whose performances they only knew of ''by hearsay evidence''.[2]

> British Embassy
> Washington D C
>
> Gentlemen.   Nov 29th 1905
>
> In reply to yours of 25th inst. I cannot help thinking there is some misapprehension of what I wish to do.
>
> I only wish to *see your machine fly*, as you yourselves say many people did on Oct 4th and 5th. I fail to see how this could prejudice you. I need not be near the machine or see its details.
>
> The War Office, I think you will admit not unreasonably, will *not* negotiate till they have seen that rapid flight is actually performed. This they can only do through me.
>
> I think you will acknowledge that it would be impossible for any purchaser to negotiate for purchase of an invention whose performances they only knew of by hearsay evidence. However I have sent the correspondence to the War Office.
>
> I am going into Kansas at once, and in case you should still see your way to arrange a flight for me to witness within the first half of December I give my address:
>
> > c/o Major Squier U.S. Signal Corps
> > Fort Leavenworth Kansas
>
> > Yours faithfully
> > H. Foster
> > Colonel   Military Attaché

---

[1] See Walker, *Early Aviation at Farnborough*, vol. II, p. 40.
[2] Wright Brothers' Papers, Colonel Foster to the Wrights, 29 November 1905.

The Wright brothers' interest in the negotiations also remained un-diminished but they were not prepared to yield the chief point at issue. Indeed, Wilbur and Orville were now more determined than ever not to exhibit their invention to anyone unless a contract was signed in advance.

In the first place the Wrights had become more apprehensive than before that some unauthorized person might observe their machine in flight if it were demonstrated to Colonel Foster. One of the witnesses they had invited to the Huffman prairie had been approached by a journalist and offered a bribe for information about the date of the next flight trials. Wilbur recorded in his diary for 17 October: "About a week after the flights of October 5th, John Tomlinson of the *Journal* offered Henry Webbert a bribe of $50 for information when we would be making another flight".[1] This development meant that the Press had been put upon the alert and it seemed to the Wrights that the vigilance of the newspapermen was increasing, as each day passed.

Secondly, their confidence in the "contingency contract" idea was even stronger than it had been before. On 4th December Wilbur explained to Chanute that Colonel Foster had written to tell them he had been instructed to visit Dayton in order to witness a flight. Wilbur added: "To tell the truth we are unwilling to show the machine to the attaché of any government without some assurance that a sale will follow a demonstra-tion that the machine can really fly as we claim. We think it a poor time to bargain as to terms after the goods have been partly delivered."[2]

In these circumstances Wilbur replied to Colonel Foster on 5 Decem-ber, in the most forthright terms. He permitted himself to criticize the British Government for its failure to act seriously in the negotiations that could enable it "to take the lead in this new art". This letter was destined to play an important part in the final decisions of the British War Office, when it was forwarded to the authorities there by Colonel Foster. Wilbur wrote:[3]

> We have your letter of November 29th. Even if there had been no other objection to showing our machine in flight, it has now become hopeless to think of avoiding observation and publicity, for the newspapers have at last begun to realize the true situation, and have been offering bribes to our friends for information of our intended movements. Under such circumstances only necessity could induce us to risk a flight to satisfy what may be only curiosity. You must admit yourself that up to the present your government has not shown

[1] McFarland, *The Papers of Wilbur and Orville Wright*, p. 516.
[2] *Ibid.*, pp. 530–1.
[3] From the copy in the Wright Brothers' Papers, Wright Cycle Co. to Foster, 5 December 1905. See also Walker, *Early Aviation at Farnborough*, vol. II, p. 42.

in its communications such indications of a serious purpose to take the lead in this new art as would justify us in assuming a very serious risk. If circumstances should hereafter lessen our objections to show the machine, we will be pleased to inform you.

Colonel Foster answered this at once, on 7 December. He concluded that a deadlock existed. His letter took the form of an exposition:[1]

> I beg to acknowledge receipt of yrs. of 5th inst, which I will send to the W.O. to shew the reason why you are not prepared to shew me a flight.
> The fact seems to be that the War Office cannot commit itself to negotiations with a view of purchasing, unless sure that your invention gives the flight it claims, while you, on the other hand, do not wish to show its flight until the W.O. have made some arrangement with you.

There is thus a deadlock.

This was the last of the exchanges between the Wright brothers and Colonel Foster. Even Percy Walker expressed some doubt about the validity of Foster's conduct, with so much at stake. Walker wrote of him: "While the conduct of the Attaché seems in many respects exemplary, we are left wondering whether it would not have been worth-while for him to have visited Dayton, irrespective of whether the Brothers were willing to show him their aeroplane or not . . . Possibly he was influenced by his impending retirement, which was due to take place on 12 December 1905, and he may have been overloaded with work in clearing up his affairs."[2]

In any case, decision now lay with the authorities in the War Office in London.

X

Owing to the complexities of the military channels through which it had to pass, it took more than three weeks for Colonel Foster's report, dated 28 November 1905, to arrive in the Directorate of Fortifications and Works. Copies of his further correspondence with the Wright brothers reached the Directorate at an even later date. During this period of time significant developments took place. These developments made it clear and obvious to many aeronautical experts in Britain that the Wright brothers did, indeed, possess a practical aeroplane, a machine they could control

---

[1] Wright Brothers' Papers, Foster to the Wrights, 7 December 1905, written from Fort Leavenworth.
[2] Walker, *Early Aviation at Farnborough*, vol. II, pp. 42–3.

perfectly in the air, a device that could be developed into an instrument of incalculable military importance.

When the Wright brothers released Octave Chanute from his obligation to keep secret the results of their recent experiments he at once advised them that he would tell Herbert Wenham, in confidence, the story of their achievements during the 1905 season. Francis Herbert Wenham was the English engineer who had greatly stimulated Chanute's interest in aviation, years before. In 1866, at the first meeting of the Aeronautical Society of Great Britain, Wenham had read a classic treatise on Aerial Locomotion. This paper, concerned with the construction of heavier-than-air machines, explained principles and phenomena not understood before. Since that time Wenham had regularly predicted that the flying problem would be solved. He argued that only technicalities barred the way. By 1905 he was looked upon in Britain as a respected pioneer, a "grand old man" of aeronautics and aviation.

On 24 November 1905 Chanute wrote to Wenham in order to acquaint him with the Wrights' epoch-making advances of that year. The situation was so sensitive and delicate that Chanute took care to tell the Wright brothers what he had done. By the time his letter to Wenham arrived in England news of the Wrights' negotiations with the French had been published in the French Press. Chanute was concerned, in these circumstances, that Wenham might reveal the contents of his confidential letter to the British authorities. He told Wilbur: "Advise me as to the status of your negotiations with the British. My confidential letter to Wenham should have reached him about Dec. 4th and he may talk to the authorities when he sees the account of French negotiations in the papers".[1]

Chanute began his letter to Wenham, dated 24 November 1905, in the most touching and sympathetic way: "I think it is due to you", he wrote, "as the pioneer of Aviation and my valued friend, to be the first to be told, confidentially, that the Wright Brothers have been in possession of a practical flying machine for the past two years and have been improving it". He went on to state: "In 1904 the British War Office intimated that it would take up the invention when sufficiently developed and this year the French War department is in the field, so that what is being accomplished has to be kept secret".[2]

Chanute proceeded to recount the Wright achievements of 1903 and 1904 and then he described the events of 1905:

> In 1905 another machine was built. Some time was spent in getting accustomed to its control and no flight made of more than 10 miles

---

[1] See McFarland, *Papers of Wilbur and Orville Wright*, p. 533.
[2] Octave Chanute Papers, Chanute to Wenham, 24 November 1905, marked "Private and Confidential".

until the last week of September. On the 26th 11 miles were covered in 18 minutes and 9 seconds; the exhaustion of the gasoline supply ending the flight. On the 29th 12 miles covered . . . On Oct 3rd the record was raised to 15 miles in 25 minutes & 5 seconds . . . On the 5th of October – 24 ½ miles in 38 minutes & 3 seconds . . .

By personal appeal to the editors all this has been kept out of the newspapers but some indiscreet friends having talked one article was published, and the experiments were stopped. I hope all this will enable you to exult to yourself without telling anybody.

Meanwhile, Samuel Cabot, who had maintained his interest in the work of the Wrights, and another Boston financier, Henry L. Higginson, fearful that the aeroplane might be lost to the United States, advised Chanute that they were prepared to offer the brothers some kind of "financial assistance". Chanute replied to Cabot that the Wrights did not require such help. Many of the troubles they had encountered, he said, arose from the entirely negative attitude and responses of the American authorities and these had to be kept a secret lest they adversely affect the negotiations that were being carried on at that very moment with the British and French governments.

"I thank you and Mr. Higginson", Chanute wrote to Cabot on 29 November, "for the patriotic interest which you take in the Wrights. They are in no present need of financial assistance . . . Our own U.S. patent office is raising difficulties and is, as well as the Board of Ordnance, pursuing the very fatuous policy which drove Hiram Maxim from the country with his inventions." Chanute went on to give expression to his own patriotic discontent: "There has been further correspondence with the Board of Ordnance and I get very indignant each time I think of it, but the Wrights do not wish to have a scandal occur at present, as both the British and French War Offices have made overtures. I have urged going to the President with the facts in order to save at least prior rights to this country, but the Wrights believe this will do no good." Shortly afterward, Cabot suggested the Wrights might like to visit him in the East in order to "talk things over". Chanute's reply to this overture was concise: "Whether right or wrong the Wrights have always expressed to me the desire to have as little talk about their matters as possible."[1]

By this time the outcry in France about the French Government's negotiations with the Wright brothers had become even more shrill than it had been earlier. A controversy raged in the French Press. One faction expressed an ardent belief in the Wrights' claims while another condemned them as mere boasters and "bluffers".

Chanute decided that since the affairs of the Wrights were receiving so

[1] Octave Chanute Papers, Chanute to Cabot, 29 November 1905, marked "Confidential", and Chanute to Cabot, 5 December 1905.

much publicity in France, it was no longer necessary for Herbert Wenham to keep secret the confidential information he had sent him about the great flights of 1905. On 28 December Chanute wrote to Wenham in order to make a suggestion:[1]

> I understand that negotiations are in progress. The French did not keep their mouths shut and it may now be useful for you to confirm to the British War Office that a practical flying machine is in existence . . .

Although Chanute did not yet know it an event had already occurred in London which confirmed beyond any reasonable doubt the fact that the Wright brothers now possessed a practical flying machine. The incident has been misunderstood in the historical literature but it was a development of some significance in the aeronautical world of that day.

It will be recalled that on 17 November the Wright brothers, in order to win a measure of publicity for their accomplishments, had despatched letters to correspondents in several countries. The letter sent to Britain was written by Orville and addressed to Patrick Y. Alexander. On 15 December 1905 Alexander read this letter to a meeting of the Aeronautical Society of Great Britain. Major Baden-Powell, President of the Society, presided at this meeting and Colonel Capper was also present.

Orville's letter was an account of the Wright experiments and flight trials for the year 1905. Alexander's audience learned from it of the astonishing flights of the previous September and October. Naturally enough, particular attention was paid, by these technical experts, to the flight of 5 October when Wilbur flew for more than thirty minutes and only landed because his fuel supply was exhausted. In addition to these exciting details Orville's letter emphasized two other aspects of the project carried out at the Huffman prairie. It explained: "We had intended to place the record above one hour, but the attention these flights were beginning to attract compelled us to suddenly discontinue our experiments in order to prevent the construction of the machine from becoming public". In conclusion the letter established the fact that the Wrights were perfectly able to fly in circles, in their machine: "In each of these flights we returned frequently to the starting point, passing high over the heads of the spectators".

Major Baden-Powell was astonished by what he heard. Here was intelligence of a machine that could remain in the air for more than thirty minutes. This aeroplane could readily perform the difficult technical manoeuvre of circular flight. Moreover, as the account made clear, spectators had been present to observe several of its trials. When Patrick

[1] Octave Chanute Papers, Chanute to Wenham, 28 December 1905.

Alexander finished his reading Baden-Powell said to the company: "I think that sounds like a remarkable statement. We have not heard much of what the Brothers Wright have been doing recently. We heard a year or two ago that they had made some successful flights, but this sounds a very successful result. I shall certainly be longing to hear more details of these flights. To remain half an hour in the air seems extraordinary."

Orville's letter and Major Baden-Powell's comments upon it were published in the *Aeronautical Journal* for January 1906. When Octave Chanute, far away in Chicago, received his copy of the *Journal* he misunderstood what Baden-Powell had said. Chanute believed, in error, that Baden-Powell did not readily accept the truthfulness of the Wright brothers' statements. He also felt a measure of annoyance with Alexander and Colonel Capper since, in his opinion, they should have defended the brothers against the "rather lukewarm remarks of the presiding officer . . .".[1]

Chanute, however, had entirely failed to understand the scene at that evening meeting of the Aeronautical Society in London. There had been no need for either Colonel Capper or Alexander to rise in defence of the Wright brothers. Baden-Powell, far from questioning the Wrights' assertions, believed them completely and was delighted to learn of what had been achieved in the rain-sodden field near Dayton. Three days later he wrote to Orville in order to offer his heartiest congratulations:[2]

> It was with the very greatest interest that we heard, at a meeting of the Aeronautical Society a few days ago, your letter read announcing that you had made a number of successful flights in your aerial machine. I beg to offer my heartiest congratulations, and hope you may continue your trials with much success.
>
> I need hardly say that we are longing to hear more details of the form and construction of your machine, but I can readily suppose that you will not wish to publish them until thoroughly sure of your ground.
>
> I should of course always be glad to hear any accounts, and to know whether the machine is similar in general principles to the glider of which you have published details. . . .
>
> Again offering my heartiest congratulations . . .

Orville Wright was delighted to receive Baden-Powell's message. His letter of 17 November had hit its British target for this was exactly the kind of reaction the brothers had hoped for when they decided to

---

[1] For Chanute's reaction see McFarland, *Papers of Wilbur and Orville Wright*, p. 688 and *n.* 4. Several aeronautical historians have accepted Chanute's understanding of this incident and have condemned Baden-Powell in consequence.

[2] Wright Brothers' Papers, B. Baden-Powell to Orville Wright, 18 December 1905.

communicate the details of their success to their various European correspondents.

When he wrote to Patrick Alexander on 17 November Orville had set out the facts of the 1905 flights and had then added: "If you think the contents of this letter would be of interest to the members of the Aeronautical Society of Great Britain, you are at liberty to communicate as much of it to them as you please."[1]

Now, as a result of their own initiative the Wright brothers knew that a company of technical experts in Britain had been made aware of their tremendous and record-breaking accomplishments at the very time that the military authorities in the British War Office were pondering upon their decision to purchase the aeroplane, or to reject the offer that had been made to them.

Orville took care to reply to Baden-Powell in order to provide more information about the new machine but he also explained: "We are sorry that we are not able to give a more detailed description . . . but business considerations forbid". In addition Orville made clear the marvellous nature of the device the Wright brothers had created. He explained:[2]

> The machine has been passing through one change after another, and it was not until the latter part of September that we had all the dangerous features overcome. From then on progress was rapid, and it is now only a matter of perfecting the mechanical details to produce a flyer that will travel hundreds of miles in a single flight.

In France the various exchanges in the Press concerning the achievements of the Wright brothers were less seemly than these British developments but they generated even more publicity, and note was taken of them in England. The Wright letter to Georges Besançon was published in Paris at the end of November 1905.

At once two factions appeared in France. One group of technical experts accepted the claims set out by the Wrights in their communication of 17 November, while another, consumed by patriotism and envy in varying amounts, denounced the brothers as frauds and "bluffers". In December and January this public discussion raged on, with increasing intensity. The names of the Dayton witnesses were published in the French Press. Inquiries were made in Dayton itself, by French agents. In January 1906 the respected technical journal, *L'Aérophile* published a long article which confirmed the veracity of the Wright brothers' accounts; set out the details of the French negotiations to purchase a Wright machine; and acknowledged the glorious triumph that had occurred, not "chez nous" as the paper put it, but far away in America.

[1] Wright Brothers' Papers, Orville Wright to Alexander, 17 November 1905.
[2] The letter is printed in Pritchard, *The Wright Brothers and the Royal Aeronautical Society*, p. 172.

This news from France quickly spread to other countries. On 29 December an article about the Wrights appeared in the London *Daily Mail*. In January 1906 a very long article in a technical London publication, the *Automotor Journal*, came to the conclusion that the Wright brothers were, indeed, the conquerors of the air. The *Automotor Journal* declared that their achievement "will . . . be regarded as epoch-making in the highest degree. We are dealing with the first reports of absolutely the first successful attempts to accomplish mechanical flight. . . ."

The fame of the Wright brothers also reached Vienna. Wilbur and Orville were pleased and amused to receive a letter from the "Austrian Association of Builders". The directors of this organization, having read the accounts in the French Press, wished to purchase the aeroplane for the Emperor Franz Joseph and present it to him as a gift from the nation, upon the occasion of his sixtieth jubilee.

By this time, however, the Wrights were no longer in a position to deal with this Austrian request. On 30 December 1905 they had signed a contract with a Frenchman named Arnold Fordyce. He represented a syndicate of wealthy men in France who wished to acquire their invention. This contract granted Fordyce an option for a short period. By its terms if certain specified sums were not paid into the Wrights' account by 5 April 1906, the contract would become null and void. Eventually the two parties failed to agree upon the details of their arrangement and the option lapsed, almost at the last moment. We will have to look more closely at this failure to secure a French connection in our next chapter because, with the passage of time, the British became very interested in it.

In the War Office the time for decision had come. A whole year had elapsed since the Wright brothers had written to Colonel Capper in the previous January. Colonel Ruck had now to consider the entire course of the negotiations and to make some judgement upon them.

The first item to pass under his review was the letter from the Wrights dated 28 November 1905. This paper, addressed to the Secretary of the War Office, set out the Wright attitude as clearly as possible. It began by summarizing the impasse reached by the Wrights in their negotiations with Colonel Foster:[1]

Your communication of November 11th (84/W/5144) is received.

Colonel Foster has informed us that his instructions limit him to the sole duty of witnessing a flight of our machine. Our answer has been that we are not willing to show the machine to the representative of any government in advance of an agreement as to terms of sale.

---

[1] Air 1/728/176/3/33. Wright Cycle Co. to The Secretary, War Office, 28 November 1905. See also Walker, *Early Aviation at Farnborough*, vol. II, pp. 43–4. Walker's ludicrous comments upon this letter may be seen at pp. 44–5.

The Wright letter went on to explain the reasons for the position they had taken up:

> We recognise that the War Office has no desire to waste time in preparing contracts which can not be fulfilled, but sight of our machine by further witnesses is not necessary to establish the fact that man can build machines which fly long distances with an operator on board, and land safely. A few hours' investigation at Simms station on the electric road between Dayton and Springfield will disclose conclusive proof that it has been done. Flights of more than twenty miles have been witnessed not only by a dozen families living in the neighbourhood, but also by a number of prominent citizens of Dayton. We refer by permission to Mr. E. W. Ellis, Mr. Torrence Huffman and Mr. C. J. Billman. Additional names will be furnished if desired.

Those named in this part of the letter had all witnessed the Wright aeroplane in flight. The reader is already acquainted with the name of Torrence Huffman, the banker. E. W. Ellis was assistant auditor of the City of Dayton while C. S. Billman was secretary of the West Side Building Association of that town. The Wright explanation continued:

> In view of the abundant evidence already available, we can not regard an actual sight of the machine by your representative a necessary prerequisite to the formulation of terms of agreement, since the necessary safeguards can be included in the contract; but, on the other hand, we do regard an agreement a necessary prerequisite to the disclosure of any part of the invention, since it provides the only guarantee that a sale on satisfactory terms will follow a demonstration that the machine is all that has been claimed for it.

The Wright brothers ended their letter with a formal proposal that each side should now proceed to action, at once:

> We are able and willing to furnish at once proper presumptive evidence of ability to fulfil a contract. When a contract has been signed, we will build a machine at our own expense and make flights as specified in the contract, in the presence of the War Office representatives, before any money whatever is paid to us. We do not ask for such advance payments as are customary in the building of battle ships, etc. nor for any assumption of risk whatever on your part.
> The invention has been carried entirely through the experimental stage, and is ready for sale to some one at once.

Ruck turned next to the Military Attaché's report dated 28 November. Colonel Foster's message to his superiors was clear and simple: "I have communicated with Messrs. Wright who are, however, not satisfactory. They *will not* let me see the flight before the negotiations are made – as I am instructed to do. I therefore can do nothing by going to Dayton. They require an arrangement first. It seems most unreasonable, as so many people have seen the flight."[1]

The authorities in the War Office now decided to refer the entire matter to the Royal Engineer Committee. The committee, in its turn, asked Colonel Capper to report to it before any decisions were taken. He offered the committee some remarkable advice.[2]

Capper began his report by stating that he believed in the claims brought forward by Wilbur and Orville Wright: "There appears to be little doubt", he wrote, "that the machine has done all that the Wright Brothers claim for it, and that it is within their power to construct a similar machine capable of going much longer distances and of carrying one or more passengers". He next added a cautionary note: "I cannot think that a machine so limited in capacity can have great practical value *except as leading to the building of better ones*, and therefore the purchase of a single one, without power to construct more on similar lines, would be of no great assistance to us."

The Wright brothers, in their letter of 1 March 1905, had proposed that the cost of the machine to the British Government should be based on a "mileage run" at the rate of five hundred pounds for each mile covered in a trial flight made in the presence of British representatives. Colonel Capper rejected this idea and suggested that the Wrights should be asked by the War Office to set a fixed price for a single aeroplane. He wrote: "It would be well, therefore, to write these gentlemen, stating that we are willing to accept the evidence before us as to the accomplishments of their machine, but that we could not accept any contract based on mileage run, but ask if they can name a fixed sum for which they would be disposed to sell us a machine to go fifty miles."

It is thus clear that Colonel Capper disagreed with his colleagues upon the need for a British representative to see the Wright aeroplane in flight before a contract could be signed. He accepted the evidence of successful powered flight adduced by the Wright brothers in their several communications with Colonel Foster and with the War Office. This, however, was not Colonel Foster's view, and as we shall see, it was not the opinion adopted later by Sir James Wolfe Murray, the Master-General of the Ordnance, and by Colonel Ruck, the Director of Fortifications and Works.

Colonel Capper finished his report in an odd way. When Percy Walker

[1] See Walker, *Early Aviation at Farnborough*, vol. II, p. 43.
[2] Capper's report is printed in Walker, *Early Aviation at Farnborough*, vol. II, pp. 45–6.

analyzed this part of it he was surprised by Capper's conclusions. Walker declared of this portion of the report: "He ends on a curious note that leaves us wondering what he *really* thinks . . . which does he feel most – regret at the prospect of losing the Wright aeroplane, or hope at the prospect of Britain producing her own?"[1] Capper had written as follows, in his conclusion:

> I am inclined to think that the sum asked will be too great for acceptance, and that we must do our utmost to build successful machines ourselves and learn their use.

Capper's attitude at this stage of the negotiations was a complicated one. All British military officers worked under severe budgetary constraints in this period and he was certainly concerned by the high cost of the Wright invention. But more was involved in the advice he offered the Royal Engineer Committee at this time.

It will be recalled that when he returned from his American visit Capper had addressed the Aeronautical Society of Great Britain, on 2 December 1904. On that occasion he predicted that news would soon arrive from America telling of successful powered flight by a gliding machine driven through the air by a motor. But he also said: "It seems to me it is rather bad for us to allow the Americans to lead us in that direction".

These remarks were one early indication among others of a fervently cherished desire. Above all else John Capper wanted to see a British aeroplane produced at Aldershot or at Farnborough, under his direction.

It is certainly true that when he received the Wright letter of 10 January 1905 with their first offer to bargain with the British authorities, Capper urged his superiors to allow him to answer it in a positive way. But this reaction was merely temporary. It was caused by Capper's intense and entirely understandable excitement when he learned of the sensational advances made by the Wrights in 1904, and by the fact that they had written to him when they sought to begin their negotiations with the British Government. Capper's report to the Royal Engineer Committee reflected his earlier and more strongly held attitude.

Later, in 1906, when his influence and authority had grown considerably, he did all that he could to prevent the authorities at the War Office from purchasing the Wright aeroplane when it was again offered to them.[2] And this pattern was repeated in 1908, as we shall see in a later

---

[1] *Ibid.*, p. 46.
[2] See Alfred Gollin, "The Wright brothers and the British authorities, 1902–1909" in *The English Historical Review*, Vol. XCV, No. CCCLXXV, April 1980, pp. 313–14. See also chapter VI, below.

chapter of our history, when the Wrights tried once more to sell their aeroplane to the British.

Colonel Capper was at once a patriot, an aeronautical enthusiast, and an ambitious man. When he first discovered the truth about the abilities of the Wright brothers he quickly grasped the tremendous military significance of their work. Even before he met them he had written to Colonel Templer, as we have seen, that: ". . . machines will fly . . . I feel convinced . . . the time is near, and that we must have a proper experimental school in England, or we shall be left behind. . . ". This reflected his attitude as a patriotic soldier, concerned for the military preparedness of his country. When he met the Wrights a few days later he asked them "to give Great Britain the first chance" to acquire their invention. Upon his return to England he was still excited by what the Wrights had done, and by what they were planning to do, but he felt it was "rather bad" for the British to be led by the Americans in this new and important area. When the Wright letter of 10 January 1905 arrived in Aldershot his patriotism and enthusiasm determined the nature of the note he wrote to his superiors at that time. However, since then his hopes for the production of a successful British flying machine had increased, and with good reason.

During the course of the year 1905 Samuel Franklin Cody had managed to build and to fly a biplane kite-glider. This work was carried out at Farnborough under Capper's direction, and with his wholehearted cooperation. Both men entertained the hope that with the passage of time the device could be developed into a practical and successful aeroplane. Indeed, Cody's experiments with his kites played some part in the decision of the War Office to reject the Wright offer.

XII

When Colonel Ruck completed his examination of the relevant papers he discussed the entire matter with John Capper. He then prepared a minute, addressed to his immediate superior, Sir James Wolfe Murray, the Master-General of the Ordnance. In this document, dated 18 January 1906, Ruck stressed the significance of the negotiations; he reviewed their history; and he condemned the Wright brothers for expecting the British War Office to negotiate with them upon what he called "hearsay evidence":[1]

---

[1] The document is printed in Walker, *Early Aviation at Farnborough*, vol. II, pp. 46–7.

An important decision is involved in this correspondence if, as I think probable, the manufacture of a flying machine for scouting purposes has actually been effected.

You will recollect that about 18 months ago Colonel Capper R. E. was instructed to visit the United States in connection with ballooning, and that he visited Messrs Wright, reporting that he thought their trials were far in advance of anything else which he had come across. He afterwards wrote the letter . . . upon which we made inquiries as to terms, and instructions were issued to Colonel Foster . . . to witness a trial. This trial was, however, refused by Messrs. Wright who thought we ought to treat with them on hearsay evidence, the terms specified being £500 for each mile of successful flight.

· Colonel Ruck proceeded to offer his own advice. He believed that the War Office should not agree to bargain under the conditions set out by the Wrights. He mentioned also that he had read in the newspapers that the Wright invention had been purchased by the French. It was at this stage of his analysis that he mentioned the significance of Samuel Cody's kites. He had also turned up an article in the *Morning Post* which described the Wright aeroplane in detail. This article was written by H. Massac Buist, a well-known journalist and "Motoring Correspondent", who was beginning to specialize in aeronautical subjects. Ruck believed that Massac Buist's article revealed the secrets of the Wright brothers, that the "details" of their machine had "leaked out":

I do not think it possible to proceed with these negotiations under these conditions, and I see it is stated in the papers that this flying machine has been purchased by France, in which case we shall no doubt hear more about it before long.

If we drop the negotiations it is all the more necessary that we should press on with our aeronautical experiments as rapidly as possible in the direction indicated by the reports from Aldershot and given effect to (to some extent) in the estimates for next year, and in the correspondence relating to Mr. Cody and his kites. I enclose a cutting from the 'Morning Post' of 9th January, giving a general description of the Wright Flying Machine, the details of which appear to have leaked out.[1]

Sir James Wolfe Murray agreed with these suggestions and conclusions. He would not accept a contract based upon hearsay evidence. He rejected the idea of an "unlimited maximum price" which turned upon a mileage run in flight trials to be carried out in the presence of British

---

[1] Ruck's remarks are printed in Walker, *Early Aviation at Farnborough*, vol. II, p. 47.

representatives. Indeed, in his opinion, the price of £25,000 which Ruck expected the Wrights to demand was too much to pay for an invention about which so little was known. He wanted the British Army to press on with its own aeronautical investigations and experiments. His final decision was: "I think we should inform Messrs Wright that their terms do not recommend themselves to us, and we should pursue our own investigations".[1]

The machinery of the War Office was now employed in order to inform the Wright brothers of the decision. Colonel Charles Hadden, the Director of Artillery, wrote in formal terms to the Wright brothers on 8 February 1906 in order to bring the negotiations to an end:[2]

84/W/5144. (A.4.)

War Office,
London, S.W.

Gentlemen,   8th February, 1906

With reference to your letter of the 5th December last, addressed to Colonel H. Foster, British Military Attaché, Washington, and previous correspondence on the subject of your flying machine; I am directed to acquaint you that the question has been given very careful consideration, and the terms and conditions specified under which you could carry out flying trials in the presence of a representative of this Department cannot be accepted.

I am,
Gentlemen,
Your obedient Servant,
C. F. Hadden
Director of Artillery

The Wright Cycle Co.,
1127 West Third Street,
Dayton, Ohio

XIII

"At the beginning of the twentieth century", a distinguished aeronautical authority has observed, "an event occurred which, in its ultimate effects, is without parallel in history. That event was the achievement of mechanical flight".[3] This noble achievement, however, was not an isolated goal in the lives and minds of Wilbur and Orville Wright. They yearned also to gather in the monetary rewards they felt they had earned. In addition they

---

[1] *Ibid.*, p. 47.

[2] Wright Brothers' Papers, Hadden to the Wrights, 8 February 1906. See also Walker, *Early Aviation at Farnborough*, vol. II, p. 48.

[3] M. J. B. Davy, *Interpretive History of Flight* (London, 1948), p. iii.

wanted to secure for themselves the acclaim of their contemporaries, and
of those who came after them, which would acknowledge and confirm the
originality of their genius.

In order to fufil all these dreams the Wright brothers realized they
would have to sell their invention, when it was at last brought to a
practical stage, to one government or another. When the American War
Department refused to treat their offers of sale seriously, the Wrights
pursued their negotiations with the British authorities for a period of
more than one year, with no success. In 1907 they found that they were
still unable to sell the aeroplane, to anyone. In that year Wilbur Wright
travelled to Europe in an attempt to interest European governments in
the aeroplane. When Patrick Y. Alexander learned that one of the
Wrights was in Europe he at once wrote to Octave Chanute in order to
discover the exact details of the excursion. Chanute, always eager to
accommodate his friend, responded as soon as he could.

In this letter Chanute explained to Alexander that in his opinion the
British had missed a "capital opportunity" when they did not secure the
aeroplane for themselves when they possessed an excellent opportunity
to do so, during the negotiations of 1905–6 which we have traced in this
chapter. The British reader may care to reflect upon Chanute's opinion,
bearing in mind that in this period he was the leading aeronautical
authority in the world, a man who knew more than anyone else of the
various developments in aviation that were taking place at the time. On
22 June 1907 Chanute wrote to Patrick Alexander:[1]

> It is Wilbur Wright who is now in Europe. I have not heard from
> him direct, but his brother wrote that he had spent two days in
> London, two days in Paris and had then gone on to Berlin. My own
> hope has been all along that he would make his first arrangement
> with the British, as I believe that a new war device would be safest in
> their hands. I think that your people missed a capital opportunity by
> not absorbing the invention at the outset and making of it a military
> secret, the dread of which would make for peace.

[1] Octave Chanute Papers, Chanute to Alexander, 22 June 1907.

CHAPTER 6

The Intervention of Colonel Count Gleichen

Outlook of the Wright Brothers – Henry Weaver in Dayton
– And at the Huffman Pasture – Captain Ferber Acts –
Arnold Fordyce Appears – The French Contract – The
French Commission – Sudden Appearance of Patrick Y.
Alexander – Alliott Verdon Roe writes to *The Times* –
Colonel Capper's Talk – Octave Chanute's Article – The
judgement of Sir Hiram Maxim – Capper's letter to the
Wrights – Why the French Negotiations failed – Effect of
the first Moroccan Crisis – The Wrights Approach the
British War Office Again – Colonel Capper's new Position –
The new British Military Attaché – Alfred Edward Wilfred
Count Gleichen – His Travels in the West – Count Gleichen
Visits Dayton – Fascinated Beyond Credibility – He Re-
ports to the Director of Military Operations – Lieutenant
John William Dunne – His Work at the Balloon Factory –
Colonel Capper's Minute – Colonel Gleichen's Despatch –
"These Figures Seem Almost Incredible" – Significance of
Gleichen's Initiative – Capper's Further Advice – His Posi-
tion in the Historical Literature – Tactics of the Wright
Brothers – Alberto Santos-Dumont – Colonel Ruck Con-
fers with Capper – They Refuse the Wright Offer – A
Tremendous Development – Colonel Gleichen Informs the
Wrights.

I

When the Wright brothers learned that the British War Office would not
purchase their invention they were disappointed, but their faith in
themselves and in the plan they had devised to sell the aeroplane
continued unshaken. They remained steady and composed in the face of
what they looked upon as a mere temporary set-back.

They saw their situation as still favourable. They had created and now
controlled a new type of weapon of such tremendous military significance
that in time one government or another would have to deal with them,
and upon their terms.

They were ready to deal with any government. Before the spring of 1906 was over they had approached the governments of Germany, Italy, Russia, Austria and Japan. The Wrights believed, with good cause, that the international situation had now become so dangerous that war was imminent. In these circumstances, they reckoned, the several powers would not dare to fall behind any of their rivals in the development of a practical Air Arm.

At the beginning of the year the negotiations which held the most promise for them were those with France. The Wrights were so sanguine that they felt that when the sale to the French Government was at last completed it would spur the American and British authorities to acquire the Wright aeroplane for themselves.

In the autumn of 1905 they had bluntly told Captain Ferber of the French Army: "With Russia and Austria–Hungary in their present troubled condition and the German Emperor in a truculent mood, a spark may produce an explosion at any time. No government dare take the risk of waiting to develop practical flying machines independently. To be even one year behind other governments might result in losses compared with which the modest amount we shall ask for our invention would be insignificant."[1]

In his negotiations with the Wrights Captain Ferber was torn by conflicting emotions. As a soldier he wanted his country to secure the first practical aeroplane in history by purchasing it from the Wright brothers. At the same time he entertained powerful ambitions. He hoped to produce an efficient aeroplane of his own. If he could accomplish this he would win for himself all the praise, glory, and rewards his fellow countrymen were only too eager to lavish upon any Frenchman who might overtake the Wrights and thus give France the lead in the new technology.

While Ferber bargained another man acted. This was an American who lived in France, Frank S. Lahm. In the autumn of 1905 he happened to meet a British friend, Patrick Y. Alexander. Lahm, a business man, was also an amateur balloonist and a member of the Aéro Club of France. Alexander tried to convince him that the Wright brothers had, indeed, made the successful powered flights that were still a subject of high dispute in French aeronautical circles. Lahm determined to find out the truth for himself.

Eventually, he contacted Henry M. Weaver, his brother-in-law, a resident of Mansfield, Ohio, and involved him in the quest. Weaver, a manufacturer of cash registers for department stores, set about the task in a straightforward and business-like way. He visited Dayton and arranged to meet the Wright brothers, in order to see for himself.

---

[1] See Kelly, *Miracle at Kitty Hawk*, p. 170.

Weaver met Orville first, at a hotel, and was at once taken to see a witness of the flights, a resident of the city of Dayton. They next travelled to the Huffman pasture and spoke to some of the farmers who lived in the immediate vicinity. When they returned to Dayton they interviewed another witness and finally went to the Wright home where Henry M. Weaver met Wilbur. The business man, as a result of these experiences, was entirely convinced that the Wright claims were accurate and true.

He later wrote a letter to Frank Lahm which was read, in translation, by Lahm on 29 December 1905 before the aviation committee of the Aéro Club of France. This letter was also published in the French Press two days later. It caused consternation in the hearts of those Frenchmen who still hoped that France, home of the Montgolfiers, would triumph yet in the race to achieve successful and practical powered flight.

Parts of Henry Weaver's letter contained anecdotes and accounts of such charm that they merit a place in any history of early aviation. Of Orville, Weaver wrote: "His very appearance would disarm any suspicion – with a face more of a poet than of an inventor or promoter. In contour, head and face resemble Edgar Allan Poe . . ." He reported about Wilbur: "The elder brother, Wilbur, I found even quieter and less demonstrative than the younger. He looked the scholar and recluse . . ."

Henry Weaver also wrote of his meeting with Amos Stauffer, a farmer who lived near the Huffman pasture, a witness of the great flight of 5 October:[1]

> On October 5, he (Stauffer) was cutting corn in the next field . . . When he noticed the aeroplane had started on its flight he remarked to his helper, "Well, the boys are at it again", and went on cutting corn, at the same time keeping an eye on the great white form rushing about its course. "I just kept on shocking corn", he continued, "until I got down to the fence, and the durned thing was still going round. I thought it would never stop". I asked him how long he thought the flight continued, and he replied it seemed to him it was in the air for half an hour.

II

Meanwhile, Captain Ferber was making progress of his own in Paris. Complicated transactions took place there; and then Ferber informed the Wrights that a "friend" would travel to Dayton with full powers to negotiate a contract for the purchase of their invention.

The "friend" turned out to be Arnold Fordyce who arrived in the town at the end of December 1905. Wilbur and Orville were suspicious about

---

[1] For Weaver's letter see, Kelly, *The Wright Brothers*, pp. 143ff.

their visitor. Fordyce, a civilian, claimed to represent a syndicate of wealthy Frenchmen who desired to buy the aeroplane so that they could present it to the government of France for the defence of the nation. Chanute advised the Wrights, however, that Fordyce might be an agent of the French Ministry of War.

The brothers, despite their trepidation, took Arnold Fordyce to see their witnesses. They answered his questions. He was quickly convinced that their claims were true, accurate, and valid. On 30 December a carefully drawn contract was signed with the Frenchman.

By its terms the Wrights would sell one machine, the lessons required to train a pilot in its use, and their secret data to the French syndicate for the sum of one million francs which in those days amounted to two hundred thousand dollars, or forty thousand pounds. This French contract called for several demonstration flights. In at least one of these the brothers would have to fly a distance of thirty miles in one hour.

The contract granted Fordyce an option for a short period. The million francs were to be paid in two instalments. As a binder the first payment was to be placed in escrow in a New York bank, J. P. Morgan and Company, by 5 February 1906, with the rest of the money due in escrow two months thereafter, on 5 April. If for any reason the French failed to make the second deposit the original payment in the sum of five thousand dollars would belong to the Wright brothers.[1] If the Wrights were unable to carry out any part of their obligations as set out in the contract they would receive nothing from the bank, which controlled the money.

Wilbur took care to inform Chanute that he was free to tell all his friends and correspondents that the French contract was not an "exclusive" one. He wanted the Americans, British, and Germans to realize that by the terms of the contract the Wrights would be free to begin negotiations with other countries three months after the delivery of a machine to France.

In time the French Ministry of War took over the Fordyce option. Their initial payment was deposited in the New York bank. Then, the French military authorities began to ask for changes in the details of the agreement. Wilbur and Orville were willing to bargain. Eventually it was decided in Paris to send a commission to Dayton to work out with the Wright brothers the alterations in the contract that were now required by the French military leaders.

The French commission was made up of military and civilian officials. The soldiers were Commandant Henri Bonel of the Army Engineer Corps and Captain Fournier, Military Attaché at the French Embassy in Washington. The civilians were Arnold Fordyce and Walter V. R. Berry,

---

[1] As we shall see, the Wright Brothers eventually received this sum from the French Government.

counsel of the French Embassy in Washington and a close friend of the Ambassador, J. J. Jusserand. They arrived in Dayton on 20 March 1906 and at once repaired to an unpretentious hotel in the town so that they would escape the notice of the local Press. The French authorities looked upon their mission as a highly secret enterprise.

There followed days of discussion and argument. Coded cable messages flew between the Dayton hotel and the Ministry of War in Paris. The commissioners were unanimously in favour of closing the deal with the Wrights but they were bound by the orders and instructions they received from Paris.

As the negotiations approached a climax Wilbur begged Chanute, by telegram, to hurry to Dayton so that he could assist the brothers in their final conference with the French. Chanute, who was immersed in his own business affairs, abandoned them so that he could lend his knowledge and his experience to his friends in this vital hour.

Despite his help, however, no agreement was reached and on 5 April the commissioners informed the Wrights that the Minister of War continued to insist upon the alterations he desired. The time limit expired. The commission was recalled. As Wilbur told Chanute on that day: "The deal is therefore off temporarily". The brothers believed that when Commandant Bonel arrived home and reported his enthusiastic reactions to his superiors the negotiations would begin, all over again.

About a week after the Frenchmen left Dayton the Wright brothers received a letter from Patrick Y. Alexander who announced that he was preparing to visit the United States, and that he hoped to call upon them in Dayton during the course of his American excursion. Alexander also informed Octave Chanute of his arrival in the United States but he made no arrangement to see the older man.

On 20 April 1906 Patrick Alexander dined with the Wright family at their home. His behaviour on that occasion shocked and startled his friends.

Their reaction was published in Fred. C. Kelly's *The Wright Brothers*. The reader should bear in mind that this biography, published in 1944 many years after Wilbur's death, was "authorized" by Orville Wright and that Orville gave "generously of his time in verifying the accuracy of various statements . . ." in the book.

According to Fred Kelly's account, Alexander, "After some casual talk . . . inquired with seeming innocence, as if just to make conversation: 'Is the French commission still here?' " Kelly's account continued:[1]

> The Wrights were startled. So great had been the secrecy about the visit of the Frenchmen that not many even in the French Government were permitted to know about their trip to Dayton. How did

[1] For the incident see Kelly, *The Wright Brothers*, pp. 154–5.

this mysterious Englishman know about it? The Wrights assumed that he must have been a volunteer worker in the British secret service. It was now obvious that he had crossed the Atlantic for no other purpose than to call on the Wrights and had hoped to burst in upon them while the Frenchmen were still there . . .

It is scarcely surprising that not many British aeronautical historians have chosen to comment upon the incident. However, one who did, Harald Penrose, a friend of Alexander and Colonel Capper in later years, wrote in his *British Aviation: The Pioneer Years* of the Wrights and Alexander: ". . . that spring the indefatigable Patrick Alexander visited the Wrights again, but was received somewhat guardedly, for Wilbur considered the trip was to discover whether there was any truth in reports that they had signed a contract with the French. To their suspicious minds it seemed that Alexander might be a spy for Capper; but if he was, it ought to have reassured them that Britain's interest was genuine."[1]

At the time Octave Chanute came to a somewhat similar conclusion. Wilbur told him that "Mr. Alexander spent a day with us and then started home . . . As near as we can make out, his trip was for the purpose of learning whether or not there was any truth in the reports that we had made a contract with the French. I think he was asked to get information on this point by the government authorities." Chanute replied in order to say: "It rather looks now as if the British will be the first to buy and the French will have to take a back seat for a year".[2]

III

Significant developments took place in England while these French negotiations were dragging on inconclusively. On 18 January 1906 Colonel Ruck had advised his superiors to reject the Wright offer because, in his opinion, the Wrights believed that the British Government should treat with them upon the basis of "hearsay evidence".

In the weeks after Ruck wrote his memorandum, however, a corpus of expert testimony, upholding all the Wright claims, appeared in the British technical Press or was presented at meetings of British technical and professional societies. The arguments and exhortations worked little or no effect upon the controlling minds in the War Office.

At the end of 1905 a young engineer named Alliott Verdon Roe, who was destined to become one of the brilliant figures in the history of British aviation, wrote a letter to *The Times* about the Wright brothers and their recent flights. Roe, at this stage of his life, was an enthusiast. He longed to

[1] Penrose, *British Aviation: The Pioneer Years*, p. 87.
[2] See McFarland, *The Papers of Wilbur and Orville Wright*, pp. 712–13.

build a successful aeroplane and thus make a contribution of his own to the new and developing technology. He also wanted to make certain that people in England learned of the Wrights' achievement, and of its significance.

His letter was not published for several weeks but it appeared at last in *The Times Engineering Supplement* of 24 January 1906. It began with an announcement: "It may be news to some of your readers", he wrote, "that flying with the heavier-than-air type of machine is an accomplished fact – I allude to the Wright Bros.' 24 ¼ miles motor-driven aeroplane flight. Although great publicity does not seem to have been given to the fact, it is nevertheless one of the greatest achievements of the time."

Roe turned next to the possibility that aeroplanes might be developed in England. He allowed himself to explain to the readers of *The Times* that he had already produced several successful model gliders and that he now proposed to attempt to win two aviation prizes, one French and the other English.

The first of these was a French award in the sum of £2,000 and was known as the Deutsch-Archdeacon Prize. The second was a prize that had been offered by Sir David Salomons, a wealthy engineer and an amateur balloonist who was also a member of the Aero Club of the United Kingdom. Sir David, in order to promote the cause of British aviation, had offered his prize for the first successful mechanically driven aeroplane to be built in Britain. Roe, in his ardour, declared: "I see no reason why a motor-driven aeroplane should not be gliding over England by the middle of the summer."

The editor of *The Times Engineering Supplement* was not impressed by the information Roe sent him; nor did he approve of his correspondent's effrontery. He sought to shrivel Roe's enthusiasm and his hopes with an editorial comment worthy of the great newspaper he served. His comment declared: "Whilst giving that encouragement to new enterprise denoted by the admission of what is patently a free advertisement to our literary columns, it is not to be supposed that we in any way adopt the writer's estimate of his undertaking, being of the opinion, indeed, that all attempts at artificial aviation on the basis he describes are not only dangerous to human life, but foredoomed to failure from an engineering standpoint."

Verdon Roe's desire to play some part in the development of British aviation was in no way diminished by the editor's harsh opinion. He meant to fight back in another organ of the public Press. *The Automotor Journal* was a London publication that had regularly reported the accomplishments of the Wright brothers since September of 1902. Roe now struck up an alliance with its publishers.

He also wrote to the Wright brothers in order to tell them what he was doing and to ask if they would agree to have him as their salesman, agent, or representative in Britain. On 3 February Roe sent an account and his proposals to the Wrights:[1]

> I believe you are prepared to sell some of your motor driven aeroplanes. I thought perhaps we could come to some terms, as I would be pleased to act as your agent or representative in this country (The British Isles). It is extraordinary how dead the interest appears to be in this country on this important subject, but I am doing my best to arouse interest and have carried out many experiments . . . I am also constantly corresponding with the press on the subject. The Automotor Journal . . . take a keen interest in aeronautical matters and have offered to help me as far as they are able. With reference to the enclosed printed letter, I sent "The Times" one to the same effect, they added a footnote stating they were of opinion that all attempts at artificial aviation on the aeroplane system are not only dangerous to human life, but foredoomed to failure from an engineering standpoint. "The Automotor Journal" this week points out the absurdness of this criticism, saying that at all times it is a gratuitous error to prophesy and more so to maintain the impossibility of what has already been done . . .

On the evening of the day Alliott Verdon Roe's letter was published in *The Times Engineering Supplement* Colonel Capper addressed the Royal United Service Institution. His subject was "Military Ballooning". His talk was looked upon as an important event. Field-Marshal Sir George White served as chairman at the meeting of this distinguished society.

Colonel Capper's lecture, which was published in the *Journal of the Royal United Service Institution* for July 1906, was divided into two parts. In the first he discussed apparatus presently available to the armies of the world. This included observation balloons and kites, captive signal balloons, and free balloons. In the second part of his talk he dealt with future developments – "dirigible balloons and motor-driven aeroplanes".

Capper made clear to the listening officers his opinion that in the next major war dirigible balloons, or airships, would be employed in order to drop explosives. He stated: "The dirigible balloon is a problem that will have to be faced in the next great war . . . Whether it will be used for offence by dropping explosives from it I cannot say. Such use is at present, I understand, barred by International Conventions. If, however, the unfortunate aeronaut, in addition to the ordinary risks inseparable from ballooning, is to be shot at and risk a violent death by his machine being blown to pieces in mid-air, I conclude he will feel himself entirely justified in making things as unpleasant as possible for people on the ground."

---

[1] Wright Brothers' Papers, A. V. Roe to Messrs Orville and Wilbur Wright, 3 February 1906.

When Capper turned to the subject of the "Flying Machine or Prop- elled Aeroplane" he adopted an even graver tone. He pointed out that aeroplanes involved "a far more important phase of aerial locomotion" than did the dirigibles; and he insisted that serving soldiers would shortly be required to learn how to employ them in actual operations of war.

Capper, as a matter of course, had to speak with care and circumspec- tion in any of his public appearances. Although he mentioned no names he referred, in his talk, to the achievements of the Wright brothers and also to Samuel Franklin Cody's machine, developed under his own direction at Farnborough in the previous year.

When Colonel Capper completed his remarks about dirigibles he began upon another topic. He said: "There is another and far more important phase of aerial locomotion which in the near future may probably have to be reckoned with, and that is the propelled aeroplane, or motor-driven kite".

Although he did not refer to the Wrights by name he explained to his audience that an aeroplane had already travelled for more than twenty miles in a single flight. He pointed out that in the early days of its development such a machine would be small and the pilot so involved in managing it in the air that he would have little or no time to look about him.

However, after practice and experience, pilots would be able to control their machines instinctively and then would be able to become useful scouts. He said also that when larger machines were built they would carry passengers who could devote all their time to observation or to offensive operations, "and then a new phase of war will be brought into being".

He concluded his remarks with a number of comments that applied most particularly to the population of the British Isles. British civilians had "slept quiet in their beds" for generations past because of the immense authority and awe-inspiring power of the Royal Navy. Because of the new invention, however, they were now about to enter a new phase of their national life and experience. When aeroplanes were fully de- veloped, Colonel Capper said, "war will be so immediately brought to the very door of the citizen as it is now brought to coast dwellers by the Navies of the world; that it will become amongst civilised nations a calamity far more real and far more dreaded than even at present . . .".

About a month after Capper delivered this lecture, on 21 February 1906 a remarkable article or essay was published in a London journal called *The Car*. The article was a lucid and masterly account of the way the Wright brothers had developed their machine from the time of the earliest trials at Kitty Hawk to the magnificent triumphs of October 1905. The author of the article was Octave Chanute.

No one could write with more authority on this subject than Octave

Chanute. If the Wright brothers had published such an account it might
be suspected that they were partisans concerned only to advance their
own cause. This was, in fact, the reaction of many Frenchmen to the
letters the Wrights had written in the autumn and winter of 1905 to their
various correspondents in France. Chanute, on the other hand, was
universally respected as the most reliable aeronautical authority of his
time.

His article had a history behind it. In January 1906 the manager of *The
Car*, G. Foster Pedley, had applied to Chanute to ask if he could send him
photographs and a technical description of the Wright aeroplane. Chanute at once approached the Wright brothers to find out if they would
object to his making "a few remarks" for publication in *The Car*.

He explained that he wanted to respond to Pedley in such a way that his
article would "forward" the Wrights' "interests". Eventually Wilbur
agreed to Chanute's request but he insisted that the article should not
reveal any of the aeroplane's technical secrets.

Chanute sent his article to Pedley together with a letter marked
"Personal", dated 5 February 1906. In the letter and in the article he did
all he could to "forward" the interests of Wilbur and Orville Wright.
Chanute's letter to Pedley made clear to him that the Wright contract with
the French was not an exclusive one; and it stated in the strongest terms
possible that Chanute believed in all that the Wrights claimed for
themselves:[1]

> I received your letter of January 5th. I referred it to Wright
> Brothers and I regret, for your sake, that no photographs or descrip-
> tions of their latest dynamic flying machine can be given out at
> present.
>
> Indeed, I doubt whether it is to the British interest that such should
> be published. The Wrights say that they have not given the French an
> exclusive contract and I believe that all the countries which purchase
> their machines will want to keep them as secret as possible.
>
> You will have seen in the Aeronautical Journal for January a letter
> from Orville Wright giving an account of recent performances which
> were characterised as "remarkable".

When he wrote this sentence Chanute had in mind Major Baden-
Powell's comment upon Orville's letter, read a few weeks earlier by
Patrick Alexander to the Aeronautical Society of Great Britain. Chanute, as we have seen, had misunderstood Baden-Powell's remarks and
sought now to confirm the validity of what Orville had written. His letter
to Pedley ended with a flourish. With respect to Orville's statement he
declared:

[1] Octave Chanute Papers, Chanute to Pedley, 5 February 1906.

I can vouch for the absolute accuracy of that account from personal investigations at Dayton and the testimony of eye-witnesses of the flights.

When Foster Pedley published Chanute's article in *The Car* on 21 February 1906 he included with it an introductory paragraph of his own which paraphrased this personal letter. The introduction thus reinforced the arguments of Chanute's essay.

The article began by calling attention to the reaction of the French to Chanute's visit in 1903 when he made known to them something of the Wrights' achievements. They were full of envy. The French, he wrote, would not incur the shame of allowing foreigners to triumph over the "native land of Montgolfier". Some of the French aviators said in print that they would "hasten to beat the Wrights".

A regular charge levelled at the Wright brothers at this time was that they were entirely too secretive. Chanute employed this account of the French reaction to explain the course adopted by his friends. "For this, and other obvious reasons", he wrote, "the Wright Brothers enjoined absolute secrecy upon all their friends and hastened on the tedious and dangerous task of perfecting their invention".

Chanute's article continued by recounting the developments that took place at Kitty Hawk during the 1903 season of experiments. He stressed the dangers and risks the young brothers faced in this phase of the work which culminated in the successful flights of 17 December.

Chanute next offered an account of the experiments of 1904 when, at the end of the year, after much trial and experiment, circular flight was achieved. "Each flight taught something", Chanute wrote, "and the season's work was brought to a close in December".

When he described the trials and experiments carried out near Dayton in 1905 Chanute revealed that the local farmers were requested not to talk about what they saw in the air and the local press was "intreated not to publish anything". He then proceeded to publish the exact details of the great flights of September and October. He took care, also, to inform the British public of the practicality and sturdiness of the Wright aeroplane: "The apparatus by this time had grown so robust through strengthening of parts that landings were frequently made at 39 miles per hour, this being the present ordinary speed in the air".

All the parts of the aeroplane, Chanute wrote, were designed by the Wright brothers. In a stirring section of his article he took care to affirm, publicly, his belief in all their claims: "They built the machine complete . . . and they took all the risks. There is no question about the perfect truth of all that they have stated about performances . . ."

Having furnished his British readers with a tolerably full and an entirely accurate and authoritative account of the history of the Wright brothers and their invention, Chanute finished his article by informing them of the future of the Wright aeroplane, as he perceived it. "It has now become evident", he wrote, "that the first practical application of this flying machine will be in the art of war . . . it is probable that the ultimate effect will be greatly to diminish the frequency of wars. This may come to pass not only because of possible additional horrors in battles but because a fast flying machine will render the enemy's disposition of forces so easy of observation and its directing minds so exposed to destruction that nations may incline more and more to universal peace."

A few weeks after Chanute's article was published *The Aeronautical Journal* for April 1906 made an announcement that was certain to arouse the interest of most of its readers. "As is notified in another part of this Journal", the editor wrote, "no less an authority than Sir Hiram Maxim has promised to address the members of the Aeronautical Society of Great Britain, on the subject of the recent experiments of the brothers Wright. . . ."

Sir Hiram Maxim, inventor of the quick-firing gun associated with his name, was an aeronautical pioneer of great distinction. One British aeronautical expert has written of him that "The most wasted talent in aviation history was undoubtedly that of Sir Hiram Maxim", while another declared that "With Maxim the real prologue of England's aeroplanes commences".[1]

Hiram Maxim was born in the United States where he became a talented and exceptionally brilliant engineer. After establishing himself in his profession he began to produce a number of inventions of his own. It has been said that he almost solved the problem of making an efficient and durable incandescent electric lamp. In 1880 Maxim emigrated to England and set up a workshop in Hatton Garden, London.

There he developed his machine-gun. It was fitted with a unique mechanism that enabled it to fire very rapidly. This Maxim gun was so remarkable that many distinguished people made it their business to visit his underground firing range at Hatton Garden to see it in action. Sales of the gun helped to establish his large personal fortune.

In 1887 Maxim decided to build a machine that would fly. He seemed well equipped for the enterprise. He was a man of great energy, remarkable scientific curiosity, and an unrivalled engineering skill. Nevertheless the task took him several years and before he was finished with it he had spent nearly twenty thousand pounds.

In 1894 he tested a machine of gigantic size at his experimental ground near Bexley Heath, in Kent. Although the huge device rose briefly into the air Maxim was unable to control it and he at once brought it to a stop

---

[1] The comments are by Gibbs-Smith in *The Invention of The Aeroplane*, p. 21 and Penrose, *British Aviation: The Pioneer Years*, p. 21.

before it smashed itself to pieces. He immediately abandoned his flying machine experiments and made no other investigations of the kind for many years.

Despite this failure he won the recognition and respect of the scientific community. His experiments with wind-tunnels and "whirling arms" advanced human knowledge. Maxim was looked upon as a technical expert who had performed valuable service in the quest to attain the dream of successful mechanical flight.

Although he became a naturalized British subject and was knighted in 1901 Hiram Maxim did not fit in. He found he often had to endure snubs and slights in the circles in which he moved. He suspected that his workmen often cheated him and he knew his domestic servants did so, on a regular basis. It is not surprising that he became overbearing, loud, and boastful. He regularly made the most ridiculous claims about the brilliance of his aeronautical achievements. When it was learned that he was to speak about the experiments of the Wright brothers everyone realized that his views would be definite, and very forcefully expressed.

Maxim addressed the Aeronautical Society of Great Britain on 27 April 1906 and his remarks were published in *The Aeronautical Journal* in the following July. His audience did not have to wait long for his opinion. He began by saying: "I think we should all congratulate ourselves on the great success of the experiments conducted in the United States by the Wright Brothers . . . It can no longer be said that flying machines are impossible; a flying machine has at last been made . . ."

With characteristic energy and insight Maxim proceeded to explain the significance of what the Wright brothers had done:

> This machine marks a distinctly new epoch . . . The first flying machine has come, and, whether we like it or not, it has come to stay. No less a genius than Edison himself has pointed out its potency as an instrument of warfare. It is impossible to over-estimate the changes that will take place during the next ten years in everything relating to civilised warfare. The flying machine must become a very important factor, and it behoves all the civilised nations of the earth to lose no time in becoming acquainted with this new means of attack and defence. The nations which do not appreciate the importance of this instrument of destruction will be very soon left in the lurch.

IV

While these public declarations were being made in England two private exchanges took place which also made clear the validity of the Wright brothers' claims. Colonel Capper was first in this field.

It will be recalled that the Wrights had written to him on 17 November

1905 when they wrote also to a number of other European correspondents to make them aware of the astonishing results of their successful flight trials of 1905. Capper took care not to reply to this letter while his colleagues in the War Office still deliberated upon their decision to purchase the Wright invention, or to reject the offer that had been presented to them.

On 8 February 1906 Colonel Charles Hadden, the Director of Artillery, informed the Wrights that their terms and proposals could not be accepted by the British authorities. Capper did not answer the Wright letter of November 1905 until he was certain they had received this official message which brought their negotiations with the British War Office to an end.

On 19 February 1906 Capper wrote to Wilbur Wright to congratulate the brothers upon their great success. He began with an apology. He admitted he had taken a long time to reply to the letter Wilbur had sent him in the previous November. Capper's object was to maintain and reinforce the friendly relationship he had established with the Wright brothers. His letter was written in his own hand from his home in South Farnborough. It could not be looked upon as an official communication:[1]

> I have been long in answering your most welcome letter informing me that you & your brother had met with such great success in the extended trials of your machine.
>
> However extended becomes the method of travel in the air by motor driven aeroplanes, you will go down to posterity as the first to make it a practical success, and will be as such honoured and welcomed by the whole aeronautical world.
>
> May I be permitted most heartily to congratulate you on the immediate advance you have made over all your predecessors.
>
> There are many rumours as to your intentions, and as to the applications made to you by foreign governments and individuals – but no authoritative statements have appeared so far in the public press.
>
> There can be no doubt though that your success will encourage far more people to experiment – and should the art be extensively practised either for war, commerce, or sport, nations will have to consider the question of proper police regulations for air travelling in their own countries, and international regulations to define the limits of travelling over other territories.
>
> It will bring about an entirely new set of circumstances, & great care will have to be taken to avoid damage to persons & property on the ground in times of peace, or an immense public outcry will be raised against the free use of such machines.

[1] Wright Brothers' Papers, Capper to Mr Wright, 19 February 1906. See also Walker, *Early Aviation at Farnborough*, vol. II, pp. 50–1.

I hope before long we may see you over in Europe.
With kind regards from Mrs. Capper & myself to you both & to Miss Wright . . .

Shortly after, Major Baden-Powell informed Octave Chanute of the interest in the Wrights' work that existed in British aeronautical circles. On 8 March he told Chanute: ". . . We have all been much interested over here in hearing of the Wrights' success. I hope we shall soon hear more about them. . . ."[1]

When he received this letter Chanute believed that the Wrights' negotiations with the French might still succeed. He therefore took care to tell Baden-Powell that by the terms of the arrangement the French would not acquire exclusive rights in the invention. He wanted to make it absolutely clear that Great Britain still possessed the opportunity to secure the Wright aeroplane for itself.

Chanute at once sent a copy of his letter to the Wright brothers. He hoped it might prove of some slight value to them when they again attempted to negotiate with the British War Office. He told the Wrights: "Having occasion to write to Major Baden-Powell . . . I have today thrown another anchor to windward by saying:[2]

> . . . The Wrights are building a new machine. It is my impression that their arrangement with the French is not yet fully closed, the government having brought forward some additional requirements which the Wrights deem unreasonable. You know, I presume, that in no case is an exclusive right to be given. . . .

V

When the French Commission was withdrawn from Dayton in April 1906 the Wright brothers were disappointed at the result but they remained as firm as ever in their conviction that they were following the correct course. They were unruffled by the French decision. They were not prepared to permit a government to force them into an arrangement that was in any way unacceptable. After an unemotional analysis of their experiences with the French they still believed the various powers would shortly have to deal with them, upon their own terms. In particular, they thought the American and British Governments would act in this way.

When the French Minister of War began to demand that the details of their contract with Arnold Fordyce should be altered in several particu-

---

[1] Octave Chanute Papers, Baden-Powell to Chanute, 8 March 1906.
[2] Octave Chanute Papers, Chanute to Baden-Powell, 7 April 1906. See also McFarland, *The Papers of Wilbur and Orville Wright*, pp. 709–10.

lars, the Wrights tried to discover and analyse the causes that lay behind his attitude. They believed the French authorities were anxious to seek changes in the contract for several reasons.

By the beginning of 1906 there was a marked sense of optimism in French aeronautical circles. French aviators seemed to be making genuine progress with their own aeroplanes and it was only natural for some French officials, in that period of intense national feeling, to hope that one of their own countrymen might succeed as a flier, within a short period of time.

Conversely, one of the commission members, Walter Berry, later told the Wrights that the French Government did not break off the negotiations because they entertained any doubts about the efficiency of the Wright aeroplane. The negotiations were dropped because the French decided that the limited period of their monopoly under the contract was simply not worth one million francs. Berry hoped the Wrights would reduce the price and he was even prepared to try to reopen the discussion if they would do so.

Wilbur and Orville soon realized that the period of exclusive French control of the invention was a key element in the negotiations. The Wrights were prepared to bargain upon this issue. They told the commissioners they were ready to sign the original contract with a new clause in it which made the exclusive period one year, instead of three months, provided that the date for delivery of the machine was extended, and on condition that the United States Government was excepted from this part of the transaction. Eventually, the parties were unable to agree upon this aspect, and the negotiations were allowed to lapse.

The French military also insisted that the aeroplane should rise to a height of three hundred meters during the trials. They reckoned that if the machine flew at a lower altitude it would at once become an easy target for fire from the ground. The Wrights at once rejected this stipulation. During their own practice they had never attempted to fly so high. They had already agreed to conditions that left them little margin for error and they felt that the time of the trials would have to be put back for a considerable period if they were to prepare themselves to operate at the three hundred meter level.

In the opinion of the Wright brothers there was yet another set of factors that helped to determine the actions of the French Government during the negotiations. In 1905 and 1906 there took place a revolution in European diplomacy. War between France and Germany seemed a possibility, for the first time since 1875. The long-standing era of peace Bismarck had fixed upon the European states seemed about to end.

During this diplomatic crisis, known as the first Moroccan crisis, the Wrights believed that the French were eager to acquire the aeroplane whenever war seemed imminent. When the danger receded they bargained, quibbled, and sought changes in the contract Arnold Fordyce had arranged.

The immediate origins of this tense international situation may be traced to the actions of the British and French Governments in 1904. In that year London and Paris composed their long-standing quarrels by concluding a series of agreements which resulted in the creation of the famous Anglo-French *Entente*. The decisive element in this reconciliation was that the two powers pledged themselves to mutual diplomatic assistance in case of conflicts with other countries arising out of their agreements over Egypt and Morocco. With respect to Morocco, the British promised to support France's aspirations for a protectorate over the greater part of the country.

The German Government did not at once react to these developments. Nevertheless, the Kaiser and his ministers were eager to demonstrate to the world that Imperial Germany could not be ignored by the other powers. They complained they had not been informed, officially, about the Anglo-French agreement that dealt with Morocco.

In March 1905 the Kaiser landed at Tangier in Morocco and there publicly proclaimed German recognition of the Sultan as an independent sovereign. This act was an open challenge to France. It caused panic in Paris, where it was feared the Germans might be planning a war. In London, as time passed, the suspicion arose that the Germans had precipitated the crisis in a deliberate attempt to test or break up the Anglo-French *Entente*.

The Imperial German Government next demanded that the Moroccan question should be submitted for solution to an international conference. The French responded with various suggestions of their own, all designed to bring the crisis to an end without recourse to a conference. Their proposals were rejected in Berlin. Tension between the powers continued.

Eventually, on 6 June, Théophile Delcassé, the French Foreign Minister, resigned his office. The reasons for his action were complex but contemporaries knew him as a chief architect of the *Entente* with England, and many believed he had been removed from his place as a result of German pressure. On the day of his resignation William II created his Imperial Chancellor, Bernhard von Bülow, a prince. The fall of Delcassé has been called "the greatest German victory since Sedan".

The Germans, after the resignation of Delcassé, continued to call for the summoning of an international conference. Early in July the French gave way, and agreed to this demand. It was a serious diplomatic defeat for France. In the months that followed there was fitful bickering between Berlin and Paris about the details of the agenda for the conference. Eventually, the concerned powers met at Algeciras, in Spain, in January 1906, in order to settle the future of Morocco.

At first, the diplomats found it impossible to discover Germany's intentions. It seemed the conference might break up with nothing accomplished. If this happened war between France and Germany might follow and this was certain to involve the other states of Europe.

It was then seen that France was supported at the conference by every one of the powers, except Germany and Austria. When this became clear Bülow lost his nerve. An agreement was signed on 31 March. By its terms the French gained most of their objects in Morocco. The Algeciras Conference ended on 7 April. Contemporaries were certainly aware of the gravity of the situation while all historians are agreed that the Moroccan issue was a turning-point in European history. It was the first of a series of diplomatic episodes which ended, eventually, in the great crisis of August 1914.

For their part, the Wright brothers were convinced that the French, in bargaining with them, had been dominated by the vicissitudes of this first Moroccan crisis. Their attitude is summed up in Fred Kelly's "authorized" biography:[1] "For some time war clouds had been gathering over Morocco and it looked as if there might be trouble between France and Germany. If war should come a flying-machine for scouting purposes would be of great value . . . But while the commission was still in Dayton the European war crisis had subsided. Even before the formal settlement of the dispute, at the close of the conference at Algeciras, Spain, on 7 April, it was known that France would still have a favoured position in Morocco, and the need for a scouting 'plane by the French Army became less pressing. The War Ministry now began to demand more and more in aeroplane performance. . . ."

VII

Indeed, Captain Ferber had already involved the Wright brothers in the Franco-German quarrel of 1905-6. As we have seen, when the Wrights began to bargain with Ferber in the autumn of 1905 they sought to convince him that the various governments would soon have to deal with them because the international situation was so bad it might result in the outbreak of war, at any time, and then all the powers would clamour for aeroplanes.

They had written to him: "With Russia and Austria-Hungary in their present troubled condition and the German Emperor in a truculent mood, a spark may produce an explosion at any time".

Wilbur and Orville were outraged when they discovered that Ferber had published this letter in *L'Aérophile*. They had looked upon it as a

---

[1] Kelly, *The Wright Brothers*, pp. 150–2.

private communication. Moreover, the editor of *L'Aérophile*, a patriotic Frenchman, had chosen to translate "in a truculent mood" to mean "*cherchant noise*" – seeking a quarrel.

The Wright brothers had expected that an article written by Carl Dienstbach would be published in Germany, at about this time. Dienstbach, the New York correspondent of the *Illustrierte Aeronautische Mitteilungen*, a paper edited by Major Moedebeck, had visited Dayton in the previous summer. It had been announced that an article giving an account of his visit would be published, but it did not appear; nor did the German paper produce a later article which included in it a statement about the great achievements of September and October 1905. Wilbur told Chanute: "The conduct of the German paper is rather strange". Chanute, on 14th February 1906, sent him a spirited reply to this remark:[1]

> I think the developments you mention in Germany are not "strange". They are mean. The Kaiser had probably made up his mind to a war with France. The taking over of your machine by the latter causes him to pause, as he may not know that the sale is not exclusive.

A few days later Chanute received a copy of the February edition of Major Moedebeck's journal. In it appeared the two letters written by the Wrights on 17 November 1905, addressed to Carl Dienstbach. The editor, however, had prepared certain comments of his own dealing with these communications. He made clear his doubt of the full truth of the Wrights' claims, he expressed his resentment of the allusion to the Kaiser as a disturber of the peace, and he roundly asserted that there were experts in Germany who could fly as well as or even better than the Wrights.

In March Chanute sent the Wright brothers a press cutting which stated that the Germans were about to undertake "the construction of war balloons and aeroplanes". According to this account the German Emperor had lent his patronage to the formation of a company which had as its object experimenting with and constructing "military aircraft".[2]

The directors of the company had dined with the Kaiser and with several generals and members of the nobility, a few nights before. These directors were Walter Rathenau, president of the German General Electric Company, Isidor Loewe, head of the Mauser rifle and machine-tool works, Paul Schwabach of the Bleichroeder bank, and James Simon, a manufacturer of woollens.

In April Major Moedebeck wrote Chanute a letter; and Chanute at once furnished the Wrights with a copy of the parts of it that referred to them. In this letter Moedebeck declared that he did not believe in the

[1] See McFarland, *The Papers of Wilbur and Orville Wright*, p. 696.

[2] *Ibid.*, p. 704 and *n.* 9.

Wrights' "pretensions",[1] nor did he admit the credibility of their witnesses. He said that if a flight was made in the presence of Chanute that would convince him. It may be mentioned that Chanute had, of course, already witnessed a flight, on 15 October 1904. Moedebeck stated also that he did not think the aeroplane would prove useful in war and he hoped Germany would not purchase Wright machines.

In 1907 Wilbur Wright travelled to Europe in an attempt to interest the various governments in the Wright aeroplane. He arrived in Berlin in August. There he received full confirmation of the hostility aroused in Germany as a result of Captain Ferber's publication of their letter with the remark in it about William II. In his diary Wilbur noted: "Herr Loewe stated . . . that there was much antagonism to us on account of the Ferber reproduction of our letter containing a reference to the Emperor, and said that he was told that the military department would not be disposed to do anything even if we should be able to do all we had claimed".[2]

During the course of their unsuccessful negotiations with the French Wilbur and Orville learned a number of lessons which determined their plan of action for the future. In March 1906, when their veracity was being challenged in Germany, they told Chanute: "We consider the fight to establish the truth of our claims practically over". In April, after the French discussions had collapsed, Wilbur declared: "Our position is constantly becoming stronger . . . and we will soon find a sale somewhere".[3]

In these circumstances, and with this attitude fixed firmly in their minds, the Wright brothers embarked upon a new phase of their enterprise. In May 1906 they wrote to Theodore Roosevelt's secretary, William Loeb, and asked for a formal interview with the president, in the White House, in Washington. At about the same time they also sent a letter to the War Office in London and again offered to sell their aeroplane and their scientific discoveries to the British Government.

VIII

Although William Loeb was prepared to arrange an interview between the Wrights and President Roosevelt the meeting did not take place. Wilbur and Orville had been planning to visit Washington and New York but they cancelled the proposed journey, and did not meet the president. They were looking elsewhere.

A few days before they approached Loeb they wrote a formal letter to

---

[1] *Ibid.*, p. 711 and *n.* 6.
[2] *Ibid.*, p. 811.
[3] *Ibid.*, p. 697 and p. 712.

the British War Office in order to reopen negotiations with the authorities there. This document, dated 8 May 1906, began by acknowledging receipt of Colonel Hadden's letter of the previous February:[1]

> Your communication of the 8th of February has been received.
>
> We are now offering to the various governments our complete invention, including (1) a flyer capable of carrying a man and supplies sufficient for a long trip, (2) instruction in the practical use of the machine, (3) data and formulae for the designing of machines of other sizes and speeds, (4) the confidential disclosure of the original discoveries in aeronautical science which for the first time made the designing of a practical flyer possible, and rendered progress certain and economical.
>
> No government has been offered or granted a permanent monopoly of the fruits of our labors. The date which can be named in any case for the delivery of a flyer and instruction will be dependent upon the limitations imposed upon us by prior contracts.
>
> If it should accord with your wishes, we would be very glad to discuss the whole subject in detail with a commission representing His Majesty's government.

Significant changes had taken place in the aeronautical organization of the British Army by the time this letter arrived in London and was taken under consideration by the authorities there. Colonel Templer had just retired and had been replaced by Colonel Capper as Superintendent of the Balloon Factory. Moreover, Capper had also been promoted in his brevet rank to full colonel. Since he continued to serve as Commandant of the Balloon School his position was stronger than it had ever been before.

As Superintendent Capper was now consulted by the authorities in the War Office as a matter of course, on all aeronautical matters. He was directly responsible to Colonel Ruck, the Director of Fortifications and Works. He took part in every phase of the negotiations that began with the receipt of the Wright brothers' letter of 8 May.

In the War Office itself certain procedural changes were adopted in order to deal with the new proposals. It was decided that in the first instance the Superintendent of the Balloon Factory would provide the Director of Fortifications and Works with technical advice and opinion. He, in his turn, would write to the Director of Artillery who was, except for the higher secretariat of the War Office, the only officer permitted to communicate directly with the Wrights. The task of the Director of Military Operations would be to send instructions for action to the

---

[1] Air 1/728/176/3/33. Wright Cycle Co. to The Secretary, War Office, London, 8 May 1906. A copy exists in the Wright Brothers' Papers in the Library of Congress. A slightly different version is printed in Walker, *Early Aviation at Farnborough*, vol. II, pp. 49–50.

Military Attaché in Washington. In the official view the Military Attaché was "the man on the spot" who would put into effect the orders sent him from London. These administrative arrangements reflect how seriously the soldiers in the War Office now looked upon the possibility of acquiring the Wright aeroplane for the British Army.

The new routines were put into train. The Wright letter was sent to Capper for his comments. He was at once business-like and cautious in the advice he returned to Colonel Ruck, on 6 June:[1]

> D.F.W.
>
> Letter dated 8th May, 1906, from the Wright Cycle Co.
> I am of opinion that this letter shows a much more practical intention of coming to terms.
> I do not know how far it would be advisable to appoint a commission to discuss the whole subject in detail with Messrs. Wright. but I do think we could ask them now what would be the price for parts I and 2 of what they propose, – (1) a flyer capable of carrying a man and supplies sufficient for a long trip, and (2) instructions in the practical use of the machine, presuming we had one such machine.
> I do not know that it would be worth while paying much for the data and formulae for the designing of machines of other sizes and speeds, nor for the confidential disclosures of the original discoveries made by the Wright Brothers.
> It must be quite easy now for the Bros. Wright to be able to quote a price and name a date by which they could deliver, and also say when they could impart instructions; and if the terms are still such as are unacceptable to His Majesty's Government, they must be told so.
> I would strongly advise their being asked for their quotation, as it commits us to nothing. . . .
>
> Aldershot   JEC
> 6.6. 6   Colonel,
>   Supt. Balloon Factory

The various Directorates in the War Office now began to deliberate upon the issues involved. It was decided, eventually, to refer the matter to the British Military Attaché in Washington. The Director of Military Operations instructed him to contact the Wright brothers and to ascertain, more exactly, the precise details of their proposal.

Meanwhile, Wilbur Wright wrote a letter to Colonel Capper in order to thank him for his message of congratulation, sent in the previous February. In this letter Wilbur made no reference to the official negotiations between the Wrights and the British War Office. However, he took care

---

[1] Air 1/728/176/3/33. Capper to D.F.W., 6 June 1906. See also Walker, *Early Aviation at Farnborough*, vol. II, pp. 52–3.

to let Capper know that the French Government had not yet purchased their invention. He explained: "The French deal is for the present at a standstill owing to a stubbornly contested difference of opinion regarding the length of the period during which they shall have exclusive use of the discoveries we have made. The time named in the original contract was very short." He also made a discreet reference to Patrick Alexander's visit of the previous April: "Mr. Alexander made us a short visit in April, which we enjoyed very much notwithstanding we were precluded from talking freely on some points. If you chance to meet him please convey to him our respects . . ."[1]

The preliminaries in this second round of negotiations were over. The initiative now lay with Colonel Foster's successor, the new British Military Attaché in Washington.

IX

Albert Edward Wilfred Count Gleichen, the new Military Attaché, was a remarkable man and an experienced soldier. He was a godson of King Edward VII and moved easily in the very highest circles of international society. Colonel Gleichen was a German count of distinguished ancestry. He was the only son of Prince Victor of Hohenlohe-Langenburg, an admiral in the British Navy. Prince Victor, for his part, was the son of Princess Feodora, the half-sister of Queen Victoria. Despite his German background Colonel Gleichen was a patriotic British officer who looked down upon the Emperor William II, a man he knew well, as "the Imperial tyrant".

Gleichen had been educated in Germany and in England. In 1880 he had entered Sandhurst and shortly after joined the first Battalion of the Grenadier Guards, at Chelsea. He saw active service in the Sudan on several occasions. In 1886 he became a member of the Intelligence Department in the War Office, which was later renamed the Directorate of Military Intelligence. During the Boer War he suffered a serious wound in the neck and heard one of his fellow officers cry out – "Poor Glick is dead!" As Gleichen explained in a charming autobiography written years later, "Luckily his remarks were only 50 per cent true".[2]

When he returned to England Gleichen became an extra equerry in Edward VII's household. He thus joined a circle described by Sir Sidney Lee, the King's biographer, as "all amiable and chivalrous gentlemen,

---

[1] Air 1/728/176/3/33. Wilbur Wright to Capper, 10 July 1906. See also Walker, *Early Aviation at Farnborough*, vol. II, pp. 53–4.

[2] Major-General Lord Edward Gleichen, *A Guardsman's Memories* (London, 1932), p. 198.

devoted to the King, endowed with discretion and diplomatic cleverness, polished, urbane, and for the most part excellent sportsmen". In 1903 Gleichen was sent as Military Attaché to Berlin, at the King's suggestion. There he outraged the Kaiser because he was too haughty to behave in the servile way the Kaiser required of those about him.

As a result of this unpopularity he was ordered from Berlin and instructed to replace Colonel Foster as the Military Attaché in Washington. King Edward did what he could to smooth the way in this new enterprise. He wrote to President Theodore Roosevelt, in January 1906: "As Lieutenant-Colonel Count Gleichen is leaving for the United States in order to take up his appointment as Military Attaché to my Embassy in Washington, I gladly take this opportunity of writing you a few lines to recommend him to your notice. He is a cousin of mine – as his father was nephew to my beloved mother Queen Victoria – and served many years in the army. Gleichen has seen much service both in Egypt and South Africa, and has held important posts, his last being Military Attaché at Berlin."[1]

When Gleichen met the President he received a warm and friendly reception. Indeed, Roosevelt wrote to the King: "Your kind letter has just been handed me by Count Gleichen. It was a pleasure to meet him; he is evidently thoroughly well up in his work. I shall talk with him freely."[2]

This was the man who now took up the negotiations for the British War Office in their dealings with Wilbur and Orville Wright. Gleichen was diligent and hard-working; cool, sophisticated and cynical. He was less stiff than Colonel Foster but, upon the evidence contained in his memoirs, it is clear he was an aristocrat who did not readily tolerate all those he was required to meet in the course of his social or official duties as a Military Attaché.

Colonel Gleichen was determined to see as much of the New World as he could during the course of his American tour as Attaché. Therefore, in May 1906, he left Washington in order to visit Mexico, as his duty required, but, as he took pleasure in pointing out in his autobiography, he travelled there "*via* Cuba".

He enjoyed the cigars in Havana and proceeded then by leisurely stages to the Mexican capital. After a pleasant round of visits with friends he started north upon a tour of the western United States. The great earthquake at San Francisco had taken place a few months earlier "so", he recorded in his memoirs, "as my military duties led me in that direction, I thought I might as well have a look at what remained of the city". During this part of his journey he fell in with an Englishman who

<hr>

[1] Sir Sidney Lee, *King Edward VII* (London, 1927), vol. II, p. 435.
[2] *Ibid.*, p. 436.

begged him to "come out salmon-fishing (in the sea)". As he put it: "I really could not resist these attractions, so on arriving at Los Angeles I 'stopped off' . . ."

When the salmon-fishing (in the sea) was done with Colonel Gleichen continued on to San Francisco. Since he planned to travel east to Washington he decided it might be a good thing to visit the Wright brothers in Dayton, during the course of the journey. Therefore, on 23 July 1906, he wrote to the Wrights, from San Francisco, in order to discover those exact details of their proposal the Director of Military Operations had instructed him to find out about a few weeks earlier. In his letter Gleichen put four questions to the Wright brothers:[1]

From   23 July 1906

    The Military Attaché   San Francisco
    British Embassy, Washington   Cal.

Gentlemen.
    My War Office has forwarded me a copy of your communication to them, dated May 8th last.
    Will you kindly inform me by letter, to reach me at Fort Riley, Kansas, by the 3rd August.
1. What would be the price of a "flyer" capable of carrying a man & supplies for a "long trip",
    a. delivered in England,
    b.   ,,   at your establishment?
2. What do you call a "long trip", as above?
    How many miles, or hours?
3. How long after the order was given would it take you to build and deliver the "flyer"?
4. When, & where, could you impart practical instruction?

                                 Yrs. truly
                                 Gleichen
                                 Lt. Col.
                                 Mil. Attaché

P.S. If necessary, I could come to Dayton for a personal interview.
                                         G.

The Wright brothers lost little time in replying to these overtures. In a letter dated 31 July 1906 they told Colonel Gleichen they could furnish the British Government with an aeroplane that could fly for "not less than one hundred miles". They also informed him that they wanted the sum of one hundred thousand dollars (twenty thousand pounds) for a single machine. They further declared that Gleichen would be welcome to visit

---

[1] Wright Brothers' Papers, Gleichen to the Wrights, 23 July 1906.

Dayton so that they could explain any points that were not clearly understood by him:[1]

> Your letter of July 27th has been received.[2]
>
> For the sum of one hundred thousand dollars we offer to furnish a flyer, train a British operator in the use of it, and grant full rights to manufacture flyers for the government's use under any patents we may secure upon its mechanical details.
>
> For one hundred thousand dollars additional we offer to impart confidentially our scientific knowledge and discoveries together with formulas and tables which make the designing of flyers of other sizes and speeds a science as exact as that of marine engineering, and enable the designer to discriminate between impossibilities and possibilities without the necessity of costly abortive experiments.
>
> If the complete invention be purchased we would agree that neither instruction nor machines should be delivered by us to any other government (the United States excepted) for a period of six months following the delivery of the machine to the British government.
>
> In case the delivery is made in England a reasonable allowance for expenses would be expected.
>
> The expression "long trip" as used in our letter of May 8th means "not less than one hundred miles".
>
> At present we could agree to deliver the machine not later than May 1st 1907, but no date can be guaranteed in advance of contract.
>
> If desired we would give instruction in England promptly after the delivery of the machine provided proper facilities were offered.
>
> The acceptance of the machine and the payment of the purchase price would be conditional upon its first making a trial flight of fifty kilometers in less than an hour in the presence of representatives of the British Government.
>
> We expect to be in Dayton till the end of August and would be pleased to have a personal conference for the purpose of explaining any points you may not clearly understand.
>
> > Yours truly,
> > (sd) Wright Cycle Co.
>
> P.S. It would be well to avoid any mention of us at the hotels in case you visit Dayton as the hotel clerks notify the newspaper reporters.

Colonel Gleichen had been ordered to obtain exact details of the Wrights' proposals. He was not entirely satisfied with this reply. He

---

[1] Air 1/728/176/3/33. Wright Cycle Company to the British Military Attaché, Fort Riley, Kansas, 31 July 1906. See also Walker, *Early Aviation at Farnborough*, vol. II, p. 55.

[2] Gleichen's letter was dated 23 July 1906.

therefore decided to travel to Dayton in order to come to grips with the brothers upon closer terms than correspondence could permit.

He arrived in the town on 8 August and was met at the railway station by Wilbur and Orville, who at once conducted him to the "paternal mansion". In his memoirs Gleichen wrote a clear account of the meeting and made obvious the entirely favourable impression the Wright brothers produced upon their distinguished visitor: ". . . after an excellent meal, presided over by Mr. Wright senior – a courteous old gentleman, bishop or dean of a local Christian church community – we had a most interesting talk. The brothers were nice modest fellows, not the least typical of the usual American inventor, and before coming to details they insisted on my seeing some of the chief representative inhabitants who had actually seen the machine in the air, 'coming along like a railroad train', as one of them expressed it. They could not show me the machine itself . . . as it had been dismantled for repairs; but they explained it at some length, telling me of their initial struggles and of their joy when it first rose into the air. Their chief preoccupation, it appeared, had been to prevent newspaper reporters from publishing fulsome reports of the new wonder before it was really ready, and all tests had to be carried out with the greatest secrecy. I expect the natural desire not to have their secrets 'jumped' had also something to do with it."[1]

Indeed, as we shall see, Colonel Gleichen was charmed and enchanted by the Wright brothers. He saw no signs of "obsession" or "excessive concern over secrecy", terms later applied to Wilbur Wright by Percy Walker, in his analysis of the visit. Walker's factual account of what occurred, leaving aside his interpretations of Wilbur's motives, made entirely clear the impression created by the Wrights on Gleichen. Walker wrote:[2]

> He arrived at Dayton on 8 August 1906. At once he was captivated – fascinated to a degree beyond credibility for those who had never met the two brothers. It was Colonel Capper's visit of 23 October 1904 all over again. There was about the brothers an indefinable aura of personality, apparently much stronger in Wilbur than in Orville.

X

When he returned to his post in Washington after his adventure in Dayton Colonel Gleichen's first duty was to prepare a report for the Director of Military Operations in order to acquaint him with the results of the

[1] Lord Edward Gleichen, *A Guardsman's Memories*, p. 302.
[2] Walker, *Early Aviation at Farnborough*, vol. II, p. 56.

meeting. However, he was so moved by his interview with Wilbur and Orville Wright that, on his own initiative, he composed a very long despatch, addressed to Sir Mortimer Durand, the British Ambassador in Washington. This letter, which Gleichen marked "Very Confidential", must rank as a significant document of early aviation history. We will examine it at a later phase of our account.

Technically, Gleichen's task in his report to the Director of Military Operations was to furnish his superiors with exact information. Nevertheless, he composed his paper in such a way that they would be able to surmise from it that he favoured the idea of acquiring the Wright aeroplane for the British Army:[1]

SUBJECT: – *Wright Bros: Flying Machine.*

From M.A., Washington   No. 054   Date 11th August 1906
Replying to your No. 53   Date 20th June 1906

D.M.O. 2.f.

I wrote to Messrs. Wright Bros. as directed, and enclose their answer, dated 31.7.06. As it did not seem to give exact answers to 3 out of my 4 questions, I stopped at Dayton on my way East, and went to see them on the 8th instant.

I gathered from them the following, which I think supplements their answer.

They will not take a penny less than $100,000 for the flyer; this includes training a British operator, and granting full rights to manufacture under patents on the mechanical details. Whether these rights are granted or not makes no difference to the price.

I gather that these rights are of little or no value, unless accompanied by the "confidential scientific knowledge", for which they demand another $100,000. That is to say that though, having bought the flyer, you could manufacture as many more exactly like it as you please, you could not, without the "scientific knowledge" of formulae etc., build any other of any other size or speed, as the formulae vary according to the size, etc.

The securing of the patents of the mechanical details is a secondary matter. The secret of the whole thing lies in the calculations and formulae, which are unpatentable, being merely mathematical and scientific deductions regarding wind-pressures on planes at different angles, dimensions of screws etc.

Regarding dates, they have got the parts of several flyers nearly ready, so that they would not take more than about a month to get one ready after signature of contract. This of course if no other contract is on hand and the contract is given soon, whilst they still have their material on hand.

[1] Air 1/728/176/3/33. Military Attaché, Washington to D.M.O., 11 August 1906. See also Walker, *Early Aviation at Farnborough*, vol. II, pp. 57–8.

They will not give any instruction until the order is definitely given, the flier has passed its trial trip, and the money paid. They have difficulties about keeping the matter secret in the U.S., and though they could get a secret place for the trial, there would be difficulties, and they would prefer the trial to take place under a Government guarantee of secrecy (Okehampton?). (For the trial and instruction in England they would charge rather more, to cover expenses, but I should think this would come cheaper in the end than having to send people over to U.S. and cart the machine perhaps several hundred miles to a place of secrecy for the trial).

The practical instruction (after money paid) would take 3 or 4 weeks, but the "confidential scientific" instructions would take several months, as a totally new set of ideas would have to be taught. For this reason they give a 6 months option. The above, I think, answers your questions.

I am writing a despatch by bag of 24th inst., going into the matter more fully, from a concrete point of view.

(sd) Gleichen
M.A.

Colonel Gleichen's report and the Wright letter of 31 July arrived in the War Office by early September. It will be recalled that during the negotiations of 1905–6 Sir Charles Hadden and Colonel Ruck had been annoyed because the Wright brothers had presumed to try to bargain with the British Government upon the basis of what these officers called "hearsay evidence". When the Wrights refused to permit Colonel Foster to observe their machine in flight the authorities in the War Office became so angry they adopted an entirely negative attitude, and eventually abandoned their negotiations for the aeroplane.

In the autumn of 1906 this notion that the Wrights were attempting to treat with the War Office upon "hearsay evidence" was no longer a factor of significance in the minds of the various directors and their associates. The idea was not brought up by any of the officers concerned in the transition. Nevertheless, they were still opposed to the suggestion that the aeroplane should be purchased by the British Government.

On this occasion Colonel Ruck and his colleagues decided that the selling price demanded by the Wrights was entirely too high for their consideration.

The administrative arrangements fixed upon to deal with this second offer of the Wright brothers required that Colonel Capper should be consulted and his advice sought as the first step in the War Office's decision-making process. Therefore on 5 September Colonel C. B. Mayne, Assistant Director of Fortifications and Works, writing for his chief, sent the appropriate papers to Capper at the Balloon Factory. There was also a covering note. In it Mayne declared: ". . . the accom-

panying copy of letters from the Wright Cycle Co., and the Military
Attaché, Washington, are forwarded for your remarks, but there appears
to be no probability of approval being given for the expenditure of the
large sum asked for".[1]

Colonel Capper was thus told, even before he could address himself to
the documents, that his military superiors believed the Wright brothers
were seeking far too high a price for what they wished to sell.

XI

Colonel Capper's reply to this request for advice played a vital part in the
further development of British military aeronautics. However, his motives in preparing his report for the Director of Fortifications and Works
were complex, and they must be examined with care if we are to
understand the suggestions he now returned to the War Office.

Earlier in 1906 Colonel J. D. Fullerton had proposed that a Committee
of Investigation on Aeronautical Matters should be set up by the British
Government. He suggested that the committee be composed of military
officers, aeronautical experts, mechanical engineers, and representatives
of the Royal Navy. Although Fullerton's idea was rejected in 1906, it
eventually bore fruit.

During the discussions that took place with respect to this proposal
Colonel Capper adopted a strong line. He insisted that such a scientific
and technical committee should be established, while he made absolutely
clear to his superiors his opinion that the flying machine was a weapon of
the very greatest importance and potential. On 10 April 1906 Capper
advised the President of the Royal Engineer Committee:[2]

> I am very strongly in favour of such a Committee being appointed.
> I am very clearly convinced that the flying machine is now a matter of
> practical politics, and will play in the future . . . a most important
> part in warfare, whether by sea or land.

However, this attitude and these firm conclusions did not mean that
Capper was now prepared to urge the War Office to come to terms with
the Wright brothers. He had struck out upon a line of his own.

At the end of May 1906 Capper was appointed Superintendent of the
Balloon Factory, in Colonel Templer's room. One of his first acts as
Superintendent was to secure the services of Lieutenant John Dunne of

[1] Air 1/728/176/3/33. C. B. Mayne to Superintendent Balloon Factory, 5
September 1906 (copy). Colonel Mayne signed this note "for D.F.W.".
[2] Air 1/729/176/4. O.C. Balloon Companies to President, R.E. Committee, 10
April 1906.

the Royal Wiltshire Regiment. Dunne's job at Farnborough was to experiment with model gliders as a first step in a series of developments that would result in the production of a power-driven aeroplane for the British Army.

Moreover, Dunne and Capper were convinced that Dunne's machines would prove to be much more valuable for military purposes than the aeroplane devised by Orville and Wilbur Wright.

John William Dunne had been born in Ireland in 1875. His father was a distinguished soldier, General Sir John Hart Dunne. During the Boer War the younger Dunne, who suffered from a weak constitution, became ill in South Africa and was invalided home. It was then that he began to concern himself with the possibilities of mechanical flight.

In Africa he had seen that the power of modern weapons made reconnaissance in the field extremely hazardous. He decided that if he could develop an efficient flying machine he would be able to overcome this problem of contemporary warfare.

He began to experiment with model gliders of his own design. As this work continued he became more and more ambitious. He established a warm friendship with H. G. Wells, who developed a genuine interest in his practice and sometimes allowed Dunne to conduct trials with the gliders in his own garden at Sandgate.

In time, Dunne was employed as a model for the aviators in several of H. G. Wells's novels. In his turn he supplied Wells with technical information that helped to make the tales as accurate as possible. On one occasion Wells sent a paper written by Dunne to the great scientist, Lord Rayleigh, in order to call attention to his friend's work. This was typical of the manner in which Dunne sought to push himself forward.

He tried regularly to attract the attention of men who might advance his prospects as a designer of aeroplanes. General Dunne was often asked to exercise his influence. When Dunne wanted advice from Major Baden-Powell, President of the Aeronautical Society of Great Britain, the General wrote to secure it and praised his son very highly at the same time. Dunne established a connection with Sir Hiram Maxim and was, after an interlude, invited by that great man to supervise his own experimental work in aeronautics.

During these years Dunne studied all the information he could secure about the Wright brothers and their gliders. He became very jealous of their achievements and convinced himself that he could produce a better military aeroplane than the one they had developed. In 1905 some of his models were shown to Colonel John Winn of the Royal Engineer Committee. Winn was so impressed with these devices that he wrote to Colonel Capper in order to call Dunne to his attention.

In June 1906, at Capper's invitation, Dunne began work at the Balloon Factory. Here the influence of General Dunne came into play. Although

Samuel Franklin Cody was still carrying out his flying experiments at Farnborough it soon became obvious that Colonel Capper was more friendly to Dunne than he was to the ex-cowboy. Cody was a foreigner and a showman. Lieutenant Dunne was a gentleman and the son of a general.

Capper quickly came to the conclusion that Dunne had before him a brilliant future in aeronautics. He readily supplied him with assistants and with a good deal of the technical resources of the Balloon Factory in order to enable him to secure his object: the development of a powered aeroplane of greater military efficiency than that invented by Wilbur and Orville Wright.

Dunne and Colonel Capper were convinced that Dunne's machine would prove to be much more valuable for military purposes than the Wright aeroplane. They believed that the Dunne aircraft could provide the British Army with an advantage over the forces of every other power, in the field of military aviation.

The Wright brothers had designed their machine to be "unstable" in the air. This meant that it could only sustain itself in flight if the pilot continually manipulated the controls in order to maintain equilibrium. Dunne, a soldier, was obsessed by other ideas. He hoped to produce an aeroplane that was inherently "stable" in the air, a machine that could maintain itself in flight and thus spare the pilot much of the work he was required to perform in flying an aeroplane of the Wright type.

Dunne later explained the military advantages of his concept to C. F. Snowden Gamble, the aeronautical historian: "The War Office idea at this time (1906) was that flight with aeroplane surfaces of the conventional Lilienthal, Chanute, and Wright kind was perfectly possible, but only as an acrobatic feat. The pilot, it was supposed, would need years of training, and, even then would be unable to control his machine in any very high wind. But it seemed probable that, with the Dunne wing-surface, a pilot would be able to fly without difficulty at the first attempt . . . so it was considered that the Power which got hold of this machine would be able to develop its air force with much greater rapidity than could any rival nation equipped with the Wright system of surface and control . . ."[1]

As military men Dunne and Capper also calculated that the pilot of a Wright aeroplane would always be busy with the controls in order to keep his aircraft in flight. The more stable Dunne machine, however, would permit the pilot to perform as an observer or aerial scout, and he would also be in a position to carry out any offensive actions that might be devised as the technology of military aviation was extended and improved.

[1] Dunne's account is printed in Snowden Gamble, *The Air Weapon*, p. 96.

This was the military secret that dominated Capper's mind in September 1906 when he received Colonel Mayne's request to supply the Directorate of Fortifications and Works with his "remarks" upon the letters from the Wright brothers and from Colonel Gleichen.

The authorities in the War Office were not aware of the possibly brilliant results that might follow from Lieutenant Dunne's experiments at the Balloon Factory. They were more concerned with those budgetary restrictions which dominated the British military mind in this period of history.

When Dunne was formally attached to the Balloon Factory in June 1906 "to assist in carrying out experiments in connection with flying machines" the War Office made it clear to him that he would serve there on half pay, with "no claim to allowances of any kind in consequence of (his) being so attached". Dunne was medically unfit and the War Office was determined not to pay him the full salary of a regular serving officer.[1]

Later, in September, Dunne found he would have to appear before an Army Medical Board. He knew he was not well enough to pass the physical examination that lay ahead of him. He appealed to Colonel Capper for help. Three days before Capper received Colonel Mayne's request for his technical advice about the Wright aeroplane Capper, in his capacity as Superintendent of the Balloon Factory, wrote to the Director of Fortifications and Works in order to tell him of the great value of Dunne's work. In this document, Capper made clear the high significance of what Dunne was accomplishing, under his direction:[2]

> I have found Lieut. Dunne a most indefatigable experimenter. He has both the time and inclination to carry out the nicest experiments; and though progress in such a matter as Flying must be slow, I think that Lieut. Dunne has learnt and been able to teach us more by his experiments since he has been here than we should have ascertained for ourselves in a long time. His services are of the utmost value to me, and I strongly recommend that if he cannot be passed as fit to join his Regiment and be allowed to be attached to the Balloon Factory on full pay, that at least his services be continued in the Balloon Factory on the present footing.
>
> I may note that Lieut. Dunne's services, which are of a highly scientific nature, are rewarded at present with merely the wages of an ordinary unskilled labourer, so the continuance of half pay to him cannot be considered in the light of an extravagance.

---

[1] For these details see Air 1/1613/204/88/17. R. H. Brade to Dunne, 15 June 1906.

[2] Air 1/1613/204/88/17. Capper to D.F.W., dated "Farnborough 3.9.1906". The document is marked "CONFIDENTIAL".

This was the condition of affairs in the Balloon Factory when Colonel Capper prepared his formal reply to the request of the Directorate of Fortifications and Works that he advise them about the contemplated purchase of the Wright aeroplane. Capper set out his technical opinions in a document entitled "Wright Bros. Flying Machine", dated 6 September 1906. He began his minute by suggesting that the Wright offer should not be taken up because the price asked by them was entirely too high:[1]

> I cannot advise any further action being taken in this matter. I consider the prices asked by the Wright Bros. are entirely out of all proportion to the benefits to be gained. One has no certainty whatsoever that their claim of having special "confidential scientific knowledge", for which they demand £20,000, is based on fact.

He next pointed out to his superiors that the Balloon Factory, as a result of Lieutenant Dunne's high abilities, would be able to produce, within a reasonably short time, an aeroplane superior to the one designed by the Wright brothers.

It should be mentioned at this point that Dunne, during his period of service with the British Army, was never able to devise a machine that could rise successfully into the air. He did succeed in this task years later, after he left the service, but it may be observed that the time factor was a matter of crucial consequence in these deliberations of September 1906. Capper's paper continued:

> As regards the Flying Machine itself: I have but little doubt that we shall be able, thanks partially to the scientific attainments and ability of Lieutenant Dunne, to turn out within a reasonable time a Flying Machine on much the same lines as that of the Wright Brothers, but we hope superior to it in several essentials, at an infinite fraction of the cost demanded by them.

The final paragraph in Colonel Capper's paper hinted at his plans for the future. Capper hoped to secure a site for the flight trials of Dunne's machine, when it was ready, at some remote place where it would be secure "from public gaze". The War Office had condemned the Wright brothers for their excessive secrecy and for their desire to bargain upon the basis of "hearsay evidence". Colonel Capper now suggested it would be necessary for the British Army to follow a similar course when the moment came to test its own aeroplane:

> There will always be in this country the difficulty of experimenting with these machines, and should we be successful in our preliminary efforts I should like to make later some definite proposals as to a site for experimenting purposes. I feel that at present, until we are

[1] Air 1/728/176/3/33. Supt Balloon Factory to D.F.W., dated 6 September 1906. See also Walker, *Early Aviation at Farnborough*, vol. II, p. 59.

perfectly certain that the machine itself is built on the proper lines – which we can be sure of after trial without great risk to anyone's life – that the training of men to guide the machine is not a matter of considerable moment. It will require special ground suitable for the purpose, and as far as possible from public gaze; but the time has not yet come to enter further into this matter.

The time came in less than a year. In 1907 Capper arranged for the secret flight of the Dunne aeroplane to take place in the hills north of Blair Atholl, a remote village in the far distant Scottish Highlands.

Colonel Capper wanted to oversee the creation of a successful British Army Flying Machine. In June 1906 he selected Lieutenant Dunne as the man who would be able to carry out the work. With this great object in mind, he was not prepared to permit anyone or anything to interfere with the course of Dunne's experiments at the Balloon Factory, where he was Superintendent. This attitude and these desires helped to decide the nature of the advice he submitted to the Directorate of Fortifications and Works in September 1906 when he was asked to furnish his superiors with his technical opinion about the proposed purchase of the Wright aeroplane by the British Government.

Unfortunately for Capper, Colonel Gleichen's letter addressed to Sir Mortimer Durand arrived in the War Office shortly after this minute of 6 September was received there. Although Gleichen's despatch was sent, in the first instance, to the ambassador in Washington it was drawn up as an official document designed to be read by the highest authorities in the War Office.

The ambassador sent Gleichen's despatch to the Foreign Office. From there it was forwarded to the Army Council, on 18 September 1906:[1]

> The Under-Secretary of State for Foreign Affairs presents his compliments to the Secretary of the Army Council, and, by direction of the Secretary of State, transmits herewith copy of the under-mentioned paper and enclosure.

Foreign Office
September 18, 1906

Description of Inclosure

Name and Date	Subject
Sir M. Durand, H.M. Ambassador, Lenox, No. 157 Confidential August 18, 1906	Flying Machine of Messrs. Wright Brothers of Dayton – Ohio. Transmits despatch from Military Attaché

[1] W.O. 32/8595. Under-Secretary of State to Secretary of the Army Council, No. 30712, 18 September 1906.

Colonel Gleichen's despatch was a document of very great length. It reflects the tremendous enthusiasm he experienced as a result of his meeting with Wilbur and Orville Wright.

There was no doubt in his mind about the fabulous nature of their accomplishments. In Count Gleichen's sophisticated view what they had achieved was "almost incredible". Their aeroplane was, in his professional opinion, a device of almost incalculable military importance.

The despatch is a document of genuine historical significance. It reveals that Colonel Gleichen did not waste his time in Dayton. He learned a very great deal about the Wrights and their work during his brief stay in the town. He acquired, during his visit, information about the brothers not previously available to the British authorities. The purpose of the despatch was to inform his military superiors of the knowledge he had acquired; and to endorse the Wright claims as warmly as possible:[1]

Very Confidential British Embassy
Lenox, U.S.A.,

His Excellency
Sir Mortimer Durand, G.C.M.G., August 17th, 1906
His Britannic Majesty's Ambassador
Washington.

Sir:–
In order to elucidate certain points connected with some previous correspondence between the War Office and Messrs. Wright Brothers of Dayton, Ohio, about their flying-machine, I stopped on the 8th instant at Dayton on my way east, and had a couple of hours' most interesting conversation with the brothers. I have communicated direct with the War Office regarding the correspondence, and venture to record here some further details in the matter.

Gleichen next provided the ambassador with a classic description of Wilbur and Orville Wright at this period in their lives:

The brothers Wright are two young men of about 30, intelligent looking, not "cranks", apparently honest – their venerable father being a bishop of some hazy denomination – and with little or none of the usual braggadocio of the Yankee inventor. Strange to say, they are modest in demeanour, and even shy.

The despatch continued with a history of the Wrights' work with flying machines. Gleichen explained they had been experimenting for nearly ten years but had only recently achieved a complete success in their endeavours. He made it clear that the Wright brothers began by em-

---

[1] W.O. 32/8595. Gleichen to Sir M. Durand, 17 August 1906.

ploying a glider which they invented, and then perfected. The experience gained with the glider was "invaluable". It enabled them to design their power-flyer, "a flying-machine driven by an engine".

Gleichen emphasized that the Wrights from the first attacked their subject "from a purely original point of view". They found that many of the conclusions reached by Maxim, Langley, Chanute, and others were incorrect. Before any of their own experiments were attempted they mastered the theoretical calculations that were a necessary prelude to success. He also explained the reasons for their caution and reticence: "They have not flown at all since last autumn, chiefly owing to the impossibility of keeping the flights secret and to the babblings of various indiscreet friends".

He made clear the mastery of the air attained by the Wright brothers: ". . . they are so certain of their machine that they constructed the last one purely from their formulae and, without even making a trial trip . . . took it . . . and flew it . . . perfectly, without a mishap. They have now made about 40 consecutive flights, the longest being 24 1/2 miles, and several others between 16 and 21 miles, without a mishap."

Gleichen explained that "by dint of numerous questions" he had gathered a number of technical details of genuine military interest:

> The present type of machine is intended to carry one man and supplies. It weighs about 750 lbs. by itself (including engine) and can carry, besides, about 160 lbs., i.e. man and fuel. For military purposes they would build one of perhaps 800 lbs., to carry over 300 lbs. in weight (i.e. 2 men and some fuel, or 1 man and complete fuel and supplies for 100 miles). They could, if required, build them larger to carry up to 4 or 5 men and supplies, and fly up to 70 miles an hour. . . .
>
> This aeroplane can go up to 40 miles an hour, even against a head-wind. It appears that the stronger the headwind the better it goes. Downwind it can go at the rate of 40 miles an hour + the velocity of the wind. These figures seem almost incredible: but I subsequently interviewed two independent witnesses, a banker and a chemist, who assured me that the machine went "like a train" and turned very handily.
>
> The aeroplane is on an even keel throughout, except when turning. Even against a high beamwind it does not heel over. What is still more extraordinary is that – so I was assured – they have discovered not only how to soar – i.e. move without motion of the wings – but also how to hover: they have remained stationary in the air for over a minute without the motor working . . .

Gleichen next informed the ambassador that the Wrights were asking the sum of one hundred thousand dollars for their Flyer. He went on to explain why Wilbur and Orville Wright felt they could demand such a sum. In their technical opinion they enjoyed a practically impregnable position. No one else, they believed, could attain their levels of proficiency for at least five years. They could afford to wait until prospective purchasers accepted their terms:

> They have been approached by various syndicates but refuse to sell to anyone except Governments for military purposes. Their reason, so they say, is partly to prevent swindles by private companies and partly because by holding it back from public use for another 5 years or so they expect to make a much larger sum. They say they are at least 5 years ahead of anyone and can afford to wait. The French Government is in negotiation with them and demands a one year's option: but this they have refused to give, and nothing has yet been settled. Neither the United States Government nor Army has taken any steps, and no other Government has done more than, so to speak, smell at it.

Colonel Gleichen concluded his despatch by setting out the military capabilities of the Wright aeroplane. In this part of his letter he refuted completely Lieutenant Dunne's curious notion that it would require "years of training" for a pilot to learn how to fly a Wright machine:

> To turn to the military aspect: they expect the flyer to be used chiefly for scouting. It can fly at any height, would not be visible till fairly close, on account of its thin wooden framework and white wings (canvas), and could fly at such a rate that it would be practically invulnerable: the man being the largest and practically the only vulnerable point to aim at. For Transport it could be packed in a railway car or, if on the march, could either be carried on or in a wagon or, better still, keep up with the column by flying slowly. For practical use it would seem best to have a 2 man size, as one could hardly expect that one man could attend both to the important duties of observation and to those of directing a novel mechanism. Messrs. Wright assured me that after a few trials it came as natural and easy as riding a bicycle!
> . . . they are now employed in perfecting their motors and constructing others and different parts of the aeroplanes, so as to have a supply handy when the demand comes.

I have etc.,
(Signed) Gleichen
Lieutenant-Colonel
Military Attaché.

Here was a formal document composed by an experienced and sophisticated Military Attaché. It had passed through the hands of the British

Ambassador in Washington and by direction of the Secretary of State for Foreign Affairs had been transmitted to the Secretary of the Army Council. It was obvious enough that Colonel Capper, despite the clear advice he had offered in his minute of 6 September, would have some further questions to answer when his superiors received their copy of Colonel Gleichen's despatch.

XIII

As a result of Gleichen's initiative the British authorities now knew everything the Wright brothers wanted them to know about their invention. His despatch was full of the most significant technical information.

Lieutenant Dunne and Colonel Capper believed it would require years of training before a pilot could achieve any degree of proficiency with a Wright aeroplane. Gleichen offered the surprising information that after a few trials it was as easy to fly the Wright machine as it was to ride a bicycle.

Colonel J. D. Fullerton had advised the War Office, in November 1905, in his "Report on Proposed Experiments with Flying Machines", that "soaring machines" of the Wright type were very "crank" in the air and therefore extremely dangerous to fly. Gleichen reported that the Wright aircraft flew well in headwinds and downwinds. Even when struck by a beamwind it did not heel over.

The Wright brothers, according to Gleichen's account, spoke of designing military aircraft that could carry four or five men aloft, with supplies, and would then fly at a speed of seventy miles an hour. In Colonel Gleichen's opinion the performance figures of the Wright aeroplane were "almost incredible". Moreover, when the brothers compared their work with that of the other aviation pioneers of the day they insisted they were "at least 5 years ahead of anyone" else. This was the device, this the scientific information, and this the opportunity they now offered to sell to the British Government.

When the Director of Fortifications and Works read Gleichen's despatch he came to the conclusion that it was a "very interesting report". He at once ordered his assistant, Colonel Mayne, to send it to Capper at the Balloon Factory.

The Gleichen despatch arrived there on 1 October. In a covering note, marked "Confidential", Mayne wrote: "The attached copy of a report from the Military Attaché to the British Embassy in America is forwarded for your information . . . Would you like to add any remarks before the question is submitted for decision".[1]

---

[1] Air 1/728/176/3/33. Mayne to Supt Balloon Factory, 29 September 1906.

Colonel Capper was embarrassed to read the Gleichen despatch. In his minute of the 6 September he had advised the War Office to take no further action in the matter of the Wright offer. He suggested at that time that he and Lieutenant Dunne, working at the Balloon Factory, would be able to produce a superior aircraft, within a reasonable time. Despite Gleichen's keen enthusiasm and the new information he brought forward, Capper refused to alter his opinion. He continued to urge his superiors to reject the Wright proposals so that they could concentrate their limited resources on Dunne's experiments. He seized also on the point that the Wrights claimed to be five years in advance of every other aircraft designer, and questioned the validity of their opinion. He asked also if it was worthwhile to pay so much for the advantages they offered. In a minute addressed to the Director of Fortifications and Works, he wrote, on 11 October 1906:[1]

> . . . I cannot add to my previous minute. I feel perfectly sure the Wrights are honest, & they possibly are 5 years ahead of the rest of the world in this matter, but the question is whether
> (1) They are so far in advance.
> (2) Whether it is worth while paying so much for the advantage.
> Unless we can experiment and manufacture far away from the public gaze, it would be impossible to keep secret the details of such a machine.

It is necessary to pause at this point in our account in order to examine Colonel Capper's attitude toward the Wright brothers, as it is presented in the historical literature. Many of the most distinguished British historians of aviation have described Capper as the Wrights' advocate, as the man who continuously urged the War Office to seize upon their various offers in order to exploit an unparalleled military opportunity, the chance to acquire the first practical and successful aeroplane in the history of the world. These writers, in dealing with Capper and the Wright brothers, regularly declare that in the secret councils of the State he was their champion – from the moment of his return from his American visit in November 1904 until the Wrights at last despaired of the British Government and sought their fortunes elsewhere.

In his classic history *British Aviation, The Pioneer Years* Harald Penrose wrote of Capper in 1905–6: "With typical drive Col. Capper sought every possible means of inducing officially sponsored aeroplane construction. Ever since his return from the United States he had been pursuing his recommendation that the War Office should offer the Wrights a contract to work solely for the British Government for four

---

[1] Air 1/728/176/3/33. J. E. Capper to D.F.W., 11 October 1906. See also Walker, *Early Aviation at Farnborough*, vol. II, p. 60.

years in return for a sum of £20,000 . . . Capper knew the Wrights were prepared to give Great Britain the benefit of all their knowledge with the honourable reservation that their country must come first if need be. . . ."[1]

In 1952 Brigadier P. W. L. Broke-Smith, himself a pioneer of British military aviation, published a series of articles in *The Royal Engineers Journal*. The articles were entitled "The History of Early British Military Aeronautics". With respect to Capper and the Wright brothers the brigadier wrote: ". . . if the British authorities had realized the possibilities of flying, listened to the advice of Colonel Capper, and taken up negotiations with the Wrights wholeheartedly, the British army might have been the first in the field in developing military aviation".[2]

In the same year Brigadier-General W. Baker Brown published the fourth volume of the official *History of The Corps of Royal Engineers*. Baker Brown had actually served as an assistant to the Director of Fortifications and Works and as Inspector of Electric Lights during the years when the Wright brothers sought to sell their aeroplane to the War Office. Nevertheless in his history he repeated the story that Capper urged the authorities to hire the Wrights at a salary of £20,000 for four years of service. He further explained: "Colonel Capper . . . recommended that the Wrights should be engaged on these or similar terms; but the proposal, which was strongly supported by Brigadier-General Ruck, who was the D.F.W. and a keen advocate for the development of the aeronautical service, was rejected. The British authorities had as yet no belief in the practicability of flying and subsequent negotiations for the purchase of a Wright machine were abandoned in 1906. The British service thus missed the chance of being the first in the field in developing military aviation."[3]

A similar account was published years before by C. F. Snowden Gamble in his brilliant work, *The Air Weapon*: "In 1904 Capper went to North Carolina and asked [the Wrights], on behalf of the War Office, if they would come over to England to continue their experiments; but the Treasury would not sanction the expenditure."[4]

How can we possibly explain the curious fact that these capable experts all made the same mistake about the official advice Colonel Capper offered his superiors between 1904 and 1906?

It may be the case that in later years, after the Wright brothers had established the entire validity of their claims and had won world-wide

[1] Penrose, *British Aviation, The Pioneer Years*, pp. 73–4.
[2] Brigadier P. W. L. Broke-Smith, "The History of Early British Military Aeronautics" in *The Royal Engineers Journal*, June 1952, p. 112.
[3] Brigadier-General W. Baker Brown, *History of The Corps of Royal Engineers* (Chatham, 1952), vol. IV, p. 287.
[4] Snowden Gamble, *The Air Weapon*, p. 90.

fame and fortune for themselves, Colonel Capper recalled, with advantages, the incidents of his visit to Dayton in 1904 and his conduct thereafter. Both Brigadier Broke-Smith and Snowden Gamble were helped by Capper when they wrote their histories while Harald Penrose, as a prelude to the preparation of his book, was able to meet "most of the twentieth-century pioneers . . . obtaining much of the material at first hand".[1]

XIV

While the authorities in the British War Office reflected upon Colonel Capper's technical advice and deliberated further upon their decision, the Wright brothers spent their time in building new and more efficient engines for their aeroplanes. Early in October 1906 Octave Chanute informed his friends that several of his correspondents believed the Wrights could not sell their machines because of the price they asked for them. "I think myself", Chanute added, "that it is very high".[2]

This comment provoked a quick response from Wilbur. He explained to Chanute the principles which guided the brothers' actions at this stage of their career. His explanation reveals the iron-hard determination of Wilbur and Orville Wright. No changes or alterations, however slight, would be allowed in the course they had fixed upon as the best method to sell their aeroplane, and thus reap in the rewards they believed they had earned.

Wilbur, in a letter dated 10 October 1906, dealt first with the question of price. He told Chanute: "Regarding the matter of price, no two persons will have exactly the same view. There is really no such thing in the world as absolute value for anything. If there were, the air we breathe would be the highest priced thing in the world instead of the cheapest."

He turned next to tactics: "From our own study of the situation and conversation with the French & English visitors we believe that the price or rather the amount of money is not directly an important issue. If it be assumed that someone else will produce a practical flier in a year or two at most, or that by refusing to buy governments can force us to sell at their own terms, then the price we ask is undoubtedly too high. But if the governments know that there is only one way to get a practical flier within five or ten years, and that there is no hope of beating down the price, then

[1] Penrose, *op. cit.*, p. 7. See also Snowden Gamble, *op. cit.*, p. vi and p. 1 of Broke-Smith's "The History of Early British Military Aeronautics" in *The Royal Engineers Journal*, March, 1952 where acknowledgement of Capper's assistance is mentioned.

[2] McFarland, *Papers of Wilbur and Orville Wright*, p. 728. All quotations in this section, unless otherwise specified, are taken from this source.

they will consider the price very low . . . It is not the amount involved but the possibility of getting it cheaper that makes them hesitate . . ."

Wilbur's letter continued: "If it were indeed true that others would be flying in a year or two, there would be no reason in selling at any price but we are convinced that no one will be able to develop a practical flyer within five years. This opinion is based upon cold calculation. It takes into consideration practical and scientific difficulties whose existence is unknown to all but ourselves. Even you, Mr. Chanute, have little idea how difficult the flying problem really is. When we see men labouring year after year on points we overcame in a few weeks . . . we know that their rivalry and competition are not to be feared for many years . . . It is many times five years . . . We do not believe there is one chance in a hundred that anyone will have a machine of the least *practical* usefulness within five years. If our judgement is correct undue haste to *force a sale* would be a mistake."

Wilbur concluded with a cold request: "We would be very glad to know exactly upon what grounds you base your opinion of the selling value of our machine, and your views of the chief elements in fixing it, and particularly why there is such need of haste as so many seem to think. We wish to make sure that no important point has escaped our attention."

The unfortunate Chanute, reeling from these blasts, struck back as best he could. He pointed out that other inventors, with the successful Wright example to spur them on, might produce a practical flyer in less than five years. He mentioned that the development of light motors would assist all the aviation pioneers in their various tasks. "I cheerfully acknowledge", he wrote, "that I have little idea how difficult the flying problem really is and that its solution is beyond my powers, but are you not too cocksure that yours is the only secret worth knowing and that others may not hit upon a solution in less than 'many times five years'? . . ."

Exchanges like these continued until 1 November 1906 when Chanute suddenly flashed word to the Wright brothers that Alberto Santos-Dumont, the Brazilian who lived in Paris, had successfully flown an aeroplane of his own design for a short distance. Chanute took care to point out that France was not the only country where significant progress seemed to be taking place. He wrote: ". . . I suppose you realize that Esnault-Pelterie, Ferber, Blériot & Voisin, Barlatier & Blanc, Vuia, Cornu, Cody and a German syndicate are all experimenting with dynamic flying machines. Some of them may develop something. See the remarks of Col. Capper in his lecture on page 62 of the *Aeronautical Journal* for October. His attitude appears to be one of expectancy, so that I do not believe that it would be wise to be very stiff as to terms should a good offer come from the British War Office."

The Wright brothers responded to the news of Alberto Santos-Dumont's activity with instant vigilance. On 13 September 1906 the young Brazilian made what technicians today call a "hop-flight". His machine travelled through the air for a distance of some seven meters before it fell back to the earth. On the 23 October Santos tried again. On this occasion his craft rushed through the air for sixty meters and won for its designer the Archdeacon prize, a silver trophy awarded for the first flight of twenty-five meters.

The Wright brothers, after reading an early report of these achievements, remained unmoved. They decided, correctly, that Santos had managed a few "powered hops", but nothing more. Wilbur blandly explained to Chanute: "This report gives such an excellent opportunity for exercising our powers as prophets that I cannot resist making a forecast before the details arrive. From our knowledge of the subject", the master continued, "we estimate that it is possible to *jump* about 250 ft. with a machine which has not made the first step towards controllability and which is quite unable to maintain the motive force necessary for flight. By getting up good speed a machine can be made to rise with very little power, and can proceed several hundred feet before its momentum is exhausted . . . Maxim made a machine lift 12 years ago, and immediately quit in despair."

However, on 12 November 1906 Alberto Santos-Dumont managed to keep his machine in the air for a distance of two hundred and twenty meters. There were plenty of spectators present at his field at Bagatelle, near Paris. Men cheered, women fainted, and Santos at once won for himself world-wide celebrity, and also a prize of fifteen hundred francs awarded by the Aéro-Club of France.

This time the Wright brothers were concerned. Wilbur told Chanute of this development: "It is the first real indication of progress that has been displayed in France in five years".

It must not be supposed that Wilbur and Orville now looked upon Alberto Santos-Dumont as a serious technical rival. They knew he was nothing of the kind. They understood he had not achieved genuine flight. The cause of their concerns lay elsewhere.

It was their belief, as we have seen, that the various governments would eventually pay the prices they required when it was at last realized that no one else could build a practical flying machine for years to come. As a result of Santos-Dumont's achievements, however, many people began to speculate that the Air age had arrived at last. The idea was widely entertained that others could take up where he left off, and improve upon what he had created.

Such a condition of affairs would have a devastating effect upon the Wright plan to collect from the various governments the high prices they were demanding. Wilbur candidly explained to Chanute the effect of Santos' triumph on the Wrights' business aspirations: "Fear that others will produce a machine capable of practical service in less than several years does not worry us. We have been over the course and understand how much remains for them to do. The real disturbing element is the general *belief* that they will accomplish wonders shortly. As a hindrance to business this is almost as bad as reality . . ."

When the Wright brothers arrived at this conclusion they decided to strike out on a new course. As a result of Santos-Dumont's accomplishments they could no longer wait until governments sought them out. They realized they would have to take more positive steps if they were to sell their aeroplane, and thus secure all their hopes and dreams.

XV

During these weeks Colonel Ruck continued to ponder upon his decision. When he received Capper's minute of 11 October 1906 he was not entirely satisfied by its arguments. He ordered Capper to come up to London and report to him the War Office. Their conference took place on 25 October. As a result of these deliberations Colonel Ruck recommended that it would not be advisable for the British Government to purchase the Wright flying machine. Two days earlier Alberto Santos-Dumont had flown in public for a distance of sixty meters and had won the Archdeacon prize. The Press in several countries had already begun to trumpet the high significance for the world of his achievement.

On the day he conferred with Capper Colonel Ruck prepared a minute, addressed to the Master-General of the Ordnance. In it he pointed out that he had discussed the Gleichen despatch with Capper. They were in agreement, he made clear to his superior, that there could be little doubt the Wright brothers had produced a practical flying machine. The cost of the machine was so high, however, that Ruck could not recommend its purchase. He argued also that the design of the Wright aeroplane could be readily imitated.

Although Colonel Gleichen had explained, in his despatch, that the Wright brothers refused to sell to anyone but governments, this significant item of information was entirely ignored by Ruck. He suggested, incorrectly, that the Wrights might soon manufacture their machines on a commercial basis and then the British authorities, like anyone else, could purchase them at a much lower price than the one presently under consideration. Wilbur and Orville, of course, had foreseen this snare and at this stage of their work were determined to sell only to governments, at a high price.

Ruck concluded his argument by suggesting that Capper's aeroplane experiments at the Balloon Factory might prove successful. For these reasons he would not recommend further action in the matter. He wrote to the Master-General of the Ordnance of the Gleichen despatch:[1]

> I have discussed this very interesting report with Superintendent Balloons and I agree with him that although there is little doubt that Messrs. Wright have constructed a successful flying machine which would be of great utility for scouting purposes, yet it would be so costly to purchase at this stage, and the design so readily imitated when seen that I do not recommend further action in this matter at present.
>
> It appears quite possible that Messrs Wright will manufacture before long and that we shall be able to purchase in common with others at a much reduced price: in the meantime we are making experiments at the Balloon Factory which seem likely to lead us in the same direction as Messrs Wrights' developments as far as we know them.

The Master-General of the Ordnance agreed with these opinions. It was arranged that instructions should be sent to Colonel Gleichen in Washington, ordering him to inform the Wright brothers that the Army Council had decided, after careful consideration, "that it would not be advisable to purchase, especially in view of the great cost".[2]

Before Gleichen could carry out these instructions Wilbur Wright sent exciting news to Octave Chanute. A tremendous development had taken place in the affairs of the Wright brothers.

On 1 December Wilbur happily told Chanute: ". . . it seems that the favorable conditions we have been awaiting for six months have now arrived and we have some opportunities we would be glad to talk over with you, the best from a financial standpoint that we have had. There is nothing definite yet, but we are to meet the people interested in New York next week."[3]

Before the Wright brothers could travel to New York and begin to bargain with the people who were "interested" they received Colonel Gleichen's message which informed them that the British Government was not prepared to purchase their invention, "especially in view of the great cost". Gleichen's letter, written on his own hand, was brief and business-like:[4]

---

[1] For his minute see Walker, *Early Aviation at Farnborough*, vol. II, pp. 60–1.
[2] *Ibid.*, p. 61.
[3] McFarland, *Papers of Wilbur and Orville Wright*, p. 741.
[4] Wright Brothers' Papers, Gleichen to Wilbur Wright, 3 December 1906.

FROM   3d Dec. 1906
THE MILITARY ATTACHÉ
BRITISH EMBASSY, WASHINGTON

Dear Sir, –

With reference to our interview at Dayton on the 8th August last, & to communications which have passed between yourselves & the British War Office, I regret to have to inform you that the Army Council has decided, after careful consideration, that, especially in view of the great cost, it would not be advisable to purchase your invention.

                                         I am, Sir,
                                         Yrs. truly
                                         Gleichen
                                         Col. M.A.

CHAPTER 7

England Is No Longer An Island

Alberto Santos-Dumont Flies – Lord Northcliffe Observes the Scene – His Tremendous Role in Early Aeronautical History – Alfred Harmsworth fascinated by technological developments – His interest in Mechanical Inventions – His gigantic Ambition – His Commercial Success – His contact with Lord Salisbury – Harmsworth launches *The Daily Mail* – Arthur Balfour's Reaction – Harmsworth acquires *The Observer* – The Godfather of the Royal Flying Corps – "The future lies in the air" – "Air power will be an even more important thing than sea power" – *The Daily Mail* Prize – An Interview with Orville Wright – Charles R. Flint – Patrick Alexander appears Again – Flint's task – "First Come first Served" – He Offers Fifty Aeroplanes to Germany – Lady Jane Taylor – Her Position and Target – Flint's Secret Code – He Offers Fifty Aeroplanes to Great Britain – And to Russia – A Firm Offer from Germany – The Offer to Great Britain – Lady Jane sees R. B. Haldane – His Conditions – The Wright Brothers React – Lord Tweedmouth Invites Lady Jane to the Admiralty – Flint approaches Lord Northcliffe – The Interest of the German Emperor – An Unfortunate Official – The Refusal of the British Ministers – The Attitude of General von Einem – Northcliffe "can put the screw on".

I

Unlike the Wright brothers, Alberto Santos-Dumont always flew in public. He was well known and widely admired by the people of Paris because of his flights over their city in the various dirigibles he had designed. After several spectacular triumphs with these lighter-than-air craft Santos, in 1906, determined to build an aeroplane.

The first test of this machine took place at the Polo Ground in the Bois de Boulogne on 21 August. Unfortunately the propeller broke at the start and the attempt was abandoned for that day. Nevertheless Santos and his experiments now began to attract publicity in France and also in England.

Later tests were made at Bagatelle in September 1906. After one or two

186

tentative starts Santos managed on 23 October to fly a distance of more than fifty metres. The spectators at once became wild with excitement and admiration. Many in the throng believed they had witnessed the first successful aeroplane flight in human history.

In the crowd at Bagatelle on that day was the great British newspaper proprietor, Lord Northcliffe. His imagination was immediately set on fire by what he had seen.

From that instant Lord Northcliffe's interest and enthusiasm became factors of the very highest significance and consequence in the further development of British aviation, military and civilian alike. He played a tremendous part in the history of early British aeronautics.

Alfred Harmsworth, who later became Lord Northcliffe, was, from an early age, fascinated by new technological developments. He was born at Chapelizod, near Dublin, in 1865, the eldest of a family of fifteen children. His father, Alfred Harmsworth, was an Englishman who came from Hampshire. The great source of strength in the family, however, lay with his mother, Geraldine Maffett. She exercised a powerful influence over her husband and over each of her children. She was the daughter of an Ulster land agent, a woman who was determined to see her husband and her sons succeed in life.

Under her prodding the family moved to London, where the elder Alfred Harmsworth began to read for the bar. He was not a very successful lawyer. Alfred Harmsworth was entirely too genial; he drank too much; and he loved to spend his time talking and discoursing in a circle of like-minded friends, where he was affectionately known as "Harmie". Geraldine Harmsworth, who dominated her sons, and was adored by them in return, wanted them to follow more practical courses than those in which their father wandered so placidly.

In his youth Alfred Harmsworth was strikingly handsome. At an early age he decided to become a journalist. He always regretted that his family had been unable to provide him with an education at Oxford or Cambridge. Nevertheless he developed into an industrious reader of classical English novels and also of popular accounts of the latest discoveries of science. Eventually, in Lord Beaverbrook's famous phrase, Harmsworth became "the greatest figure who ever strode down Fleet Street". He achieved wealth, fame, and fortune. By the first decade of the twentieth century he was approaching the zenith of his influence and power.

Developments in technology played a part at almost every turn of his upward flight. He was intensely interested by new mechanical inventions. His first genuine opportunity in journalism came in 1886 when the great publishing firm of Iliffe, in Coventry, offered him the editorship of a periodical called *Bicycling News*. Harmsworth, a bicycling enthusiast, had predicted shortly before that the bicycle would "revolutionize modern life".

At this time, as a result of advances in technology, the bicycle was developing into its modern, efficient form. Coventry was the centre of a booming trade in the manufacture of these machines. Harmsworth fixed his grip upon *Bicycling News* and within a few months, under his direction, the paper's circulation increased eight-fold. His uncanny insight into popular tastes suggested to him that photography might become a part of the pleasure of riding in the countryside. He gave this subject plenty of space in *Bicycling News* and in this way helped to popularize the camera.

Harmsworth's gigantic ambition did not permit him to remain in the provinces for long. He was consumed by the desire to own his own periodicals. He realized that the Education Act of 1870 had created a new class of people in England who now knew how to read but were in no way attracted by the established journals of the day. He meant to exploit these new readers by providing them with publications of an entirely different kind. In 1888 he produced a magazine called *Answers to Correspondents on Every Subject Under the Sun*. After a time *Answers* became a commercial success. Other publications of this calibre followed: *Comic Cuts*; *Chips*; *Forget-Me-Not*; *Funny-Wonder*; *Home Sweet Home*; the *Halfpenny Marvel*; *Union Jack*; the *Sunday Companion*; *Home Chat*; the *Comic Home Journal*. In all these enterprises Harmsworth was proud of the fact that his organizations used more new mechanical devices – typewriters, mimeograph machines, and telephones – than did his contemporaries. He lived and flourished in an atmosphere of technical innovation.

A new departure came in 1894. In that year Harmsworth entered the field of daily journalism for the first time when he acquired the *Evening News*.

Although the *Evening News* could boast of reasonable circulation figures it was steadily losing large sums of money as a result of poor management. Harmsworth looked upon the paper as a professional challenge. In a short time the *Evening News*, under his guidance, began to produce a profit and within a year it was announced that the paper had secured the largest sale of any evening newspaper in London. The *Evening News* had been closely connected with the Conservative party. When he became its owner Harmsworth established contacts with several prominent Conservative politicians including Lord Salisbury, the party leader. His ambition, fortified and sustained by genuine commercial success, now began to swell and grow and his horizons became wider than those of a proprietor of weekly or monthly magazines of the quality of *Answers* or *Comic Cuts*.

In 1895 Alfred Harmsworth decided to stand as the Unionist candidate for Portsmouth in the General Election of that year. Despite tremendous efforts his campaign was a disaster, and he was beaten badly at the poll. It soon became obvious to him that a public platform could not be his arena.

The next significant step in this remarkable career followed almost at once. Harmsworth launched the *Daily Mail* in May 1896. His object was to secure nothing less than the largest circulation in England. The new paper was an instant triumph. Within three years its average daily sale was more than five hundred thousand copies. No other daily in England could sell even half this number. Harmsworth told Kennedy Jones, one of his colleagues, "We've struck a gold mine".

The first edition of the *Daily Mail* emphasized that "new inventions" had been employed in order to make certain of the paper's success. The *Daily Mail*'s leading article proudly explained: "It is no secret that remarkable new inventions have just come to the help of the Press . . . It is the use of these inventions on a scale unprecedented in any English newspaper office that enables the *Daily Mail* to effect a saving of from 30 to 50 per cent and to be sold for half the price of its contemporaries. That is the whole explanation of what would otherwise be a mystery."

These statements were typical of Harmsworth's professional attitude. When the official *History of The Times* sought to analyse his character after his purchase of that paper it declared of him: "Old fashioned printing types . . . he could not bear: an old printing-press was to him an outrage on the progress of the craft."[1]

The great success of the *Daily Mail* and Harmsworth's other publications outraged the high Liberal Establishment of the day. Later, the Liberal historian R. C. K. Ensor wrote of Harmsworth in his classic *England 1870–1914*: "His papers bore the stamp of their uneducated founders. . . . But the public which liked them was extremely wide and by no means all poor. The business class, which had become so important in England, comprised enormous numbers of men who had not had even a secondary education. Outside the matters in which they made their money they had the minds of children. Existing newspapers ignored their naïve tastes, while assuming an amount of critical intelligence which they simply did not possess. . . ."[2]

Ensor, in his account, took care to include Lord Salisbury's famous gibe that the *Daily Mail* was "written by office-boys for office-boys". But this was at best a misleading comment. The highest authorities in the Conservative party were immediately aware of the power that Harmsworth now held in his hand. Arthur Balfour, the aloof aristocrat, Salisbury's nephew and heir-apparent to the Tory leadership, made certain he wrote to Harmsworth about the *Daily Mail* a few days after its first appearance. In a letter sent from 10 Downing Street and dated 7 May 1896 Balfour explained to Harmsworth:[3]

---

[1] *History of The Times* (London, 1951), vol. III, p. 577.
[2] R. C. K. Ensor, *England 1870–1914* (London, 1949), p. 313.
[3] B.M. Add. MSS (Northcliffe Papers) Arthur Balfour to Mr Harmsworth, 7 May 1896.

Though it is impossible for me, for obvious reasons, to appear among the list of those who publish congratulatory comments in the columns of the "Daily Mail", perhaps you will allow me privately to express my high appreciation of your new undertaking. That, if it succeeds, it will greatly conduce to the wide dissemination of sound political principles, I feel assured; and I cannot doubt it will succeed, knowing the skill, the energy, the resource, with which it is conducted.

You have taken the lead in newspaper enterprise, and both you and the Party are to be heartily congratulated.

This cordial association was kept up and maintained. In 1904 Balfour, by then Prime Minister, saw to it that a baronetcy was conferred upon Harmsworth; and in December 1905 Sir Alfred was raised to the peerage as Baron Northcliffe of the Isle of Thanet in the County of Kent on Balfour's recommendation. Although Balfour, in his patrician way, often claimed that he never bothered to read newspapers he was especially vigilant with respect to the Press and did everything he could to secure newspaper support for the Conservative party.

Later, in 1909, as we shall see, Lord Northcliffe invited Balfour to visit Pau in France so that he could personally observe the work of Wilbur and Orville Wright, who were flying in public there. Northcliffe's motive, at that time, was to enlist Balfour's powerful support in pressing R. B. Haldane, the Secretary of State for War, to show more interest in the military possibilities of flying machines.

When the success of the *Daily Mail* was assured Alfred Harmsworth and his brothers became men of tremendous wealth. By the turn of the century Harmsworth's personal income amounted to almost £150,000 per year while his net capital worth was estimated at £900,000. Despite this phenomenal affluence he continued to work hard in each of his businesses. He wrote one of the earliest books on motoring, *Motors and Motor-driving*, published by the Badminton Library in 1902. His newspapers, for some time, had emphasized a "coming revolution on the roads". He argued that Britain's archaic laws, which severely limited the use of motor vehicles, were absurd and out-of-date because they denied all incentive to British engineers and inventors while they allowed the French and Germans to take the lead in developing internal combustion engines.

Although his restless energy and his great ambitions were in no sense diminished, Harmsworth began to lose his youthful elegance and slimness and he became a chronic worrier about his health. It has been well said that he developed into a Titan among men, or at least among newspaper men.

By 1903, when his ample fortune was secured, Harmsworth began to crave for political power, but found that his several newspapers and all the publications of his Amalgamated Press could not secure it for him. When these organs of his popular Press failed him he decided to purchase *The Observer*, a venerable and respected Sunday newspaper that could attract the attention of that small but powerful public which counted for so much in Edwardian England.

It was his proud boast that his *Daily Mail* was the greatest "whispering gallery" in the nation. "After all", he once explained, "if a newspaper that goes every day into one household in every six in this country cannot move the people, nothing can".[1] Despite this awareness of his power, hard experience revealed to him that the *Daily Mail* lacked certain of the attributes that were necessary to affect the mind of the public in the way that he now desired.

When he secured control of *The Observer* in May 1905 he at once offered the editorship of the paper to J. L. Garvin, the man he looked upon as "the greatest journalist in England". Garvin, an expert political journalist and an outstanding moulder of public opinion, was at that time editor of *Outlook*, a weekly publication, and for that reason he declined Harmsworth's generous offer.

Harmsworth turned next to Leo Amery and invited him to become editor of *The Observer*. Amery was a brilliant young writer who worked for *The Times*. When G. E. Buckle, editor of *The Times*, mentioned his hope that Amery might one day succeed to his own highly coveted place, the young man told Harmsworth he would not accept his proposal.

In this way Harmsworth was twice disappointed in his efforts to acquire for *The Observer* men of a calibre unlike that of the able heads of departments who controlled his other publications. Nevertheless still desiring the kind of political power which had escaped him thus far, he decided he would have to bide his time. His confidence in his own great abilities, and in his splendid future, remained undiminished.

Lord Northcliffe had not reached these heights without making bitter enemies. He took pleasure in hectoring and badgering his employees without mercy. The Liberals despised his political outlook. He was once dismissed by one of them as "a footpad of politics and an enemy of the human race". Moreover, he was unlike the other members of the Establishment of his day. His power and his influence were resented because he was different. He had made his own way, without the benefits of family connection or those of class. The traditional rulers of Britain were ruthless enough in conducting their affairs. Northcliffe had to be harder, tougher, and more obviously brutal, or else he would be pulled down by those who looked upon him as an upstart and an outsider. He had beaten his way to an Olympian position by exploiting novel methods

---

[1] B.M. Add. MSS (Northcliffe Papers) Northcliffe to T. Gibson Bowles, 14 December 1911.

and new techniques. He was not ready to abandon them in the hour of his ambition.

This was the formidable figure who was so aroused by Santos-Dumont's aeroplane flight at Bagatelle. He now determined to launch a massive campaign in the *Daily Mail* that would make clear to his fellow countrymen the high significance of what had occurred on that October day in the field near Paris.

This campaign, and those which followed it, produced tremendous results. An unsigned and undated document, preserved in the House of Lords Record Office, and written during the First World War, suggests something of Lord Northcliffe's contribution and achievement:[1]

> . . . We are in normal times a slow thinking people and Lord Northcliffe's meteoric swoops and pounces on the decrepit working of the old party machines left the nation interested but puzzled. Here and there, however, there emerged the outline of some pregnant achievement. The foundations of British aviation were laid on Northcliffe's indomitable perseverance in the face of obstruction, indifference, and ridicule.
>
> He almost alone believed in the conquest of the air, turned the power of his press and his purse over to the men who would invent and risk their lives on the experiment, when everyone else looked askance at the future of the aeroplane.
>
> Imagination had taken him beyond his contemporaries and made him the God-father of the Royal Flying Corps. As we follow the swift flight of our aeroplanes over the German lines . . . let us not forget the man who saved our air-service from limping hopelessly behind that of our French Allies or our German enemies.

II

Lord Northcliffe was a man of extraordinary vision and enthusiasm. He possessed the kind of imagination that was usually lacking in the high military leaders who occupied the most important places in the War Office or in the Admiralty. Moreover, as an independent advocate he did not bear any responsibility for spending significant sums of public money to secure or develop untried and relatively unknown mechanical devices for the service of the State. He was more free than the soldiers in the War Office who had shown themselves hesitant or reluctant to purchase the Wright aeroplane for the British Government. Immense responsibilities, it has been said, tend to breed conservative ideas.

[1] HLRO, Beaverbrook Papers, C/261, "Lord Northcliffe", undated and unsigned.

In April 1906 Northcliffe read, in his *Daily Mail*, an account about the wife of a London patent attorney, Mrs Griffith Brewer. She was the "first lady to cross the Channel in a balloon". At once he summoned a young journalist named Harry Harper to his headquarters at Carmelite House in London, where he told him: "Make no mistake, the future lies in the air, and that's why I sent for you." He decided to make Harper the "first Air Correspondent".[1]

He wanted a journalist who would do nothing "but watch and describe the efforts of the pioneers of the air . . ." At first, Harper's assignments dealt wholly with ballooning, in those days a popular sport among the wealthy.

Alberto Santos-Dumont's flights in the autumn of 1906 changed the nature of his calling, forever. The *Daily Mail* of 25 October published a brief account of Santos-Dumont's "Triumph" of two days before. But this was only a beginning. When Northcliffe returned to London from Paris he ordered Harry Harper to visit France in order to interview Santos and to find out more about him and his work. This was a preliminary move in a campaign Northcliffe had decided to launch in the *Daily Mail*, a campaign "to make the nation air-minded".

Lord Northcliffe was convinced that Britain was falling behind other countries in aeronautical research. His nimble intelligence grasped the fact that if this trend was not altered the nation would be exposed to grave, if not immediate, danger.

On 12 November 1906 Santos-Dumont flew again at Bagatelle. After a few disappointing hops his machine, on its fourth trial, covered a distance of 722 feet through the air. On the next day the *Daily Mail* published a brief factual account of these developments. Northcliffe was outraged. He immediately made one of those telephone calls which were a regular and continuing source of terror to his employees. He told his editor that the news was not that "Santos-Dumont flies 722 feet", but, "England is no longer an island . . . It means the aerial chariots of a foe descending on British soil if war comes".[2]

As a result of Northcliffe's telephone call a leading article in the *Daily Mail* of 14 November declared: ". . . M. Santos Dumont has solved one of the great problems which have for more than a century baffled human intelligence . . . he has made of the aeroplane a practical machine".

On the next day the *Daily Mail* produced an even more startling

[1] For these quotations and those in the following paragraphs, see Graham Wallas, *Flying Witness. Harry Harper and the Golden Age of Aviation* (London, 1958), pp. 23ff., hereafter cited as Wallas, *Flying Witness*.

[2] Wallas, *Flying Witness*, p. 52 and Reginald Pound and Geoffrey Harmsworth, *Northcliffe* (London, 1959), p. 301.

conclusion. Its first leading article stated of the aeroplane: ". . . New difficulties of every kind will arise, not the least serious being the military problem caused by the virtual annihilation of frontiers and the acquisition of the power to pass readily through the air above the sea. The isolation of the United Kingdom may disappear . . . They are not mere dreamers who hold that the time is at hand when air power will be an even more important thing than sea power."

III

By 16 November the *Daily Mail* campaign was moving forward with the speed Lord Northcliffe always required in such matters. On that day the paper was able to print an account of Harry Harper's interview with Santos-Dumont. The young inventor claimed that within a year he would be able to fly for a distance of one hundred miles.

He was then asked when he would be prepared to fly across the English Channel. He replied with a challenge: "To a great extent," Santos declared, "it is a matter of inducement, for, as I told you, the expense of these experiments is very heavy. You English are practical, but you don't encourage inventors or beginners. You wait to reap the fruit of other people's brains. Now, as you know, the *Matin* is offering a prize of £10,000 for an aerial race from Paris to London in 1908. Let the English show their appreciation of the efforts now being made by offering a like sum and advancing the date to 1907, and you will see . . . a serious attempt to cross the Channel with aeroplanes and airships will be made even before 1908."

Here was an opportunity to create a sensation. Northcliffe, a master in the art of attracting attention to his projects, at once seized upon it. The first leading article in the *Daily Mail* for 17 November, entitled "Our Offer to Aeronauts", explained that aeronautical research was very expensive and extremely dangerous; but that it was also "vital for national reasons". In such circumstances the *Daily Mail* was "prepared to offer the sum of £10,000 to the first aeronaut who accomplishes with success a journey by aeroplane from London to Manchester".

This gigantic sum was only the first of a number of awards, all on a princely scale, that Northcliffe offered to aviators. At once his enemies attacked the proposal as another of those "stunts" he regularly employed to boost the circulation of his newspapers. The *Star* and *Punch* ridiculed the idea and dismissed it as a mere publisher's trick. It is certain that Lord Northcliffe would resort to almost any device in order to sell more newspapers; but it is also clear that in this instance he was moved by patriotic motives and by a genuine desire to encourage and to stimulate the further development of aeronautical science.

The leading article in the *Daily Mail* of 17 November took care to explain the vital "national reasons" involved: "We have already adverted to the stupendous changes which will be worked should aviation, or flight through the air, become general. The disappearance of British insularity would be one of those changes, and not the least important from the political standpoint . . . we shall have time to adapt ourselves to the transformation, but it is fast coming upon us . . ." This analysis and prediction became a regular theme of Northcliffe's campaigns.

In the days that followed the *Daily Mail* was able to announce, with pride, that its offer had attracted favourable notice in Britain, Germany, Italy, France, Switzerland and Denmark. When news of the prize was published in New York Augustus M. Herring[1] spoke to the *Daily Mail* correspondent there and told him he believed the Wright brothers could win the prize with the machine they already possessed. Herring also said that if the Wrights did not try for the award he would do so, in the following spring. He claimed that he had flown a power-driven machine in October 1898; and he boasted that he had solved the problem of equilibrium, a problem, he said, that Santos-Dumont did not even comprehend.

Northcliffe was delighted by the interest he had aroused. Lord Montagu of Beaulieu, a motoring enthusiast, added £1,000 of his own to the sum the *Daily Mail* had offered; and *The Car* promised to present the winning aviator with a trophy worth £525.

On 24 November the *Daily Mail* published an interview with the "well-known aeronautical expert", Patrick Y. Alexander. He told the paper's representative that a British competitor was certain to win the prize. "Great Britain and the British Empire", he said, "stand easily in the van of progress. We know more about the science of aeronautics than any other country in the world . . . the first great aerial battleship will be built by a citizen of the British Empire . . . Britain's aerial fleet will rule the air as her ironclads have ruled the seas". The *Daily Mail* also printed a rumour that Alexander was preparing to leave England for the United States in order to visit his friends, "the mysterious Wright brothers".

As time passed the *Daily Mail* concentrated more and more of its attention upon the work of Wilbur and Orville Wright. On 29 November the paper printed long accounts from the *New York Herald*, which had begun an investigation of the Wrights and their achievements. Northcliffe, however, was not a man who relied on second-hand reports. When he wanted information he usually received it or the lives of his subordinates were made unbearable. At last, on 10 December 1906, the *Daily Mail*

---

[1] The reader will recall that Herring was an unscrupulous rival of the Wright brothers. He will appear again in our account.

published an interview with Orville Wright which had been secured by the paper's New York correspondent.

The account of the interview began by stating that the *Daily Mail*'s New York correspondent had received information that the Wright flying machine was about to be purchased by the American Government. By the terms of this arrangement, the correspondent explained, the American authorities would acquire not only the Wrights' present inventions but also "all the future achievements of the gifted brothers". These were to become "the absolute and exclusive property of the nation". A "huge lump sum" was to be paid to the Wrights to compensate them "for all they might hope to gain . . ."; and they were also to be provided with "permanent Government positions similar to those of British naval constructors".

The correspondent reported that President Roosevelt was keenly interested in the Wright aeroplane, and that he was determined to secure it for the United States. His account went on to say that he had met Orville Wright in New York and had succeeded in obtaining an interview with him: "There is no sign of the bragging air . . . about Orville Wright that one looks for . . . in a man boasting without achievement. What impressed me most was that he spoke rather with affection for his flying machine than pride in his own achievement. His words and manner would have convinced me that the machine had really accomplished all that he claimed for it even if from other sources one had not already been convinced of what was accomplished . . ."

Orville did not confirm, in this interview, that the Wrights were prepared to sell their aeroplane to the United States. Instead he explained that the brothers had decided, after months of reflection, that their best course would be to sell it to a "great Government".

When the *Daily Mail* correspondent suggested that the Wrights could reap an "immense fortune" from the commercial exploitation of their invention, Orville provided him with a candid reply. The Wrights were afraid lest their secrets might be stolen from them if they tried to sell their machine in the open market. On the other hand, if they sold it to a government they would secure the fame and fortune they desired without the risks involved in a commercial transaction: ". . . we do not despise money", Orville said, "but there is something else. We shall have sufficient money to go on with. Nor do we despise the fame of being the first men to fly. We would greatly like the fame of winning the 'Daily Mail's' magnificient prize, but it would interfere with all our plans. We shall get fame, too, in the way we propose."

They turned next to technical details. It will be recalled that Colonel Capper and Lieutenant Dunne believed that their proposed aeroplane would be of greater military value than the Wright machine because they could train pilots to fly it in a very short period of time. In their view no one could learn to fly the Wright aeroplane without a great deal of practice. The authorities in the British War Office accepted this technical analysis and calculated that the Dunne machine would enable them to create a military air force more quickly than any of the other powers. Nevertheless when Orville was asked: "Is it difficult to guide the machine?" he replied in terms that should have alerted the British authorities to the true nature of the situation. He said: "No more difficult than guiding a bicycle. I could teach any young man within three days."

No one in the British War Office paid any attention to this revelation. Capper and Dunne were allowed to continue with their own secret preparations. When it published this conversation between its New York correspondent and Orville Wright the *Daily Mail* declared: "The scientific importance of this interview is very great indeed." We may conclude that its importance was even greater than the *Daily Mail* conceived.

IV

Wilbur and Orville Wright were in New York for a good reason, in December 1906. Their visit, at that time, was the first development in a significant and remarkable episode in the history of early British military aeronautics. Nevertheless, the episode has been misunderstood or entirely ignored by some of the most capable aeronautical historians. The Wrights, as a result of this visit to New York, now became involved in an amazing and almost unbelievable series of negotiations that was designed to sell their aeroplane to almost every major power on the earth.

At the end of 1906 the Wright brothers, having failed to sell their invention in any country, attracted the notice of Charles Ranlett Flint, an immensely wealthy New York business man, banker, and dealer in armaments. In December they travelled to New York in order to begin negotiations with several of Flint's colleagues and associates. Eventually, Flint and his company agreed to act as their business representatives for the sale of the aeroplane.

In the early months of 1907, in close collaboration with Flint and his company, the Wrights made the most strenuous efforts to sell their machine and all its secrets. Urgent representations were made, at that time, to R. B. Haldane, the Secretary of State for War, and to Lord Tweedmouth, First Lord of the Admiralty. The offers were not accepted by these high British authorities but the Wright brothers cannot be blamed for their decision.

Nevertheless, when Percy Walker analysed their situation after the War Office had refused to purchase their aeroplane for the second time, at the end of 1906, he declared:[1]

[1] Walker, *Early Aviation at Farnborough*, vol. II, pp. 61–2.

After being told for the second time that the British War Office could not accept their proposals, and that the great cost was now the main obstacle, the Wright Brothers did nothing by way of bargaining . . . They did not, in fact, approach the British War Office again until nearly two years later – in April 1908.

It was not only Britain that had difficulties in reaching agreement. Not until the spring of 1908, after protracted negotiations, were contracts at last reached with the United States and France, while Germany was still in a state of uncertainty . . . Regarded collectively . . . the universality of unsuccessful negotiation does bear out the belief that subconsciously the Wright Brothers did not want to sell their aeroplane; and especially does this appear to have been so in the course of the negotiations with Britain.

No analysis could be more invalid than this one. Charles R. Flint, the go-between in the negotiations of 1907, offered an entirely different conclusion. In his memoirs he wrote: "After the United States Government failed to take advantage of the Wright discovery, they asked me to offer their aeroplane to England . . . the Wrights . . . without any reservations whatsoever, gave England the opportunity to be the first to establish a navy of the air."[1]

Flint's statement, however, was not entirely accurate. In 1907 he and the Wright brothers sought to sell the aeroplane to several governments. In their view, the British were only one of a number of potential customers.

V

The Wrights became acquainted with Flint at the end of 1906. One of his associates, a New York business man named Ulysses S. Eddy, visited them in their home in Dayton in November. Eddy had read several articles about their work in the newspaper Press. He believed that Flint's company, an organization constantly seeking new inventions that could be exploited for military purposes, might be interested in the Wright aeroplane. Flint, as a result of Eddy's initiative, now developed an "intense interest" in the Wrights and in their work.

It was arranged, after several discussions, that the Wrights should travel to New York in order to negotiate an arrangement with Flint's colleagues. Wilbur and Orville were genuinely excited by the tremendous possibilities that now at last lay before them. Charles R. Flint was one of the world's leading arms dealers. He dealt on a personal basis with high

---

[1] Charles R. Flint, *Memories of an Active Life* (New York, 1923), p. 246, hereafter cited as Flint, *Memories*.

officials in almost every country. In those places where his own influence
did not reach, his associates, American and foreign, were employed as
agents or emissaries in order to contact important government authorities. Flint was connected with the Rothschilds and with the great banking
firm of J. P. Morgan. He was a personal friend of President Theodore
Roosevelt and he saw to it, as a matter of good business practice, that he
met United States senators and congressmen as often as was convenient.
He sold guns, warships, and submarines to anyone who could pay for
them. On one occasion he purchased, equipped, and manned an entire
fleet for a South American country. Wilbur Wright, spartan and fasti-
dious, was not attracted by such a voracious money-maker; once he
referred to Flint and his colleagues as "mere hustlers". Nevertheless,
Charles Flint "hustled" only at the highest levels.

Before the Wrights could travel to New York they received a letter
from Patrick Y. Alexander who informed them that he would visit
Dayton early in December. The rumour published earlier in the *Daily
Mail* thus turned out to be accurate.

On 5 December 1906 Alexander, in Bishop Milton Wright's phrase,
"dined and supped with us, and at 10.00 p.m. he and Wilbur and Orville
started to New York . . ." Later, Wilbur Wright told Chanute of Alexander: ". . . he told us that the last *Aérophile* contained a full account of our
French negotiations with the names of the commissioners . . . Also that
he had talked with one of them . . . We suspected that he was trying to
draw us out and were not very responsive. It is very strange that he should
have made such statements to us."[1]

As a result of their preliminary negotiations in New York Flint and
Company offered the Wright brothers the sum of five hundred thousand
dollars for their rights outside the United States. This gigantic payment
was to be made in cash upon the delivery of one machine, after a
demonstration flight of fifty kilometers. Wilbur and Orville, suspicious
and cautious, now applied to Octave Chanute for his advice. They
believed that the price and the terms were satisfactory but they were less
certain about the character of the men they had dealt with in New York.
Upon their return to Dayton, they asked Chanute to tell them if Flint and
Company were "safe people to deal with under proper precautions?"[2]

Flint was equally careful in this first phase of the bargaining. Unknown
to the Wrights, he, too, approached Chanute for intelligence about them.
Chanute at once informed the brothers of these enquiries and then, on 26
December, wrote to Flint about Wilbur and Orville:[3]

[1] McFarland, *Papers of Wilbur and Orville Wright*, p. 746.
[2] *Ibid.*, p. 743.
[3] Octave Chanute Papers, Chanute to Flint, 26 December 1906.

I may say . . . . that I have followed their work since 1900, have seen all their machines and witnessed a short flight of one quarter mile in 1904 with their power machine. The long flights of 1905 I did not see being then in the East, but had abundant information of their length (about 24 miles) from eyewitnesses in Dayton.

From somewhat intimate acquaintance I can say that in addition to their great mechanical abilities I have ever found the Wright Brothers trustworthy. They tell the exact truth and are conscientious, so that I credit fully any statement which they make.

Chanute explained to the Wrights that Charles Flint was a very rich merchant who had extensive dealings with South American republics and with European war departments. He further told them that the terms and the price Flint offered were much better than he had thought possible. However, a moral question was involved in the transaction. Chanute was afraid that the invention might pass into the hands of a single government. In particular, he feared that Tsarist Russia, the great despotism of that era, might secure the first practical aeroplane in history. In that case, Chanute predicted, there might be a new Russian war against Japan and much bloodshed.

Wilbur assured Chanute that if Flint obtained the foreign rights in the aeroplane the brothers would see to it, by means of their reservations, that the Russians would not gain exclusive control of the invention. Chanute was entirely correct in his prediction. Flint, who had previously sold submarines to the Russian Government, was thinking of a special arrangement with the Tsar but the Wright brothers objected to this course, and he was forced to abandon it.

By the end of January 1907 new arrangements were adduced by Flint and Company. Some of Flint's European associates had objected to the original proposition, the outright purchase of the foreign rights in the aeroplane for the sum of five hundred thousand dollars. Instead, it was suggested that the Flint Company should act as the Wrights' business representatives, on a commission basis, in all countries except the United States. While negotiations for such foreign sales were being carried out the Wrights would be allowed to draw upon the Flint firm for their expenses, up to the sum of ten thousand dollars. These terms were eventually agreed upon.

It was now Charles Flint's task to sell the aeroplane in all countries except the United States. This was the type of challenge in which he took delight. He already possessed, in his New York offices, an organization that had been built up, trained, and equipped to carry out exactly this kind of enterprise. He produced a grandiose plan. Later he boasted: "We offered the Wright aeroplane to every minister of war in the world . . ."[1]

---

[1] Flint, *Memories*, p. 249.

This statement only slightly exaggerated the course upon which he now embarked. He proposed that he would personally conduct negotiations with the Russian Government. In the case of Germany and Austria he would employ the services of Isidor Loewe of the Mauser rifle and machine-tool company. In England he expected to cooperate with a large gun company. There were to be approaches to Flint's associates in France and in Italy.

Flint was distinguished by a certain largeness of outlook. It had contributed to his phenomenal success as a merchant. He would not sell the aeroplane in single units. Instead, he planned to offer each of the governments an entire air force, at one stroke. He proposed to offer fifty machines to each minister of war. If they hesitated to commit themselves to this number he would offer twenty machines at a time. If this proved too bold a proposition he was ready to sell ten machines to each of his clients. This daring attitude impressed the Wright brothers. They approved of the new concept.

When Flint wrote in his memoirs that the Wrights ". . . without any reservations whatsoever, gave England the opportunity to be the first to establish a navy of the air" his statement was not correct. As soon as he became the sole agent for the Wright brothers in all countries except the United States, he decided to offer the aeroplane to the governments of Germany, England, Belgium, and Russia. In the earliest stages of his agency he also toyed with the idea of applying to some business men in France who might be interested in the Wright invention. Shortly after, he also approached representatives of Japan and of China and tried to sell the aeroplane to them.

Despite what has been written to the contrary, the Wright brothers accepted this plan of action. By the terms of their arrangement with Flint they, alone, would deal with the Government of the United States. With respect to all the other nations, however, they concurred in the course he proposed. On 11 February, after several of his arrangements in various countries had been put in train, one of Flint's staff explained his tactics to Wilbur and Orville. He wrote with respect to the Russians: ". . . we thought it wise to give them the same opportunity of purchasing as we give to England and Germany. We have also taken the same view in regard to the King of Belgium and think we deal fairly by all parties when we adopt the principle of '*First come first served*.' & it's good business . . ."[1]

Nevertheless, Flint made his most positive advances in Germany and in England. He was not pleased by the first German response to his proposals. He hoped the British would react more favourably. It was in this way that England secured the opportunity to "be the first to establish a navy of the air".

[1] Wright Brothers' Papers, Charles R. Flint to Messrs. Wright Brothers, 11 February 1907.

VI

On 5 February 1907 Wilbur Wright travelled to New York for a series of final conferences with Flint and his colleagues. A few days later he was able to report to Orville that the German Government, through the offices of Isidor Loewe, had been offered the opportunity to purchase fifty machines. Until the Germans replied, Wilbur explained, no further advances would be made to the Russians.[1]

However, Charles Flint, bursting with energy, had already made certain arrangements in Great Britain which were designed to secure a sale of aeroplanes there. Originally he had planned to employ the services of a large English gun company. Later he changed his mind; he decided to write to a friend in London, Lady Jane Taylor, the elderly widow of a distinguished British general, Sir Richard Taylor, and a person of high aristocratic connection in her own right.

There were good reasons for Flint's success as an arms salesman. He knew how to get things done. He understood the nature of society in Edwardian England. On 11 February 1907 one of his staff explained his change of course to the Wright brothers:[2]

> After thinking over our connections in England we finally decided that we would be likely to get quicker results and higher influence by addressing our Senior's friend Lady Jane Taylor. Lady Jane Taylor, although a woman of remarkable intelligence, will undoubtedly avail, as may be desirable, of the influence of the different members of her family. Her brother, Sir John Hay, is a full Admiral and is very active in affairs. Her eldest brother, the Marquis of Tweeddale, is a man of great influence, and her family includes the Duke of Wellington, Sir Robert Peel and the Earl of Dalhousie.

On 27 January Flint had written to Lady Jane Taylor to invite her to become his agent for the sale of Wright aeroplanes to the British Government. Her particular target was to be R. B. Haldane, the Secretary of State for War in Sir Henry Campbell-Bannerman's Liberal ministry. If she succeeded in the task Flint's firm would reward her with a commission.

In order to render their communications secure Flint sent Lady Jane his company's commercial code. She was instructed to employ it to send and receive coded cablegrams which would pass between her home in London and Flint's offices in New York during the course of the negotiations.

[1] McFarland, *Papers of Wilbur and Orville Wright*, pp. 751–2.
[2] Wright Brothers' Papers, Charles R. Flint to Messrs. Wright Brothers, 11 February 1907. All further letters from Flint and his staff to the Wrights reproduced in this work are drawn from this source.

Flint was particularly proud of his firm's secret code. In his office there were special printed forms that were employed in connection with it. A clerk was required to initial the form whenever he coded or uncoded a cabled message. A second clerk initialled the form to certify that he had checked and verified his colleague's work. The cabled messages were reproduced on the form in two columns. The left hand column consisted of meaningless groups of letters in code. The right hand column corresponded to these coded groups and contained the decoded message.

Flint waited for nearly a fortnight to make certain that his letter and the code arrived safely in London. Then he produced an explosion of activity. At four a.m. on the morning of Sunday 10 February he sent the first of his coded cablegrams to Lady Jane Taylor. The decoded message read as follows:[1]

TO LADY JANE TAYLOR . . . REFERRING TO––LETTER OF JANUARY 27th WE . . . ARE APPOINTED SOLE AGENTS [FOR] WRIGHTS MAKE FIRM OFFER OF 50 AEROPLANES 2,000 POUNDS STERLING EACH COLONEL CAPPER BADEN POWELL HAVE SEEN.   FLINTCO.

A few hours later, at one p.m. on 10 February, Lady Jane's coded reply was received in Flint's office. The British negotiations had begun. Lady Jane's message declared:

RANFLINT N.Y. THANKS ACCEPT TERMS HOPE TO SEE HALDANE TUESDAY AFTERNOON.   JANE TAYLOR.

VII

On the same day that she despatched her cablegram Lady Jane wrote a letter to Flint to explain her plans in greater detail. "Your cable", she said, "made quite a flutter in the dovecote . . . I have never used such a code before so comprehensive and so bulky . . . Then I said I hoped to see Haldane on Tuesday 12th. Perhaps this being the day before opening of Parliament and tomorrow the opening day, he will not have time, and so our meeting will be later. Rest assured, that I will not delay, and shall work hard to promote your sale of Aeroplanes . . ." Lady Jane further

---

[1] Wright Brothers' Papers, FLINTCO to LADY JANE TAYLOR, 10 February 1907, 4 a.m. All cablegrams reproduced in this work between Flint and his agents or associates are drawn from this source.

explained that she had already written to Haldane asking for an interview with him.[1]

Meanwhile the negotiations with Russia were reopened. Flint's associate in St Petersburg was a brash and ambitious American salesman named Hart O. Berg. His headquarters were in Paris but he plied his trade in several European countries. He sold electric automobiles, submarines, and anything else that could bring him a good profit. On 10 February Flint sent him a coded cablegram to make the situation clear. Flint, according to the cablegram, had planned to treat with a Russian admiral of his acquaintance but the Wright brothers would not consent to the deal he proposed for the Russians. Instead, they offered to sell them fifty aeroplanes at a cost of ten thousand dollars each. Berg was instructed to make such a proposal to the Russian authorities. He was also warned to do nothing in England because Flint's firm was already in communication with the British Minister of War.[2]

On the morning of 11 February Flint received Isidor Loewe's[3] cabled reply to his offer. Loewe declared that it would be impossible for him to purchase fifty aeroplanes. Instead, he proposed that he should buy one machine for the sum of ten thousand dollars. If this aeroplane proved to be satisfactory he desired an option that would enable him to acquire forty nine more, at the same price. Flint, of course, was not prepared to accept such an arrangement. He told the Wright brothers: "You will note that the 'Walk into my parlor says the spider to the fly' proposition of Germany we respectfully decline . . ."[4]

Flint was too brilliant a dealer to be disappointed by Loewe's proposal. He realized at once that he could make good use of it in his dealings with the British. By 1907 relations between Britain and Germany were becoming strained. Many informed people in England were seriously worried about the growing menace of Imperial Germany and some of them feared that the Liberal Government of the day, relying for political support upon Radicals and pacifists, and concerned with its own programme of domestic social reform, was not prepared to respond adequately

[1] Wright Brothers' Papers, Copy, Jane Taylor to Flint, 10 February 1907. All the correspondence between Flint and Lady Jane Taylor reproduced in this work is drawn from this source. Flint took good care to send all the appropriate letters and cablegrams to the Wright brothers throughout the course of the negotiations. When the first batch was sent Flint wrote to the Wrights, on 11 February 1907: "Some of this correspondence . . . is of a very personal character, and while we know that all will be treated as confidential, we beg that you will treat this with special reserve."

[2] See Wright Brothers' Papers, FLINTCO to HARTOBERG, 10 February 1907, for these details.

[3] The reader will recall that Loewe was Flint's associate in Berlin.

[4] Loewe's proposal is contained in a coded cablegram dated 11 February 1907. A copy is preserved in the Wright Brothers' Papers.

to the German challenge. Flint hoped to excite British enthusiasm for a deal by suggesting to them that the Germans might be the first to acquire a Wright aeroplane.

Three hours after Isidor Loewe's message arrived in his office Flint sent this information to Lady Jane Taylor by cablegram. In his cablegram he also suggested that her brother, Sir John Hay, a retired admiral, should approach the British Admiralty about the aeroplane. His cable further informed her that the Wright aeroplane could take off from and return to a war vessel's deck. His coded message, composed with care and ingenuity, stated:

> THIS IS CONFIDENTIAL AND FOR YOUR PERSONAL GUIDANCE ONLY WRIGHTS HAVE RECEIVED THIS MORNING FIRM OFFER OF GERMANY THEY WILL DE-LAY SO THERE WILL BE AN OPPORTUNITY . . . FOR HALDANE   SIR JOHN MIGHT SEE NAVY DEPARTMENT GREAT BRITAIN   CAN START AND RETURN TO WAR VESSEL(S) DECK.

On the same day that this cable was despatched Flint's staff wrote a letter to Lady Jane so that they could present her with a fuller account than a cablegram allowed. The letter, dated 11 February, explained:

> In our cable of even date . . . you will note that we suggest it may be desirable for you also to see the Minister of Marine and that the Wright Power Propelled Aeroplane can start from the deck of a vessel and return thereto. We only suggest this idea in the event of your not making satisfactory progress with the Minister of War.
> . . . Having received information that the British Admiralty are much interested in the subject of aeronautics we thought it well to mention this feature to you. If in the event of your not succeeding with the Minister of War and in the event of your having taken up the subject, or desiring to take it up with the Minister of Marine, you will send us a cable (&) we will send you specific information in regard to the use of these machines as scouting adjuncts to vessels of war.

On the same 11 February Flint's staff sent two further letters to Lady Jane Taylor. In one of these they informed her that if she succeeded in inducing Haldane to accept the Wright brothers' proposal, she would receive two per cent of the amounts paid by the British Government for the aeroplanes. Furthermore, if she rendered other services she would be paid an additional amount, this sum to be decided upon by Charles Flint himself. The second letter of 11 February 1907 set out the exact details of the Wright offer to the British authorities.

Dear Lady Jane: February 11, 1907

We . . . now detail the Messrs. Wright Brothers' proposition to sell to the British Government as follows:

50 Power Propelled Aeroplanes capable of a flight of 30 miles, alighting at the point of departure within one hour after starting, each having a carrying capacity of two men and surplus fuel.

PRICE   £2,000 each, or a total amount of £100,000 payable as follows:

£25,000 (25 per cent.) payable on demonstration of efficiency as herein stated, and immediate delivery of the machine which makes this demonstration.
£60,000 in payments of £15,000 on each delivery of 10 machines.
£15,000 on delivery of the remaining 9 machines.

The demonstrations to be made at some agreed upon point in England. Each machine to have the same demonstrated efficiency as the trial machine, and two English subjects to be taught to operate them before the second payment is made.

Awaiting your further advices, we have the honor to remain

Your obedient servants,

Lady Jane Taylor
16 Eaton Place, LONDON.

Flint's tremendous energies were not exhausted even by this furious pace. On 11 February he wrote yet another letter to a friend in London. His object, in this case, was to employ a tactic he often used in his business dealings. He wanted to make certain that his offer to Haldane did not remain a secret. If Haldane rejected Lady Jane's initiative Flint wanted other people in Britain to know of the Secretary of State's decision. Therefore he wrote to a friend, Colonel Robert Baring, a brother of Lord Revelstoke who was a senior partner in the great banking firm of Baring Brothers. If Colonel Baring knew of Flint's proposals and told his friends about them, Haldane might be affected by the pressure of this select opinion. Flint wrote to Baring in his cynical way:[1]

When you are drinking "high balls" with some of the "high Flyers" at the Army and Navy Club bring up the subject of Aeronautics . . .
I am offering to your Minister of War fifty flyers subject to flying 30 miles returning to the starting point.
. . . I venture to say that if I was Minister of War considering the large weekly expenditures by England for the Army and Navy and the advantages of flyers for scouting and other purposes I would close for the "real thing". . . .

[1] Wright Brothers' Papers, Copy, Flint to Colonel Robert Baring, 11 February 1907.

I hear that Col. Capper and other officers in your service are very progressive and *way up* in Aeronautics but they haven't yet flown; that the greater "powers that be" take more time to ponder deliberate and reflect than the German Emperor and that England is more likely to follow Germany and France than to lead in this important field of enterprise.

I enclose a cutting from the Scientific American and if when you are telling of the Wright flyers some forward youth should offer to bet two to one that they can't fly and return to the starting point say for 30 miles or more take him up to £10,000 for my a/c and I'll cable the cash.

VIII

The initiative in the British negotiations now lay with Lady Jane Taylor. She acted with great speed. By the afternoon of 12 February a cablegram reporting upon her activities arrived in Flint's offices. It declared: "HALDANE HAS BEEN INFORMED CONFIDENTIALLY . . ." Unfortunately, the rest of her message was less clear because there were mistakes in the transmission. It seemed certain, however, that the Secretary of State was not prepared to take any action in the matter unless the plans and specifications of the Wright machine were submitted to him and then examined by Major Baden-Powell and by others. Haldane also required that the Wrights should demonstrate their machine in a public competition.

Flint at once sent a copy of this message to Dayton in order to keep the Wright brothers informed of the progress of the negotiations. He also sent them, on 12 February, a copy of his reply in which he explained to Lady Jane that "We positively will *not* furnish" the detailed plans and specifications that Haldane had requested. He further asked the Wrights to send him information about the *Daily Mail* or Harmsworth prize, as he called it, and information about any other aviation prizes that were being offered in Europe. He suggested to the brothers: "We might try to combine *public* & military trial".

Flint took care to make certain that his messages and instructions could not be interpreted to mean that he proposed to break off the negotiations with the British Government. On the 12th he sent another cabled message to Lady Jane Taylor: "See Minister of War. We are negotiating Germany & England; but we wait until hear further from you."[1] On the

---

[1] 12 February was Lincoln's Birthday, a public holiday in the United States. Flint, who was not in his office on that day, sent a draft of this coded cablegram to the Wrights, for their information. The message is preserved in draft in the Wright Brothers' Papers in the Library of Congress. No copy of the actual cablegram itself is preserved in this collection.

next day Flint instructed Lady Jane to seek out Lord Northcliffe and to ask him to send the particulars of the prizes he offered to Flint's office in New York.

By 15 February Lady Jane Taylor realized that some of her cabled messages to Flint were not composed carefully enough and that they might not convey the information she desired to send, in the clearest terms. Therefore, she wrote him a letter on that day in order to explain exactly what she had accomplished, thus far. When she met Haldane, she reported, he was "most amiable but firmly refused to have anything to do with Wrights or any one else's proposals until their superiority was established over all comers by public trial and competitions after which he said there would probably have to be further military tests before he could countenance the adoption of any particular system". Haldane, at their meeting, had suggested that the Wrights should try to win the *Daily Mail* prize for an aeroplane flight between London and Manchester.

In compliance with Flint's instructions Lady Jane visited Carmelite House in order to see Lord Northcliffe. The great man was away, however, and she was received by George Augustus Sutton, his right hand and closest subordinate. At her request, Sutton sent the details of the *Daily Mail* prize to Flint, on 15 February.[1]

By this time Wilbur and Orville Wright were ready to respond to Haldane's suggestion that they should compete for the Harmsworth prize. They told Flint: "We might consider going for the Harmsworth prize in case government previously guaranteed substantial order for machines to winner, but not otherwise. We have no intention of going for this prize in the near future merely for the sake of the prize. We are willing to enter public competition, or make reasonable trials before military board if Haldane wishes, but only with the agreement that substantial business on satisfactory terms shall follow in case we meet requirements." On the day following, the brothers sent Flint a more detailed proposal. They made clear what they looked upon as substantial business: "Haldane's willingness that we should show England how to fly by competing for the Harmsworth prize is very kind. . . . If he would guarantee us an order for machines amounting to $500,000, conditional upon winning the Harmsworth prize, it might be worthwhile to sacrifice the chances of selling secrets on the continent, and go for it . . . It has always been our policy to take up prizes only after it should be found impossible to deal with governments at any price or on any terms . . ."[2]

Flint reacted to this information at once. On 16 February he despatched a coded cablegram to Lady Jane Taylor:

[1] Wright Brothers' Papers, George Sutton to Messrs. C. Flint Co., Copy, 15 February 1907.

[2] These letters, dated 15 and 16 February 1907 are preserved in the Wright Brothers' Papers.

WILL BUILD FOR HARMSWORTH TRIAL TRIP BY JULY 1st IF GREAT BRITAIN SECRETARY . . . OF WAR AND GREAT BRITAIN SECRETARY OF NAVY (MINISTER OF MARINE) IS (*sic*) WILLING TO PURCHASE 50 AT 4,000 EACH.

Two days later Flint sent the Wright brothers a complete budget of news about the course of his negotiations in Britain, Germany, and France. He revealed that Ulysses S. Eddy would try to sell the aeroplane to Latin American countries; and he suggested it would be of great assistance to him in his task as agent if he could state to his potential customers that he had personally witnessed the aeroplane in flight. He explained that he was planning to visit Europe and he advised the brothers that they should hold themselves in a state of readiness so one of them could sail with him, upon receipt of his telegraphic request.[1]

He made clear the latest developments in the English negotiations. It seemed wise to him to increase the price offered to the British Government because the requirements of the Harmsworth prize were far more rigorous than those of the trials he had first proposed to the authorities in London: "We . . . deemed it desirable to increase the price to the British Government, feeling that an increased price for a machine of increased efficiency would cause them *to take us more seriously*. . . ."

In Germany, he reported, Loewe was making little progress. In order to encourage him, Flint had promised to double his commission as soon as he sold fifty machines. In France, Flint explained, Hart O. Berg had joined the French Aero Club "to widen his sphere of influence . . ." Berg, however, was worried because he was not certain that the Wright brothers had adequately protected themselves with patents. Furthermore, Berg could not see how a government which was not awarded exclusive control of the invention would be justified in paying a very large sum for it: "If any Government was engaged in war", Flint explained, "or anticipated an early engagement, the fact of getting the first machines would be very important for which they would pay well, but no such conditions exist at the present time or are immediately prospective".

Flint concluded his budget by bringing up again the question of a demonstration flight: "If entirely agreeable to you, I feel that it will be desirable for Mr. Ulysses Eddy to accompany me when I meet your appointment to witness a flight as it will facilitate him in his negotiations with Latin American countries and while my secretary, Baron Zglinitzky, has no technical knowledge, the fact of his having been for five years an officer of Emperor William's favorite Artillery Regiment, and that he will

[1] See Wright Brothers' Papers, Flint to Messrs. Wright Brothers, 18 February 1907 for the details in this and the following paragraphs.

either precede or accompany me to Europe, makes it also desirable for him to be present."

This planning and these speculations were interrupted on 19 February when another cablegram arrived from Lady Jane Taylor:

GREAT BRITAIN SECY. NAVY (MIN. OF MARINE) APPOINTS INTERVIEW NEXT SATURDAY.

Lady Jane had persuaded Lord Tweedmouth, the First Lord of the Admiralty, to see her so that they could discuss Flint's proposal that the British Government should purchase Wright aeroplanes. Tweedmouth had written to her:[1]

Feb. 19, 1907

Dear Lady Jane:–
  Tomorrow in the morning we have a cabinet and in the afternoon I go down to Devonport where I have a naval function on Thursday, but if you could come to my office here on Saturday 12 I should be very glad to see you and hear about the aeroplane.

Truly Yours,
Tweedmouth

IX

Edward Marjoribanks, second Baron Tweedmouth, was a Liberal politician of considerable experience but his contemporaries did not look upon him as a capable First Lord of the Admiralty. It was known that he was determined to maintain Britain's naval superiority but he possessed little technical knowledge, had few strong opinions of his own, and rarely interfered with his technical advisers, the Sea Lords. In the latter part of his life Lord Tweedmouth experienced serious and embarrassing financial problems and suffered also from a brain ailment which resulted in his death, in 1909. Nevertheless, he was a pleasant and amiable man. When he saw Lady Jane Taylor at the Admiralty, on Saturday, 23 February 1907, he showed her every courtesy.

Lady Jane realized, by this stage of the bargaining, that her coded cablegrams had to be supplemented by fairly lengthy letters if Charles Flint, directing matters thousands of miles from the scene, was to understand every detail of her negotiations. As soon as she returned

[1] Wright Brothers' Papers, Copy, Tweedmouth to Lady Jane Taylor, 19 February 1907.

home from her visit to the Admiralty on 23 February she prepared a long report of the episode and at once sent it to Flint in New York.

In her report Lady Jane explained that her reception at the Admiralty had been "most kind and encouraging". Lord Tweedmouth, she declared, "appeared much interested and examined the printed account of Wright's Aeroplane that you sent me at the first". Early in the interview Lady Jane told the First Lord of the "firm offers" from Germany to purchase the Wright invention.

At this stage Tweedmouth offered some curious opinions of his own about the possibilities of employing aircraft for naval purposes. Lady Jane reported:

> . . . he pointed out that the Admiralty is provided with a direct wireless telegraphy code and apparatus which is by degrees being affixed to all their ships which would entirely supersede the necessity for despatch bearing, by Aeroplane. He suggested, however, that if it were made strong enough and powerful enough to carry several shells your instrument would become most useful, especially on land, for said he, A sea aeroplane would hardly have time to drop the shell on board before the ship had passed from under the aeroplane . . . He was struck by the promised trip starting from a ship's deck and returning to it . . . *I* think that if the Wrights could make their aeroplane a weight-carrier for men or shells, it would greatly influence the War Office in making a decision. Lord Tweedmouth's manner toward the invention was *much* more cordial than Haldane's. . . .

Lady Jane told Flint that the proposed purchase of the aeroplane was to be discussed at a meeting of the Board of Admiralty. Sir John Fisher, the dynamic and influential First Sea Lord, was to attend this meeting. Haldane, she declared, was determined to reduce expenditures at the War Office but the British Navy was not so hampered in its ability to secure funds for its projects: "I feel sure", she concluded, "that by patience and perseverance something must come out of all these negotiations."

Meanwhile Flint continued to try to sell the aeroplane in other countries. At the end of February 1907 he travelled to Washington D.C., in order to seek out the representatives of several foreign governments. He spoke first to Commander Shigetoshi Takeuchi of the Imperial Japanese Navy. Takeuchi, who had been one of Admiral Togo's officers during the Russo-Japanese War, showed genuine interest in the Wright invention. During this visit to Washington Flint also approached the Chinese minister. This official explained to Flint that he did not possess any authority to negotiate for aeroplanes but he assured him that he could always count on his "friendly offices" in case a Chinese military commission was ever sent to the United States in order to take up the question of acquiring aircraft for the Chinese Government. Flint had also planned to call upon the Military Attaché at the German Embassy but he found that this officer was away from Washington. Flint was not disturbed by this development because he wanted to receive more advice and information from Isidor Loewe before he pressed forward with his German negotiations. While he was in Washington Flint received news from his colleagues in New York that Lady Jane Taylor had informed them that Lord Tweedmouth proposed to bring up the question of purchasing the aeroplane at a meeting of the Board of Admiralty, on 4 March.[1]

Flint's lively intelligence did not permit him to rest. He was determined to sell the Wright aeroplane. When he reflected upon the situation in Great Britain it occurred to him that if he could interest Lord Northcliffe in the negotiations he would secure the services of a powerful ally.

As Flint saw it, Northcliffe, the aeronautical enthusiast, could exert his personal interest in the highest quarters and he could also "use his newspapers to create a progressive public sentiment". Flint was so eager to draw Northcliffe into the affair that he was prepared to pay him for his efforts, in case they succeeded.

On 26 February he prepared a letter to Northcliffe and sent it to Lady Jane Taylor. She was instructed to deliver it to Northcliffe if she agreed that Flint's idea was a valid one. Flint told her: "In case you feel it is desirable that he be compensated in the event of success for his efforts in the Wright interest we will be glad to receive your recommendation by cable or letter, and I would arrange a definite commitment to that end."

Flint was occasionally confused by the styles and titles of his British correspondents. His letter to Lord Northcliffe was addressed to "My dear Sir Alfred"; but there was nothing confused about the proposals he now set out for Northcliffe's attention:[2]

> I . . . write to further the interest of Messrs. Wright Brothers of Dayton, Ohio, who as you know, have invented a successful Power Propelled Aeroplane.
>
> I have a letter from your Mr. Sutton, copy herewith, and I have read the cutting he enclosed from the Daily Mail which seems to be very clear that the person who is first to "get there" by a flight from a point within five miles of your office in London to a point within five miles of your office in Manchester, gets £10,000. It is the kind of proposition that I would expect you to make, being straight and to the point and without the complications, which characterize some of the propositions emanating from the other side of the channel.

[1] For these details see Wright Brothers' Papers, Flint to Messrs. Wright Bros., 25 February 1907.

[2] Wright Brothers' Papers, Flint to Sir Alfred Harmsworth, 26 February 1907.

The Wrights are ready to make a practical demonstration by a long flight such as you propose, but the prize offered by you is not as attractive as some other propositions made them for a *first* demonstration. It has occurred to me that the *winning* of your prize might be made the basis of a proposition for a considerable Government purchase of machines for both military and naval use, to which the Wrights' machine is fully adapted and it seems to me that you would get much additional satisfaction from thus not merely opening the era of aerial navigation but opening it in a manner which will establish it from the date of such demonstration as an entirely practical business operation. It would give your Government the prestige resulting from the first practical application of this revolution in navigation, and I feel sure that with your recognised knowledge and forwardness in these matters you can, if you approve, materially assist Lady Jane Taylor in bringing about a situation where the successful fulfilling of the requirements of your competition shall be the basis for an order from the Ministers of War and Marine in your country.

I am sending this letter to Lady Jane Taylor in order that she may become apprised of its contents. She is duly authorised to act and in case my suggestion interests you she will be able to give you full information and confer with us freely by cable, or will if you prefer, place our cable code at your disposal.

On the day after this letter was despatched startling news arrived from Isidor Loewe in Berlin. His information completely changed the situation. He told Flint that the German Emperor was now interested in acquiring the Wright aeroplane. On 27 February 1907 Loewe sent a coded cablegram to Flint. It declared:

THIS IS CONFIDENTIAL AND FOR YOUR PERSONAL GUIDANCE ONLY. (FULL STOP) I HAVE NO DOUBT (THAT) EMPEROR OF GERMANY WILL FEEL INCLINED (TO) TAKE INTEREST WRIGHT INVENTION AND TO ASSIST TRIAL(S) IF PROPER(LY) APPROACH(ED) I (AM) NOT IN A POSITION TO TAKE STEPS FOR THE PRESENT OWING TO LACK OF COMPLETE DETAILS AND INFORMATION.

X

In London, Lady Jane Taylor continued with her own negotiations. She discovered that "Haldane and Tweedmouth will consult together probably at a future cabinet meeting before they give a firm reply". She reported this information to Flint on 1 March. The two ministers were close personal friends. Haldane, according to his *Autobiography*, "spent every autumn at Guisachan, the Highland home of my great friends, Lord and Lady Tweedmouth".[1] The Secretary of State possessed a more powerful personality than that of his colleague at the Admiralty. There can be no doubt that he used his influence with Tweedmouth to determine the nature of his reply to the Wright brothers' offer.

In her report of 1 March Lady Jane also told Flint that the British authorities had now developed a warm interest in their coded cablegrams. "You will be amused to hear", she said, "that I have been interviewed by order of the Post Office Officials to find out whose code I am using, what the meaning of certain words is, and in fact to give the show away".

An unfortunate official of the Post Office had called on Lady Jane, in her home, in order to press these enquiries. Lady Jane Taylor was outraged by this effrontery. She was a Scots aristocrat who expected people to do her bidding, as a matter of course. Ordinary public servants did not tell her what to do. She would not tolerate such an impertinence. She explained to Flint:[2]

> The official sent, left me much discomfitted by the impracticability of my replies and fully persuaded of the truth of the Scotch saying "Ye can sit on a rose, ye can sit on a shamrock but ye canna sit on a thistle".

By this stage Lady Jane believed that her negotiations with the British Government were about to come to a successful conclusion. In her patriotic enthusiasm she now made another suggestion to Flint: "I should much like to have something more to do for you when this is over. Why not the French Government? Of course I have access here to the Ambassador and should go in at the top as I have done with the present Government of Gt. Britain."

Unfortunately, all these hopes were dashed to pieces by 7 March 1907. On that day Lord Tweedmouth wrote: "I have consulted my expert advisers with regard to your suggestion as to the employment of aeroplanes, and I regret to have to tell you, after the careful consideration of my Board, that the Admiralty, whilst thanking you for so kindly bringing the proposals to their notice, are of opinion that they would not be of any practical use to the Naval Service."[3]

[1] See Richard Burdon Haldane, *An Autobiography* (London, 1929), p. 91, hereafter cited as Haldane, *Autobiography*.

[2] Flint was so amused by this episode that he printed an account of it in his *Memories*, at p. 247. For the letter see Wright Brothers' Papers, Copy, Jane Taylor to Flint, 1 March 1907.

[3] Tweedmouth's letter is printed in Snowden Gamble, *The Air Weapon*, p. 101. Gamble does not identify the recipient of this letter and makes no mention at all of any of the negotiations with Lady Jane Taylor.

On this day Lady Jane sent Flint a cablegram to inform him that both Haldane and Tweedmouth "REFUSE TO ENTERTAIN THE PROPOSITION". Despite this double rebuff and her genuine disappointment, Lady Jane Taylor was in no way prepared to abandon her quest. Instantly, she hit upon a new course of action. She decided to enlist the help of Lord Northcliffe in securing her object.

On 21 March Flint instructed Hart O. Berg, by cable, to visit Lady Jane in London and there to place all his experience at her disposal. After their meeting in her home she reported to Flint, in defiant terms, on 25 March: "I am most grateful to you for having introduced me to Mr. Hart O. Berg. We had a long conversation . . . upon the best means of promoting the desired adoption of the Wright's machine by our Government and we have agreed to hold hard for the present, until I can formulate for Harmsworth's paper a statement of the accomplished work of the Wrights . . . I am expecting a note from Mr. Hart O. Berg with suggestions on the same lines and shall then put myself immediately into communication with the Daily Mail . . . I am not confident of success with Mr. Haldane . . . I build my hopes upon the enlightened and expert views of the board of Admiralty. It is not bound down by dread of the Treasury . . ."

In New York, Flint adopted an equally sanguine attitude. Early in April he prepared another of his budgets of news for the Wright brothers. It seemed to him that the negotiations in Germany and in England were proceeding in reasonably good order.

On 8 April he informed the Wrights that Isidor Loewe had met with the German Minister of War, General Karl von Einem. Loewe had proposed to the Minister that the Wrights should come to Berlin and demonstrate their machine in the presence of high-ranking German officers.

According to Flint's account, General von Einem had given his "positive assurance" that "anything that his assistants . . . would see or learn from the demonstration, would be kept absolutely secret and that nothing could be used against the interest of Wright". Flint told the Wrights: "I have not the slightest question but what this assurance on the part of the Minister of War is sincere and that every means would be taken to live up to that understanding . . . We should also suppose that the opening of the era of aerial navigation in Berlin would be pleasing to the Emperor . . ." The Wright brothers accepted Flint's conclusion. Later, Wilbur explained to Octave Chanute: "We had a pledge from the Minister of War, Gen. von Einem, that if we would come to Germany we would receive fair treatment."[1]

When he dealt with the English negotiations in his letter of 8 April Flint called the attention of the Wrights to Hart O. Berg's impression. In

[1] McFarland, *The Papers of Wilbur and Orville Wright*, p. 819.

Berg's view by "constant knocking the door of success will eventually open". Flint pointed out that Berg and Lady Jane Taylor were "following up the idea of bringing pressure to bear on Minister Haldane and Lord Tweedmouth under a proposed arrangement with Lord Northcliffe, to excite action through his newspapers to have their Excellencies put in a position before the public so that the responsibility of doing nothing may be greater than the responsibility of giving an order".

It thus came about that the success of the Wright brothers' protracted negotiations with the British Government in 1907 turned, in good part, upon the attitude of Lord Northcliffe, the man who had already warned his fellow countrymen that with the appearance of the first practical aeroplane in history "England is no longer an island". Lady Jane Taylor had attempted to see Northcliffe a few days after Haldane and Tweedmouth had rejected her proposals. Unfortunately he was travelling abroad at that time. Lady Jane, angry and obstinate, believed that he would solve all her problems. On 10 April she told Flint: "When Lord Northcliffe arrives he can put the screw on . . ."

CHAPTER 8

The Mystery of Lord Haldane and the Failure of Lady Jane Taylor

I

It was not easy for Lady Jane Taylor to accept the situation that confronted her in mid April 1907. R. B. Haldane, at the War Office, and Lord Tweedmouth, at the Admiralty, had each rejected her overtures. Lady Jane was accustomed, from birth, to having her desires gratified. She was born Lady Jane Hay, a daughter of the eighth Marquis of Tweeddale. Her husband, General Sir Richard Taylor, had pursued a successful career in the Army and at the end of it had served as Governor

of the Royal Military College, Sandhurst. She would brook opposition
from no one. She was a diligent practitioner of the old British adage which
holds: "You cannot expect people to look up to you until you look down
on them".

Although she told Charles Flint that she built her hopes for the
successful sale of the Wright aeroplane "upon the enlightened and expert
views of the board of Admiralty" she could not forget, or forgive, the
treatment she had received from R. B. Haldane. She was determined to
force him to reverse his decision. She decided to approach Haldane again,
even before Lord Northcliffe returned from his foreign travels.

In the United States Flint and the Wright brothers agreed that a
demonstration of the machine in flight would help to overcome official
reluctance to purchase it. The Wrights, however, still held fast to their old
rule: they would not demonstrate their aeroplane to anyone until a
"contingency contract" was first agreed upon, and signed. In these
circumstances Flint suggested to Lady Jane Taylor that the Wrights would
now agree to exhibit the aeroplane in the presence of the British
Ambassador in Washington, the famous historical scholar, James Bryce,
later first Viscount Bryce. Flint was prepared to pay all the costs of such a
demonstration, provided that a "contingency contract" was signed in
advance by a representative of the British Government.

Lady Jane seized upon these proposals and at once used them in order
to approach Haldane, yet again. When she explained Flint's proposition
to the Secretary of State she was so eager to secure the arrangement she
said that the Wrights "being of English birth" were eager for the British
Government to be the first to acquire their invention. The Wright
brothers, of course, were born in the United States. On 10 April Lady
Jane wrote to Haldane in formal terms:[1]

> Dear Mr. Haldane:　　　　　　　　　　　　　　　April 10, 1907
> 　　I have been waiting upon events since your last letter reached me
> . . . I feel that the time has come to renew the claim which I brought
> before you some time ago of the Messrs. Wrights' Aeroplane to be
> taken into consideration by the English Government, that is by the
> Secretary of State for War. This aeroplane appears by a consensus of
> expert opinion to be the most advanced and most practical of all
> competitors known as yet.
> 　　In addition to the various offers which I was authorised to put
> before you by Messrs. Flint & Co. who are sole agents of the Messrs.
> Wrights' Aeroplane, and in response to your suggestion that they
> should make a public trial by entering for the Harmsworth competi-
> tion and so test public opinion in this country, I have had the

---

[1] From the Copy in the Wright Brothers' Papers, Jane Taylor to Haldane, 10
April 1907.

following communication from Messrs. Flint. Wright Brothers say that if a contract is made with Great Britain they will make a private preliminary exhibition in America in the presence of the British Ambassador. In case it was not convenient for His Excellency to witness the flight they would arrange with him to name some party in his confidence to do so. Messrs. Wright Brothers are ready to meet any reasonable proposition. They will also pay all expenses of a full and complete demonstration made under conditions to be fixed by contract. They also undertake to train a certain number of British subjects in the management of their Aeroplane. The Wrights being of English birth are anxious that the British Government should have the first advantage in this new and unique machine which is exciting so much attention on the continent.

I am,
Yours truly,
Jane Taylor

At an early stage of these negotiations of 1907 the Wright brothers had mentioned Colonel Capper's name to Flint as one of those in the British Army who was familiar with their work. Flint, as a matter of course, sent this information to Lady Jane Taylor. She at once sought Capper out, and tried to enlist his support in her attempt to sell the Wright aeroplane to the War Office. As a highly placed aristocrat with substantial military connections she was in a position to exert considerable pressure on the colonel. Despite her status, however, the matter was too serious for him to intervene in it, in any way. Capper tried, almost desperately, to avoid becoming involved in her schemes. Finally, however, on 11 April, he was forced to respond to her various advances. He informed her in tones that bordered on exasperation that the Secretary of State for War was the one she should address:[1]

Highcliffe,
S. Farnborough, Hants.

11/4/07

Madam:

I fear you have somewhat misunderstood my former communication.

I can as a private individual who is interested in flying machines, see you on the subject of Wright's Aeroplanes, or any other similar matter, and such interview would of course be absolutely private.

I cannot however think that this is Mr. Flint's intention.

If, as I presume, he wishes you to see me with a view to interesting

---

[1] From the Copy in the Wright Brothers' Papers, Capper to Lady Jane Taylor, 11 April 1907.

His Majesty's Government in the Wright Aeroplane it will be necessary for him, or yourself, to address the Secretary of State for War on the subject.

I can only, under these circumstances, see you if I receive orders from the War Office to do so, and I should be bound to communicate the result of our interview to my official superiors, in the form of a confidential report, which would be dealt with only by high officials.

> I am,
> Yrs. truly,
> J. E. Capper

Lady Jane Taylor dealt with Capper's letter in a summary way. She continued to insist that he should visit her in her home in order to discuss the Wright aeroplane:[1]

Sir:–

I only wish to see you as a private individual and if in the course of conversation about Mr. Flint, or Wright's Aeroplanes I pass outside of the limits of unofficial life, in *your estimation* I shall take a hint from you to cease that line of conversation. I shall be glad to hear from you the day and hour when it will be convenient for you to call here.

> I am,
> Yours truly,
> Jane Taylor

While these courtly exchanges were taking place in England the Wright brothers prepared a lengthy paper for Flint in order to try to convince him that they were correct when they still hesitated to agree to make a demonstration flight before the representatives of any government. In their paper they discussed the negotiations which had taken place thus far with the governments of Germany, France, Italy, and Great Britain. Their attitude, as revealed in this paper, helped to determine the early development of the Military Air Forces of each of these countries.

The Wrights were convinced that any demonstration was a "serious and risky proposition". They were only prepared to make one if they were protected by a binding contract, drawn up in advance. In case they were unable to secure such a contract from any government, they now offered an alternative suggestion for Flint's consideration. "We think", they explained, "that if one of us could have a long talk with Berg, Loewe, Lady Jane Taylor, and afterwards with some of the government officials, it would be much easier for all of us to plan the best way of proceeding in

[1] From the Copy in the Wright Brothers' Papers, Lady Jane to Capper, 12 April 1907.

this business. We can convince them in a very short time that the government that means business and finally deals with us will have cause for regret if we make a practice of giving demonstrations to all who ask for them. The less other governments know, the more it is worth to the purchaser. At present we are able to give positive assurance to any government that other governments have not seen the machine."[1]

Their paper also stated: ". . . We ought to think a long time before showing our machine to a government which after the case is fully explained persists in displaying no interest in anything but a preliminary demonstration".

It was for this reason that the Wrights rejected, out of hand, Haldane's requirement that they should compete for the Harmsworth prize, without a prior contract of some kind with the British Government. They suspected that the British were not genuinely interested in purchasing their invention.

In their view Haldane had suggested that they compete for the *Daily Mail* prize for one reason only. If such a course were followed it would allow the British authorities to discover all the technical details of their aeroplane, without paying anything at all for the privilege.

Finally, they proposed to Flint in their paper that they would like a little more time, and his own final judgement on the question, before they accepted or rejected the idea of a demonstration flight, in any country.

On the same day that the Wrights drew up this paper R. B. Haldane sent Lady Jane Taylor a reply to her latest proposal. His letter, dated 12 April 1907, declared in the clearest terms:[2]

> I have nothing to add to my last letter to you. The War Office is not disposed to enter into relations *at present* with any manufacturer of Aeroplanes.
>
> (Signed) R. B. Haldane

II

Richard Burdon Haldane, later first Viscount Haldane of Cloan, was one of the great twentieth-century servants of the State. He reformed the British Army in the period after the Boer War and successfully prepared it for the ordeal of 1914. Later, Field-Marshal Lord Haig, with good

[1] For these views and those set out in the following paragraphs see Wright Brothers' Papers, the Wrights to Flint, 12 April 1907.

[2] See Wright Brothers' Papers, Lady Jane Taylor to Flint, 17 April 1907. Haldane's letter is appended to this, as a postscript.

cause, referred to him as the "greatest Secretary of State for War England has ever had".

No man did more to determine the nature of Britain's Air Force in its earliest phases than did Haldane. Percy Walker called him "the . . . saviour of British aviation . . ." So complicated were his contributions to the development of British military aeronautics that Walker also stated: "Haldane's actions behind the scenes may never be known with certainty . . ."[1]

Haldane came from an old landed Scottish family. From an early age he planned for a career at the English Bar. He was educated at Edinburgh University where he easily won all the prizes and scholarships and at Göttingen where he conceived an admiration for Germany which remained with him throughout his life.

He was a man of enormous physical powers. He could study for prodigious lengths of time; and he was a great walker. Once, with his younger brothers, he walked from their home at Cloan to the top of a nearby mountain, covering a distance of seventy-three miles, within twenty-three hours. Later, when he worked in London, he often walked from Brighton to London in thirteen or fourteen hours. This tremendous energy enabled him to take up and to discharge tasks which would have broken a more ordinary man.

He was called to the Bar in 1879 and after the usual indifferent start he began to develop into an outstandingly brilliant lawyer. He attributed his success to his high intellectual abilities and to his capacity for hard work. In 1885 he was elected Liberal Member of Parliament for East Lothian. He now began to combine his busy life at the Bar with the work of an active, concerned, and dedicated politician. He was often forced to labour until midnight in his rooms at Lincoln's Inn and then, as he put it in his *Autobiography*, he would "dine on a chop at the old 'Cock Tavern' in Fleet Street". He wrote a letter to his mother every day of his life when he was away from home.

Haldane was a gentle and shy man. in 1890 he proudly announced his engagement to Miss Valentine Munro Ferguson, a sister of his friend, Robert Munro Ferguson, who later became Lord Novar. Within a month, however, the lady changed her mind and cancelled the arrangement. Haldane was stunned and shocked by this unexpected development. He suffered something like a nervous breakdown. He never married.

When he recovered from his disappointment Haldane plunged into his legal and political work with renewed zeal and devotion. He showed himself to his contemporaries as a bland, elegant and imperturbable

[1] For Walker's remarks see *Early Aviation at Farnborough*, vol. II, p. 273; and vol. I, p. 254.

advocate; and as a tireless politician who would go to almost any lengths in order to secure the results he and his friends desired.

He became famous for the intimate political dinner parties he gave at his home in London. He offered his guests the finest foods and the best cigars obtainable. He developed a reputation as a political intriguer.

His Tory opponents liked to say of him: "Haldane is like the boa-constrictor. First he slobbers all over you and then he swallows you whole." Many Liberal politicians concurred in this view. When Haldane fixed upon a political goal he would not rest until it was secured. This unrelenting determination to gain his own way, and the tactics he employed to do so, produced enemies in each of the great Parties. Nevertheless, his conduct was carefully examined by an expert watcher of men in this period. Lloyd George, who belonged to a different wing of the Liberal Party and who was not Haldane's friend, offered his own opinion in his *Memoirs*. Lloyd George wrote: "Haldane was a baffling personality. In private he talked incessantly – in public he talked . . . at interminable length on any subject . . . Nevertheless, with all his loquaciousness he was a doer of things . . . this garrulous lawyer was a man of action . . . He had boundless energy. He always wanted to be doing something. A combination of ideas and energy is tiresome to the complacent. He was, therefore, viewed with distrust by that class of politician . . . The sterile and indolent cannot distinguish between intrigue and action – so Haldane passed for an intriguer. Of all the great political personalities he was the kindliest I met. . . ."[1]

At the end of the nineteenth century Haldane and many other political leaders in Britain were frightened by the future. They feared that the British leadership in trade, commerce, and power which had marked out the Victorian era was now slipping away owing to developments in Germany, Japan, and the United States. It seemed certain that the hammer blows of these rivals would eventually destroy the foundations of British power. Haldane, and his friends, known as the Liberal Imperialists, believed that these trends could be altered and reversed if their countrymen would only abandon their habits of smugness, lethargy, and complacency. They urged that Britain could restore her position if more attention was paid to science, to technical education, and to a novel system of organizing British resources, a system of organization by the State. Haldane and his political allies stood out as leaders in the movement for "National Efficiency", as contemporaries called it.

Haldane, in particular, believed that British businessmen were neglecting the latest developments in technology, higher education, and the application of new scientific techniques. He became an advocate of

---

[1] David Lloyd George, *War Memoirs* (London, *n.d.*), vol. I, pp. 603–4, hereafter cited as Lloyd George, *War Memoirs*.

educational reform and sought to develop new institutions and new universities to prepare his country for the twentieth-century test.

He was eager to cooperate with anyone, regardless of party affiliation, in order to work the changes he believed were needed. He collaborated with Arthur Balfour, the Conservative leader, and with Sidney Webb, the Fabian Socialist. He successfully applied to Alfred Beit of the great firm of Wernher, Beit & Co., for funds for the new Imperial College of Science. He lunched with Cecil Rhodes in order to interest him in a scheme for the reconstruction of London University. He secured contributions from Sir Ernest Cassel and from Lord Rothschild. He believed that technical training, the creation of a new class of managing technologists, and exploitation of the applied sciences could help to save his country. He looked upon Germany as Britain's most formidable rival.

It was the Boer War that revealed Britain's inadequacies to the entire world. The British War Office showed itself to be incompetent. The blunders of the armies in the field shocked the nation. Continental rivals wondered, with good cause, if the Empire was built upon foundations of sand. Britain's position of diplomatic isolation, previously a source of national pride, was now looked upon as a frightening condition which would have to be altered if the dangers that loomed in the new century were to be avoided.

Many political leaders were distressed by these signs of national incompetence. One of them, Joseph Chamberlain, the dynamic Secretary of State for the Colonies in Arthur Balfour's Conservative Government, decided to act. Chamberlain was a patriot. He believed he could save his country.

In 1903 he launched his famous campaign for Tariff Reform and Imperial Preference. His idea was to fashion a more unified and more powerful Empire by binding the Colonies into a closer political union with the Mother Country. He would do so by introducing a system of Imperial Preferences or tariffs which would keep foreign goods out of the United Kingdom market while Colonial products were allowed in, free of all duties. Once these economic bonds of Empire were tightened Chamberlain believed he could go forward and create, in concert with the Colonial leaders, those Imperial diplomatic, military, and naval arrangements which were his object, in the first place. If he succeeded he believed he could establish an organized and unified Empire that need fear no power on the earth.

Chamberlain's initiative resulted in one of the most exciting political campaigns of recent British history. It was carried on in the years between 1903 and 1906. The Liberals, almost to a man, fiercely rejected his plan. They still believed in the Free Trade system which did not permit the imposition of most tariffs. They argued that Britain had grown rich as a result of Free Trade. They saw no reason to abandon it for an untried and untested solution of the kind Chamberlain proposed. Both sides realized that the fate and future course of the nation and the Empire would be determined by the result of Chamberlain's activities. If his scheme were put into effect Britain would abandon the traditions and practices it had followed for almost a century.

Haldane's reaction to the Chamberlain campaign was unlike that of most of his Liberal colleagues. He looked upon himself as a philosopher in action. Unlike many Liberals, he was not a devoted believer in the *laissez-faire* Free Trade system. He did not object to State controls and organization by the State if they produced a more efficient national and Imperial community.

His attitude at this time merits our careful attention because he followed similar principles when he helped to create the Air Force, after he became Secretary of State for War at the end of 1905.

The key to Chamberlain's policy was the establishment of a system of protective tariffs designed to keep foreign products out and to give a preference in the British home market to Colonial imports. Both British parties looked upon Germany as Britain's most dangerous competitor. In his *Autobiography* Haldane explained his own reaction to Chamberlain's ideas in the most careful terms. He rejected Chamberlain's policy of Protection. He stated: "Our cardinal point was that what was threatening our industrial position was want of science among our manufacturers. We pointed to case after case, particularly in the industries which required chemistry, where business was being lost to this country by the deficiency of our people in the use of science . . . Our real danger was not one of German invasion, but one of German permeation of our markets by the employment of scientific knowledge. This was one of the features in the case for the increase we were struggling for in the number of teaching Universities of Great Britain. . . . The campaign in which we were engaged against the policy of Protection . . . was our opportunity for pressing the counter-case for science and organisation."[1] These themes of science and organization became the principles which guided Haldane's actions when he became responsible for the creation of Britain's Air Force.

III

Chamberlain's great campaign split the Conservative Party into quarrelling factions. As a result, and after many tactical delays, Arthur Balfour, the Tory prime minister, resigned in December 1905. Sir Henry Camp-

---

[1] See Richard Burdon Haldane, *An Autobiography* (London, 1929), pp. 151–2, hereafter cited as Haldane, *Autobiography*.

bell-Bannerman, the Liberal leader, was now faced with the task of forming a government.

Sir Henry Campbell-Bannerman did not like Haldane. They belonged to different wings of the Liberal Party. Campbell-Bannerman knew also that Haldane had tried for years past to rob him of his power and authority in the party.

The new prime minister possessed a sardonic sense of humour. He regularly mocked those colleagues who disagreed with him by assigning them nicknames. Knowing of Haldane's great interest in German philosophy, he contemptuously nicknamed him "Schopenhauer". Nevertheless Haldane counted for so much in the party that Campbell-Bannerman decided, after calculation, that he would have to offer him a place in the new ministry. Eventually he decided to invite him to become Secretary of State for War.

There was plenty of malice in the appointment. The problems of the War Office seemed insoluble. They had ruined the political reputations of several of Haldane's predecessors. The prime minister thoroughly enjoyed the situation. "We shall now see", he placidly remarked in a phrase that later became famous, "how Schopenhauer gets on in the Kailyard".

Haldane responded to the challenge. One of his admirers once wrote of him that he possessed ". . . the greatest intellect that had ever been devoted to the State in our day and generation".[1] He immediately applied this fabulous power in order to prepare the British Army for war. His achievements in this sphere were immense. He turned an inefficient organization into a crack army. He was responsible for the creation of the Expeditionary Force, trained and prepared to fight on the European Continent. He helped to establish the Territorial Army which served as a second line and also as a unit for home defence. He instituted a General Staff, a "thinking department" for the army, as he liked to call it. These reforms, carried out over a period of several years, won Haldane a place in history as one of the most effective servants of the State in the pre-1914 era.

High intellectual capacity was not the sole source of Haldane's success at the War Office. He employed tact and guile at every step. On the day after he received his seals of office the generals of the Army Council came for their first interview with the new Secretary of State. They were suspicious of this Liberal politician who had not previously shown much interest in military affairs. They wondered about the military reforms he proposed to submit to the Parliament. Haldane murmured a response which at once won over his visitors. "My reply", he wrote in his *Autobiography*, "was that I was a young and blushing virgin just united to

---

[1] See J. H. Morgan, "The Riddle of Lord Haldane" in *The Quarterly Review*, vol. CCX/II, January 1929, p. 170.

a bronzed warrior, and that it was not expected by the public that any result of the union should appear until at least nine months had passed. This was reported by the generals to the king, who accompanied with mirth his full approval of the answer."[1] In time the soldiers in the War Office came to look upon Haldane with affection. They called him "Uncle Richard". Sir Charles Harris, head of the Finance Department in the War Office, later described Haldane as an "inspiring and ideal chief to work under".[2]

Haldane also managed to repair his relationship with Sir Henry Campbell-Bannerman. The Liberals had won the General Election of January 1906, in part because they had promised the nation a programme of strict economy in the field of military expenditure. Haldane recognized and respected the delicate situation of Campbell-Bannerman's government after the election. He realized that many of its supporters, Radicals and social reformers, would not tolerate or countenance excessive Army Estimates. He carefully avoided any significant financial increases in his military budgets. The prime minister was charmed by his skilful performances in the House of Commons. Haldane managed to get all his reforms passed without bruising the consciences of his fellow Liberals and Radicals. His deftness in action won Campbell-Bannerman's respect. The two former enemies now became friends.

Haldane's great military reforms established his reputation. His initiatives and accomplishments in the field of military aviation, however, have been criticized very severely. Even some of his closest subordinates in this aspect of his work as Secretary of State have condemned the courses he adopted and the decisions he made.

As we shall see, most of these criticisms were undeserved. In spite of his tremendous abilities and achievements it is not unreasonable to say that R. B. Haldane lived and worked under an unlucky star.

For example, during the first World War he was driven from office because of base and groundless charges that he was a pro-German, an enemy of his own country. In that crisis of his political and private life his closest friends failed to stand by him. They allowed him to resign from the government in disgrace. Haldane certainly admired many aspects of German culture and society but he was a sincere patriot who did not deserve the vicious attacks that were hurled against him in 1915. The best comments about Haldane in this general connection were made by the great French historian, Halévy. He wrote of "the restless Haldane, who dressed his window with German goods but sold merchandise of a very

---

[1] For this classic incident see Haldane, *Autobiography*, p. 183.
[2] Sir Charles Harris, "Lord Haldane at the War Office" in *Viscount Haldane of Cloan, O.M.* Reprinted from "Public Administration" (London, October 1928), p. 11.

different character . . ." He said also: "Haldane . . . prepared by German methods to wage war with Germany".[1]

In the same way that his contemporaries falsely condemned him as a pro-German, some of those he worked with and several aeronautical historians have denigrated his activities and achievements in the earliest days of British military aeronautics. However, these adverse opinions were largely incorrect. Haldane entirely deserved the title of "saviour of British aviation".

IV

When he began his period of service at the War Office R. B. Haldane gathered about him a select group of officers. They furnished him with information and with technical assistance. He was grateful for their expert help. Nevertheless, by the summer of 1906, before he worked out any of his great military reforms, he felt that he required more knowledge.

He knew Germany well and admired that genius for organization which made the Germans such formidable rivals. The creed of scientific preparation and organization dominated his mind. He decided that if he could observe the German Army at work much could be learned from the experience.

Discreet overtures were begun. After a time, Major Ostertag, the German Military Attaché in London, and Count Metternich, the German Ambassador, were consulted. Eventually, Haldane received an invitation from the German Emperor himself. He was invited to visit Berlin and also to attend the great annual manoeuvres of 1906. Haldane demurred. He explained to the emperor that he was merely a portly civilian and that not even an Imperial Command from the All Highest would induce him to get on the back of a horse. Finally, it was arranged that he should attend the manoeuvres in an open carriage. He was also invited to visit the German War Office in order to observe it in the routine performance of its duties.

When news of the proposed visit became known the French Press at once became alarmed. The Secretary of the British Foreign Office urged that Haldane should cancel the arrangement, and stay at home. Haldane, however, believed that this German excursion was so important that he was prepared to resign his office if the consequences of the journey turned out to be harmful.

Some British Army officers were later convinced that the experiences

---

[1] Halévy's comments are in his *History of the English People*, vol. VI, Book I, p. 123, and p. 173.

of this visit to Berlin, in the summer of 1906, determined Haldane's outlook when he began to build up a British Air Force. It was believed that during his visit to Berlin Haldane became convinced of the high military potential of Count Ferdinand von Zeppelin's huge airship. It was also believed that Haldane came to the conclusion that aeroplanes would be of less value than airships, for military purposes.

One of his closest subordinates in this work became critical of his attitude and outlook. In February 1911 a major step in the development of the British Air Force was taken when, by an Army Order, a unit known as the Air Battalion of the Royal Engineers was created. The battalion was assigned the task of training a "body of expert airmen".

The Air Battalion's first commander was an officer of Royal Engineers, Major Sir Alexander Bannerman, Bart. Unfortunately, Sir Alexander was not a successful leader. He knew little about aeroplanes. He was a balloon expert who had served in the South African War and had gained further experience with balloons in the Russo-Japanese War. In 1919 Bannerman blamed Haldane for some of the difficulties he experienced in the Air Battalion, in the pre-war period. He fixed upon Haldane's visit to Berlin in 1906 as a chief cause of the problem. He made this point in an official interview:[1]

> Sir Alexander pointed out that they had great difficulty in obtaining aeroplanes for the Air Battalion . . . Lord Haldane (then Mr. Haldane – Secretary of State for War) returned from Germany very impressed with the Zeppelin, and apparently of the opinion that we should develop the airship for military purposes. It is to this fact that Sir Alexander attributes his difficulty in obtaining aeroplanes . . .

Sir Alexander Bannerman's conclusions were incorrect. Haldane did develop an interest in the military possibilities of dirigible airships. However, he was also very eager to secure an efficient aeroplane for service in the British Army. He paid closer and more serious attention to aeroplanes than any other member of the Liberal Government.

V

Shortly before Haldane made his visit to Berlin, at the end of August 1906, the British Army began highly secret experiments of its own that were designed to provide it with aeroplanes that could be used effectively in war. It was in June of that year that Lieutenant Dunne began his work

[1] See Air 1/735/100/1. "Record of an interview with Sir Alexander Bannerman, Bt. on November 25 1919, respecting the Air Battalion of the Royal Engineers", and marked "*STRICTLY CONFIDENTIAL*".

at Farnborough, under Colonel Capper's direction. S. F. Cody was also engaged in experiments of a similar kind at this time. The plan was to experiment with gliders that could eventually be developed into powered aircraft.

Dunne's work was carried out in the strictest secrecy. The separate parts of his machine were built in the main workshops at the Balloon Factory but each individual worker was not allowed to see what his colleagues were doing. Dunne assembled the components by himself in a locked room. Later, he explained to Snowden Gamble, the aeronautical historian, the conditions under which he was required to work in 1906: ". . . it was decreed that the experiments should be carried out with the utmost secrecy. The machine was built piecemeal in the shops, and the parts were put together by myself and one assistant in a locked room. I was forbidden to wear uniform; and my name remained in the Army List as an invalided officer on half-pay."[1]

In those days the aeroplane was looked upon as a military secret. Dunne had convinced himself, and Colonel Capper also, that he could produce a machine that was infinitely more valuable for military purposes than was the Wright aeroplane. In his opinion no pilot could learn to control a Wright aeroplane in flight except after an extremely long period of training; but pilots would be able to fly his "stable" aircraft at once, with almost no training at all. This was the glowing military advantage that inspired him and Capper to carry their work forward as quickly as they could. They believed the Dunne aeroplane would permit the British Army to produce an entire corps of trained aviators before any other nation could do so.

In June 1906 the War Office's Royal Engineer Committee authorized the expenditure of the sum of £600 for experimental gliders. This was recognized as the first step in the production of a power-driven aeroplane. In December authority was given for the acquisition of an *Antoinette* engine, at a further cost of £550. Cody was sent to Paris in order to purchase it. Dunne was also encouraged to press forward with his own work. Percy Walker has concluded that the support Lieutenant Dunne received at this time from the War Office in London and from the Balloon Factory at Farnborough was "impressive".[2]

Although aeronautical historians have not recognized the fact, R. B. Haldane soon developed a very keen interest in Dunne and in his work. As a matter of course the Secretary of State received official information about the Farnborough experiments. It may also be that Dunne's champion, friend, and advocate, H. G. Wells, drew Haldane's attention to the young officer and to his exciting ideas about a "stable" aeroplane.

---

[1] Snowden Gamble, *The Air Weapon*, p. 96.
[2] See Walker, *Early Aviation at Farnborough*, vol. II, p. 163.

Although Wells and Haldane did not always agree they had known each other for several years. Both were ardent believers in the movement for "National Efficiency".

In 1902 Sidney and Beatrice Webb, always eager to promote the cause of the welfare state, proposed the formation of a small dining club, to meet at regular intervals for serious discussions and to formulate or propose political policy. It was decided to call this society the "Coefficients". The name was chosen to emphasize that the keynote of the new group was efficiency.

The Webbs, with their Fabian outlook, proposed to collect politicians from each of the parties, and invite them to join the "Coefficients". Among the Liberal Imperialists, Sir Edward Grey, later the Foreign Secretary in Campbell-Bannerman's government, and R. B. Haldane were selected. W. A. S. Hewins, the economist, and Leo Maxse, Editor of the *National Review*, represented the Tories. Bertrand Russell joined the group. Leo Amery, an expert on the conditions of the army, and Carlyon Bellairs, a naval officer, also became members. This was exactly the kind of select circle that always appealed to Haldane's political instincts, to his desire to get things done by exploiting the best talent available.

H. G. Wells was asked to join this society because he was capable of original thoughts on every subject. Wells was an especially active member of the "Coefficients". He always argued to his fellow members that mankind, having moved beyond the era of pre-scientific superstitions, would be guided by logical and scientific reasoning in seeking solutions to its problems. The first meeting of the "Coefficients" took place at Haldane's home in December 1902. After a brief interval the society abandoned immediate political goals but it continued to meet as a dining club for the discussion of serious national and Imperial problems, for a period of five or six years.

In any case, Dunne's work in the Balloon Factory at Farnborough progressed according to a logical plan. For several months he experimented with model-sized gliders. Early in 1907, however, construction began on his first full-sized machine, an aircraft that was supposed to be capable of carrying a man into the air. This large glider was built in such a way that it could easily be converted into a powered aeroplane.

It was exactly at this time that Lady Jane Taylor had burst in upon Haldane, in February 1907, with her proposal that the War Office should purchase Wright aeroplanes. Despite his firm refusal to treat with her she persevered in her efforts, as we have seen, until an exasperated Secretary of State wrote to her on 12 April in order to say: ". . . The War Office is not disposed to enter into relations *at present* with any manufacturer of Aeroplanes".

Later, Haldane was severely criticized for this decision. An aviation historian, E. Charles Vivian, wrote of this development:[1]

> . . . let it be set down that in 1907, when the Wright Brothers had proved the practicability of their machines, negotiations were entered into between the brothers and the British War Office. On April 12th, 1907, the apostle of military stagnation, Haldane, then War Minister, put an end to the negotiations by declaring that "the War Office is not disposed to enter into relations at present with any manufacturer of aeroplanes". The state of the British air service in 1914, at the outbreak of hostilities, is eloquent regarding the pursuance of the policy which Haldane initiated.

Later still, Lord Haldane sought to defend himself from these brutal charges. During the first World War when England was being bombed by Zeppelins he explained his actions in a debate in the House of Lords, in May 1916; and in his *Autobiography*, published in 1929, he produced a fuller defence of the course he adopted at this time. In his *Autobiography* he explained he had interviewed several inventors, including the Wright brothers, but he dismissed them all as "clever empiricists". He wrote: ". . . I saw that those whom I interviewed were only clever empiricists, and that we were at a profound disadvantage compared with the Germans, who were building up the structure of the Air Service on a foundation of science . . ."[2] Haldane, in this account, so compressed his narrative of events that it became misleading. We should point out that he did not interview the Wright brothers in 1907. He met them for the first time in the War Office in London, in 1909.

Marvin McFarland, the American expert who edited the two-volume work *The Papers of Wilbur and Orville Wright* for the Library of Congress, subjected Haldane to devastating criticism in an article published in *The Air Power Historian* in October 1955. McFarland believed, incorrectly, that Haldane had "never set eyes" on the Wright brothers. In his article McFarland concentrated upon those developments which took place in 1907. He explained that when Charles Flint contacted Haldane in 1907 the Secretary of State "took a high ministerial tone. He was not interested in acquiring a new plaything for the Army. There was, he said, no public demand for aeroplanes . . ."[3]

McFarland then attacked Haldane's statements in his *Autobiography*.

---

[1] E. Charles Vivian, *A History of Aeronautics* (New York, 1921), p. 176.

[2] For Haldane's speech in the Lords see *Parliamentary Debates*, House of Lords, 5th ser. vol. 22 (24 May 1916), cols 145ff. See also Haldane, *Autobiography*, pp. 232–3.

[3] For these remarks and those in the next three paragraphs see Marvin W. McFarland, "When The Airplane Was A Military Secret" in *The Air Power Historian*, vol. II, Number IV, October 1955, pp. 78–9.

When Haldane sought to defend the course he adopted in 1907 his explanation, according to McFarland, "not only reads like an apology, but is so contrived as to put the unwary off the scent".

When Haldane wrote about "empiricists" and about the "Germans, who were building up the structure of the Air Service on a foundation of science" he was not telling the truth. According to McFarland, Haldane's errors in chronology confused the true sequence of events. As McFarland put it Haldane was "Lumping together, anachronistically", the events of the period 1909–1912, and was not really dealing with those of the years before 1908, "with which we are concerned here".

Haldane, according to McFarland's analysis, so telescoped his account that it could only be dismissed as misleading: what he did in the years between 1909 and 1912 when the Germans were hurrying forward their own scientific preparations for an Air Service did not bear upon his decision of 1907 when he refused to purchase the Wright aeroplane at the time it was offered to him. McFarland came to the conclusion that in 1907 "Haldane, and so England, missed the aviation bus as completely as Neville Chamberlain was to miss another bus at a subsequent stage of world history".

How can we explain Haldane's actions in 1907 and his remarkable defence of them in his *Autobiography*? The answer is not so much that he "missed the bus" in 1907, but that he "backed the wrong horse" in that year and was later unwilling to admit his mistake. He was fascinated by the military possibilities of Lieutenant Dunne's aeroplane.

Dunne's full-sized machine was assembled during the very weeks that Lady Jane Taylor pressed the cause of the Wright brothers upon the War Office. In order to preserve Dunne's secrets it was decided to test his aircraft in a remote part of the Scottish highlands. Haldane personally intervened at this stage. He asked his friend the Marquess of Tullibardine, the eldest son of the Duke of Atholl, if he could assist the military authorities with their problem. As a result of this initiative, the duke placed a lonely grouse moor at the disposal of the War Office so that flight trials could be carried out there. The grouse moor overlooked Glen Tilt, near Blair Atholl.[1] The duke owned all the land in this area. The security of the trials was thus guaranteed.

In the summer of 1907, as we shall see, the dismantled parts of the Dunne aeroplane were dispatched to the north, by rail.[2] At the same time a party of soldiers from Farnborough, who were required to wear civilian clothes in order to avoid the notice of the curious, was also sent to Blair Atholl. These troops afterwards formed the nucleus of the "Aeroplane Section" of the Air Battalion of the Royal Engineers, commanded so

[1] For these details see Snowden Gamble, *The Air Weapon*, p. 97.
[2] Lieutenant Dunne's aeroplane experiments are dealt with in subsequent chapters of this history.

unhappily by Sir Alexander Bannerman. Haldane, as we shall demonstrate later, was so interested in this work that he actually travelled to Blair
Atholl in order to observe the secret experiments for himself.

In the light of Haldane's special and particular concern with the Dunne
aeroplane the meaning of his letter of 12 April 1907 to Lady Jane Taylor
may be interpreted somewhat differently than has been done by a number
of aeronautical historians.[1] When Haldane informed Lady Jane Taylor
that "The War Office is not disposed to enter into relations *at present* with
any manufacturer of Aeroplanes" he was not expressing his opposition to
the invention, as has sometimes been supposed. His was not the statement of a short-sighted politician who was misapplying the power and the
authority of his office. In 1907 R. B. Haldane, the apostle of science and
organization, had backed an empiricist of his own choice, Lieutenant
Dunne, who, in the event, failed to produce the results expected from him
by his military superiors in the Balloon Factory at Farnborough and in the
War Office, in London. Haldane's letter to Lady Jane was most probably
composed in the way that it was in order to protect a military secret.

VI

Lady Jane Taylor possessed no knowledge of Lieutenant Dunne's secret
activities. She believed that Haldane's every action as Secretary of State
for War was determined by his need to economize in order to satisfy the
Radical tail of pacifists and social reformers that played so important a
role in the politics of the Liberal Party at this time.

Lady Jane was outraged by Haldane's curt letter of 12 April. She meant
to pay him back for the way in which he had dismissed her proposals. She
decided that Lord Northcliffe was the man who could render her anger
effective. He was so powerful that he might be able to force the Secretary
of State to negotiate with her, on an official basis.

On 16 April Lady Jane called on Northcliffe in order to lay before him
every detail of her attempts to sell the Wright aeroplane to the British
Government. She brought with her a copy of Wilbur Wright's memorandum, parts of which we have noticed earlier in this work, entitled "*Wright
Brothers' English Negotiations*". It was Wilbur's account of the Wrights'
adventures with Patrick Alexander, Colonel Capper, and Colonel Count
Gleichen. It was a summary of their English negotiations up to the time
when they decided to ask Charles R. Flint to try to sell their invention to
the British Government.

Wilbur's memorandum, however, was much more than a mere summary. It was the Wright brothers' interpretation of the several incidents

---

[1] See the critical comment in Geoffrey Dorman, *Fifty Years Fly Past: From
Wright Brothers to Comet* (London, 1951), p. 23.

that had occurred between them and their various British visitors in the years between 1902 and 1906.

Lady Jane read this paper to Northcliffe during the course of their meeting. The document began by mentioning Patrick Y. Alexander's visit to Dayton in 1902:[1]

MEMORANDUM BY W. WRIGHT, ESQ.   February 8, 1907

WRIGHT BROTHERS' ENGLISH NEGOTIATIONS

In 1902 Mr. Patrick Alexander, a supposedly wealthy English amateur, visited us at Dayton. It is suspected that he may have some secret connection with the Government.

The Memorandum turned next to the activities of Colonel Capper:

In 1904 Colonel J. E. Capper, Chief of the Aeronautical Department of the British Department [*sic*] visited us in Dayton and requested us, when we felt that our machine had been brought to a practical stage, to give Great Britain the first chance. We told him that we were not yet ready to talk business.

Wilbur then set out the details of the Wrights' initiative of 1905:

In the Spring of 1905 we wrote to Colonel Capper the results that had been obtained and said that we would be pleased to take up the matter with the Government if it wished. The Government requested us to make a proposition, which we did. The substance of the proposition was that we would furnish a machine to carry one man and that the price of the same should be dependent upon the distance which would be covered in a trial flight . . . but the Government to be under no obligations to accept the machine unless a distance of at least 10 miles was covered. This matter remained unacted upon until after we had privately made known to Colonel Capper the results of our experiments of September and October 1905. The Government then replied that the conditions did not seem to it such as to justify a contract.

The memorandum next touched upon their association with Colonel Gleichen:

We then wrote to the War Office stating that we were prepared to make a new proposition. The War Office instructed the Military

[1] This memorandum is preserved in the Wright Brothers' Papers. The accounted presented above of Lady Jane's meeting with Northcliffe is based on her coded cablegram to Flint, dated 16 April 1907, and on her letter to Flint, written on the next day. Both these documents are preserved in the Wright Brothers' Papers and contain her reports of the interview.

Attache at Washington (Colonel Glichen) [*sic*] to visit us at Dayton
and obtain a proposition from us. We prepared a brief offer, the
substance of which was similar to that of our French offer, but in
which the total price was $200,000, but we offered to divide it into
two parts:

The machine to be delivered for————————$100,000, and
Scientific information, formulae, etc.
                    for additional————————$100,000.

After some delay Colonel Glichen [*sic*] replied that he had been
instructed by his superiors to say that the Government was not
prepared to make a contract at this time at the price named. This
communication has not yet been answered by us.

Wilbur concluded his paper by giving clear expression to the Wright
brothers' suspicions of Patrick Y. Alexander:

During these negotiations we have been visited at somewhat
frequent intervals by Mr. Alexander and feel convinced that he has
some connection with the Government and that the Government has
some reason for his watching very closely what we are doing.

When Lady Jane Taylor saw Northcliffe on 16 April he was in a
wrathful mood. In this period of his life he was suffering from an eye
illness and he was terrified that he might lose his ability to see. The
condition irritated his already uncertain temper. Later, when he met the
Wright brothers he fell, like so many others, under the spell of their
charm; at this time, however, he told Lady Jane he was "most sceptical
about everything concerning the Wright Brothers. They are always going
to do, and do nothing that can be seen or appreciated."

Lady Jane responded to these aspersions by reading to Northcliffe a
firm offer Flint had authorized her to make. The Wrights, according to it,
were prepared to carry two hundred and fifty pounds, fuel, and an
operator for a distance of two hundred miles. Furthermore, they would
bear all the expenses of such a demonstration. Northcliffe said this was
the first practical proposal he had heard of with respect to the Wright
brothers. "This", Lady Jane reported to Flint on 17 April, "mollified him
extremely and his ruffled feathers were entirely smoothed".

Northcliffe bristled again when he learned of the Wrights' suspicions of
Patrick Y. Alexander. Lady Jane told Flint: "As to Mr. Patrick Alexander he said he is nothing but a rich booby who passes his time looking after
new inventions. He said the idea of his being an emissary of the British
was a perfectly childish illusion." Northcliffe declared of the Wright
brothers: "they are never ready to talk business".

It was no light thing for the Lady Jane Taylor to listen to the bluntly expressed opinions of one who disagreed with her. Such a practice was quite alien to her nature, and to her experience. Nevertheless, in this instance she exercised a remarkable patience. She carefully explained the details of her own association with Charles R. Flint and also told Northcliffe of "all that has passed between . . . me and the two officers of state, which I read out with the dates of each point as it occurred . . ." She observed during the meeting that Lord Northcliffe was deeply interested in the developing science of aeronautics and that he strongly hoped someone would win his *Daily Mail* prize.

She learned, also, that Northcliffe planned to visit Paris in the immediate future so that he could see Alberto Santos-Dumont again. In his opinion, Santos possessed "a fair chance of winning the £10,000". Lady Jane came away from her meeting with Northcliffe convinced that he was now at last prepared to act. As she told Flint: "He was quite convinced that Wright Bros. mean business and that . . . he had some concrete offers to deal with".

Unfortunately, this sanguine mood did not last for long. After the meeting Lady Jane at once sent Northcliffe a carefully composed summary of their conversation and a detailed account of exactly what the Wright brothers were prepared to offer. She requested an early reply to this letter but Northcliffe took no notice of it. No answer came from Carmelite House. "If in a fortnight he has said nothing", she reported to Flint on 22 April, "I propose to write to him again or to see Mr. Sutton about it. I perceive that there is over here a good deal of . . . waiting upon events and it seems generally thought that nothing will come of all the inventions for a few years to come". This report of 22 April was lacking in the high enthusiasm that had marked out her conduct in the affair up to this point. She ended on a forlorn note: "If you think of any wise moves toward making Harmsworth speak please tell me on receipt of this".

Lady Jane, despite her great energy and her devotion, was unable to rouse Lord Northcliffe to an active course. Early in May she met with Hart O. Berg in order to obtain his advice about the best strategy to follow at this stage of her mission. Berg, at this time, was actively engaged in trying to sell the Wright aeroplane in France. He believed that Henri Deutsch de la Meurthe, a very wealthy and patriotic member of the Aéro Club of Paris, might buy the invention "in order to get ahead of Harmsworth".[1]

Armed with this intelligence Lady Jane Taylor called on Northcliffe again, on 13 May. Later on that day she reported to Flint: "I was much disappointed today, when I had an interview with Lord Northcliffe, to find that the elaborate letter which I wrote him the other day, about three

[1] Wright Brothers' Papers, Coded cablegram, Berg to Flintco, 10 May 1907.

weeks ago, of which you know, has been entirely forgotten, ignored, and I am not quite sure that he ever read it."

Northcliffe, suffering still from his eye ailment, was in a terrible frame of mind. He now demanded a typewritten statement, signed by the Wright brothers, "stating what they can do, will do, where they will do it, and what remuneration they demand and in what form". When Northcliffe received such a document, he declared, he would present it to R. B. Haldane and "Mr Haldane's answer shall be the final answer".

When Lady Jane reflected upon these singular developments she was unable to come to any definite conclusion about them. She wondered if Northcliffe had already shown her letter to the Secretary of State for War. She told Flint in apologetic terms:

> Well now, my private opinion is that Lord Northcliffe may have already shown my letter, and that he may wish to see the same things repeated and signed by the Wrights; but it is quite possible that he has really lost the sheet of paper, and therefore knows nothing at all about it.
>
> I am very sorry that this has been delayed so many days – first by his carelessness, if it be so, and secondly by the sight of his eyes, which is a very serious matter for him poor man.

In New York, Charles Flint had already fixed upon a new course of action. His restless nature did not permit him to wait upon events. Lady Jane Taylor and his other agents in Europe had failed to achieve a single positive result. No government had offered to buy the Wright aeroplane. Flint now decided that one of the Wright brothers should at once travel to Europe in order to visit London, Paris and Berlin.

In these circumstances Lady Jane Taylor's services were no longer needed. Her remarkable adventure, a curious episode in British aeronautical history, was now coming to an end.

VII

While Lady Jane strove to win over Lord Northcliffe, Charles R. Flint continued to furnish the Wright brothers with news of the activities of his various agents in different parts of the world. The Wrights, at home in Dayton, analysed this information and then sent Flint their impressions of each new development, as it arose. Flint found that he often had to give way to Wilbur and Orville whenever there was a disagreement between him and his office staff upon the one hand and the Wrights upon the other. The Wright brothers remained fixed in their resolve to see to it that all was done exactly as they desired. No other course was acceptable to them.

The first account of Lady Jane Taylor's meetings with Lord Northcliffe was sent to Flint in a coded cablegram which was received in his New York office on 16 April 1907. The deciphered cablegram was despatched to Dayton at once. There were so many errors in the transmission that much of her message was unclear. However, it seemed from the text that Northcliffe had suggested that Colonel Capper should be invited to witness a demonstration of the Wright aeroplane in flight.

On 17 April the Wright brothers wrote to Flint in order to repeat their old rule that a "contingency contract" would be required before any demonstration flights were made, anywhere. They held fast to the idea that their secrets would not be revealed until a contract was signed:

> The cable from Lady Jane Taylor is rather obscure, and we do not quite make out whether the pronoun "he" in some cases refers to Harmsworth or Capper. We have no objection to Col. Capper, nor to Harmsworth or any one whom the British Government may appoint, so long as the contract precedes the flight.

We must now take up again, in the present context, the charges levelled against the Wright brothers by some of their contemporaries and by several aeronautical historians.

These complaints hold that the Wrights followed a policy of such "excessive secrecy" that no government, anywhere, could come to terms with them, or even bargain upon a reasonable basis for the purchase of their invention; that the "contingency contract" idea was simply "Wilburian rigmarole"; that the brothers "subconsciously . . . did not want to sell their aeroplane"; that they adopted the contingency plan in order to conceal the fact that they were incapable of genuine powered flight in the period 1903–1907, and that they only achieved this capability in the year 1908.[1]

Charles Flint and his employees and associates were concerned with making money. They were hard-headed men of business. They were experienced in selling new inventions to all kinds of purchasers. They were not men prepared to pander to the self-esteem of the Wright brothers nor would they involve themselves with an aeroplane incapable of powered flight.

In 1907 they did not believe the Wrights were too secretive or that they were mentally unbalanced or that they really did not want to sell their aeroplane. On the contrary, they entirely agreed with the prudence, caution and business acumen of Wilbur and Orville Wright; in effect, they disagreed with historical critics like Percy Walker, Oliver Stewart and others who, over the years, have condemned the Wrights for "excessive secrecy".

---

[1] See Chapter V above for some discussion of these charges.

During the course of the 1907 negotiations Flint, Lord Northcliffe, Haldane, the German authorities and others all urged the Wrights to grant them the opportunity to see the Wright machine in flight, before any contract was signed. The brothers steadfastly refused to comply with these requests; and the firm of Flint & Co., with years of experience in such transactions, upheld them in this decision.

As early as 14 February 1907 Flint himself wrote to the Wrights: "I see that there is a strong desire on the part of parties to get information regarding your machine and as it is not fully covered by patents and you expect to deal to a considerable extent with Governments, I see the soundness of your policy of withholding information . . ."

Later, when Haldane and then Lord Northcliffe suggested that Colonel Capper should be allowed to witness a flight before a contract was signed, Flint's associates wrote to the Wright brothers, on 19 April 1907, in order to make clear their own firm opposition to this British request:

> It seemed to us that we were justified in interpreting the suggestion of Capper witnessing a flight before a contract as a "Walk into my parlor said the spider to the fly" proposition and we therefore cabled immediately that we were not able to show to Capper as he is a competitor.
>
> We also wanted the English to appreciate that "there are others" and that it was impossible for us to wait. We offered to fly in the presence of Northcliffe or the British Ambassador to the United States during the first half of June or to have a trial trip in July in London and emphasized our "C.O.D." (cash on demonstration) proposition . . .
>
> If you think, in view of all the correspondence, that it is desirable that we should cable that we are willing to have Capper present in the event that the contract precedes the flight, we will do so, but we think our advices to that effect by letter are sufficient. From what we have written they should certainly appreciate that we are willing that all or any experts they desire should be present provided the contract precedes the flight.

VIII

In this same letter Flint and his associates furnished the Wrights with information about their future plans for the sale of the aeroplane to the French, British and German Governments. They also suggested that one of the brothers should prepare to visit London in order to be able to confer there with Hart O. Berg and Lady Jane Taylor:

> It is true that we have not tested the sentiment in France, but we hope that by exciting the interest of Germany and Great Britain, and

the French getting the "secret information" that the German Emperor is regarding the obtaining of your inventions very seriously, they may realize the necessity of securing a power propelled dirigible aeroplane of demonstrated efficiency . . .

In the event that Loewe does not succeed in arranging a preliminary exhibition . . . (and we will consider it a remarkable accomplishment if he does) or in the event that we cannot arrange for an exhibition under similar conditions in the presence of Lord Northcliffe or the British Ambassador to the United States, it seems to us the next move should be for one of you to proceed to London at the earliest possible date to confer personally with Mr. Berg and Lady Jane Taylor, and our Senior would follow in case you and our European associates deem it desirable after conference.

The Wright brothers, who knew well the power of their own personalities, entirely agreed with this last proposal. They did not, however, accept the implications contained in the final paragraph of this letter. Flint and his colleagues were aware that in France in the early months of 1907 several inventors were trying desperately to overtake the Wrights. They wrote:

ENTRE NOUS.

We are becoming afraid of the concentration of "grey matter" on the perfection of power propelled dirigible aeroplanes and are anxious that you "should do it first".

The Wright brothers responded at once to this challenge. They knew, better than anyone else, the immense difficulties involved in the production of a fully controllable powered aeroplane. They were not afraid of any of their French rivals; they decided to make this attitude known to Flint and his colleagues, in the clearest terms possible.

The Wrights were diligent students of the aeronautical literature of their day. By studying it they learned the exact nature of the achievements of their French competitors. They were well informed about the work of Blériot, Archdeacon, Voisin, Esnault-Pelterie, and the other French pioneers.

They realized that the Frenchmen had entirely failed to grasp that a successful aeroplane required a control system that would be instantly effective in the air. These French aviators sought to force their machines aloft by exploiting brute power. They had never considered, adequately, what they would have to do with their machines once they were airborne and exposed to the mysteries and caprices of the air. Moreover, they flew with the most primitive and inefficient propellers and engaged in no research designed to improve them. As a result of their studies, and their own experiences, Wilbur and Orville were entirely confident that not one of the French fliers was in a position to equal their own achievements, for a long time to come. This was the source of their unwavering determination to have their own way.

As a result of these convictions the Wrights prepared a long and remarkable letter for Flint and his colleagues so that they could grasp the true nature of the situation in 1907. This exposition, dated 24 April 1907, deserves to rank as a classic document of early aeronautical literature.

An uninformed contemporary might look upon it as a reflection of the arrogance of the Wright brothers. From our point of view, the letter may be regarded as a clear explanation of the factors that determined their course in this period of aeronautical history. The Wrights knew they possessed a tremendous device that existed nowhere else in the world. For this reason the various governments would have to accept their terms or forfeit the opportunity to acquire a practical aeroplane. This stark and rigid attitude determined the history of aeronautics in every country.

The Wright exposition of 24 April began by acknowledging receipt of Flint's letter of the 19th. The brothers went on to declare:

> The concentration of grey matter to which you refer is not a matter to cause immediate worry. We know the various difficulties involved in this complex problem and how few of them these new experimenters have essayed to meet and overcome. It requires years of time to work out such a problem. They have barely made a start; their practice of giving out pictures and descriptions of their machines enables us to know just where they are, and saves us a world of anxiety.

The Wrights next pointed to the "real" problem that confronted them:

> Our real trouble will not come from real competition but from the false hopes aroused by the partial successes which long precede practical results. So far no one has come near equalling our records of 1903, nor, so far as control is concerned, our records of 1901, on a glider. It must be remembered that Capt. Ferber, Archdeacon, Voisin, Esnault-Peltier [*sic*] and a number of other Frenchmen experimented with gliding machines in 1899, 1900, 1901, 1902, 1903, 1904, 1905, and 1906, but after eight years of work our records of 1901 yet remain unequaled by them in distance, duration, and in the velocity of the winds encountered. In less than a year, in 1903, we designed and built with our own hands the first motor flyer, solved the problem of the theory of screw propellers, and demonstrated the soundness of both our theory and our practice by a flight of 59 seconds in a wind of twenty miles an hour. Capt. Ferber has been working on motor machines since 1902: the Archdeacon-Voisin-Delagrange machine is now in its fourth year: sixteen months have

elapsed since Santos Dumont boasted that within three months he would be flying all over France, etc. etc.

The Wrights then explained what developments in France might serve to alarm them. They were especially scathing of Lord Northcliffe's demand that they must instantly demonstrate their machine or lose all hope of recognition and reward:

> When our gliding records are equaled, and our motor flyer records of 1903 are equaled, and other machines begin to lift fifty to seventy pounds to the horse-power, instead of ten to fifteen pounds as at present, and we see from the designs of the machines that they are beginning to provide means of overcoming troubles whose existence they have not even got far enough to discover yet, then it will be up to us to do something before they flounder through the final difficulties which cost us the years 1904 and 1905, and overtake us. But when a man like Harmsworth who knows nothing whatever of the difficulties of flight sends word to us that unless we make our machine public immediately we will be lost, we find it hard to make the cold chills run up our backs in the way he wishes.

At this stage of their exposition the Wrights described the "actual situation", as they saw it. In their opinion there was no reason for them to deviate by a jot from the policy they had adopted:

> The actual situation is this:- We can furnish governments practical machines with which they can begin the creation of a highly trained corps of aeronautical scouts *now*: no one else can. There is no certainty that any one else is within three years of us . . . When novices whose capacity is yet to be proven, boast that they will do in a few months what required years of our time, it is well to take a look at the past and see whether in our early experiments, where comparison is possible, we advanced only one third or one fourth as fast as our competitors. If the facts are quite to the contrary, why should it be assumed that the relative rates of progress in the power machine will be so marvelously different?

Wilbur and Orville ended on a defiant note. They made clear to Flint and his colleagues there was no valid reason to fear they could be overtaken by the French aviators:

> The motor flyer has cost us four years of hard work, a hundred and sixty trial flights, and changes in construction and methods of control almost innumerable. Yet we made a flight of a minute in a high wind before the end of our first year. Has any one done better in his first year? The progress made by others since the announcement of our final success at the end of 1905 is as rapid as could reasonably be

expected, but it by no means indicates that others will reach the goal in less time than we required. Our lead is sufficient for our purposes, if properly conserved.

IX

Charles Flint was impressed by the arguments contained in the Wrights' letter of 24 April. As soon as he received it he caused a copy to be made and this was instantly despatched to Hart O. Berg, in Paris.[1] Lady Jane Taylor did not receive a copy. By this stage she no longer counted for much in Flint's calculations.

Hart O. Berg, travelling regularly between Paris and London, had by now come to the conclusion that there were too many difficulties to be encountered in trying to sell the aeroplane to a European government. He decided that a more effective method would be to form a European Wright Company. Under the arrangement he contemplated the Wrights would receive cash payments, royalties on the sale of each machine, and a large block of stock. Berg believed that Henri Deutsch de la Meurthe, the wealthy and patriotic French oil magnate, would be very interested in such a proposal.

At the end of April Flint had further talks with the Military Attachés of Germany and Russia. Major Körner, the German Military Attaché, expressed a "general" interest in the aeroplane. He planned to leave for Berlin in June and promised to discuss the matter with Flint again, before his departure. By this time, however, Flint had decided that one of the Wright brothers should travel to Europe in order to make his presence felt at the scene of action.[2]

On 16th May 1907 the Wrights received a telegram from Flint asking that one of them should go to Europe, at once. After some discussion the brothers decided Wilbur should make the journey while Orville stayed at home. Wilbur wanted to remain in Dayton in order to work on their new engines but Orville insisted that he should go. In his diary for 16 May Bishop Milton Wright wrote: "Wilbur got a telegram from Flint and at 10:00 p.m. started for New York to take ship for London. He goes to talk with agents in London, Paris, and Berlin . . ."[3]

On 18 May Wilbur Wright sailed for Liverpool on the *Campania*. It was arranged that he would be met in London by Hart O. Berg; and that Frank Cordley, one of Flint's colleagues, would join them there.

---

[1] See Wright Brothers' Papers, Flint to Messrs. Wright Brothers, 1 May 1907.
[2] For these details see Wright Brothers' Papers, Flint to Messrs. Wright Brothers, 1 May 1907.
[3] See McFarland, *The Papers of Wilbur and Orville Wright*, p. 759; and p. 803.

Flint and his associates realized that when they separated the brothers in this way it would be especially painful for the one who remained at home. On 22 May Ulysses S. Eddy wrote to Orville in order to give him Wilbur's address in London. The letter was tactfully composed. He wrote: "I meant to write this to you on Saturday but it slipped my mind, for which I must apologize". He added:[1]

> We shall have constant cable advices from England on and after his arrival, of which you will be kept fully informed. I believe that his journey is made at the psychological moment and have great hopes of important results.

The *Campania* arrived in Liverppol on 25 May and Wilbur took the special train for London. There he was met at the station by Hart O. Berg. Wilbur produced a profound impression on the salesman. Berg sent a marvellous report of their meeting to Flint:[2]

> At 12:30 yesterday I met Mr. Wilbur Wright at Euston Station. I have never seen a picture of him, or had him described to me in any way, still he was the first man I spoke to, and either I am a Sherlock Holmes, or Wright has that peculiar glint of genius in his eye which left no doubt in my mind as to who he was . . . He arrived with nothing but a bag, about the size of a music roll, but mildly suggested . . . he thought it might be advisable for him to buy another suit of clothes . . . he came to the conclusion that he'd "guess he'd better have a swaller-tail coat". We spent the entire afternoon together. . . .

When they began to discuss their business affairs Berg quickly discovered the unbending firmness of his new friend:

> The company idea did not seem to please him very much, as he first wanted to know himself exactly what the attitudes of the several governments were. After a long talk . . . I believe, please note that I say distinctly "I believe", that I made something of an impression as regards the impossibility of getting any sort of action in the near future from any government. He agreed he did not think the British Government would do any business. He also stated that perhaps it would be very hard to do anything with the French Government . . . There was only the German Government left, and even there I assured him that the government would do nothing, but we must look to the power greater than the government, that is, the Emperor himself. . . .

[1] Wright Brothers' Papers, Ulysses S. Eddy to Orville Wright, 22 May 1907.
[2] For Berg's report see Kelly, *Miracle at Kitty Hawk*, pp. 205–7.

About 5 o'clock in the afternoon, I think, you will distinctly note
that I say "I think", I brought about some sort of action in his mind
and I think he was on the point, you will note that I distinctly say that
"I think he was on the point", of veering around from the government to company methods . . .

At the conclusion of his report Berg offered a concise account of his
reaction to Wilbur Wright. His opinion was very much like those of
Colonel Capper and Count Gleichen, when they first made the acquaintance of the Wright brothers:

I am much pleased with Wright's personality. He inspires great
confidence and I am sure that he will be a capital Exhibit A.

Lady Jane Taylor's experiences with R. B. Haldane and with Lord
Northcliffe convinced Flint and Berg that the British Government was
not, at that time, prepared to negotiate for the purchase of the Wright
aeroplane. Flint still hoped for a favourable response in Berlin and in St
Petersburg. Hart O. Berg, for his part, believed that the best opportunity
lay in Paris where Deutsch de la Meurthe had arranged to see Wilbur
early in the following week. Berg therefore proposed that he and Wilbur
should quit London in order to travel to Paris, a day or two after Wilbur's
arrival in the British capital. "I think", Berg told Flint in his report, "'he
agreed', to go to Paris with me on Monday. I am to see him again at 1
o'clock today, Sunday, and I think I shall be able, you will kindly note that
I distinctly say that 'I think I shall be able', to get a more distinct
expression from him of what he wants than resulted in my efforts of
yesterday."

Wilbur decided to fall in with Berg's plans. On 27 May they left for
Paris. Wilbur saw no British officials during his brief visit to London. In
this way the British Government in 1907 lost its opportunity to acquire his
invention.

CHAPTER 9

Aeronautical Developments in 1907

Work in The Balloon Factory – Influence of the Wright
Brothers – Evidence of the Hon. C. S. Rolls – The Reason
for the Wrights' Reticence – Attitude of the Wright
Brothers – Renewed American Negotiations – A Sensitive
Theme – Orville Responds to the Board – Patrick Alexan-
der Seeks Information – 'Do Not Break your Neck' –
Wilbur Wright in Paris – Rumours About the British Gov-
ernment – The Decision of General Picquart – Senator
Humbert, a Scoundrel – He Demands a Bribe – The
Wrights Begin to Rely upon Colonel Capper – Orville
Arrives in Paris – The Wrights Put Their Faith in Capper –
Patrick Alexander Learns Wilbur has Gone to Russia – He
Checks Up – Cordial Attitude of the Germans – The
Barnum and Bailey Circus – Treachery of Captain Ferber –
Independence of the Wright Brothers – Orville Visits Eng-
land – Capper Convinces Him – Nulli Secundus I – Dirigible
Airships – Capper and Cody Fly to London – A Disaster –
Lieutenant Dunne's Aeroplane – The Strictest Secrecy –
Alexander Reveals the Secret – Failure in the Highlands –
The Marquess of Tullibardine Attacks the Liberal Govern-
ment – Colonel Capper's Problem – Haldane Visits Blair
Atholl – Decision of the Army Council – The Second Hague
Peace Conference – Its Predecessor – Military Employment
of Balloons – The Hague Conference and Aerial Naviga-
tion – A Failure of Definition – The War in The Air.

I

During the course of the year 1907 the British War Office was responsible for a good deal of aeronautical activity. In the Balloon Factory at
Farnborough Lieutenant Dunne continued to improve his gliders. S. F.
Cody worked zealously upon his own machine. The goal of each of these
experimenters was to create a powered aeroplane that could be employed
in the field as a new and revolutionary military weapon.

Colonel Capper and Cody were also engaged in the construction of a
dirigible airship, known later as the *Nulli Secundus I*. Capper and his

superiors in the War Office believed that their country could not be allowed to fall behind in this area of aeronautical achievement. The French and Germans had already made significant progress with dirigible airships. The authorities in the War Office were convinced that such dirigbles, with the passage of time, might develop into a grave danger for the people of the British Isles. They resolved to produce a British Army airship of their own design.

In these months the British maintained a fitful and intermittent contact with the Wright brothers. Despite the failure of their negotiations with them, they were intensely interested in what the Wrights did. As Percy Walker put it, "for some years the Wright Brothers dominated Farnborough's thinking, and they were closely bound up with the country's aviation policy".[1]

As we have seen, Britain's highest military authorities had neglected to purchase the Wright invention when it was offered to them because the brothers refused to demonstrate their aeroplane before a contract for its sale was signed. This was a significant factor in Haldane's decision to reject Lady Jane Taylor's overtures. It also played a part in the negative conclusions reached by the several authorities in the War Office who concerned themselves with the matter.

Nevertheless, an impressive explanation and defence of the Wright brothers' policy had already been published in the London Press. In this instance the Wrights' advocate was the Hon. C. S. Rolls, a man who was universally respected and admired in Britain as a gallant and dashing racing car driver and founder of the newly established firm of Rolls-Royce, Ltd.

Charles Stewart Rolls was the third son of Lord Llangattock. He had been educated at Eton and at Trinity College, Cambridge, where he obtained a first class degree in Mechanics and Applied Science. His contemporaries looked upon him as a brilliant sportsman and as a technical expert of proven abilities. In 1906 the Rolls-Royce car was kept constantly in the public eye in order to boost its sales. Rolls competed in and won some of the most important trials and rallies of the day. He regularly demonstrated the technical superiority of his firm's car in competition with British and foreign rivals. He was an enthusiastic balloonist. He was also keenly interested in aeroplanes.

At the end of 1906 he travelled to the United States in order to drum up American sales for the Rolls-Royce car. While he was in New York Patrick Alexander[2] introduced him to the Wright brothers who were there to negotiate with Charles Flint and his colleagues. When Rolls returned to London he sent a letter about his American visit to the editor

[1] Walker, *Early Aviation at Farnborough*, vol. II, p. xvi.
[2] It will be recalled that Patrick Alexander was in New York with the Wrights in December 1906.

of *Ballooning and Aeronautics*, a London periodical. His letter was published in its edition of April 1907.

Ballooning and Aeronautics explained to its readers that Rolls' communication contained several "interesting passages". Rolls declared that he had interviewed the Wrights and some independent witnesses who had seen the various flights of their machine. "The result is", he wrote, "that I am quite convinced and perfectly satisfied that they have attained in flight even more than has been published in the newspapers."

Rolls devoted several paragraphs of his letter to a defence of the Wright policy of "excessive secrecy". He declared: "I might mention that the reason for the reticence of these gentlemen in the matter of their experiments is quite clear, and it is, I think, grossly unfair upon them to deprecate the value of the work they have done by reason of the policy of silence which they have adopted."

Rolls went on to state: "It is true that their machine is covered with numerous patents, but once the public were able to watch the experiments closely and have photographs taken of the machine, it would then be comparatively easy for men experienced in the subject to construct a machine like it; and it would take endless time and much money to fight the patents in the law courts. It is, therefore, obviously much simpler and safer for them to keep their machines to themselves and thus prevent other people from copying them, than to rely upon their patents, whether these could be upheld or not."

His defence of the Wrights' policy continued: "This, of course, only applies to matters in their present stage, for when once they have sold their invention to some Government or other powerful body, they would then have no object in keeping their experiment secret. . . ."

Rolls concluded this part of his letter to *Ballooning and Aeronautics* by explaining: "These remarkable men are extremely modest, and it is very difficult to get them to talk at all about their achievements or to claim anything, but when pressed on the point, they admitted that their machine was certainly capable of covering the distance involved in the *Daily Mail* prize . . ."

Later, as we shall see, C. S. Rolls purchased a Wright aeroplane. He then offered his services to the British Government so that they could benefit from the experience he gained while flying it. The government, at that time, accepted his remarkable proposal after it had been discussed at a secret meeting of the Committee of Imperial Defence. In the early spring of 1907, however, no one in authority paid any attention to his opinions about the Wright machine or to his defence of their plan not to demonstrate the aircraft until its sale was completed.[1]

---

[1] The details of Rolls' remarkable arrangements with the British Government are set out in subsequent chapters of this work.

II

In 1907 Wilbur and Orville Wright entered upon a new phase of their remarkable career. Some of their contemporaries looked upon them as mere "mechanics", unscientific bicycle repairers who had wandered, ignorant and ill-equipped, into a new and awesome field of technology. Nevertheless, it was at this stage that the Wrights began to treat, on a personal basis, with high officials in the American, French, and German Governments.

The Wright brothers' attitude at this time was determined by their realization that they controlled a device that would change the destiny of the world. They knew that not one of their rivals had yet mastered the secrets of successful mechanical flight. They understood, better than anyone else, the significance of what they had done. Two later writers declared of their invention: "It would mark a dividing line in the history of civilisation. Mankind would have as complete control of the air as it now had of land and water; the hidden corners of the globe would become accessible; warfare would be revolutionised. Such an invention would be worth untold millions of dollars."[1] This was an exact reflection of the Wright attitude in 1907 when they hawked their machine before quibbling military and civilian authorities in Paris, Berlin, and Washington.

The Wrights, who were not warlike men, believed the aeroplane would be employed at first for military purposes. In their opinion it would serve, eventually, as a carrier of civilian goods and passengers but in the beginning it would be most valuable for military scouting. Moreover, the brothers hoped their invention would actually prevent wars, and they based this hope on two sets of reasons. Firstly, they thought the aeroplane would be such a destructive instrument that no government would readily expose its people to the terrors that might be rained upon them from the air. Secondly, they calculated that the very possibility of air bombing had introduced a new and significant element. The persons chiefly responsible for wars would now be exposed to attack, in a way that had not existed before. The Wrights thought that kings, presidents, ministers, and legislatures might pause if they knew that bombs could be dropped from the air on their palaces, homes or places of assembly. These beliefs helped to convince them that they should approach governments first, in their attempts to sell the aeroplane.[2]

Even before Wilbur set out for Paris in the company of Hart O. Berg and Frank Cordley, tentative negotiations for the sale of their machine had begun again with the authorities in Washington, D.C. When Wilbur left Dayton for London in May 1907 he undertook to carry out the

[1] See Morris and Smith, *Ceiling Unlimited*, p. 67.
[2] These opinions of the Wright brothers are set out in Kelly, *The Wright Brothers*, p. 165, *n*. 1.

European phase of the Wright's business while Orville dealt with the American phase of it. By the terms of their agreement, Flint and Company played no part in the Wrights' bargaining with the American Government.

The renewed American negotiations began early in April 1907. On one of his visits to New York Wilbur discovered that Congressman Herbert Parsons had already called President Theodore Roosevelt's attention to the Wright aeroplane. Congressman Parsons hoped the United States Army would secure control of the invention and develop it for military purposes.

Herbert Parsons was an influential Republican leader in New York City and in Washington, D.C. His brother-in-law, Courtland Field Bishop, President of the Aero Club of America, was a man who knew all about the Wrights' achievements and was particularly impressed by them. In order "to get aeronautical matters moving in the United States",[1] Bishop, early in 1907, suggested to Congressman Parsons that the Congress should pass a bill appropriating the sum of one million dollars for the purchase of aeronautical equipment for the Army. Eventually, it was decided that such a course was not feasible. Parsons, however, was a close friend of President Theodore Roosevelt. He acquainted him with the situation and pressed him to see to it that the War Department acted. Early in April 1907, at Parson's request, the Wrights sent him copies of all their correspondence with the United States Army's Board of Ordnance and Fortification.

Wilbur enabled Octave Chanute, who was very interested in these new departures, to follow them in detail. He regularly informed Chanute of each new development, as it arose. Early in April he told Chanute he believed the officials in the United States War Department would welcome an initiative from the Wrights so that the American negotiations could be reopened. However, Wilbur explained, "we are inclined to let them make the first move". He emphasized to his friend that "Negotiations are in progress with several foreign governments. . . ."[2]

Chanute saw at once that the Wright brothers were now treading upon extremely dangerous ground. He was sorry they were not more eager to negotiate with the American Government. On 2 May he took care to warn them about the possible consequences of a sale to a foreign power: "I was called on a few days ago by a newspaper reporter who said that the

---

[1] This phrase is Orville's. He employed it when he described the situation to Octave Chanute, in May 1907. See McFarland, *The Papers of Wilbur and Orville Wright*, pp. 762–3.

[2] For the exchanges between Wilbur and Chanute at this time, mentioned in this and the following paragraphs, see McFarland, *The Papers of Wilbur and Orville Wright*, pp. 754–9.

American people will mob you if you sell your invention abroad and it is used against the United States. . . ."

Here was a sensitive theme. At this stage the Wrights had before them prospects of sales in England, France, Germany, and also in Tsarist Russia. They would not readily abandon the possibility of reaping in such glittering European rewards. Wilbur composed a reply to Chanute's warning with particular care: "We offered our flyer to the U.S. Government before offering it elsewhere, and repeated the offer before entering upon the French negotiations of 1905-6. We also some weeks since expressed to Mr. Parsons, who was in communication with the War Department, a willingness to have a conference . . . if it at any time seemed desirable, but declined to make the first move again. Our consciences are clear, and we will keep them so."

Later in May the Wright brothers suddenly received a communication from the Board of Ordnance and Fortification, in Washington, D.C. The communication informed them that the Board had under consideration several proposals for the construction and testing of flying machines; and that the Wrights could take any action in the matter they deemed desirable. The Wrights learned also that the initiative behind this communication lay with President Theodore Roosevelt. He had instructed his Secretary, William Loeb, to direct the attention of the Board to the Wright aeroplane. A copy of Loeb's letter accompanied the message from the Board of Ordnance and Fortification. It requested the Board to look into the Wright invention.[1]

Wilbur and Orville were thus confronted by a delicate problem. Before they reached a final conclusion about how to deal with it they received Flint's telegraphic signal requesting one of them to travel to Europe, upon the instant. As Wilbur rushed eastward by train to New York he sent Orville clear instructions about the manner in which he wanted the problem dealt with. En route to New York he offered his brother the following terse advice: "In the U.S. correspondence be careful not to give them any chance to put us in a bad light as very unreasonable, etc."[2] The Wright brothers were prepared to bargain with the United States authorities; but they would not readily abandon the possibilities that gleamed before them in the various European capitals because of what they looked upon as a rather tepid overture from the U.S. War Department.

Orville responded to the Board's initiative on the day after Wilbur's departure, 17 May. He informed the American authorities that the

---

[1] Loeb's letter went originally to W. H. Taft, the Secretary of War, who sent it to the Board. See Kelly, *The Wright Brothers*, pp. 131–2.

[2] McFarland, *The Papers of Wilbur and Orville Wright*, p. 760. The following paragraphs, above, are based on this source and on Kelly, *The Wright Brothers*, pp. 132ff; and Kelly, *Miracle at Kitty Hawk*, pp. 208ff.

Wrights possessed several machines in the course of construction and that they would be pleased to sell one or more of them to the United States War Department. He explained that these aeroplanes were capable of carrying two men and a supply of fuel for a flight of two hundred kilometers. He also proposed a conference with the War Department so that the proposition could be discussed in detail. If a formal proposal was preferred by the military authorities instead of a conference, the Wright brothers were prepared to submit one.

In due course the Board replied requesting the Wrights to submit a formal proposition. The suggestion about a conference was not taken up. The board also declared that it would be interested in witnessing a machine in flight and that its members would be prepared to visit the Wright establishment in order to do so.

Orville had no intention of showing the aeroplane to anyone before a contract was signed. He decided he would offer to sell one machine to the United States Government for the sum of one hundred thousand dollars. On 29 May he cabled to Wilbur in Paris naming this price. He quickly received the reply he wanted: "It is satisfactory. Full power has been given to you."[1]

With the ground thus cleared, Orville sent his proposal to the Board of Ordnance and Fortification, on 31 May 1907. The Wright brothers, he declared, were prepared to furnish the War Department with one aeroplane, for the sum of one hundred thousand dollars. They would also teach an operator to manage the machine in flight. The device would be capable of carrying two men and a supply of fuel sufficient for a flight of two hundred kilometers, at a speed of at least fifty kilometers to the hour. He further explained that many features of the aircraft were secret, and not protected by patents. In these circumstances it would not be prudent to show the machine in advance of a contract. However, in order to protect the purchaser from any and all risk, the Wrights agreed that the contract should provide for a demonstration of the aeroplane's capabilities in the air and for evidence of its substantial construction. Furthermore, Orville proposed that no part of the purchase price should be paid until a trial flight demonstrated that the Wright aeroplane could meet all the requirements set out in the contract.

While these American negotiations lurched forward by slow degrees, the newspaper Press in Europe and in the United States began to mention the Wright brothers more and more frequently. Rumours about their activities were published in a variety of journals. In London, Patrick Y. Alexander did what he could to obtain accurate details about them. He did so by corresponding with the Wrights, on occasion, and by writing more frequently for news about them to Octave Chanute.

[1] McFarland, *The Papers of Wilbur and Orville Wright*, p. 765.

When he responded to a letter Alexander wrote on 8 May Chanute said: ". . . I shall be glad to learn what is being done in England to develop a flying machine".[1]

Now, it is certain that Lord Northcliffe was entirely correct when he told Lady Jane Taylor that Alexander was nothing more than a rich booby who amused himself by indulging a feverish and amateurish interest in new inventions. Nevertheless, Alexander's enthusiasm for aeroplanes had made him known to every one of the aeronautical pioneers of his day. Colonel Capper was entirely prepared to exploit Alexander's contacts in order to acquire intelligence that might be of value to the British Army.

As we shall see, Capper now decided to permit Alexander to learn the vital secrets of Lieutenant Dunne's aeroplane. In return for this exciting and privileged association with the work at Farnborough, he expected Alexander to furnish him with any information he could obtain about the activity of the Wright brothers. Under Capper's direction, even a rich booby was pressed into service for the sake of Britain's developing Air Arm.

In May 1907 Alexander was not yet prepared to allow Chanute to learn anything about the Dunne aircraft and the high hopes entertained for it in the British War Office. He replied to Chanute's request for information by sending him the details of one of his own machines, together with a number of photographs. Octave Chanute's response is of considerable interest, for several reasons:[2]

> I have your letter . . . and your superb photographs. I note therefrom that you have been experimenting on screws and I do hope that you will publish the results. I also hope that you are proceeding in the manner which I have indicated so often, i.e. to learn the management of the machine down a hillside before putting on a motor and propeller. In my judgement that is the only safe way and our French friends who are making such haste to beat the Wrights will come croppers.
>
> I see in the Aerophile for April that five English aviators are having flying machines built at Battersea in profound secrecy. I conjecture that the British Government is one and that you are the other four. . . .
>
> I wish you good luck in all your own experiments. Break as many machines as you like but do not break your neck.

Early in June Alexander again wrote to Chanute to ask which of the Wright brothers was in Europe. Later in the month Alexander learned from an article in the London *Evening News* that the Wright invention

---

[1] Octave Chanute Papers, Chanute to Alexander, 21 May 1907.
[2] Octave Chanute Papers, Chanute to Alexander, 27 May 1907.

had been sold to the French Government. He at once asked Chanute to confirm this report. Octave Chanute knew a good deal about the Wrights' negotiations in Paris but he was unable to satisfy his friend's curiosity on this particular point. On 24 June he told Alexander:[1]

> I have just received your note of 11th with clipping from "London evening News", stating that Wright Brothers aeroplane has been purchased by France.
>
> In answer to your enquiry I beg to say that I do not know whether the report is true or not. I wrote you on the 22nd giving the information which I had up to that time.

III

Wilbur Wright's adventure in Paris was a painful one. It served to make the brothers even more suspicious than they were before. They realized yet again that ceaseless vigilance was required if they were not to be robbed of the fruits of their genius, hard work, and devotion.

Wilbur, Berg, and Cordley arrived in the French capital on 27 May 1907. On the next day Wilbur and Berg met the French oil magnate, Henri Deutsch de la Meurthe. Deutsch declared that he was very interested in the Wright aeroplane. He was ready to join in the formation of a company to exploit the invention as soon as a proposition of sound business character was put before him. He also volunteered to see the Minister of War in order to inform him about the aeroplane. When Deutsch met the Minister, General Georges Picquart, one of the heroes of the Dreyfus affair, Picquart declared that the matter was of obvious military importance. If machines were for sale he was prepared to buy some.

After Wilbur obtained Orville's consent to the formation of a company, he set to work to arrange the details with Berg and Deutsch. Eventually, it was decided the Wright brothers would receive two hundred and fifty thousand dollars in cash and a half interest in the company which would control the European rights in their invention. The French War Ministry required that the machine should be able to fly to a height of three hundred meters; they also insisted upon a period of exclusive control of the aeroplane and its technical secrets.

For Wilbur, a key element in the arrangement was the power, political and economic, of the other stockholders. Deutsch agreed to take seventy thousand dollars of the stock while Isidor Loewe of Berlin was to have an equal amount. Flint and Company were also eager to be associated with

---

[1] Octave Chanute Papers, Chanute to Alexander, 24 June 1907.

the new enterprise. The founders were not interested in small stockholders. They expected to secure other large subscribers in England, France, and possibly in Austria. As Wilbur later told Octave Chanute, "With such men in it the company would have been strong enough to command the respect of any government or person disposed to pirate our inventions . . ."[1]

While these details were being worked out, Wilbur met Courtland Field Bishop of the Aero Club of America. Bishop was visiting Paris at this time. He reported that C. S. Rolls had told him that the British Government was now willing to pay the sum of twenty five thousand dollars for a single machine. According to Bishop, if the aeroplane showed evidence of being practically useful in war the British Government was prepared to order thirty machines at a price of ten thousand dollars each. "I do not attach much importance to the rumor", Wilbur wrote in his diary, "beyond its indication of interest in England".[2]

Orville, stern and resolute in his bicycle shop in Dayton, was unwilling to accept the height requirements demanded by the French Ministry of War. He believed more time would be needed if the Wrights were to train themselves to fly at an altitude of one thousand feet. Nor would he readily allow the French a period of exclusive control of the Wright secrets. Then, an even worse blow fell upon the developing scheme.

Arnold Fordyce, the French agent who had travelled to Dayton in December 1905, suddenly discovered that the Wrights were negotiating with Henri Deutsch de la Meurthe. Fordyce worked for Henri Letellier, proprietor of the prominent Paris newspaper *Le Journal*, and for his son.

In 1905, it will be recalled, Fordyce had signed a contract with the Wright brothers which, among its other clauses, granted him an option for a short period of time. The younger Letellier had assigned this option to General Picquart's predecessor in the French Ministry of War, but the authorities there had allowed it to lapse. They did not complete the deal Fordyce had arranged. As a result the French Government paid the Wright brothers, after some quibbling, the sum of five thousand dollars, as the Fordyce contract required. Now, however, Letellier became very angry. He insisted that he should be the sole French member of the new corporation to invest in it on a large scale. He demanded that Deutsch should at once withdraw from the company.

Wilbur and Hart O. Berg suggested that Letellier be allowed to subscribe the same amounts as those offered by Henri Deutsch. Letellier refused to entertain their proposal. Now, Wilbur became very worried. If Deutsch withdrew from the arrangement it would mean that Isidor Loewe would not proceed. Furthermore, Flint and his friends had no

[1] See McFarland, *The Papers of Wilbur and Orville Wright*, p. 837.
[2] *Ibid.*, p. 778.

respect for the younger Letellier and no confidence in any business fostered by him. As a result, all Letellier's demands were refused.

Letellier, in a rage of anger and frustration, now seized the initiative. He went to General Picquart and roundly told him he had spent a good deal of money in sending Arnold Fordyce to Dayton, in 1905. As a result, he had secured an option to purchase the Wright aeroplane and had then assigned the option to the previous minister. Letellier did not propose to allow Henri Deutsch to enter the affair at this late stage and reap all the credit, the renown of securing for France the first practical aeroplane in history. He claimed further that Picquart's predecessor had given a paper to Fordyce which awarded him certain rights in the matter. He demanded that the business of purchasing the Wright aeroplane should be put in his hands.

General Picquart had endured more than a reasonable share of political trouble and tribulation, at an earlier stage of his career. He knew that Letellier's father owned *Le Journal*, a newspaper of considerable political consequence in the capital. He informed Deutsch that he wanted the business done through Letellier.

Now it was Deutsch's turn to be upset. He at once withdrew from the project. For a considerable period he believed the Wrights were, indeed, bound to Letellier and that they were culpable in coming to him at all. Only later did Wilbur find an opportunity to explain the true nature of the situation to him, that the Fordyce option had been allowed to lapse months earlier. Then Henri Deutsch became quite friendly again, but for a time the good name of the Wright brothers had been tarnished in the high French circles where Berg had introduced them. This feeling rankled. Wilbur and Orville were jealous of their reputation and suffered when it was called into question.

Wilbur Wright was now forced to reconsider his position. There was no longer a company of powerful European stockholders to support him in the venture. He decided two courses lay open. He could try to secure a deal with France by selling a machine to the French Government, or he could abandon the French altogether and try his hand in Germany.

However, he soon realized he could not give up his French negotiations so easily. It had become known that he had bargained with Henri Deutsch and that Deutsch had approached the Minister of War in order to interest him in the Wright aeroplane. Wilbur decided it would be hopeless to make advances to the Germans after the government and the private capitalists of France had refused to sign a contract with him. The value of what he had to sell had been seriously reduced. In these circumstances he decided to approach the French once again. He knew that General Picquart wanted to acquire aeroplanes for the French Army.

Unfortunately, Wilbur and Berg were not permitted to deal directly with Picquart. The French bureaucrats insisted that all negotiations must be carried out by Arnold Fordyce but these produced no result.

By the beginning of July Wilbur received a cablegram from Orville refusing his consent to the requirements brought forward by the French Government. Orville would not grant the French exclusive rights in the invention; and he was uneasy about the height at which they wanted the aeroplane to fly. At the same time Wilbur learned that the French had also turned him down. With so much at stake the tension between the brothers rose to an almost unbearable level. On 2 July Wilbur wrote to Orville: "I confess that I am a little hurt that you should refuse this job yourself and then turn [down] my recommendations after I supposed you had given your assent to every important point. . . . I have cabled to you for instructions, so that an offer can be made to Germany."[1]

At this depressing stage the French suddenly expressed a renewed interest in the Wright aeroplane. But grave difficulties remained. Neither Wilbur nor Berg were allowed to communicate directly with the French War Ministry. They were forced to deal with Fordyce, and with Charles Humbert, a member of the French Senate and secretary of its budget committee.

Humbert was a scoundrel. When the first approach to the French had been made Berg and Wilbur were told that Humbert insisted upon a bribe of two hundred and fifty thousand francs, if they wanted their proposals to be accepted. He demanded that this extra sum should be inserted in the contract offered to the French Government.

Such a suggestion was intolerable to a man of Wilbur Wright's character. When he reported the incident to Orville he wrote in guarded terms because he feared his letter might be intercepted. Nevertheless, he roundly declared: "I will not countenance any crookedness".[2]

Wilbur sought to solve his problem in a way that was typical of the Wright brothers: "There would be no objection to having the contract call for more money than the Wrights were to receive, said Wilbur calmly, *but* the contract must give the name of the man who would receive that additional sum".[3]

Senator Humbert's attempt to obtain a bribe from the Wright brothers was not the only notorious incident of his career. He was later involved in the infamous Bolo Pasha affair.

During the first World War Paul Bolo, a French financier of dubious reputation, travelled to the United States, where he accepted huge sums of money from German agents. He was supplied with these funds so that he could secure a controlling interest in *Le Journal* and thus publicize the views of those defeatists in France who sought to undermine the desire of

---

[1] See McFarland, *The Papers of Wilbur and Orville Wright*, pp. 784–5.
[2] See McFarland, *The Papers of Wilbur and Orville Wright*, p. 781, *n.* 3.
[3] Kelly, *The Wright Brothers*, p. 162.

the French people to continue the struggle against Germany. Bolo Pasha's treachery was discovered when the French Government, under Clemenceau, embarked upon a vigorous course of hunting down treasonable conspiracies. In 1918 Bolo was tried by court-martial and found guilty of treason. He was sentenced to death and shot at Vincennes.

Senator Charles Humbert was one of the principle figures in the case, for, by the time Bolo sought to gain control of *Le Journal*, he had become its proprietor. After Bolo's conviction Humbert was arrested and tried for high treason. This was the man who sought to obtain a bribe from the Wright brothers in 1907 and then said of them: ". . . he had no faith in the Wrights . . . they were frauds".[1]

In these circumstances, it is scarcely surprising that the Wrights were unable to effect a sale of the aeroplane in France, in 1907. As Wilbur later told Octave Chanute: "After the second attempt we decided . . . to get out . . . the more we saw of the inside of French official life, the less we felt like taking any risks with such people . . ."[2]

The Wright brothers decided it would be necessary to visit Berlin if they were to carry their business forward. They did not entirely despair of the French but they were uncertain of their ability to guide the negotiations to a succesful issue; and they were uneasy about some of the Frenchmen they met during their various consultations with them. As a result of these bleak experiences in Paris they became more vigilant than ever before in their further negotiations with the German, French, American and British Governments.

However, by this stage of their adventure they were able to take comfort from the fact that the Americans seemed more interested in the aeroplane than they had been earlier. President Roosevelt's initiative was beginning to produce results in the American War Department.

Furthermore, Wilbur and Orville felt they were now on such friendly terms with Colonel Capper that they might be able to appeal to him to arouse the British Government to positive action of some kind. As we shall see, they were in error when they came to this conclusion; but the idea played some part in their calculations during their European visit of 1907.

IV

Several Frenchmen, inside and outside the government, continued to hope their country would be able to secure the Wright aeroplane. By

---

[1] These phrases are taken from Orville Wright's diary. See McFarland, *The Papers of Wilbur and Orville Wright*, p. 812.
[2] *Ibid.*, pp. 838–9.

mid-July, despite his various disappointments, Wilbur believed the prospects of a sale in France were still good. He decided to call up his reserves.
He sent a cable to Orville urging that he and Charlie Taylor come to Paris;
and he asked them to crate up a dismantled aeroplane and ship it to
France.

The French negotiations were not terminated but they produced no
positive result. By the end of July Wilbur told Fordyce he would not
proceed further until Orville arrived in France.

Both brothers were now genuinely annoyed with Flint, Berg, Cordley,
and their associates. The Flint group, despite all its efforts, had failed to
sell a single aeroplane. Moreover, the Wrights felt they were so greedy
and grasping that a new agreement would have to be worked out with
them. Furthermore, the possibility of selling the aeroplane to Great
Britain had become a factor of high significance in their plans. By the
terms of the new agreement, which was signed somewhat later, Wilbur
and Orville assumed all responsibility for the sale of their invention in
Great Britain. Flint and Company were excluded from this area of the
business, in the same way that they were denied all connection with the
American negotiations.

The Wright brothers, in arriving at this decision, put their faith in
Colonel Capper. They believed their friendship with him was more
significant than any influence that might be exerted in London by Flint's
friends, however highly they were placed.

Meanwhile, Orville arrived in Paris at the end of July; and Charlie
Taylor appeared there early in August. By this time, Wilbur and Berg
decided to leave for Berlin. They reached the German capital on 5 August
and at once began negotiations for the sale of the aeroplane.

The man they dealt with first was Isidor Loewe of the Mauser gun
company. He agreed to introduce them to those German military leaders
who were concerned with and responsible for aeronautical developments.

It was Orville's task to remain in Paris to continue to treat with Arnold
Fordyce and with Cordley. During these anxious days of bargaining and
negotiation the Wrights strove in vain to preserve the secrecy of their
activities. Orville told his father: "A *Daily Mail* reporter was in to see us
the other night. He says we are recognized among the newspapermen as
the toughest proposition they have run up against. He said that we were
being watched very close, by all the papers . . ."[1]

When Berg and Wilbur departed from Paris in an easterly direction on
4 August it was thought by some of those who watched them that their
destination was St Petersburg. There was reason for such a conjecture.
Charles Flint believed the Russians were ready to acquire aeroplanes at

[1] See McFarland, *The Papers of Wilbur and Orville Wright*, p. 816, n. 9.

this time. His contact in Russia was the famous Admiral Abaza, a man who enjoyed a close relationship with the Tsar himself.

Aleksei Mikhailovich Abaza was a naval officer of considerable experience. In 1903 he had been appointed Director of the Committee for Far Eastern Affairs. In this position he possessed the privilege of personally reporting to the Sovereign. Abaza gained so much influence he managed to displace the Ministry of Foreign Affairs in the conduct of much of its diplomacy, especially in its negotiations with Japan. He was convinced, like so many others, of the military weakness of Japan and as a result he pursued an extremely provocative policy. His attitude helped bring about the Russo-Japanese War. When Flint became the Wrights' agent he at once wrote to Admiral Abaza to offer him their invention; but the brothers refused to consent to the terms he proposed, and that particular deal was abandoned as a result of their opposition to it.[1]

In the event, Berg did travel to St Petersburg, after his visit to Berlin. Wilbur Wright, however, did not venture beyond the German capital. Patrick Alexander was one of those who believed both men had gone to Russia. He quickly sought confirmation of this intelligence from Octave Chanute. Chanute told Alexander:[2]

> I have your welcome letter of 13th. It is news to me that Wilbur Wright has gone to St. Petersburg. I had supposed that the French would close an arrangement with him and send him to Casablanca to soar over the Moors and incline them to peace. Great Britain has more of that kind of constituency than any other nation, and it is for that reason, – the moral effect, – that I have all along, favored that she should take up the Wright machine. . . .

Wilbur Wright made two visits to Berlin in 1907. The all important autumn manoeuvres prevented him from accomplishing much, on the first of these excursions, but he was very favourably impressed by the Germans. They seemed more straightforward than their French counterparts.

During the second visit Orville joined him. Significant progress was made in discussions with civilian and military officials. At the start Wilbur met Isidor Loewe, who was most cordial, helpful and friendly. Another German industrialist who expressed warm interest in the invention was Walter Rathenau, head of the Allgemeine Elektrische Gesellschaft. Among the soldiers they encountered were the Chief of the Great General Staff, von Moltke, who was favourably impressed with their proposals; and General von Einem, the Minister of War. Von Einem

---

[1] For Flint's approach to Abaza, see Wright Brothers' Papers, FLINTCO to HARTOBERG, 10 February 1907.

[2] Octave Chanute Papers, Chanute to Alexander, 29 August 1907.

gave them a pledge. If they dealt with Germany, he said, they would receive fair treatment.

Eventually, the Wrights decided to wait until the following year before they sold an aeroplane in Berlin. They planned to spend the winter months building several new aeroplanes, in Dayton. They chose not to deliver a machine at the very end of the flying season and thus permit German imitators to manufacture copies of it, during the winter of 1907-8.

It is clear enough that the Wrights were as vigilant as ever in their exchanges with the Germans. While the Berlin negotiations were taking place, Orville made two visits to England. There, the Wrights completely misread the situation. Colonel Capper managed to gull them into the belief that he could obtain, from the British War Office, an order to purchase their aeroplanes; and that he was prepared to assist them in their business dealings with the British Government.[1]

When the Wright brothers visited Europe in 1907 they were possessors of a device of incalculable significance and importance. They had devised a machine they could fly into the air. In addition, they were able to control it in flight after it became airborne. At the time no one else knew how to fly in that way. Octave Chanute made this point as clearly as he could in a letter he sent to Major Baden-Powell, in July 1907. Flying machines were the subject of his discourse. He declared:[2]

> . . . I note . . . from the Journals that the French are most active in this direction and I have compiled a list of no less than 24 aviators who are said to have built or to be building flying machines. My judgement is that they have not done as yet sufficient experimenting in gliding to learn the control of their machines in the air and so will meet with accidents. . . .

Nevertheless, no government was prepared to buy the Wright invention. In September 1907 the brothers, in these circumstances, were reduced to speculating upon a bizarre idea that came to them from Flint and Company.

Flint arranged for one of the Wrights to meet the controller of the Barnum and Bailey circus. This worthy, in cooperation with Flint, was ready to offer them fifty thousand dollars and a percentage of the profits he contemplated, if the Wrights would fly their aeroplane inside an enclosure where an admission fee could be charged. The Barnum and Bailey circus representative travelled to England to discuss the details of the arrangement. Orville met him there to look into this grotesque proposal but no deal was arranged, and the strange plan was quietly abandoned.

---

[1] See below for the establishment of these points.
[2] Octave Chanute Papers, Chanute to Baden-Powell, 8 July 1907.

Shortly after, Orville made another trip to England. His object on this occasion was to seek out Colonel Capper in order to talk to him about the sale of the aeroplane to the British Government. In this instance the Wrights proposed to themselves an approach that was unlike anything they had ever contemplated in their dealings with the Americans, French or Germans. They relied, for results, upon an earnest and sincere discussion with the British colonel, who was their friend.

On 22 October Wilbur explained their plan to his sister, Katharine: "Orville . . . will go on to England to see Jack and if possible have a 'heart-to-heart talk' with him".[1]

This belief in and reliance upon Colonel Capper was entirely misplaced. It was also very uncharacteristic of the Wright brothers.

In France, they found they could trust no one. Captain Ferber, their disciple there, had turned on them in a spasm of jealousy, after Wilbur's arrival in Paris; and they were aware of his treacherous attitude.

When Ferber met Wilbur Wright for the first time, in June 1907, he wrote to the editor of *L'Aérophile*: ". . . I grasped his hand and looked upon him with great emotion. Just think that without this man I would be nothing . . . Think that, without him, my experiments would not have taken place and I should not have had Voisin as a pupil. Capitalists like Archdeacon and Deutsche de la Meurthe would not . . . have established the prizes you know of. The press would not have spread the good seed on all sides . . . Without this press campaign, Santos-Dumont, the great balloonist, would not have realised the moment had come . . . Delagrange would have kept on sculpting delightful statues and not have ordered an aeroplane from Voisin. . . ."[2]

After further experience in France Wilbur discovered that Ferber was his implacable enemy. In his diary for 3 July Wilbur wrote: "Ferber evidently is double-faced, but at bottom bitterly hostile". Later, he reported to Octave Chanute: "I have met Capt. Ferber several times, but we are not very intimate . . . he became infected with ambition . . . and was largely responsible for the failure of the final negotiation in March 1906. Since then he has done all he could to prevent us from doing business here". Chanute replied: "I have surmised the facts about Capt. Ferber to be as you state and I have no doubt many of the people with whom you have to deal are intensely jealous of you".[3]

Above all else Wilbur and Orville Wright had been trained by their

---

[1] See McFarland, *The Papers of Wilbur and Orville Wright*, p. 825. Percy Walker was surprised Wilbur could refer to a British colonel as Jack. In his view this implied "more than a casual friendship". See Walker, *Early Aviation at Farnborough*, vol. II, p. 66.

[2] See McFarland, *The Papers of Wilbur and Orville Wright*, p. 780, *n.* 2.

[3] For these see McFarland, *The Papers of Wilbur and Orville Wright*, p. 786, pp. 807–8, and p. 812.

parents to rely upon themselves. This attitude of self-reliance was reflected in all their enterprises. Their aeroplane was the product of their own theoretical reflections, experiments, and practice in the field. When they discussed the formation of great companies to sell their invention they refused to accept the advice of the business men they dealt with. They roundly disagreed with Flint, Cordley and Hart O. Berg, the business experts, whenever they decided they were not being treated fairly. Although they were only bicycle repairers they would not blindly accept the counsel of H. A. Toulmin, their patent attorney in Ohio. They told him what to do whenever they felt he was being lax in his preparation of technical papers and blueprints for them. In their own eyes they were early twentieth century American business men. It followed that it was their business to see to it their affairs were dealt with as they wished. If a mistake was made they would blame only themselves for the lapse.

When Wilbur left Dayton for Europe his father warned him to be especially vigilant and alert. Bishop Wright wrote to his son:[1]

> It behooves you to be watchful of your interests, and to be certain in any move you may make. And you may be sure that all dealing with you will try to reach into you as far as possible. Men of wealth generally have exercised their shrewdness pretty well.

Wilbur felt he was in no need of such hard advice. He told his sister: "You people at home must stop worrying! There is no need of it. Orville & I can take care of ourselves all right, and we will be found on top when the smoke has cleared away."[2]

The only European who managed to slip under their guard was the British colonel, John Capper. He sought to convince them, for his own arcane purposes, that he was devoted to their interests and that he would help them to sell their aeroplane to the British Government.

We know exactly what Colonel Capper told Orville when he visited England, in the autumn of 1907. The Wright brothers quarrelled so frequently and so spiritedly with Hart O. Berg about their business affairs that, on 6 November, they prepared formal notes of one of their conversations with him. When the discussion turned to the English market for aeroplanes the following was recorded:[3]

> BERG. . . . . Referring to what Orville said about England relying on Germany and would follow in their lead, I think it only right we should have England.

[1] Kelly, *Miracle at Kitty Hawk*, p. 218.
[2] *Ibid.*, pp. 223–4.
[3] For these "Notes of Conversation between Wilbur and Orville Wright and Hart O. Berg", dated 6 November 1907, see McFarland, *The Papers of Wilbur and Orville Wright*, pp. 826ff. and especially pp. 831ff.

ORVILLE WRIGHT. I think we could get an order there now. Capper told me that he thought he could do it. He said the war department would do it if we put in a proposition.

BERG. Yes, I know – the same as every military attaché on the continent would. . . .

ORVILLE WRIGHT. That is partly why I went to England. I wanted to see him – we were told he was an inventor and was interested in what he was doing himself – and whether he'd oppose us. But he wants us to make a proposition there. I thought he would not.

Later, Orville wrote to his sister: "When I was in England last week I was out to the Cappers from Saturday noon to Sunday noon. Mrs. Capper wants to send you a climbing rose. I told Will to get it if he goes out to see them on his way home".[1]

Early in 1908 the Wright brothers offered to sell a flying machine to the British War Office. As we shall see, Colonel Capper was involved in the decision to accept or to reject their proposal. Percy Walker, no friend of the Wrights, wrote of Capper and this proposed transaction: "There is more than a trace of suspicion . . . that rejection is what Colonel Capper wanted; that he was deliberately making things difficult with a view to improving the prospects for his Farnborough designs."[2]

VI

At Farnborough, Colonel Capper was extremely busy in the autumn of 1907. He closely supervised Lieutenant Dunne's secret work; and he was involved in the construction of the British Army's first dirigible airship, later known as *Nulli Secundus I*.

The dirigible airships of this period were divided into three categories or classes. Non-rigid airships possessed no framework. They were great bladders which maintained their shape by gas and air pressure. The semi-rigid airship also maintained its shape in this manner but it was fitted with an interior spar or keel. The third category, the rigid airship, had a framework which was covered by fabric. It retained its shape permanently, even when the gasbags which supplied lift were withdrawn from the interior of the vessel. Count Zeppelin's gigantic dirigible was an example of this latter type.

Contemporaries envisaged a variety of uses for these huge craft which were being developed in several countries at this time. They could be

[1] *Ibid.*, p. 833. According to Penrose Orville saw models of Dunne's machine on this visit. See Penrose, *British Aviation, The Pioneer Years*, p. 115.

[2] Walker, *Early Aviation at Farnborough*, vol. II, pp. 70–1.

employed as troop carriers or as vehicles to transport civilian passengers. They might be used as aerial scouts over the land, or the sea. Offensively, they might be employed to drop bombs, shells, or other explosive missiles on a variety of targets. Some of those concerned with airships also looked upon them as weapons that might serve the purposes of Aerial Defence. It was thought that in this capacity they might be effective in attacking other airships.

Work upon a British dirigible was begun in 1903 by Colonel Templer. In order to acquire information about this class of vessel, he visited France, where he interviewed Colonel Charles Renard, the officer in charge of the great French Balloon Establishment at Chalais-Meudon. He discovered, to his dismay, that the French spent vastly greater sums than did the British on their Aeronautical Establishment. Templer also met Alberto Santos-Dumont, a technical expert of the highest quality in this sphere, during a visit to Paris.

After Colonel Templer retired work on the British Army airship languished. Meanwhile, in France the firm of Lebaudy produced a genuinely successful dirigible named *La Patrie*. In Germany, Count Zeppelin made remarkable advances with his large rigid airship. Early in 1907 the War Office ordered Capper to bring Templer's work to fruition, as quickly as possible. The British public had become concerned that their country was falling behind in this new area of competition among the several great Powers.

On 5th August 1907 Major William Anstruther-Gray, the Unionist member for St Andrews Burghs, brought the matter up in the House of Commons:[1]

Aerial Flight

Major Anstruther-Gray (St. Andrews Burghs): To ask the Secretary of State whether, in view of the progress made by Foreign Powers in the solution of the problems of aerial flight, he will consider the desirability of increasing the grant for research on this subject.

(Answered by Mr. Secretary Haldane.)
The importance of this subject is recognised and experiments are in progress. It is not considered necessary or desirable to increase the grant of money available this year for the subject. My advisers and I are fully aware of the nature of the work that is being done elsewhere.

The House turned next to an infinitely more important subject. Anstruther-Gray enquired if the Secretary of State had seen to it that steps had been taken to secure a sufficient supply of horses for military

---

[1] *Parliamentary Debates*, 4th Series, 5th August 1907, vol. (179), col. 1517.

purposes, in case of war. Haldane dealt with this question in his usual imperturbable way.

By 10 September the *Nulli Secundus I*, a semi-rigid dirigible,[1] made its first tentative flight before a large crowd at Farnborough. Before the month was out Capper and Cody, who acted as his chief assistant in the work, made a few more flight trials. They were successful. In these circumstances Colonel Capper decided upon a bold forward step. Among the newspapers of the day the *Daily Express* stood out as a journal of genuine enterprise in the sphere of military aeronautics. On 1 October 1907 the *Daily Express* reported the events of the previous day: "The Nulli Secundus, the British military airship, performed a series of marvellous evolutions this afternoon. So successful were the trials that at their conclusion it was stated that the Nulli Secundus would fly to London in the near future, and circle over Buckingham Palace for the King's inspection. . . ."

On 3 October another trial flight took place. Two days later Capper decided to fly to London, and to return. He has been criticized severely for this decision. It has been said that he really did not understand how the expandable airship was supposed to work; that he was deficient in his scientific knowledge; that he was extremely careless in his technical preparations. "It must always be a matter of opinion", Percy Walker has written, "whether Colonel Capper's flight to London was an act of courage or of rashness".[2]

On the morning of Saturday, 5 October, *Nulli Secundus* lifted aloft and set out for London. On board and in control of the airship were Colonel Capper and S. F. Cody. They proceeded in a north-easterly direction at an average speed of about twenty four miles per hour, aided by a reasonably strong following wind. Lieutenant C. M. Waterlow, Royal Engineers, raced after them by road, in command of a ground crew of sappers. Waterlow travelled in Cody's motor-car because no official vehicle was provided for, in the experiment.

By noon the brave fliers reached London. Once there, John Capper revealed a capacity for showmanship which set at defiance his usual reputation as a stern military disciplinarian.

He flew over Kensington Palace. He advanced to Hyde Park. Next, flying at a few hundred feet, he passed over the lawns of Buckingham Palace. He then proceeded in an easterly direction in order to show himself to his superiors in the War Office, in Whitehall. There, the manoeuvres of *Nulli Secundus I* were watched by several members of the Army Council including General Sir William Nicholson, Chief of the

---

[1] See Robin Higham, *The British Rigid Airship, 1908–1931* (Westport, 1975), p. 13, hereafter cited as Higham, *The British Rigid Airship*.

[2] Walker, *Early Aviation at Farnborough*, vol. I, p. 207.

General Staff, and Major-General Hadden, the Master-General of the Ordnance. Thousands of their fellow citizens rushed into the streets in order to observe the remarkable spectacle.

The airship proceeded along Whitehall to Trafalgar Square and then, via Fleet Street, it arrived above St Paul's Cathedral, where it circled the dome. Capper's triumph seemed complete.

However, he and Cody found they could not return to Farnborough. An adverse wind sprang up. They were forced to descend in the grounds of the Crystal Palace, at Sydenham.

The British Press was delighted by Colonel Capper's remarkable achievement. On the next day *The Observer* declared: "All doubts as to the capabilities of the British military airship Nulli Secundus were dissipated yesterday by its making a wonderful voyage from Aldershot to London . . ." On 7 October *The Times* stated: "The military airship Nulli Secundus accomplished a fine performance on Saturday, travelling from Aldershot to London . . ."

A more serious note was struck on the leader page of the *Pall Mall Gazette* for 8 October: "Colonel Capper and Mr. S. F. Cody are to be congratulated on the successful flight. . . . Things are still in their incipient stages with regard to the conquest of the air. It is pleasant to know that we are now well in the flying, instead of being outsiders as we were a year ago . . . So far the Zeppelin balloon is the most elaborate which has been brought to public notice . . . Perhaps someone will say Why should not we, as a nation, be able to compete with our foreign rivals in matters of this sort? Exactly so. Why not? We have been up to the last decade or two *facile princeps* in matters of invention. Why should we latterly take retrograde steps or be left standing still while others go forward? The answer is very simple. In all these foreign attempts at aerial navigation the inventors have been supplied freely with money from the State . . . For want of sufficient funds no one will deny that Colonel Capper has been heavily handicapped. Let us hope that in future he will get a little more encouragement. . . ."

An even more ominous point was made in the *Daily Express* for 7 October. Referring to the crowds of Londoners who watched the flight of *Nulli Secundus*, the paper reported: "More than one suggested how easy it might be for the occupants to drop a score of shells and destroy the city. . . ."

Disaster struck the *Nulli Secundus* a few days later. The airship remained at the Crystal Palace until Thursday, 10 October, unable to leave because of adverse weather conditions. On that day the winds increased in strength and a severe gust struck the tethered dirigible. The front picketing stakes were torn loose and the airship, still inflated, began to thrash and heave in its efforts to break loose. The escape valves were opened in order to release hydrogen but this proved to have little effect.

No officer was present. A resourceful corporal named Ramsay rushed up and slit the envelope with a knife. But the harm was done. The understructure was smashed and the vessel collapsed, an almost total wreck.

Attempts were made at the time and later to soften this blow to British pride. In the official history, published in 1922, Sir Walter Raleigh wrote: ". . . to avoid damage by a squall, the ship was deflated, packed up, and returned to Farnborough by road".[1] This account was misleading. The *Nulli Secundus I* was severely damaged. It never flew again.

VII

While work on the *Nulli Secundus I* went forward, Colonel Capper was also concerned with the aeronautical experiments of S. F. Cody, and with those carried out so secretly at the Balloon Factory in Farnborough by Lieutenant John Dunne. Capper was especially interested, indeed excited, by the potential of Lieutenant Dunne's several flying machines.

Dunne concentrated his talents upon the creation of a "stable" aeroplane. His concept possessed a particular appeal for the military mind, for several reasons.

Pilots of a Dunne aeroplane would not require a lengthy period of training because the machine would be able to maintain itself in flight without much guidance from its operator. Moreover, it was believed that the task of flying a Wright aeroplane, which was "unstable" in the air, would exhaust any pilot who tried it. In addition, Dunne's machine would permit a pilot to perform several tasks in the air. He would, of course, be required to direct it in flight from time to time, but he would also find himself with plenty of leisure to observe enemy dispositions or to carry out any other warlike tasks.

Another set of factors was involved. Lieutenant Dunne was extremely jealous of the Wright brothers. Colonel Capper's chief object was to overtake them and to provide the British Army with a more efficient aircraft, one designed, constructed, and tested at Farnborough, under his direction. It was for these reasons that Capper urged his superiors in the War Office to reject every proposal the Wright brothers submitted for their consideration.

In July 1907 the dismantled parts of Dunne's aeroplane, together with experimental gliders and other devices, were despatched to Blair Atholl in the Scottish highlands. Lieutenant Francis Westland, R.E., commanded a support party of Farnborough sappers who were to assist in the

---

[1] See Sir Walter Raleigh, *The War in The Air*, vol. I, p. 157. See also Harald Penrose, *British Aviation, The Pioneer Years*, pp. 104–5, for another misleading account.

experiments. The strictest secrecy was maintained during the entire course of the operation.

Aeronautical historians have been unable to agree about who secured the Blair Atholl site for the British Army's secret aeroplane trials of 1907. Percy Walker states that Colonel Capper wrote to the Marquess of Tullibardine, the Duke of Atholl's son; Harald Penrose writes that the Director of Fortifications and Works, Colonel R. M. Ruck, made the arrangement. Snowden Gamble is clear that R. B. Haldane, the Secretary of State for War, asked Tullibardine if he would help the Army to carry out flight trials at one of his father's remote grouse moors. In any case, Tullibardine acted as host when the party arrived in the highlands.

The first experiments at Blair Atholl in 1907 were made with gliders. Miniature models and full-scale Dunne machines were employed in these tests. On one occasion, the Marquess of Tullibardine was pressed into service as a glider pilot. The plan was to launch him off a cliff in one of Dunne's primitive and untried man-carrying machines. Before he started the Marquess turned his glass on a white spot he had noticed far below, in the proposed landing area. He saw that it was a doctor spreading out a ground-sheet and getting his appliances ready. Fortunately for the heir to the Atholl dukedom the glider was blown over by a gust of wind before the trial even began, and he never made the flight.

Later, Colonel Capper acted as glider pilot. He wore a fencer's mask to protect his face in case of an accident. The glider, on this occasion, lifted into the air for a few seconds but almost at once it began to descend very rapidly. It smashed into a nearby wall. Mrs Capper, who was present, rushed forward to help her husband. Blood poured from his face where the mask had cut his ear. Luckily, he was not seriously injured.

With this much proven, the decision was made to repair the glider and also to convert it, without any further significant tests, into a powered aeroplane. This was achieved by fitting the two *Buchet* engines which had been brought along for the purpose.[1]

While the British experts carried on in this curious way, Patrick Alexander decided to reveal the secrets of the Dunne aeroplane to Octave Chanute. In his letter he stated boldly that the Dunne aeroplane was far more efficient than the Wright machine. No one who did not possess full information about Dunne's secret work could have written as Alexander did. When Chanute received this startling intelligence he was stunned and shocked. He replied to Alexander:[2]

---

[1] Harald Penrose, *British Aviation, The Pioneer Years* states at p. 102 that the engines were not fitted to Dunne's glider in 1907. It is clear enough that they were.
[2] Octave Chanute Papers, Chanute to Alexander, 24 September 1907.

Mr. P. Y. Alexander   Sept 24th 7
   82 Victoria Street, Westminster

Dear Mr. Alexander,
   You fairly took my breath away by announcing that there is in
England a machine far away ahead of the Wrights and their type of
machine. It seems hard to believe unless it has been tested in actual
flight, for the merit of the Wright machine lies in its perfection of
control and I hope that no accident will occur when the British
machine is tried. . . .

                                                   Yours truly
                                                   O. Chanute

   Meanwhile, the Press in Britain sought to discover what was happening
in the Scottish highlands. The lead in this endeavour was taken by the
Special Correspondent of the *Daily Express*. He was particularly
efficient, and several other publications reproduced or summarized his
reports in their own columns. He knew what took place in the Balloon
Factory at Farnborough. On 6 September the *Daily Express* reported that
the experimental work of the Balloon Factory had been divided into three
parts: Balloons, including the airship *Nulli Secundus*; Man-lifting kites;
and Aeroplanes: "The aeroplanes are of a new and interesting type. All
the parts have been made separately so that only the highest officials who
have the plans in their possession know what the completed figure will
resemble . . ."
   By the end of the month the *Daily Express* correspondent was at Blair
Atholl. He could only observe the Dunne machine from a great distance
but he was eventually able to interview the Marquis of Tullibardine, in an
attempt to glean further scraps of information from him. On 27 September large headlines in the *Daily Express* proclaimed: "BRITAIN'S
FIRST AEROPLANE. EXPERIMENTS WITH AERIAL FIGHTING
MACHINE. SUCCESS ASSURED. WORK IN SECRECY IN THE
HIGHLANDS."
   Two articles followed. In the first the *Daily Express* explained: "Experiments have been carried on for more than a week . . . with the new
aeroplane for the British Government, which it is believed will surpass
any other machine of the kind in existence. The aeroplane must not be
confused with the airship Nulli Secundus . . . It has no gas bag, and is built
on the heavier-than-air principle. Its lifting power is derived from motors.
. . . It is essentially a fighting machine."
   In the second article the Special Correspondent reported that he had
seen the Dunne aeroplane "through a pair of powerful field glasses". He
stated: "So confident are the inventors of the new aeroplane of its success
and of its superiority over all its predecessors, that they are sparing

neither pains nor expense to maintain absolute secrecy . . . Sentries are posted in the flanking hills . . .''

On the next day the *Daily Express* contained another report. Although success still seemed certain an excuse, in case of failure, was also offered: "The trials are hampered by the parsimony of the Government . . . But for the generosity of the Marquis of Tullibardine, who has granted the site and paid all the expenses of cartage, the aeroplane would not have gone beyond Lydd, where it was arranged originally for the experiments to take place. . . . All that ingenuity, experience, and mechanical skill can devise has been brought into operation but another £5,000 or £6,000 is wanted to ensure a definite triumph.''[1]

Unfortunately, the Dunne aeroplane of 1907 proved to be a lamentable failure. It did not fly at all. In the final experiment the machine was poised on a raised track pointing down the hillside. The engines were opened up and the vehicle rushed along the track and at once pitched into the ground, on its nose. It was badly damaged but not beyond repair. However, the last trial of the 1907 season had taken place. Cold weather, with ice and snow, was expected in the highlands at any time. The contingent of Royal Engineers packed up its equipment and returned to Farnborough. Dunne and Capper had to be content with making plans for the next year's trials.

No one knows who attempted to fly the powered aircraft at Blair Atholl in 1907. Generally Dunne was not allowed to fly because of his delicate health but he may have been the pilot on this occasion.

It must be borne in mind that Colonel Capper and Lieutenant Dunne looked upon the Wright brothers as their most formidable rivals; and it should be mentioned in this connection that when the Wright brothers flew the dates and exact times of flight were always carefully recorded. The direction and force of the wind was measured and set down, as a matter of course. The name of the pilot and those of any witnesses always appeared in the Wrights' logs or diaries. Air temperatures were set down. The distances covered in glides or in power-driven flights were measured exactly, and then written into the diaries. Any vagaries of the weather were described in detail. None of these procedures or practices was followed by Dunne or by his party of Royal Engineers during their trials of his aeroplane in Scotland, in 1907.

[1] Octave Chanute regularly received Press cuttings that dealt with the subject of aeronautics: from Britain, and from other countries. By the end of October 1907 his "British clippings" furnished him with a few details about the "Government flying machine designed by Mr Dunne. . . ." See Octave Chanute Papers, Chanute to Alexander, 25 October 1907.

VIII

In later years the Marquess of Tullibardine attacked the Liberal Government, R. B. Haldane and the War Office in very bitter terms because of what happened at Blair Atholl in 1907. He argued that Lieutenant Dunne failed there because he did not receive adequate support from his superiors. His criticisms, in so far as the experiments of 1907 were concerned, were not wholly accurate.

Tullibardine, in adopting this course, acted as a political partisan. He was an active Conservative politician. He sought to injure the Liberal Government in any way he could.

In Britain the years between 1908 and 1914 were marked by terrible and almost intolerable political disagreements. The Conservative and Liberal Parties opposed each other with an almost unprecedented savagery.

The Tories believed the Liberal Government had adopted an entirely inadequate programme of National Defence. They adopted Joseph Chamberlain's policy of Tariff Reform and Imperial Preference as the rallying cry of their cause. The Liberals felt the course Chamberlain advocated would result in the ruin of Britain's international position and in the destruction of her prosperity. There were terrible political battles over the Lloyd George Budget of 1909 and the famous Parliament Act of 1911. When a Home Rule Bill for Ireland was introduced in 1912 many Conservatives were outraged and a few of their leaders actually planned to defy the law in case the Bill was ever passed by the Liberals and their Irish Nationalist supporters in the House of Commons.

In November 1911 Arthur Balfour was forced from the leadership of the Conservative Party by the actions of his disappointed and angry followers. They believed he was not vigorous enough to continue to serve as their leader. Balfour, the aristocrat, found their criticism tedious, and even boring. He decided it would be more convenient for him to resign his place than to continue to attempt to deal with their factious carping.

His replacement was a tough, hard politician of Scots and Canadian background, Andrew Bonar Law. His great object was to restore the unity of his Party. He could only do so by giving full rein to its extremists or they would tear him down in the same way they had worn out Balfour. Bonar Law was a proponent of what his contemporaries called the "new style" in British politics. His motto was: "Cut the cackle". He planned to lead his party as vigorously as he could. In these circumstances he resolved to offer no quarter to his Liberal enemies, and to ask for none from them. The Marquess of Tullibardine was one of his followers.

Early in March 1912 Tullibardine prepared to oppose the Liberal Government's Army Estimates for the year. He wrote to Bonar Law so that he could act in concert with his leader in their Parliamentary attack on the Liberal proposals. In his letter he mentioned Haldane's reaction to the aeroplane experiments which had taken place at Blair Atholl in 1907. His charge about Haldane and aeroplanes was taken up in several quarters:[1]

                                                      84 Eaton Place, S.W.
Dear Bonar Law,   2 March 12
    Herewith the rest of the Army notes. You will find it straightfor-ward reading. . . .
    If you have a moment to spare you might let me know the chief points you are going for as then I can rub it in afterwards & prepare beforehand. Anyhow I am quite confident that I can flatten Seely[2] on any point he chooses to raise including Aeronautics – as I was in charge of the Govt. experiments 5 years ago when Haldane made the memorable announcement to us (not publicly) that aeroplanes would never fly.
    I don't know of course if I shall be called but it might be a good thing if I came on fairly early in the debate. . . .

                                                      Yours
                                                      Tullibardine

In August 1913 the Marquess of Tullibardine made further charges about the War Office and aeroplanes. He wrote a letter to the *Daily Mail* in order to refer to Dunne's experiments at Blair Atholl in 1907, and in 1908. His letter was published in the *Daily Mail* for 19 August 1913. It appeared below large headlines which stated: "BRITAIN'S LOST CHANCE. DISCLOSURE BY LORD TULLIBARDINE. HOW WE MIGHT HAVE LED THE WORLD IN FLYING. THE WAR OFFICE FAILURE." Tullibardine's letter declared:

    . . . At that time our War Office was very sceptical as to the future of flying, and in consequence parcimonious [*sic*]. . . .
    In 1907 the aeroplane was finished, but the War Office would only stand us a 20.h.p. Green engine, which, good engine though it was, had only sufficient power to drive the machine along the ground. Dunne's suggestion that he should have at least a 50.h.p. engine was scouted, and it was pointed out that if aeroplanes required such terribly expensive engines there could be no future for them. Even-tually the conclusion was come to by the War Office of that time that machines that were heavier than air would never fly, and both the machine and Lieutenant Dunne were scrapped in consequence. . . .

[1] HLRO, Bonar Law Papers 25/3/5, Tullibardine to Bonar Law, 2 March 1912. See also Stephen Koss, *Lord Haldane* (New York, 1969), p. 144, hereafter cited as Koss, *Haldane*.
[2] The Rt Hon. J. E. B. Seely, later Lord Mottistone, succeeded Haldane as Secretary of State for War in Asquith's Liberal Government in 1912. Before that, he served as Under-Secretary in the War Office.

Some of these statements were inaccurate in their conclusions about the experiments of 1907. The authorities who have written about them agree that two *Buchet* engines were employed in the 1907 tests. Percy Walker makes the point in his authorized history. Snowden Gamble refers to two *Buchet* motors in his account. Harald Penrose argues that a motor was not installed at all in the 1907 trials but he does mention twin *Buchet* engines in his analysis of the 1907 adventure in the Scottish highlands.[1]

However, far more was involved in Lord Tullibardine's charges than these technical niceties suggest or imply.

When Colonel Capper returned to his headquarters in the Balloon Factory at Farnborough he realized that he was confronted by a very serious problem. Despite the time and money expended upon it, the Dunne aeroplane of 1907 could not fly. Indeed, it had been unable to leave the ground despite several attempts to force it into the air.

As we have seen, in the previous September Capper had formally reported to the Director of Fortifications and Works, Colonel Ruck: "I have but little doubt that we shall be able, thanks partially to the scientific attainments and ability of Lieutenant Dunne, to turn out within a reasonable time a flying machine on much the same lines as that of the Wright Brothers, but we hope superior to it in several essentials, at an infinite fraction of the cost demanded by them."

With good cause, Colonel Capper now feared that his superiors in the War Office, confronted with such dismal results, might abandon the work and also remove Lieutenant Dunne from his place in the Farnborough establishment. Capper was determined to avoid such a development.

On 2 November 1907 he sent a report to the War Office in order to explain the high significance of Dunne's achievements at Blair Atholl. The main object of his account was to secure official permission to continue with his aeroplane experiments at Farnborough and to retain Lieutenant Dunne as one of his subordinates in the enterprise. When Capper in his report described the trial in which he flew as a glider pilot and crashed into the wall, he wrote: "The result, though to an unskilled eye disastrous, in effect showed that Lieutenant Dunne's calculations were entirely correct, the machine being poised for eight seconds."[2]

When Percy Walker analysed Capper's report in his history, he explained: "Most important is the information that at least one trial of the glider was witnessed by two leading men from the War Office: the

---

[1] See Percy Walker, *Early Aviation at Farnborough*, vol. II, p. 200; C. F. Snowden Gamble, *The Air Weapon*, pp. 98–9; and Harald Penrose, *British Aviation, The Pioneer Years*, p. 102. Dunne himself stated that two *Buchet* engines were employed in the 1907 tests. See Walker, *Early Aviation at Farnborough*, vol. II, p. 205.

[2] See Walker, *Early Aviation at Farnborough*, vol. II, p. 204.

Master-General of the Ordnance and the Director of Fortifications and Works."[1]

While it is correct that these authorities, Major-General C. F. Hadden, and Brigadier-General R. M. Ruck, did attend at least one of the trials, it must be made clear, for the purposes of the present analysis, that an even more important visitor also observed the scene at Blair Atholl. This was the Secretary of State himself. R. B. Haldane was so fascinated by the Dunne aeroplane and its military possibilities that he travelled to Scotland in order to see it in action.

In the autumn of 1908 the Liberal Prime Minister, H. H. Asquith, concerned about aeronautical developments in foreign countries, appointed a sub-committee of the Committee of Imperial Defence, to examine the entire subject and to find out the dangers to which Great Britain might be exposed, as a result of the new technology.

The chairman of this sub-committee was the distinguished military authority, Lord Esher. One of the expert witnesses called to give evidence was Colonel Capper. He was examined by Lord Esher on 15 December 1908. The following exchange took place, at that time.[2]

Evidence of Brevet-Colonel J. E. Capper, C.B., R.E.

525. Where has the experimental work been carried on? Has it been carried on exclusively at Aldershot? – No. There has been an experiment with one particular aeroplane on the Duke of Atholl's property at Blair Atholl. Mr. Haldane saw the experiments there last year.

Haldane's interest in the potential of the Dunne aeroplane was so great that he went to Scotland to observe its performance for himself. He was keenly disappointed by what he saw at Blair Atholl. Nothing very significant took place there. There was no obvious advance in technological development. The Secretary of State, a shrewd lawyer, realized he was confronted by failure. It may well be that in these circumstances he told Tullibardine that "aeroplanes would never fly".

However, the War Office, under his direction, adopted an entirely different policy in 1907. Colonel Capper's report about the Blair Atholl experiments, with its plea that he should be permitted to carry on with his aeroplane work at Farnborough, was sent to the War Office early in November 1907. Even before it arrived Haldane's Army Council considered the entire subject, on 24 and 25 October, and reached the following

[1] *Ibid.*, p. 204.
[2] Cab. 16/7. "Report and Proceedings of a Sub-Committee of the Committee of Imperial Defence on AERIAL NAVIGATION", 28 January 1909, and marked "*SECRET*".

decision: "15. The Council were of opinion that experiments with dirigible balloons and aeroplanes should be continued".[1]

Later, in 1908, Lieutenant Dunne and his machine were again despatched to Blair Atholl for further trials, as we shall see. These trials produced no valid results. The Dunne aeroplane could not be persuaded to fly, at that time.

After this second failure, Haldane despaired of the possibility that Dunne was the man who could give Great Britain the lead in the air. Then he took radical action and reorganized the Air Service with an iron hand. In 1907, however, he was still prepared to support Capper, Dunne, Cody and their Farnborough colleagues in their efforts to produce an efficient flying machine for service with the British Army.

IX

While Capper, Dunne, and their contingent of Royal Engineers laboured in the Scottish highlands in 1907, the Second Hague Peace Conference met in the Netherlands. Among the many issues dealt with was the question of aerial bombardment. Recent progress in aeronautical technology made the matter a topic of genuine interest and concern.

The First Hague Peace Conference had been called in May 1899, at the suggestion of the Russian Tsar. Such was the condition of international relations at the time that no nation welcomed the Tsar's initiative with any degree of enthusiasm. Eventually, however, twenty-six States sent representatives to the Hague.

The British Naval Delegate in 1899 was Admiral Sir John Fisher. At the Hague he had an opportunity to study, for the first time, the behaviour of German military officers of high rank. He came away from the conference convinced that Germany, not France, would be Britain's opponent in the next great European war. The German representatives adopted an equally stiff attitude. When a proposal to restrict armaments was brought forward Colonel Gross von Schwartzkopf, the German delegate, rejected the idea out of hand. The other delegates, aware that the suggestion could not be adopted owing to the German attitude, at once voted in favour of submitting it to the conference for further consideration.

In 1899 when the first Hague Conference assembled aircraft capable of navigating the air and carrying bombs had not yet been invented. Nevertheless, the forward march of aeronautical science justified the expectation that in the near future dirigible balloons able to discharge bombs and torpedoes might soon appear in the skies over Europe.

---

[1] W.O. 163/12. "Minutes of Proceedings and Precis Prepared for The Army Council for The Year 1907", 96th Meeting, 24–25 October 1907.

The attention of the 1899 conference was therefore directed to this mode of warfare. At first, a subcommission voted almost unanimously for the permanent prohibition of balloons for military purposes. Later, however, Captain W. Crozier, an American representative, moved that the prohibition be limited to a period of five years.

Crozier argued that the prohibition of the use of balloons "for the hurling of projectiles or other explosive materials" could not be justified on humanitarian grounds. When these devices were perfected, he said, they might be employed at a critical point in the field of battle and thus decide the victory. They would localize, at important points, the destruction of life and property and thus spare the sufferings of "all who are not at the precise spot where the result is decided". "Such use", Captain Crozier declared, "tends to diminish the evils of war and to support the humanitarian considerations which we have in view". He continued:[1]

> . . . The balloon, as we know it now, is not dirigible; it can carry but little; it is capable of hurling, only on points inexactly determined and over which it may pass by chance, indecisive quantities of explosives, which would fall, like useless hailstones, on both combatants and non-combatants alike. Under such conditions it is entirely suitable to forbid its use, but the prohibition should be temporary and not permanent. At a later stage of its development, if it be seen that its less desirable qualities still predominate, there will still be time to extend the prohibition; at present let us confine our action within the limits of our knowledge.

As a result of these reflections a declaration was adopted forbidding for a period of five years the discharge of projectiles and explosives by balloons. An article (No. 25) was also added to the Hague Convention respecting the laws and customs of war on land, forbidding the bombardment of undefended towns, villages, habitations, and buildings. The First Hague Peace Conference achieved nothing with respect to disarmament or limitation of armaments. A Permanent Court of Arbitration was provided for but it was realized that much had been left undone.

In 1904 President Theodore Roosevelt was asked to convene a second Peace Conference to take up those subjects postponed or neglected at the Hague. President Roosevelt agreed to this request but when the Tsar allowed it to be known that he would like to call for the Conference himself, the President gladly accepted his suggestion.

There were several postponements before the various nations would agree to return to the Hague. During this time progress in the art of aerial navigation was noteworthy and even remarkable. In France, the airship

---

[1] See William I. Hull, *The Two Hague Conferences* (New York, 1970), pp. 77–8. The original edition of this work was published in 1908.

La Patrie, "made in the shape of a cigar, dirigible at will", was capable of successful flight. Genuine advances with dirigible aircraft were also taking place in Germany. While the various Powers squabbled, the matter was raised in the House of Commons on 19 April 1907 by an old Radical champion, Sir Charles Dilke:[1]

The Hague Conference and Aerial Navigation

Sir Charles Dilke (Gloucestershire, Forest of Dean): To ask the Prime Minister whether in view of the expiration of the five years' term for which the launching of explosives from airships was by agreement of the Powers prohibited, and the possible absence of present unanimity and difficulty of enforcement of any new agreement, he can give the House general information as to any decision of the Defence Committee upon the subject; whether defensive airship experiment and construction is treated as the exclusive concern of the Army, or how far the Admiralty is being consulted with regard to it.

(Answered by Sir H. Campbell-Bannerman.) As the question of the renewal of the agreement will doubtless be considered at the coming Conference at the Hague, I think it better to say nothing on the subject of renewal at the present moment. The Naval and Military Departments are watching such progress as has been made with aerial navigation, but experimental work, so far, has been confined to the War Office.

The Second Hague Peace Conference met between June and October 1907. Sir Henry Campbell-Bannerman's Liberal Government had already committed itself to a policy of reduction of Britain's military and Naval budgets and to an attempt to secure a general European limitation of armaments.[2] The Imperial German Government, however, obstinately opposed any discussion of arms limitation at the Second Hague Conference and refused, in advance, to take any part in such discussions if they were raised there.

The Germans believed the British proposal to limit armaments was merely a cunning trick, an attempt to preserve British naval superiority, at German expense. When the British Government made known their plan to bring up their ideas at the Hague the German Chancellor, Von Bülow, in a speech to the Reichstag announced that the German delegates would not participate in such deliberations.

As a result of this attitude, the question of reducing expenditure on

[1] *Parliamentary Debates* 4th Series, Vol. 172, 19 April 1907, col. 1268.
[2] See in this general connection M. W. Royse, *Aerial Bombardment and The International Regulation of Warfare* (New York, 1928), p. 53, and pp. 118–19.

armaments was not even discussed at the Second Hague Peace Conference. This was a disaster of the first magnitude. From that instant the Anglo-German naval rivalry dominated the future of Europe, with fatal consequences for the several European nations.

In these circumstances the Second Hague Conference turned to a variety of lesser matters. One of these was the question of throwing projectiles and explosives from balloons. There was considerable discussion of the subject at the conference.

The five years' prohibition of the military employment of balloons, imposed by the first conference, had expired in 1904. The Belgian delegation now proposed to renew the prohibition of 1899 for another period of five years. Their initiative was supported by Lord Reay of Great Britain. The Russian and Italian representatives urged that a permanent prohibition be placed upon the bombardment, by airships, of unfortified cities and towns. This proposal, however, was withdrawn when it was decided to have been already included within the laws and customs adopted for war on land.

The French delegation then brought forward the argument that these laws and customs made unnecessary any regulations concerning warfare in the air. The Belgian proposal, however, now received a considerable measure of support in the subcommission and commission of the conference especially concerned with the deliberations about aerial warfare. These bodies voted to adopt the Belgian idea.

In the plenary session of the conference Britain's delegation offered an amendment to the Belgian proposition. Their amendment urged that the prohibition should be extended until the end of the third Peace Conference. This was accepted although there was a significant number of the Powers that decided to abstain from the vote. Many States which in 1899 approved the prohibition declined to do so in 1907. They were unwilling to surrender the advantages of a mode of warfare whose possibilities had been so fully demonstrated since the time of the First Conference. Among the States who refused to sign the declaration were Germany, France, Russia, Spain, Italy, Japan, and Sweden.

As a result, the declaration could not be looked upon as a universally binding regulation. Nevertheless, there was general agreement among the Powers in favour of imposing restrictions or limitations upon the practices of aerial warfare.

The Italian and Russian delegations proposed, in place of the temporary renewal of the prohibition of 1899, a declaration forbidding the discharge from balloons of projectiles or explosives against undefended towns, villages, houses or dwellings. Their proposal was not adopted in the form submitted. However, it found its way into the Convention that dealt with the laws and customs of war on land. Article 25 of this Convention reads: "The attack or bombardment *by any means whatso-*

ever of towns, villages, habitations or buildings which are not defended is forbidden."[1] In effect, this article was a renewal of Article 25 of the Convention of 1899, with the addition of the words "by any means whatsoever". The article clearly covered aerial bombardments, "as it was undoubtedly intended to do".[2]

These words were added upon the initiative of the French delegation, for a particular purpose. The object was to remove all doubt as to the illegality of aerial attacks upon undefended places; moreover, unlike the prohibition of 1899 this prohibition was of unlimited duration.

Unfortunately, grave problems about the restriction arose in the period after 1907. It was argued that the prohibitory clause of the Land War Convention was merely declaratory of an existing rule of customary law and was therefore binding, independently of the status of any convention. More significantly, Article 25 of the Land War Convention, the only rule in existence before the outbreak of war in 1914 which touched upon the subject of bombardment from the air, did not define the word "unde-fended". The latitude of interpretation which the word admits rendered the Article ineffective, so far as bombardment from aircraft was con-cerned. The Hague Conference of 1907, despite its considerable exer-tions, did not define what were and what were not legal targets for attack by aircraft.

This failure produced considerable public discussion by learned au-thorities in Britain in the years that followed. Unknown to the public, however, as we shall see, the British Government took up the matter in secret, within a year of the ending of the Hague Conference in October 1907.

X

A striking episode in these general developments took place in 1907. The British people were forced to recognize that the very nature of war was about to change. No longer would they be isolated from the scenes of carnage and battle.

For many generations they had looked upon themselves as being more fortunate than their European neighbours because the English Channel was no mere land frontier easily crossed by invading armies. Rather, the Channel was a boon of Providence which had enabled them to develop their own peculiar institutions and traditions, unhampered by the disas-

---

[1] See James W. Garner, *International Law and The World War* (London, 1920), vol. II, pp. 466–7, an excellent account.

[2] *Ibid.*, p. 467.

ters and catastrophes the various Continental nations regularly inflicted upon each other. In 1907 H. G. Wells wrote *The War in The Air*.

The War in The Air and Particularly How Mr. Bert Smallways Fared While it Lasted began to appear as a serial story in the *Pall Mall Magazine* in January 1908. The novel is an account of the first major air war in history, a war which results in nothing less than the destruction of civilization in every part of the world. Mankind, after the war ends, is forced to live a kind of feudal existence typical of life in the Dark Ages. The various nations employ gigantic airships and aeroplanes to destroy each others' cities.

The Wright brothers are mentioned in the story. Before the war begins the hero, Bert Smallways, meets a soldier, a Royal Engineer:

> 'I tell you they *are* flying', the soldier insisted. 'I see it myself.'
>
> 'We've all seen it,' said Bert.
>
> 'I don't mean flap up and smash up; I mean real, safe, steady, controlled flying, agains the wind, good and right.'
>
> 'You ain't seen that!'
>
> 'I 'ave! Aldershot. They try to keep it a secret. They got it right enough. You bet – our War Office isn't going to be caught napping this time . . .'
>
> 'I tell you they got nearly a square mile fenced in – a sort of valley. Fences of barbed wire ten feet high, and inside that they do things. Chaps about the camp – now and then we get a peep. . . .'
>
> 'Flying's going to break out,' said the soldier. 'When it does come, when the curtain goes up, I tell you you'll find every one on the stage – busy. . . .'
>
> '. . . have you noticed what one might call the remarkable case of the disappearing inventor – the inventor who turns up in a blaze of publicity, fires off a few successful experiments, and vanishes? . . . .'
>
> '. . . . You get anybody comes along who does anything striking in this line, and, you bet, he vanishes. Just goes off quietly out of sight . . . Gone – no address. First – oh! it's an old story now – there was those Wright Brothers out in America. They glided – they glided miles and miles. Finally they glided off the stage. Why, it must be nineteen hundred and four, or five *they* vanished!'

These are mere preliminaries. The chief object of *The War in The Air* was to inform the British people of the disasters that lay in store for them in the altered circumstances resulting from successful mechanical flight. Years later Wells explained his purpose, in his *Autobiography*:[1] "Already in 1908 in *The War in The Air* written before any practical flying had occurred, I reasoned that air warfare . . . would abolish the war front and with that the possibility of distinguishing between civilian and combatant.

[1] H. G. Wells, *Experiment in Autobiography* (New York, 1934), p. 569.

. . . This I argued, must . . . alter the ordinary man's attitude to warfare. He can no longer regard it as we did the Boer War . . . as a vivid spectacle in which his participation is that of a paying spectator at a cricket or base-ball match."

Bert Smallways was forced to learn this lesson when he looked down upon New York, "a furnace of crimson flames, from which there was no escape":

> He had glimpses of what it must mean to be down there – glimpses that such disasters were not only possible now in this strange, gigantic, foreign New York, but also in London . . . that the little island in the silver seas was at the end of its immunity, that nowhere in the world any more was there a place left where a Smallways might lift his head proudly and vote for war and a spirited foreign policy, and go secure from such horrible things.

The War in The Air carried these ideas to Wells's countrymen in the most frightening tones. One character in the novel declares:

> Think of it . . . there's war everywhere! They're smashing up their civilization. . . . No place is safe – no place is at peace. There is no place where a woman and her daughter can hide and be at peace. The war comes through the air, bombs drop in the night. Quiet people go out in the morning, and see air-fleets passing overhead – dripping death – dripping death.

The impact of *The War in The Air* was tremendous. Later in 1908, as we shall see, some of Wells' ideas were brought up by Lloyd George, the Chancellor of the Exchequer, at a secret meeting of a sub-committee of the Committee of Imperial Defence. The problem of the Air Defence of Great Britain had by now become a new factor in the life of the nation.

CHAPTER 10

The Wright Brothers Try Again

British Interest in Aeronautics – Articles Published in
Service Magazines – Henri Farman's Circular Flight –
Response in *The Times* – Reaction of the Wright Brothers –
Captain Ferber Speaks in London – The Wrights and The
American War Department – "If we can obtain assurances"
– Wilbur Interviewed by American Officers – The New
Wright Aeroplane – U.S. Army Signal Corps Advertises
for Bids – Reaction of the Newspaper Press – "The most
epoch-making Invention in the History of Civilisation" –
Augustus Moore Herring Again – Octave Chanute Informs
the British – A French Syndicate – Orville Approaches the
British War Office – Colonel Capper Reports to the Direc-
tor of Staff Duties – The Interest of General Douglas Haig –
Capper on Dirigibles and Flying Machines – He mentions
the Wright Brothers – Formidable Dirigible Balloons –
Military Flying Machines – Wilbur Wright's Report to the
Germans – General Sir William Nicholson – His Opposition
to Military Aviation – His Feud with Admiral Fisher – 'Old
Nick' as Chief of the General Staff – Colonel Capper's
Projects at Farnborough – Nulli Secundus II – The Dunne
Aeroplane – Success of Samuel Franklin Cody – Capper
Reports to the Director of Fortifications and Works – The
Wright Brothers at Kitty Hawk – "The Greatest Act of the
Ages" – The Hon. C. S. Rolls Entreats the Wright Brothers
– A Remarkable Episode – Slyness of Colonel Capper –
Inexperience of Colonel Rainsford-Hannay – No Positive
Result – Success of Count Zeppelin.

I

By the beginning of the year 1908 many serving officers in Britain's
Armed Forces began to develop a serious professional interest in aeronautics. The officers of the Corps of Royal Engineers were not the only
ones to concern themselves with the subject. Its significance was recognized elsewhere, as well. From 1908 onward articles about aeronautics

and aviation began to appear, upon a regular basis, in such publications as: *The United Service Magazine*; *The Journal of the Royal Artillery*; *The Journal of the Royal United Service Institution*; and in *The Royal Engineers Journal*.

One early entrant in this field was Captain C. DeB. Boone, the Essex Regiment. In January 1908 he published an article entitled "Aerial Navigation in War" in *The United Service Magazine*.

The captain's object was to review the most recent aeronautical discoveries and to forecast, for his readers, the probable developments that might take place in the next few years. Time, perseverance, and the researches of science, he explained, had "worked wonders" and it seemed to him that man was now at last on the verge of the "conquest of the air". His purpose was to discuss the military significance of this remarkable achievement.

Captain Boone fixed upon three aeronautical devices in order to carry his theme forward: the spherical balloon; the dirigible airship; and the flying machine. He argued that each of these would prove its value in wartime.

Balloons, he explained, had already rendered such excellent service on the field of battle that all the European Powers had provided themselves with Balloon Corps. Nevertheless, they had serious limitations. They were at the mercy of the winds. Furthermore, he argued, experiments carried out in Germany on captive balloons demonstrated that they could be shot down by shell fire and by concentrated volleys, at elevations up to forty five hundred feet.

When he turned to the dirigible airship Captain Boone declared that its power as an engine of war was as yet unknown. He pointed out that Count Zeppelin had achieved significant success with his airship and that he had already remained in the air for a period of seven hours, in a single flight. The French airships, *La Patrie* and *La France*, were capable of carrying thirty torpedoes, each weighing more than twenty pounds. These dirigibles, however, also possessed serious defects. They could not be employed in foggy weather, or at night. They could operate only in the most favourable atmospheric conditions. He believed airships would be most valuable for the purposes of observation, reconnoitring, and communication. He was bold enough to write that "a few air-ships could take the place of the Cavalry screen". He warned also that the light German field howitzer of the day could endanger airships at heights up to sixteen hundred meters and that balloon cannons for use against them were already being produced in Germany. It seemed to him that the airship would be particularly valuable for harbour defence because it would enable the aeronaut to see submarines or mines even when they were submerged to considerable depths. The possibility of attack by airship, he predicted, would affect the construction of field works and greater attention would have to be paid, in the future, to overhead cover when such works were built.

Finally, Captain Boone discussed aeroplanes or, as he put it in his article, "The flying-machine, aeroplane, or kite, propelled by motive power, and heavier than air". He recognized the pre-eminence of the Wright brothers in this field, but he referred to them as "Otto and Wilbur Wright". The secret of their invention had been well kept, he reported, but he believed the American Government had now decided to purchase the Wright machine, together with all of its technical innovations. According to his account, the Wrights claimed it would be easy for them to design a practical and durable flyer capable of a flight of more than five hundred miles, at a speed of fifty miles per hour. He believed the most efficient employment of such aeroplanes in war would be as "Aerial scouts".

II

On 13 January 1908 one of the great French pioneers, Henri Farman, made the first circular aeroplane flight in Europe, before a number of official witnesses. The ability to fly in a circle was a basic and essential requirement for any practical aeroplane. The Europeans, in their ignorance of what the Wrights had achieved years earlier, hailed Farman's accomplishment as nothing less than an epoch-making event in the history of mankind.

In London, *The Times* took particular note of the development. An article by the paper's Paris Correspondent was published on 14 January: "In the domain of the air . . . the number 13 would seem to bring good luck. In any case, today has been an epoch-making date, that of the victory before official witnesses of human intelligence in its efforts to solve the problem which brought Icarus to grief . . . Mr. Henri Farman succeeded in rising on . . . a machine of his own invention, in flying over a kilometre towards a goal previously fixed, which he rounded in perfect conditions of stability, and in returning to his starting point . . . Nothing of the kind has ever before been accomplished. Mr. Farman thus wins the 50,000f (£2,000) prize of aviation offered by MM. Henry Deutsch and Archdeacon. But he wins as well a unique fame. . . ."

We must be clear that the machine Farman flew in January 1908 was not the answer to the flying problem. A British expert, C. H. Gibbs-Smith, has written of Farman's circular flight: "European aviation was still in such a parlous state that the first achievement of this essential manoeuvre for any flying machine – carried out in the aerodynamically worst manner

– was heralded as a literally epoch-making event. . . ."[1]

Before he left France Wilbur Wright, on 9 November 1907, had witnessed one of Farman's public flights made before a large crowd at a field near Paris. As a result of this experience the Wright brothers were convinced yet again that they had nothing to fear from their European rivals. In its turn this conviction of their own technical superiority had an effect upon their further negotiations with the Americans, the French, the Germans, and also with the British War Office.

What Wilbur saw on 9 November has been described as follows: "The construction of Farman's plane . . . was surprisingly amateurish when compared with what the brothers . . . had done. Its makeshift propeller . . . was woefully inefficient. Its aerodynamic design was a polyglot of ideas, some good, some defective. For lateral balance it possessed only a dihedral angle in the wings . . . Turns – when Farman got around to trying them – were to be effected by movement of a big box-kite rudder at the rear, without putting the machine into a bank, the same idea Henson had contemplated sixty years before. The Wrights left France more convinced than ever that they had nothing to fear in the way of actual competition. . . ."[2]

After their return to the United States the Wright brothers were approached by Stanley Y. Beach, of the *Scientific American*, who asked for their opinion of the Farman machine and its performance. They replied, on 16 January 1908: "In the matter of control, the Farman machine uses nothing but the dihedral angle for lateral control . . . we believe that almost every experimenter who has operated in winds has been compelled to discard it. Farman in an interview attributed to him is reported to have said that some other method would probably be necessary. . . . He is now face to face with new problems which others have only solved by new inventions which are of a patentable nature. Mr. Farman has not yet found *any* solution of these problems, much less one free from infringement."[3]

Shortly after this exchange took place Captain Ferdinand Ferber of the French Army travelled to London. There on 7 February he delivered a remarkable lecture before the Junior Institution of Engineers at the Royal United Service Institution, in Whitehall. His topic was "Aerial Navigation".

Ferber began his talk by referring to Farman's circular flight of 13 January. He said Farman had "realised a dream which has occupied the minds of men in all ages". Gibbs-Smith, in his analysis of Ferber's discourse, has dismissed it as a paper which "exhibits an almost

[1] C. H. Gibbs-Smith, *The Rebirth of European Aviation*, p. 261.
[2] Walsh, *One Day at Kitty Hawk*, pp. 209–10.
[3] McFarland, *The Papers of Wilbur and Orville Wright*, pp. 852–3.

monumental naïveté . . . It provides . . . a fascinating microcosm of the floundering Continental failure to conquer the air. . . ."[1]

Ferber pointed out that "such a wonderful result" as that achieved by Farman was not brought about by any scientific calculations. Rather, he said, it was "due to three causes, moral, sporting, and commercial . . ." Later, in his survey, he mentioned the achievements of Octave Chanute. According to Ferber, Chanute had "trained two remarkable pupils, the brothers Wright, whose works, published up to 1903, have assisted my own progress . . . We must . . . tender them their due, although pitying them for not having understood that there is no secret in a flying machine, and that the skill required to drive it is not worth a million. But we should perhaps excuse them, because, blinded by a great and legitimate pride, they have believed, as they have often told me in letters, that they were ten years ahead of other workers."

Ferber also boasted about the two hundred and sixty "aerial glidings" he claimed to have made. Gibbs-Smith commented: "It is particularly interesting to find Ferber here implying that he was a master of gliding flight, whereas he had never built a successful glider, and therefore had never really mastered glider flight in any serious sense."

It was in this general climate that the Wright brothers prepared themselves for business in what they called the flying season of 1908. In 1908 they hoped to sell their aeroplane in the United States, in France, in Germany, and also in Great Britain.

III

In their new venture, the brothers looked first to the American War Department. Orville had already made some progress in the Wrights' American negotiations before his visit to Paris, in the summer of 1907. A decisive turn in these developments was taken on 30 October 1907.

On that date Orville, who was in London, addressed a letter to the Board of Ordnance and Fortification in Washington, D.C. His letter was a document of significance because it clearly reveals the Wrights' attitude about the sale of their invention to the American Government. They were at once eager to sell the aeroplane to their own country-men and also apprehensive that they might lose everything in the attempt.

Orville began by referring to the conference he had proposed in the

---

[1] For Ferber's talk and Gibbs-Smith's comments, see the latter's *The Rebirth of European Aviation*, pp. 265ff.

previous spring. He explained: "When we suggested a conference in one of our letters to you last spring, we hoped that by a frank interchange of views, misunderstandings could be removed, and a basis of agreement satisfactory to both parties arrived at".[1]

He next set out the details of the course the Wright brothers had followed in their dealings with governments: "Our course in asking from governments large sums for the first machine has been based upon an impression that governments often appropriate inventions useful in warfare, and tell the inventor to prosecute a claim under the law. . . ."

Orville's letter then suggested that the Wrights were prepared to make concessions, including a reduction in the price asked for the aeroplane, if they could be convinced that they would receive fair treatment from the American authorities:

> If we can obtain assurances that we shall receive fair treatment, and that our patents will not be palpably disregarded by the government officials, we on our part will make every reasonable concession in order to provide a basis of agreement which it will be possible for your Board to accept. We care much more for an assurance of fair treatment than for an extreme price on the first machine.

Orville emphasized that the Wright brothers were eager to sell their invention to the Americans:

> Our European business will demand our presence here next spring, but if arrangements can be made for doing business with our own government before that time one of us will return to America and provide for making demonstrations in one of the southern states. During the past eighteen months all of our offers to foreign governments have contained provisions giving us liberty to furnish machines to our own government absolutely without restriction. Nothing would give us greater pleasure than to furnish the *first* machine to it.

Wilbur Wright now took over the initiative in these American negotiations. He returned from France at the end of November while Orville remained in Paris so that he could arrange for a French firm to build several engines for the Wrights, in preparation for the European season of 1908.

[1] Orville's letter is printed in McFarland, *The Papers of Wilbur and Orville Wright*, pp. 825–6.

Upon his arrival in New York Wilbur conferred with Frank Cordley[1] in order to discuss the Wrights' European business in the coming year. Then he travelled to Washington, where he was interviewed by General William Crozier, Chief of Ordnance, General Allen, the Chief Signal Officer of the United States Army, and by Major Lawson Fuller, of the Ordnance Department, on 25 November.

At this meeting Wilbur informed the assembled officers that the Wright brothers now wanted the sum of twenty-five thousand dollars for their aeroplane. He also explained the performance capabilities of the Wright machine to his listeners. Wilbur was not favourably impressed by the attitude shown by the two generals. Nevertheless, he was invited to appear before the Board of Ordnance and Fortification at its next meeting, already fixed for 5 December.

When Wilbur came away from the meeting of the Board he was convinced that the American authorities were not prepared to pay the sums he required. His impression, however, was not an accurate one. The members of the Board of Ordnance and Fortification, after their interview with him, had come to an entirely different conclusion.

The Board formally recommended that the Chief Signal Officer should be asked to draft a specification for a military flying machine; that he should secure proposals for its construction; and that these should be submitted to the Board for consideration at a subsequent meeting. The specification for the military flying machine was to be based upon Wilbur's statements about the performance capabilities of the Wright aeroplane.

The machine the Wright brothers now offered to the United States Army was radically different from those they had flown in the years between 1903 and 1905. This aeroplane was the forerunner of an entirely new type of aircraft.

In writing of this machine Gibbs-Smith has stated that it represented ". . . not only the culmination of the Wrights' achievement, but the type of Wright machine which was first seen in public, and which directly inspired the last and triumphant phase of world aviation in which the powered aeroplane was to be established as a new and practical vehicle . . ."[2]

The new Wright aeroplane was more valuable for military purposes than any of its predecessors. In the earlier machines the pilot lay prone on the lower plane with his head raised so that he could see where he was going. "I used to think", Orville Wright once said, "the back of my neck would break if I endured one more turn around the field."[3]

[1] It will be recalled that Cordley was an associate of Charles R. Flint.
[2] Gibbs-Smith, *The Rebirth of European Aviation*, p. 271.
[3] Kelly, *The Wright Brothers*, p. 174.

Now the brothers proposed to fit their machine with two upright seats on the front edge of the lower wing. As a result of this alteration the pilot would not find his task so exhausting while his passenger would be enabled to observe the scene below or to carry out any other warlike tasks that might be assigned to him. As a further result, it will be observed, several of Lieutenant Dunne's criticisms of Wright aircraft were rendered meaningless and invalid.

The capabilities of the new Wright aeroplane were revealed on 23 December 1907 when the Signal Corps of the United States Army advertised for bids for an aeroplane. The specifications which the machine had to satisfy were as follows: it would have to fly at a speed of at least forty miles per hour; the machine would have to be capable of carrying two persons having a combined weight of three hundred and fifty pounds and sufficient fuel for a nonstop flight of one hundred and twenty five miles; the duration of the flight would have to be at least one hour; the machine had to be controllable in flight in any direction and it had to be able to alight at its starting point without damage so that a further flight could be undertaken promptly.

At once, the American Press began to attack the War Department for its folly in assuming that any such device existed, anywhere. The New York *Globe* declared:[1]

> A machine such as is described in the Signal Corps' specifications would record the solution of all the difficulties in the way of the heavier-than-air airship, and, in fact, give mankind almost as complete control of the air as it now has of the land and water. It would be worth to the world almost any number of millions of dollars, would certainly revolutionize warfare . . . in short, be probably the most epoch-making invention in the history of civilization.
>
> Nothing in any way approaching such a machine has ever been constructed (the Wright brothers' claims still await public confirmation) and the man who has achieved such a success would have . . . no need of competing in a contest where the successful bidder might be given his trial because his offer was a few hundred or a few thousand dollars lower than that of some one else. If there is any possibility that such an airship is within measurable distance of perfection any Government could well afford to provide its inventor with unlimited resources and promise him a prize, in case of success, running into millions.

To everyone's surprise no less than forty-one aspirants sent in proposals in response to the Signal Corps' advertisement. On 27 January 1908 the Wright brothers produced a bid of their own, and this was accepted by

---

[1] *Ibid.*, p. 170.

the War Department on 8 February. The Wrights undertook to deliver a machine in two hundred days and they asked for the sum of twenty-five thousand dollars in payment for the aeroplane, when it was shown to be capable of meeting the advertised specifications. The "contingency contract" idea had triumphed at last.

Most of the other bidders soon dropped out of the competition but one of them refused to do so. This was Augustus Moore Herring, a man who had plagued the Wrights in the past.[1]

Herring did not know how to build a machine that could fly but he was determined to secure the Army contract for himself. He had devised a rascally plan of his own in order to achieve his object.

Herring submitted a bid in which he asked for the sum of twenty thousand dollars and promised delivery of a machine in one hundred and eighty days. He calculated he could win the contract in consequence of this lower bid. He then planned to sublet his contract to the Wrights, in return for a commission. He was bold enough to travel to Dayton in order to make this proposal to Wilbur and Orville. They refused to fall in with his disgraceful scheme.

Although Herring was thwarted on this occasion he was not yet done with the Wright brothers. He meant to make money from the newly developing technology of aviation. He continued to mark the Wrights' course for years afterward. His actions clearly demonstrate that the Wrights could not be too cautious, or too vigilant, whenever or wherever they tried to sell their aeroplane.

IV

The Wright brothers had not flown since 1905. They now had to complete the machine they would demonstrate before a panel of American Army officers, and also renew their skill as pilots by a further course of training, in the air.

During this period they continued to correspond with Octave Chanute. By this time Chanute had convinced himself that the Wrights were asking too much money for their invention. In addition, Chanute had become jealous of his friends' achievements. He began to believe that he had made significant technical contributions to their aeroplane, and that the brothers were deliberately ignoring the part he had played in advancing their work.

Chanute took care to keep his British friends informed about the Wrights' negotiations with the United States Army. Early in February he wrote to Colonel J. D. Fullerton, now the Secretary of the Aeronautical

---

[1] See above, Chapter III, section II.

Society of Great Britain, and promised to prepare a paper for him on the development of aeronautics in the United States. In addition, he wrote to Herbert Wenham, the great British pioneer of aviation, in order to inform him of the Wrights' activities:[1]

> . . . The screw used by Wright brothers has an efficiency of about 75 per cent of the power at the shaft. I suppose that you have followed the gossip there has been about them in the newspapers and know that the authenticity of their flights is now generally acknowledged. I think however that they have been holding out for dour prices and unacceptable conditions and are in some danger of being supplanted by other experimenters, for which I shall be very sorry.
>
> Our military signal service has recently asked for bids for dirigible balloons and for a flying machine. You will be amused if you see the specifications as they are crude and I believe there will be a pretty row when the bids are opened. . . .

When the bids were at last opened Chanute made it his business to warn his friend, Colonel William Glassford of the United States Army Signal Corps, about Augustus Moore Herring:[2]

> . . . Herring you will remember as my assistant in the 1896-1897 experiments in gliding. He thought that the problem of stability and control was solved and left me in order to reap all further benefits. He has now built two light motors . . . which he proposes to use to run two propellers . . . The Wrights stand the best show of winning out and I sincerely hope that they will meet with no untoward accident. . . .

Wilbur and Orville decided that if they were to win out it would be necessary for them to return to Kitty Hawk in order to engage in some practice flying as a necessary prelude to the American trials, which were to be held in the summer. In March, their preparations were interrupted. Wilbur was suddenly summoned to New York for a conference with Flint and Company.

There Wilbur learned of great developments in the European area of the Wrights' business. Hart O. Berg had continued to persevere in his efforts to sell their aeroplane in France. Now he had come to a tentative arrangement with a powerful French syndicate. Flint and Company wanted one of the Wrights to approve the terms of a new contract that would dispose of the French rights in their invention.

Berg had dealt with several French capitalists. Their idea was to form a

---

[1] Octave Chanute Papers, Chanute to Wenham, 25 January 1908. Chanute wrote to Colonel Fullerton on 8 February.

[2] Octave Chanute Papers, Chanute to Colonel Glassford, 10 February 1908.

syndicate to purchase the Wrights' French patents and the rights to manufacture, sell, or license Wright aeroplanes in France, and in the French colonies. The leader of this group was a wealthy Frenchman named Lazare Weiller. Henri Deutsch de la Meurthe was another member of the syndicate. The group was prepared to spend a great deal of money in order to establish itself as the sole supplier of Wright aircraft in France.

In order to make the arrangement valid there was to be a series of demonstration flights in France. When these flight trials proved the capabilities of the Wright aeroplane a company, La Compagnie Générale de Navigation Aérienne, would be formed in order to take over the Wright patents, and to sell machines in France. The "contingency contract" idea had worked again. In this instance very serious sums of money were involved.

The Wright brothers were to receive five hundred thousand francs (one hundred thousand dollars) in cash upon the delivery of their first aircraft. They would also be given fifty per cent of the founders' shares of stock in the company and twenty thousand francs for each of four extra machines they were to deliver. By the terms of the arrangement they would be asked to instruct a number of French operators in the use of their aëroplanes.

On 23 March 1908 the Wrights learned that Lazare Weiller had accepted their terms. In the opinion of Wilbur and Orville only one problem remained to mar these triumphant results.

The brothers had tried, without success, to sell their aeroplane in several countries, for a period of years. Now they were worried that in order to fulfil the terms of their contracts one of them would be required to fly the aeroplane in France while the other would have to demonstrate the machine's qualities in the United States.

On 6 April Wilbur left Dayton for Kitty Hawk, where he began to prepare a camp. Orville remained at home to attend to business. He would follow his brother to North Carolina, shortly.

The business that concerned Orville Wright at this time was another attempt to sell the Wright invention to the British Government. On 10 April 1908 Orville wrote to the Secretary of the War Office in London to call his attention to the Wright aeroplane yet again, and to offer it to the British authorities.

V

On the day after Orville Wright sent his letter to the British authorities Colonel Capper prepared two papers and despatched them to the Director of Staff Duties in the War Office. These papers were entitled the

"Role of Dirigibles in War" and "The Role of Flying Machines in War".

At the end of March 1908 Capper had been summoned to the War Office in order to discuss these topics with the Director of Staff Duties there, Major-General Douglas Haig. The general's object was to seek expert technical guidance from the Director of the Balloon Factory at Farnborough.

In 1908 Douglas Haig was already recognized as one of the brightest luminaries in the higher ranks of the British Army. His nickname, with good cause, was "Lucky Haig".

Haig came from a Scots family of great antiquity. He had been educated at Clifton College, at Oxford and at Sandhurst. He served with distinction in the Sudan and later performed with conspicuous skill in the South African War. In time he came to be referred to as "the best brain" in the British Army. He was posted to India as Inspector General of Cavalry in 1903.

In 1905 King Edward VII invited him to visit Windsor. There, he met the Hon. Dorothy Vivian, one of the Queen's Maids of Honour, and at once proposed to her. When the king learned of this development he expressed delight but he asked Miss Vivian, in the most serious tones, to promise she would do nothing to interfere with the military career of "my best and most capable general".[1]

When R. B. Haldane became Secretary of State for War Lord Esher regularly and insistently urged him to bring Haig home from India so that he could assist in the great military reforms that were being carried out in the War Office. A place was eventually found for Haig as Director of Military Training. This title was misleading. Haig's Department dealt also with War Organization and Home Defence so that, as the general put it in a letter to his sister, "it is the most important Directorate in the General Staff at the present time".[2]

Haldane himself has testified to the invaluable guidance Haig provided. He became one of the Secretary of State's principal advisers in working out the military reforms of 1906 and 1907. In November 1907 he was transferred from the post of Director of Military Training to that of Director of Staff Duties. The work of determining policy, however, was at once removed from the one place to the other[3] so that Haig maintained his very close association with Haldane. On 30 March 1908 he summoned Capper to an interview in the War Office in order to learn about the possible employment of aircraft for military purposes.

It is thus clear that the subject was of genuine interest at the highest

[1] Duff Cooper, *Haig* (London, 1935), vol. I, p. 104.
[2] *Ibid.*, p. 105.
[3] See John Gooch, *The Plans of War* (New York, 1974), pp. 112–13, hereafter cited as Gooch, *The Plans of War*.

levels in the British Army. In those early days of aviation even the technical experts were uncertain if aeroplanes or dirigibles would prove to be more effective as engines of war. Each class of vehicle had its partisans and advocates.

Colonel Capper, after his meeting with Haig, sent him three separate papers, prepared with very great care. The first of these documents was a covering letter.[1]

In his covering letter Capper dealt briefly with the subject of Captive Balloons and then turned to the "Uses of Dirigible Balloons". He pointed out that these vessels could easily keep a course, even at night. He explained it would be difficult to see them from the ground when they flew in clouds, in misty weather, or at night. He took care to make clear that he possessed only a theoretical knowledge of dirigibles; but he stated also that he had studied the subject very closely.

When he touched upon flying machines he declared, candidly, that he could claim no practical experience with them. Of the flying machine, he wrote, "At the present moment it is in the chrysalis state; but no one who has studied the subject can doubt but that it has a great future, though the period of development may be longer than some of us at present are inclined to think".

Although Capper did not mention the Wright brothers by name, he now called General Haig's attention to them:

> I have discussed the subject with two men who have actually flown for half an hour, covering a distance of over 20 miles in one flight; and these men are serious men who have accepted a contract to supply the U.S.A. Government this year with a machine to go 100 miles carrying a passenger (besides the operator) and there is every prospect of their contract being literally fulfilled.
>
> I can claim in this case no particular weight for my opinions.

Having thus prepared the ground for his two principal papers, Capper concluded his covering letter with an earnest, if unsoldierly, appeal to higher authority. He wrote:

> I have written this covering letter, as I know we are by nature conservative and doubtful of the utility of anything new and strange, and venture to express a hope that my views may be discussed in all seriousness as those of a practical soldier, and not hastily put aside as the vapourings of an irresponsible enthusiast.
>
> J. E. Capper
Colonel,
>
> S. Farnborough,   Supt. Balloon Factory
11th April, 1908.

[1] See Air 1/729/176/4/3, dated 11 April 1908, for Capper's papers, addressed to the Director of Staff Duties.

Capper's paper on the "Role of Dirigible Balloons in War" was composed in such a way that it was certain to attract attention. It began by setting out exactly what such dirigibles could be expected to accomplish:

It is promised as practically certain that –
(1) A Dirigible Balloon can be constructed which will go at a speed of 40 miles per hour in still air.
(2) That such a balloon can remain in the air for several days during which period it can cover a distance (assuming winds neither favourable nor unfavourable) of nearly 3000 miles.
(3) That it can manoeuvre at heights up to 10,000 ft., i.e. well above ordinary clouds or artillery fire.
(4) That it cannot be seen at night at a height of 1000 ft. for more than a mile.
(5) That it can carry necessary fuel, crew, and ballast, for the above journey, and still be able to carry from 5 to 10 tons of high explosive.
(6) That explosives can be dropped in large quantities from heights of 1000 ft. or less, with fair precision, and without causing the balloon to rise so rapidly as to endanger it. . . .

There followed some startling conclusions about the military effectiveness of the balloons Capper had thus described. Anyone reading this part of his paper could see that the British Isles were particularly in his mind:[1]

Such balloons would be a very serious menace to the very vitals of a nation. The effect of considerable quantities of high explosives judiciously dropped in dockyards, arsenals, storehouses, workshops, railway junctions, etc., would probably be very material; whilst attacks on these points could not fail to keep a nation in a high state of tension.
Important bridges might also be attacked, and no army would dare to embark in fragile transports with the probability of encountering a fleet of such balloons. . . .
The balloons might possibly prove also dangerous enemies to ships of war, who would at night find it difficult to locate and destroy them.
The course for such balloons to follow would appear to be to proceed to the point to be attached at high altitudes during the day time, sinking closer to the ground at night, and attacking only in the night time. . . .

Colonel Capper turned next to the means of defence that would be required against these formidable dirigible balloons. He seemed to

---

[1] This part of Capper's paper has been summarized in Higham, *The British Rigid Airship*, p. 36, *n.* 2.

suggest that other airships would be most effective against them. He did not believe that artillery fire could drive them away. He predicted that aeroplanes, when they were more fully perfected, would be able to destroy airships; but he emphasized that aeroplanes, or flying machines, were not yet able to compete with dirigibles in the air, especially at higher altitudes. This conclusion, although Capper did not realize it when he wrote his paper, had a most serious effect upon the thinking of his superiors in the War Office. His treatise concluded as follows:

> It would appear to be impracticable to defend oneself against the attack of such balloons without similar equipment on one's own side.
> However artillery may be developed for firing into the air, it cannot be expected that everywhere at all hours the gun crews would be ready prepared to fire at these vessels if they came into view, whilst often the vessels would be out of sight above the clouds. . . .
> The true flying machine when perfected will probably prove the greatest enemy to such vessels, but at present the development of the balloon is far in advance of that of the flying machine, and it is doubtful how far the latter will be perfected to such an extent as to be able to pursue the balloon at great heights. . . .

Colonel Capper's second paper reinforced these negative conclusions about aeroplanes. This document, "The Role of Flying Machines in War", began by pointing out that aeroplanes, at their present stage of development, were only capable of very short flights. Capper added: ". . . it must be at present doubtful as to whether the human frame can stand the mental strain of long flights until use has made these flights second nature".

Capper went on to suggest that the first military flying machines would be employed tactically as scouts, flying at comparatively low elevations. The pilot, he surmised, would not be able to perform as an observer. A passenger would be required for this purpose. The radius of action of the first machines would be about fifty miles. He estimated that their speed would be from twenty-five to forty miles per hour.

He concluded by suggesting that the first aeroplanes would not be able to destroy dirigibles in the air:

> They may be of use against dirigible balloons if they can be in the air in time when the balloons are trying offensive action . . . but it is probable that a dirigible can, unless injured severely, always escape . . . by ascending to heights where it is practically harmless for offence. . . .
> When ultimately perfected, they should have enormous offensive capacities, great speed, and drive dirigible balloons entirely from the

air; but until the first ones have been tried it appears useless to speculate on the possibilities of larger craft.

Colonel Capper's report provided the chief authorities at the War Office with the best technical advice available. As Superintendent of the Balloon Factory he had carried out some work with an airship; and he had supervised the aeroplane experiments of Lieutenant Dunne and S. F. Cody. Moreover, he was a trained soldier and a prudent military administrator who understood the Army's requirements with respect to these vehicles. He was not one of those "air enthusiasts", as contemporaries called them, who believed that flying machines or airships would at once revolutionize the conditions of warfare on land or at sea. His clear advice was that in 1908 dirigibles were more efficient than aeroplanes, and that their "development" was "far in advance of that of the flying machine".

The Director of Staff Duties in the War Office was not the only soldier interested in such technical comparisons. The German military authorities were also eager to acquire information on the subject at this time.

When Wilbur Wright began to negotiate with the Germans in the summer of 1907 one of Isidor Loewe's first acts was to ask him to prepare a paper comparing the military effectiveness of aeroplanes and dirigibles. After revision, Wilbur's composition was despatched to Berlin in July 1907.[1]

Wilbur Wright was a partisan with a particular cause. His conclusions differed completely from those offered to General Haig by Colonel Capper.

In his paper Wilbur argued that airships were very costly to construct and to maintain and that they were so delicate it would be impossible to save them from destruction in a gale. The aeroplane, or flyer as he called it, was much smaller and therefore cheaper to construct. Wilbur argued that the cheap aeroplane could be supplied in such great numbers that if the enemy managed to destroy one the loss would be insignificant.

Cost, Wilbur explained, was merely one factor to be considered. The great advantage of the aeroplane lay in its enormously greater speed. He declared that speeds up to seventy-five miles an hour could be attained easily, even by small machines. Another matter of military consequence was that a small aeroplane moving at great speed would be much less vulnerable to fire from the ground than a bulky dirigible. "It comes and goes", he wrote, "before the gunners can train their pieces and get the range". Wilbur's conclusion was straightforward. It was quite different from the advice Colonel Capper presented to General Haig:

> Attention is . . . called to the fact that the flying machine is in its infancy, while the airship has reached its limit, and must soon

[1] See McFarland, *The Papers of Wilbur and Orville Wright*, pp. 799ff.

become a thing of the past. The future is for the speedy, cheap, and hardy flyer. The results already attained with flyers make it manifest that the airship will be superseded within a few years and that money spent in attempts to improve the latter will be practically wasted. Every recognised scientific student of aeronautics in the world favors aeroplanes as against airships.

VI

In April 1908 at the time Capper prepared his several papers for the Director of Staff Duties the prospects for the future of aeronautics in the British Army suffered a devastating blow. In that month General Sir William Nicholson was appointed Chief of the General Staff.

Nicholson was a brilliant administrator but he was bitterly opposed to military aviation, in any form. As Percy Walker put it: "To him balloons, airships, and aeroplanes were almost equally reprehensible and unwanted by the British Army".[1]

William Gustavus Nicholson had never distinguished himself as a commander of troops in the field. Nevertheless, he was a veteran of scores of bitter battles waged in Whitehall and its immediate environs. He meant to have his own way in his quarrels with the Treasury, with the representatives of the Admiralty, and with those colleagues in the War Office who presumed to disagree with him.

Much of his early military career had been spent in India. In 1901 Lord Roberts appointed him Director-General of Mobilisation and Military Intelligence. In this post he was entrusted with the preparation of detailed plans for the military defence of the Empire. He threw himself into the work with great energy. He was a strategic planner. Unlike some of his fellow officers in the British Army, he wanted the War Office to study in peacetime problems that might arise in war.

When he asked for more officers to assist in the work of his department the Chancellor of the Exchequer refused because of the additional cost. Nicholson would not abandon his object. Eventually a compromise was worked out. The Treasury gave way, in part at least. Nicholson's course was set.

He often presented the Army's views at meetings of the Committee of Imperial Defence, where he regularly clashed with Admiral Sir John Fisher, the Navy's most formidable champion. This ugly feud began in 1903 and coloured the relationship between the two services for years after. Fisher found that Nicholson was a disagreeable opponent who could strike back with telling effect.

---

[1] Walker, *Early Aviation at Farnborough*, vol. II, p. 292.

Admiral Fisher was one of the great letter writers of the Edwardian era. He often exploited this skill to give expression to his hatred of the general. In 1907 a sub-committee of the Committee of Imperial Defence was appointed to investigate the possibility that Great Britain was vulnerable to invasion. Fisher was outraged when he learned Nicholson was to be a member. He wrote to Lord Esher to find out "why that double dealing arch-fiend Nicholson is hauled into it".[1]

This was merely a ranging shot. A heavier broadside followed. In October 1907 Fisher wrote to Esher again: "Pray, what are you going to do with this Sub-Committee. . . . That d – d Sea Lawyer, Sir William Beelzebub (Mr. Haldane and his friends call him 'Old Nick', I believe! He'll sell them all. He's *hairy about the hocks!*), will trot out reams of foolscap and miles of railway sidings at Hamburg and Bremen, and millions of German soldiers who can get in and out of a train in 5 seconds, but what the hell does he know about the Navy or invasion? NOTHING!"[2]

Haldane, the Secretary of State, fixed upon Nicholson as his personal choice to become Chief of the General Staff even though he knew that not everyone would approve of the appointment. Haldane was determined to have his way in the matter because of his high opinion of Nicholson's abilities. Later he wrote: 'Nicholson was one of the cleverest men I ever came across, both in quickness of mind and in capacity for expressing it . . . He was not by nature a soldier in the field. I used to tell him, laughingly, that he was born to be a lawyer and that if he had gone to the Bar he might have become Lord Chancellor."[3]

R. B. Haldane was certainly aware of some of Nicholson's faults but he derived amusement from them. When the general, on one occasion, savaged the technical arguments of Sir Arthur Wilson, the First Sea Lord, the Secretary of State did not interfere. He observed their exchanges rather complacently and later commented about Nicholson: ":He had a . . . too sharp tongue, and I remembered that on a previous occasion Sir John Fisher had said to me that he wished that I would enjoin 'Old Nick' not always to stamp his hoof on his (Sir John's) toes".[4]

Sir William Nicholson, for reasons he never explained adequately, set his face sternly against any and all aeronautical development in the British Army. The new Chief of the General Staff had convinced himself that aircraft were useless for military purposes.

Nicholson believed that an observer in an aeroplane or airship would

[1] See Ruddock F. Mackay, *Fisher of Kilverstone* (Oxford, 1973), p. 383, hereafter cited as Mackay, *Fisher*.

[2] Quoted in Arthur Marder ed., *Fear God and Dread Nought* (London, 1956), vol. II, p. 145, hereafter cited as Marder, *Fear God and Dread Nought*.

[3] Haldane, *Autobiography*, p. 198.

[4] *Ibid.*, p. 227.

be either too high, or moving at too great a speed, to observe accurately, or to perform any other valid military function. No argument could change his mind. His attitude was destined to have very serious effects in the months after he became Chief of the General Staff. He was a man of tremendous vigour. He did not readily tolerate opposition to his ideas, theories, or opinions.

Many years afterward, during the First World War, Haldane wrote of a meeting of the Air Committee: "I heckled my old friends the generals and pointed out to them that when we were making a start with an air service and establishing the air factory at Farnborough the prophecies they made then had now proved to be in nearly every case wrong".[1] At the time, however, as Secretary of State, Haldane had to pay close attention to the advice given him by Nicholson, and the generals of his school. Nicholson, in the opinion of the Secretary of State, was in this period "perhaps the most powerful personality in the army".[2]

VII

While Sir William Nicholson settled in as Chief of the General Staff and First Military Member of the Army Council, Colonel Capper and his staff were engaged upon three highly important tasks in the Balloon Factory at Farnborough. In April 1908 the immediate future of British military aeronautics turned upon the success or failure of these several undertakings.

The first of these projects was the construction of a dirigible airship. The War Office had assigned the highest priority to this work. Parts of the damaged *Nulli Secundus* were used to create a new dirigible called *Nulli Secundus II*.

In due course the vessel was completed and a few brief flights were made in it but this airship could not be looked upon as a success. Percy Walker's comment, though harsh, was entirely correct: "*Nulli Secundus II* was never any use at all".[3]

In August 1908 the envelope of *Nulli Secundus II* was deflated and the airship was not flown again. It may be that Colonel Capper acquired valuable experience during the course of constructing and flying *Nulli Secundus II* but no one could regard this aeronautical project as a positive achievement.

The second major work of the Balloon Factory in April 1908 was concerned with Lieutenant Dunne's powered aeroplane, the machine that had failed to fly at Blair Atholl in the previous year. Dunne's patron,

[1] See Sir Frederick Maurice, *Haldane* (London, 1939), vol. II, pp. 21–2.
[2] See Gooch, *The Plans of War*, p. 98.
[3] Walker, *Early Aviation at Farnborough*, vol. I, p. 220.

Colonel Capper, was especially anxious for his success. Such a result would vindicate his own sponsorship of all Dunne's experiments at Farnborough.

The 1908 expedition to Blair Atholl was planned more carefully than the excursion of 1907. Dunne and his fellow officers were required to keep a diary of events.[1] Early in September 1908 a party of Royal Engineers from Farnborough arrived at Blair Atholl and a series of gliding trials was begun. The experimenters were greatly encouraged by the results of these preliminary tests.

The next task was to assemble the powered aeroplane. In due course this machine was made to run along the ground, on several occasions. Although a jump of some forty yards was accomplished in December, the Dunne machine proved incapable of sustained flight. The experiments when then abandoned by the War Office. Later Dunne succeeded in building an aeroplane that was able to fly; but this exploit was accomplished as a civilian, by one who was then entirely unconnected with Farnborough, the War Office, or the British Army.

The third major undertaking at Farnborough involved the development of Samuel Franklin Cody's aeroplane. Cody was regularly ordered to abandon his aeroplane experiments because his skills were needed in building the airships *Nulli Secundus I* and *Nulli Secundus II*. In this period he also worked for the Navy and trained sailors in the operation of his man-lifting kites. Nevertheless, in the months between October 1907 and January 1908 Cody managed to produce his aeroplane. It was this machine that made the first successful and sustained powered flight in Great Britain, on 16 October 1908.

Percy Walker has called the Cody aeroplane a "masterpiece".[2] Aeronautical historians have regularly enquired about the sources upon which Cody drew that enabled him to create an aeroplane capable of powered flight. Examination of the evidence has revealed that the influence of the Wright brothers was paramount, that Cody copied many of their ideas after studying information about their gliders.

The technical authorities have also sought to discover how Samuel Cody managed to learn the details of the various Wright machines that served as his inspiration. It has been argued that Colonel Capper supplied Cody with articles published in technical periodicals. Capper was a great collector of such material. Furthermore, Capper had interviewed the Wright brothers in Dayton, in 1904, where they spoke quite freely to him not only about gliders but also about their powered machines.

We may point to yet a third source of information. Patrick Y. Alexander told Cody a good deal about the Wright aeroplane. On 27 April 1906 a

[1] The diary is preserved in Air 1/1613/204/88/10.
[2] Walker, *Early Aviation at Farnborough*, vol. II, p. 86.

meeting of the Aeronautical Society of Great Britain was held at the Society of Arts. On this occasion, Colonel J. D. Fullerton enquired about the details of the Wright aeroplane. He was answered by Samuel Franklin Cody. Their exchange was published in *The Aeronautical Journal* for July 1906:

> Col. Fullerton: I should like to ask . . . what the actual surface of the Wrights' machine is.
> Mr. Cody: I have been told by Mr. Alexander that it weighed about 900 lbs., had about 600 feet of lifting surface, and had a 13 or 14 h.p. engine on it.

On 16 October 1908 Cody decided the time had come to fly his aeroplane into the air. He had been accused of merely "jumping" his machine. On this day he began by driving it along the ground on Farnborough Common. He then managed to fly for a distance of almost fourteen hundred feet, in twenty-seven seconds. Unfortunately, when he tried to turn the machine crashed into the ground. Luckily the brave aviator was unhurt.

In referring to this flight Gibbs-Smith has stated that Cody "was an ingenious and indefatigable pioneer, but he only influenced aviation history indirectly, by helping to make Britain airminded. . . ."[1] Percy Walker came to a different conclusion. He called the Cody aeroplane "one of Farnborough's greatest achievements".[2]

On the day of Cody's flight Colonel Capper sent three letters about it to Colonel Frederick Rainsford-Hannay, the new Director of Fortifications and Works, who had been appointed in April 1908. These reports were drawn up in a curious way.

Capper composed his letters in such a manner that in Rainsford-Hannay's mind the account of Cody's record flight was reduced "to the status of an accident report".[3]

Although Capper explained that the machine had flown steadily, the nature of Cody's achievement was buried in a mass of inessential detail. When Rainsford-Hannay sent his own report to his superior, the Master-General of the Ordnance, he explained: "Please see three letters herein from the Superintendent of the Balloon Factory . . . Reporting an accident to the experimental aeroplane . . ."[4]

Colonel Capper did not like Cody. At this stage he still hoped Lieutenant Dunne, far away in the Scottish Highlands, would succeed in flying his own powered aeroplane. By this time, also, as we shall see, the British

---

[1] Gibbs-Smith, *Rebirth of European Aviation*, p. 257.
[2] Walker, *Early Aviation at Farnborough*, vol. II, pp. 136–7.
[3] *Ibid.*, p. 271.
[4] *Ibid.*, p. 271.

Government had undertaken a major examination of the entire problem of "Aerial Navigation". Early in 1909 the Master-General of the Ordnance recommended to the Secretary of State for War that the engagements of both Cody and Dunne should be terminated.

However, before these negative conclusions were reached another development took place. Orville Wright's letter, dated 10 April 1908, arrived in the War Office.

This document came into the hands of the Director of Fortifications and Works on 28 April. The Inspector of Electric Lights, Major W. Baker Brown, at once sent it to Colonel Capper at Farnborough and asked him to supply the War Office with his recommendations. Capper was asked if the British Government should now purchase a Wright aeroplane.

VIII

When Wilbur Wright arrived in Kitty Hawk in April 1908 he found the old camp in ruins. The fierce storms that occur regularly on the North Carolina coast had demolished almost everything the brothers had left behind. Shortly after, Wilbur was joined at his camp site by Charles Furnas, a Dayton mechanic who had been engaged to assist the brothers in this phase of their work. As one storm followed another Wilbur found the conditions almost intolerable. Nevertheless, he and Furnas, assisted by some local residents who were paid for their help, put up buildings designed to house the machine and to shelter themselves.

By 25 April Orville reached the camp. Shortly after, the brothers began to assemble the parts of their aeroplane. The object of this visit to the Kill Devil Hills was to revive their flying skills and to test the new control systems which were to be installed so that a pilot and a passenger could fly in a sitting position.

There now began a period of great tension which took its toll upon the Wright brothers in the weeks and months that followed. There were technical problems. A new system of controlling levers had to be installed in order to accommodate their new design arrangements. "The sitting position for the operators", Wilbur confided to his diary, "will probably be more comfortable but will require practice before we can tackle high winds."[1] Indeed, before Wilbur mastered the new controls he crashed into the ground on one flight and suffered cuts and bruises which bothered him for days after.

Although the brothers always strove to present a calm, self-reliant, and confident appearance when they dealt with others, they were very much aware of the great challenges that now lay immediately before them.

[1] McFarland, *The Papers of Wilbur and Orville Wright*, p. 871.

At Kitty Hawk they would train and practise with their new aeroplane. Then, in order to meet the terms of their contracts, one would rush off to France to arrive there in time for the French trials while the other would report to Fort Myer in Virginia to satisfy the requirements and stipulations of the American arrangement.

In this period they were also concerned about their English patents. The Hon. C. S. Rolls had begun a steady and regular correspondence with them in order to urge that he be permitted to acquire one of their machines or to purchase their English patents.[1] The brothers were uneasy about the patents and feared they might lose business in the English market if an error had been made in the drawing up of these important documents.

Augustus Moore Herring lurked upon the fringes of their enterprise and twice tried to speak to Wilbur, who managed to avoid him. Others began to build flying machines which infringed upon their American patents. Although the Wrights received some financial support from Flint and Company they now began to worry about money. They felt they might not be able to bring all to a satisfactory conclusion before their funds were exhausted, or at least seriously diminished.

Early in May the Wrights' preparations were complete. They began to fly. On this occasion, however, several journalists had been alerted to their activities and were secretly camped in the woods nearby.

The party of newspapermen included some prominent New York reporters, and also D. B. Macgowan, a representative of Lord Northcliffe's *Daily Mail*. Macgowan was an old hand at this work. He had visited Octave Chanute's glider camp at Dune Park in 1897. As we shall see, he knew every trick of his trade.

Even before their first flight was made a false report of their activity had been published in the Press. It produced a telegram of congratulations from their vigilant friend in London, Patrick Y. Alexander. Wilbur recorded in his diary: "A telegram from Mr. Alexander congratulates us – we suppose on the fake report of a flight. This would indicate that the report has been cabled abroad. We have not yet seen the report."[2]

In August and September 1908 Wilbur and Orville Wright flew separately before large crowds, in France and in the United States. They then won for themselves the acclaim of the civilized world and an undying fame. What the assembled newspapermen saw at Kitty Hawk in May was an overture, a prelude of what was to come.

One of these journalists was the star reporter for the *New York Herald*, Byron R. Newton. He later became Assistant Secretary of the Treasury,

---

[1] The Wrights' exchanges with Rolls are dealt with in detail in subsequent sections of this history.

[2] *Ibid.*, p. 872.

and afterwards Collector of Customs in New York. His recollection of one of the flights, seen from a distance at Kitty Hawk at this time, provides us with the reaction of a sensitive contemporary to a phenomenon most human beings had never seen, to a development people of that day believed to be impossible:[1]

> . . . and then we saw the machine rise majestically into the air, its white wings flashing and glistening in the morning sun. On it sped at an altitude about fifty feet from the ground. I have never experienced another moment with like sensations. It was like standing in the presence of some overpowering calamity. I recall the one utterance that escaped our lips; Jimmie Hare, in his richest Cockney flavor, merely said: "My Gawd!"
>
> On sped the great white craft straight toward one of the high sand dunes. Then to our bewildering amazement we saw the wings on one side warping slightly, saw the operator pulling at the levers and the craft heeled over slightly, turned in a graceful curve and came straight toward where we were hiding. . . .
>
> No wonder that we were paralyzed and dumb with the wonder of it all. It was something that few mortals had believed to be within the scope of possibility. Again and again the machine wheeled about over our heads and as it came closer on the second circuit we were still further amazed to discover that two men were in it. They were Wilbur Wright and a mechanic.
>
> There was something weird, almost uncanny, about the whole thing. Here on this lonely beach was being performed the greatest act of the ages, but there were no spectators and no applause save the booming of the surf and the startled cries of the sea birds. . . .

After observing scenes like this there was a great rush on the part of the assembled journalists to reach a telegraph station and send the amazing story to their various newspapers. The only telegraphic communication was a line maintained by the United States Weather Bureau. Here, D. B. Macgowan came into his own.

He meant to flash his account to the *Daily Mail* and to hamper the others in their attempts to send the story to their newspapers. Lord Northcliffe, had he known of it, would have been proud of the course Macgowan adopted.

Macgowan put into practice an old device known as "keeping the wire". He reached the Weather Bureau station before his colleagues and at once filed seven or eight hundred words. By the time Alpheus W. Drinkwater, the officer in charge of the station, had sent Macgowan's message, the other journalists arrived. It was then that Macgowan picked

---

[1] His account is paraphrased in Mark Sullivan, *Our Times, The United States 1900–1925* (New York, 1935), pp. 610–11.

up a magazine, marked a page of it, and told Drinkwater to send it while he prepared more copy.

The assembled reporters were outraged. Violence was threatened. As Drinkwater put it, "had it not been for the cool heads of Mr. Newton and Mr. Salley some one would have got hurt". Drinkwater now asserted his authority. He declared he would transmit their despatches but each man would be allowed thirty minutes of his time, and no more.[1]

Byron Newton was so impressed by the flights he saw in May 1908 at the Kill Devil Hills that he predicted, in his diary, that one day the Congress of the United States would erect a monument there.

In November 1932 the Wright monument on top of Kill Devil Hill, ordered by Act of Congress, was dedicated. It has been said that this monument is the most impressive memorial ever built anywhere in the world to honour someone still living.[2] The monument towers sixty-one feet above the Kill Devil Hill. At its top there is a beacon light which may be seen for miles. At the four sides of the base there is a legend: "In Commemoration of the Conquest of the Air by The Brothers Wilbur and Orville Wright, Conceived by Genius, Achieved by Resolution and Unconquerable Faith".

The reports of the Wright achievement published in May 1908 attracted some attention but there was no great outburst of public enthusiasm. The brothers proceeded with their practice, under considerable pressure.

Time was now running out. The Weiller group demanded Wilbur's presence in France. On 17 May he left the camp. He was so pressed that he travelled at once to New York and boarded a ship there. He had no opportunity to return to Dayton before his European excursion began.

His sister, in the parental home in Dayton, packed his trunks and sent them to New York in order to assist him in these arrangements. On 21 May Wilbur sailed for France. His task was to fulfil the requirements of the French contract and at last reap the rewards the brothers had worked and planned for with such diligence and dedication.

During this period the Wright brothers were in regular communication with the Hon. C. S. Rolls. He was determined to attach himself, in some way, to the Wrights and to their business activities. As early as November 1907 Rolls had written to Wilbur Wright, in Paris, to enquire if the Wright patents were for sale. At the end of March 1908 Rolls again wrote to Wilbur, from London, asking the Wrights to "bear in mind that I trust you will give me an opportunity of representing you in any way you may desire in this country". He said also: "I would much like the opportunity of operating one of your machines if it is possible for me to get one in this

---

[1] The charming story is told in Sullivan, *op. cit.*, pp. 612–13, *n.* 1.
[2] Orville was still alive in 1932.

country".[1] It seems clear enough there was no question in his mind about the capabilities and the potential of the Wright brothers' aeroplane.

While the brothers were practising at Kitty Hawk there was no opportunity for them to attend to correspondence of this kind. When Orville returned to Dayton he sent a full account of the Wrights' activities to Rolls. In this way C. S. Rolls learnt the exact situation of the Wright brothers before anyone else in England. In his letter, dated 27 May 1908, Orville explained to Rolls:[2]

> Your letter was received just as we were leaving for our experi-ment station in North Carolina. We were not able to attend to any correspondence while there, and as a result your letter has remained some weeks unanswered, for which I am very sorry.
>
> While we have had some correspondence with some of the officials of your government in regard to flying machines, we have just begun to get things in shape to do a commercial business, and we would like to get the business moving in England.
>
> Wilbur sailed for France a few days ago. . . . I know he would be very glad to see you any time you get over in France.
>
> Our late experiments at Kitty Hawk prove our flyer capable of carrying two men with fuel supplies for long flights, as we had anticipated. Its behaviour in high winds was better than we looked for. With only a few minutes practice we began making flights in 20 mile winds.

IX

We come now to a remarkable episode in the history of British military aeronautics. In the Balloon Factory at Farnborough, Colonel Capper was determined to thwart the sale of a Wright aeroplane to the British Government. He hoped a practical aeroplane could be produced in England, under his own direction.

Orville Wright's letter of 10 April 1908 was sent to Capper by the Inspector of Electric Lights in the War Office at the end of April. Orville's letter, addressed to the Secretary of the War Office, declared:[3]

> The increased interest now taken in the different countries in aeronautics prompts us to again call your attention to our aeroplane. The machines as now designed are suitable for military scouting, being capable of carrying two men . . . and sufficient fuel for long flights.

[1] Wright Brother's Papers, Chas. S. Rolls to Mr Wright, 26 March 1908.
[2] Wright Brothers' Papers, Orville Wright to Rolls, 27 May 1908.
[3] For the letter see Percy Walker, *Early Aviation at Farnborough*, vol. II, p. 68.

We are prepared to undertake the manufacture of one or more of these machines under contract; or, if the Government would prefer to build machines for itself under our British patent, we will grant license to operate on payment of suitable royalties on machines so manufactured.

The United States Government has lately entered into contract with us for one of our two-men machines.

While the Wrights were practising at Kitty Hawk, Colonel Capper deliberated upon the reply he should send to his superiors in the War Office. His principal recommendation was straightforward: he advised that the Wright brothers should be asked to fix a price for one of their machines and for the cost of instructing two officers in its use.

He further advised that the Wrights should be sent a *Specification for a Military Flying Machine* he had recently drawn up. This document declared among other requirements that the machine should be able to carry two men, each weighing one hundred and seventy pounds; and enough fuel to permit the aircraft to make a flight of four hours' duration. Some of the other requirements of the *Specification*, as we shall see, were rather loosely drawn.[1]

The new Director of Fortifications and Works, Colonel Rainsford-Hannay, accepted Capper's advice. On 6 June the Director of Army Contracts caused a letter to be sent to the Wright brothers; enclosed with it was Colonel Capper's *Specification*. The letter requested the Wrights to name a price for one of their machines, a machine that could meet the requirements of the *Specification*. The price, the Wrights were advised, should include the cost of teaching two officers how to operate the machine.

Percy Walker commented on this letter: "The wisdom of introducing a specification at this stage is seriously open to question. The aeroplane had been offered as an existing design and – most important – a successful one. . . . Colonel Capper's specification, moreover, was loose and ambiguous, and the Brothers would have been fully justified in rejecting it as a contractual document. There is more than a trace of suspicion, however, that rejection is what Colonel Capper wanted; that he was deliberately making things difficult with a view to improving the prospects for his Farnborough designs. The inexperience of the new War Office Director, Colonel Rainsford-Hannay, was unfortunate; and his predecessor, Colonel Ruck, might well have acted very differently."[2]

Late in July Orville, who was very busy preparing for his United States Army trials at Fort Myer, replied to the War Office letter. Orville asked

[1] A copy of Capper's *Specification* is preserved in W.O. 32/8596. See also Appendix B in Walker, *Early Aviation at Farnborough*, vol. II, pp. 336–7.
[2] *Ibid.*, pp. 70–1.

for a clarification of some of the requirements in Colonel Capper's *Specification*. Capper had suggested that the machine should be able to rise from and descend upon an open space of ten acres. Orville wanted to know if such a field could be surrounded by high trees or other obstructions. Capper had further stipulated that the aeroplane should be capable of remaining in the open in all ordinary weather for a period of one month without material deterioration. Orville, experienced in such matters, prudently enquired if a tent would be allowed. He also asked where the British wanted the machine delivered; and what conditions would govern the trial flights.

Upon receipt of Orville's enquiries the War Office, in accord with its usual procedures, turned to Colonel Capper for further advice. He now prepared a singular report, dated 12 August 1908, and despatched it to the Director of Fortifications and Works.[1] After some remarks about the ten-acre field, Capper explained that waterproof sheets could be used to cover the picketed aeroplane but that a tent would not be allowed.

Colonel Capper included with this report a new schedule of flight tests, some six pages of foolscap, on which acceptance of the aeroplane should be based. As Percy Walker put it, this document "was open to the serious objection that it introduced a number of conditions that should have been incorporated in the specification, and which were not to be found there".

It was at this stage that Capper exercised his very considerable ingenuity. He slyly introduced in his new schedule a stipulation that completely ruled out the Wright aeroplane. He took care, moreover, not to explain the significance of this novel prerequisite to the inexperienced Rainsford-Hannay.

The new condition Capper proposed declared: "On all trials the machine must rise from the ground under its own power, without special starting devices outside its own construction".

Capper knew, even if Colonel Rainsford-Hannay did not, that the Wright brothers employed a special starting device, their "derrick" with weight attached, which was used to hurl their machine into the air at the start of every flight.[2] It was certainly possible for a Wright machine to rise without the use of the "derrick" but at this stage the Wrights depended upon it as a basic part of their aeronautical equipment. Their first flights at Kitty Hawk in 1903 were made without the "derrick" and its accompanying track but, in the interests of efficiency, the device had been employed by them ever since, in all their flights.

When the War Office received Colonel Capper's report and his new

---

[1] See *Ibid.*, pp. 72–3 for this Report, and Walker's various comments on it, cited below.

[2] For the Wrights' starting device or "derrick", as they called it, see above Chapter III, Section VI.

schedule a letter was prepared there for despatch to Orville Wright. Percy Walker, regularly critical of the Wright brothers throughout his history, states of this letter: "In his report to the Director, Colonel Capper made no mention of the fact that his flight-test schedule virtually nullified the negotiations. In good faith, therefore, the schedule was enclosed with the War Office letter to the Wright Brothers, ostensibly merely answering the points raised by Orville. The letter, moreover, like the previous one, was signed on behalf of the Director of Army Contracts – a sure indication that the War Office as a whole had accepted the purchase of a Wright aeroplane as a foregone conclusion, and were now only seeking reasonable terms".

The War Office letter, dated 24 August 1908, read as follows:[1]

Gentlemen,   24th August 1908
    With reference to your letter of the 27th ultimo, I have to forward herewith confidentially for your information a copy of Tests for Military Flying Machines.
    As regards the third paragraph of your letter under reply I have to inform you that a regular tent would not be allowed, but that you would be permitted to use a light water-proof cover. . . .
    Delivery would be required to be made at the trial ground in England selected by the War Department.
                                    I am, Gentlemen,
                                    Your Obedient Servant
                                    J. M. Bull
                                    for Director of Contracts.

Two comments on this letter are pertinent to the present history. Percy Walker wrote: "Apart from any question of ethics, such a letter is clearly absurd. Here the War Office were arguing about a triviality such as a waterproof sheet, without mentioning specifically the radical changes that were implicit in the document they were enclosing. Much more serious, however, was the dubious ethics that seem to have lain behind the whole business: first in introducing conditions not incorporated in the previously agreed specification; and secondly, in the surreptitious way in which the changes were hidden in a lengthy document. . . . The War Office directors concerned in this affair were clearly unaware of these sinister implications. Colonel Capper, on the other hand, cannot be so readily exonerated, since ignorance of the facts cannot be claimed on his behalf. . . ."[2]

When the War Office letter of 24 August together with Colonel Capper's new schedule of flight tests arrived in Dayton, neither of the

---

[1] See *Ibid.*, p. 74.
[2] *Ibid.*, p. 74.

Wright brothers was at home. Wilbur was in France and Orville was in Washington, D.C. In these circumstances the letter was opened by Bishop Milton Wright. He at once sent news of it to Wilbur. The gentle old clergyman, startled by the new British requirements, told his son: "Some Specifications (confidential) came to Orville's address here, after he was away. They were from the British War Department. . . . They only ask that an applicant should jump over the moon! through a hoop!! six times!!!"[1]

Colonel Capper had done his work well. Orville Wright's initiative of 10 April 1908 produced no positive result. The aeroplane work at Farnborough marched forward, under Capper's direction, without the distractions that might have been caused by the acquisition of a machine that could fly successfully in the air.

X

Meanwhile, Octave Chanute laboured to fulfil his promise to Colonel J. D. Fullerton of the Aeronautical Society of Great Britain. He prepared an article for Fullerton which dealt with the recent development of aeronautics in the United States. The article was published in *The Aeronautical Journal* for July 1908 under the title "Recent Aeronautical Progress in the United States".

Although Chanute surveyed the entire American aeronautical scene for his British readers, a good part of his article was devoted to the work of the Wright brothers. "The performances of Wright brothers", he wrote, "have been viewed with incredulity because of the mystery with which they have been surrounded in the hope of a rich monetary reward, yet it is now generally conceded that they have accomplished all that they have claimed. . . ."

Chanute further explained that the Wrights had signed a contract with the United States Government to furnish a flying machine that would have to perform under very "formidable specifications". He revealed that the Wrights had established themselves in their old camp at Kitty Hawk where they were practising, in preparation for their United States Army trials. Chanute concluded his article by stating: "Wright Brothers stand a fair chance of passing the tests and having their machine accepted. They may be defeated by some accident . . . but the present writer is sure that all the members of the Aeronautical Society of Great Britain will join him in the hope that the best of luck will attend the demonstration."

Chanute published a similar article in the *Illustrierte Aeronautische Mitteilungen* in July 1908. This publication, which dealt with the subject

---

[1] See Kelly, *Miracle at Kitty Hawk*, p. 306.

of aviation in America, aroused the anger of Orville Wright. Orville told Wilbur: ". . . I notice that Chanute has written an article for the *Mitteilungen*, in which he again criticises our business methods, says we have spent two years in fruitless negotiations because we have asked a ridiculously high price, but that now we have gone to the other extreme in making a price to our own government. He predicts that Herring will fail, but that we will succeed. . . . He has also become a convert to airships, and thinks they are going to have great value in war. He says the use of the flyer is greatly overestimated. . . . He seems to be endeavouring to make our business more difficult. . . ."[1]

Chanute was not entirely incorrect in these various predictions. Exactly at this time Count Zeppelin began to achieve astonishing and even spectacular results with his gigantic rigid airship.

At once, interest in aeronautics shifted from the United States to Germany. In Britain there was genuine agitation. The Germans, it seemed, had discovered a powerful new weapon. To contemporaries, the prospect of an air invasion of the British Isles now seemed a genuine possibility of the future.

[1] McFarland, *The Papers of Wilbur and Orville Wright*, p. 908, n. 6.

CHAPTER 11

The Zeppelin Menace

Count Zeppelin – His early Career – Hostility of the Kaiser – Zeppelin's difficulties – His Fortunes Turn – Admiral Tirpitz and the Air – Zeppelin's Historic Flight – The Reaction in Britain – Fear of Invasion and the Menace of Imperial Germany – The Invasion Problem – Bolt from the Blue and Blue Water Schools – The Need for a Higher Authority – New developments of Consequence – Arthur Balfour and the Committee of Imperial Defence – The Invasion Enquiry – Balfour's Declarations – Lord Roberts Intervenes – His Interest in the Air – Second Invasion Enquiry – Fear of the Power of Germany – The Anglo-German Naval Rivalry – Tirpitz and the German Fleet – The Crisis of 1908 – A Pattern is Set – "The German Peril" – Privy Councillor Rudolf Martin – He holds that the future of Germany lies in the Air – A Warning in *The Times* – Lord Northcliffe and F. W. Wile – The Invasion of England – A Teutonic Vision – Major Baden-Powell Responds – *The Daily Mail* Urges Caution – An Article in *Marine-Rundschau* – The Director of Naval Intelligence Intervenes – The Admiralty Decision – Captain Reginald Bacon – His Scheme – An Arrangement with Vickers Sons & Maxim – Exchanges with the Treasury – The Admiralty's New Departure – Command of the Air – The Zeppelin Destroyed – Lloyd George Observes the Scene – The Miracle of Echterdingen – Effect upon Lloyd George – The Peril from the Air or from Under the Sea – Effect of Zeppelin's Flight.

I

The story of Ferdinand August Adolf, Count von Zeppelin was a saga of triumph over adversity, ill-will, and misfortune. At an early stage of his career as an airship designer Zeppelin was dismissed as "the crazy Count". Later, he became the great hero and symbol of the entire German nation. On 1 July 1908, after many unsuccessful trials, he flew in his huge rigid dirigible for a distance of two hundred and forty miles,

315

remaining in the air for a period of twelve hours. This achievement far exceeded the endurance record of any other airship in history.

At once, the alarm signals began to ring in every European capital. The British, fearful for their ancient insularity, were especially concerned, and with good cause. Zeppelin, and his airships were now to plague the lives of the British people for more than a decade.

Count Zeppelin, a native of the south German state of Württemberg, was born in 1838. At the age of fifteen he entered the Army as an officer of cavalry. In 1863 he was granted leave to travel to the United States so that he could observe the fighting in the American Civil War. Upon his return he saw active service in the war of 1866 fought out between Prussia and Austria for the mastery of Germany. In this conflict the kingdom of Württemberg ranged itself on the Austrian side, and suffered defeat at Prussian hands. Later, Zeppelin fought against France in the great war of 1870–71.

The defeat of France meant the triumph of Prussia in Germany. A German *Reich*, dominated by the Prussians, was established by Bismarck. Württemberg became a part of the new German Empire. According to Bismarck's design, however, the southern German states were permitted a measure of fictional independence. They were allowed to maintain embassies at the Prussian court, in Berlin.

In 1885 Zeppelin became Württemberg's plenipotentiary in Berlin and two years later he was appointed Ambassador Extraordinary and Minister Plenipotentiary at the Prussian court. He carried out his duties with such zeal and energy that many of the Prussians he dealt with became annoyed with him. There was genuine anger at his "Swabian pig-headedness" in the Berlin salons and offices where he was encountered.

In 1890 this Prussian resentment resulted in the ruin of Zeppelin's military career. In that year, as a matter of routine, he gave up his diplomatic post in order to return to service with the Army. Unfortunately, no Württemberg unit was available and Zeppelin was given command of a Prussian cavalry brigade.

In this position Zeppelin acted as a keen soldier, devoted to improving the military efficiency of his command. He introduced changes based upon his American experiences and upon his adventures in the Franco-Prussian War. These innovations were frowned upon by his Prussian superiors.

Then, in March 1890, Zeppelin prepared and sent a strongly worded memorandum to the Prussian Foreign Secretary, protesting against Prussian dominance over the soldiers and officers of the King of Württemberg. Prussian practices, he declared, had turned the southern king into a "mere rubber stamp". They were not justified by the terms of the Imperial Constitution or the military convention signed with Prussia.

In Berlin, the Kaiser was outraged by "these particularist ideas". At the autumn manoeuvres Zeppelin was severely criticized for the manner in which he handled his brigade. He was informed that he was unfit for high command and that he could not expect to be given command of a division.

Thus at the age of fifty-two the count found himself unemployed. His military career was over.

Count Zeppelin was a man of tremendous energy. He was also a patriot. He would not contemplate an inactive retirement.

For several years he had brooded upon the fact that the French had produced remarkably successful airships, designed for military reconnaissance. He now conceived the idea that it was his patriotic duty to create for the Fatherland a huge rigid dirigible, an "air cruiser" the size of a large ship, a vessel that would give Imperial Germany the first place in the air. Such was his nature that once this idea became fixed in his mind he would permit no one and nothing to bar him from his chosen goal.

In 1891 Zeppelin established a design department so that he could investigate the technical problems that lay in his path. Engineers and workmen were engaged to carry the project forward. Preliminary experiments and trials were begun at Lake Constance, near his home. Zeppelin, a soldier at heart, believed the military authorities would assist him in his project when they were made to realize the immense possibilities of the airship he contemplated.

He turned first to Count von Schlieffen, Chief of the Great General Staff in Berlin. He explained to Schlieffen that his controllable aircraft would be capable of journeys of twelve hours' duration. They would enable the Army to carry out reconnaissance missions deep in an enemy's territory. They could serve as troop carriers. They would permit the German military authorities to bombard hostile fortresses or troops with concentrations of projectiles dropped from the air. Zeppelin asked von Schlieffen to see to it that a government commission was appointed to examine his plans and designs. If they found his airship practical he hoped the War Ministry would purchase his creation and thus establish the German Empire in the forefront of military aeronautics.

Eventually, the desired commission was created. Its members included a famous physicist, a distinguished meteorologist, two professors of engineering, and military officers from the Prussian Airship Battalion and the War Ministry. Unfortunately this expert body found it impossible to recommend Zeppelin's design to the authorities.

Zeppelin would not accept their negative opinion. At once bitter enmities were formed, and diligently nourished thereafter. Charges of ignorance, bias, and bad faith filled the air. Zeppelin would not give in. Professor Müller-Breslau, a civilian, became the chief target of his attack. The commission, as a result of the count's urgings, was reconstituted so that the entire matter could be examined yet again. Count Zeppelin now submitted a revised design. The commissioners found, after study, that they were still unable to recommend the Zeppelin airship to the War Ministry. Zeppelin angrily brought his case to the attention of the Kaiser himself. The highest authority now decided that the government would take no further action in the affair until a demonstration airship was completed, at private expense.

There followed a period of several years during which the count made almost endless appeals in his efforts to raise private capital so that he could build his demonstration airship. In May 1898 Zeppelin established, in Stuttgart, the "Joint Stock Company for Promotion of Airship Travel". In order to launch this organization he drew deeply upon his own personal fortune. Within a month work on the dirigible began. The airship he contemplated was to be four hundred and twenty feet in length with a diameter of thirty-eight and one half feet, a vessel of truly monstrous size. It was designated LZ1 (*Luftschiff Zeppelin* 1).

LZ1 flew first on 2 July 1900. Two further short flights were made in this craft but the government, acting upon information supplied by a military commission of investigation, refused to purchase it. The authorities now recognized the potential of the airship but they concluded it was not yet suitable for military purposes. The funds of the company were exhausted. It went into liquidation and LZ1 was dismantled.

At just this time the French began to make genuine and significant progress with their semi-rigid Lebaudy airships. Count Zeppelin, in a fever of patriotic alarm, made further almost frantic appeals for private funds. These produced no significant result. A German engineer was impertinent enough to tell Zeppelin to his face that "the monster will never rise again".[1] Zeppelin was now ridiculed in Germany as the "crazy inventor".

These pleasantries, and others like them, were not enough to turn the count from his chosen course. The King of Württemberg authorized a State lottery which realized some of the funds needed for further construction. The Government of Prussia contributed a modest sum. The count raised a considerable amount by mortgaging his wife's estates. In April 1905 construction of LZ2 was begun.

In the new airship two huge Daimler engines were installed to provide the power LZ1 had lacked. When this Zeppelin was towed from its shed in November 1905 an accident occurred and the ship was badly damaged before it could take to the air. Undeterred, Zeppelin made preparations to try again. In January 1902 LZ2 rose from her moorings and ascended to an altitude of fifteen hundred feet, but then a series of accidents occurred. The vessel lost power and was driven, at the mercy of the winds, in a

---

[1] See Douglas Robinson, *Giants in the Sky* (Henley-on-Thames, 1973), p. 29, hereafter cited as Robinson, *Giants in the Sky*.

north-easterly direction. Zeppelin, the pilot, managed to bring his ship down safely but during the night she was smashed against the ground by high winds. There was considerable damage and Zeppelin reluctantly decided his airship would have to be dismantled. For the moment his stubborn optimism abandoned him. He declared publicly that he would build no more airships.

Ambition, pride, and patriotic enthusiasm did not permit Zeppelin to remain inactive for long. Within a short time he was again seeking funds to enable him to build yet a third aircraft.

By this time, the military authorities in Berlin were seriously concerned by the advances made in France with the Lebaudy airships employed by the French Army. A military commission, appointed to study the entire question, recommended that the Kaiser should present Zeppelin with a gift of one hundred thousand marks so that he could carry on with his work. Permission was granted for Zeppelin to hold a lottery in the State of Prussia. Interest-free loans were arranged.

Work began on the LZ3 in the spring of 1906. In October this airship, with eleven passengers on board, flew for more than two hours. A second successful flight was made and then the vessel was dismantled for the winter. Now a feeling of enthusiasm for Zeppelin and his work began to spread throughout Germany. The tide of his aeronautical fortunes had turned at last.

II

As a result of the new attitude the Reichstag voted to provide the count with the sum of half a million marks. A new floating shed, known as the Reichshalle, was built on Lake Constance. The Minister of the Interior decreed that Zeppelin would have to make an uninterrupted flight of twenty-four hours, and then the government would purchase one of his airships.

Throughout the summer of 1907 work on the LZ3 went forward. In September, a flight of more than four hours was made. Then, on 30 September 1907 LZ3 remained airborne for seven hours and fifty-four minutes. On board was a representative of the German Navy, *Fregatten-kapitän* Mischke.

Until this time the German Navy had not shown much interest in rigid dirigibles or in other aircraft. The Kaiser's brother, Admiral Prince Henry of Prussia, was an enthusiast but his suggestions were largely ignored owing to the opposition of the Navy Minister, *Grossadmiral* Alfred von Tirpitz.

Tirpitz was the founder of the new German Navy. He meant to create a fleet that could challenge Britain's supremacy at sea. As early as 1906 he had shown a slight measure of interest in the airship as a naval scouting weapon. However, he was firmly convinced that the great issues of the twentieth century would be decided upon the surface of the sea. He was desperate to secure the money he required for the building of an adequate number of warships. He would not readily squander his limited funds on aviation or aeronautics. He preferred, for a time, to watch the Army's experiments with aircraft, as an observer.

When Mischke, after flying in the LZ3 for almost eight hours, prepared his official report, he admitted that Zeppelin was still confronted by several serious problems but he stressed also that "Count Zeppelin had enjoyed a decisive success, which showed that the path he was following would lead to his goal".[1] Shortly after, in April 1908, Tirpitz' Dockyard Department Chief reported that in his view the Zeppelin airship was especially suited for strategic scouting at sea. He further reported: "also they will eventually be able to be used with great success for independent operations against the enemy coast (attack on vital objectives thereon by dropping shells, etc.)".[2]

These reports produced no immediate result. Later, Tirpitz explained: "As a naval officer who had got to know the force of the wind and the malice of squalls on sailing ships, I never promised myself much from the airships. . . . I set much greater expectations on the development of the aeroplane. During the Zeppelin craze which passed over Germany I kept myself in the background as much as possible, without appearing a wet blanket. . . ."[3] Upon the evidence contained in the second volume of his Memoirs, these statements were not entirely accurate. Nevertheless, they reflect Admiral Tirpitz' attitude in the earliest days of Count Zeppelin's endeavours.

Meanwhile, the military authorities in Germany reacted more favourably. General von Moltke, Chief of the General Staff, made the point that only in the Zeppelin airship did Germany possess an aerial vessel potentially superior to those already employed by the French Army. It was decided that Zeppelin should be granted the sum of four hundred thousand marks so that he could build a fourth airship, one that could fly for the stipulated period of twenty-four hours.

In November 1907 construction of LZ4 began. This Zeppelin had a length of four hundred and forty-six feet with a diameter of more than forty-two feet. Improved Daimler engines were installed to make certain the vessel possessed adequate power. The first flight of LZ4 was made on 20 June 1908. Two further trial flights were successfully completed and

---

[1] Quoted in Douglas Robinson, *The Zeppelin in Combat* (Henley-on-Thames, 1971), p. 19, hereafter cited as Robinson, *The Zeppelin in Combat*.

[2] *Ibid.*, pp. 19–20.

[3] Grand-Admiral von Tirpitz, *My Memoirs* (London, *n.d.*), vol. I, p. 139.

then Count Zeppelin decided to make a major effort, a journey over Switzerland with twelve passengers and a fuel supply that could last for twelve hours. On this record-breaking journey of 1 July 1908 Zeppelin remained in the air for twelve hours; he achieved a maximum altitude of twenty-six hundred feet; and he covered a distance of two hundred and forty miles. The German people, as a result, became wild with enthusiasm. They eagerly awaited Count Zeppelin's next aerial foray.

The reaction in Britain was completely different. There, many people believed a new era in the history of the world had begun. For the British people, Zeppelin's triumph fused two vital themes which were their particular concern. The first of these was their age-old fear of invasion. The second was their more recently developed but growing anxiety about the menace of Imperial Germany.

III

Sir Walter Raleigh, in his official history *The War in The Air*, took pride in pointing out that the English were less "excitable" than the Germans when they contemplated the military potential of aircraft in the years before 1914.

"Conservative and humorous minds", Sir Walter explained, "are always conscious chiefly of the immutable and stable elements in human life . . . Those who were responsible for the naval and military defences of the country preserved great coolness, and refused to let judgement outrun experience. They knew well that the addition to man's resources of yet another mode of travel or transport does not alter the enduring principles of strategy."[1]

Despite these sage reflections it must be pointed out that the British from ancient times always feared an invasion of their home islands. Moreover this fear sometimes produced panics and alarms which knew neither sane nor reasonable limits. Often, though not always, advances in technology or new inventions were responsible for these episodes in British history. The success of the Zeppelin airship in 1908 resulted, as we shall see, in yet another classic instance of this recurring trend or tendency of British life. The Zeppelin was responsible for a new series of alarms in what Arthur Balfour called "this eternal and most important question of our safety against invasion".

In modern times the problem of an adequate defence against invasion threw up two schools of thought in Great Britain. The highest authorities in the Army and the Navy were sometimes unable to agree upon this fundamental issue of national life and existence.

[1] Raleigh, *The War in The Air*, pp. 2–3.

Upon the one hand were those who placed their faith in the Navy as the supreme barrier to any invading force. Upon the other was the "military school". These experts held that the Navy was not invincible, that despite every precaution a mistake might be made in the country's naval arrangements which would put all at hazard. They feared, in their patriotic enthusiasm, that the fleet might be decoyed from the Channel and that an invading army, as a result, could be thrown successfully upon the British shore.

These planners urged the value of a "second line" of defence. They wanted the government to build extensive fortifications at key points along the coasts and to organize behind these works a large home army whose task would be the destruction of an invading force.

Since the funds available for national defence were strictly limited, an almost unending quarrel arose. The advocates of naval defence demanded the bulk of the country's resources for her ships of the line, and for the ancillary vessels that might be needed. The technicians of the "military school" urged significant expenditures for fortifications and an adequate home army.

During the early part of the nineteenth century concern over the possibility of invasion resulted in a clear-cut policy. The defence of the British Isles was assigned to the Navy supported, if need arose, by the militia. The Army, according to this design, was to be prepared to serve as an overseas striking force. By the 1840s, however, these arrangements for the national defence were subjected to a rude shock.

Technical advances were responsible for the invasion panic of 1848. Steam power was not the sole cause of the alarm. By the early 1840s there were several developments in marine engineering, in particular the appearance of the screw propeller, which resulted in a widespread fear of sudden assault by France upon the British coast. In 1846 General Sir John Burgoyne, an engineering officer who was especially concerned with military fortifications, sounded a warning which resulted in the "scare".

Burgoyne argued, without explaining how it could be done, that the French might obtain naval control of the English Channel and then land a force of one hundred and fifty thousand soldiers in England. According to his analysis, the regular Army in Britain did not possess enough men to deal with such an invading force. He urged that it was necessary to increase at once the number of regulars stationed in the United Kingdom. In January 1848 the *Morning Chronicle*, a leading newspaper of the day, published a letter written by the Duke of Wellington, Britain's greatest soldier, which concurred in General Burgoyne's startling conclusions.

The panic of 1848 soon subsided but a precedent had been set and a pattern for further alarms and excursions created: a warning had been sounded, based upon questionable technical assumptions; a great public figure had given his support to the outcry; no analysis from the enemy's point of view had been attempted; the most frightening conclusions had been accepted as valid possibilities of the immediate future. The notion of a successful "Bolt from the Blue" had been fixed firmly in the official and in the public mind.[1] General Burgoyne's patriotic initiative became an example which was diligently followed by many of the alarmists who came after him in the decades which followed.

In the 1850s and 1860s the "Bolt from the Blue" school of strategic thought played the major role in Britain's defensive arrangements. The public began to doubt the ability of the Navy to protect the country from invasion. In 1859 a Royal Commission was appointed to report upon the best means of defending the country. The Commission, after study, decided the fleet might be rendered ineffective by storm, defeat in battle, or by a ruse that drew it away from the British coast. It recommended significant expenditures for fortresses, land defences, and floating batteries. In this period the military view dominated. The awful possibility of a "lightning invasion" with which the Navy could not deal became a major cause of concern.

The issue was so vitally important that it could not be left alone. In 1867 the views of the "Bolt from the Blue" thinkers were challenged by Sir John Colomb, an expert on the subject of Imperial defence. He sought to return Britain to her more traditional reliance upon naval power as the chief source of national defence.

Invasion, he argued, was only likely after a naval defeat and a successful blockade of the British Isles. The Navy, in his view, was Britain's "shield" while the Army was her "spear to strike", valuable chiefly for offence. As long as the fleet was maintained in adequate numbers it would dominate the seas and make a successful invasion impossible. His opinions, and the arguments of those who agreed with him, were soon labelled the "Blue Water" school of naval theory.

By the 1880s these theorists had developed into a powerful and influential faction. Their message to the British Government and people was clear and simple. As long as Britain controlled the seas invasion was impossible. Money spent on a large Army for home defence was a disgraceful waste of public resources. If the fleets were beaten at sea fortifications or other passive defences would be of no value because the British could be starved into submission by a naval power in control of the sea lanes, a power that would be in a position to cut the country off from its sources of overseas supply upon which all British life depended.

During the 1880s the battle between the "Bolt from the Blue" theorists and those of the "Blue Water" school flared intermittently. In May 1888 Lord Wolseley, the distinguished soldier, issued a grave warning in the House of Lords. Britain, he argued, lived under the menace of an attack

[1] John Gooch, *The Prospect of War* (London, 1981), pp. 2–3.

from France. The country lay open to the serious danger of an invasion.
The Duke of Cambridge lent powerful support to his suggestions. The
"Blue Water" enthusiasts replied with a vigorous public response of their
own. The partisans of the Army and Navy now became locked in a bitter
contest to decide which Service would play the major role in the defence
of the country.

Their spirited clashes, as might be expected, resulted in nation-wide
apprehension and anxiety. Eventually, the Navy triumphed. A major
step was taken with the passage of the Naval Defence Act of 1889. The
new law provided funds to build eight battleships, thirty-eight cruisers,
and more than a score of gunboats.

However, the ascendancy of the "Blue Water" school was not entirely
complete. Many concerned observers were impressed most by the fact
that the War Office and the Admiralty seemed unable to cooperate
effectively. The partisans on each side urged such contradictory courses
and policies it seemed impossible to work out a logical, unified, and
coherent programme of national defence.

The suggestion was now put forward that some kind of higher authority
should be created to coordinate the business of national defence. The task
of such a body would be to impose a rational policy upon the two Services,
for the greater good of all. In 1890 a Royal Commission under the
chairmanship of an eminent political figure, Lord Hartington, reported
there was little cooperation between the Army and the Navy. The
commission recommended, as a remedy, the formation of a naval and
military council, composed of the political leaders of each Service,
assisted by their highest technical advisers, and presided over by the
Prime Minister himself. This proposal was not acted upon for several
years. Eventually, however, it resulted in the creation of the Committee
of Imperial Defence.

Two further developments of consequence took place in late
nineteenth-century England and these significantly altered the nature of
the public debate. The Education Acts of 1870, 1880, and 1881 created for
the first time a literate proletariat in Britain. At the same time the Reform
Acts of 1867 and 1884 gave the vote to large segments of the working
classes and furnished them with a measure of political power, however
limited.[1]

In earlier times there had been plenty of sensational Press comment
about the menace of invasion. Works of fiction had been written to
exploit popular interest in the theme. Now, however, Alfred Harmsworth and publicists like him realized that lurid fictional accounts could

---

[1] See for these themes an excellent unpublished Ph.D. thesis preserved in the
University of London Library, Howard Roy Moon, "The Invasion of the United
Kingdom: Public Controversy and Official Planning 1888–1918".

be employed to increase the circulation of their popular journals, maga-zines, and newspapers. "Invasion fantasies", as they have been called, became an almost regular ingredient in publications of this type. These sensational stories attracted the notice of large segments of the British people and influenced their attitude. The result was an aroused public interest and a strident national clamour for heightened vigilance against the possibility of a sudden brutal blow upon the coast by some scheming and envious foreign enemy.

IV

The disasters of the South African War revealed to everyone concerned with such matters that significant changes in the defence arrangements of the Empire were now a basic requirement of British policy. In July 1902 Arthur Balfour became prime minister. He looked upon himself as a philosopher. He was not content with the haphazard methods that had determined matters in the past. He wanted to procure for the State an analysis of the Empire's strategic position, furnished by the most capable civilian and military minds available for the purpose.

Arthur Balfour was a great Conservative and aristocratic leader but he was also a man of narrow Tory outlook. In domestic affairs he struggled, without respite, to preserve the well-being of his own class and order, the class he represented in politics. It is no wonder that he early took up, as prime minister, the question of the defence of the home islands against invasion. His duty, as he saw it, was to preserve and protect the nation and the Empire, to make certain that no abrupt or radical changes in their condition took place.[1]

Lord Salisbury, Balfour's predecessor, had established a Defence Committee of the Cabinet in 1895. This body, like similar organizations appointed in the nineteenth century, was not particularly effective in discharging its duties. However, Balfour fixed upon it as the base which would enable him to advance toward his own goals. In December 1902 the Defence Committee was tentatively reconstituted as the Committee of Imperial Defence.

Balfour proposed to employ this committee in order to make clear to the Army and Navy exactly what their respective responsibilities were. He would eliminate rivalry and confusion and replace them with an ordered system.

---

[1] It may be mentioned that Lord Sydenham of Combe, a man who knew about such things, wrote of Balfour's interest in these themes in the strongest terms. See Lord Sydenham of Combe, *My Working Life* (London, 1927), p. 188: "No Prime Minister has ever given so much personal study to Imperial Defence in all its aspects. . . ."

Eventually a scheme was worked out whereby the prime minister became the "invariable President" of the Committee of Imperial Defence with "absolute discretion" in the selection of its members. In practice, Balfour and those who succeeded him summoned cabinet ministers, the chiefs of the Fighting Services, and others concerned with the wider aspects of strategy to meetings of the Committee of Imperial Defence. In time, under Balfour's direction, a "Permanent Secretariat" was created to record and preserve the discussions, memoranda, and decisions of the committee. These initiatives have been called "one of the most significant steps of his premiership".[1]

There now existed for the first time a forum in which the politicians, those responsible for the final decisions, could listen to the technical arguments of each of the Services, and weigh the evidence put before them. The first subject submitted to the Committee of Imperial Defence for its consideration was the invasion question.

In February 1903 a special sub-committee began its investigations. The War Office and the Admiralty presented their several points of view over a period of months. Eventually the "Blue Water" school triumphed. It was established that an invasion of the British Isles could not succeed unless an army of seventy thousand men was employed for the purpose. Such a force, however, would require so many transports and so much time to assemble that the Navy would have ample warning to sound the alarm and to gather enough ships to engage and destroy it.

Arthur Balfour took particular care to make these technical conclusions known to the British people so that they would be reassured that his government, unlike its predecessors, had studied the matter adequately and had made all necessary preparations to deal with it. In November 1903 he publicly explained that Britain's home defences no longer needed to be a source of concern for the people of Britain.

In May 1905 Balfour made an even more authoritative declaration. In a speech to the House of Commons he took up at length the roles of the Army and Navy in any attempted invasion of the British Isles. He assured his audience that, provided the Navy was efficient, "serious invasion of these islands is not an eventuality which we need seriously to consider". Some of the subtleties of his argument were lost by those who listened to him but the prime minister's message seemed clear enough.

Despite these pronouncements by the highest authority, the fear of invasion was not laid to rest in Great Britain after 1905. Apprehension and anxiety were revived as more and more people became concerned with what contemporaries called the "German Peril".

In December 1905 Arthur Balfour resigned office. In the Liberal

---

[1] Nicholas d'Ombrain, *War Machinery and High Policy* (Oxford, 1973), p. 1, hereafter cited as d'Ombrain, *War Machinery and High Policy*.

Government that succeeded him R. B. Haldane, the new Secretary of State for War, at once accepted the "Blue Water" doctrines of the previous administration. Nevertheless, a serious agitation soon developed, fixed once again upon the possibility that Britain lay naked to a sudden surprise attack from the sea. This time the alarmists were led by an outstanding champion, the great hero of the Boer War, Field-Marshal Lord Roberts, the most revered British soldier then alive.

Lord Roberts, an advocate of conscription, drew a formidable company of associates to his side. The most capable of these was the brilliant military correspondent of *The Times*, Lieutenant Colonel Charles á Court Repington. Roberts, Repington, and their friends decided it was their patriotic duty to force the Liberal Government to reopen the invasion question and to examine it anew, bearing in mind recent developments in Germany, and in particular, the emergence of a powerful new German navy.

In 1907 the Roberts group scored a tremendous victory. They persuaded Balfour, now Leader of the Opposition, that the invasion enquiry should be taken up yet again by the government. Balfour, as a result of their urging, sent certain papers Lord Roberts and his friends had drawn up to the secretary of the Committee of Imperial Defence "with a view to their being submitted to expert investigation if such a course was considered advisable by the Prime Minister".[1]

Balfour was sometimes criticized for this apparent reversal of course in 1907. Such criticisms, however, were not justified. In 1903 when the Committee of Imperial Defence examined the question of the possibility of a successful invasion of the British Isles Balfour explained to the committee that the subject was of such overmastering importance that no decision about it could ever be considered final. Balfour made his position absolutely clear at that time when he prepared and submitted to the committee a "Draft Report on The Possibility of Serious Invasion", dated 11 November 1903:[2]

> The Committee of Defence have felt it to be their imperative duty to come to some decision of this protracted controversy. No decision can, indeed, be final. In a matter which concerns national existence the arguments on either side must be made the subject of constant revision and reconsideration. . . .

[1] Cab. 3/2. C.I.D. 44A. "Report of a Sub-Committee appointed by the Prime Minister to reconsider the question of Oversea Attack", dated 22 October 1908 and marked "*SECRET*".

[2] Cab. 3/1. C.I.D. 18A. "Draft Report on The Possibility of Serious Invasion" by A.J.B., dated "November 11, 1903", and marked "*CONFIDENTIAL*".

Lord Roberts and his friends were motivated by similar reflections, in part at least. Their movement was inspired by their fear of Germany; by their hostility to the Liberal Government of the day; by their desire to see a system of National Service imposed upon the manhood of the country; and by concern about what contemporaries regularly called Britain's "deplorable condition of national unpreparedness". However, they were also afraid that some technical innovation might, even if only for a moment, upset those deadly balances upon which England's safety depended. In 1907 they were not yet worried by the possibility of a sudden German attack from the air. But this idea became a part of their armoury within a couple of years.

Early in 1909 R. P. Hearne, a journalist who worked for *The Car* magazine, published a book entitled *Aerial Warfare*. Hearne was closely associated with Lord Northcliffe[1] and shared with him a fear of Germany's developing power in the air. *Aerial Warfare* at once attracted the attention of Lord Roberts.

Roberts and his friends always feared the Germans might strike at England before they issued a formal declaration of war. They believed the Germans were ruthless enough to cast such a formality aside if that course could materially assist them in the carrying out of a successful invasion. In *Aerial Warfare* R. P. Hearne linked these themes together. He wrote in his book:[2]

> . . . In a critical time, before war were declared, an aerial fleet might be massed some forty or fifty miles away from our coasts, and on receiving a wireless message *could strike within two hours of war being declared*! . . .
>
> Sheerness, Portsmouth, and Rosyth would all be open to . . . attack, whilst another section of the aerial fleet could make destructive raids on London, the midlands, the manufacturing districts, Liverpool, and other great commercial ports, where no defences exist. . . .
>
> The German aerial fleet, by crippling our naval forces . . . would open the way for a German naval raid covering an expeditionary force. The landing of a German army on our shores would be possible in no other way – and it would be the last chapter of the war!
>
> . . . It is not easy for the British public to accept these possibilities, for the majority of experts do not yet admit them, and the idea of the invincibility of the 'blue-water' policy cannot be knocked out of their heads. But in a very few years the advance in aeronautics will be so evident that these theories will have to be seriously considered. . . .

[1] See B.M. Add. MSS. (Northcliffe Papers) R. P. Hearne to Northcliffe, 30 March 1909; and Hearne to Northcliffe, 27 April 1909.

[2] See R. P. Hearne, *Aerial Warfare* (London, 1909), pp. 169ff. The book was published with an introduction by Sir Hiram Maxim.

When Lord Roberts read *Aerial Warfare* he was "shocked to find out how little I knew about flying machines and the progress of aerial navigation". From this moment he began to pay very special attention to them. He at once wrote to his former subordinate, Sir William Nicholson, who had recently become Chief of the Imperial General Staff, but that high soldier did not encourage him to pursue his new interest in aeronautical developments.[1]

In 1907 Lord Roberts and his allies continued to press the Liberal Government about the possibility of a successful invasion of England. Germany was their particular concern. Eventually the prime minister, Sir Henry Campbell-Bannerman, gave way to their demands. On 27 November 1907 the Committee of Imperial Defence began its second invasion enquiry. They were still deliberating upon this vital question when Count Zeppelin made his brilliant twelve-hour flight on 1 July 1908.

V

Count Zeppelin's successful flight also contributed to Britain's general anxiety about the might and purpose of Imperial Germany. By 1908, as Halévy has written, "the dominant sentiment in England was fear of the power of Germany".[2]

For years past many people in England had observed developments in Germany with growing concern. German business men seemed to be more efficient than their British rivals. Native British industries were already feeling the power of those great trusts and cartels which had been formed in Germany, and in the United States. Abroad, the British were impressed by the vitality and energy of German exporters and salesmen who sought to compete almost everywhere, even in markets previously looked upon as closed British preserves. At the time of the Boer War an outburst of anti-English feeling had made itself evident in the German Press, and in the attitude of German public opinion.

By the beginning of 1908, however, the master issue that separated the two peoples and the two governments was the Anglo-German naval rivalry. For many in Britain this was looked upon as the most vital question of their time. Britain depended for life itself upon the power and efficiency of her Navy.

In June 1897 Admiral Tirpitz, the man who created the modern German Navy, presented a "Very Secret" memorandum on the subject

---

[1] See David James, *Lord Roberts* (London, 1954), p. 436.

[2] See Halévy, *History of The English People*, vol. VI, Book II, p. 403. See also in this general connection Paul M. Kennedy, *The Rise of The Anglo-German Antagonism 1860–1914* (London, 1980), pp. 441ff.

to the Kaiser, in which he declared: "For Germany the most dangerous enemy at the present time is England. It is also the enemy against which we most urgently require a certain measure of naval force as a political power factor. Commerce raiding and transatlantic war against England is . . . hopeless . . . Our fleet must be so constructed that it can unfold its greatest military potential between Heligoland and the Thames . . . The military situation against England demands battleships in as great a number as possible. . . ." The brilliant historian of this new German departure has concluded that Tirpitz and the Kaiser were determined "to wrest from Great Britain her exclusive hegemony over the world's oceans".[1]

The result of Tirpitz' formidable initiative was passage of the first and second German Navy Laws of 1898 and 1900 which provided for the creation of a powerful new fleet. In England these laws were not at first regarded as an especial cause for apprehension. By the end of 1902, however, the Admiralty became convinced that the German fleet was being built so that it could engage in a naval war against England.

Diplomatic developments contributed to the increase of tension between the two Powers. After the first Moroccan crisis, which we have touched on in an earlier chapter, both sides became more concerned than ever before about the potential of the German Navy. Later, the failure of the Second Hague Conference to check the competition in naval armaments served to increase the British sense of insecurity.

At the end of 1907 the German Press suddenly forecast the appearance of a new supplementary law which would reduce the age of ships on active service and mean a genuine acceleration in the German building programme. In January 1908 this law was accepted by the Budget Committee of the Reichstag. Sir Henry Campbell-Bannerman's Liberal Government had sought to limit or reduce the naval rivalry, without success. Now observers waited with heightened interest for the appearance of the British Navy Estimates for 1908, since this pronouncement of the Liberal Ministry would make clear the nature of Britain's reply to Germany.

In 1908 the guiding force at the Admiralty was Admiral Sir John Fisher, the great genius who had early recognized the meaning of Germany's naval challenge and had begun to make preparations to meet it. As First Sea Lord it was Fisher's duty to see to it that the Navy Estimates provided enough funds for the Board of Admiralty to build ships in sufficient numbers in 1908 to make certain Britain maintained her maritime supremacy over Germany.

However, the situation which confronted Fisher at the beginning of the

---

[1] The Tirpitz memorandum is reproduced in the outstanding work of Jonathan Steinberg, *Yesterday's Deterrent* (New York, 1965), pp. 209ff; the conclusion cited is at p. 201.

year was extremely complicated. Inside the Liberal Cabinet a powerful block of Radicals led by Lloyd George, John Burns, and "Lulu" Harcourt were determined to reduce the amount of the 1908 Estimates. They argued that the Liberals had been elected in order to curtail expenditure on armaments. They refused to tolerate any policy save that of retrenchment. They warned Fisher in the strongest terms that they were not prepared to accept the Estimates his Board had submitted to the Cabinet.

Moreover, Admiral Fisher's extensive reforms had created a formidable opposition to his policies, inside the Navy itself. Admiral Lord Charles Beresford and a faction of officers who agreed with him were demanding a formal enquiry into Fisher's conduct as technical head of the Navy. Talk about such an enquiry had begun in 1906. Now, Beresford and his followers were determined that their charges and allegations should be heard by a panel composed of the highest officers of the State. Beresford hoped that such an enquiry would force Fisher to resign from his post as First Sea Lord. It was not without reason that Lord Esher, Fisher's friend, sent a famous letter to the Secretaries of the Maritime League at this time. Esher's letter declared: "There is not a man in Germany from the Emperor downwards who would not welcome the fall of Sir John Fisher."

The situation in the House of Commons made Admiral Fisher's position even more uncertain. There, the landslide election of 1906 had brought into the House significant numbers of Liberals and Radicals who had never expected to win seats in the first place. These "cranks", as they were sometimes called, were resolved that Campbell-Bannerman's Liberal Ministry should fulfil its election promises and seriously reduce the sums spent on the Navy so that funds would be available for social reforms. These men were less amenable to party discipline than the more usual politicians; the Whips would have less effect on the way they voted if they were asked to violate their consciences in order to approve Navy Estimates in 1908 which had not been reduced below the level of those for 1907.

Admiral Fisher laboured under awesome burdens. He realized that if his fleets were beaten by the German Navy there would be no chance to muddle through to eventual victory, in the usual British way. An initial defeat of the Navy in a war with Germany would mean the extinction of England's defences, certain invasion, and the consequent destruction of the Empire.

Fisher was a savage fighter. In order to get his own way over the Estimates he would not hesitate to force a major political crisis upon a reluctant Liberal Cabinet. He was the first admiral to make significant use of the Press to present the public with information about the Navy he desired it to have.

In 1908 Admiral Fisher strengthened his relationship with J. L. Garvin, recently appointed as editor of *The Observer*. Lord Northcliffe had purchased *The Observer* in 1905 in order to acquire a journal that could win for him political influence and power of a kind the *Daily Mail* could not provide. He looked upon J. L. Garvin as the "most powerful journalist in England".

Fisher now proceeded to supply Garvin with confidential and secret Admiralty documents. These papers enabled the editor to publish a series of sensational articles about the Navy and the Naval Estimates which astonished contemporaries. The king, the prince of Wales, the leaders of all the Parties, and a significant number of readers of *The Observer* were presented with amazing accounts that explained the situation from Admiral Fisher's point of view. Lord Northcliffe repeated the arguments and information contained in Garvin's great articles in his *Daily Mail* and in the columns of his other newspapers. The rest of the British Press found it had to pay very careful attention to everything published in *The Observer* dealing with the condition of the British Navy.[1]

Garvin wrote in the tones of an alarmist. His articles contributed significantly to the naval crisis of 1908. Admiral Fisher managed to win his battle for the 1908 Estimates but it was done in an atmosphere of panic and fear. Moreover, a pattern was now set.[2] After 1908 the struggle over Britain's Naval Estimates each year was usually carried out in the most heated political circumstances. The country was regularly warned each January, February, and March of the German menace, the danger of invasion, and the German determination to outstrip Britain in the building of warships, especially *Dreadnought* battleships on which the fate of the naval battle was expected to turn. In 1909 as a direct result of these developments there occurred the "greatest navy scare in English history".[3] The origins of the 1909 "scare" were established at this time.

As a journalist, J. L. Garvin did not confine his activities to *The Observer*. He regularly wrote for other journals and periodicals in this period. Often he employed a pseudonym – "Calchas", "X", or "Ignotus" – when he published articles about the German Empire; and these sometimes aroused the wrath of the Kaiser himself.

In July 1908 Garvin published a tremendous article in the *Quarterly Review*, entitled "The German Peril". Although the article was unsigned his friends soon learned who the author was. The impression produced by this article was remarkable. The German Chancellor, Prince von Bülow, was seriously irritated by it. He complained that the nervous-

---

[1] For these developments see Alfred Gollin, *The Observer and J. L. Garvin* (London, 1960), pp. 28ff.

[2] See D. W. Sweet, "Great Britain and Germany, 1905–1911" in F. H. Hinsley ed., *British Foreign Policy Under Sir Edward Grey* (Cambridge, 1977), p. 221.

[3] See Arthur Marder, *From The Dreadnought to Scapa Flow*, vol. I, p. 149.

ness shown in the piece was more worthy of the French than the British Press.[1] Many in England, however, expressed their thanks to Garvin for his warnings about Germany, for years after.

In form "The German Peril" was a review of a number of recent books dealing with Germany. In fact, it was a strident warning about German hostility to England. "Year by year", Garvin wrote, "silently, ceaselessly, proceeds the automatic expansion of a colossal military strength . . . nothing can be more certain than that the German Government and the whole German people . . . regard the strength of England and the existence of her maritime supremacy as the first and chief obstacle to the realisation of their ambitions by land and sea . . . In face of the permanence and the increasing urgency of the German peril, let us be certain, not only that eternal vigilance has become the price of Empire and the necessity of national existence, but that no forewarning will avail us unless the crisis finds us forearmed. We can only aggravate it and precipitate it by our weakness. We may postpone, we may even avert it, by our strength. . . ."

Garvin placed particular emphasis upon the danger of invasion. His article explained:

> Nor, in case of war, will Germany remain on the defensive. Her General Staff does not accept the theory that an invasion of this country is impossible. Nothing can be much more certain than that, if we are locked in a life-and-death struggle with Germany, she will attempt invasion. Her naval officers have sounded and sketched our harbours and studied every detail of our coasts. Her military officers have carried out staff-rides in this country. They have examined, as it were, every inch of our surface through a military microscope. . . . There are, in this country some 50,000 German waiters; and a large number of these are employed in connection with the hotels at railway stations. Many keepers of public-houses near our forts are German. The nakedness of our land is spied out. . . . Germany does not rely upon the chance success of a sudden thrust. She relies upon the ultimate power of the naval organisation she is creating to battle down our own. . . . And then? We shall pay the penalty. . . .

It is no wonder that when Halévy surveyed the British scene in 1908 he was impressed by the national fear of Germany. He came to the conclusion that in England in 1908, the "peril of invasion was the staple topic of conversation. . . ."[2]

---

[1] See Halévy, *op. cit.*, pp. 394–5, for Bülow's reaction.
[2] *Ibid.*, p. 394.

VI

Garvin wrote his *Quarterly Review* article before Count Zeppelin made his record-breaking flight in July 1908. However, when the news of Zeppelin's success burst upon the world Garvin used the information he had acquired in preparing "The German Peril" in order to explain the meaning of Zeppelin's accomplishment in *The Observer*.

It was Garvin's custom to place a column called "The Week" next to his great editorials on the leader page of *The Observer*. "The Week" was not another leading article. It consisted of brief unconnected paragraphs and notes about recent items of interest. It was a key feature of *The Observer*, especially appreciated by Lord Northcliffe. On 5 July 1908 "The Week" was given over to the Zeppelin. Its first paragraph declared:

> "The Week"
> By far the most remarkable event of the week, and perhaps of the year, is the epoch-making voyage of the German airship. For the first time a flying machine has risen in one nation and sailed over the territory of another. As the airship has already crossed mountains, lakes, and international boundaries, we cannot doubt that it will yet cross seas and oceans, kingdoms, and continents, and revolutionise the political relations of the world. . . .

It will be recalled that in form "The German Peril" article was a review of books. One of the books listed at the top of the article was *Die Zukunft Deutschlands: eine Warnung* by *Regierungsrath* Rudolf Martin, published in Leipzig in 1908. Martin was a former German official who wrote fictional accounts about Germany and her relations with the other Powers. He was especially concerned, in these works, with Anglo-German relations; and he fixed upon German advances in the air as a key to the future. In the next paragraph of "The Week" Garvin concentrated his readers' attention upon Privy Councillor Martin, and his aggressive attitude toward England:

> A decade ago the German Emperor electrified his people with the famous phrase: "Our future lies on the water". His subject, Councillor Martin, was much ridiculed for the series of books in which he maintained, on the contrary, that "the future of Germany lies in the air". This writer, an ex-official, well acquainted with the drift of thought in German governing circles is a financial expert, as well as a daring visionary, and if any are still inclined to laugh at him, it will be just as well for this island to refrain. Herr Martin points out that even in the early stages of air navigation the narrow seas at least will be negotiable, and he demands that the Fatherland should from the first maintain its air-fleets at a Two-Power standard. . . .

A final paragraph was devoted to the future, in the new age of airships:

> . . . By dropping explosives airships may ultimately be able to destroy battleships and docks, and in many other ways to spread panic and injure the credit of an enemy. . . . We do not realise how rapidly the world is changing. Any State which means to survive in the twentieth century will have to grapple by land and sea and air alike with the forces of the three elements.

An even more pointed warning appeared in *The Times* a few days later, on 13 July. In an article entitled "The Conquest of The Air" a special writer sounded the alarm about England's danger:

> . . . During the past week there has been an effort made through the Press to point out that England is only a third-class Power as regards her equipment for aerial warfare. . . .

> . . . We are lagging behind the other Powers to such a degree in this respect that, when the possibilities and dangers are fully realised, our backwardness is sufficient to cause anxiety. . . .
> The old cry that England, being an island, is only secure from attack by the upkeep of a powerful Navy is fully recognised by all grades of society and all denominations of politicians, but it is not yet realised that England's safety as an island will vanish if not ensured against aerial attack . . . Airships, before aeroplanes, are undoubtedly going to prove enormously powerful factors in any war of the future . . . if England is to be prepared against all emergencies, money and plenty of it must be promptly devoted to the building of airships. . . .
> 'Wake up England' must be the watchword again. . . .

It remained for Lord Northcliffe to carry these warnings to an even more extreme stage. He at once took up the theme of Garvin's article in *The Observer* and arranged for the *Daily Mail* correspondent in Berlin to seek out Privy Councillor Rudolf Martin, and to interview him about the international consequences of Count Zeppelin's achievement.

At this time the *Daily Mail* correspondent in Berlin was a brilliant American journalist named Frederick W. Wile. He had established himself in Berlin in 1902 and represented several British and American newspapers in the German capital until he was chased out by the authorities upon the outbreak of war in 1914. Lord Northcliffe looked upon Wile as an outstanding member of the *Daily Mail* staff.

Wile was convinced that the Germans loathed England and he saw to it that his articles for the *Daily Mail* reflected this German animosity. In 1907 he learned that the British Ambassador in Berlin was annoyed with the articles he sent to London. In April 1907 Wile reported to Northcliffe from the *Daily Mail* office on the Friedrichstrasse in Berlin: "It was intimated to me today, indirectly, that the British ambassador in Berlin is not pleased with the 'zeal' with which the 'Daily Mail' has followed the inception and course of the reigning spell of Anglophobia in Germany . . . I can readily understand that diplomats would prefer that we pay no attention to the press campaign against England that has been so incessantly in progress here, but I have never been able to reconcile their desires with my obligation to report glaringly obvious facts."[1]

Wile was exactly the kind of agent Northcliffe wanted to serve him in Berlin. Lord Northcliffe was convinced the Germans meant to usurp Britain's place in the world and he believed it was his patriotic duty to warn his countrymen of the German ambition and their intention to fulfil it.

Since 1906 Northcliffe had employed Wile to find out about aeronautical developments in Germany. He and Wile resorted to a simple tactic in their efforts to obtain confidential and even secret information about German airships. Northcliffe instructed Wile to contact the officials of German companies which were building airships and to inform them that his employer in London, the great British newspaper magnate, was eager to purchase a German airship. This device enabled Wile to discuss German airships with their builders, on several occasions. For example, on 8 February 1908 Wile reported to Northcliffe: "The Siemens-Schuckert company advise me today that their airship expert will call on me Monday or Tuesday to discuss the subject matter of your recent letter. I shall take up with them roughly the question of price and all other details of interest. . . ."[2]

When F. W. Wile saw Privy Councillor Rudolf Martin in Berlin in July 1908 the result was a sensational interview.

Wile discovered that Martin was not thinking about an isolated bombing raid or two, to be carried out against English targets by Zeppelin airships of the future. Martin contemplated nothing less than an invasion of England.

He told Wile that in case of a world war the Germans would transport three hundred and fifty thousand troops from Calais to Dover, in half an hour, employing airships for the purpose.

Wile's report of the interview was published in the *Daily Mail* for 11 July 1908. Large headlines appeared above his account:

[1] B.M. Add. MSS. (Northcliffe Papers) Fred W. Wile to Northcliffe, 29 April 1907.
[2] B.M. Add. MSS. (Northcliffe Papers) Wile to Northcliffe, 8 February 1908. See also in the same source Wile to Northcliffe, 19 November 1906.

COMMAND OF THE AIR
GERMANY AS THE AERIAL POWER
TEUTONIC VISION
A LANDING OF 350,000 MEN
(From Our Own Correspondent)

. . . Herr Rudolf Martin, author of books on war in the air and "Is a World War Imminent?" points out how England is losing her insular character by the development of airships and aeroplanes.

"In a world war", he said to me, "Germany would have to spend two hundred millions sterling in motor-airships, and a similar amount in aeroplanes, to transport 350,000 men in half an hour during the night from Calais to Dover. Even today the landing of a large German army in England is a mere matter of money. I am opposed to a war between Germany and England, but should it break out today, it would last at least two years, for we would conclude no peace until a German army had occupied London.

"In my judgement it would take two years for us to build motor-airships enough simultaneously to throw 350,000 men into Dover via Calais. During the same night, of course, a second transport of 350,000 men could follow. The newest Zeppelin airship can comfortably carry fifty persons from Calais to Dover. The ships which the Zeppelin works in Friedrichshafen will build during the next few months are likely to be considerably larger . . . and will carry one hundred persons. . . .

"The development of motor-airship navigation will lead to a perpetual alliance between England and Germany. The British Fleet will continue to rule the waves, while Germany's airships and land armies will represent the mightiest Power on the Continent of Europe."

A second brief despatch from Wile was printed directly below the account of his interview with Martin. This despatch declared: "It is reported here that if Count Zeppelin's Airship IV makes a successful twenty-four hour flight twelve more airships will be ordered from him by the German authorities. . . ."

Lord Northcliffe decided the judgement of a British expert on the subject was required, in order to balance Wile's account. He knew Major Baden-Powell well. Earlier in 1908 Northcliffe had discussed airships with Baden-Powell and had even agreed to pay the major to construct a small airship in the grounds of his beautiful country home, Sutton Place.[1]

When Wile's despatches arrived in London a *Daily Mail* reporter was at once sent to Baden-Powell to secure his technical opinion. The account of the interview with Baden-Powell, described in the *Daily Mail* of 11 July as

[1] See B.M. Add. MSS. (Northcliffe Papers) B. Baden-Powell to Northcliffe, 28 February 1908.

"the well-known aeronautical expert", was as sensational as the report sent from Berlin.

Major Baden-Powell declared that the British Government should at once allocate the sum of one hundred thousand pounds for aerial research and the construction of "aerial ships of war". He also said: (*Daily Mail*, 11 July 1908):

> The one fact that must be impressed upon our legislators is this: The use of a practical airship in time of war has ceased to be the fantastic creation of an inventor's brain. In the next great European war it will become an accomplished fact. . . .
>
> What this great revolution means is this, so far as we are concerned, although the fact is insufficiently realised. In time of war we should no longer be an island and our mighty fleet would cease to be our first line of defence. A dozen great Dreadnoughts would be helpless when faced with the task of repelling a swift fleet of foreign airships sailing high above the earth.
>
> In the near future, too, machine guns of light construction may be mounted upon these aerial ships of war, in addition to the explosives which may be carried to drop death and destruction upon an enemy. . . .
>
> Instead of tying its purse strings . . . the Government should, in order to preserve our supremacy, be building not one craft as efficient as Count Zeppelin's, but two. . . . At the present moment also we should be busy upon the construction of special guns adapted to fire a projectile high into the air against a hostile airship.
>
> Only a year or so ago, our authorities were talking of aerial navigation in its relation to war as 'an interesting and instructive study'. Now we must reckon it as the gravest problem of the moment. . . .

The first leading article in the *Daily Mail* for 11 July took up the story of German progress in the air. It referred to Rudolf Martin as "the German official who has made a special study of the probable effects of aerial navigation upon war". However, the *Daily Mail* criticized both Martin and Major Baden-Powell for their alarmism. Their "terrifying" predictions could refer only to the future, the *Daily Mail* suggested.

The leader went on: "The destructive power of existing airships has been exaggerated. Their lifting power is not yet great; Zeppelin No. IV can only raise two tons of dead weight. . . . This would enable her to carry sufficient explosives to do a good deal of damage to great industrial centres and dockyards but she could not attack battleships with any prospect of success."

Having rendered these sober judgements the *Daily Mail* concluded with a stern warning to the British Admiralty and War Office: "Yet what Zeppelin No. IV cannot accomplish may be, and probably will be, within the range of Zeppelin No. X or No. XX, and it is for this reason that the British Admiralty and War Office would be well advised without further delay to appropriate money to enable us at least to keep abreast of Continental enterprise."

Until this moment, as we have seen earlier, the War Office had shown more interest in aeronautics than the Admiralty. However, exactly at this time the Admiralty began to take steps to inform serving officers about the military potential of airships. Moreover, Captain Reginald Bacon, the Director of Naval Ordnance, having received instructions to draw up a programme that would enable the Admiralty to take over the construction of airships for the British Government, now produced a set of recommendations to achieve this object.

VII

In July 1908 Captain Neumann, Instructor in the German Air-ship Battalion, published in the *Marine-Rundschau* a long article entitled "The Possibility of Making Use of Balloons and Motor Air-Ships in The Navy". This article attracted the attention of the British Admiralty. A translation was prepared for the Admiralty and permission to publish it secured from the editor of the *Marine-Rundschau*.

The authorities at the Admiralty saw to it that the translation was widely disseminated. The Director of Naval Intelligence, one of the most important officers concerned with the formulation of British naval policy, sent the translation to the editor of the *Journal of the Royal United Service Institution* and it appeared in that periodical in two parts, beginning with the edition for November 1908. In this way the Admiralty took a definite step designed to make certain that many serving officers became acquainted with the latest facts in the development of airships for naval purposes. The *Journal of the Royal United Service Institution* made it clear that Neumann's article had been communicated to it by the Director of Naval Intelligence.

Captain Neumann, a technical expert, began his article in suitably cautious tones. He was not an enthusiast of Privy Councillor Martin's quality. "The present great interest universally taken in the navigation of the air", he wrote, "can only be advantageous for further military development . . . provided it does not lead to excessively optimistic expectations, fantastic conclusions, and impossible schemes, as now happens occasionally with regard to motor air-ships . . . As regards their utilisation in the Army and Navy, there is a certain danger in the readiness with which too favourable, and therefore false, suppositions can be made, these being followed by disappointment, as a result of which development may easily be undeservedly hampered."

In such circumstances Captain Neumann believed it would be of value if he prepared a cautious estimate of the "various possibilities of our newest instrument of war – the motor airship". There followed a long and technical account of the problems associated with the employment of airships.

Neumann suggested that airships in the earliest phases of their development might be most effective, for the Army as well as for the Navy, as aerial scouts. He admitted that the endurance in the air of these vessels was still an "open question". He concluded, therefore, that the first employment of naval airships would confine them to activities near their own coasts.

However, he emphasized that with the passage of time and the advance of aeronautical technology, airships could also be used for purposes of offence by the Navy. He wrote:

> . . . in the near future air-ships will come into prominence for naval reconnoitring; in addition, they may occasionally have opportunities for destroying, amongst other things, ships, naval establishments, docks, and, perhaps, also coast fortifications which are not bomb-proof. Moreover, the moral effect of airships, capable of being used offensively, in proximity to a blockading squadron, to a squadron lying in a harbour, or to coast works, must not be overlooked.

Meanwhile, in the Admiralty the decision was made to come to closer grips with the possibility of employing airships for use with the Navy. The formal entry of the British Navy into the field of aeronautics was prepared with some care.

On 13 July 1908 the *Daily Mail* reported that John Gretton, the Conservative Member of Parliament for Rutland, planned to ask the prime minister a question about aeronautics in the House of Commons on the following day. Sir Henry Campbell-Bannerman had died earlier in the year. The new prime minister was the powerful Liberal Imperialist politician, H. H. Asquith.

In the event Gretton did not ask his question on 14 July. His initiative was postponed for a week, perhaps with good cause. On 21 July the following exchange took place in the Commons:[1]

Aerial Navigation and National Defence

Mr. Gretton (Rutland): I beg to ask the Prime Minister if questions of aerial navigation have received consideration by the Committee of National Defence; whether naval officers have been called into consultation; and if it is intended to entrust all experiments and construction to the military authorities.

---

[1] *Parliamentary Debates 4th Series*, vol. 192, col. 1735, 21 July 1908.

The Prime Minister and First Lord of The Treasury (Mr. Asquith, Fifeshire, E.): This is a matter which presents both naval and military aspects, and it is not desirable to say any more at present than that it is engaging the attention both of the naval and military authorities who have been, and are, in consultation with one another on the subject.

On this same 21 July Captain Reginald Bacon, the Director of Naval Ordnance, submitted a "confidential" programme to the First Sea Lord. The object of Bacon's paper was to bring forward for the attention of his superiors a scheme whereby the Admiralty would take over the construction of airships for the government.

Reginald Bacon was a brilliant officer of proven ability. A few years earlier he had been appointed Inspecting-Captain of Submarine Boats. His task in this post was to introduce submarines into the British Navy. He was given a free hand to develop and organize this new branch of the Service. He performed his duties with notable skill. Working in conjunction with the great firm of Vickers Sons, and Maxim, Bacon was responsible for the appearance of submarines of genuine quality. Admiral Fisher was particularly pleased by Bacon's achievements with the first British submarines.

Bacon, moreover, was one of Fisher's closest disciples. In the contemporary phrase he was "in the Fish pond", one of a select group of officers who worked intimately with Fisher and had been selected by him for high advancement in the Service. Indeed, Fisher considered Bacon to be "the cleverest officer in the Navy".

However, Fisher's enemies in the Service looked upon Captain Bacon somewhat differently, and with good cause. He was the author of the so-called "Bacon letters". In the spring of 1906 when Bacon was serving in the Mediterranean under Admiral Lord Charles Beresford, Fisher asked him to keep him informed about what was taking place in Beresford's command. Rumours about "espionage" in the Fleet began to circulate in naval circles as early as the autumn of 1907. Eventually proof was obtained that Bacon had written to the First Sea Lord to tell him of developments in the Mediterranean Fleet. This outraged officers and contemporary politicians alike when they learned of it. Beresford's followers sometimes referred to Bacon as one of "Fisher's jackals".

Admiral Fisher, throughout his career, was always keenly interested in new technical developments. A small group of enthusiastic officers had believed for some time that the Navy should prepare to equip itself with airships. Fisher instructed Bacon to formulate proposals that would turn their ideas into reality.

On 21 July Bacon, in compliance with these instructions, sent Fisher a paper, marked "Confidential". In it, Bacon proposed a programme that became the first significant step taken by the Admiralty in the newly developing field of aeronautics.

Less than a month before Count Zeppelin had achieved his notable triumph in the skies over Switzerland and Germany. It seemed clear that the British Navy could no longer afford to lag behind the Germans in the technology of the air. Bacon wrote:[1]

> First Sea Lord,
>
> In accordance with verbal instructions to submit a programme for the Admiralty taking over the construction of airships I submit the following remarks and procedure:–
>
> As regards airships there is nothing in their construction which is of the nature of an invention or which is not a straightforward application of scientific and engineering principles. . . .

Bacon went on to point out to Admiral Fisher that his experience with submarines would help him in airship work. "There is nothing", he boldly declared, "which will not yield to scientific investigation and sound mechanical construction. No country has a monopoly of the Laws of Nature. Their economical application depends solely on organisation and procedure. It will be remembered that in introducing submarines into the Navy the knowledge of submarine navigation was hardly more advanced than aerial navigation is at the present moment but in the space of three years we were able to design boats which fully fulfil all their functions and which, so far have never been surpassed. . . ."

Captain Bacon went on to suggest that the procedures followed in developing submarines should be employed again, in the case of airships. He proposed that he should be given authority to arrange for the construction of an airship with the firm of Vickers Sons, and Maxim, the company that had built the first British submarines. Indeed, even before he drew up his paper for Fisher, Bacon had "discussed the problems of manufacture with a Director of Vickers Sons and Maxim Limited, Lieutenant A. Trevor Dawson, (later Sir Arthur Trevor Dawson, Bart.)."[2]

Bacon concluded his paper with a number of concrete recommendations. These reflect his long experience as an administrator. They reveal that he knew how to get things done in the Whitehall of his day:

---

[1] F.O. 371/27367. R. H. Bacon D.N.O. to First Sea Lord, dated 21/7/08 and marked "Confidential".

[2] For this point see a privately printed work, H. E. Scrope, *Golden Wings, The Story of Fifty Years of Aviation By the Vickers Group of Companies 1908–1958*, p. 7.

For the present therefore I submit for approval:
(1) That covering Treasury sanction be obtained to proceed with the design and construction.
(2) That Messrs Vickers should be approached with a view to carrying out the design and manufacture in precisely the same manner as with submarine boats.
(3) That I shall select a Naval Assistant whose name will be submitted later.
(4) That as soon as the design has been worked out and an estimate of the cost obtained that this be forwarded to you for approval.
(5) The War Office should be requested to place the present Military Superintendent of Ballooning in close touch with myself so that we may benefit by each other's experience.

As soon as the above is approved I am prepared to start without any delay.

R. H. Bacon
DNO. 21/7/08.

When Admiral Fisher received this paper he acted at once. He prepared a Minute for his political chief, the First Lord of the Admiralty, Reginald McKenna. Asquith had replaced the unfortunate Lord Tweedmouth by appointing McKenna to his post, a few months earlier. McKenna, a tough financial expert, soon fell under Fisher's spell and helped him in every way possible. Fisher's Minute, dated 22 July, declared: "First Lord. I concur in enclosed and suggest Captain Bacon being authorised to obtain Mr. Haldane's concurrence in the proposed letter to the Treasury if you approve it". On 28 July McKenna signified his approval.[1]

On the next day the Secretary of the Admiralty despatched a letter, marked "Confidential", to the Treasury:[2]

My Lords have had under consideration the necessity of investigating the possibilities of aerial navigation especially as applied to offence and defence against Fleets at sea. As a result of these deliberations they propose to commence an experimental airship with a view to obtaining definite experience.

It is not probable that any payment will fall due this financial year. The exact sum will be communicated as soon as ascertained.

My Lords have been in communication with the War Office with a view to ensure . . . cooperation and the absence of overlapping in functions so that duplication and any consequent waste of labour and money will be avoided.

[1] F.O. 371/27367. Minute signed by J. F. 22.7.08 and initialled by R. McK. 28.7.08.
[2] F.O. 371/27367. Secretary of The Admiralty, to The Secretary, H.M. Treasury, marked "*Confidential*", Draft.

My Lords will therefore be glad to hear that the Lords Commissioners of H.M. Treasury concur in the above arrangement.

In due course the Treasury sent a provisionally favourable reply to the Admiralty. This letter, dated 4 August 1908, was marked "CONFIDENTIAL".[1]

In reply to your letter of the 29th ultimo, I am directed by the Lords Commissioners of His Majesty's Treasury to request you to inform the Lords Commissioners of the Admiralty that They concur generally in the proposals made therein with regard to the projected experiments in aerial navigation.

My Lords note that no appreciable expense will be incurred in the present financial year and They will be glad to be supplied with further information in connection with the preparation of the Navy Estimates 1909–10.

Admiral Fisher watched over this correspondence with very great care. On the day the Admiralty approached the Treasury for its sanction of Bacon's proposals, Fisher applied his own deft touch to the exchange. He wrote to Lord Knollys, King Edward's private secretary. In his letter Fisher suggested that the initiative in the airship proposals had come from Asquith, the prime minister. This suggestion was probably not strictly accurate. Fisher's great object, however, was to see to it that the king learned of the Navy's bold new departure.

On 29 July Fisher told Knollys: ". . . I am only writing to say that I think the King will like to hear that the Prime Minister spoke to me the other day about the Navy undertaking the airship business (*in which this country is lamentably behind*), and the Admiralty have agreed, on the clear understanding that we have absolutely a free hand as we had with submarines . . . I have handed the business over to Captain Bacon, who His Majesty will remember as the first Captain of the *Dreadnought* and who brought our submarines to their present pitch of perfection . . ."[2]

It will be seen that the officials concerned with the project placed the greatest emphasis upon the experimental nature of the proposed British naval airship. When the Secretary of the Admiralty approached the Treasury for its sanction he stressed the necessity of investigating the potential of aerial navigation "especially as applied to offence and defence against Fleets at sea".

---

[1] F.O. 371/27367. J. Murry to The Secretary to the Admiralty, 4 August 1908, marked "*CONFIDENTIAL*".

[2] A. J. Marder, ed., *Fear God and Dread Nought*, vol. II, p. 186. There is a good summary of these developments in Higham, *The Rigid British Airship*, pp. 36ff.

However, it may be observed that other factors were also involved in this new departure by the Admiralty. The suggestion that airships might be employed to drop bombs on dockyards and coastal installations had already been mentioned in the technical Press, and noticed by the Director of Naval Intelligence and his colleagues. An air attack upon the United Kingdom had now been recognized as a definite possibility of the future, however remote or distant. Thus, an entirely new element was introduced. Until this year the leaders of the British Navy could take comfort from the often quoted words of Admiral Lord St Vincent to a group of nervous fellow peers at the time of the French invasion danger early in the nineteenth century: "I do not say they cannot come, my Lords, I only say they cannot come by sea." Now, as a result of unprecedented technological developments it was possible for a vigilant and forward-looking observer to contemplate an air assault upon Britain that would put St Vincent's pithy maxim in an entirely new light.

VIII

While these sober preparations went forward in England there was very great excitement in Germany, where Count Zeppelin made ready for the final test of LZ4, a flight of twenty-four hours' duration to comply with the requirements established by the German Government. The Kaiser ordered that a gun salute should be fired for Zeppelin when his great dirigible appeared in the air over Strasbourg. This mark of Imperial favour was looked upon as a "unique honour".

The German people awaited the flight with tremendous enthusiasm. They were especially interested by the English reaction to Count Zeppelin's experiments. On 13 July the *Daily Mail* published a report by F. W. Wile on this theme: "Germany is ablaze with airship enthusiasm and [the] trip is awaited with breathless interest. The country's concern has been materially heightened by the alleged 'nervousness' of England over the rapid development of the German aerial fleet and by Major Baden-Powell's vigorous call to arms in Saturday's *Daily Mail* which is widely reproduced in the Press, and interpreted as flattering evidence of British 'uneasiness' over Germany's bid for command of the air. The attention which England is bestowing on aerial affairs gives impetus to Herr Rudolf Martin's project for the organization of a German aerial navy league. The league will not only carry on an agitation for the creation of an Imperial fleet of airships and aeroplanes, but itself acquire and operate such craft. Its fleet will serve as 'auxiliary cruisers' of the Imperial aerial fleet in war time."

This question of the "command of the air" was raised a few days later in the House of Commons where Dundas White, the Member for Dunbartonshire, asked the Secretary of State for War about the amounts of public money allotted to aeronautical work during the past five years. He also asked: ". . . in view of the paramount importance of the command of the air, what steps are being taken for the further development of this branch of the service"? Haldane calmly replied that "Such steps as are considered necessary are being taken in connection with the further development of this work".[1]

After one or two false starts Count Zeppelin made his bid to remain in the air for twenty-four hours on 4 August 1908. The LZ4 flew above the Rhine valley on this flight and in the cities along the route great crowds rushed into the streets in order to watch the passage of the gigantic dirigible. Guns boomed in salute while people waved handkerchiefs and hats to acknowledge the new hero of Germany. After one or two minor mishaps the ship landed on the Rhine river, having been in the air for more than eleven hours. Zeppelin's enterprise was far from over. The damage was quickly repaired. Shortly after, the LZ4 rose from the surface of the waters and continued her journey. However, when the airship arrived in the vicinity of Stuttgart further troubles were encountered. Count Zeppelin decided to bring his vessel down so that the forward engine could be repaired at the Daimler works in nearby Untertürkheim. At 7.51 a.m. LZ4 safely settled to earth south west of Stuttgart, near the village of Echterdingen.

Huge crowds came together to gaze with awe at the tremendous airship. Troops were sent from Stuttgart to preserve order and to act as a ground crew. Daimler engineers set to work to correct the problems encountered in the forward engine. All seemed to be in order. Then, before dawn, a storm appeared. A sudden gust tore the ship's moorings from the ground and the Zeppelin began to drift away. The frantic soldiers tried desperately to hold her but were unable to do so. LZ4 drifted for a half mile and then came down into some trees. There was a flash and within seconds the entire Zeppelin burst into flames and was reduced almost at once to a mass of blackened wreckage.

Crowds of distressed citizens assembled at the scene of the disaster. In their midst was a man who was later to become Germany's implacable enemy, one who did almost more than anyone else to break the power and destroy the life of Imperial Germany. In August 1908 Lloyd George, Chancellor of the Exchequer in Asquith's Liberal Government, went on a visit to Berlin. He had travelled to Germany to study, at first hand, the German system of industrial insurance as a prelude to the preparation of his own great insurance schemes for the working people of Great Britain.

In Berlin, Lloyd George met the German leader von Bethmann-

---

[1] For this exchange see *Parliamentary Debates 4th Series*, vol. 193, cols. 1481–1482, 29 July 1908.

Hollweg, regarded by contemporaries as a relatively moderate figure. Lloyd George, at this phase of his career a Radical opposed to significant expenditure on armaments and a critic of Admiral Fisher's policies, was astonished by Bethmann's hostility to England. Much of it was revealed after a remarkable dinner in the Zoologischer Garten when great tankards of beer were consumed and tongues loosened, as a consequence. Later, Lloyd George wrote in his *War Memoirs*: "I left Berlin gravely disturbed by the expressions of distrust and suspicion I had encountered in so high and friendly a quarter". His account went on:[1]

> At the other end of the scale, I was also deeply impressed by a scene I witnessed at Stuttgart during the same tour. On our arrival there we learnt that a "Zeppelin" was about to make an exhibition flight. We went along to the field where the giant airship was moored, to find out that by a last-minute accident it had crashed and been wrecked. Of course we were deeply disappointed, but disappointment was a totally inadequate word for the agony of grief and dismay which swept over the massed Germans who witnessed the catastrophe. There was no loss of life to account for it. Hopes and ambitions far wider than those concerned with a scientific and mechanical success appeared to have shared the wreck of the dirigible. Then the crowd swung into the chanting of "Deutschland über Alles" with a fanatic fervour of patriotism. What spearpoint of Imperial advance did this airship portend? These incidents were cracks in the cold surface, through which the hot, seething lava of unrest could be seen stirring uneasily underneath.

Lloyd George had witnessed the beginning of what his German contemporaries called the "miracle of Echterdingen". As might be expected, Zeppelin's spirits were crushed when his marvellous dirigible was destroyed. However, a spontaneous wave of enthusiasm instantly swept every corner of the Empire. Rich and poor alike began to send money to Zeppelin so that his work could be continued. The German people took an iron vow to see to it that the Zeppelin, already looked upon as a symbol of national greatness, would not disappear from the skies. A total of six million marks in voluntary contributions was received at the count's headquarters. Astonished at this reaction of the populace, Zeppelin decided to carry on.

It was not only Lloyd George who noticed the effects and the significance of the "miracle of Echterdingen". The high excitement of the Germans was remarked upon everywhere in England. The *Daily Express*, a journal that disagreed completely with Lloyd George's political views, revealed the attitude of many Conservatives in England in its first

[1] See *War Memoirs of David Lloyd George* (London, *n.d.*), vol. I, pp. 18–19, hereafter cited as Lloyd George, *War Memoirs*.

leading article published on 7 August 1908. This article, entitled "Love of Country", linked the Zeppelin and the German people together as yet a new element in the awesome power of Imperial Germany, a power the British people had to prepare to defend themselves against, or give up their established position in the world. "Love of Country" declared:

> The Zeppelin airship was wrecked on Wednesday. Today it has been announced that eighty thousand pounds has been subscribed to build its successor. Could anything more fully exhibit the temper of the German people? 'Deutschland Über Alles' is the living maxim of the German people. The whole nation is concerned with national greatness. It is not the Kaiser who desires an invincible navy, it is the German people. It is not Count Zeppelin whose ambition it is that Germany should rule the air, it is the ambition of the German people. . . .
> It is the realisation of the great qualities of Germany that causes us to fear her as a potential foe. . . . If we are not ready to defend ourselves we must inevitably fall under the yoke of a greater and more virile people. . . .

IX

The effect of "Echterdingen" upon Lloyd George merits further attention. Lloyd George was already looked upon as the leader of the British people in their struggles against the established order. As the great historian George Dangerfield put it: "He wanted the poor to inherit the earth, particularly if it was the earth of rich English landlords". The General Election of 1906, as all sophisticated observers knew, foreshadowed basic changes in British life and society. Lloyd George, the hero of the Radicals, was in the forefront of this surge. His was a democratic voice in the land. Although Asquith succeeded Sir Henry Campbell-Bannerman as Prime Minister in April 1908, many in Britain looked upon Lloyd George as their champion. In 1908 Lloyd George became Asquith's first lieutenant when he was appointed Chancellor of the Exchequer. It was already obvious that he carried in his hands much of the fate and future course of British Liberalism. He was a leader. His attitude counted in the life of the State.

In his *War Memoirs* Lloyd George made plain the effect upon his outlook of his visit with Bethmann-Hollweg and also the effect of the bizarre scene he had witnessed at Echterdingen. The conclusions he set down were not those of a Radical "Little Englander", unconcerned with the danger of foreign enemies. After describing the German crowd at Echterdingen Lloyd George wrote:[1]

---

[1] *Ibid.*, p. 20.

After these few glimpses of our foreign problem, I was drawn back during the succeeding years into the anxious preoccupations of domestic affairs. I understood, nevertheless, that there was a growing menace to peace abroad, and social order at home, which we must strive to avert if possible by peaceful methods, though I realised that we could not altogether rule out of account the possibility of a failure of such methods.

Echterdingen awoke in Lloyd George a fear that some new device of science, invention, or technology might result in an irretrievable disaster for the British people. He now began to pay attention to aeronautical developments and to reflect upon their significance. In October 1908, as we shall see, Asquith appointed a sub-committee of the Committee of Imperial Defence to examine the entire question of "Aerial Navigation". Lloyd George agreed to serve on this body even though he was at that time deeply engaged in preparations for a tremendous political battle with his Tory enemies, preparations which resulted in the production of his famous "People's Budget" of 1909.

Later in 1909 the first great aviation meeting in history was held by the French on the plain of Bétheny, near Reims. The Reims meeting was a milestone in the history of aviation.

At Reims the public was enabled to observe dozens of aviators in the air, demonstrating the several qualities and capacities of their various machines. French fliers and aviators from abroad competed for prizes. They revealed to the world that flying was no longer the preserve of some daring individual inventor or pilot. Flying machines were shown to exist in several forms and types. The public now began to accept them as practical vehicles. As a result of the Reims meeting, they were recognized as adjuncts to civilization in a way that had not occurred before.

Lloyd George took care to travel to Reims so that he could observe this aeronautical scene. He was not a technician but he granted interviews to reporters representing the *Daily Mail* and the *Morning Post* so that his impressions received wide publicity in the British Press. Lloyd George told the journalists he did not believe aeroplanes were formidable weapons of war as yet, but he also recognized that Britain was lagging behind in the new technology. "I am", he said to the *Daily Mail* correspondent, "more than glad I came . . . I only wish we could hold such a meeting in England, say on Salisbury Plain. I sincerely hope we shall have something of the kind organised before long."[1]

In 1910 Lloyd George embarked upon a new political course which has been recognized by historians, after a good deal of dispute, as one of the most profound and dramatic incidents of his long and exciting career in politics.

[1] *Daily Mail*, 23 August 1909.

In 1910 Lloyd George was the most formidable political partisan then alive. His brilliant and slashing attacks on the Tories were almost without precedent in the annals of British political history. They had aroused the fervour of his supporters and the savage enmity of his opponents. Nevertheless, in 1910 Lloyd George paused in these headlong assaults in order to step back so that he could survey the British scene with the eyes of a statesman.

He saw that partisan strife between the political parties was tearing Great Britain apart. At the same time the country was confronted by terrible and awesome problems, at home and abroad. The energies of her best leaders were consumed in these party struggles. The national destiny was subordinated to the caprices of party strife.

Lord Roberts and his friends warned that the Germans could land a large force in England and capture London, as a result. They argued, in increasingly strident tones, that only a policy of conscription could render the nation safe from this deadly menace. Many Conservatives accepted their analysis of the situation as valid. The Liberals, almost to a man, would not accept the idea of National Service.

Other grave issues separated the parties. None had been solved and they became more complex and more divisive with the passage of time. The Liberals were already contemplating Home Rule for Ireland. The Tories vowed never to accept such a course. Indeed, civil war had already been mentioned as a possibility of the future if a Home Rule Bill was forced through the legislature.

Britain's trade was severely hampered by the competition of foreign rivals. The Liberals held fast to the doctrines of Free Trade while the Tories insisted that only a policy of Tariff Reform and Imperial Preference, protection, could save the nation from economic disaster and collapse.

British workers, suffering from low wages and almost intolerable conditions at home and in their factories, were becoming sullen, angry, and hostile to the established order. The parties would not work together to discover the correct course to follow in dealing with this ominous situation.

Lloyd George believed the British countryside was suffering from neglect and that the life of the workers in the towns was being poisoned by excessive indulgence in alcohol.

The political battles between Liberals and Conservatives had resulted, by 1910, in a terrible constitutional crisis. The position of the House of Lords in the political life of the State was now at hazard. Many Liberals and Radicals meant to curb its powers so that it could no longer tamper with the legislative decisions of the elected representatives of the people, who sat in the Commons. The Tories were preparing a sullen resistance to such a revolutionary departure from accepted practices and traditions.

Lloyd George was especially impressed by the failure of the parties to deal adequately with any of the issues. The best national leaders devoted all their energies to partisan strife. No one was prepared to cooperate with his political opponents to try and seek out solutions that would affect the national destiny.

As a result of this analysis Lloyd George decided upon a radical course of his own in 1910. In order to secure the cooperation of the leading party statesmen in a settlement of these national problems he proposed to the prime minister the formation of a National or Coalition Government. The most capable leaders in each party would be invited to join such a Ministry to deal with matters of urgent national importance. Party strife, according to his plan, would be set upon one side for a period of several years so that these great objects could be secured.

The Lloyd George plan of 1910 has been analysed and studied by large numbers of historians. However, they have paid less attention to the factors which first impelled him to proceed in such an unexpected way.

Despite this lapse by the scholars, Lloyd George made his position absolutely clear in his *War Memoirs*. Advances in science, technology, and invention contributed greatly to his radical decision to propose a National Government in 1910. In the section of his *War Memoirs* which follows his description of the "massed Germans" at Echterdingen, Lloyd George wrote:[1]

> I had for some time past been growingly concerned with the precariousness of our position in the event of our naval defence being broken through. . . . But the rapid march of scientific discovery, constantly revealing the existence of hitherto unsuspected forces . . . made me feel that it was quite within the realm of possibility that one day there might be an invention which would neutralise our superiority, and reduce us to equality with, if not inferiority to, our neighbours. Inventions which portended such a menace had already appeared. Whether the peril would come from the air or from under the waters, I knew not; but no one could feel assured that such possibilities were altogether out of the reckoning. . . .
>
> There were ominous clouds gathering over the Continent of Europe and perceptibly thickening and darkening. The submarine and the Zeppelin indicated a possible challenge to the invincibility of our defence. . . .
>
> It was with these thoughts in my mind that I ventured in 1910 to submit to the leaders of both political parties in this country a series of proposals for national cooperation over a period of years to deal with special matters of urgent importance.

The German people in their pride rightly believed that the "miracle of

[1] Lloyd George, *War Memoirs*, vol. I, pp. 20–21.

Echterdingen" had saved the Zeppelin airship for the Fatherland. It also produced another significant effect. It helped to alert the most formidable British politician of the day to the Zeppelin menace, and to the dangers which faced his country from the increasing might and ambition of Imperial Germany. When Count Zeppelin flew in 1908 the results were more intricate, complicated and profound than many of his contemporaries, in Germany and in other countries, could realize.

CHAPTER 12

"... Wilbur Wright is in Possession of a Power which Controls the Fate of Nations ..."

Wilbur Wright in France – C. S. Rolls – Patrick Y. Alexander – The War Office Pronouncement – Wilbur is Scalded – His First Flights in France – Reaction of the French Experts – Acclaim in the British Press – Lord Northcliffe Proposes a Channel Flight – Wright Influence on European Aviation – A New Concept of Control – C. S. Rolls bargains for an Aeroplane – German Interest in the Wright Machine – Orville Wright at Fort Myer – His Sensational Flights – British Reaction – Augustus Moore Herring – More Capable Rivals – A Bitter Contemporary Situation – Alexander Graham Bell and the Aerial Experiment Association – Glenn Curtiss – Orville Alarmed – The Crash of the 17th September – Unauthorized Persons Examine the Wreckage – The Wrights are closely watched by the Germans – Count Gleichen Again – Wilbur Wright's Flights at Auvours – His British Visitors – Reaction of Major Baden-Powell – The Aero Club Gold Medal – Baden-Powell Reports to the War Office – The British Military Attaché in Paris – His Aeronautical Despatch – Wilbur's Response – Dr F. W. Lanchester – His Analysis – The Initiative of H. H. Asquith.

I

While Count Zeppelin's spectacular adventures riveted the world's attention upon aeronautical developments in Germany, Wilbur Wright quietly proceeded with his own preparations in France. His business there was to make a number of observed flights and so meet the conditions of his arrangement with the syndicate of French capitalists led by Lazare Weiller.

Wilbur now entered upon a period of very great tension and anxiety. Occasionally in his letters to his family during these months he wrote of his fear that he might break down under the terrible pressures imposed upon him by his life in France.

The challenge was tremendous. Several of the French pioneers were already flying successfully. Wilbur knew they were unable to control their machines in the air in the masterly way he and Orville had devised for their aeroplane. Nevertheless he was still inexperienced in the use of his new controlling levers. He had crashed his aeroplane at Kitty Hawk only a short time earlier and brooded upon the fact that one mistake in the air might ruin in seconds everything he and Orville had sought to achieve for years past.

He was also worried about the historical record. As businessmen the Wrights were resolved to make a great deal of money from their invention. They were also very jealous of their reputations. They could not bear the thought that someone else might receive credit for ideas, systems, devices, or methods that had originated with them. Indeed, it soon became clear that commercial success might depend upon historical accuracy.

Before he sailed from New York Wilbur told Orville: ". . . it is my opinion as firmly as ever that we need to have our true story told in an authentic way at once and to let it be known that we consider ourselves fully protected by patents. . . . It is important to get the main features originated by us identified in the public mind with our machines before they are described in connection with some other machine. A statement of our original features ought to be published and not left covered up in the patent office. . . ."[1]

When Wilbur was in New York he visited the offices of a publication called *The Century Magazine*. This periodical had offered the Wrights the sum of five hundred dollars for the first popular account of their experiments written by themselves. Wilbur was unable to contribute to the preparation of the article because business required him to travel to France. Orville's time was taken up in getting ready for his own flight trials at Fort Myer in Virginia.

Eventually it was decided that a true account of their work was a matter of such significance that Orville had to write it. Glenn Curtiss, an American competitor, together with his associates, had already built an aeroplane they called the "June Bug". This machine exploited information contained in the Wright patents. The brothers were outraged not merely by Curtiss's effrontery but also by the fear that he would rake in monetary rewards which were properly their own. Their bitter battles with Curtiss, which were to last for years, began at this time.

From France, Wilbur sent Orville detailed instructions about what should be included in *The Century Magazine* article. In particular, he wanted Orville to call attention to the fact that the revived European interest in aviation dated from the time Octave Chanute lectured in Paris

---

[1] McFarland, *The Papers of Wilbur and Orville Wright*, pp. 882–3.

in 1903 after he had been their guest in the camp at Kitty Hawk. Wilbur instructed Orville to emphasize that Chanute's full account of their work, illustrated by photographs, was the spur that had roused the French to action.

Orville managed to complete the article before the end of June. It was published as a joint composition of the brothers in *The Century Magazine* for September 1908 with photographs supplied by the authors. In time this article, "The Wright Brothers' Aeroplane", became a classic of aviation literature. It set out in the clearest terms exactly what the Wrights had done, ending with a promise about a future and more technical publication and with a bold statement of the Wright claim: "As soon as our condition is such that constant attention to business is not required, we expect to prepare for publication the results of our laboratory experiments, which alone made an early solution of the flying problem possible."

Wilbur's first task in France was to discover a suitable field where the flying trials could take place. He proposed to employ, in these tests, the machine Orville had sent to France in a crate in the previous year. It had been purposely left in the country for the brothers' use in the 1908 flying season.

Hart O. Berg, who acted as a kind of business manager, now introduced Wilbur to Léon Bollée, a wealthy automobile manufacturer whose factory was situated at Le Mans, some one hundred and twenty miles north of Paris. Bollée suggested that a flying-ground might be found in the Le Mans area, where there were great stretches of open country. He further offered to set aside space in his factory so that Wilbur would have a place to assemble his aeroplane.

Eventually Wilbur and Berg selected the racetrack at Hunaudières near Le Mans as the field where the flight trials would take place. It was at this site that Wilbur Wright was shortly to perform feats in the air the civilized world looked upon as nothing less than miraculous.

In due course the crated aeroplane was despatched from the port of Le Havre to the Bollée factory so that Wilbur could begin upon the task of assembly. In time, the Hunaudières racecourse was secured when Wilbur and Berg worked out an arrangement to rent it from its owner, on a monthly basis. As these preparations advanced Wilbur was able to report to Orville that the French, suspicious for the most part until this time, were beginning to show a more friendly spirit. Wilbur was particularly grateful for Léon Bollée's courtesies and kindness.

When information about Wilbur Wright's project became known in Europe the various governments at once displayed a serious interest in his activities. Russian officers appeared in Paris. Requests for an arrangement were received from the Italian authorities. The Germans began to pay careful attention.

Men in England were also fascinated by Wilbur's preparations in France. The Hon. C. S. Rolls had begun a regular correspondence with the Wrights. He was determined to secure one of their machines for himself and to use it to become the first man to fly a Wright aeroplane in England. Wilbur and Orville welcomed his initiative. They had to exercise their rights under their English patent within a reasonably short time or else forfeit their position in what they looked upon as "the English market". Up to this point they had been unable to sell their invention to the British Government. They now hoped to sell machines in Britain upon a commercial basis.

On 11 June Wilbur met Rolls at the latter's hotel in Paris. He told Rolls that the Wright brothers were prepared to supply him with an aeroplane but Orville would have to be consulted first with respect to the price and the date of delivery. When Rolls returned to his office in Conduit Street in London he wrote to Wilbur to ascertain the exact terms of their proposed bargain.

C. S. Rolls was well known in England as a man who did not readily part with his own money. This tendency was reflected in the proposal he now made to become the first man in England to secure a Wright aeroplane. On 16 June 1908 he wrote to Wilbur to outline a deal whereby he would be given a Wright machine without paying anything at all for it:[1]

> This is a reminder to ask you to kindly write to your brother to know exactly on what terms I could obtain one of your machines to carry two persons for use in England.
>
> Rather than have to pay you a cash sum for purchasing the machine outright, which would be a little difficult for me, I would prefer to have – if possible – an arrangement by which I used the machine as your representative or agent in this country and would in return carry out your wishes as to any special demonstrations you might require to be made. I think it possible that after some practice which I am going to have with a "Voisin" machine, followed by a little practice on your machine, I should be able to operate it for demonstration purposes in a manner which might save you the necessity of making visits to England when any particular demonstration is required and when it might be inconvenient for you to come over.

Wilbur had already suggested to Orville that it would be prudent for the Wrights to sell a machine to Rolls. On 14 June he informed his brother: "I saw Mr. Rolls the other day. He wishes to be the first to fly one of our machines in England. He did not propose to buy one himself but thought he could get a wealthy friend to buy one if we would sell one, and let him

[1] Wright Brothers' Papers, Chas. S. Rolls, to Wilbur Wright, 16 June 1908.

run it. If we can get an order I think it might be well to take it. When could you have a machine ready to ship? And what should be our price without training operators? What do you say to $10,000 each? We ought to do something in England. Do not fail to inform me when our patent there must be worked."[1]

While these important negotiations were still in their earliest stages Patrick Y. Alexander again chose to intervene in the business of the Wright brothers. He contacted Hart O. Berg and told him he planned to visit Paris shortly. He also informed Berg that people in England were not seriously interested in the possibilities of the Wright aeroplane: ". . . We have been getting all sorts of accounts about Wilbur Wright, none of which seems to be very optimistic. I think it is only fair to tell you that over here the machine is looked upon as an interesting toy. Scarcely anyone beside myself, seem [*sic*] to appreciate the years of labour that has [*sic*] been expended by the Wright Bros. I seem to fear that they have made their machine public a little late in the day. However, it will be a deep disappointment to me if they do not succeed in getting all they deserve."[2]

On 21 June Alexander arrived in Paris, where he saw Berg in his offices in the Avenue des Champs-Élysées. The American business man was astonished by the behaviour of his British visitor. Berg instantly reported to Wilbur:[3]

> I had the visit this morning of Mr. Patrick Y. Alexander. I hardly know what to make of this peculiar quantity. He arrived here this morning, leaves at 7.22 p.m. by the Orient Express for Vienna, arrives in Vienna tomorrow, Monday, afternoon at 6 o'clock, leaves Vienna at 9 o'clock, Tuesday morning to be back here in Paris Wednesday morning, and takes the Wednesday morning train and boat for London. It seems to me that he is a natural flyer. I could not quite make him out – he seems to be posted about everything that is going on. He knew more about what other people are doing than I have ever thought of, and while he has great faith in what you will accomplish, I could gather from his talk that there would be others in the field. . . .

Berg also took care to tell Wilbur, in this letter, that Alexander had tried to secure technical information about the Wright machine during the course of their interview in Paris. He assured Wilbur he had revealed nothing of significance in the conversation.

It may be that Patrick Alexander's opinions about the Wright aero-

---

[1] See Kelly, *Miracle at Kitty Hawk*, pp. 271–2.

[2] Wright Brothers' Papers, Patrick Y. Alexander to Hart O. Berg, undated, but written in June 1908.

[3] Wright Brothers' Papers, Hart O. Berg to Wilbur Wright, 21 June 1908.

plane were a reflection at second or even third hand of Sir William Nicholson's attitude. Nicholson and the generals of his school in the British War Office did not believe in the summer of 1908 that aircraft of any kind could become factors of significance in the immediate future. A semi-official pronouncement was therefore issued to the Press by the War Office. It appeared in the *Daily Mail* for 23 July 1908. The object of this arrogant statement was to reassure the British public that there was nothing to fear from airships or aeroplanes for a long time to come. The War Office communication declared:[1]

WAR AIRSHIPS
"Nothing to be feared for a long time"
OFFICIAL VIEW

In the highest military circles in Great Britain it is accepted that so far airships are a failure.

The military authorities have had experts employed in watching the flights of the various airships and aeroplanes, and the impression is that for a long time to come there is nothing to be feared from them.

The Government has not stinted the necessary funds for experiments at Aldershot and elsewhere, but the Royal Engineers, on whom has devolved the task of finding out at least a dirigible balloon, are contenting themselves with cautious experiments. From time to time reports are received of the performances of various airships and aeroplanes on the Continent, and in every case details of mechanism and construction have been available. The Army Council is therefore thoroughly aware of all that is taking place both on the Continent and in America in aerostatics.

Consultations have been held at the War Office with expert artillerists as to how aerial attacks can be best met, and the plan of campaign in which the principal feature will be the use of high-angle fire with high-explosive shells has been evolved.

The military authorities point to the fact that nowhere has any machine designed for flight in the air proved effective. . . . All this points to a lack of practical working in the various designs . . . When it is possible to cross the Channel, say with a party of excursionists, and to land at any fixed point, the War Office may be prepared to regard recent experiments seriously.

Those in Britain who feared their country was lagging behind in aeronautical developments might find a measure of relief in the statement that experts were employed by the War Office to watch foreign airships and aeroplanes. However, it was obvious that the chief burden of the

[1] The War Office *communiqué* is printed in Snowden Gamble, *The Air Weapon*, pp. 109–10, and also in R. P. Hearne's book at pp. 77–9.

announcement was to make clear the opinion of Britain's highest military leaders: in their view aircraft were not yet a matter of any consequence in their planning.

Wilbur Wright, busily preparing for the supreme test of his life in Le Mans, laboured under an entirely different impression. As the hour for his flight trials approached he became more and more tense and this uneasiness was reflected in some of his letters to Orville. Among the several developments which annoyed him at this time was Orville's failure to keep him informed about the Wright negotiations with the British War Office. Wilbur, it will be recalled, had left this phase of the business in his brother's hands. Now he wanted exact information about what had occurred. On 5 July he told Orville in tones that clearly reflected his anxieties: ". . . You have never sent me a copy of your letters to British war dept. I ought to see them. I have asked you to tell me the date when British business must be worked to hold patent, but you seem to never notice requests or instructions. To think it is only a month away. . . ."[1]

II

In the Bollée factory Wilbur set to work to assemble his aeroplane. The fate of the Wright brothers would turn upon the performance of this particular machine.

However, when Wilbur opened the crate which had been shipped through Le Havre he received an unexpected shock. The Wrights were distinguished by the care they exercised in everything they did: all was ordered, planned in advance, and carried out with meticulous attention to detail. But the opened crate revealed a scene of utter confusion. Parts of the machine were broken. Other components were stored in the wrong places. Nothing was secured in the required manner. The cloth for the wings was torn and dirty. Confronted with this evidence of slovenly workmanship Wilbur quickly expressed his sense of outrage. He told Orville: "I opened the boxes yesterday and have been puzzled ever since to know how you could have wasted two whole days packing them. I am sure that with a scoop shovel I could have put things in within two or three minutes and made fully as good a job of it. I never saw such evidences of idiocy in my life. . . . Ten or a dozen ribs are broken and as they are scattered here and there through the surfaces, it takes almost as much time to tear down and rebuild as if we could have begun at the beginning . . . The radiators are badly smashed; the seat is broken; the magneto has the oil cap broken off . . . and I suspect the axle is bent a little. . . . It is going to take much longer for me to get ready than it should have done if things had been in better shape."[2]

[1] McFarland, *The Papers of Wilbur and Orville Wright*, pp. 906–7, *n.* 5.
[2] *Ibid.*, p. 900.

Orville was not the culprit. He had packed the aeroplane in the standard Wright manner. At Le Havre, however, when the French customs officials examined the machine they failed to replace the parts in the places where they found them. Nothing was fastened down after their inspection. The result was the mess that confronted Wilbur when he opened his boxes.

At the Bollée factory Wilbur's personality and the manner in which he carried himself produced a curious effect. He dressed in a workman's clothing. He laboured for ten hours a day like the other employees. He ate his lunch with his fellow workers and showed none of the aloofness that had been expected from the inventor of a flying machine. The modest, reserved and outwardly calm American now began to impress the Frenchmen he met as a remarkable man, as one who merited their sympathy, admiration, and good will.

As he laboured to repair the damaged aeroplane Wilbur found himself confronted by a host of problems. His inability to speak French complicated every phase of his work. His assistants were unable to understand his simplest requests or instructions. He worried that his time was running out and that the Weiller syndicate might try to abandon their arrangement with him if the flight trials did not take place shortly. From Dayton, Orville reported that Glenn Curtiss and his friends were abusing the Wright patents. At the end of June Orville explained to Wilbur: "Curtiss et al are using our patents, I understand, and are now offering machines for sale at $5,000 each, according to the *Scientific American*. They have got good cheek!"[1]

On 4 July 1908 Wilbur decided to test his engine to make certain it could produce the power he needed for the impending trials. The engine was run up to fifteen hundred revolutions per minute while Wilbur stood in front of it to check the speed. Suddenly, a rubber hose jerked loose and a jet of boiling water, under pressure from the pump, struck Wilbur on his bare forearm and on his left side. The agony of this scalding blast was so intense that Wilbur fainted. Léon Bollée rushed forward to help his stricken friend.

The injuries Wilbur sustained were serious. A blister more than a foot long formed on his arm. It was feared blood poisoning might set in. All realized that if his wounded arm did not heal quickly he would be unable to fly his aeroplane in the trials that were to take place in a matter of weeks. Some of his French critics refused to believe that Wilbur was seriously hurt. They argued that the accident was merely another ruse to avoid a public demonstration of the Wright aeroplane. One Paris newspaper declared: "*Le bluff continue*".[2]

The scalding produced another grave consequence. It will be recalled

[1] Kelly, *Miracle at Kitty Hawk*, p. 279.
[2] See Kelly, *The Wright Brothers*, p. 189.

that years earlier when Wilbur was smashed in the face with a hockey stick the shock to his system was so serious that he decided, at the time, that his heart had been weakened. This old fear now recurred. On 9 July, when he described the incident in a letter to his father, Wilbur explained: "My forearm was bare and suffered the worst though the scald over my heart had more dangerous possibilities".[1]

Wilbur took care not to reveal his anxieties to anyone in France. He quickly returned to his work in the Bollée factory. His scalded arm hampered him in everything he did but he maintained an air of quiet self-confidence which impressed all who met him. His French rivals – Farman, Delagrange, and Blériot – were now flying in the presence of large and enthusiastic crowds. Wilbur, in these circumstances, felt he could not relax his efforts.

A shed was built at the Hunaudières racecourse and on 4 August, after it became dark, the aeroplane was moved there from the factory. The machine, assembled at last, was placed on a cart and towed to its destination by Bollée's automobile. Wilbur established himself in the shed so that he could guard his invention at all times. He installed a cot, a chair, a wash basin, and a petrol stove that would enable him to cook his meals in the shed whenever he chose to do so. He was like some trooper of old who slept tethered to his horse on the eve of battle.

Wilbur's wounded arm did not heal quickly. Nevertheless on 8 August he decided that his time had come. His preparations had been made with exquisite care. The starting rail and "derrick" catapult were positioned exactly as he wanted them. As spectators gathered to observe his performance on that day Hart O. Berg harangued the crowd by means of a loudspeaker. He warned the audience that the taking of photographs would not be allowed.

In the afternoon the doors of the shed were opened and the Wright aeroplane was drawn out into the sunshine, where all could see it. The machine was moved, on a cart, to the starting catapult. There Wilbur tested the engine and made his final adjustments.

The object of this first flight in France was merely to try out the machine and to give its pilot some experience in handling it. It was not Wilbur's intention to fly for a long period or at a great height. His every move was watched by the French technical experts and reporters who had assembled to observe the scene.

They were thrilled by what they saw. The engine was started, Wilbur released the weights and the aircraft rushed forward on its track. Fleury, Berg's chauffeur, steadied the right wing until he was left behind by the moving vehicle. The aeroplane leaped into the air. Wilbur ascended to a height of thirty feet and then executed a turn in the air of a kind never seen

---

[1] McFarland, *The Papers of Wilbur and Orville Wright*, p. 905, *n.* 4.

before in Europe. The crowd gasped in astonishment. He flew twice around the field and then brought his machine back to the earth. Hundreds of spectators, overjoyed by the grace and quality of his flying, rushed forward to offer congratulations. No one had believed it possible that a flying machine could be manoeuvred as Wilbur had just man-oeuvred his. The Wright aeroplane turned and banked easily, in a way that differed completely from the lumbering evolutions of the French machines.

The French experts were awestruck by what had taken place. Louis Blériot said: "I consider that for us in France, and everywhere, a new era in mechanical flight has commenced, I am not sufficiently calm after the event to thoroughly express my opinion. My view can be best conveyed in the words, 'It is marvellous!' "[1]

René Gasnier, another French pioneer, declared: "It is a revelation in aeroplane work. Who now can doubt that the Wrights have done all they claim? My enthusiasm is unbounded. . . . We are as children compared with the Wrights."

Paul Zens expressed himself in even stronger terms: "I would have waited ten times as long to see what I have seen today. Mr. Wright has us all in his hands. What he does not know is not worth knowing. This machine proves that travel by aerial means is at hand. . . ."

Surcouf, the airship designer, was the most enthusiastic of all. A few days later, after Wilbur had flown again, he told a reporter: "It is marvellous. Wright is a titanic genius. The flights . . . demonstrate his enormous lead over the rest of the world. . . . Mr. Wright's control is beyond all praise . . . Mr. Wright has solved the problem of flight. . . . The machine is beyond criticism – that is to say, I defy anyone for the moment to say how it can possibly be improved."

III

On 10 August Wilbur flew again. On this occasion some two thousand spectators had assembled at the race track. They were astonished at the technical capabilities of the Wright aeroplane. Its ability to turn in tight and graceful circles seemed unbelievable to those who saw it. The enthusiasm was so intense that a police cordon had to be formed to protect the pilot from the hosts of his admirers after landing.

Wilbur Wright was a man who knew how to press his advantage. In the afternoon he performed a manoeuvre never seen by the Europeans. He flew his aircraft in a tightly controlled figure of eight and thus demons-trated a mastery in the air that none of his French rivals could even

[1] The remarks of the various French authorities are printed in Gibbs-Smith, *The Rebirth of European Aviation*, pp. 286–7.

approach. Léon Delagrange, one of the leaders of French aviation, declared: "We are beaten! We just don't exist!" The flights continued. On 12 August Wilbur rose to a height of ninety feet. No French pilot had yet come close to this altitude.

Later, Wilbur proudly reported to his brother: "The excitement aroused by the short flights I have made is almost beyond comprehension. The French have simply become wild. Instead of doubting that we could do anything they are ready to believe that we can do everything." In this letter Wilbur also revealed that an English firm had approached him with an offer: "The English crowd, Daimler Mercedes, is ready to make a contract similar to the Weiller contract but at a higher price. However I fear that they are more interested in selling stock than in doing regular business and I am waiting to make further investigations. . . ."[1]

Some of the French authorities soon recovered from their initial enthusiasm. Delagrange, Voisin, Archdeacon and others took care to point out, in the days that followed, that their countrymen still had a chance to overtake the Americans. In England, however, a wave of excitement dominated the Press. It was realized that something tremendous had occurred in the field at Le Mans.

A leading article in *The Times* of 10 August declared: "Immense enthusiasm has been called forth in France by the successful flight achieved . . . by Mr. Wilbur Wright at Le Mans . . . M. Blériot considers that a new era in mechanical flight has begun with the remarkable exhibition of complete control over the flying machine which has just been witnessed. . . ." More soberly, however, *The Times* leader continued: "The world may come to 'airy navies grappling in the central blue', but some of us may cherish yet awhile the comfortable belief that the prospect chiefly concerns posterity".

A report in the *Daily Telegraph* of 10 August said: "Mr. Wilbur Wright is the hero of the hour. . . ." On the 13th an article in the *Daily Telegraph* explained: ". . . As Mr. Wright multiplies his experiments, the superiority of his machine over other aeroplanes becomes more and more apparent. . . . Anyone who has seen M. Delagrange, Mr. Farman, M. Santos Dumont, M. Blériot, and others practise with their machines . . . will at once see the immense superiority of the Wright method. . . . It is no wonder . . . that such experts as M. Delagrange . . . admit that they have been beaten by the Wrights. . . ."

In *The Morning Post* a correspondent reported on 13 August that Wilbur Wright "flew with the greatest ease and mastery of his apparatus". This *Morning Post* report was accompanied by a long article which told the history of the Wright brothers and their work. The article ended by referring to claims Wilbur had made as early as 1906: ". . . even in the existing state of the art it is easy to design a practical and durable flyer that

[1] Kelly, *Miracle at Kitty Hawk*, pp. 296–7.

will carry an operator and supplies of fuel for a flight of over five hundred miles at a speed of over fifty miles per hour".

A leading article in *The Observer* of 16 August was more reflective than most accounts. *The Observer* explained to its readers that much of the recent comment on the future of aerial flight had been "excited and extravagant". "It is wrong", *The Observer* continued, ". . . to err upon the side either of premature expectancy or obstinate denial, but in this case the dreamers seem more likely to be justified than the doubters . . . The American brothers, whatever may be the measure of their success in the future, have shown an astonishing capacity for the profound silence and concentration which have characterised immortal inventors . . . It is less than fifteen years since the first important experiments with a machine heavier than air were made in Kent by Sir Hiram Maxim . . . For a long time flying machines may be small and the chauffeurs of the air may be few: but to our age . . . another miracle is added."

Lord Northcliffe, the aeronautical enthusiast, was overjoyed by the news that Wilbur Wright had flown successfully. His suspicions of the Wright brothers, made so brutally obvious at the time Lady Jane Taylor had called upon him in the previous year, now disappeared completely. The *Daily Mail* was made to reflect his high excitement. On 10 August a special correspondent's report about Wilbur's flight of the 8th was published in the paper. "The scoffer and the sceptic are confounded. Mr. Wilbur Wright last evening made the most marvellous aeroplane flight ever witnessed on this side of the Atlantic. . . . A bird could not have shown a more complete mastery of flight. . . ."

Years of experience had taught Northcliffe that his readers always desired to learn something of the "personality" of the great men they read about in their newspapers. He saw to it that this information was supplied in a special article published in the *Daily Mail* on 17 August. The article, written by the paper's Paris Correspondent, was entitled: "Mr. Wilbur Wright. The Fanatic of Flight". In it the correspondent wrote of the American flier he had met outside his shed on the Hunaudières racecourse:

There was something strange about the tall, gaunt figure. The face was remarkable, the head suggested that of a bird, and the features, dominated by a long, prominent nose that heightened the birdlike effect, were long and bony. A weird half-smile played about the clean-shaven chin and puckered lips, and the skin was deeply tanned with wind and sun. From behind the greyish blue depths of his eyes there seemed to shine something of the light of the sun.

From the first moments of my conversation with him I judged Wilbur Wright to be a fanatic of flight, and I had no longer any doubt that he had accomplished all he claimed to have done. He seemed born to fly.

Northcliffe was not content with newspaper articles. Months earlier, as we have seen, he had publicly offered a tremendous prize for the first aeroplane flight from London to Manchester. He now invited Wilbur to make the attempt when his work in France was finished. On 24 August Northcliffe sent a letter to Wilbur in order to open the matter up with him:[1]

> I should very much like to see you in regard to the London to Manchester aeroplane test, in which we should be most happy to assist you in every way possible. I should like to know your movements. My own are as follows: I shall be in Paris next Monday at the Hotel Ritz. Then I shall be in Germany till the 21st. September, after which I shall be in London for a fortnight before leaving for the United States. I think I could find you an absolutely private practice ground in my own park, and I have a fairly well equipped machine shop there.

Northcliffe had reason to believe Wilbur would be interested by his proposal. The *Daily Mail* Paris Correspondent had already discussed the London to Manchester flight with him when they met at the Hunaudières racecourse. An account of their conversation was published in the *Daily Mail* for 15 August. According to this article Wilbur said of the trial: "I am firmly resolved to compete at no very distant date – perhaps after I have finished my business in France". However, Wilbur later wrote an article for the *London Magazine* in which he clearly stated that he and Orville were not interested in competing for the prize. "The men", he wrote, "who perform exceptional feats with pianos, typesetting machines, automobiles etc., are never the inventors. The inventor is always more interested in the development of the machine than in contests of skill or daring."[2]

Inventor or not, Wilbur was attracted by another of Lord Northcliffe's proposals. In October 1908 he told Orville that the *Daily Mail* was offering a prize of twenty-five hundred dollars for a flight across the English Channel. Moreover, the paper "has offered to privately give me $7500 extra, $10,000 in all, if I will go for the prize and win it. The latter is confidential. . . . I am personally inclined to chuck the prize business and get home as soon as possible. What do you think? . . ."[3]

Before Orville could reply Wilbur sent further details of the *Daily Mail* proposition and also explained the reasons why it attracted him: "The

[1] Wright Brothers' Papers, Northcliffe to Mr Wright, 24 August 1908.

[2] See Wilbur Wright, "Flying From London to Manchester" in *London Magazine*, February 1909, p. 617.

[3] These exchanges between Wilbur and Orville on this subject are printed in Kelly, *Miracle at Kitty Hawk*, pp. 324–333.

Daily Mail offers $12,500 for a cross channel flight and half the net receipts of an exhibition of the machine at a big hall in London. If I felt sure of decent weather I would go for it as such an exhibition would practically end the necessity of further demonstrations next year, and cause all the parliaments of France, Germany & England to vote credits at their winter sessions. . . ."

Orville Wright vetoed the idea. On 14 November 1908 he told his brother in the clearest terms: "I do not like the idea of your attempting a channel flight, when I am not present. I haven't much faith in your motor running. You seem to have more trouble with the engine than I do."

Lord Northcliffe's interest in an aeroplane flight across the English Channel was no transitory whim. He knew that tremendous excitement would be generated when plans for such a project were announced. He could see to it that the preparations for a flight across the Channel were reported in detail in all his newspapers. The circulation of his journals would increase in consequence. When the flight was attempted popular interest would be so great that the *Daily Mail*, the sponsor of the plan, the newspaper with exclusive access to the pilot, would secure a journalistic triumph of the first order. Furthermore, enthusiasm could be maintained after the flight was over at the proposed *Daily Mail* exhibition of the flying machine; and at dinners, luncheons, and banquets to honour the successful flier and to commemorate his achievement. Northcliffe, master of the "newspaper stunt", knew exactly what he was doing when he offered Wilbur Wright large sums to fly across the Channel.

However, much more was involved in the scheme. Circulation figures were not the only factor in Northcliffe's calculations. He was, in his own phrase, "determined to make the nation air-minded". A successful cross-Channel flight would symbolize Britain's vulnerability to attack from the air.

Lord Northcliffe was convinced that his country lay open to such an attack. It was not, in his opinion, an immediate cause for concern. What worried Northcliffe was that the British authorities were failing to make adequate preparations. His lively imagination enabled him to envisage that day in the future when an air attack upon the British Isles would be technically feasible. Yet, as we have seen, the War Office had published an arrogant statement, in his own *Daily Mail*, on 23 July 1908. According to this account the highest military authorities in the country laboured under the impression that there was "nothing to fear" from aircraft "for a long time to come". Two weeks after this opinion of the Army Council was published Wilbur Wright astounded the civilized world by flying in such a way that even his French rivals declared that a new era in mechanical flight was at hand.

For someone who analysed the situation as Northcliffe did in the summer of 1908 no comfort could be found in the conclusion of the War

Office statement of 23 July. It declared in cavalier tones: "When it is possible to cross the Channel, say with a party of excursionists, and to land at any fixed point, the War Office may be prepared to regard recent experiments seriously".

A flight across the English Channel was well within the technical capacity of the Wright aeroplane. Furthermore, Wilbur had already spoken of flying machines capable of carrying five or six passengers.

It is not possible to say if Wilbur Wright could have been tempted to make the flight, as Lord Northcliffe desired. Orville's veto, delivered in the autumn of 1908, made it certain that he would refuse to involve himself in the proposal. When a successful cross-Channel flight was accomplished almost everyone in Britain looked upon it as a development of consequence in the life of the country. But the Wright brothers, despite Lord Northcliffe's efforts, played no part in this notable aeronautical achievement, an achievement which made clear to the British people that the English Channel could no longer serve them as a barrier against attack in the same way it had served for ages past.

IV

In the summer of 1908 Wilbur Wright's business was in France. Soon it became clear that the racecourse at Hunaudières was not large enough to accommodate the great crowds now flocking to Le Mans. Moreover, Wilbur planned to make longer and more intricate flights in order to satisfy his contractual obligations. A huge field was available at the French Army's artillery testing grounds at Auvours, some ten miles from Le Mans. After negotiation, a shed was erected there and Wilbur began a further series of flights from this new field.

The aeronautical world was changed completely as a result of Wilbur's activities at Auvours in 1908. One British authority, Snowden Gamble, has argued that the Admiralty authorities were correct in their refusal to purchase the Wright aeroplane when it was offered to them in 1907 because it was soon superseded by other more efficient aircraft. Snowden Gamble explained: ". . . having saddled itself with an obsolescent device, the Department would probably have kept on trying to improve it. Failure would have been probable, and so the general progress of naval and military aeronautics in this country would have been delayed."[1]

It is difficult, and perhaps idle, for the historian to argue about probabilities. However, it is certain that the condition of aeronautics at this time was more complex than Snowden Gamble's comments suggest. In America, Glenn Curtiss was already flying an aeroplane which was

[1] Snowden Gamble, *The Air Weapon*, p. 102.

based upon the technical innovations and discoveries of the Wright brothers, and with the passage of time he and his associates succeeded in improving it.

The Wrights' European rivals, for their part, managed to create more efficient aircraft but they were only capable of doing so after they learned the details and the significance of the Wright secrets. They were then able to greatly advance aviation technology and carry it far beyond the point reached by the Wright brothers. The best analysis of Wilbur Wright's gigantic influence upon the ideas of the European pioneers may be found in Gibbs-Smith's *Aviation*. He wrote:[1]

> When Wilbur got in his stride . . . at Auvours, the effect on the whole world of aviation was indeed revolutionary. It was not just the achievement of duration and height records that made such an impression: it was the flying of an aeroplane as it should be flown, smoothly, expertly, and with complete mastery of manoeuvre . . . a flying technique undreamt of in Europe. . . .
>
> Two general achievements soon emerged as dominant in aviation, and came to condition all future flying. The first was effective control in the air, control in three dimensions – in pitch, yaw and roll. This stemmed direct from the Wrights, and involved the understanding of control in roll and its co-ordination with both directional and longitudinal control, not only to preserve equilibrium, but equally important, the dynamic employment of this co-ordinated control to *initiate* manoeuvres. Until Wilbur Wright flew in France in 1908, the Europeans had looked upon flight-control in a spirit of passivity; as a technique of simply remaining intact in the air by corrective action. It had been the chauffeur's attitude . . . in which the pilots saw themselves as driving their winged automobiles off the ground and keeping them in equilibrium on the aerial highway; and only steering them cautiously to right or left when necessary. Then, in 1908, the Europeans saw Wilbur using his flying controls actively and dynamically as an airman. . . . it meant the difference between a rider whose whole effort is devoted passively to staying on the horse's back, and one who actively rides and commands the horse, and bends it to his will.

The Europeans learned an entirely new concept of control from Wilbur Wright but something else occurred when the visitors came to the field at Auvours to observe his remarkable aeroplane in flight. Wilbur became the hero of France. Men and women of every rank and class were charmed by his modesty and integrity. The acclaim and adoration of thousands did not change his habits or his outlook. When he was invited to receive an award at a formal dinner of the Aéro-Club de la Sarthe he

---

[1] See Gibbs-Smith, *Aviation*, pp. 132ff, and pp. 139ff.

agreed to attend upon the condition that he would not be required to speak at any great length. In their enthusiasm the diners pressed him to deliver a speech. The Press was delighted by his response. Wilbur said: "I know of only one bird, the parrot, that talks, and it can't fly very high." Wilbur's admirers were overjoyed by this typical Wright rejoinder.

The technical experts were more critical. Some praised him. Others were full of envy. Yet all benefited from the knowledge and insight they gained by studying the aeroplane and its pilot in action.

The European governments were extremely interested in his demonstrations. The Press regularly referred to the presence of Russian officers. The Italians were convinced their Armed Forces needed Wright aeroplanes. Isidor Loewe in Berlin, pressed forward by Hart O. Berg, began a new series of negotiations with the German authorities.

The most persistent of the Europeans was C. S. Rolls. He never abandoned his efforts to secure a Wright aeroplane. He did not, however, reveal all his plans to Wilbur. Rolls had decided that when he obtained a Wright machine he would then offer his services to the British Government so that they could benefit from his experiences with the aeroplane, and also help to defray his costs in flying it.

In July, before Wilbur's first flights in France were made, he suggested to Rolls that he could obtain a Wright machine by having it built in England. The Wrights were prepared to allow this to be done by granting a license to a British firm to exploit their patents in return for royalties. Rolls was attracted by the proposal. On 25 July he informed Wilbur:[1]

> In reference to your letter of the 10th inst. I think the idea of my having a machine built here is quite feasible, but could you let me have proper working drawings. . . .
>
> I quite agree as to giving you a share of any financial profit I might make, and the general idea suggested by you seems good. Could we, therefore, go into further details? Are you likely to be in London soon or possibly I could go to Le Mans, as I ought to have a good deal of coaching from you as to methods of construction etc.
>
> Needless to say the working drawings above referred to . . . or blue prints, I should treat as confidential, and only make use of them for the purpose of getting the work carried out.

Wilbur was not convinced Rolls could carry out the bargain he had proposed. At the end of August he told Orville: "I have talked with Rolls but doubt whether he is in a position to do anything".[2] Rolls, however,

---

[1] Wright Brothers' Papers, Chas. S. Rolls to Wilbur Wright, 25 July 1908.
[2] See Kelly, *Miracle at Kitty Hawk*, p. 299.

did all he could to keep the negotiations alive. He regularly sent Wilbur letters in an attempt to secure an arrangement. For example, on 14 August he told Wilbur:[1]

> As soon as you are in a position to treat for the British rights, please let me know as I think I am in touch with the best people, & would also like to be connected with it myself.
> I have heard of one or two people who are going over to see you, but you will no doubt exercise great care.

As we know, Hart O. Berg was allowed no part in the Wrights' British negotiations. However, when Wilbur began to fly in France Berg urged Isidor Loewe in Berlin to renew his approaches to the German Government. In August Berg sent Loewe photographs of the Wright machine in flight so that he could employ them to re-awaken German interest in the aeroplane.

On 24 August 1908 Loewe reported on this new phase of his agency in the German capital. The officer he saw first was Major Hans Gross, one of the foremost aeronautical experts in the German Army. Gross was delighted by Wilbur's triumph over his French rivals. Loewe's report was not written in an elegant English style but his message was clear enough. According to it Major Gross said: ". . . he had followed with great interest Mr Wright's trials in France and was glad to see that all went so well. He personally had never doubted that Mr. W. would do what he claimed to have done already for years. In his opinion the Wright aeroplane was no doubt the best of all known so far. The machines of Delagrange, Farman, Ferber and others were in his eye only inferior imitations of Mr. W's machine. The Major got quite enthusiastic over W's performances and said he had enjoyed very much to see the French, who had always opened their mouth so wide, entirely beaten by W."[2]

Loewe revealed that Gross had promised to discuss the aeroplane with Count von Moltke, Chief of the General Staff. According to Loewe's account Gross promised that he would "make soundings this weekend when he would see some members of the Staff. One of its members, Count Moltke, was a man with very modern ideas . . . and he would put the matter before him also . . ."

They next discussed the height at which Wilbur had flown his aeroplane in his demonstrations at the Hunaudières track. Gross insisted that at a height of thirty or fifty metres the pilot could be brought down easily by massed infantry fire. The matter of height, Gross declared, would be

[1] Wright Brothers' Papers, C. S. Rolls to Wilbur Wright, 14 August 1908.
[2] For Loewe's memorandum or report addressed to Hart O. Berg and reproduced in this and the following paragraphs see "Memorandum for Hart. O. Berg, Esqre., Paris" dated 24 August 1908, preserved in the Wright Brothers' Papers.

"Der springende Punkt" in negotiations with the German Army. Loewe, in response, informed Major Gross that the French Army had placed the Camp d'Auvours at Wilbur's disposal for his further trials. At this, "the Major replied that the German authorities would naturally also gladly furnish any facilities in the way of a field and guard same by soldiers".

As we have seen, Colonel Capper at Farnborough was critical of the Wright starting device or "derrick", as they liked to call it. Major Gross entertained a different opinion: "We also came to speak about the method of starting the machine, the major liked the Wright method well and thought it very effective. He agreed with me that wheels as used by the French up to the present would soon be smashed on rough grounds . . . The major should like very much to have some fotos showing the launching device in detail. . . . He was also much interested in the way the apparatus could be transported. . . ."

Loewe concluded on an encouraging note: "En résumé, I am glad to say that the Major follows with the keenest interest the trials in France, he was much pleased with the fotos you sent him and he would with great pleasure hear further from us".

In this way the Wright negotiations with the German Army were begun again. It will be observed that the attitude of Major Gross and his superiors differed completely from the opinions published by the British War Office in its aeronautical pronouncement of 23 July 1908.

V

While these developments were taking place in Europe Orville Wright was busily engaged in attempting to fulfil the requirements of the Wright brothers' American contract. Orville arrived at Fort Myer in August. Charlie Taylor and Charles Furnas, his mechanics, were already upon the ground.

On 3 September Orville made his first flight. It was a brief excursion in the air and lasted less than two minutes. A crowd of spectators, civil and military, gasped in astonishment when they observed the miracle of flight. As soon as Orville brought his machine back to the earth a group of journalists rushed up to congratulate him. Orville was astounded to see that several of these hard-bitten professionals had tears streaming down their faces. They had witnessed a feat they had earlier believed to be impossible. When Orville flew again on the second day of his tests thousands were present to observe his wonderful performance.

Thereafter Orville began to attack the height and endurance records established earlier in Europe. On 9 September he remained in the air for more than an hour. On the same day he flew with a passenger for six minutes. On the 10th Orville flew for more than an hour in great circles above the field and rose to a height of two hundred feet. On the 12th he flew for one hour and fifteen minutes. The Wright brothers, each in a different continent, awed the civilized world with their achievements. They demonstrated, for all to see, a mastery of mechanical flight which had not been dreamed of before.

In Britain Orville's activity excited much enthusiasm. The *Daily Mail* for 10 September reported: "All previous aeroplane exhibitions pale into insignificance before the marvellous performance of Mr. Orville Wright's machine. . . . He flew for 66 min. 31 sec., maintained a speed of more than forty miles an hour, and came to earth as lightly as a feather. . . ." A later account in the same edition stated: "Mr. Wright flew again this evening, and kept his aeroplane aloft for one hour, two minutes and thirteen seconds. This time he had a most brilliant company of spectators: Mr. Taft, the Secretary for the Navy; Mr. Metcalfe, the Assistant Secretary of War; Mr. Oliver, the Assistant Secretary of the Treasury . . . and a formidable array of Army officers in uniform, among them several generals." The first leading article in the *Daily Mail* for 10 September was devoted to Orville's achievements. It was entitled "The Aeroplane's Victory".

On 11 September the *Daily Mail* reported further triumphs. The military potential of the Wright aeroplane was emphasized in this account: "Mr. Orville Wright's epoch-marking flights are the one topic of conversation today from the Atlantic to the Pacific. Army and Navy experts are especially interested, and predict that the flights will vitally modify the conditions of warfare in the future." A naval officer, the official observer for the United States Navy, told the *Daily Mail* correspondent that Orville's aeroplane could be flown from an American cruiser: "It could", he said, "fly over the advance column of the enemy's fleet, drop explosives, and secure valuable information". An army officer who flew with Orville was equally enthusiastic about the military value of the aeroplane.

The *Daily Mail* of 11 September also published the proud reaction of Wilbur Wright. He was delighted with his younger brother's triumph. Interviewed at Le Mans, Wilbur announced: "Now we are going, Orville and I, to beat all the world's records . . . and to show people what we are really capable of".

On 14 September full and excited accounts of Orville's work appeared in the *Daily Telegraph*: "The remarkable demonstration given by Mr. Orville Wright on his aeroplane . . . when he broke all records by making the longest sustained aeroplane flight and in another attempt, carrying a passenger . . . was the culminating point of an epoch-making week in the history of aerial navigation". The passenger, on this flight, was Major George O. Squier, Acting Chief of the United States Army Signal Corps. He spoke in terms of the highest praise when he described Orville's ability to control the machine in the air. Among the observers at Fort Myer was Colonel James Templer, the former head of the British Army's Balloon Factory. His presence at Fort Myer suggests that the War Office was continuing to watch aeronautical developments in foreign countries. According to the Reuter's despatch in the *Daily Telegraph*, Colonel Templer said: ". . . he was convinced, as a result of the exhibition, that Mr. Wright could fly on the machine he was now using from Washington to New York and back without replenishing his fuel".

The Times devoted a leading article to Orville's flight on 12 September: "We cordially congratulate Mr. Orville Wright on the success which has attended his efforts, and the world will look forward with the greatest interest to the future developments of his invention. For the first time in history the conquest of the air appears to have been brought fairly within the compass of practical mechanics, and the first steps in the direction of that conquest have been made." Wilbur Wright was especially pleased by this article. He wrote to his sister: "Tell 'Bubbo' that his flights have revolutionized the world's beliefs regarding the practicability of flight. Even such conservative papers as the London *Times* devote leading editorials to his work and accept human flight as a thing to be regarded as a normal feature of the world's future life."[1]

Orville Wright's flights at Fort Myer were not an unalloyed triumph. Soon after he arrived in Washington Augustus Moore Herring boldly announced that he planned to fly his own aeroplane from New York to the scene of the trials and there win the United States Army Signal Corps' contract for himself. Herring did not possess a machine that could fly nor did he know how to construct one. This in no way deterred him from making the most extravagant claims. Herring was entirely without scruples. He reckoned that if he held on for long enough, if he refused to withdraw from the aeronautical arena, something might turn up and so enable him to cheat someone or some organization and thus realize his object which was a monetary reward of some kind. Herring's activities make it clear that the Wright brothers were correct in the intricate and secretive courses they adopted when they sought to sell their aeroplane.

Herring's first step was to request a postponement of his trials. He claimed he had injured himself in an accident which shook his engine to pieces while it was being tested. He asked for more time to build a new engine. This reprieve allowed him to observe Orville Wright in action. When Orville flew at Fort Myer Herring at once boasted to the correspondent of the *Daily Mail* that his aeroplane was superior to that of the Wrights.[2]

Despite several tricks and stratagems which extended his association

---

[1] McFarland, *The Papers of Wilbur and Orville Wright*, p. 926.
[2] See the *Daily Mail*, 11 September 1908.

with the United States Army for a very considerable period of time, Herring never produced a machine that was capable of flight. Undeterred, he later managed to form an association with Glenn H. Curtiss, who was devious enough in his own way in these early days of aeronautics. But Herring failed to contribute anything of value to their joint enterprise. An associate of Curtiss later dismissed Herring in terms that would outrage any American if they were applied to him: "He sized Herring up as 'a fourflusher and a faker' and bluntly informed Curtiss that he did not wish to be connected with a business in which Herring had any part. As he afterward avowed, he also told Curtiss: 'I thought it a great mistake for him to have become associated with Mr. Herring; that Mr. Herring had attained a very bad reputation for himself by the manner in which he had taken a contract with the government, and the manner in which he had failed to carry out the provisions of the contract. . . .'"[1]

VI

Augustus Moore Herring was not the only one to plague Orville's course at the Fort Myer trials. Other more capable rivals were also active there. The behaviour of these men further illustrates the merciless competition and the ruthless ambitions of the earliest pioneers of aviation.

The policy the Wright brothers adopted in their dealings with the British Government, and with other governments, cannot be understood unless this bitter contemporary situation is made clear. The Wrights were determined to acquire great wealth from their invention. Furthermore, they would not compromise in any way their valid claim to be recognized as the discoverers of the principles of controlled flight and the inventors of the first practical aeroplane in history. They realized, from the earliest stages of their work, that they would have to guard against competitors, infringers, and other aspirants who might seek to benefit, unjustly, by exploiting the results of their genius, dedication and hard work. This inflexible attitude helped to determine the early history of almost every contemporary Air Force in the world.

In 1907 Alexander Graham Bell, the inventor of the telephone, in company with several associates in Nova Scotia, formed a society they called the Aerial Experiment Association. The object of the group was to create a practical aeroplane. Bell, a man of great energy and broad outlook, was convinced that a brilliant future lay before anyone who could produce an aircraft driven by its own motive power. He had already carried out extensive experiments with kites of his own design.

---

[1] For these pleasantries see C. R. Roseberry, *Glenn Curtiss, Pioneer of Flight* (New York, 1972), p. 219, hereafter cited as Roseberry, *Curtiss*.

An early recruit to Bell's circle in Canada was Lieutenant Thomas Selfridge, an artillery officer in the United States Army. Selfridge was fascinated by the subject of aviation. He knew about Alexander Bell's work with kites. Early in 1907 he asked to meet Bell in order to learn more about his ideas and theories. At an interview in Washington, D.C., Selfridge impressed the older man with his energy and enthusiasm. Dr Bell, a scientist of international reputation, wrote to President Theodore Roosevelt and arranged for Selfridge to be sent to his home in Nova Scotia as an observer for the United States Army. Selfridge's assigned task was to watch the kite experiments and also to assist Bell and his colleagues in their work.[1]

Another recruit to Bell's group was Glenn H. Curtiss, who was especially proficient in the design and building of petrol engines. For several years Curtiss had distinguished himself as a brilliant racer of motorcycles. He owned his own factory in Hammondsport in New York where he produced hundreds of motorcycles each year. After a time he developed an interest in aeronautics because the pioneers of the day were prepared to pay very high prices for the light but powerful engines they wanted and he was able to build.

Dr Bell, as his experiments progressed, proposed to install a motor in one of his man-carrying kites. He applied to Curtiss to assist him in this aspect of his work. In the summer of 1907 Curtiss agreed to join Bell's group so that they could benefit from his expert knowledge. When the Aerial Experiment Association was formed later in the year Lieutenant Selfridge became its Secretary and Curtiss was given the title "Director of Experiments". Lieutenant Selfridge received no salary but Curtiss was paid five thousand dollars per year for his part-time appointment.

The Wright brothers met Glenn Curtiss for the first time in 1906. Shortly after he became "Director of Experiments" in the Aerial Experiment Association Curtiss wrote to the Wrights to tell them he wanted to present them with one of his engines, free of charge. This offer was prudently declined. In his letter Curtiss mentioned that Dr Bell had read out to the members of the Aerial Experiment Association an account of the recently published United States Government's specifications for a flying machine. Curtiss added: "You, of course, are the only persons who could come anywhere near doing what is required".[2]

Soon after, on 15 January 1908, Lieutenant Selfridge in his capacity as Secretary of the Association wrote to the Wright brothers to inform them that his group had recently begun to experiment with gliders. He asked

[1] For these details see J. H. Parkin, *Bell and Baldwin* (Toronto, 1964), pp. 33ff, hereafter cited as Parkin, *Bell and Baldwin*.
[2] See Kelly, *The Wright Brothers*, pp. 233ff for the Wrights and their adventures with members of the Aerial Experiment Association.

for information about their own scientific experiments and for technical advice. The Wrights, addressed by an officer of a scientific association, supposed the information would be exploited for scientific purposes only. They at once drew Selfridge's attention to Wilbur's addresses delivered before the Western Society of Engineers in 1901 and 1903, and published in the Journals of the Society. They furnished Selfridge with information about their own scientific experiments and also referred him to the specifications in their United States patent. Selfridge replied to say he had secured a copy of the patent and was trying to obtain the other references they had provided for his information.

In the summer of 1908 Glenn Curtiss began to fly an aeroplane the Aerial Experiment Association called the "June Bug". Later, in public statements about their work, no mention was made of the contribution of the Wright brothers to their results. Orville sent a letter of complaint to Curtiss. He pointed out that when the Wrights furnished Selfridge with information about their machines they "did not intend, of course, to give permission to use the patented features . . . for exhibitions or in a commercial way".[1] In reply, Curtiss explained that he did not expect to do any exhibition flying and that his flights had been made in connection with the work of the Aerial Experiment Association. He added that he had referred the matter of the patent to the Secretary of the Association.[2]

Earlier, when Wilbur was in New York before his departure for France he had attempted to alert Orville to the activities of the Aerial Experiment Association. On 20 May 1908 he sent him a letter together with a number of Press clippings: "One of the clippings which I enclose intimates that Selfridge is infringing our patent on wing twisting".[3]

Orville was now thoroughly alarmed. On 29 July he reported to Wilbur: "I sent you a few days ago copies of my letters to Curtiss . . . I have a reply from Curtiss that he is not intending entering the exhibition business as has been reported by the papers, and that the matter of patents has been referred to the secretary of the Aero. Experiment Assn. A Mr. Todd, who is connected with *World's Work* and who is preparing a series of articles for that magazine, was here several days ago . . . He had just been at Hammondsport. . . . He explained a great deal of the details of their machine, and spoke of several features which he thought especially ingenious . . . I showed him one patent which contained all the special features to which he had referred."[4]

[1] *Ibid.*, p. 235.
[2] Parkin in *Bell and Baldwin* was naturally anxious to protect the reputations of the subjects of his book. He wrote at p. 63: ". . . it is a matter of record that Selfridge wrote to the Wrights . . . and later obtained a copy of the patent issued to the Wrights . . . It can only be assumed that Selfridge did not show the patent to the others".
[3] See McFarland, *The Papers of Wilbur and Orville Wright*, p. 882.
[4] *Ibid.*, p. 909.

Alexander Graham Bell did not believe the Wright patent could affect the further work of his society but he was more cautious than his colleagues in the Aerial Experiment Association. Despite Orville's warning to Glenn Curtiss some of them proposed to exhibit and race their machine at an aeronautical show in St Louis. The promoters of the event had offered a large sum of money if the "June Bug" was demonstrated at their exhibition. Bell, however, refused to allow his associates to carry out their plan. His strictures merit careful attention:[1]

> ... Dr. Bell slapped them down ... Bell said it was "tempting" to race the *June Bug* ... "Such propositions, however, cannot be entertained by us.... If we authorize public exhibitions ... involving pecuniary transactions or emoluments, we at once lay ourselves open to attack from numerous inventors who will claim that we are infringing their patents, and we will be obliged to defend ourselves. The letter from Orville Wright ... indicates clearly what would happen, and the Wright Brothers would not be the only aggressors ... So long as we are an Experiment Association carrying on experiments, not for gain but simply to promote the art of aviation ... there can be no possible ground for legal action of any kind. But the moment we begin to make money, look out for trouble."

Glenn Curtiss, we should notice, had not involved himself with the Aerial Experiment Association merely to promote the art of aviation. His object was to make money. He was a business man and not a scientist. He was determined to gain his object despite the sage arguments of Dr Bell and the outraged protests of the Wright brothers.

Glenn Curtiss and Lieutenant Selfridge arrived at Fort Myer while Orville was still demonstrating his aeroplane there. Dr Bell appeared at the site of the trials shortly after. Selfridge was the first to arouse Orville's suspicions. The United States Army was testing a dirigible at Fort Myer at this time. The engine for this vessel had been supplied by Glenn Curtiss. On 6 September Orville reported to Wilbur: "Curtiss was here Thursday and Friday. They have not been able to make the motor ... on the ... dirigible run more than a minute or two ... Ours runs without a miss. Selfridge has been trying to find out how we do it! ..."[2] He also explained about Selfridge: "... I don't trust him an inch. He is intensely interested in the subject, and plans to meet me often at dinners, etc. where he can try to pump me. He has a good education and a clear mind. I understand that he does a good deal of knocking behind my back. ..."[3]

[1] See Roseberry, *Curtiss*, p. 116.
[2] See McFarland, *The Papers of Wilbur and Orville Wright*, p. 918, *n*. 3.
[3] See Kelly, *Miracle at Kitty Hawk*, p. 303.

Before Dr Bell reached Fort Myer Glenn Curtiss sent him an appraisal of the Wright aeroplane. It was written in the tones of a competitor: "The launching device . . . does not seem to be very well liked, and I believe that all who have seen our machine and the Wrights' prefer our method of starting on wheels, to skids".[1]

On 17 September Orville prepared for another flight. The military authorities decided that on this occasion his passenger would be Lieutenant Selfridge. His experience with the Aerial Experiment Association had qualified him as a technical expert of genuine quality. It is most probable that his superiors looked upon Selfridge as an officer with a great future in the newly developing field of military aeronautics.

On the 17th, the machine with its two occupants rose to a height of more than one hundred feet and circled the field several times. Then, disaster struck. Something in the aircraft broke and Orville found he was no longer able to control its flight. He instantly shut off the engine and tried to glide back to the earth. He almost managed a successful landing but the machine smashed into the ground with a terrible impact. Selfridge's skull was fractured and he died a few hours later. Orville was badly injured.

On the day following the accident some parts of the damaged aeroplane were taken to Orville as he lay in a hospital bed. He hoped to discover the cause of the crash by examining these bits of wreckage. The aeroplane was then dismantled and put in a crate for shipment to Dayton.

Katharine Wright had rushed to Washington to be with her injured brother. They were now told that unauthorized persons had examined the aeroplane while Orville was still confined to his hospital bed. According to the information they received Dr Alexander Graham Bell had entered the aeroplane shed at Fort Myer and taken measurements of the Wright machine. Octave Chanute was at Fort Myer. They at once applied to him to help them to find out more details. On 29 September Chanute wrote to Katharine Wright: [2]

> I am inclined to believe that the account which reached you was greatly exaggerated. I met Sergeant Downey after I left and spoke to him about the occurrence.
>
> He says that Dr. Bell went into the shed after almost everything was packed up, but there was no cover on the aeroplane box. That a dispute arose about the width of the wing and Dr. Bell said, "Well, I have a tape in my pocket and we will measure it". That this was the only measurement taken is what I gathered, but you had better see Sergeant Downey when opportunity serves and get an understanding of what occurred.

[1] See Roseberry, *Curtiss*, p. 125.
[2] See McFarland, *The Papers of Wilbur and Orville Wright*, p. 929.

The editor of *The Papers of Wilbur and Orville Wright* commented: "Alexander Graham Bell's relationship to the Aerial Experiment Association, which was already building machines that infringed the Wrights patents, made it difficult for Orville and Katharine to believe that his interest in taking measurements had been entirely due to momentary curiosity."[1]

The Wrights, now unable to fulfil the terms of their contract with the United States Army, were forced to ask the authorities for a postponement of their trials. In these circumstances Dr Bell, with the concurrence of his colleagues in the Aerial Experiment Association, now wrote to President Roosevelt to offer to make available to the Army their machines and their knowledge. The Assistant Secretary of War expressed appreciation for the offer and stated an officer would be ordered to witness their flights if he was told when they would take place. [2]

Meanwhile, in Paris, Hart O. Berg had received another report from Isidor Loewe. In Berlin, Loewe had seen Major Gross again. The topic of their conversation was the separate aerial achievements of each of the Wright brothers. Gross revealed to Loewe that the German military authorities were paying very careful attention to their work, in France, and also in the United States. Loewe informed Berg: [3]

> ... The Major showed me a report, quite a dossier, on flying machines which he was making up for the War Department. ...
> ... I could notice that the Major takes the greatest interest in the performances of the Wrights and that they are closely watched.

VII

Wilbur Wright was immensely proud of his brother's achievements at Fort Myer. When he first received news of Orville's record flights he wrote to their sister: "'You ought to seen it! You ought to seen it! Great big sing!' I refer to the excitement roused by Orville's dandy flights ... When I made my first flight over here the sudden change from unbelief to belief roused a furor of excitement I had not expected to see renewed, but the news from America seems to have been sufficient to repeat the stir ... Well, it was fine news all right and lifted a load off of my mind."[4]

Wilbur's flights at this stage of his work had been hampered by his engine. It failed to perform well enough to permit him to remain in the air for long periods of time. He now addressed himself to this problem. He

[1] See *Ibid.*, p. 929, *n.* 1.
[2] For these details see Parkin, *Bell and Baldwin*, p. 73.
[3] Wright Brothers' Papers, Memorandum, Loewe to Berg, 11 September 1908.
[4] McFarland, *The Papers of Wilbur and Orville Wright*, pp. 922–3.

was preparing for a long flight of his own when he received word of the tragedy at Fort Myer. By chance, his old friend Count Gleichen, the former British Military Attaché in Washington, arrived upon the scene shortly after Wilbur learned of the accident. Gleichen described the terrible result produced by the cabled message in his Memoirs:[1]

> On a visit to the French manoeuvres in 1908, I went to see my friend Wilbur, for he had promised to give me a fly . . . but when . . . I arrived on the ground, I was met by the Wrights' agent who told me that Wilbur had had a cable with very bad news . . .
>
> I caught sight of Wilbur sitting in his tent, with his head in his hands; tears were streaming down his face, his shoulders were trembling convulsively, and when he looked up he could not speak, while his outstretched hand was shaking like an aspen.

As we have seen, Percy Walker regularly condemned and disparaged Wilbur Wright's character in his authorized history of the Royal Aircraft Establishment. Walker noticed Count Gleichen's account of this incident at Auvours and wrote of it in his book that it was a "very human story illustrative of the high regard in which the Wright Brothers were held by men of the British Army with whom they came into contact. . . ."[2]

Wilbur revealed the extent of his agony in a letter to his sister: "The death of poor Selfridge was a greater shock to me than Orville's injuries, severe as the latter were. I felt sure "Bubbo" would pull through all right but the other was irremediable. . . ." He also explained to his sister the nature of the difficulties that confronted him and Orville as they went about their dangerous work separated from each other by thousands of miles. The visitors who came to see Wilbur Wright perform in the air all remarked upon his self-confidence, his iron will, and the calm appearance he presented to the world. These impressions were not entirely accurate. Wilbur told Katharine: "The worry over leaving Orville alone to undertake those trials was one of the chief things in almost breaking me down a few weeks ago . . . A half dozen times I was on the point of telling Berg that I was going to America in spite of everything. . . . I do not mean that Orville was incompetent to do the work itself, but I realized that he would be surrounded by thousands of people who with the most friendly intentions in the world would consume his time, exhaust his strength and keep him from having proper rest . . . A man cannot take sufficient care when he is subject to continual interruptions and his time is consumed in talking to visitors . . . Here Berg helps to act as a buffer and gives me some chance to be alone when I work . . . When we take up the American demonstrations again we will both be there. It is much easier to do things

[1] Lord Edward Gleichen, *A Guardsman's Memories*, p. 303.
[2] See Walker, *Early Aviation at Farnborough*, vol. II, p. 75.

when you have someone at hand in whom you have absolute confidence."[1]

Now Wilbur decided to attack the established endurance records for aeroplanes. He would show his competitors that the Wright brothers were years in advance of any rival in any country. On 21 September he flew for more than one hour and thirty minutes and set a new world distance record of forty-one miles. On 28 September he flew for more than one hour. On 10 October he flew a distance of forty-six miles. These great flights at the Auvours camp culminated on the last day of 1908 when Wilbur remained aloft for two hours and twenty minutes and covered a distance in the air of more than seventy-seven miles.

No princes or kings had adorned the bleak scene at Kitty Hawk when the brothers made their first pioneering flights. Now distinguished visitors from every country rushed to Auvours to witness this miraculous activity.

The members of the Aeronautical Society of Great Britain were unable to resist the spectacle. C. S. Rolls, Major Baden-Powell, Sir Hiram Maxim, Patrick Alexander, Colonel Fullerton, Dr F. W. Lanchester, and others travelled from London to observe Wilbur Wright in the air. Each went to France with a secret ambition. Wilbur often carried a passenger on his flights. The members of the British contingent hoped they would be fortunate enough to be invited to fly with the master.

Wilbur Wright obliged. The first Englishman to fly with him was Griffith Brewer, the London patent attorney and balloonist who later became an intimate friend of the Wright family. C. S. Rolls was allowed to fly and so was Major Baden-Powell. When Baden-Powell first saw Wilbur in the air he was awe-struck. He sought to warn his fellow countrymen of the significance of the Wright achievement. He told a representative of the Paris edition of the *New York Herald*: [2]

> If only some of our people in England could see or imagine what Mr. Wright is now doing I am certain it would give them a terrible shock. A conquest of the air by any nation means more than the average man is willing to admit or even think about. That Wilbur Wright is in possession of a power which controls the fate of nations is beyond dispute.

C. S. Rolls was also excited by the flight he made with Wilbur Wright. He continued to try to secure a Wright aeroplane for himself. On 14 October he wrote to Wilbur: [3]

---

[1] See McFarland, *The Papers of Wilbur and Orville Wright*, pp. 925–6.

[2] The major's remarks were published in the Paris edition of the *New York Herald*, 6 October 1908. See also Kelly, *The Wright Brothers*, p. 198.

[3] Wright Brothers' Papers, Chas. S. Rolls to Wilbur Wright, 14 October 1908.

I did not half thank you for giving me that ride, it was the realisation of several dreams & I could think of nothing else for a long while. . . .

You will of course keep private the fact of my negotiating for a machine etc. as such things are so quickly apt to get into the Press which can do no good at any rate at present. . . .

Formal British recognition of the Wright achievements soon followed. C. S. Rolls was one of the founders of the Aero Club of the United Kingdom. The purpose of this distinguished society, which began its work in 1901 and later became the Royal Aero Club of the United Kingdom, was to promote the development of aerial navigation. On 27 October Rolls told Wilbur the Club had conferred a signal honour upon him and his brother:[1]

We awarded you the Aero Club Gold Medal at today's meeting of the Cttee. & the letter will be sent to you thro' Brewer.

We are anxious for you to come to our annual dinner & have it presented, & what I am writing for is to ask you to stay with me at my father's London house if you do come over. . . .

If you come you are to be the guest of the Club during your stay. . . .

I shall have a motor car at your disposal so that you can go about wherever you want.

VIII

We come now to an episode previously unnoticed in British aeronautical history. It will be recalled that when Wilbur went to France Orville Wright took charge of the negotiations with the War Office for the sale of the Wright aeroplane to the British Government. When Orville crashed and injured himself at Fort Myer Percy Walker concluded: "Negotiations between the British War Office and the Wright Brothers ended with this tragedy."[2] This was not the case.

Major Baden-Powell travelled to Auvours with all the fervour of an enthusiast who had dreamed for years of the possibility of successful mechanical flight. Another motive also lay behind his visit. His purpose was to prepare for the British Government a full report upon the Wright aeroplane. Upright and honest soldier that he was, he made this aspect of his mission clear to Wilbur Wright during the course of his stay at

[1] Wright Brothers' Papers, Chas. S. Rolls to Wilbur Wright, 27 October 1908.
[2] Walker, *Early Aviation at Farnborough*, vol. II, p. 75.

Auvours, which lasted from 3 to 9 October. Upon his return to London Major Baden-Powell explained to Wilbur:[1]

> I have at last got back home, & must write you a line to thank you for affording me such a very interesting sight of, and experience with, your machine. It will always remain one of the events of my life.
> I am hard at work writing up my report for the Government, & I sincerely hope they may waken up & get one of your machines. . . .
> I hope you will find an opportunity of coming over to England. . . .

Baden-Powell also wrote to Octave Chanute to tell him of his wonderful experience in France: ". . . Then I went over to Le Mans, and not only had talks with Wilbur Wright, but he very kindly gave me a trip in his machine . . . It is marvellous to see that which one has so often imagined, actually going and going so *very* well & steadily. I am sure it will not be long now before such machines are common. . . ."[2]

By 24 October Baden-Powell's report was completed. He sent it to the War Office together with two covering notes:[3]

32, Princes Gate. S.W.
Oct 24 '08

Sir
>   I have the honour to enclose herewith some notes on Wright's Aeroplane, which may possibly prove of some interest.

I have the honour to remain
Your obedient Servant
B. Baden Powell
Major

The Secretary
The War Office

The second covering note explained to the authorities that the "following notes were made chiefly from personal observation though some of the facts were given by Mr. Wright or his associates. Most of the figures are therefore only approximate." Baden-Powell further explained he had made two flights with Wilbur Wright during the course of his visit.

The report itself comprised eight typewritten pages. It dealt in minute detail with every aspect of the Wright aeroplane. It was divided into

[1] Wright Brothers' Papers, B. Baden-Powell to Wilbur Wright, 11 October 1908.

[2] Octave Chanute Papers, B. Baden-Powell to Chanute, 18 October 1908.

[3] For this report see W.O. 32/8596. "Some Notes on W. Wright's Aeroplane Taken by Major B. Baden-Powell on Oct. 3 to 9 1908 at the Camp d'Auvours, near Le Mans". The note is dated 24 October 1908.

sections. The first dealt with the "Main Planes". There followed descriptions of the "Fore-Planes"; the "Vertical Rudders"; "Steering Devices"; "The Motor"; "Propulsion"; "Accessories"; the "Starting Device"; and "Manipulation". In his conclusion Major Baden-Powell stated: "The machine travels very steadily, often going for long distances within two or three feet of the ground so steadily that one could easily imagine it was running on wheels."

Colonel F. Rainsford-Hannay, the Director of Fortifications and Works, sent these documents to Colonel Capper, at Farnborough: "The annexed letter with notes on the 'Wright' aeroplane, received from Major B. Baden-Powell, is forwarded for your information and early return please".[1] There is no record of Colonel Capper's reply. However, other results soon followed.

On 25 November 1908 Colonel H. C. Lowther, the British Military Attaché in Paris, wrote to Wilbur Wright in order to ask if he would sell aeroplanes to the British Government:[2]

> November 25th 1908 British Embassy,
> Paris.
>
> Sir,
>   I am directed by my government to enquire from you whether you are prepared to sell aeroplanes such as you now have in use, but with such recent modification, as you may have approved. If so what would be the price and when could it or they be delivered. I presume that delivery would be made complete in every respect.
>   I originally addressed Mr. Weiller on this subject, but that gentleman informs me that he only has the French rights and cannot sell for use outside this country, so he referred me to you.
>
> Believe me, Sir, Yours faithfully
> H. C. Lowther
> Lieutenant Colonel
> Military Attaché

On the same day he approached Wilbur Colonel Lowther sent a long despatch to George Grahame of the British Embassy in Paris. Grahame was an experienced diplomat who had earlier served in Berlin and in Buenos Aires. Shortly after, this letter was forwarded to the Army Council by the Under-Secretary of State for Foreign Affairs.

Lowther had been extremely diligent in discovering information about the Wright aeroplane and about the interest shown in it by other

---

[1] W.O. 32/8596. F. Rainsford-Hannay to Superintendent, Balloon Factory, 29 October 1908 and marked "Confidential".
[2] Wright Brothers' Papers, H. C. Lowther to Wilbur Wright, 25 November 1908.

governments. His letter to Grahame revealed that C. S. Rolls had at last secured a Wright machine for himself; that the French Government had ordered Wright aircraft for use with the Army; that the Russian Government had set aside a large sum for the purchase of Wright aeroplanes; and that the German Emperor himself had personally written to Wilbur Wright in order to ask him to allow the Counsellor of the German Embassy in Paris to fly with him as a passenger so that the Counsellor could send a report about the aeroplane to Berlin as quickly as possible.

The source of Colonel Lowther's information was Lazare Weiller, the French capitalist who headed the syndicate that had contracted to purchase the French rights in the Wright invention. Lowther's letter to Grahame was a document of significance. When the Army Council received it Britain's military leaders learned a great deal about the aeronautical plans of other countries. The letter stated:[1]

> I have the honour to inform you that I had today an interesting conversation with Mr. Weiller, who owns the French rights in the Wright aeroplane.
> In the course of the conversation I gathered the following items of information.
> Mr. Weiller has *only* the French rights and the terms of his contract do not permit him to sell for use outside this country. I understand that patent laws do not allow of machines made here being used in England.
> Wright himself retains the rights in all other countries: I am in communication with him regarding the price he asks for his machines.
> Weiller's contract is so stringent that he was not allowed to make a present of two machines, as he wished to do, to the King of Spain and the Hon C. S. Rolls. But by special permission of Wright he has eventually been allowed to send one to the latter under very strict conditions.
> So far Weiller has received 58 orders from private customers. He is not permitted to state how many have been ordered by the French Government, but I know the number to be 30 for the present. He further informed me that the use of aeroplanes had been approved in principle for the French Army, and that to the best of his belief 10 per army corps were talked of.
> The Russian government has taken over the patent in Russia for its own use. (Not the *general* patent rights in the country). Forty million roubles have been allotted for this purpose, but probably a large proportion of this sum will stick to the fingers through which it passes.

[1] W.O. 32/8596. Lowther to Grahame, 25 November 1908 and Foreign Office transmission form dated 1 December 1908 addressed to the Army Council.

As soon as the weather settles down after the winter Weiller hopes to see six of his aeroplanes cross the Channel, and he was good enough to intimate that there would not be difficulty in obtaining a place as a passenger.

By February he intends to have completed an aeroplane carrying four persons and flying at the rate of 150 kilometres per hour.

Wright had an autograph letter from the German Emperor in which he requested that Herr von Lanken the councillor at the German Embassy here, should be taken up as a passenger, for he wished to have a personal report on the machine as soon as possible. It will be remembered that Herr von Lanken was one of the very first to accompany Wright on a flight. . . .

Wright is quarreling with his manager, Hart O. Berg just now, and all communications regarding purchase or patent rights should be made direct to Wright at the Hotel du Dauphin at Le Mans.

In due course Wilbur Wright replied to Colonel Lowther's letter. He offered a straightforward proposition:[1]

Replying to your letter . . . we could furnish flyers similar to those used at Le Mans and Washington at a price of one thousand pounds each.

With an order of 5 machines we would teach an operator to use them without additional charge. Flyers could be delivered in about six months from the placing of the order.

IX

Not all the British visitors who travelled to Le Mans were as impressed by the Wright aeroplane as were C. S. Rolls and Major Baden-Powell. Dr F. W. Lanchester, a prominent member of the Aeronautical Society of Great Britain, went to France and interviewed Wilbur Wright about his invention. Lanchester recognized the originality of the Wright design but his impressions were not entirely favourable. Gibbs-Smith in his *The Invention of The Aeroplane* has pointed to three mistakes made by the Wright brothers in the construction of their aeroplanes. Lanchester became aware of some of these facts as a result of his visit to France in 1908. Gibbs-Smith wrote:[2]

It is . . . important to note – albeit with the wisdom of hindsight – three of the Wrights' mistakes. . . . The first of these was in deliberately adopting an inherently unstable machine, instead of a com-

---

[1] Wright Brothers' Papers, Wright Bros to Lowther, 3 December 1908.
[2] Gibbs-Smith, *The Invention of The Aeroplane*, p. 35.

promise between sensitivity of control and inherent stability. The second was the adoption and retention of the forward elevator which is always far less satisfactory than a rear one, although there was a good reason for their having such a forward surface in their early days of gliding. The third mistake was to retain the skid undercarriage and accelerated take-off device long after they had outlived their usefulness. . . .

. . . As we see it today, they did not adopt a good configuration, but it was a workable configuration, and a cohesive one, and they triumphed with it. They mastered the theory and practice of aviation, construction and flight control, and – amazingly enough – added the mastery of design and construction of both propellers and engines. No other aviation pioneers came anywhere near such accomplishments.

Frederick William Lanchester was well known to his contemporaries as an engineer who had made pioneering contributions to the development of the motor car. He was also interested in the theory of flight. In 1907 and 1908 he published two brilliant books upon the subject. These works have been criticized because even specialists found them difficult to understand.

On 8 December 1908, at about the time Colonel Lowther's despatch was delivered to the Army Council, Lanchester read a paper entitled "The Wright and Voisin Types of Flying Machine" before the Aeronautical Society of Great Britain. This paper was published in *The Aeronautical Journal* for January 1909.

In his talk Lanchester identified the "most successful types of flying machine" as "those constructed by the Brothers Orville and Wilbur Wright, of the U.S.A., and by M M. Voisin frères of Billancourt, on the outskirts of Paris". Lanchester explained to his audience that he had observed both types of machine in flight and had collected enough data about them to "permit of an intelligent comparison being made between the two systems".

Lanchester began his lecture by paying a high tribute to the Wright brothers. He stated that after years of work they had "achieved, for the first time in history, free flight in a man-bearing machine propelled by its own motive power".

Later in his talk he pointed out that the Voisin machine was much heavier than the Wright aeroplane. The reason, he explained, was that the Voisin aircraft was fitted with four wheels mounted to swivel freely while the Wright design was equipped only with a pair of light wooden runners of comparatively little weight. Lanchester concluded: "If the runners of the Wright machine would do all that can be done by the Voisin mounting, then this additional weight would not be justified, but they will not do so. The Voisin machine can rise by itself from any reasonably smooth surface, the Wright is unable to take flight without its launching gear. . . ." In a footnote in the published version of his account Lanchester pointed out that the Wright aeroplane had undergone alterations which enabled it to rise from the ground by its own power. The Wright brothers knew, long before they demonstrated it in France, that their aeroplane could be fitted with wheels. At Kitty Hawk the skids or runners were more effective in the sand. Later Wright machines, of course, were equipped with wheels and in time the runners were abandoned.

Lanchester declared that the Wright propellers were more efficient than those used by Voisin. He also explained that the "Voisin machine is . . . slightly less efficient considered as a glider, that is to say, its gliding angle is not quite as good as that of the Wright machine – the machine is *aerodynamically* less efficient".

Lanchester was particularly critical of the instability of the Wright aeroplane in flight. He said:

> In the case of the Wright machine it is claimed by Mr. Wright himself that the stability depends entirely on the skill and address of the aeronaut; in fact . . . he does not believe in the possibility of safety, under ordinary weather conditions, being achieved by the inherent properties of the machine. He says that sooner or later the fatal puff must come that will end the flight.
>
> The author's own observations on the flight of the Wright machine fully confirms the statement that *Mr. Wright does depend entirely upon his manipulative skill*. . . .
>
> In brief, not only does Mr. Wright design definitely for hand-controlled equilibrium, but he has no belief in the possibility of making a machine safe by its own inherent stability. The success of the Wright method shows that *there is at least more than one way to fly*.
>
> In the Voisin machine, on the contrary, it has been the intention of the designer that the machine should be automatically and inherently stable. . . .
>
> . . . The author believes that the future of flight as a useful and practicable means of aerial navigation will depend definitely upon the abolition of hand-maintained equilibrium and the substitution of automatic stability, and already the Voisin machine goes a considerable way in this direction.

Aside from these valid technical criticisms of the Wright design another more subtle element played a part in the conclusions Dr Lanchester arrived at as a result of his meeting with Wilbur Wright. Orville and Wilbur were always keenly sensitive about their origins and background. Neither had received a university education. Many professional men they met refused to accept them as anything more than mere "mechanics". It was for this reason their sister insisted they should try to avoid appearing in public while they wore their working clothes. She always urged them to don starched collars, ties, and coats when they flew in the presence of others.

In 1909 Wilbur met a famous American architect named Cass Gilbert. The architect recorded his impressions of the meeting in a memorandum. This document clearly reflects the condescension the Wright brothers sometimes encountered in their dealings with formally trained scientists or members of the professional classes. Cass Gilbert described Wilbur as follows: "His personality interested me very much. . . . He seemed to be quite unostentatious and without any pose of manner. Very simple and direct and of few words, modestly spoken. He smiled occasionally with a sort of half smile that did not give the impression of much exuberance of spirit but rather of a provincial boy who had an underlying sense of humour and perfect confidence in himself but with a slightly provincial cynicism as to how seriously the other man might regard him or his views. He was totally impassive . . . but probably very keenly sensitive, and on the whole rather the type of high grade, intelligent and well read mechanic whom I occasionally meet in connection with building work. He looked like the student and shop man rather than the man of affairs or the pushing administrator of a factory. . . ."[1]

Dr Lanchester reacted to Wilbur in a somewhat similar way. He had rushed to Auvours to ascertain by personal observation the quality of the Wright invention. He sought further information by questioning Wilbur closely with respect to the theoretical and technical aspects of his machine. He seemed unable to understand that Wilbur Wright was not prepared to tell everything about his aeroplane to a visitor who was a complete stranger.

Years later when J. Laurence Pritchard analysed Lanchester's lecture in his *The Wright Brothers and the Royal Aeronautical Society* he wrote: "Lanchester had been over to France to watch Wilbur Wright fly and to ask all the questions, though he didn't get all the answers!" [2]

The French aeroplanes were beautifully finished machines. The Wright brothers were more interested in function and in mechanical efficiency than in outward appearance and their aircraft reflected this predilection. Lanchester's condescending attitude was made obvious in his lecture when he touched upon the "constructional methods" he had observed during his visit to France. He seemed surprised that the Wright aeroplane could fly at all. He said:

> The constructional methods employed by Wright and Voisin present a striking contrast. The Wright machine is astonishing in its

[1] The Cass Gilbert memorandum is printed in Walsh, *One Day at Kitty Hawk*, p. 289.

[2] Pritchard, *The Wright Brothers and the Royal Aeronautical Society*, p. 778.

simplicity – not to say in its apparent crudity of detail – it is almost a matter of surprise that it holds together. The Voisin machine has at least some pretensions to be considered an engineering job.

. . . the author feels (perhaps wrongly) that there is a considerable amount of the Wright "mechanical detail" that might be revised with advantage . . . However, "the proof of the pudding is in the eating", and in spite of the . . . aggressive simplicity of the constructional detail of the Wright machine, it appears not to come to pieces, but continues to fly day after day without showing any signs of weakness or disintegration.

The entire matter was more complex than Lanchester's various remarks suggest. In his analysis of the condition of aeronautics in the first half of the year 1909 Gibbs-Smith has written: ". . . it was the biplane which in the eyes of professional and amateur alike, still represented the only tried and reliable species of aeroplane during the first six months of the year; but even here, only two makes were fully established, the manoeuvrable two-seat Wright, with its rightful aura of fame; and the limited but reliable single-seat Voisin, already obsolescent, on which almost anyone in their right mind could become safely airborne in straight-hop flights in calm weather . . ." Gibbs-Smith continued: "But, by the close of the Reims meeting[1] . . . the *Henry Farman* biplane . . . had blazed its way into acceptance as the leading biplane of the day – and the morrow – with a highly attractive compromise between Wright-like manoeuvrability and Voisin-like stability . . . Close runner-up in this class of biplane, and superior in speed, was the Glenn Curtiss 'Reims machine'."[2]

However, contemporaries looked upon Dr Lanchester as a professional engineer of the highest accomplishments. In Britain his Lanchester Engine Company enjoyed a formidable reputation in every part of the country. Moreover, his theoretical treatises on the theory of flight were accepted as pioneering works of consequence. His opinions counted.

In 1909, as we shall see, R. B. Haldane decided, as he put it, to build up "the structure of the Air Service on a foundation of science. I therefore took the matter largely out of the departmental hands of the Master-General of the Ordnance, and going to the Prime Minister, got his authority to add a special section to the National Physical Laboratory at Teddington. There we installed a permanent Scientific Committee, paid for its work, including our best experts, both theoretical and practical."[3] This was the origin of the famous Advisory Committee for Aeronautics

[1] The Reims aviation meeting took place in August 1909.
[2] See Gibbs-Smith, *Aviation*, p. 140.
[3] Haldane, *Autobiography*, p. 233.

which did such splendid work for British aeronautics in the decades that followed. The first president of the committee was an eminent and distinguished scientist, Lord Rayleigh. Dr F. W. Lanchester was appointed as one of its founding members and worked with it for years thereafter. He was exactly the kind of man Haldane wanted to advise the chief political authorities in the State about the new technology of aeronautics and aviation.

Meanwhile, other developments in the world of aeronautics impelled the prime minister to embark upon an initiative of his own. In October 1908 Asquith appointed a special sub-committee of the Committee of Imperial Defence to look into the entire matter of "Aerial Navigation". He wanted its expert members to ascertain the dangers to which Britain might be exposed by the further development of airships and aeroplanes.

CHAPTER 13

The Aerial Navigation Committee

The British Press and Aviation – Privy Councillor Rudolf
Martin and an Air Invasion of England – Another *Daily
Mail* Prize – Ten Thousand Zeppelins – The French Ac-
quire Wright Aeroplanes – The Prime Minister Reacts – He
Appoints a Committee – An Event of Great Consequence –
Lord Esher as Chairman – Captain Bacon, The Admiralty
Representative – Sir William Nicholson – R. B. Haldane's
Remarkable Course – Lloyd George's Interest – The War
Office Documents – Situation of Aeronautics in Various
Countries – Use of Dirigible Balloons for Destructive Pur-
poses – Expenditures on Aeronautics – Russian Activity –
Sir William Nicholson Dominates – Haldane's Analysis –
Captain Bacon's Opinion – Sir Charles Ottley on the
German Attitude – Air Bombardment by Dirigibles –
C. S. Rolls Interviewed – "The French Have Been Train-
ing Men to Drop Explosives" – Airships Are Capable of
Causing an Immense Amount of Destruction – Lloyd
George Asks if they can "Set Towns on Fire?" – "England
Will Cease to be an Island" – Major Baden-Powell's
Evidence – Colonel Capper Examined – Sir Charles
Hadden Interrupts the Proceedings – A Letter from
Lieutenant Dunne – Sir William Nicholson's Idea – Lord
Esher Informs the King – Winston Churchill Intervenes –
Sir Hiram Maxim Interviewed – Effect of Air Bombard-
ment on London – The Final Report – The Proposal
of C. S. Rolls – He Volunteers to Obtain Information from
the Wright Brothers – Winston Churchill Objects – A New
Course.

I

In the autumn of 1908 as the Wright brothers astounded the world by their
magnificent flights in France and in the United States the Press in Britain
paid more and more attention to the development of aeronautics in every
country. Several themes were stressed. It was pointed out that Britain
lagged far behind her continental rivals in the new technology. Some

newspapers urged the government to purchase Wright aeroplanes and so make a start in this area of the nation's defences. The hostility of Imperial Germany and German interest in aeronautics were combined in several analyses of the contemporary situation and the conclusion was offered that a new German threat to British life had now emerged. The possibility of a forthcoming flight across the English Channel was sometimes mentioned to highlight and make more immediate the nature of the danger.

However, not all the comments were negative. Some articles speculated upon the non-military aspects of successful mechanical flight and discussed the various contributions to human civilization that aeroplanes might make in the future. The Wright brothers had aroused men's interest in flying as it had not been aroused before. As a result a good deal of meditation, reflection, and conjecture followed upon their several triumphs in the air.

Lord Northcliffe saw to it that his *Daily Mail* took up and maintained a prominent role in this trend or development. Articles concerned with aeronautics and aviation appeared in its pages upon a regular basis. When Orville Wright crashed his machine at Fort Myer, R. P. Hearne was invited to write a special article about the tragedy in the *Daily Mail* for 19 September. Hearne argued that the mishap was no cause for discouragement. Lessons would be learned as a result of the accident and the technology of flight would advance as a consequence. "It will not", he explained, "have the least effect on the principles or progress of aeronautics, as to every intelligent man it has now been amply demonstrated that flight is practicable and that the Wrights have several grand secrets which enable them to make more rapid progress than their rivals."

Hearne stressed, in his article, that the future of flying was bright. However, he took care to end his essay upon a dismal note. He took up a theme which dominated Lord Northcliffe's appreciation of the situation. Aeronautical progress was being made in several countries but in Britain there was only stagnation, lethargy, and failure. Hearne's article concluded by pointing out: "The one note of regret in all this advance and activity is that so little is being done in England. Our War Office has dismantled its second dirigible balloon after a short and inglorious career, and so far not a single successful aeroplane has been flown in the United Kingdom. We are painfully backward in every branch of aerial navigation; and yet for naval and military reasons it is most essential that we should lead the world in the new science."

It may be observed that the negative attitude expressed in this article was typical of the outlook of many in Britain in the period after the Boer War. Edwardians, unlike their predecessors in Victorian England, were not confident about the future of their country. A sense of insecurity and uneasiness dominated their generation. The Army had performed incom-

petently in the South African War. It was no longer possible for manufacturers to look for that inevitable increase of British exports which had
marked out the great days of the Victorian era. British agriculture seemed
to be in an even worse condition than her manufactures. Her workers
were grumbling and discontented. The failure to maintain the pace set by
foreign rivals in the field of aeronautics seemed, to many, to be yet
another part of this dismal pattern, another indication that Great Britain
was falling behind in those areas of national activity where previously she
had been the leader among the nations of the world. Some despaired of
this development. Others, like Northcliffe, meant to see to it that Britain
forged ahead in aeronautics and overtook the Germans, the French, the
Americans and any other competitors in order to become yet again a
world leader, in a technology that was certain to be immeasurably
significant in the years to come.

Northcliffe also saw to it that his Berlin correspondent, F. W. Wile,
kept a vigilant eye upon the activities of Privy Councillor Rudolf Martin,
the German enthusiast who believed that Britain lay open to an invasion
from the air. Martin, president of the newly formed German motor-
airship league, was now pressing for the establishment of a German
aeroplane fleet. He also proposed, according to Wile's account published
in the *Daily Mail* of 25 September, to travel to Le Mans in order to induce
Wilbur Wright to attempt a flight across the English Channel from Calais
to Dover: "Herr Martin will assure Mr. Wright that if he accomplishes
this, 'public opinion in Germany will forthwith demand the acquisition of
an enormous number of Wright aeroplanes for military purposes'. If Mr.
Wright entertains Herr Martin's proposal the latter will 'accompany' him
over the Channel in a fast motor-boat and embody his impressions in a
brochure dealing with the landing of a German army in England by means
of airships."

On 28 September the *Daily Mail* began to publish an entire series of
articles entitled "Man in The Air". The paper explained to its readers that
while the science of aviation was still experimental such rapid progress
had been made of late that the problems remaining were almost exclusively mechanical. In such circumstances aerial navigation was certain to
become a general means of locomotion and the time had therefore
arrived to "survey the immense social changes it will bring". The first
article of the series argued that it could be taken for granted that the
future lay with aeroplanes and not with dirigible airships. In subsequent
articles it was predicted that giant aeroplanes would carry large numbers
of passengers. When this occurred an international authority of some
kind would have to be appointed to regulate traffic in the air, to make
laws, and to see to it they were enforced. This international board, with
the passage of time, would grow to an immense size: "Beginning tentatively with subsidies, it will become rapidly the most independent and

wealthy of corporations, levying its dues and rates in the uttermost parts of the earth".

On 5 October the *Daily Mail* offered another of its aviation prizes. The proprietors of the paper undertook to pay the sum of five hundred pounds to the first person who flew across the English Channel in an aeroplane, from France to England or from England to France. The paper pointed out to its readers that the shortest distance across the channel was twenty one miles and that both Wilbur Wright and Henri Farman had already exceeded this distance in their machines.

Clearly, the offer of this prize was aimed not only at the daring aviators who might attempt to win it but also at those authorities in the British War Office who had haughtily explained in their pronouncement of 23 July 1908 that they might be prepared to regard recent aeronautical experiments seriously when it became possible "to cross the Channel, say with a party of excursionists, and to land at any fixed point. . . ."

In Berlin, Privy Councillor Rudolf Martin continued to advocate the construction of a huge fleet of Zeppelins that could be employed for the invasion of England. F. W. Wile reported his latest exploits in an article published in the *Daily Mail* on 9 October. At a public meeting in the German capital Martin "fired the imagination of his hearers . . . with a plan for the conquest of England by airships. He asserted that the principal duty of aerial navigators was to induce the combined Continental Powers to construct a fleet of 10,000 'Zeppelins', each to carry twenty soldiers, which should land and capture the sleeping Britons before they could realise what was taking place."

The account of this meeting was not written in alarmist tones. Wile made clear that before he ended his talk Rudolf Martin's audience began to laugh at some of his notions and theories. Martin predicted that the ships of the British Fleet would instantly abandon the coasts when the airships came into view so that they could avoid the shells that might be dropped upon them from the skies. He also believed that artillery and cavalry could be landed in England as easily as his proposed force of two hundred thousand infantrymen. Wiles wrote: "Before he finished his alluring sketch of Great Britain's fall his audience was rocking with merriment, but not altogether at the expense of England."

On 13 October the *Daily Mail* struck a more serious note when it informed its readers that one hundred Wright aeroplanes were to be built in France. Fifty of these machines would be purchased by the Ministry of Marine for service with the coastguard. Moreover, the paper explained, the French military authorities were about to acquire Wright aeroplanes for the Army. When Joseph Reinach, at this time a member of the Army Commission of the Chamber of Deputies, witnessed one of Wilbur Wright's record-breaking flights he declared: "There is no time to waste, no reason to wait. The Wright aeroplane is sufficiently practical to be used by the Army. It will make a wonderful change in scouting. I shall speak of it to the Army Commission."

The *Daily Mail*, on the next day, published a report that the British War Office had not failed to take note of Wilbur Wright's successful experiments at Le Mans. The paper correctly pointed out that the Lazare Weiller syndicate had acquired the French rights in the machine but that the British rights had not yet been sold. It further declared: "There is ample margin in the Estimates for the War Office to buy these rights the moment it is considered desirable. The British Army authorities will not be slow to move at the proper moment, and it may be taken for granted that they are very much awake to the advantages which a perfect aeroplane will confer."

Lord Northcliffe's object in publishing a news item like this one was to force the authorities in the War Office into an active course. He wanted a valid start of some kind to be made by the British Army in the field of aeronautics. In his view they had already delayed for too long.

Everyone knew, by this time, that the Army's *Nulli Secundus* airships were a failure. There was reason to hope that S. F. Cody might succeed with his aeroplane. Less information was available about Lieutenant Dunne's experiments in Scotland. The key for Northcliffe, and he was not alone in this opinion, was that the Army had now at once to advance along positive lines or else fall even further behind the French and the Germans. This could only be done by purchasing Wright aeroplanes. These machines flew more successfully than any others. There could be no doubt that more efficient aircraft would be produced in the future. However, Northcliffe's point was that the British military authorities could no longer afford to wait upon events.

A Military Air Service had become a requirement for the national defence. Hesitation to establish one would endanger the country. As Northcliffe saw it a genuine beginning in this new sphere could be made only if the War Office purchased Wright machines as quickly as possible.

This was the condition of aeronautical affairs when the prime minister decided to act. By October 1908 Asquith had determined that the time had come when the British Government was required to examine, as thoroughly as possible, the entire question of "Aerial Navigation". He turned to the Committee of Imperial Defence to carry out this duty:[1]

---

[1] See Cab. 16/7. "Report and Proceedings of A Sub-Committee of the Committee of Imperial Defence on Aerial Navigation", dated 28 January 1909 and marked "*SECRET.*" There is an excellent account of this sub-committee's work in Percy Walker, *Early Aviation at Farnborough*, vol. II, pp. 284ff. Extracts from its report are also published in Captain S. W. Roskill ed., *Documents Relating To The Naval Air Service*, Volume I (London, 1969), pp. 5ff. This work is hereafter cited as Roskill, *Naval Air Service*.

SECRET.

AERIAL NAVIGATION

Terms of Reference

Several of the Great Powers are turning their attention to the question of aerial navigation, and are spending large sums in the development of dirigible balloons and aeroplanes.

It is probable that for countries with land frontiers immediately across which lie potential enemies the development of airships has hitherto been more important than it is for Great Britain, and that we have been justified for this reason in spending less money in experiments than some of our neighbours.

The success that has attended recent experiments in France, Germany, and America has, however, created a new situation, which appears to render it advisable that the subject of aerial navigation should be investigated, and the Prime Minister desires that a Sub-Committee of the Committee of Imperial Defence, consisting of –

Lord Esher (Chairman)	Captain Bacon,
Mr. Lloyd George,	Sir W. Nicholson,
Mr. Haldane,	Major-General Ewart,
Mr. KcKenna,	Sir C. Hadden
	Sir C. Ottley (Secretary).

should meet and report as to –

(a) The dangers to which we would be exposed on sea or on land by any development in aerial navigation reasonably probable in the near future.

(b) The naval or military advantages that we might expect to derive from the use of air-ships or aeroplanes.

(c) The amount that should be allotted to expenditure on aerial experiments, and the Department to which it should be allotted.

October 23, 1908

II

The establishment of this sub-committee of the Committee of Imperial Defence was an event of the very greatest consequence, a landmark in the history of British military aeronautics. It was obvious that the significance of the subject was recognized even though practical aeronautics in 1908 was still in its infancy. Some of the most powerful and important members of the government were asked to involve themselves in the work of the sub-committee.

Lord Esher, the chairman, was recognized by his contemporaries as a strategic thinker of the highest quality. He was also a courtier of long experience, an intimate friend and adviser of the king. Esher moved easily and elegantly among the leaders of each of the great political parties. He knew all the chief officers in the Army and the Navy. He had been largely responsible for the reform of the War Office in Balfour's administration and had played an important role in the creation of the Committee of Imperial Defence itself. He was a man of influence – at the Palace, in the War Office, and at the Admiralty. Esher always sought to avoid the formal trappings of office but he meant to act with those who fashioned the destiny of the State. It was his habit to work discreetly, behind the scenes. He knew how to get things done in the highest circles of British life.

The soldiers who were asked to serve on the sub-committee included the Chief of the General Staff and some of his closest associates and subordinates. We have already noticed the warm admiration of the Secretary of State for Sir William Nicholson's abilities and capacities. In 1908 Nicholson became Chief of the Imperial General Staff.

Captain Bacon, the Admiralty representative, was one of the most brilliant officers in his Service. He possessed the complete confidence of Admiral Sir John Fisher, the powerful First Sea Lord, and acted throughout on his instructions during all the meetings of the sub-committee. It may well be that Fisher was not asked to serve himself because of his well-known hostility to General Sir William Nicholson, "Old Nick" as the Admiral liked to call him. Nevertheless, Fisher's presence was felt throughout the course of the sub-committee's deliberations. Reginald Bacon was his vigilant agent, deputy and surrogate. He saw to it that the Admiralty obtained what it wanted when the final decisions were made.

Rear-Admiral Sir Charles Ottley, the secretary of the sub-committee, was a naval officer noted for his tact, patience, and ability to persuade others. He was also secretary of the Committee of Imperial Defence at this time.

The prime minister, it is clear, had assembled a formidable team. Nevertheless, when Percy Walker analysed the work of this sub-committee he wrote and with good cause: ". . . the report of the sub-committee was indeed open to much adverse criticism".[1]

One reason for the failures of this sub-committee was that only two men who served on it knew exactly what they wanted to obtain as a result of its deliberations and conclusions.

The first of these was the chief army representative, General Sir William Nicholson. Owing to his high rank he often dominated the meetings of the Aerial Navigation Sub-Committee. Sir William was firm

---

[1] Walker, *Early Aviation at Farnborough*, vol. II, p. 327.

in his convictions. He was unable to see that much of military value could be secured by the employment of any device of aeronautical technology. He condemned almost equally kites, observation balloons, dirigible airships, and aeroplanes. General Nicholson, as we know, was always aggressive and quarrelsome in debate. He followed his usual course in these deliberations. He was not anxious for the British Army to involve itself in aeronautics at all and he impressed this opinion upon his colleagues at every meeting of the sub-committee. His ideas were reflected in the final report.

The second man who knew what he wanted was the naval representative, Captain Bacon. At this time Admiral Sir John Fisher was determined to secure for the British Navy a large rigid dirigible of the Zeppelin type. He believed that such airships could perform invaluable service for the fleets as scouts. Bacon's assigned task was to see to it that the committee recommended construction of such a dirigible. An unpublished Admiralty paper, a history of "Rigid Airships of Zeppelin Type", preserved in the Public Record Office in London, states: "Lord Fisher instructed Admiral Bacon to press for the construction of Rigid Airships for Naval purposes at the meetings of a sub-committee of the C.I.D., which held their first meeting in December 1908 . . . . Bacon presented the Naval point of view with much lucidity."[1] The Aerial Navigation Sub-Committee, in its final report, recommended that funds should be included in the Naval Estimates for the construction of a dirigible airship of a rigid type.

The other members of the sub-committee had no fixed objectives in their minds. Lord Esher, the chairman, performed his duties in his usual devoted, bland, and efficient way. He sought to ascertain the separate opinions of the representatives of the Army and the Navy. He hesitated to put forward positive conclusions of his own.

Richard Burdon Haldane's position was the most significant and the most curious of all. Percy Walker has variously described it as "cryptic" and "devious". Walker also wrote of him in this period: "Haldane's actions behind the scenes may never be known with certainty."[2]

Haldane was keenly interested in the entire subject of aeronautics. He was very much aware of the military potential of dirigibles and aeroplanes. But he never disagreed with Sir William Nicholson's ridiculous comments and never opposed any of his ludicrous suggestions about aircraft which were poured forth regularly and freely at each of the sub-committee's meetings.

[1] See Air 1/2442/6/4. "Rigid Airships of Zeppelin Type". This paper was written in 1916 and was originally a part of the collection of Admiral Sir Murray Sueter, a pioneer in the British Navy's work with dirigibles.

[2] See Walker, *Early Aviation at Farnborough*, vol. II, p. 273, and p. 328, and vol. I, p. 254.

As Secretary of State Haldane had paid careful attention to the aeronautical experiments carried out at Farnborough under Colonel Capper's direction. In his enthusiasm, as we have noted, he had even travelled to Blair Atholl in 1907 to observe Lieutenant Dunne at work with his machines. But now he had had enough of amateurs like Capper, Cody and Dunne. They were mere "empiricists". During the third meeting of the Aerial Navigation Sub-Committee Lord Esher, in the course of the deliberations, asked Haldane if he would like to see Dunne in order to question him about aeroplanes. Haldane's exasperation was made obvious when he replied. He snapped back about Dunne: "I have had long talks with him, and I do not think you will get any more from him".[1]

Haldane desired to strike out upon an entirely different course. He believed that the problems of artificial flight were too complex to be solved by non-scientific enthusiasts like Capper or Dunne. He wanted to embark, as we shall see, upon a programme of systematic scientific research. He wanted to secure for the government the services of qualified scientists who could discover the principles of flight, in the first instance. When these were established they could then be exploited to produce efficient military aircraft for employment with the Armed Forces.

When the Aerial Navigation Sub-Committee recommended that the British Army should at once abandon its experiments with aeroplanes Haldane did not object or disagree. Shortly after, he got rid of Capper, Cody, and Dunne. They were removed from the official Farnborough scene.

Within the year, however, Haldane saw to it that a scientific body, the Advisory Committee for Aeronautics, was established and that Mervyn O'Gorman, an experienced mechanical engineer, was appointed in Colonel Capper's room as Superintendent of the Balloon Factory. O'Gorman was aided and supported by the advice and recommendations of an organized body of scientists who were paid on a regular basis to make technical contributions to the further development of British military aeronautics. The generals of Sir William Nicholson's school objected to this course of action but O'Gorman was placed directly under the Secretary of State with access to him so that the authorities in the War Office could not interfere with his work. Haldane carried out these tremendous changes in a mysterious way. He never offered a clear explanation of the courses he adopted. Percy Walker has written of him,

---

[1] For the remark see Cab. 16/7. "Report and Proceedings . . ." etc. All further quotations in this chapter, unless otherwise indicated are drawn from this source, The Report and Proceedings of a Sub-Committee of the Committee of Imperial Defence on Aerial Navigation, 28 January 1909, "*SECRET*".

probably correctly, that: "A . . . likely explanation . . . is that he saw in the Committee's recommendations an opportunity to rebuild Farnborough to his own design. The decision to abandon aeroplane work there was a purely military one, and could be reversed at an opportune time – as indeed it was – and he himself was, after all, Secretary of State."[1]

A second politician who served on the sub-committee was Reginald McKenna. He had recently been appointed First Lord of the Admiralty, the political head of the British Navy. McKenna was a financial expert and a man who knew how to fight for his own views. At the Admiralty he soon fell under the sway of Sir John Fisher and then did all he could to help Fisher in his work. During the meetings of the Aerial Navigation Sub-Committee McKenna took care to placate General Nicholson, at discreet intervals, so that a dispute between the two Services did not arise.

Lloyd George was the most powerful political figure. He did not attend all the sub-committee's meetings. He revealed a particular interest in the possibility that British towns might be bombed from the air. He was also concerned that aircraft might be employed in an invasion of the British Isles. The impressions he had formed at Echterdingen still lingered in his mind.

The two soldiers who served with Sir William Nicholson on the committee were Major-General Sir Charles Hadden, the Master-General of the Ordnance, and Major-General J. Spencer Ewart, the Director of Military Operations. They were careful to support their chief throughout.

The sub-committee held four formal meetings. It interviewed several expert witnesses. At the end of its deliberations it produced a report and the minutes of its meetings. Together with a number of appendices the Report and Proceedings amounted to ninety eight printed foolscap pages, a document of tremendous size. This paper was to influence British strategic thought for a long time to come. The printed minutes of the sub-committee, it may be mentioned, present a fascinating picture of Britain's military leaders in council, deliberating upon the best methods to adopt and the best procedures to employ in order to ensure the safety of their country.

III

The Admiralty submitted no documents to the sub-committee but the War Office produced a number of papers which dealt with various aspects of the subject of Aerial Navigation. These were later printed as appendices to the report. Some of the War Office papers were produced before

---

[1] Walker, *Early Aviation at Farnborough*, vol. II, p. 274.

the committee began its work and others appeared during the course of its deliberations.

The long letter written by Colonel H. C. Lowther, the British Military Attaché in Paris, which had been transmitted to the Army Council ón 1 December 1908 was not included in this collection of papers. It will be recalled that in this letter Colonel Lowther revealed that the French Government had already ordered thirty Wright aeroplanes for service with the Army; that the Russian Government had set aside large sums for the purchase of these machines; that Lazare Weiller, head of the Wright syndicate in France, planned to fly six of his machines across the English Channel; and that the German Emperor himself had requested Wilbur Wright to demonstrate his aeroplane to an official of the German Embassy in Paris so that a report about its performance could be sent to Berlin as quickly as possible. The Aerial Navigation Sub-Committee was not presented with any of this information although many of the papers submitted to it were prepared or received in the War Office after Colonel Lowther's letter arrived there.

The first of the War Office documents was a memorandum dated 27 November 1908, prepared by the General Staff, entitled "Memorandum by the War Office on Progress in Aerial Navigation". This paper was printed as Appendix II in the report. It was a survey that dealt with aeronautical developments in France, Germany, Italy, Russia, the United States, and the United Kingdom.

An introductory paragraph stated: "The Governments of the countries which have as yet taken the matter up, have approached the subject from the military point of view. The question is of importance to the United Kingdom, for substantial success in aerial navigation might materially modify our defensive policy."

In France, the memorandum explained, experiments had been carried out with dirigible balloons and with aeroplanes. Lebaudy and other airships had been employed and the French War Office had recently acquired additional land for an "aerostatic park". Trials of aeroplanes designed by French officers were being undertaken. The most successful aeroplane used in France, the War Office memorandum declared, was that invented by the Wright brothers.

In Germany experiments had been almost entirely devoted to the development of dirigible balloons. The memorandum listed several of these including the Zeppelin, the Parseval airship, the Gross airship, and a dirigible built by the Siemens-Schuckert firm. The memorandum revealed that the Parseval airship had been taken over by the German military authorities. Experiments were being made with it to determine the best method of dropping projectiles from airships. The memorandum offered the conclusion that at that time projectiles could not be dropped from a dirigible "with any approach to accuracy".

One military dirigible balloon had been constructed in Italy. Considerable public interest in the subject of aeroplanes had been aroused in that country and the British General Staff believed that a military machine was being built there.

In Russia, the memorandum reported, aeronautics had received little attention. However, the military authorities were becoming more interested in the subject and a dirigible balloon, the "Uchebeni", had begun its trials in September 1908.

The United States Government was actively engaged in experiments with dirigibles and aeroplanes. The War Office memorandum pointed out that the U.S. Signal Corps had expended the sum of one thousand pounds on aeronautical developments in 1902 but it was asking for an appropriation of two hundred thousand pounds for the year 1909. The Americans had established an "aeronautical park" in Omaha where experiments in photography and wireless telegraphic communication were made "on a large scale". The Wright aeroplane figured prominently in this section of the War Office memorandum: "This machine is the result of eight years' secret experiment by the Brothers Wright. The trials at Washington were undertaken by O. Wright, but were cut short by a serious accident . . . otherwise it was thought that his machine would have fulfilled the conditions laid down . . . The advantages claimed for the Wright machine are solidity and easy control; the disadvantage urged is that this control is not automatic. This difficulty may possibly be surmounted."

In the United Kingdom the most serious aeronautical work had been undertaken, the memorandum said, at the Army Balloon Factory at Farnborough. Experiments had been carried out there with dirigible balloons. Although S. F. Cody and Lieutenant Dunne were not mentioned by name reference was made to their activities in the War Office memorandum: "An aeroplane has been tried. It promised to be at least as successful as the 'Delagrange' or 'Farman' machines, though possibly inferior to the 'Wright'. An accident in turning has, however, stopped further experiment at present. Another aeroplane of new design has been constructed, and will, it is understood, be tried shortly."

The survey ended at this point. The memorandum then offered the following thoughtful conclusions of the General Staff. They bear upon the early history of the Air Defence of Great Britain:

> The question of the employment of dirigible balloons and aeroplanes in war depends so much on their mechanical development that it is idle to dogmatize. Under favourable atmospheric conditions the dirigible balloon has achieved a certain measure of success, and it may be assumed that the intention is to use these machines for destructive purposes as well as for reconnaissance in war. The German Plenipotentiaries did not sign the Agreement come to at the second Hague Conference to prohibit the use of explosives dropped

from balloons, and Germany is therefore in no way bound by that Convention. Consequently, if the mechanical development of these machines admits of it, it is conceivable that they might eventually be used for the purpose of attacking dockyards, arsenals, and railway centres, and possibly also for the creation of panic among the civil population of great cities.

While the use of dirigible balloons for destructive purposes remains as yet but a possibility, it is contended by our experts that the success achieved in France and Germany has been sufficient to make dirigible balloons a necessary adjunct of modern armies for extended reconnaissance. But as it is understood that no reconnaissances have hitherto been attempted, their value for military purposes cannot be predicted.

As regards the vulnerability of these large vessels, it seems probable that, should they move at a great height and at a rapid pace, they would form an extremely difficult target for artillery. On the other hand, if they were to move at a slow pace and low altitude, they could probably be hit without much difficulty.

It will be observed that the conclusions of the General Staff presented in this memorandum of November 1908 were far more prudent than the observations made in the War Office pronouncement published on 23 July 1908.

Two enclosures were attached to this General Staff memorandum of 27 November 1908 and included in Appendix II of the final report of the sub-committee. The first was a note prepared by the War Office dealing with the expenditure by foreign Powers on aerial navigation. The War Office readily admitted that the figures it supplied could not be looked upon as exact. They were intended to serve as a guide.

The United States had not spent much in the period 1902 to 1908 but the sum of two hundred thousand pounds was requested for aeronautical purposes in 1909. Since 1906 the French Government had spent more than forty thousand pounds per year for military ballooning but it was expected that this amount would be almost doubled in 1909. In Germany the government had steadily increased its expenditures in this field. In 1908 more than one hundred and thirty thousand pounds had been voted for airships, balloon materials, and ancillary services. Furthermore, private enterprise played a considerable part in the estimate of total German expenditure. The Zeppelin Air-Ship Fund had collected two hundred and sixty five thousand pounds. In Italy about fifteen thousand pounds had been spent in 1907 and 1908 for work connected with aerial navigation.

The second enclosure was a despatch, dated 15 December 1908, from Colonel Guy Wyndham, the British Military Attaché in St Petersburg. It was entitled: "The Development of Aerial Navigation in Russia".

Wyndham revealed that the Russian Government was subsidizing private experiments with aeroplanes. In its budget for the year 1908 the sum of £216,950 had been granted for dirigibles. Colonel Wyndham presented his superiors with a further revelation in his despatch: "Mr. Wilbur Wright in Paris has for some time been negotiating with the Russian Government, and has already received an order for ten aeroplanes. The arrangement includes instruction in their use. Four officers have been sent from Russia to receive this instruction."

IV

The first formal meeting of the Aerial Navigation Sub-Committee took place on 1 December 1908. All the members save for Lloyd George were present. On this occasion no expert witnesses were examined by the committee but W. A. Bland of the Financial Department of the War Office was interviewed at the end of the meeting. He supplied members with certain pertinent financial information dealing with British expenditure on aerial navigation in the period 1902–1908.

At this first session the committee members discussed the subject among themselves, at some length. They took up the issue of the military value of captive observation balloons. They dealt also with the possibility of employing airships, or dirigible balloons as they were sometimes called, for purposes of reconnaissance over the land and the sea and examined the question of using airships as offensive weapons, as machines that could be used to drop projectiles upon enemy targets.

General Sir William Nicholson dominated much of the discussion. We know that he was a brilliant officer who favourably impressed Haldane and others in the highest circles of the British Government. He was regularly able to cross swords successfully with anyone who disagreed with him. He was so capable, in debate, that he could defy an opponent as formidable as Sir John Fisher, whenever he chose. The significance and the quality of his achievements were recognized by the State. In 1911 he was promoted to the rank of Field-Marshal and in the following year he was raised to the peerage as Baron Nicholson.

Nevertheless, Percy Walker, the technical expert and aeronautical enthusiast, was so distressed by Nicholson's performance as a member of the Aerial Navigation Sub-Committee that in his authorized history he wrote of him in the harshest terms: "In the interests of British aviation it was most unfortunate that a man in such an exalted position should be opposed to aerial activity in all or any of its forms . . . On the face of things, here was a man who, having reached the normal retiring age, was in deadly earnest in opposing any innovation that might render him personally obsolescent. Such an attitude especially in the somewhat decadent Edwardian age, is perhaps understandable, but it takes more than elderly prejudice to explain many of the things he has to say. His logic is usually faulty; most of his alleged facts are spurious; and his arithmetic would scarcely be tolerated in a young schoolboy."[1] At the first meeting of the Aerial Navigation Sub-Committee the logic and the arithmetic, we may observe, were most certainly tolerated when they came from the Chief of the General Staff.

Although Lord Esher was chairman he allowed R. B. Haldane to make the opening statement at the first meeting of the committee. In these preliminary remarks Haldane indicated the nature of his own attitude. What he said amounted almost to an exact prediction of the course he chose to follow later on:

> 1. MR. HALDANE: I think it is a great advantage that we have got the Admiralty here to consider this question in conjunction with the War Office, because at the root of the whole thing there are big questions *in limine* which, I think we ought to clear up before we go further – such questions as what we want these things for, what they can do, and (which I think the most important one of all) the conditions under which alone we can reckon on real progress being made in the investigations. . . . what has struck me – is the little attempt which has been made, at any rate so far as the War Office is concerned, to answer these questions. You are new to this, Captain Bacon, and I think you will concede that there are a great many things as to the conditions which have to be ascertained before successful control can be established. In ship-building, I think you would consider yourselves very incompletely equipped unless you had an experimental tank for working out your problems with models. If ever there was a question which required experimental work on models it is this. . . . I do not feel sure whether one of the things we should consider is not the recommendation of a small Commission or Committee to look into this. The Explosives Committee, for instance, under Lord Rayleigh, took up the question of cordite, with, I think, very good effect. I am not sure whether we do not require systematic scientific guidance in our work. Here is a question I should like this Committee to consider: whether there should not be a very small Commission, say, with an expert from the Admiralty (someone with the knowledge of Captain Bacon) and one expert from us of standing, and somebody presiding over it like Lord Rayleigh, or Lord Justice Fletcher Moulton, or Sir George Darwin. . . . This seems to me a very important preliminary to any real progress, otherwise we may go pottering on and accomplish very little. . . . before we can make real progress, I should like to know what scientific work has been done on the Continent, and whether we are or not in a position to do the proper scientific work.

[1] Walker, *Early Aviation at Farnborough*, vol. II, p. 292.

Lord Esher then took charge. The discussion soon turned to an analysis of the value of captive balloons for observation in war. Haldane looked upon them as "very useful and necessary things". The Chief of the General Staff disagreed. After an exchange between Haldane and Nicholson, Lord Esher summed up: ". . . Sir William Nicholson's view is that, from the point of view of military needs, these captive observation balloons are a waste of money".

Next, Lord Esher introduced the subject of navigable or dirigible balloons. Sir William Nicholson at once made it clear that these airships, in his opinion, were of little value for warfare on land. Sir Charles Hadden expressed his agreement with this view. Sir William further argued that ". . . you can use wireless telegraphy to a balloon, but . . . you cannot use wireless telegraphy from a balloon, because there is a great danger that the gas in the balloon would at once explode because of the spark".

Shortly after, Captain Reginald Bacon intervened for the first time. His orders from Admiral Fisher were to do what he could to secure a large rigid dirigible for service with the Navy. He presented his case with some care. Bacon suggested that large airships could be employed as scouts over certain waters. He wanted a very large vessel because he expected these aerial scouts to be in action for several days at a time. They had to be equipped with places where the men could rest when they were replaced on duty by relief watches. Furthermore, Bacon disagreed with Haldane about the value of an advisory committee. In his view the task of airship development should be put into the hands of one man. "Anybody who undertakes this work", Bacon said, "has open to him the work of scientific England, which he has only got to tap; but if you put anything into the hands of an Advisory Committee, it will never make any progress . . . if you put anything like the building of an air-ship into the hands of a Committee, it will largely lead to disappointment". Discreetly, Bacon also corrected Sir William Nicholson with respect to wireless telegraphy from an airship: "In regard to the other point of wireless telegraphy, I think we get over the difficulty, as far as our purposes are concerned, by inclosing the spark; that is a detail."

Eventually, Lord Esher summed up:

> 105. LORD ESHER: The broad conclusion I have come to is that, from the naval point of view, in reconnaissance these dirigible balloons, if they fulfilled certain conditions . . . would be of value; but from the military point of view, whatever conditions are fulfilled, in reconnaissance they would not be of much material value. That is the conclusion which I have come to listening to what Sir William Nicholson and Captain Bacon have said.

Haldane was uneasy with these statements. He believed airships could be of great value in assisting the British military authorities in home defence against invasion. He said: ". . . supposing we had the naval balloon perfected in this country – I can conceive that they might give us enormous help for military purposes for home defence; I mean the assistance of the naval balloon might be very great in locating the point to which an invading force was coming, or where they were if they landed. . . ."

Having established these conclusions about the reconnaissance value of airships, the sub-committee next took up the question of the destructive potentialities of these aerial vessels. Lord Esher first requested Sir William Nicholson's opinion. The general argued that no one, as yet, knew very much about the subject but he believed that if the airships flew at a considerable height they would be unable to hit a target with any degree of accuracy. Furthermore, he explained, he did not believe that the physical effect of explosives dropped from a height would be very great. In this connection Haldane made a telling point. He said: "The moral effect might be very great, while the physical effect might be very little."

Earlier in the meeting when they were still discussing airship reconnaissance Major-General Ewart had presented a somewhat different point of view to the committee. Ewart argued that foreign Powers were building airships not chiefly for purposes of reconnaissance but because of their destructive power as aerial bombers. He remarked:

> Sir William has asked me what I think about it. I do not know that I go quite so far as Sir William does, because I see that foreign Powers are devoting very large sums of money to the development of these air-ships for military purposes. . . .
> I do not think anything very much is known, but I think at present they are paying more attention to the destructive aspect of the thing than they are to reconnaissance.

Eventually, Lord Esher called upon Sir Charles Ottley to read out portions of the Hague Conference declaration dealing with air bombing, the declaration we noticed in an earlier chapter of this history. Ottley did so and also let it be known that he took a much more serious view of bombardment from the air than did Sir William Nicholson. He was especially concerned by the attitude of the Imperial German Government. He pointed out about the Hague declaration of 1907:

> This is a declaration relating to the firing of large projectiles and explosives from balloons. . . . The important thing is to know those who did not sign. First and foremost, Germany distinctly refused to sign. I should very much like, if I might be allowed to say so, to give the Committee an idea of the sort of argument that was used by the German Delegates to me personally on this question . . .

Here, Lord Esher interrupted to enquire if the British Government had signed the declaration. He was answered in the affirmative. He then asked: "To what extent does that bind us?" Ottley explained that the British were only bound if they became involved in a war with another signatory Power. "We have", he said, "absolutely a free hand if we are at war with Germany." He then continued with his account of his own experiences at the Hague Conference in the previous year:

> The question of the use of these things was undoubtedly very fully considered by the Germans, and my friend and colleague, Admiral Siegel, who was of course my great opponent at the Hague on all these technical questions, said that Germany could not hear of throwing away her power to do this. He said that Germany quite believed there was a future in this form of warfare, and that, true to the conviction which Germans had that every form of warfare which would make war more horrible is legitimate – within very wide bounds, at all events – he would refuse to sign altogether. . . . The Germans also laid great stress on the fact that after all this is not such a very frightful violation of ethics. You see your enemy below you, you drop this explosive upon him. If you hit him, you hit him; if you miss him, the thing goes off, and it is not like a poisoned well, it does not leave a tale of horrors behind it for years to come. . . .

The discussion of air bombardment by dirigibles continued until W. A. Bland of the Financial Department of the War Office arrived. He was asked about the sums Great Britain had spent upon aeronautics in the recent past. In 1902, he replied, the British had spent about eighteen thousand pounds. In the fiscal year 1907–8 the sum of seventeen thousand pounds had been expended upon aeronautical development. At this point Lord Esher, after a long day, adjourned the first meeting of his sub-committee.

V

The second meeting of the Aerial Navigation Sub-Committee took place on 8 December. On this occasion all the members were present. Two expert witnesses appeared to answer questions. They were the Hon. C. S. Rolls and Major B. F. S. Baden-Powell. Rolls revealed a remarkable knowledge of balloons, semi-rigid airships, rigid airships, and aeroplanes. Major Baden-Powell, when he was examined, was able to supply the sub-committee with valuable technical opinions that supplemented Rolls's testimony. Unfortunately for the future of British aviation not much of their advice was followed when the committee made its final recommendations.

At this meeting the sub-committee came to close grips with many of the problems of the Air Defence of Great Britain. They were striking out into unknown areas. Nevertheless, it is astonishing that interrogations and discussions like these could have taken place as early as the year 1908. It was at this meeting of the sub-committee that Lloyd George mentioned the work of H. G. Wells. There were warnings that Britain could be bombed from the air. It was pointed out that high-angle guns would have to be devised to fire upon attacking aircraft. The suggestion was made that aeroplanes would prove to be the deadly enemies of airships. Rolls told the committee in authoritative tones on this 8 December 1908 that as a result of the future development of aeroplanes "England will cease to be an island".

Each member of the sub-committee pursued his own particular interests when he questioned the expert witnesses. Lord Esther sought to elicit technical information. Lloyd George was concerned about the possibilities of an air invasion of the British Isles and the bombing of British towns from the air. R. B. Haldane continued to press for a scientific approach to the entire problem. Reginald McKenna contributed little to the discussion. Sir William Nicholson and his supporting generals were generally hostile to the whole subject. Captain Bacon sought to advance his case for a large rigid dirigible for the Navy.

Lord Esher began the questioning. C. S. Rolls had been informed in advance about the kind of information the members of the sub-committee desired to learn from him. The first point they wanted to know about was concerned with observation from the air. Lord Esher wanted to find out what could be seen of the earth from a considerable height, from an altitude of three thousand feet. Rolls, an experienced balloonist, replied that from the air the ground looked rather like a map. In England haze and fog complicated the problem of aerial observation but Rolls assured the sub-committee "it is quite feasible, and you can see quite fairly from an ordinary balloon".

When Rolls was asked if he had made many ascents in dirigible balloons he replied he had made one flight in a French Army airship, a semi-rigid called the "Ville de Paris". But he knew a good deal about what the French military authorities were doing in this sphere. He assured the sub-committee that the French had been training men to drop explosives from their dirigibles and that satisfactory results had been attained. The key to securing accuracy in this work was practice.

When Lord Esher turned to the subject of aeroplanes Rolls expressed the most definite opinions. Like everyone else involved in these exchanges he believed the Wright aeroplane was the most efficient machine then in existence. He did not think these aeroplanes were powerful enough to carry significant weights of explosives into the air for bombing purposes; but they were capable of such high speeds that they would be of very great use for reconnoitring and for delivering despatches.

Throughout these discussions all the members of the sub-committee were concerned about the possibility of bombing raids upon the United Kingdom. Aeroplanes, in Rolls' view, were as yet incapable of such attacks. However, he pointed out that dirigibles could menace the very vitals of the country. He suggested that a fleet of enemy airships could be poised in the air just off the British coasts, in peacetime. When a declaration of war was made they could then instantly rush upon their targets and produce devastating results. He said:

> With regard to dirigible balloons, the sort of thing that strikes one about them is that in the case of a declaration of war at any time, a foreign country would get a certain number of dirigible balloons within a certain distance of the coast – they might work them pretty close to the Channel, for instance, just beforehand, so that on receiving their orders to go ahead, and they would probably be in wireless communication with their headquarters, they would then be possibly only a few hours' run from London. These machines have already done trips which show that their ability to come over to London is a thing quite possible in actual warfare. It is not as though it were entirely a matter of guesswork of what might happen, for they have actually travelled such distances as 200 and 300 miles. . . . They would choose a starting point whence the direction of the wind was most suitable, and so would get across and reach London, our naval bases, and places of that kind in a very short time. It seems to me that the defending side, unless they made special arrangements to defend themselves against attacks of this kind, would be very handicapped . . . a balloon would be an extremely difficult thing to hit at all. If you were to arrive with one of these air-ships over a naval base with a number of docks each containing several battleships huddled close together I cannot see what there is to prevent an immense amount of destruction being done. . . .

After further questioning Rolls explained that the airships could arrive over their British targets very quickly. Nothing could prevent them from carrying out their attacks. When they appeared over London "the whole place would in a sense be at their mercy". He could conceive of only one possible defence and that was the construction of similar airships capable of attacking and destroying the invaders.

Lord Esher then returned the interrogation to the subject of aeroplanes. The French Government, Rolls said, was particularly interested in Wright machines. They were about to purchase aeroplanes from the French company which had been formed to take over the Wright patents in that country. "The rights for England", Rolls made it clear, "are at present available, that is to say, they have not been taken up by anybody, and the Wrights are wishing to sell these patents for England for a sum of money which they have told me about, with a royalty on the machines. . . ."

Now Lloyd George intervened. He was interested in the possibilities of air bombardment. He wanted to know the weight of explosives that could be carried by one of these Wright aeroplanes. When Rolls explained that they could not carry very much Lloyd George asked about the type of machine that was capable of bombing Britain's naval bases. Rolls explained that when he spoke about a bombing attack upon British targets he had in mind a dirigible balloon of the Lebaudy type, already in service with the French Army, and capable of carrying thirteen hundred pounds of explosives. Lloyd George then enquired if the French were prepared to drop their bombs on enemy installations. Rolls said that in France they had made up their minds, they were training men to carry out this class of work, and that "the whole thing is so entirely different that it is opening up a new branch altogether in the service, so they are giving them bigger allowances and so on".

Rolls further pointed out that the French were thinking of discharging petrol bombs and bombs containing inflammable liquid. Could these, Lloyd George asked, "set towns on fire?" Rolls answered with one word – "Yes".

R. B. Haldane was the next member of the sub-committee to examine Rolls. Haldane suggested that before Rolls produced his firm's motor cars a period of scientific preparation intervened when tests were made and ideas were worked out. Rolls agreed that this was the procedure followed. Haldane then enquired about aeroplanes. He received a very clear reply to his questions:

> . . . It seems to me that it is a military question principally; the utility of aeroplanes will be enormous for military purposes. . . .
>
> Such a high average speed across the country will be attainable in these things – speeds that can hardly be realized now – that they will reduce distance immensely, and, from an aeronautical point of view, England will cease to be an island, for it makes not the slightest difference to the speed of these machines whether it happens to be water underneath or land underneath; and therefore we come immediately on the fact that we lose in that way much of the benefit of our being an island. We shall be liable to attacks in different parts of the country – in the capital and in various naval places; and before the Navy . . . would ever see the enemy . . . these things would be going on in the heart of the country – possibly in London itself.

Haldane and Rolls soon reached a significant phase in their exchanges. Haldane's attitude was clear enough. He hoped the British Government would not plunge into aeronautical development until its theoretical and scientific preparations were completed. Once such a solid base was established the authorities could then move forward upon a certain course and avoid the errors and false-turnings encountered by empiricists and enthusiasts. Rolls suggested an entirely different method. He urged that the British Government should at once purchase a Lebaudy airship and a Wright aeroplane. "Then", said Rolls, "they would have straight-away two machines which have been proved to be successes. That would be better than continuing experiments year after year, which are liable to cost a great deal of money without producing any great results." His idea of making progress was to purchase specimens of the very best type without further delay.

Here was a serious difference of opinion. R. B. Haldane was determined to hold fast and to carry out the policy he advocated. People like C. S. Rolls, Lord Northcliffe, and others were very critical of this approach to the problem. As time passed and Britain continued to fall behind her continental rivals in the development of aeroplanes and airships the disagreement became public and was transformed into a political issue of some significance. After a time, the government was subjected to serious public criticism for its failure to keep up with the progress in aeronautics made in the United States, France and Germany.

Now Sir William Nicholson and his generals took over the questioning. It is not known if theirs were the "conservative and humorous minds" which Sir Walter Raleigh praised so highly in his official history. In any case they displayed a stubborn hostility to almost all the suggestions Rolls made. Until this stage the members of the sub-committee had treated their expert witness with every mark of respect. The atmosphere of the meeting changed, however, when Nicholson began to ask his questions.

General Nicholson wondered if men could breathe at the altitudes at which the aeroplanes and airships would fly. He argued aircraft would not be needed for reconnaissance in civilized countries because they had all been mapped and contour maps of them were in existence. He also declared aviators would not be able to see much of enemy troop movements on the ground because they would be travelling too fast to see anything at all.

Rolls tried to parry these points as best he could. He had made scores of balloon ascents and knew his subject well. He told Nicholson difficulty in breathing occurred at heights above eighteen thousand feet but that it was certainly possible to continue to greater altitudes if oxygen was used. He explained that aerial reconnaissances would not be made to discover ground contours but to spy out enemy troop dispositions which would not be shown on any standard map. He argued that plenty could be seen from the air even if the aircraft travelled at great speeds.

When Rolls returned to his office in Conduit Street he decided to reinforce the oral evidence he had supplied by sending a letter to Sir Charles Ottley. This document, dated 11 December 1908, was printed as

Appendix IV in the sub-committee's final report. In it, Rolls took up one
of Nicholson's objections: "I did not have an opportunity of answering
the objection raised by one of the members of the Committee against the
possibility of making observations of any value from an aeroplane when
the speed must of necessity be over 30 miles an hour. He mentioned that
observations could not be made from a motor-car travelling at such a
speed; but this simile does not in the least apply for rushing along the
surface of the ground on a motor-car is entirely a different thing to
travelling at the same speed in an elevated position of 500 or 1,000 feet
from the ground. I have travelled at 50 miles an hour in a balloon and have
had no difficulty whatever in taking in all useful particulars of the
surrounding countryside. In the case of an aeroplane if it cannot take in
all the information it requires in one passage it has only to circle round
again – say, in the opposite direction."

General Nicholson was interested by one piece of information which
Rolls revealed when he spoke to the sub-committee but this item of
intelligence concerned war at sea and not land warfare. Rolls explained
that if aeroplanes could rise above dirigibles they could easily destroy
them. The great value of dirigibles, he insisted, was as weapons of
offence. They could also be employed, he said, to detect and follow
submarines, even when the submarines were under water. Nicholson was
astonished. "That", he said, "is something new and very interesting. Is
there a means of observing a submarine under water?" Rolls answered:
"Yes. It is one of the peculiarities of travelling over water, that you can
see through the water, and that you can see to the bottom of a river or
sometimes to the bottom of the sea, if it is a calm day. . . ."

When the sub-committee finished with Rolls he withdrew and Major
Baden-Powell then gave his evidence. He remarked to the sub-committee
that he had already made calculations for the construction of a rigid dirigible that would be the size of the ocean liner *Lusitania*. When Lloyd George
began to question Baden-Powell he took up this point. Lloyd George
wanted to know what damage aircraft could inflict on the British Isles:

451. MR. LLOYD-GEORGE: Would a balloon or aeroplane be
of very much use in discovering whether troops, ships, and *matériel*
had been accumulated at a given port, say, for the invasion of this
country; supposing Germany, for instance, were accumulating ships,
matériel and troops? – I think it would, decidedly.

452. Did I understand you to incline rather to the building of the
larger-sized balloons? – Yes . . . the larger the better.

453. Of the size of the "Lusitania", which is rather Mr. H. G.
Wells' idea?[1] – Yes. . . .

[1] The reference is to the H. G. Wells novel *The War in The Air*, mentioned
earlier in this history. Wells described his fictional German airships as follows:

455. Do you think it very likely in the future that we may have these huge machines? – I hardly think so, because I cannot help thinking that the aeroplane machine is going to entirely cut out the dirigible balloon. . . .

461. . . . What damage could a continental enemy inflict upon us by these machines? – I think myself that aeroplanes might be used for invasion in this way: A small machine, such as the Wright type, capable of carrying three or four men, is very easily made and is very cheap comparatively, and a continental nation might easily have several thousand of them made. Then there is no doubt about it they could come over to England. . . .

Two days after his interview Major Baden-Powell sent the sub-committee some written remarks upon C. S. Rolls's evidence. His paper, dated 10 December 1908, was printed as Appendix III in the final report. In it Baden-Powell argued that the British would soon need guns, both on shore and in their ships, to protect themselves from aircraft. He suggested that rockets to ignite the gas in dirigibles might prove to be effective. Dirigibles, he wrote, would be unable to operate where there were guns and this would limit their use in warfare. With respect to aeroplanes Baden-Powell argued that their management in the air would not be as difficult as was sometimes suggested. He made a novel point in his paper. He predicted that a hundred small aeroplanes operating at night could be employed to provision a place under siege. This paper completed the information supplied to the sub-committee at its second formal meeting.

The questions asked and the answers supplied at this meeting carried the committee members a considerable distance. They were grappling with very modern problems. All present were, in a sense, nineteenth-century men but they were now at grips with twentieth-century themes. These themes, in time, would decide the destiny of their country.

VI

The third meeting of the Aerial Navigation Sub-Committee was held on 15 December. All the members were present but Lloyd George and Reginald McKenna took almost no part in the proceedings. The expert witness interviewed on this day was Colonel J. E. Capper. When Lord Esher asked for information about his aeronautical experiments Capper explained that these had been carried out at Aldershot, for the most part. One aeroplane experiment, he said, had been conducted at the Duke of

"The . . . huge German airships, big as the biggest mammoth liners afloat. . . ." He also wrote that they varied in length from eight hundred to two thousand feet.

Atholl's property at Blair Atholl: "Mr. Haldane saw the experiments there last year".

When Lord Esher enquired about the value of dirigible balloons in war Capper said they would prove to be of inestimable value for reconnaissance. He had further thoughts about the military potential of such airships:

> I should like myself to try it if one had these weapons at one's disposal, for carrying small parcels of incendiary bombs or high explosives of sorts, and at night making a raid on some particular object like a bridge . . . or a big store yard, or arsenal which was within reach. . . . At any rate, it would create quite a scare. I think there is no doubt about it that a few bombs coming down into these places, even if they do not do very much material damage, would keep people always on tentacles, [sic] and would give them a great deal of anxiety and trouble. . . . I take it that the fear of these things would keep quite a number of people always on the *qui vive* looking out for them, and that they would be very harassing in that way, even if the actual material effect was not very great. Under favourable circumstances I think that you might get very important results by using them. Dirigible balloons of the large sizes now, I understand, contemplated on the Continent, may, in my opinion, be used on a larger scale for similar purposes against dockyards, arsenals, stores, etc. in an enemy's country up to a distance of 500 miles, or, perhaps even further, from their base. . . .

When Lord Esher asked about the degree of accuracy that might be attained in such air bombardments Capper replied that the French had succeeded "with very considerable accuracy". The French dropped bombs from dirigibles at heights of one thousand or fifteen hundred feet. Capper's idea was to attack at night from considerably lower altitudes. As a result of this tactic, he said, "you can make sure". He argued that determined aviators, attacking at night, could descend to such low levels that it would be impossible for them to miss their targets even if they suffered some losses in the assault.

R. B. Haldane wanted to know if aeroplanes, in Capper's opinion, could take the place of dirigibles or if both types would be required in modern warfare. Capper thought there would be room for the employment of both. The Wright aeroplane, he argued, was "the most successful . . . undoubtedly" but neither Orville nor Wilbur had flown very high, as yet. In order to satisfy their contractual obligations neither of the Wrights had to fly at great altitudes but Capper was uncertain about the ability of their machines to ascend to heights which would render them safe from fire from the ground. Capper told Haldane Wilbur Wright had said he could fly at twenty five hundred feet: "he is a man of his word, but he has not done it yet".

The Secretary of State for War was especially interested in this matter of vulnerability to ground fire. He recalled his adventure at Blair Atholl in the previous year: "I saw your aeroplane from below . . . at Blair Atholl", he said, "and I was struck with the extraordinary target which the unfortunate operator astride on the bicycle saddle presented . . ." Colonel Capper disagreed. He said that an aeroplane moving at thirty miles an hour at a range of seven hundred yards distance would not be an easy target to hit from the ground.

When Sir William Nicholson began to interrogate Colonel Capper the entire meeting degenerated into a ludicrous squabble about the military value of captive observation balloons. The Chief of the General Staff argued that the captive balloons were not significantly helpful in directing artillery fire. Capper, with much experience of this work, declared that they were of immense value and that they enabled artillery observers to perform their tasks most efficiently. Nicholson would not accept this opinion and badgered the unfortunate Capper without mercy. Sir Charles Hadden took care to agree with his superior. It is small wonder that Lloyd George and Reginald McKenna remained silent while the soldiers bickered in this way. Nicholson would not allow the subject of captive observation balloons to be dropped. He returned to it throughout the course of Capper's interview.

General Nicholson was a man who would not readily give in. On 29 December he sent a letter to several of the most important generals in the British Army to ask for their opinions about the value of captive balloons in war. His letter was composed in such a way that negative responses were almost certain to be returned to the War Office by the generals who were consulted. These included: Sir Neville Lyttelton; Sir John French; Sir Arthur Paget; and Sir H. Smith-Dorrien. Their correspondence was reproduced as Appendix VI in the final report of the sub-committee. Sir Arthur Paget, writing from Headquarters, Eastern Command, reported that captive balloons had rendered valuable service in the Boer War but some of the other returns were less favourable in their conclusions about the balloons.

It is obvious from the minutes of this third meeting that Colonel Capper did not make a good impression when he presented his evidence to the sub-committee. It was only after he withdrew that they began a preliminary discussion of their conclusions. Capper, as we know, commanded a military unit, the Balloon Schools, and he was also in charge of the Balloon Factory where experiments with aeroplanes and dirigibles were carried out. Haldane now suggested that basic changes in these arrangements should be made:

737. MR. HALDANE: It might be desirable that we should keep up the balloon school and a balloon course for such purposes as we

have been speaking of – artillery, observation, and so on; but that is quite a separate thing from the question whether at Aldershot we should go on making these experiments. My present impression is that if there is to be any real development of this, it must be done on a much larger scale.

Lord Esher was also concerned about the experimental work carried out by Colonel Capper and his associates. He said:

> 744. LORD ESHER: In regard to the particular point as to the money to be spent on experiments, the question arises whether you think the State ought to spend any money at all on experiments, or whether the experiments ought not to be left entirely to private enterprise. There, of course, comes in the very great distinction between dirigible balloons and aeroplanes. With regard to dirigibles, I do not suppose that any private funds would ever be likely to be devoted to the purpose of experiments, but the aeroplane is a different matter. . . .

A remarkable development now occurred. Sir Charles Hadden, the Master-General of the Ordnance, interrupted the proceedings at this point. He had with him, he explained, a letter Lieutenant Dunne had sent to his father, General Sir John Hart Dunne.

The younger Dunne was still in Scotland experimenting with his British Army aeroplane at Blair Atholl. His letter, dated 9 December 1908, described his activities there in some detail. The lieutenant, however, had not written the letter merely to inform his father about his experiments. He had another object in mind when he wrote it.

Several private investors, Dunne told his father, had bound themselves by contract to build a Dunne aeroplane. Two thousand pounds had already been subscribed for the purpose. Dunne wanted to know at once if the War Office had decided to abandon its aeroplane experiments because such information would greatly assist him in his dealings with these investors.

If the War Office abandoned its interest in Dunne's latest machine the investors would build an aeroplane based on its design. If the War Office maintained its interest in his 1908 machine the investors, led by Lord Howard de Walden, would construct an older model Dunne aeroplane for their business. Construction was to begin within a month. Clearly, it was vital for Lieutenant Dunne to discover which of his inventions he could place in his friends' hands.

This was an astonishing request. There is no evidence to suggest that Colonel Capper, Dunne's commanding officer, knew anything about the letter. Hadden did not mention it until after Capper had withdrawn.

Nevertheless, no member of the sub-committee objected when Hadden gave the letter to Lord Esher who at once read it out.

Sir Charles Hadden, an accomplished military administrator, introduced the matter in an adroit way. He said: "I do not know whether you would like to see a letter to General Dunne, which he got from his son within the last few days, stating exactly what he has done up to date, and also his wishes. Lieutenant Dunne wants to know what we are doing, because Lord Howard de Walden is building to his design."

The Dunne letter Lord Esher now read to his colleagues was later printed as Appendix V of the sub-committee report. It informed General Dunne that his son's experiments were almost completed. The lieutenant believed that his machine was "worth all the other aeroplanes in the world put together". He claimed that it possessed the "most wonderful power of self-balance – perfectly automatic". Its ability to manoeuvre appeared to be far greater than that of any existing aeroplane "including that of the Wrights".

However, in a later paragraph of his letter Lieutenant Dunne offered a slightly different conclusion. It was as modest as his earlier claims: "From what I have seen and heard, there are, I think, only two military aeroplanes worth considering – the Wrights and our own. Each represents a different class of machine. . . . I believe that both types should be adopted by the War Office, as they will hold their respective fields for probably ten or fifteen years to come."

Having made this suggestion about the course his superiors in the War Office should adopt, Lieutenant Dunne then expressed his hope that the authorities there would at once inform him of their intentions:

> If the War Office have definitely decided to give up aeronautical work, I hope they will let me *know at once*. Because, at the present moment Howard de Walden, Huntingdon, and the rest have got 2,000£. subscribed to build my *old* aeroplane (by War Office permission). They would, of course, abandon that for this design if the latter were in the market. They are bound by contract to build one of mine. In a month's time, however, they will be well started on the construction of the old one, and it would be too late for me to offer them this invention as the construction is entirely different.

Obviously, in 1908 it was helpful to an inventor of aeroplanes if his father was a general in the British Army. Two days after he wrote this letter Lieutenant Dunne sent his father another message. It, too, was printed in Appendix V of the sub-committee report. Lord Esher read it out to his colleagues. It was a brief note of triumph: "Dear Father, We did 40 yards this evening. We have been off the ground eight times altogether. . . ."

When Lord Esher finished reading these letters R. B. Haldane permitted himself an observation. He said: "It appears from that that Lieutenant Dunne has made his machine fly".

There now followed a very significant episode, one of the most significant in the history of this sub-committee. Sir William Nicholson argued that if the British continued to experiment with aeroplanes and improved them as a result, it would be disadvantageous to their own country because foreign Powers would at once copy the new British designs. He believed the government should not incur the great expenditures involved in such experiments. Haldane then remarked that aeroplanes might in time prove to be effective instruments of war. If this happened and the foreigners made them while the British did not, the British might find themselves in difficulties. Nicholson offered a simple solution to this problem. He declared the British could imitate the aeroplanes produced by the foreigners. R. B. Haldane at once expressed agreement with the general's straightforward idea; and this curious attitude came to dominate the War Office outlook for a considerable period thereafter. The record is quite clear on this point:

> 752. SIR W. NICHOLSON: The question is shall we be any better off supposing we have these machines? Are we to engage in an endeavour to improve a thing which will not be to our advantage? As soon as we have got, at great expense, and made a very good aeroplane, other nations will make aeroplanes in the same way, and we shall be no better off than we were before.
> 753. MR. HALDANE: Still, suppose they make them, and suppose it should turn out that by mechanical contrivances you can make observations at that rate of travelling, which I think is quite possible, should we not be in an awkward position if we did not have them too?
> SIR W. NICHOLSON: No; because we should imitate the ones they made.
> 754. MR. HALDANE: That is quite a definite policy – to leave other people, private inventors to go on with the aeroplane. I think there is a good deal to be said for that, and I have always said it. The dirigible is another question. I have been very much impressed with the possibility of the dirigible being a very potent factor in war, I do not mean in dropping explosives, but in surveying.

Haldane thereupon turned to Captain Bacon in order to discuss dirigibles. He wanted to know how the government should proceed: "Are we to go to Aldershot", he asked, "or are we to start *de novo* on a much larger scale?" Bacon supplied a ready answer: "I should go straight to Vickers". The third meeting of the sub-committee was adjourned at this point.

VII

After this third meeting a draft report of the sub-committee's work was prepared. The draft was produced by Captain M. P. A. Hankey, a Royal Marine officer who had been appointed Assistant Secretary of the Committee of Imperial Defence in January 1908. Sir Charles Ottley tentatively accepted Hankey's draft but his paper also required Lord Esher's approval before any further action could be taken. On 21 December 1908 Hankey sent the draft to Lord Esher for his comments:[1]

Committee of Imperial Defence
2, Whitehall Gardens, S.W.

21 December 1908

Dear Lord Esher,

I enclose a draft for the Committee on Aerial Navigation. The draft summary of conclusions at the end is rather sketchy and will certainly require amendment, but it is only intended to show the general trend of the report. Sir Charles has been quickly through the paper and approves its general tenor. We shall do nothing more until we hear from you.

Yours sincerely,
M. P. A. Hankey

Esher studied the paper for a month. Before the final report was submitted to the Committee of Imperial Defence for its approval Esher decided to inform the king of certain of its recommendations and thus secure his support for the policies suggested by the Aerial Navigation Sub-Committee. His letter, dated 20 January 1909, was the deft touch of a master:[2]

Windsor Castle

Viscount Esher, with humble duty, thinks Your Majesty may be interested to see what the Defence Committee recommends should be done in regard to Aerial Navigation, which is making such immense strides abroad. The gist of the Report is on page 5, and is to the effect that all experimental work should be transferred *to the Navy*.

It would then be placed under Captain Bacon, who is second to none in scientific attainments and enterprise.

If the Report is agreed to by the Government, and if the Chancellor of the Exchequer will find the necessary funds, i.e. about £50,000,

---

[1] Esher Papers, ESHR 5/28. M. P. A. Hankey to Lord Esher, 21 December 1908.

[2] Royal Archives. RA W41/85 Lord Esher to the King, 20 January 1909.

this country will not be for long behind France and Germany in this novel domain of science.

20 Jan. 1909.

Lord Esher's careful preparations were interrupted at this stage by a new and powerful development. Winston Churchill, President of the Board of Trade and a member of Asquith's Cabinet, now intervened. Although he was only thirty-four Churchill was already recognized as a politician of very great promise. He had begun his professional life as a soldier but by this time his enthusiasm had been captured by the idea of social reform. His restless and formidable energies were caught up in the desire to advance the cause of Britain's working classes. In alliance with Lloyd George Churchill had become a daring and ardent Radical who dreamed of reforming almost every aspect of English life.

Despite his new course and his new associations Churchill always maintained a keen interest in military affairs. Unlike some of his colleagues, he recognized at once that aeroplanes were certain to play a significant role in all future wars. He now began to bombard R. B. Haldane with letters on this subject. He urged the Secretary of State for War to consult Sir Hiram Maxim in order to ascertain Maxim's views about aeroplanes.

On 22 January a weary Haldane wrote to Lord Esher in order to send him one of Churchill's letters and to suggest that the Aerial Navigation Sub-Committee should interview Maxim before it concluded its work. Haldane's letter to Esher reflects the power of Churchill's enthusiasm and his persistence. "The enclosed is the 3rd letter I have had from Winston about Maxim & aeroplanes. I think we had better call him before closing the evidence. Otherwise we shall never hear the end of it. If you approve will you arrange this." Haldane added a postscript to his letter: "If Maxim cannot come on Thursday so much the better. We shall have asked him."[1]

When Percy Walker analysed the work of the Aerial Nagivation Sub-Committee he wrote: "It must always be somewhat of a mystery why the Committee thought fit to interview Sir Hiram Maxim . . ."[2] The answer to the mystery is that Winston Churchill forced Haldane and Esher to hold a fourth committee meeting, after their report was written, so that Maxim could appear before them.

Churchill's letter which Haldane sent to Lord Esher was a plea to the Secretary of State to urge him to pay careful attention to the tactical and strategical significance of aeroplanes. Churchill warned Haldane to reject reassuring statements about aircraft from the Army or Navy unless they

---

[1] Esher Papers, ESHR 5/29. R. B. Haldane to Esher, 22 January 1909.
[2] See Walker, *Early Aviation at Farnborough*, vol. II, p. 317.

were supported by solid arguments. Sir Hiram Maxim, arrogant as ever, had convinced his young friend that he could build a better aeroplane than the one produced by the Wright brothers. In order to impress Churchill Maxim had repeated the old canard that Wilbur Wright's great successes were due to his personal skill as a flier and did not result from the quality of his invention. Churchill eagerly informed Haldane:[1]

> I have just had an hour & a half with Maxim on aeroplanes. I think you should certainly see him yourself. No one can doubt his ability or dispute his achievements. He declares that Wilbur Wright's successes are due to his brain & nerve more than to the efficiency of his aeroplane; that he is in fact a great artist rather than a great inventor; that better chemistry, more perfect mechanism, a higher science, added to Wright's skill, would produce far better results; that improved patterns will largely discount the need of personal skill; and that such improvements are at hand . . . Such a machine, which he declares himself capable of constructing within a year . . . would lift and carry half a ton exclusive of the engines, of its own weight & the weight of the driver, would travel at a maximum of 55 miles an hour & at a minimum of 32 miles an hour. Its total cost wd. be £2000 (or 1/1000th part of a Dreadnought). . . .

Churchill went on to explain the military significance of the Maxim aeroplane:

> Its most obvious military use wd. be, in conjunction with others, to destroy naval bases by dropping nitro-glycerine bombs upon the docks, lockgates, vessels in the basins, & workshops. Other uses will occur to you. He suggests that the difficulty of hitting the object aimed at will be greatly reduced by lowering the bombs upon a piano wire to within a moderate distance of the ground. . . .

He concluded his letter by urging a searching and authoritative investigation into the entire matter:

> Of course I do not touch upon the tactical or strategical aspects, except to say that they appear to me very serious, & that I shd be very much disinclined to accept reassuring statements from military and naval quarters, unless supported by solid argument. But upon the purely mechanical question there can I think be little doubt that a very searching & authoritative investigation is required.

On 28 January 1909 the Aerial Navigation Sub-Committee met for the fourth time in order to examine Sir Hiram Maxim. Lloyd George did not attend this final meeting.

[1] Esher Papers, ESHR 5/29. Winston S. Churchill to Haldane, 19 January 1909.

The great success of Wilbur and Orville Wright had rekindled Maxim's interest in flying machines. In April 1906, as we have seen, Maxim told a meeting of the Aeronautical Society of Great Britain that the Wrights could fly. At that time he declared that the aeroplane was a potent instrument of war. He told his audience: "It is impossible to overestimate the changes that will take place during the next ten years in everything related to civilised warfare."

In 1908, however, after the Wrights had flown in public and the marvellous nature of their invention made clear in dozens and scores of eyewitness acccounts, Sir Hiram changed his mind. He travelled to France in order to observe Wilbur Wright's performances for himself. Now he no longer thought in terms of a decade. By the end of the year 1908 Maxim believed the aeroplane could be employed to carry out a full-scale air invasion of England.

Maxim was certain that aeroplanes could be used to bomb targets in Britain. But the ancient British fear was the fear of invasion. Maxim reckoned that the appearance of a successful aeroplane had turned this age old nightmare into a modern reality.

He advanced the theory that an invading army of one hundred thousand men could be transported to Britain in a single night "by a kind of aerial ferry of 5,000 aeroplanes". He calculated that each of the five thousand aeroplanes could carry six men and make four trips in a period of twelve hours "between sunset and sunrise". In his opinion an airborne invasion of England was no longer a matter for conjecture. It was a distinct military possibility.[1]

The themes of H. G. Well's *The War in The Air*, it will be observed, were no longer subjects for novelists and novels. One of Britain's most eminent practical engineers was now suggesting developments very similar to those that had been sketched out in Wells's book, scarcely twelve months earlier.

We have remarked earlier that Maxim, although he possessed a formidable reputation and had amassed a large personal fortune by sales of his machine-gun, was never accepted in British society. He remained an outsider, significantly unlike his fellow citizens in the country of his adoption. One result of this situation was that Maxim became intolerably boastful and arrogant. His outrageous claims about his scientific and technical achievements turned him into a laughing-stock. Lord Esher was the first to question Maxim at the fourth meeting of the Aerial Navigation Sub-Committee. He must have been shocked at Maxim's replies to his first questions:

> 763. LORD ESHER: We wish to have the benefit of your experi-
> ence in regard to aerial navigation if you will be kind enough to give it

[1] For comment on Sir Hiram Maxim's idea see *The Times*, 21 December 1908.

to us. First, have you ever built an aeroplane? – Certainly. All the machines that raise themselves from the earth are made on my lines exactly.

764. You have constructed one yourself? – Yes. I was the first man in the world ever to make one that would lift its own weight.

It is scarcely surprising that Esher and Haldane were the only committee members to question this remarkable witness. The bizarre examination soon turned to a discussion of the Wright aeroplane because all concerned believed it to be the most efficient flying machine then in existence. When Lord Esher asked if Maxim claimed that he could improve on "the Wilbur Wright machine" the inventor replied: "I should be very sorry if I could not make a better job than that. Some of the French machines are beautifully made, but their design is atrocious. The Wrights have got the right thing – you understand, they went into it in the right way; but their machine, as everyone who has seen it will tell you, is an extremely rough job."

It soon became clear that Maxim wanted financial support from the British Government. If he secured such support he would then build flying machines for it that were better than any others. Sir Hiram declared: "I have some reputation as a mechanic, and it would be for me a simple thing to make flying-machines, and a very simple thing to make them much better than anybody is making them at the present time, because I understand the whole theory better than any one else does, as I have spent more money on it and studied it longer." It is doubtful if the high authorities of the State who sat on the Aerial Navigation Sub-Committee were ever subjected to an experience quite like this one.

Despite his bombast, Maxim, in the course of his various replies, furnished the committee with a technical analysis of genuine quality. He predicted that aeroplanes of the future would be able to ascend to a height of one mile without any difficulty. As we have seen, the committee members were doubtful if aeroplanes would be able to hit their targets with any degree of accuracy during bombing raids. Maxim brushed these opinions aside. He told the committee in the clearest terms that aeroplanes could produce devastating effects. He explained his conception of the result of a bombing raid by aeroplanes:

If you were going to bombard a town, you might have a thousand of these machines, each one carrying a large shell, because it is the large shell that does the business. If a thousand tons of pure nitro-glycerine were dropped on to London in one night, it would make London look like a last year's buzzard's nest.

Eventually, Maxim's interrogation was concluded. The Aerial Navigation Sub-Committee had completed the first phases of its work. The next
task was to present its report to the Committee of Imperial Defence.

VII

The final report of the sub-committee was a document of seven printed
pages. Before it produced the sub-committee's conclusions the report
summarized the evidence on which these conclusions were based. It thus
provides us with valuable insights. The official British attitude with
respect to aeronautics at the beginning of the year 1909 was made very
clear in this account.[1]

Part I of the report began by pointing out that four types of "air-ships"
were studied by the sub-committee. These included: captive balloons,
kites, dirigible balloons, and aeroplanes.

Kites and captive balloons were dealt with summarily. These devices,
the report explained, were employed in land warfare for two purposes –
reconnaissance and observation of artillery fire. Their value, the report
declared, echoing Sir William Nicholson's opinions, was "limited".

The evidence dealing with dirigible balloons was presented next. The
report stated that great progress had been made by France and Germany
in this branch of aeronautics. It was considered that a large rigid dirigible
would be most useful for the purposes of naval warfare; and that
non-rigid dirigibles could serve best for warfare on land. The subject of
Air Defence was touched upon for the first time at this stage of the report:
"It has . . . been suggested that the dirigible might form a potent agent for
destruction in naval warfare, if employed for dropping explosives and
incendiary bombs on to the decks of men-of-war, and on to the more
vulnerable portions of dockyards. At present there is no evidence to show
whether accuracy can be obtained in dropping explosives. No experiments in this direction have been made in this country, though it is stated
that the question has been taken up seriously both in Germany and
France. It would appear that, in order to be sure of hitting the object
aimed at, an air-ship would have to descend very low, in which case it
should be possible to find means to deal with it. . . ."

The report suggested that aeroplanes had not yet emerged from the
experimental stage. "It is true", the report declared, "that successful
flights have already been made for periods up to a few hours in France,
particularly in the machine invented by the Wright Brothers. It has yet to

---

[1] For the final Report see Cab. 4/3. C.I.D. 106-B. "Aerial Navigation. Report
of a Sub-Committee of the Committee of Imperial Defence appointed by the
Prime Minister", dated 28 January 1909 and marked "*SECRET*".

be shown, however, whether aeroplanes are sufficiently reliable to be used under unfavourable weather conditions, and it is not quite certain whether they can be employed for flights at high elevations. . . ."

Aeroplanes might become useful in land warfare for reconnaissance purposes and they might be employed in the future to assail dirigibles with hand grenades, bombs, machine-guns and revolvers. However, the future of this class of vehicle was not clear: "Until these machines have proved their ability to ascend to great heights, a point concerning which expert opinion appears divided, this method of employing them must remain in the region of speculation."

Aeronautical development in Britain was then summarized. The report admitted that the British had made "little progress" in aviation save for the work done in the military establishment at South Farnborough. The two dirigibles built there were dismissed as vessels of "small dimensions and low power". S. F. Cody's aeroplane was mentioned but no comment on its capacities was included in the report. Great stability was claimed for Lieutenant Dunne's aeroplane: "At present, however, the machine has no practical value".

Part II of the report presented the sub-committee's "Conclusions". The first of these dealt squarely with the problem of the Air Defence of Great Britain:

> Although in the existing state of aerial navigation Great Britain is not exposed to any serious danger by land, it would be improvident and possibly dangerous to assume that the rapid developments which the art of aerostatics has recently made may not entail in the future risks by land and sea.
>
> Invasion of Great Britain in air-ships on a large scale may be dismissed as unlikely for many years to come . . . It is conceivable, however, that these machines might be employed for conveying a small raiding force for such a purpose as inflicting a damaging blow to an arsenal or a dockyard.
>
> Furthermore, attacks upon war-ships and dockyards by dropping explosives and incendiary bombs on to them from dirigible balloons, though at present in an experimental stage, cannot be dismissed as an impossible operation of war, and it is doubtful whether our men-of-war and coast defences at present possess adequate means to ward them off. . . .
>
> The evidence before the Committee tends to show that the full potentialities of air-ships, and the dangers to which we might be exposed by their use, can only be ascertained definitely by building them ourselves. This was the original reason for constructing submarines, and in their case the policy has since been completely vindicated.

The second conclusion of the sub-committee was concerned with the military advantages that might be derived from the employment of airships or aeroplanes. The sub-committee decided that it was very important to construct a dirigible airship for use as a naval scout. Such vessels might also be employed, in the future, "for the purpose of attacking foreign war-ships, dockyards and canal gates and locks". The committee decided that the rigid type of airship should be adopted for the Navy.

The Army would be served best, the committee recommended, if it exploited non-rigid airships. The report urged that the War Office should be granted funds to continue its experiments with non-rigids, and to purchase in the open market "either a complete dirigible balloon or such component parts as may be required".

When the report dealt with aeroplanes there was a startling recommendation. It reflected Sir William Nicholson's triumph in the deliberations of the sub-committee. The report declared: "There appears to be no necessity for the Government to continue experiments in aeroplanes, provided that advantage is taken of private enterprise in this form of aviation". The Secretary of State for War had emphasized, throughout, that systematic and organized scientific research into the principles of flight was a vital necessity of the British future. The report baldly rejected his approach to the problem when it dealt with aeroplanes.

The third conclusion of the report fixed the amounts to be allotted for expenditure on aerial experiments. Here, Captain Bacon's arguments were accepted in their entirety. The committee recommended that a sum of thirty five thousand pounds should be allotted to the Admiralty for the purpose of building a dirigible balloon. The Admiralty would invite "some firm of standing" to contract for the work. The War Office was to receive the sum of ten thousand pounds for its experiments with non-rigids, and for the purchase of such airships or their components parts.

The report ended with a concise summary of its recommendations:

(a) The Committee are of opinion that the dangers to which we might be exposed by developments in aerial navigation cannot be definitely ascertained until we ourselves possess air-ships.

(b) There are good grounds for assuming that air-ships will prove of great value to the navy for scouting and possibly for destructive purposes. From a military point of view they are also important.

(c) A sum of from 35,000£. should be included in the Naval Estimates for the purposes of building an air-ship of a rigid type. . . .

(d) A sum of 10,000£. should be included in the Army Estimates for continuing experiments with navigable balloons of a non-rigid type, and for the purchase of complete air-ships or their component parts. . . .

(e) The experiments carried out at the military ballooning establishment with aeroplanes should be discontinued, but advantage should be taken of private enterprise in this form of aviation.

IX

The full Committee of Imperial Defence considered this report at a meeting held on 25 February 1909. H. H. Asquith, the prime minister, presided. Reginald McKenna, Winston Churchill, the Earl of Crewe, and Haldane were the political leaders who attended the meeting. Rear-Admiral E. J. Slade, the Director of Naval Intelligence, represented the Admiralty. The soldiers present were Sir William Nicholson, Sir John French, and Major-General J. S. Ewart. Lord Esher also took part in these deliberations.[1]

The report of the Aerial Navigation Sub-Committee was the third item on the agenda for that day. Lord Esher introduced the subject in a very strange way: "LORD ESHER read to the Committee a letter that he had received from Mr. C. S. Rolls in which the latter stated that he had purchased a 'Wright' aeroplane, and hoped that the Government would give him facilities for experimenting with it on Government ground. Mr. Rolls also offered his services to the Government in the event of their wishing to benefit by the experience that he gained. Lord Esher thought that we should avail ourselves of this offer, and put the military authorities in touch with Mr. Rolls."[2]

When Percy Walker read this account he was shocked. He wrote in his history: "If the report of the sub-committee was indeed open to much adverse criticism its reception by the parent committee was an appalling travesty. Here was a document that was to influence Britain's defensive strategy for many years to come. Yet Lord Esher does not lead off by introducing it with due solemnity, but reads instead what many would regard as a preposterous letter from C. S. Rolls. . . . Now Rolls, despite his many excellent qualities, had a reputation for extreme closeness in financial matters and had never been known to have paid for anything he could get for nothing. In Lord Esher's vicarious generosity there seems just a hint of influence in high places, and we are left wondering whether the proposed facilities are to be granted to Rolls the famous aeronaut or to Rolls the wealthy son of Lord Llangattock."[3]

Rolls had indeed secured the promise of a Wright aeroplane for

---

[1] For this meeting see Cab. 2/2. Committee of Imperial Defence, Minutes of 101st Meeting, 25 February 1909, marked "*SECRET*".
[2] Cab. 2/2. C.I.D. Minutes of 101st Meeting.
[3] Walker, *Early Aviation at Farnborough*, vol. II, pp. 327–8.

himself. This was accomplished after the most lengthy and secret negotiations. In January 1909 Rolls revealed something of his plans to the Wrights. He assured them he would do his best to keep the details of their machine a secret when he received it. He explained to Wilbur:[1]

> . . . I should hate to think that by reason of my possessing a machine over here I was in any way a stumbling block (at some future time) to you, or was using it in any way that caused difficulties to you or your negotiations. For instance, you might fear the machine being used for copying, and I would undertake if you wished so far as in my power not to let the Aldershot authorities or anyone else take dimensions in my shed, they are all friends of mine in the W.O., but this would not make the slightest difference if I had given the promise. . . .
>
> I expect to keep it under the care of Short Bros. . . . in a separate shed. They will do anything for me in the way of guarding it, for I originally brought them to the notice of aeronauts at a time when . . . they were struggling for existence in a wee workshop.

The Short brothers mentioned by Rolls were originally balloon makers. After one of them saw Wilbur Wright fly at Le Mans in 1908 they decided to become builders of aeroplanes because they realized that flying machines would soon take the place of balloons in the sporting community they served. The Shorts established themselves at Shellness on the Isle of Sheppey and soon began to prosper in their new line of work. Eventually, with the agreement of the Wrights, they built a Wright aeroplane for C. S. Rolls. In time Shorts took over the Wright patents for Great Britain and moved their factory to Eastchurch, which then became a great centre of British aviation. As the years passed the firm of Short Brothers developed into one of the most important builders of aircraft in British history. This great enterprise took its first positive steps when the Wrights agreed to allow the Shorts to build one of their machines for C. S. Rolls.

Although Rolls had promised the Wrights he would do all in his power to preserve the secrets of their machine he now offered his "services" to the British Government if they would provide him with facilities for experimenting with his Wright aeroplane. Despite his letter to Lord Esher Rolls did not, as yet, possess a Wright aeroplane and he did not secure one for several months. Later, in March 1909, Rolls offered to become an agent for the British War Office. He suggested to Lord Esher that he might travel to France in order to see the Wrights ". . . on behalf of the W.O. . . . This would enable me to draw them & get definite information . . . which it must be important for the W.O. to have."[2]

[1] Wright Brothers' Papers, C. S. Rolls to Mr Wright, 6 January 1909.
[2] See Esher Papers, ESHR 5/29. Chas. S. Rolls to Lord Esher, 22 March 1909.

When R. B. Haldane learned of Rolls' original proposition at the meeting of the Committee of Imperial Defence held on 25 February 1909 he at once said that he "considered that Mr. Rolls' offer was a good one, and that we should give him such facilities as he had asked for, and at the same time place officers under him to be instructed".[1]

Haldane was prepared to carry out this policy to the letter. Griffith Brewer, the Wrights' patent agent in England, later told them of Haldane's arrangements with Rolls in a letter dated 24 March 1909:[2]

> I had lunch with Mr. Rolls today, who is going to Paris by the night train and purposes seeing you tomorrow. . . . Mr. Haldane – the Minister of War in England – is giving Rolls every facility in the way of using Government land, and erecting a shed for him at Government expense, providing labour and tools etc., so that they may have the benefit of his experience in flight. It is therefore important from a military point of view in England that Rolls should be able to get his machine. . . .

One of those who attended the Committee of Imperial Defence on 25 February could not agree with Rolls' curious proposition. Winston Churchill objected in spirited tones:[3]

> MR. CHURCHILL thought that there was a danger of these proposals being considered too amateurish. The problem of the use of aeroplanes was a most important one, and we should place ourselves in communication with Mr. Wright himself, and avail ourselves of his knowledge. He agreed, however, that the recommendation of the Sub-Committee that we should encourage private enterprise was a good one.

This sound advice was instantly rejected by Churchill's colleagues. The prime minister now returned the discussion to the report of the sub-committee. Asquith declared that ". . . the Report of the Sub-Committee discouraged military experiments with aeroplanes, and he considered that the recommendation that they should be discontinued is a good one". This remark ended the debate. The printed conclusion of the Committee of Imperial Defence read as follows.[4]

> The Committee approve the Report of the Sub-Committee, and decide that the offer made by Mr. Rolls, to place a Wright aeroplane

[1] See Cab. 2/2. C.I.D. Minutes of 101st Meeting.
[2] Wright Brothers' Papers, Griffith Brewer to Orville Wright, 24 March 1909.
[3] See Cab. 2/2. Minutes of 101st Meeting. Churchill's remarks are published in Walker, *Early Aviation at Farnborough*, vol. II, p. 329; and in Randolph S. Churchill, *Winston S. Churchill*, volume II, Companion, Part 3 (London, 1969), p. 1874.
[4] Cab. 2/2. Minutes of 101st Meeting, Conclusion.

at the disposal of the Government for experiments, on the understanding that facilities will be provided by the State, shall be
accepted.

The first major deliberations of the British Government concerned
with these entirely novel issues thus ended in a questionable way.
Nevertheless, Asquith and his colleagues had struck out on a new course
in discharging their responsibilities for the nation's defences. The entire
subject of aeronautics had been taken firmly in hand. If the report of the
sub-committee was indeed open to much adverse criticism, a beginning
had been made because this report, C.I.D. Document No. 106-B, was
henceforth to serve as the basis for further official investigations into the
subjects of air power and air defence.

CHAPTER 14

1909: The Year in Which Britain's Vulnerability To Attack From The Air Was Recognized

Vickers Sons, and Maxim Begin Work – Inspecting Captain of Airships – Cody and Dunne are Dismissed – Contact maintained with C. S. Rolls – Colonel Capper at the Balloon Factory – The Navy Scare of 1909 – Lord Northcliffe's Plans – He Invites Arthur Balfour to Visit Wilbur Wright – He Writes to Haldane – And to Lord Esher – The *Daily Mail* Campaign – The Naval Crisis – Questions in Parliament – Haldane's Remarkable Pronouncements – Lord Montague of Beaulieu Speaks in the Lords – Our Insularity is not what it was – The Vote of Censure – Arthur Du Cros Attacks the Government – The Aerial League – The Mansion House Meeting – Response to it in the Press – Lord Montagu's Further Contribution – British "Nerve Centres" lie open to Attack from the Air – The Aeronautical Agreement – Formation of the Parliamentary Aerial Defence Committee – Arthur Lee – His Early Life – His Association with Northcliffe – His Plan to "stir up the Government" – The Wright Brothers Arrive in London – British Reaction to their Visit – Haldane's Initiative – Reaction of the British Press – A Clever Politician's Trick – Haldane's Revolutionary Plan

I

Asquith's Liberal government now proceeded to put the decisions of the Committee of Imperial Defence into effect. The position of Ministers in this period was a difficult one. Their Radical followers in the House of Commons and in the country were furiously opposed to any increases in armament expenditures. They were ferocious in their demands that the Military Estimates be reduced.

The Tory opponents of the government followed a different course. They were convinced the Liberal leaders would sacrifice anything, even the safety of the nation, in order to hold on to their places. In the

Conservative view Asquith and his colleagues, self-seeking jacks-in-office, would never challenge the Radicals lest their majority in the Commons be put into jeopardy. In 1909 distrust of Asquith, Lloyd George, Haldane and Churchill dominated the Tory outlook.

Haldane, bland and skilful in debate, managed to parry all the attacks made upon the War Office even though his policies were roundly and regularly condemned by Lord Roberts and the National Service League, who urged that only a programme of conscription could save the country. The naval plans of the Liberal government met with such disapproval that a vote of censure on this subject was moved in the House of Commons in March. The menace of Imperial Germany loomed over all to so great a degree that political tensions rose to unprecedented heights in the early months of 1909. Air Defence, in this year, became a subject of controversy in British politics for the first time in history.

In conformity with the recommendations of the Aerial Navigation Sub-Committee the Admiralty at once pressed forward with its arrangements to secure a large rigid airship for the Navy. Their proposals were met with enthusiasm by the directors of Vickers Sons and Maxim.

In March 1909 even before the Naval Estimates were approved in Parliament the board of Vickers authorized an expenditure of five thousand pounds in order to begin the project. Later, Vickers increased this sum by allotting a further fifteen thousand pounds. Their tender was accepted early in May and construction of Britain's first rigid airship was begun in the huge Cavendish Dock at Barrow-in-Furness. The work was carried out in the greatest secrecy.

As soon as the order was placed a special branch was formed at the Admiralty to deal with all matters relating to the construction of the vessel. Sir John Fisher's first idea was to put Captain Bacon in charge of the new branch. However, in April 1909 Fisher's enemies published two of the notorious "Bacon letters" which we have mentioned earlier in this history. After the publication of these documents Bacon was so roundly criticized as Fisher's "jackal" and "spy" that he found it convenient to resign from the Service.

At this, Fisher and Rear-Admiral Sir John Jellicoe, the new Director of Naval Ordnance, offered the post to Captain Murray F. Sueter. This officer, like Bacon, had been a pioneer in the establishment of the Navy's submarine service. He was now given the title of "Inspecting Captain of Airships". Sueter and his staff were carried on the books of H.M.S. *Hermione*, a cruiser that was sent to Barrow to serve as a depot ship for the airship project.

Murray Sueter was an aeronautical enthusiast. He plunged into his new work with tremendous energy. Reginald McKenna, the First Lord, supported his activities at Barrow in every way possible. Thus began, as the Aerial Navigation Sub-Committee had recommended, the construction of the ill-fated *No. 1, Rigid Naval Airship*, popularly known as the *Mayfly*, a gigantic aerial vessel that never flew because she was destroyed in 1911 in an accident, even before her first trials began.

The attitude in the War Office was more ambiguous and less straight-forward than the course followed by the Admiralty. There, R. B. Haldane was not yet prepared to adopt a definite aeronautical policy for the British Army. His plans for a Military Air Service had not yet matured to the point where he was ready to act.

At the end of January 1909, when the report of the Aerial Navigation Sub-Committee had been completed but not yet approved by the Committee of Imperial Defence, Sir Charles Hadden, the Master-General of the Ordnance, recommended that Cody and Dunne should be dismissed from their places in the Balloon Factory at Farnborough. The Secretary of State agreed to his proposal at once in conformity with the sub-committee's recommendation that military experiments with aeroplanes should be abandoned.

In time Lieutenant Dunne became a civilian designer of aeroplanes and formed, in company with several wealthy friends, the Blair Atholl Syndicate in order to exploit his designs on a commercial basis. S. F. Cody was less fortunate. However, with the help of a far-seeing officer, Sir Horace Smith-Dorrien, Commander-in-Chief of the Aldershot Command, he was enabled to continue his aeroplane experiments. Arrangements were made to permit Cody to practice with his machine on Laffan's Plain, an open space of ground under the control of Aldershot Command.

Haldane took care to maintain contact with the Hon. C. S. Rolls so that the War Office did not lose all touch with aeroplane developments. Before he obtained his Wright aeroplane Rolls wrote regularly to Wilbur and Orville in order to ask them about every aspect and detail of their invention. After one of their machines was delivered to him Rolls began to fly with it. Whenever he was unable to understand the machine's performance in the air he described his difficulties to the Wrights and asked them to set out for him the proper course he should follow in order to become a more proficient pilot. The Wright brothers' collection of papers contain scores of letters from Rolls dealing with these subjects. Rolls picked their brains with an unswerving diligence.

C. S. Rolls was not concerned with technicalities only in this correspondence. He sought, persistently, to convince the Wrights that they should reduce the price of the machine they had sold to him. He told the brothers that whenever he purchased a motor car he was given a discount because he was "in the trade" and it seemed proper to him that a similar course should be followed when it came to aeroplanes.

Colonel Capper was allowed to remain temporarily at his post in the Balloon Factory. He had worked out a scheme to produce a few small dirigibles for the Army and his superiors, in conformity with the recommendations of the Aerial Navigation Sub-Committee, permitted him to experiment with these until October 1909. In that month Mervyn O'Gorman took Capper's place as Superintendent of the Balloon Factory. Capper continued to serve at Farnborough as Commandant of the Balloon School, the military unit concerned with captive observation balloons and kites. For some time he cooperated with O'Gorman as a test pilot and flew British Army dirigibles for a period of several months. Eventually, however, he left Farnborough for good in order to return to his regular duties as an officer of Royal Engineers.

By 1909 several small private firms in England began to build aeroplanes. Most of these British pioneers learned to fly abroad but they returned home in the hope that a domestic market might soon appear that would enable them to create a prosperous native aircraft industry. Aeronautical shows and prizes stimulated their efforts. In February 1909 the Aero Club of the United Kingdom opened its first aerodrome at Sheppey. The British manufacturers of aeroplanes were far behind the French in every phase of the business but as a result of their efforts a definite start had been made in establishing the industry in the United Kingdom.

In 1909 the first catalogues and lists of aircraft accessories began to be printed in Britain. Moreover, publications devoted solely to aviation now appeared on the news-stands. In January a magazine called *Flight* was published for the first time and in May *The Aero* began its life. In its very first edition *Flight* declared on 2 January 1909: "The flying world is about to grow up; we are preparing to grow up with it."

II

Apprehension about Imperial Germany was another factor that helped to determine aeronautical progress in the United Kingdom in 1909. In the early months of the year the menace of Germany's developing Navy produced a crisis that was unrivalled in its intensity. An American scholar has offered an excellent analysis of the famous Naval Panic of 1909: "Despite invasion and espionage scares and the agitation of conscriptionists, the vast majority of the public still looked to the navy as the guarantor of national security. As long as the navy was supreme in the North Sea and the Channel they could 'sleep safely in their beds'. When this supremacy was questioned . . . in the spring of 1909, the mass feeling of insecurity built up by successive spy and invasion scares rose abruptly to panic proportions."[1]

[1] Oron James Hale, *Publicity and Diplomacy* (New York, 1940), p. 341, hereafter cited as Hale, *Publicity and Diplomacy*.

It was only in 1909 that the tragedy of the failure of the Hague Conference became apparent on a national scale. For some months officials at the Admiralty and in the Foreign Office had been worried that the Germans were secretly accelerating their battleship building programme beyond the figures published by the German Government. There were reports which indicated the Germans had not only increased the rate of construction of their *Dreadnoughts* but that guns, gun mountings, instruments and other essential parts of big warships had been assembled in advance. As a result of these new factors it was feared the Germans would be able to complete some of their big ships more quickly than their own published time-tables suggested. It was also known that the armament firm of Krupp in Essen, the chief contractors in Germany for the construction of guns and gun mountings, had issued new bonds in the summer of 1908 in order to finance an extension of plant to increase the capacity and output of the firm.

The Admiralty authorities in these circumstances feared that Germany might, by a sudden spurt in shipbuilding, overtake the British superiority in Dreadnoughts. Moreover, technical experts in every Navy in the world believed that victory or defeat in the next war at sea would turn upon capital ships of this type or class.

These anxieties were intensified by the novelty of the situation. No one in authority had any genuine experience of this kind of arms race. When the idea of German acceleration found its way into the popular Press a national panic was the result. There were no sane limits to the fears expressed in Britain in March and April 1909. The Liberal Ministers were roundly condemned as traitors who had abused the trust placed in them by the nation. Some sections of the Press proclaimed that Britain's centuries-long condition of superiority at sea was now, at last, about to be lost to the Germans. It was widely believed that deadly balances were being altered and that Britain, owing to the lack of vigilance of the Liberal Government, was in mortal peril of a naval defeat and a consequent German invasion.

This *hysteria germanica* only began to recede in April, most authorities agree, after Lloyd George had introduced his revolutionary Budget of 1909. It is usually argued that the novel taxes Lloyd George proposed in this Budget gave people something else to think about.

Nevertheless, a genuine nervousness still continued throughout the country. On 8 May, for example, the Home Fleet was suddenly alerted, by urgent telegrams, to a possible German attack, and this unnecessary and unwarranted alarm continued for several days.[1]

Historians, of course, have written extensively about the great Navy

---

[1] For this point see Marder, *From The Dreadnought to Scapa Flow*, vol. I, pp. 181–2.

Panic of 1909. However, they have neglected another aspect of the national nervousness of this period which marched hand in hand with British fears about the German Fleet. In 1909 many people in Britain believed the country lay open to a German attack from the air because the Liberal Government, in addition to neglecting the country's naval defences, had also made inadequate provision for its Air Defence.

III

By the beginning of 1909 Lord Northcliffe was convinced that the British future would be changed more significantly than that of any other country as a result of the successful development of the aeroplane. Once this determination was fixed in his mind he proposed to act. He decided he would force the War Office, by various means at his disposal, to purchase a Wright aeroplane.

On 1 January 1909 when the *Daily Mail* reported Wilbur Wright's record breaking two-hour-and-twenty-minute flight of the previous day, the paper also announced that it was renewing its offer of a prize for the first aeroplane flight across the English Channel and that the amount of the award was increased from five hundred to one thousand pounds. Northcliffe's idea was to make the channel flight the symbol of Britain's vulnerability in the air.

Later, when Wilbur Wright moved his base of operations from Le Mans to Pau on the edge of the Pyrenees, Northcliffe decided to visit him there to observe his activities in the air at first hand. In addition, Northcliffe invited Arthur Balfour, the powerful Conservative leader, to accompany him on the visit. He calculated that he and Balfour, in concert, would then be in a position to press Haldane into a positive course of action with respect to Wright aeroplanes.

A final weapon in this armoury of persuasion was the Northcliffe Press itself. Northcliffe was determined to use his newspapers to batter at Haldane and the War Office until he secured his goal. Here, he proposed to act on familiar ground. In 1907 when Haldane sought to win recruits for his new Army he made effective use of the popular Press. A special department at the War Office supplied the newspapers with information that favoured Haldane's policies. The *Daily Mail* came forward to act as his chief publicity agent and later the Secretary of State publicly thanked the newspaper for its patriotic efforts. R. B. Haldane was a man who understood the political significance of the newspaper Press and no one was more aware of this than Northcliffe, the greatest newspaper proprietor of their day.

Northcliffe's aeronautical campaign of 1909 was not a panic-monger's effort. Early in the year people in Britain were seriously worried about the possibility of a German invasion of their homeland. Several writers now suggested that huge dirigible airships could be employed to carry a large force of armed men through the air and thus avoid Britain's naval defences. Northcliffe did not believe that such an attack was technically feasible, in 1909. He therefore caused a special article entitled "Aeronautics. The Problem of Invasion" to be published in *The Times* on 15 February.

The special article pointed out that even the largest dirigibles of that day did not possess a lifting power of more than a few tons. It would be impossible for such airships to transport guns, stores, ammunition and horses. For this reason, the article argued, "invasion by airship must remain impracticable. . . ."

However, other forms of aerial attack were looked upon as definite possibilities. The *Times* article pointed out that airships might be employed successfully in "raids, demonstrations, and secret service expeditions". The writer suggested it would be quite possible for airships to make a sudden raid upon important British naval bases where great damage might be caused and units of the fleet sunk at their anchorages. He also explained that an air attack might be employed to assist an invading force to secure a lodgement on Britain's shores: "Twenty large dirigibles and a hundred auxiliary aeroplanes . . . might wreak terrific destruction, and, even if they were all destroyed eventually, they might possibly have made an opening whereby the full naval fleet of the enemy might push home a real invading force that would be sufficient to overrun the country."

By this time Northcliffe was actively engaged in his campaign to force the War Office to acquire Wright aeroplanes. The *Times* article therefore concluded with pointed references to the Wright brothers. Orville, recuperating from his injuries suffered at Fort Myer, had travelled to France with his sister Katharine. It was known that the Wrights planned to visit England before they returned to the United States. The *Times* article declared: "It is much to be regretted that the forthcoming visit of the Wright Brothers to England will be too short to allow them to give any demonstrations here, as, if these were witnessed by the heads of the Government and by the naval and military authorities, a more accurate opinion could be formed of the utility of the aeroplane. Unfortunately, too, we have no really successful machine to show to the Wrights. . . . It is something of a humiliation not to be able to exhibit a machine which has flown as far as various aeroplanes in France, Germany, Italy, America, and Belgium. . . ."

This article was merely an opening salvo. When it was published Northcliffe was already in France with the Wright brothers. He and Arthur Balfour had now resolved that their next move would be a frontal assault upon the Secretary of State for War himself.

IV

A key element in Lord Northcliffe's design was to associate Arthur
Balfour with his scheme. Balfour, a former prime minister, was leader of
the Conservative Party in 1909 and a man of tremendous influence in
Parliament and in the country. It was known that he possessed a particu-
lar interest in all matters that touched upon the defence of the nation.
One great reason for Haldane's record of successful achievement at the
War Office was that Balfour, at critical junctures, had given him his
support by persuading the Tory legions in the Commons not to oppose the
Liberal government's military policies too strenuously. Balfour regularly
moderated or frustrated Tory attacks upon the Secretary of State for
War. Here was a powerful ally who was certain to be listened to whenever
he chose to offer Haldane advice.

It was Balfour's patrician habit to visit Biarritz during the winter
months. Early in the year Northcliffe suggested to him before he departed
from Britain that he could arrange an excursion from Biarritz to Pau so
that they could observe Wilbur Wright and his aeroplane. On 7 January
1909 Balfour accepted this invitation. "I should like much to see Wright's
aeroplane", Balfour wrote to Northcliffe, "and gladly accept your kind
suggestion".[1]

Balfour, elegant, aloof, and aristocratic, seldom permitted enthusiasm
to guide his actions. Nevertheless, he quickly revealed something more
than his usual tepid interest in affairs when he wrote to Northcliffe again
about their proposed outing. He made it clear he was prepared to endure
a certain measure of discomfort in order to be able to see Wilbur Wright
and his flying-machine. On 6 February he told Northcliffe: "I am greatly
looking forward to my visit to Pau. I shall bring a servant but no
secretary."[2]

Northcliffe made certain that Arthur Balfour's visit to Pau was reported in the *Daily Mail*. On 12 February the paper's Special Correspondent at Pau wrote that Balfour was enchanted by the Wright aeroplane.
When the time came to haul up the derrick's weight so that the machine
could start there were not enough men present to do the job. Balfour at
once rushed forward to help. He insisted to Wilbur that he must not be
denied the privilege of "taking part in a miracle".[3] According to the *Daily
Mail*'s account, Balfour exclaimed: "If volunteers are wanted, I offer
myself. . . ." After he helped to haul on the rope the great Conservative
statesman then asked Wilbur if he could fly with him but since the day was

---

[1] B.M. Add. MSS. (Northcliffe Papers) Balfour to Northcliffe, 7 January 1909.
[2] B.M. Add. MSS. (Northcliffe Papers) Balfour to Northcliffe, 6 February
1909.
[3] See Kelly, *The Wright Brothers*, p. 203.

stormy his request was refused. According to the *Daily Mail* Balfour said, after Wilbur had flown for a few minutes, "It is the most wonderful sight. It is something worth coming far to see. I wish I could be flying with him." Afterward, in conversation, Wilbur explained to Balfour the great significance of aeroplanes as military scouts. A single aeroplane, he declared, would be of more value for scouting purposes than an entire regiment of cavalry.

Northcliffe also took care to alert his other newspapers to the importance of Wilbur's flights. On 12 February he wrote to J. L. Garvin of *The Observer*: "I am sorry you are unable to come to Pau. This bird-man here is an interesting individuality and doing a wonderful thing."[1]

Northcliffe, during his visit to Pau, developed a warm friendship for Wilbur, Orville, and Katharine Wright. He corresponded with them for years after this first meeting. The suspicions he had entertained in 1907 when Lady Jane Taylor sought to interest him in the Wright aeroplane were now entirely erased. Nevertheless, his keen insight soon picked out a flaw in the Wrights' attitude. They believed their machine was "the last as well as the first word in flying". Northcliffe realized that progress beyond the Wright achievement was certain to come.[2]

Despite this impression Northcliffe was convinced that the Wright brothers controlled a device that would alter the nature of warfare. He felt also that the military authorities of his own country were not paying enough attention to it. On 19 February, while he was still at Pau, he composed a carefully prepared letter and sent it to R. B. Haldane at the War Office. In Northcliffe's mind this communication dealt with matters of the very highest national significance. As we shall see later, Haldane did not pay as much attention to it as Northcliffe hoped. The Secretary of State for War was eventually to pay a bitter price for this neglect. Northcliffe's letter declared:[3]

Hotel Gassion
Pau
19th February 1909.

My dear Mr. Haldane,

 . . . . I wonder if I may bore you on the subject of aeroplanes, which I have been studying for close on six years. I notice that the

---

[1] Garvin Papers, Northcliffe to Garvin, 12 February 1909.

[2] For this point see Hamilton Fyfe, *Northcliffe, An Intimate Biography* (London, 1930), pp. 74–5. Fyfe was a close associate of Northcliffe's for many years.

[3] B.M. Add. MSS. (Northcliffe Papers) Northcliffe to R. B. Haldane, 19 February 1909.

Germans and French[1] have both military representatives here watching the Wrights' machine, which Mr. Balfour came to see, and of which he will speak to you.

As I am constantly being chaffed by these foreign gentlemen with regard to the British army aeroplane,[2] which they have nicknamed the "steamroller", it occurs to me that, if it is worth the while of Germany and France to be on the spot, one of your young men might be down here to find out why it is that this aeroplane gets off the ground, and can fly for ten minutes or ten hours if it chooses, and your Aldershot aeroplane, which is a very bad copy of the bad French aeroplanes, is unable to leave the ground.

The American army has already three partially trained aeroplane pilots. The French Army is training one here. The Austrian army is getting a French machine (a mistake). . . . These aeroplanes can fly at any height up to about a mile, and the military men with whom I have talked here agree that it is almost impossible to hit them, but, as Mr. Wright says, if out of ten aeroplane scouts you lost four, what matters? Compare the loss with that of ordinary scouting operations.

Pray pardon this long effusion, but I think it is the duty of everyone who can to help, and I do happen to know something about aeroplanes.

Northcliffe was so concerned that he also took care to write to Lord Esher while he was still at Pau in order to complain about the negligent attitude of the War Office. In his letter to Esher he employed much harsher language than he had used in his missive to the Secretary of State. This letter, dated 26 February 1909, also railed bitterly against the aeroplane S. F. Cody had produced at Farnborough:[3]

. . . . I have been here some time making a study of the aeroplane. Our national muddle-headedness has rarely been seen to worse disadvantage than in this particular matter, aviation. Here, some seven hundred and fifty miles from London, is a machine which can fly perfectly at forty miles an hour, at any height up to about a mile. It is stated by the German and French officers here to be practically "unhitable"; provided with wireless telegraphy, the operator can scout an enemy's positions in a way possible by no other means. Despite the fact that this machine is only twenty-two hours distant,

[1] The military representatives were Captain Paul-Nicolas Lucas-Girardville, a pupil of Wilbur Wright who was trained to fly by him at Pau; and Captain Alfred Hildebrandt of the German Army who visited the United States in 1907 in order to check upon the Wrights' accomplishments. In 1909 he flew with Orville Wright in Berlin.

[2] The reference is to S. F. Cody's aeroplane.

[3] The original of this letter is preserved in the Esher Papers. It is published in Maurice V. Brett ed., *Journals and Letters of Reginald Viscount Esher* (London, 1934), vol. II, pp. 371–2.

nobody has been here from the War Office, although the following countries have made arrangements for procuring Wright aeroplanes: United States, France, Germany, (tentatively) Italy, and (almost certainly) Spain. The English aeroplane arrangements have been put in the hands of an American who, on his own statements, knows nothing about aviation. He got the appointment because he knew something about kites. I see at length that his machine has proceeded seven hundred yards in a direct line, a feat that was accomplished on the Continent long ago. . . . His machine is unwieldy, a bad copy of many aeroplanes . . . I might as well attempt to produce my newspapers by the aid of a man who confessedly knows nothing of printing, having carefully chosen old-fashioned machines to begin with.

When Northcliffe returned to England he at once went to see Lord Esher in order to discuss Britain's aeronautical situation. On 20 March Esher recorded in his journal: "Today I have been with Kennedy Jones and this evening 2 hours with Northcliffe on Navy and then Aeroplanes".[1]

In March a series of articles in the *Daily Mail* carried Lord Northcliffe's campaign to its next stage. On the 10th the paper reported that Wilbur Wright was shortly to visit England and while there he would "give the War Office an opportunity of judging the efficiency of his aeroplane". The paper stated flatly that the War Office had "every intention of purchasing one of his aeroplanes". The *Daily Mail* also revealed that King Edward, who was at Biarritz, was planning to visit the aerodrome at Pau so that he could see Wilbur Wright's flights for himself.

This edition of the *Daily Mail* took care to report the first successful flights of "The Imperial Airship Zeppelin I", the first Zeppelin airship built with funds supplied by the Imperial German Government. This vessel, the *Daily Mail* explained, made three ascents on the previous day. While Count Zeppelin took part in the first of the flights the other two were carried out with "a purely military crew".

On 11 March the first leading article in the *Daily Mail*, entitled "Aeroplanes for Britain", was devoted to the Wright aeroplane and to a criticism of the policy adopted by the War Office.

> Satisfaction at the announcement that Mr. Wilbur Wright is coming to England is tempered only with regret that we should be so late in securing the presence of the inventor of the aeroplane. Mr. Wright may not have conquered the air, but he has come so near to harnessing that unstable element to his chariot that even official Whitehall is beginning to show interest. Accordingly, he has re-

[1] *Ibid.*, p. 378.

ceived an invitation to give the War Office proof of what everybody knows. . . .

Hope may be extracted from the tardy confession that the War Office is prepared not merely to inspect but to buy one of these machines, which promise to introduce a new factor into national defence. It is incredible, yet true, that Parliament, whose vision ranges from China to Peru – from naval programmes to parish pumps – should never have deigned to look up into the air. . . .

. . . Mr. Wright will have no difficulty in convincing even official scepticism that he has outflown the experimental stage and attained the higher region of practical art. France and Germany require no visit to awaken them to the importance of this art. . . .

On 15 March the *Daily Mail* announced that the Wright brothers had given an order to the firm of Messrs Short Brothers, of Battersea, for the immediate construction of six Wright aeroplanes. In order to carry out the work Short Brothers were building a large factory at the new Aero Club flying-ground at Shellbeach in the Isle of Sheppey. One of the Shorts declared that the new factory would be able to produce one Wright aeroplane every fortnight. The construction of these machines, it was explained, would be carried out in the greatest secrecy.

The meeting of King Edward and the Wrights took place on 18 March. The *Daily Mail* reported: "The King exclaimed in admiration as the flight proceeded". With his usual courtesy and charm King Edward said he hoped to see the Wrights in England and Wilbur promised that when he finished some demonstration flights in Rome he, Orville, and Katharine would take care to visit London before their return to the United States.

The great success of the German Government's "Zeppelin I", which occurred exactly at this time, was also commented upon at length in the *Daily Mail*. On 19 March this military airship succeeded in making a flight of nearly four hours with twenty-six passengers on board. F. W. Wile reported from Berlin that the German military authorities considered this flight to be immensely significant from a strategic point of view. The weight carried on this occasion suggested that the military Zeppelins might soon be able to serve as transports for troops or as carriers of artillery and ammunition.

Count Zeppelin, according to Wile's despatch published in the *Daily Mail* of 22 March, announced that improvements were possible whereby his airship would be able to carry much heavier weights than had ever been borne aloft before. Another item in the *Daily Mail* of 22 March revealed there was reason to believe that the new German military dirigibles were about to be equipped with aerial torpedoes. One hundred of these torpedoes armed with dynamite or gun-cotton had been ordered by the firm of Krupp from the inventor of the device.

Northcliffe, throughout his career, was always accused of promoting "scares" of various kinds in order to increase the circulation of his newspapers, despite the deplorable effects and consequences of these journalistic excursions. When he began to warn his countrymen about the dangers that might come to them from the air the charge was made that he meant to exploit the situation not from motives of vigilant patriotism but only because he wanted to sell more newspapers. Lord Northcliffe, as a matter of course, would do whatever he could to enhance his circulation figures but there can be no doubt that he was keenly and genuinely alert to the dangers and the significance of the arrival of the air age for his country. He must have been gratified to receive a letter of support for his new course, at this time, from Sidney Low, later Sir Sidney Low, a former editor of the *St. James' Gazette* and one of the most respected practitioners of the "old journalism" in England. Low wrote to Northcliffe:[1]

> You have no doubt more papers than you or any man can reasonably want; but can you not add to them by giving us a first-rate aviation journal? I am not suggesting that I could help you in this, as I am not an expert; but I have been watching the subject for some years past and have found great difficulty in following it owing to the absence of a first-rate newspaper dealing with the subject more closely and scientifically than either the engineering or motoring newspapers ordinarily do. A journal of this kind would do much to assist England in gaining the position which she has so deplorably lost in connection with this momentous development.

V

Meanwhile, the Liberal government struggled desperately in its efforts to have the Navy Estimates for the year accepted in the Parliament. There had been a serious crisis in the Cabinet. Early in February Lloyd George, the leader of the anti-armament Radicals in the Cabinet, had warned the prime minister not to accede to the higher Estimates demanded by the Board of Admiralty because if he did so scores of the most loyal Liberals in the House of Commons would be so shocked they might turn against their own Ministry. He begged Asquith to pay careful attention to the arguments put forward by himself, John Morley, Churchill and other cabinet ministers who were not prepared to tolerate the Admiralty's request for increased Estimates.

In the country there were millions of Liberals who were beginning to

[1] B.M. Add. MSS. (Northcliffe Papers) Sidney Low to Northcliffe, 7 April 1909.

lose confidence in the government. If large Navy Estimates were presented, Lloyd George predicted, the disaffection of these Liberals would explode into open opposition and the usefulness of the Parliament elected in 1906 would be at an end. One of the great historical triumphs of their party would be cast aside, for no valid purpose.

Late in February Asquith hit upon an ingenious solution which satisfied most of his colleagues: only four Dreadnoughts would be commenced in the financial year 1909-10 but if the necessity for them was proven four additional capital ships would be laid down no later than 1 April 1910. Ministers, though distressed, found they could agree upon this compromise.

The situation of the government was still a dangerous one, however. Ministers could expect the Tories to attack them from one side and their own Radical followers to attack from the other. The debate in the Commons began on 16 March and the result was a fierce agitation to secure all eight capital ships at once, in order to assure the country's naval superiority over the Germans. All were surprised at the ferocity of the Conservative assault and partly for this reason many Radicals failed to press their own case for reduced Estimates. It was at this time that George Wyndham, an eccentric Tory stalwart, coined the phrase "We want eight and we won't wait".

The situation seemed so terrible that on 19 March Arthur Balfour gave notice of a vote of censure in the Commons because the government's naval arrangements did not "sufficiently secure the safety of the Empire". On 24 March the Conservative *Daily Telegraph* declared: "Since Nero fiddled there has never been a spectacle more strange, more lamentable than the imperilling of the whole priceless heritage of centuries to balance a party Budget."

While the naval agitation dominated the British political scene in these months those few members of Parliament who were concerned about the nation's weakness in the air began to make their voices heard, by slow degrees but with increasing effect. Their tactic was to ask questions of the Service ministers. R. B. Haldane was their particular target.

On 18 February 1909 Arthur Fell, the Conservative Member for Great Yarmouth, asked the First Lord of the Admiralty if the government proposed to construct a dirigible balloon for service with the fleet. McKenna replied that the matter was "under consideration". Fell then turned to the Secretary of State for War in order to enquire about the War Office's experiments with aeroplanes. He wanted to know if men of greater skill than those already employed should not be entrusted with the work. He also asked if the War Office planned to build dirigible balloons like those flying so successfully in France and in Germany. Haldane was not to be drawn. He said: "I may state that the future policy as regards aeroplanes and dirigible balloons is now receiving very careful attention, and, accordingly, at the present moment I am not in a position to give the hon. Member any further information on the subject."[1]

It must not be supposed that all members of Parliament participating in these early exchanges were aeronautical enthusiasts or advocates of a more vigilant national policy in the air. Haldane, when he was questioned in the House of Commons, found he had to brace himself to treat with enquiries that represented every point of view, as the following exchanges of 23 February indicate: [2]

> MR. J. T. MACPHERSON: I beg to ask the Secretary of State for War how much public money has been expended by the War Office . . . on experiments with aeroplanes and dirigible balloons; and whether he will put an end to further waste of public money on such experiments by ordering their instant abandonment?
> MR. HALDANE: The expenditure on dirigible balloons and aeroplanes has amounted to about £19,000. As I recently informed the House, the future policy is under consideration.
> MR. ARTHUR H. LEE: Have any steps been taken to acquire the services or assistance of the Wright Brothers?
> MR. HALDANE: I would rather not answer that.
> MR. STANLEY WILSON: Can the Army aeroplanes fly yet?

Haldane refused to reply to Stanley Wilson's question. However, in the debate on the Army Estimates on 4 March he permitted himself to reveal a slight amount of information about the government's aeronautical policy.

He explained to the House that the entire question had been referred by the Committee of Imperial Defence to "the Army and Navy experts". These authorities had deliberated, the Secretary of State said, for a considerable period of time. The Navy, he declared, was considering the production of a "pattern of dirigible balloon". The Army planned to experiment with dirigible balloons and "we are considering the best pattern as regards aeroplanes". Haldane announced that the War Office had entered into negotiations with private inventors of aeroplanes because it was believed that more rapid progress could be achieved by working with them than if the experiments were carried out by the Army's own technicians who did not possess the facilities available to the private inventors. Haldane then argued that aeroplane development was a matter that must take time. These machines, he said, could not yet be considered efficient instruments of war but the War Office proposed to experiment with them in the coming year.[3]

[1] *Parliamentary Debates*, 4th Series, 18 February 1909, cols 231–4.
[2] *Parliamentary Debates*, 4th Series, 23 February 1909, col. 585.
[3] *Parliamentary Debates*, 4th Series, 4 March 1909, col. 1619.

On 15 March Haldane was asked by the Member for St Albans if he would not advise the government to vote a substantial sum in the Estimates for the year "for the purpose of carrying out experiments with aeroplanes". In response, the Secretary of State made a firm but peculiar declaration. He said: "I have nothing to add to the statement which I made in introducing the Estimates. The Army Council propose during the ensuing year to consider the machines of private inventors and to direct the attention of special officers to the study of the subject. What experiments may be made or machines bought as the result it would be premature to forecast."[1]

These pronouncements by the Secretary of State in the House of Commons were remarkable utterances. They merit our attention. Haldane, as we have seen, had little faith in or respect for the work of private inventors. When the achievements of the Wright brothers were called to his attention he dismissed Wilbur and Orville as mere "empiricists", an opinion he retained until the end of his life. He spurned the approaches of other private inventors for the same reason. Haldane, as a responsible officer of the State, refused to traffic with them when the opportunity to do so was presented to him.

Nevertheless, he was passionately interested in the subject of aeroplanes. When Lord Esher allowed him to make the opening statement at the first meeting of the Aerial Navigation Sub-Committee in December 1908 Haldane made his philosophical position entirely clear.

Aviation, he said upon that occasion, was a subject which required a great deal of experimental work. The important preliminary to genuine progress, he suggested, was the establishment of a scientific committee, created and paid for by the State, including representatives of the Army and Navy, and presided over by an eminent scientific authority or by a distinguished judge.

Later in 1909, in May, Haldane brought into being the Advisory Committee for Aeronautics, a body which was an exact reflection of the suggestions he had brought forward in December 1908 at the first meeting of Lord Esher's sub-committee. The Advisory Committee represented the kind of institution that could, in Haldane's view, save his country in the trying conditions of the new century. This type of concept, in his mind, could be applied with equal effect and validity to Britain's conduct of her foreign trade; commerce; industry; her system of education; and also to her military affairs and enterprises.

Nor was it merely a matter of Haldane's philosophic speculations and ruminations that was involved in his curious conduct in the House of Commons at this time. R. B. Haldane was a keen student of men and affairs. He admired his young colleague, Winston Churchill, and liked to

---

[1] From the report in *The Times*, 16 March 1909.

work with him. He realized also that Churchill was a politician with a brilliant and powerful future, a man who might one day become a political ally of very genuine significance. On 26 January 1909 Churchill took his place for the first time at a meeting of the Committee of Imperial Defence. He was already known to this contemporaries as a bold, ardent, and even brash partisan who firmly believed in himself and in his own ideas. Nevertheless, even he was impressed by his surroundings on this occasion. Lord Esher observed on 26 January: "I came up late and attended the Defence Committee. . . . Winston [Churchill] made his first appearance, but was quite subdued".[1] Only a few weeks later, however, the Committee of Imperial Defence met to discuss the recommendations of its Aerial Navigation Sub-Committee. Churchill, at this meeting, was so surprised at the courses proposed with respect to aeroplanes that he was emboldened to speak out in the strongest terms even though he found himself in a minority of one in that select circle.

When the Committee of Imperial Defence on 25 February 1909 accepted C. S. Rolls' remarkable proposal to place his "services" at the disposal of the government provided they furnished him with facilities to experiment with his Wright aeroplane, Churchill was shocked. He felt, as we have seen, that the idea was entirely too "amateurish" and he urged his colleagues on the committee to put themselves in communication with Wilbur Wright himself instead of bargaining with a novice like Rolls.

Haldane, on that occasion, despite Churchill's obvious distress, did not allow himself to say a single word in support of his young friend's arguments. He preferred, in effect, to deal with what we might reasonably call a second-hand "empiricist". His ideas about a scientific approach to the subject were abandoned in favour of accepting the lame recommendation of the Aerial Navigation Sub-Committee. It is no wonder that Percy Walker later wrote that "Haldane's actions behind the scenes may never be known with certainty".

VI

Despite Haldane's cautious statements in the Commons the Parliamentary probing into the details and nature of the government's aeronautical policy continued. As the naval crisis rose to serious heights of intensity a new development took place on 16 March. On that day Lord Montagu of Beaulieu, a highly respected motoring authority, rose in his place in the

---

[1] Maurice V. Brett, ed., *Journals and Letters of Reginald Viscount Esher*, vol. II, p. 367.

House of Lords in order to deliver a carefully considered speech attacking
the government's aeronautical arrangements.[1]

Lord Montagu of Beaulieu had established himself as a motoring
expert of distinction and more recently had begun to study aeronautical
developments. He was already recognized by contemporaries as a man
who knew a great deal about aeroplanes and airships.

After the usual courtesies that mark out debates in the House of Lords
he began his speech by pointing out that there was a school in the War
Office that believed nothing practical had yet been evolved in the field of
aeronautics. Although no names were mentioned it was clear he referred
to Sir William Nicholson and his followers. Lord Montagu of Beaulieu
told the Peers that military aviation had already attained such results that
it was "absolutely imperative for this country to give it more attention and
to devote more money to it than it is at present receiving. Great progress
has been made by foreign countries, especially by France and Germany,
in the direction of fitting up dirigible balloons and aeroplanes for war
purposes."

He then said that the British Army's arrangements at Aldershot were
altogether inadequate to secure genuine progress. He explained that he
had watched Wilbur Wright fly in the previous autumn. The French
military authorities saw to it that Wilbur flew from a large field and that he
was assisted by troops whose business it was to keep curious spectators far
away from the immediate scene of his experiments. The situation at
Aldershot was entirely different: "Our military aviators, on the other
hand, labour in an atmosphere of discouragement, and the work they can
do is of a limited kind".

Montagu next proceeded to attack the policy R. B. Haldane had
advocated in the House of Commons. He declared: "As a country we
ought not to leave this to private enterprise, but ought to take an active
part from the point of view of science. . ."

At this stage he argued that it was vitally necessary for Great Britain to
at once reflect upon its vulnerability to attack from the air:

> I may be asked by my critics, can airships or aeroplanes become
> dangerous to this country? Why need we take any notice of the
> question from the military point of view? I am one of those who
> believe that within a year or two Germany and France will have a
> considerable fleet of speedy dirigible balloons . . . They will be
> capable of carrying six or eight men, or the equivalent in weight of
> explosives. One does not want to be an expert to know that high
> explosives . . . weighting 900 lbs. may do very serious damage; and
> when it is remembered that the balloon can be arrested in its flight

[1] For his speech see *Parliamentary Debates*, 4th Series, *House of Lords*, 16
March 1909, cols 456ff.

and remain stationary over a given point while the explosive is dropped on that site – be it a Government office, railway bridge, bank, or dockyard – it is obvious that airships may be very dangerous instruments indeed. Only last week the new Zeppelin airship flew thirty five miles an hour, and . . . manoeuvred with ease and satisfied the very critical authorities on the spot.

He informed the House that London was especially vulnerable to such an attack by airships:

I should like to tell the House how near as the crow, or as the dirigible flies, this country is to important points on the Continent. London is only 320 miles from Emden; or, to put it another way, in ten hours a fleet of dirigible balloons could come from Emden and be over London. That, surely, must make us think. . . .

I say, without hesitation, that today the insularity of this country is not what it was, and I feel quite certain that when the War Office and His Majesty's Government realise the progress that has been made abroad they will see the necessity of devoting attention to this important question.

He concluded with a straightforward attack on the policy of the War Office:

I beg your Lordships' pardon for having detained the House some time, but I think I have put enough facts before you to show that in this matter we must display as a nation more energy than we have been doing. No one who considers the rapid march of the science of aviation nowadays can help to a certain extent, blaming the permanent officials and the Army Council for their slackness in the past. It has been the traditional attitude to wait until private inventors or foreign nations have perfected their arrangements and then to come in with a rush. But shall we be able in this matter to come in with a rush? This question . . . cannot be deferred and with all sincerity I ask His Majesty's Government to give it their most careful attention.

The Earl of Crewe, Lord Privy Seal and Secretary of State for the Colonies in Asquith's Ministry, replied for the government. He blandly acknowledged that Montagu of Beaulieu was an expert in these matters and he expressed his gratitude for the information he had supplied and the advice he had offered to the House. However, he denied that the government was treating the matter too lightly. He pointed out that the subject had been submitted to the Committee of Imperial Defence, where it had been studied very seriously. He blamed the Treasury for the government's failure to expend large sums on aeronautical experiments. He repeated Haldane's stated policy that progress could be made most rapidly by dealing with private inventors of aeroplanes. He agreed that the conditions of warfare might be "revolutionised" by airships and aeroplanes. Finally, he assured Lord Montagu of Beaulieu that the Departments concerned would not "ignore this matter or allow it to slip". If it was found in the future that increased expenditures were necessary, he said, "the money will be forthcoming".

The great debate on the censure of the government because of its naval programme was held before a packed House of Commons a few days later, on 29 March 1909. The principal speaker on the government side on this occasion was Sir Edward Grey, the Foreign Secretary. Grey, a great Whig, was so steeped in tradition that he enjoyed the respect of even the most partisan Tories.

Grey's speech ranged over every aspect of the Anglo-German naval rivalry. A chief burden of his address was an appeal to the House to trust the government to do what was right in the emergency which confronted it. Few were converted by the debate and the censure resolution was lost by more than two hundred votes.

Historians have analysed this debate very closely but one aspect of it has been neglected. Arthur Du Cros, the newly elected Unionist Member for Hastings, attacked the government not simply because of its naval failures. He introduced another critical charge. The Liberal government deserved to be condemned, he argued, because of its gross neglect of the nation's aeronautical position.

Arthur Du Cros was one of those Members of Parliament who were convinced that the government's aeronautical policy could lead to a national disaster. At this time he was actively engaged in doing all that he could to alert the country to the dangers that menaced it from the air.

In the debate of 29 March he began his attack on ministers by explaining that Sir Edward Grey had appealed to both sides of the House "to trust the Government to do what was right in the emergency with which we are dealing today". He continued by warning the House that the Germans already possessed a dirigible airship, the Zeppelin, that could enable them to drop great weights of explosives on England whenever they chose to do so while the British, owing to the carelessness of the government possessed neither knowledge nor experience of such an aerial vessel. He said:[1]

> I wish to call attention to a phase of the subject which has not yet been referred to – I mean the question of aeroplane supremacy. . . .
> Here is a case where the greatest initiative has been shown and progress made by Germany. Special factories have been constructed at great expense for the building and equipping giant airships of the

---

[1] *Parliamentary Debates*, 4th Series, 29 March 1909, cols 108–9.

Zeppelin design. I do not refer to aeroplanes or small dirigibles. . . .
In Germany they already have in commission one of these large
vessels, and at the end of this year four more will be complete, while
next year and in the years to follow Germany will be in a position to
produce one of these vessels in any six weeks of the year. . . . Only
the other day a journey was made from Friedrichshafen to Constance
and back, a distance of 140 miles, in four hours. The distances which
have been accomplished . . . are equivalent to a voyage to England
and back, and the vessel can carry supplies for a journey of twice that
distance. In addition to the crew . . . they have lifting power
sufficient to carry between one and two tons of explosive matter. . . .

Having explained these facts Du Cros launched into his attack on the
government:

> In the face of that, I say, that British initiative and enterprise have
> never appeared to less advantage. We possess absolutely no know-
> ledge or experience of this type of vessel. Our experiments have been
> confined to smaller vessels, such as the aeroplane or the non-rigid or
> semi-rigid dirigible, which have so far been conspicuous by their
> failure and utter inadequacy. . . . Contrast that with the action of
> Germany, where they have already spent about half a million of
> money . . . and in the danger period we are discussing they will
> possess a fleet of between 24 and 30 of these vessels. Can anyone
> believe that these people are wasting and squandering their money
> or energy in these experiments. . . . It is a fact that should not be
> ignored that in the year 1912 there will, or can be, in existence a fleet
> of 24 of these vessels, capable of carrying explosives in large quanti-
> ties and of travelling long distances. . . . In the face of the total
> failure of this country to attempt anything to combat this state of
> things, it is idle to deny that this is a consideration which should cause
> us grave concern. The Foreign Secretary appeals to us to trust the
> Government; but here is a case in point where the Government has
> not shown initiative. . . . I earnestly hope the matter will not be
> further neglected, but that some proper and comprehensive steps
> will be taken to place Great Britain in a line with her rivals upon this
> great and important question.

Du Cros's speech in the debate of 29 March was not an isolated
initiative. He and his friends were now contemplating a great campaign of
propaganda to bring the air threat to Britain to the attention of every one
of its inhabitants. In the next stage of their campaign they planned to
carry the matter outside Parliament in order to present it to the country in
the most striking manner possible.

VII

Early in Janury 1909 a society known as the Aerial League of the British Empire was founded in London. Its objects were similar in character to those of its predecessor, the more famous Navy League. This Aerial League described itself as a "strictly non-party organisation". It was a patriotic association whose members desired to stimulate British interest in aeronautics by disseminating information on the subject which would demonstrate the "vital importance to the British Empire of aerial supremacy, upon which its commerce, commmunications, defence, and its very existence must largely depend; and to urge these matters upon Parliament, public bodies, and public men".

By April 1909 the officers of the Aerial League of the British Empire decided to take a dramatic step forward in order to accomplish the objects of their society. They approached the Lord Mayor of London, Sir George Truscott, and asked him to permit them to hold a large meeting in the Mansion House, on 5 April. The object of the proposed gathering was to call public attention to the urgent need to begin a great national movement in Britain concerned with furthering aeronautical development in the country.

When the Lord Mayor considered the request he was at first reluctant to accede to it. However, the supplicants quickly changed his mind. They convinced him that London was so close to the British sea frontier that it was a prime target for aerial attack. The metropolis lay open to bombardment from the air. Eventually, in consequence of these arguments the Lord Mayor agreed to permit the meeting to be held in the Mansion House. Indeed, he further decided, in his newly awakened enthusiasm, to serve as chairman at the gathering.

The metropolitan Press was alerted to the forthcoming event and the newspapers, in response, gave it wide publicity. On the day of the meeting at the Mansion House several journals published articles about it, in advance. These accounts emphasized British unpreparedness in the air at the same time that they published reports of the most recent airship developments in Germany. There, experiments with the Zeppelin, Gross, and Parseval dirigibles were proceeding at a rapid pace. The Press revealed also that the Germans were planning to try out, at their army manoeuvres in August, certain "airship destroyers", guns mounted on motor cars and so positioned that they could fire vertically upwards. These guns were to be supplied with special shrapnel shells already constructed by the firms of Krupp and Ehrhardt. The tone of these articles all suggested Teutonic efficiency in aeronautical development and British backwardness in the new technology.

The Mansion House meeting of 5 April attracted a large audience.

Several generals and admirals sat on the platform in company with Lord Montagu of Beaulieu, Colonel Templer, Sir Philip Magnus, Sir Hiram Maxim, Major Baden-Powell and other eminent men. The proceedings were opened by Sir George Truscott. He said: ". . . he had been asked by the Aerial League to grant the use of the Mansion House in order that the subject of aerial navigation might be brought before the citizens of London . . . He confessed that at first he was rather doubtful as to the value of airships and . . . he could hardly conceive that in the thin and invisible air around and above us ships could be made to float which would be a menace to us if they belonged to an enemy. . . . But wonderful things were happening every day. Indeed, the navigation of the air had become a reality . . . in navigating the air it would appear that we are very much behindhand. . . . The Aerial League wanted to arouse the nation to the importance of this matter. . . ."[1]

As was the custom at such gatherings several letters were then read out from sympathizers who were unable to be present. Prince Louis of Battenberg, Commander-in-Chief of the Atlantic Fleet and one of the most respected and brilliant officers in the Royal Navy, wrote: "It is time we woke up, seeing what is being done on the Continent". Letters written by Winston Churchill and Lord Curzon, the former Viceroy of India, were also read to the company. They expressed warm support for the objects of the Aerial League.

Lord Montagu of Beaulieu proposed: "That this meeting of the citizens of London . . . regards with considerable anxiety the rapid development of the science and practice of aerial navigation by other nations and deplores the backwardness and apathy shown by this country regarding this new means of communication, which is of vital importance from a commercial as well as from a national defence point of view and pledges itself hereby heartily to support the objects of the Aerial League of the British Empire".

In urging support for the resolution Lord Montagu of Beaulieu asked: ". . . Did we realise that within a short period, say five years, the insularity of this country, as we understood it, might be destroyed . . . He referred to the latest achievements of the Zeppelin airship, and said that after that no one could say military aviation was merely a thing of the imagination". These remarks were received with cheers by the Mansion House audience.

The resolution was seconded by Vice-Admiral Sir Percy Scott, the crack gunnery expert of the British Navy. He revealed that he was cooperating with a firm of gun-makers to design a gun that could be effective against aerial ships. However, he predicted that such aerial vessels would attack at night, and he added "he had not yet met any

[1] This account of the Mansion House meeting is based on the report in *The Times* for 6 April 1909.

gunnery person who could teach him how to hit an object that one could not see. . . ."

The resolution was then carried unanimously and a vote of thanks was accorded to the Lord Mayor. Other speakers endorsed these various remarks and urged that the Aerial League should give lectures and organize demonstrations to arouse public opinion in every part of the country.

The response to this meeting at the Mansion House was tremendous. In the days after it took place a chorus of support appeared in the newspaper Press. Leading articles in the *Daily Telegraph*, the *Morning Post*, the *Daily Graphic* and other journals endorsed the objects and goals of the Aerial League. Although the League stressed that it was a "strictly non-party" organization, several of the newspapers were severely critical of the failures of the Liberal government in this sphere and all of them expressed concern about Germany's aeronautical advances. The *Daily Telegraph* declared: ". . . it behoves this country to wake up at once, and become alive to the facts of the situation. . . . Great Britain must at once set about building an aerial navy. Though there is no need for scare, there is abundant need of careful preparation, and we cannot suppose that the British Government will require much pressure to induce them to increase the paltry sum . . . which was set aside in the Army Estimates for aerial experiments. It is manifestly inadequate, in view of the Zeppelin successes, and the enormous importance attached to these airships by the German military authorities. No Englishman can read the telegrams from Friedrichshafen without feeling a keen sense of patriotic regret that we have nothing similar to show. . . ."

An even more spirited attack on the government's aeronautical policies appeared in the first leading article in *The Times* on 6 April. *The Times* leader denounced Asquith's Ministry in the severest tones:

> While other nations are prosecuting the construction of airships as a matter of serious business . . . they seem still to be regarded in this country as merely interesting toys . . . The influential meeting held yesterday at the Mansion House . . . will at least make known to the people of this country that there is in existence an Aerial League of the British Empire, and that it contains many men of science . . . men of distinction in the public services. The collective views of such a gathering are worthy of serious public attention. . . .
>
> Mr. Wright's machine is a practicable flyer. . . . If we turn to the other type depending upon flotation, the progress made is perhaps even more suggestive. . . .
>
> The Zeppelin airship can carry several tons weight in addition to all that is needed for the crew . . . We have only to suppose its load to consist of high explosives in order to get some notion of its possibilities . . . Yet with all these possibilities ready at very short notice to

become actualities, this country is doing nothing worth naming to meet the danger. Probably we shall again be told that the Government policy is one of masterly inactivity combined with economy, and that, when we have seen the best that other nations can do, we shall be better able to do something for ourselves. It is a beautiful policy for dreamers. . . .

The members of the Aerial League were not content to rest upon the achievements of the Mansion House meeting. They planned a further vigorous propaganda campaign. The League's chairman, Colonel H. S. Massy, a former Commandant of the 19th Bengal Lancers, was especially active. He proposed to deliver lectures on aviation wherever he could secure an audience to listen to him. He approached the mayors of several provincial towns for the purpose and turned also to clergymen in London and in the country in order to ask them to mention his lectures to their congregations at the conclusion of services each Sunday. The League suggested to the Secretary of State for War that special companies in the Territorial Army should be trained in the defence of seaport towns against attack by airships. The League also wanted Haldane to provide funds for the establishment of a technical college that would train aviators and airship pilots.[1] It soon became known that Lord Roberts, the Marquess of Salisbury, Lord Esher and H. G. Wells endorsed the purposes and objects of the Aerial League.

It remained for Lord Montagu of Beaulieu to make a further contribution of significance at this stage of the agitation. On 21 April he read a paper to the members of The National Defence Association, a society jointly composed of civilians who were interested in military affairs and of officers in the Army and the Navy. He had something new to say. In his address Lord Montague of Beaulieu explained that London lay open to a strategic air attack that might produce devastating results.

He suggested that in a highly civilized country like Britain there were certain vitally important places he called "nerve centres". These "nerve centres" included the government buildings, the Houses of Parliament, the railway stations, the telephone and telegraph headquarters, the Stock Exchange, and also all the main communications systems of the nation. According to his concept, a single powerful blow from the air aimed at these "nerve centres" could cripple the country.

Airships, he said, "would come so swiftly and strike so directly at the centres that the nation would be almost paralysed before armies or navies could come to her aid". In his opinion "war airships" were not to be feared because they could land an invasion force on the coast or because they could attack the fleet. It was his idea that airships were a great

---

[1] For these latter points see the *Daily Mail*, 13 April 1909.

danger to Britain because they could almost instantly destroy "the nerve centres and all the main communications of this country. . . ."

It will be seen at once that Lord Montagu of Beaulieu's concept was far more sophisticated than the ideas already advanced by Privy Councillor Rudolf Martin or those of Sir Hiram Maxim. Privy Councillor Martin believed that airships could carry an invading German force with its artillery, horses, and stores across the Channel and thus effect a successful invasion of England. Most technical authorities of the period realized that the airships of that day were incapable of lifting such tremendous weights. Sir Hiram Maxim had argued that a thousand aeroplanes could land an invading army in England but his suggestion contained no plan for the provisioning of such a force.

Lord Montagu of Beaulieu's idea was different, and quite novel. He recognized, as Rudolf Martin and Hiram Maxim did not, that the great recent advances in aeronautics introduced entirely new possibilities for an enemy of Great Britain. His argument was that Britain was in danger because it possessed no system of defence that could enable it to disrupt or even hamper bombardment from the air, bombardment from vessels already capable of such an attack. As he saw it there was no need for an enemy to occupy any part of the British Isles in order to compel the government to sue for peace. British ability to resist could be broken or very seriously diminished even though no enemy soldier occupied even a yard of British territory. Rudolf Martin and Hiram Maxim were still thinking along traditional lines. Lord Montagu of Beaulieu saw the matter in en entirely different light. London, in his view, was an almost unique target for bombardment from the air because so many of Britain's vital "nerve centres" were concentrated in that one place where they could be attacked relatively easily, and destroyed as a result.

An account of this talk was published prominently in *The Times*, on 26 April.[1] In this way Montagu's remarkable analysis of Britain's vulnerable condition was presented to a wide audience in the country. However, the campaign to stimulate British interest in aeronautics now took another turn. Lord Montagu's friends in both Houses of Parliament reckoned that further organization was required if the air danger to the country was to be met while time remained. The politicans at Westminster therefore decided to form a group they called the Parliamentary Aerial Defence Committee.

---

[1] For an excellent comment see Neville Jones, *The Origins of Strategic Bombing* (London, 1973), p. 27, hereafter cited as Jones, *Origins of Strategic Bombing*.

VIII

In April 1909 the leaders of the Aero Club of the United Kingdom, the Aeronautical Society of Great Britain, and the Aerial League of the British Empire came together in order to work out an agreement defining the nature and scope of the activities of each of their societies. They acted in this way for a good reason. They desired to avoid the "lamentable waste of effort and much unnecessary friction" that had resulted from the competition of British organizations concerned with advancing the cause of motoring in the United Kingdom. "By a judicious and reasonable agreement", they declared, ". . . . a working scheme can be contrived . . . which will prevent a similar occurrence in the development of aeronautics. . . ." A further great object was to induce the government "to take up the subject seriously, and to spend sums of money . . . for the purpose. . . ."[1]

In order to achieve these goals it was recognized by those concerned that public opinion had to be educated and roused. It was decided also that a parliamentary committee should be formed "consisting of members of both Houses, with the strict understanding that the whole question is one entirely outside party politics".

The leaders, after deliberation, agreed that the Aeronautical Society would be regarded as the "paramount scientific authority on aeronautical matters"; that the Aero Club would be looked upon as the "paramount body in all matters of sport, and the development of the art of aeronautics"; and that the Aerial League would be recognized as the "paramount body for patriotic movements and for education".

These leaders, R. W. Wallace of the Aero Club, Colonel Massy of the Aerial League, and E. P. Frost of the Aeronautical Society believed that "at the present moment an opportunity offers itself which may never occur again". The War Office had been consulting their members for advice for several months past "with a view to dealing with the pressing question of national aerial defence". They realized that if they combined and defined their efforts they could help the government more efficiently than if they continued to act as separate and uncoordinated organizations. As a result, they drew up and signed an agreement which recognized the "respective spheres of each separate body".

In order to help the parliamentary committee that was to be formed it was further agreed that each of the societies would nominate three of its members "to advise and assist [it] when required". All concerned believed that their agreement would greatly benefit their country and help it to face the dangers and the opportunities of the new air age.

---

[1] For the details set out in this and the following paragraphs see the account in *Flight*, 8 May 1909.

Early in May 1909 a meeting of several Members of Parliament was held and it was decided that a permanent committee should be established, on strictly non-party lines, for the "purpose of co-operating with the Government on aeronautical questions affecting the defences of the country". Arthur Lee, later Lord Lee of Fareham, the Conservative Member for the Fareham division of Hampshire, was appointed chairman of this Parliamentary Aerial Defence Committee. Cecil Harmsworth, Lord Northcliffe's brother and Liberal Member for Droitwich, was selected as vice-chairman, and Arthur Du Cros was appointed secretary of the new organization. It was eventually decided that members of the House of Lords would be permitted to join and Lord Montagu of Beaulieu came forward to assist the work there.

IX

The chairman, Arthur Lee, was a remarkable man. Lord Northcliffe had already picked him out as the parliamentary leader who could carry forward a positive aeronautical policy in the House of Commons. On 10 April Lee and his wife were invited to Sutton Place, Northcliffe's country home, where "After dinner . . . there was a Cinematograph performance, with the most interesting pictures of Wilbur Wright and his aeroplane, a graceful bird-like thing in flight".[1]

Arthur Lee had suffered through a terrible childhood. He was the son of a Dorsetshire clergyman who died when the boy was still an infant. Since his mother was almost without funds she was forced to hand him over to the care of strangers. Before he was four he was "practically adopted" by a wealthy woman who devoted her life to bringing up the children of "poor gentlefolk". Although this lady was generous she was also a strict disciplinarian and a "cruel tyrant" who never allowed Lee to forget that he existed only because of the charity of others. She plagued his life upon a regular basis. When Lee was sent to school he was flogged without mercy by several of his schoolmasters. The result was that he grew up to become a sensitive man who was also irascible, combative, and pugnacious. When he was selected as chairman of the Parliamentary Aerial Defence Committee it was practically certain that he would employ the new organization for partisan objects.

Despite the expressed intention of its founders that the committee was

---

[1] For this incident see Alan Clark ed., *A Good Innings, The Private Papers of Viscount Lee of Fareham* (London, 1974), p. 101, hereafter cited as Clark ed., *Lord Lee of Fareham*. The details of Lee's early life in the above account are drawn from this source.

to be "non-party", we must be clear that Arthur Lee was incapable of acting in an even-handed way. He was a bitter Tory stalwart, eager to attack the Liberal government at any time and for any purpose.

When he was still a boy Arthur Lee decided he could escape from his unpleasant condition of life by becoming an army officer. After training at the Royal Military Academy at Woolwich he was posted, at his own request, to the Royal Garrison Artillery in Hong Kong, in 1888. He was, in his own words, determined to "emerge from the ruck". In Hong Kong he quickly learned that the British authorities there were very interested in the new Russian fortifications recently completed at Vladivostock. Lee decided that "here was my predestined opportunity". He resolved to smuggle himself into Vladivostock and spy out the Russian emplacements, bringing back sketches and plans, and thus attracting the favourable notice of his military superiors.

After a time he obtained leave and travelled to Japan where he struck up an acquaintance with a British sea captain whose ship travelled regularly to Vladivostock. This patriot decided to help Lee in his bold enterprise and smuggled him ashore in the vicinity of the Vladivostock forts. Lee carried out his self-appointed mission almost without incident. Once, however, when he was crouching behind an eleven-inch gun he was almost spotted by a Russian sentry who passed close by: but the soldier never even glanced in his direction. Lee was so elated by his narrow escape that when the danger was past, in a marvellous display of bravado, he flicked his visiting-card down the gun's muzzle and then retreated to the safety of his friend's ship.

The military authorities in London were delighted with the results of this adventure. In the Foreign Office, however, Lord Salisbury was less enthusiastic. He believed such escapades could damage those friendly relations with other countries it was the business of the Foreign Office to preserve. Nevertheless, the young officer was soon posted to the gunnery school in the Isle of Wight, a distinct advance in his military career. Later, Lord Wolseley chose Lee to become the British Military Attaché in Washington. In time Lee married an American heiress of gigantic fortune and returned to England in order to take up a political life.

In 1903 when Arthur Balfour reorganized his faltering government he invited Arthur Lee to join it as Civil Lord of the Admiralty. Lee accepted the preferment with pleasure. He believed, in his innocence of such matters, that his "foot was really on the ladder at last" and that a great political career now lay before him.

Lee's quarrelsome personality soon made him a score of enemies at Westminster. Moreover, he was never accepted by the high Tory leaders who controlled the destinies of his Party. They subjected him, throughout his political life, to a series of cruel insults and slights. Bonar Law once said to him: "The trouble with you is that your wife has too much money."

Sir Edward Carson told him: "The trouble with you, Lee, is that you are getting to be a fat little round old man".

From the start, the Liberals in Parliament despised him. Sir Henry Campbell-Bannerman conceived "an almost rabid dislike of me which I did not hesitate, being young and combative, to return with interest. . . ." Years later when Arthur Lee presented his great country house, Chequers, to the nation as a residence for the prime minister, his contemporaries at once suspected the reasons which lay behind this magnificent gift. Several of them hastened to declare the gift was not a disinterested act but was motivated by the hope that it could restore his badly damaged political fortunes.

Early in February 1905 Lee went to his constituency in Hampshire in order to deliver a speech at an annual dinner of railwaymen there. It was a humdrum affair of the kind politicans always have to attend if they hope to retain the loyalty, and the votes, of those they represent in Parliament. Lee's tactless remarks on this occasion provoked an international incident. He said: "If war should unhappily be declared, under existing conditions, the British Navy would get its blow in first, before the other side had time even to read in the papers that war had been declared. . . ."

These remarkable observations caused considerable distress in Germany. The *Berliner Tageblatt* pointed out that the speech was made by a member of the British Government and described it as a "threat of war in a time of peace". The German Emperor was outraged. He called the speech an "open threat of war". He summoned the British Ambassador, Sir Frank Lascelles, and told him Lee was a "revenge-breathing corsair". If he were not immediately disavowed by his government there would be a storm of protest in the German Press and a "colossal" programme of warship construction in Germany.[1]

Lee's speech also resulted in domestic complications. In Parliament, Sir Henry Campbell-Bannerman, the leader of the Opposition, referred to ". . . the most improper speech made by a subordinate member of the Board of Admiralty, who, apparently tired of his obscurity, resolved to make a name for himself". Even Lee, pugnacious as he was, was shaken by the bitterness of this attack. He rushed out of the House when Campbell-Bannerman was finished and sought to avoid meeting even his friends in the lobby.[2]

Lee, a junior minister, had embarrassed the government. On 8 February he wrote to Arthur Balfour, the prime minister, in order to apologize

---

[1] For the Emperor's remarks see E. L. Woodward, *Great Britain and The German Navy* (Oxford, 1934), pp. 95–6, *n*. 1, hereafter cited as Woodward, *Great Britain and The German Navy*. See also Jonathan Steinberg, "The German background to Anglo-German relations, 1905–1914" in F. Hinsley ed., *British Foreign Policy under Sir Edward Grey*, p. 577, *n*. 26.

[2] See Clark ed., *Lord Lee of Fareham*, pp. 89–90.

for the effect of his speech. Fortunately for Lee, the Press had not reported his remarks with any great accuracy. This enabled Balfour, who could not afford any more resignations from his tottering Ministry, to gloss over the matter. On 9 February he wrote to Lee from 10 Downing Street:[1]

> I do not think you need give another thought to the incident referred to in your letter of yesterday.
> You were grossly misreported, and no man can be made responsible for anything which he never said. The Germans are ludicrously sensitive.

This was the man Lord Northcliffe "took up" in 1909 so that he could cooperate with a parliamentary leader vigorous enough to force the Asquith government into a more active aeronautical policy. Northcliffe offered positive inducements to encourage the relationship. He promised to see to it that Lee would be provided with "special publicity" and "other favours" in his newspapers. Later, Lee wrote that while he and his wife became very friendly with the Northcliffes, "I made it a cardinal principle never to come under any personal obligation to him . . ."[2]

Despite this assertion we should notice that on 30 March 1909 a long article by Frank Dilnot, the *Daily Mail*'s parliamentary correspondent, was published on the paper's leader page. It was called "A Specialist in National Defence: Arthur Lee: An Impression". Dilnot, in his article, could not ignore Lee's blunder of February 1905 when he was Civil Lord of the Admiralty in Balfour's government. He wrote of Lee: "He has made political mistakes in his time . . . he will make others in the future". He also told his readers that Lee was "one of the picturesque personalities of the Unionist Party . . . with the exception of his leader, Mr. Balfour, Mr. Lee is a more interesting personality than any other occupant of the Opposition front bench . . . Mr. Lee has force of will as well as more ornamental gifts, and will yet go far".

When Arthur Lee became chairman of the Parliamentary Aerial Defence Committee in the beginning of May he was already cooperating with Northcliffe on air matters. He took care to tell him about the new committee and made it clear that while it was a "strictly non-party concern" he proposed to use it to press the Liberal government in a manner that had not been attempted before. He explained to Northcliffe:[3]

[1] Lord Lee of Fareham Papers, Arthur James Balfour to Lee, 9 February 1905.
[2] See Clark ed., *Lord Lee of Fareham*, p. 102.
[3] B.M. Add. MSS. (Northcliffe Papers) Arthur Lee to Northcliffe, 13 May 1909.

The particular Committee of which I have been elected Chairman is called the "Aerial Defence Committee", and consists solely of members of the House of Commons.[1] It has, of course, been started as a strictly non-party concern; but I intend that it shall be used as a lever to stir up the Government in the direction not of theory but of effecting practical results. The immediate point that we are aiming at is to force the Government to acquire, by purchase, specimens of as many as possible foreign dirigibles and aeroplanes which have given practical results, in order that we may at least profit at this late hour by the experience which has been gained abroad.

I have an interesting scheme in this connection which I think might be effective in forcing the hands of the Government, and I am very anxious to discuss it with you at the earliest possible moment. . . . I am looking forward to seeing you at Sutton. . . .

The Tories were battling the Liberals on several fronts at this time. The struggle over the government's naval policy had blended into a fierce party fight concerned with the passage of Lloyd George's radical Budget of 1909, introduced in the House of Commons by the Chancellor of the Exchequer only a few days earlier. Lee told Northcliffe he proposed to play a prominent role in the naval controversy in addition to preparing to carry out his plan to "stir up" the Liberal government to adopt a more "practical" aeronautical programme:

I am just starting off on a long series of meetings in different parts of the country in support of the "eight Dreadnoughts"; . . . it will be tiring work; but it is of vital importance that the country should not be allowed to go to sleep about the Navy simply because it is agitated about the Budget.

Lord Northcliffe was in Berlin in May 1909 so that he could receive treatment for his eyes from a German specialist whom he consulted upon a regular basis in these years. Even though he was unwell and far from home he maintained a firm grip upon the policies of his newspapers. When he learned that his brother, Cecil Harmsworth, had been chosen as an officer of the Parliamentary Aerial Defence Committee he at once wrote to Arthur Lee to let him know that he looked forward to their continued cooperation:[2]

I shall be in London at the end of the month, and hope to meet you as soon as possible. . . .

I was glad to see that my brother Cecil is working in connection

[1] Peers were later allowed to join.
[2] B.M. Add. MSS. (Northcliffe Papers) Northcliffe to Lee, 13 May 1909.

with you. He is a very nice fellow – "quite a human Harmsworth" someone once said about him. . . .'

I wired "The Daily Mail" to look after the reporting of your speeches.

The time would come in later years when Northcliffe and Arthur Lee quarreled, when Northcliffe sent his editors the firm order that "I wish no member of the staff to see or in any way communicate with Lord Lee. . . ." But this was not yet. In the spring of 1909 they were planning to work together to see to it that ministers were driven to adopt policies that would at last enable the British to compete in the air with their French and German rivals.

X

Meanwhile, on 2 May the Wright brothers, accompanied by their sister, arrived in London. The British Press greeted them as heroes. As we have seen, the Aero Club of the United Kingdom had voted to award them a gold medal. In November 1908 the Council of the Aeronautical Society of Great Britain decided to present the Wrights with the Gold Medal of their society. Now Wilbur and Orville had come to England to accept these symbols of high distinction and regard.

Several newspapers employed the occasion of the visit to warn the Liberal government that a dangerous situation was developing owing to its inadequate aeronautical policies. A leading article in the *Morning Post* of 4 May was typical of these expressions. The paper said: "The splendid success which the Messrs. Wright have won is the result of long years of courageous and laborious effort. They have met and overcome incredible difficulties. If their triumph today is splendid and complete it has been obtained by the exercise of the highest qualities of mind and character . . . combined with unusual fertility and quickness of intellect. As yet the science of aviation is in its infancy, but in view of the results already obtained it would be the height of folly to depreciate the potential powers of aeroplanes and to ignore the problems created by their development. To Englishmen, perhaps, more than to any other nation the question of the navigation of the air is a matter of vital concern. . . . It is by no means impossible that in a few years time the United Kingdom will have lost, for purposes of defence, many of the advantages conferred by its insular character. . . . The greatest danger may come, in the near future at least, less from aeroplanes than from dirigible balloons. . . . It will be dangerous for the British nation to wait passively till a successful type of airship is evolved by some foreign nation, and then seek to profit by the experience of others. . . ."

The Wrights were entertained handsomely at lunches, dinners and banquets and were presented with their gold medals. They called in at the Short brothers' factory in Battersea and also travelled to Sheppey to inspect the Aero Club's flying-ground there. Their first formal interview, however, was a visit to the War Office where they spoke to the Secretary of State for War for half an hour, on 3 May.

The initiative for this meeting had been taken by R. B. Haldane himself. His private secretary wrote to Wilbur:[1]

> War Office
> Whitehall
>
> 1 May '09
>
> Dear Sir,
>   Mr. Haldane asks me to say that it would give him great pleasure if you and Mr. Orville Wright could call upon him at the War Office on Monday at 11 am. From a telegram which I received from Mr. Brewer of the Aero Club I understand that you will be free at that time.
>
>   I am Sir,
>   Yours faithfully,
>   A.E. Widdows
>   Private Secretary

After the Wrights met Haldane at the War Office they were taken to see Sir Charles Hadden, the Master-General of the Ordnance, and conferred with him for thirty minutes. His department, it will be recalled, controlled British military aeronautics in this period. Thereafter Hadden, Colonel Sir Edward Ward, the Permanent Under-Secretary for War, and General Gerald Ellison, one of Haldane's closest military advisers, accompanied Wilbur and Orville to a formal luncheon at the Carlton Hotel.

The British Press, having observed these developments, at once decided the Wrights had been invited to the War Office so that an arrangement could be made whereby they would sell aeroplanes to the British Army and train British military pilots in their use. This was a universal impression.

On 4 May the *Morning Post* reported the Wright visit to the War Office and explained:

> There is every indication that the presence of the brothers in town . . . points to some more important business than the mere interchange of amenities. . . . In point of fact . . . they are here to communicate with the War Office in regard to approaching official trials of their machines with a view to their adoption by the British

---

[1] Wright Brothers' Papers, A. E. Widdows to Wilbur Wright, 1 May 1909.

authorities. It is known that they have building at Shellbeach, Sheppey, machines which will soon be ready for trial, and Messrs. Wright yesterday had a formal interview with a number of leading War Office officials on the subject. Reticence is naturally preserved . . . but we learn that as a result there may be further negotiations, and we are further informed it is quite certain that the Brothers Wright will be returning to London again soon for another visit.

The *Daily Telegraph* of 4 May reported:

The famous American aeronauts, the brothers Wilbur and Orville Wright, called by appointment at the War Office yesterday, and had a long conversation with Mr. Haldane. The Secretary of State for War displayed keen interest. . . . It is understood that certain questions were asked which give an indication that the Government may make an offer to the Wright brothers. . . . the whole matter is being seriously considered by the authorities.

The *Daily Mail* of 4 May declared:

British aviators, discussing this visit to the War Office, and re-marking upon the fact that it was the first call the brothers made in London, declared that the Government intends at last to take a tangible interest in the Wright machine.

When *Flight*, a weekly publication, discussed the visit in its issue for 8 May it commented:

Happily, now there are not lacking practical signs that the author-ities of the War Office, and the Government . . . appreciate the significance of flying machines. On Monday Messrs. Wilbur and Orville Wright paid a visit to Mr. Haldane, and while it is needful and fitting to preserve secrecy . . . it may be taken as assured that our Government will duly acquire Wright aeroplanes and that the famous American brothers will themselves instruct the first pupils in England.

Despite his invitation to Wilbur and Orville Wright to visit him at the War Office R. B. Haldane had no intention of coming to an arrangement with them. His initiative of the 1 May was merely a clever politician's trick.

By that time the Liberal government was in serious trouble as a result of its aeronautical policy. Qualified speakers in and out of Parliament had warned the public that Britain was now vulnerable to attack from the air because it had allowed other countries to seize the lead in the new technology. Writers in the Press had repeated these opinions and had broadcast them in every part of the nation. The Wrights' visit to London made the government's neglect even more glaring because they were, in themselves, the most eminent living symbols of the new age of the air, an age that was certain to affect Great Britain's defensive arrangements more profoundly than those of any other State.

Haldane could blunt the effect of their appearance in London in one way only, by pretending to show official interest in them and in their invention. By this tactic he could hope to mollify his critics and keep them quiet until he was ready to reveal his own great plans for the further development of British military aeronautics. His object in seeing the Wright brothers in the War Office on 3 May was to play for time.

For weeks before the arrival of the Wrights in London Haldane had been working upon a profound aeronautical programme of his own. In this scheme the Wright brothers, mere "empiricists", would be allowed to play no part at all. Indeed, there was no reason for the Secretary of State to deal with them. The War Office authorities had already made their arrangements with C. S. Rolls. He would reveal all the secrets and details of the Wright aeroplane to them as they became known to him.

As a result of R. B. Haldane's design all the negotiations between the British Government and Wilbur and Orville Wright now came to a definite term. Haldane's new purpose was to turn the development of British military aeronautics in an entirely different direction. In this way the first chapter of a novel phase of British life came to an end, in May 1909.

Index

compiled by Geoffrey Jones